Integrated IT Performance Management

I thank these reviewers for their valuable suggestions and contributing remarks. Their encouraging words are very much appreciated.

I am impressed with Ken Bainey's approach to integrated IT performance management. His practical approach to accountability for results by aligning strategy to execution using a performance measurement dashboard is revealing and insightful. This book provides that understanding of how to apply results-based management and results-based budgeting to transform your IT organization into a culture of performance excellence.

Ken Maharaj
Former CIO, Bishop's University, Sherbrooke, Canada

This book is well written by a respected IT professional. It could serve as a textbook or an easy read for any professional. Although this book is written from an IT perspective, there is something in it that would appeal to professionals in any field of performance. More specifically, it could very easily be applied to project management world especially team performance. This book appeals to both new and experienced managers and project managers.

Sami Fahmy
Adjunct Professor, University of Alberta-Engineering, Alberta, Canada

An excellent body of knowledge on integrated IT performance management that integrates strategic management, IT operational management and performance management. The readers will understand how IT strategic directives align with the outputs, outcomes and performance measures in the IT performance measurement dashboard. This understanding via practical applicability will be of tremendous value to IT and business decision makers in managing, measuring and monitoring the delivery of IT services.

Qing Tan
Associate Professor, PhD, School of Computing and Information Systems, Athabasca University, Alberta, Canada

Already a published author, Ken has produced an amazing comprehensive collection of his experiences in IT leadership, represented by an integrated IT performance management framework-body of knowledge. His logical approach with practical "real-life" scenarios and dashboard implementation provides clarity to this complex discipline of performance management, which is perceived quite differently in practice and academic research. I believe that this framework can be used in the design and implementation of performance management systems or the start of a new body of knowledge-Performance Excellence Body of Knowledge (PEBOK).

Eugene Sears
Former Vice-President, Information Technology Services, Ontario, Canada

Ken has created the first IT performance management body of knowledge, from my research and awareness. The ideas, strategies, and processes covered in this book are very well articulated, with innovative and practical insights into the alignment and integration of performance measurement results-accountability for results, processes, and tools. His integrated IT performance management framework provides a clear, consistent, and complete picture with key insight suitable for the academic, private, and business sectors. I believe this framework will inspire many IT leaders to assess and transform their performance management practices.

Stanley Boodram
Professor, DSc, American Military University, Pittsburgh, Pennsylvania

Ken's book is a thoughtful collection of his extensive experiences and research to integrating performance measurement and management practices. He is an author with "hands-on" IT leadership and consulting experiences. This book is a must-read for those responsible for managing the performance of their IT organization.

Ashvanee Bisonauth
IT Director, Government of Alberta, Canada

Writing a book about concepts such as performance management that is perceived quite differently in practice requires experience, research, and wisdom. Assembling experience, research, and wisdom into an integrated performance management framework of clarity, consistency, and completeness is even more challenging and daunting. Ken has developed a logic model to bridge strategies with practical IT operational execution, represented as an integrated IT performance management framework (IPMF-IT), with discussion of positive and negative views. I am sure you will reflect on your own views and experiences for improvements after reading this book.

Myles Diamond
Senior Performance Manager, Edgeware Inc., Alberta, Canada

IT projects are notorious for cost overruns, delays, and failure to deliver value. Ken Bainey has gifted the IT industry with a valuable compedium of models and insights for delivering outstanding returns on investments in IT.

Touraj Nasseri
Professor and IT Director, Government of Alberta, Canada

This is one of the best books on performance management that I have ever read. Ken Bainey has done an excellent job of illustrating accountability for results-based management, linking strategy with IT operational execution using an integrated IT performance measurement dashboard, and transforming an IT organization to a culture of performance excellence. His discussions are logical, his scenarios are real, his graphical representations are practical, and his writing is inspirational.

Edson Roopnarine
Specialist, IT Governance, Government of Alberta, Canada

This is a must-read for business and IT leaders who are serious about improving their understanding of performance management integration, accountability, transparency, sustainability, and transformational change, in order to optimize the utilization of IT resources and to enable and support organizational excellence.

Michael Frenette
Senior Partner, Sierra Systems Consultant, Nova Scotia, Canada

Almost fifty percent of major IT projects fail because of significant cost overruns, much longer delivery time, or because they do not meet their original objectives. One of the reasons for this is a lack of adequate performance management protocol, poor coordination, and integration during the project life cycle, and failure to implement appropriate monitoring and reporting systems. Far too often we have text books written by authors who do not have enough hands-on experience regarding the subject matter. Ken Bainey, however, has done a marvelous job presenting his over 35 years of proven practical experience and expertise in *Integrated IT Performance Management Framework*, which provides a blueprint to enable the delivery of value-based IT services by linking strategic and operational management with outcomes-driven performance management. This book will not only benefit university students but also serve as an excellent reference guide for practicing IT and engineering professionals.

Jay G. Ramotar
Deputy Minister (retired), Government of Alberta, Canada

Integrated IT Performance Management

Kenneth Bainey

CRC Press
Taylor & Francis Group
Boca Raton London New York

CRC Press is an imprint of the
Taylor & Francis Group, an **informa** business
AN AUERBACH BOOK

CRC Press
Taylor & Francis Group
6000 Broken Sound Parkway NW, Suite 300
Boca Raton, FL 33487-2742

Printed on acid-free paper
Version Date: 20150827

International Standard Book Number-13: 978-1-4822-4253-9 (Hardback)

Library of Congress Cataloging-in-Publication Data

Bainey, Kenneth R., author.
Integrated IT performance management / Kenneth Bainey.
pages cm
Includes bibliographical references and index.
ISBN 978-1-4822-4253-9 (alk. paper)
1. Management information systems. 2. Information technology--Management. 3. Performance--Management. I. Title.

HD30.213.B355 2016
004.068'3--dc23 2015027120

Visit the Taylor & Francis Web site at
http://www.taylorandfrancis.com

and the CRC Press Web site at
http://www.crcpress.com

To my wife, Carol Bainey, who has been a partner in life since 1974, my two wonderful sons, Kevin and Kristian, and my brothers and sisters, whose encouragement, emotional support, and suggestions made this a much better book than it otherwise would have been. My deceased parents would have been proud of this accomplishment.

Contents

Preface

Before you start some work,
always ask yourself three questions –
Why am I doing it, What the results might be and
Will I be successful.
Only when you think deeply and
find satisfactory answers to these questions, go ahead.

—Chanakya

This book is a compilation of my extensive information technology (IT) management, performance management, project management, enterprise architecture and applications development knowledge, skills, and industry experiences gained over more than 35 years as an IT professional in the private, public, and academic sectors in Canada and the United States. It is *not* intended to be another theoretical book on human resources performance management, as there are many excellent books on this topic, some of which are mentioned in the "Recommended Readings" section at the end of each chapter. If you are in search of a book on human resources performance management, then this may not be the book that will interest you. The focus is within the context of a *results-driven* performance measurement and accountability framework that is *outcomes-based.* This book assumes a certain level of understanding of basic IT performance management concepts and theory.

However, if you are in search of real-world practical scenarios of IT performance management practices, with a desire to obtain examples of strategic directives, accountabilities, outcomes, and performance measures for managing IT services, with an interest toward how performance management integrates with strategic and operational management, then this book may be the magical solution for your performance management knowledge needs. The objective of this book is to provide an Integrated IT Performance Management Framework (IPMF-IT)™ that integrates strategic, IT operational, and performance management components based on a *results-driven* performance measurement and accountability framework. This book also demonstrates the applicability of this framework, within the context of the entire IT services delivery life cycle, using a *model-centric* approach. A unique and innovative approach of this model is the alignment of *outcomes measures with outputs measures,* which focuses on the effectiveness and efficiencies of output measures to the management, measurement, and delivery of IT services.

During my 35 years as an IT professional, I have had the opportunity of experiencing both high excellence and less desirable practices in performance management, according to the Capability Maturity Model Integration (CMMI)® of the Software Engineering Institute, Carnegie Mellon University. Certainly, performance management requires human resource management skills, but these skills alone are definitely not sufficient for IT organizational excellence. The Balanced

Scorecard (BSC) framework, originally created by Kaplan and Norton in their book *The Balanced Scorecard*, published by Harvard Business School Press, identifies human resource–employee management as one of the four major areas of measurements required for effective and efficient organizational excellence. Some senior managers strongly believe that human resource management talent is the only solution to performance management excellence to resolve the integration, communications, accountability, and transformation change problems internal and external to organizational excellence. This view that human resource management talent is the only skill requirement of managers is often expressed by executives and senior management staff who may have limited knowledge, skills, and experiences in integrated performance management processes. Managers who do not demonstrate the confidence and ability to apply or objectively challenge executive management directives and provide valuable suggestions or recommendations usually lack the required performance management knowledge, skills, and processes, as defined by Six Sigma®, *The Balanced Scorecard*, or similar performance measurement frameworks.

The effective applications of modern performance management principles in this technologically advancing world require professional managers with generalized strategic integration, specialized performance measurement risk management, quality improvement, and excellent transformational change management skills. By measuring success through the achievement of outcomes rather than counting human resources efforts and activities, we will be further ahead in determining how outputs are aligned with outcomes to delivering the desired result. We need to shift from performance measures that are primarily focused on accountability for effort and activities to accountability for results and outcomes. We may look busy but may be producing the "wrong" results.

The key to solving the problems of integration, communications, accountability, and transformational change, internal and external to an organization, is the establishment and deployment of consistent performance measurement processes that focus on measuring results, outputs, and outcomes, rather than only measuring human resources efforts and activities. Employing an integrated performance measurement dashboard to align strategy formulation with operations execution using outputs, outcomes, and performance measures will provide a framework for resolving integration and accountability issues. Effective transformational change requires an understanding of people/culture, politics, process, and performance, with actions for improvements. It is not only about communications, but it is also about improving performance.

As a result of these real-world experiences, I decided to compile, in a single volume, the performance management problems and challenges that I have experienced in both the highly excellent and less desirable performance management practices and to provide a set of real-world solutions, with an emphasis on the integration of strategic, IT operational, and performance management processes.

The real-world solutions presented in this book demonstrate a results-driven performance measurement and accountability framework to managing IT services that focus on the three major modern performance management skills requirements of strategic integration, quality improvement, and transformational change, as discussed in William A. Howatt's book *9 Elements for Integrated Performance Management.*

In order to progress in this dynamically changing information technology industry, we need to apply modern performance management talent in managing IT services using strategic integration, quality improvement, and transformational change management skills, rather than the traditional performance management skills based on measuring human resources efforts and activities and financials. These traditional performance measures are normally applied by human resource managers, financial auditors, sales executives, and business management specialists. There is no widely adopted performance management body of knowledge for information technology management. The Project Management Institute (PMI®) may consider adding a performance management knowledge area to their Project Management Body of Knowledge (PMBOK®) framework. To start transitioning performance management in your organization, you need to

- Establish and implement an IPMF-IT to enable accountability for achieving the results of IT services, to optimize resource utilization efficiency, and to ensure that IT services are aligned with the goals and objectives of the business while improving performance, demonstrating value, and implementing transformational change effectiveness.
- Employ professional managers with strategic value integration, performance improvement, and transformation change management skills who can achieve the four major performance management goals of accountability, transparency, transformational change, and service excellence, while optimizing the utilization of IT resources—people, process, financials, and technology—and ensuring accountability for results.
- Educate senior and executive management on performance management integration principles to assist them in making logical and accurate evidence-based decisions.
- Demonstrate to senior and executive management the value of performance management by showing them how the integration of strategic management, IT operational management, and performance management is essential in enabling strategic and operational performance improvements—organizational excellence.

The lack of standards and an integrated body of knowledge for performance management leave room for interpretations, flawed assumptions, and confusion. The concept of performance management is perceived quite differently in practice and academic research. It is still in the formation stages with no unified body of knowledge outlining its structure, results, processes, and boundaries.

This book provides that body of knowledge from the perspectives of integrating strategic, IT operational, and performance management results—outputs, outcomes, and processes. It uses a logic model to enhance performance through outcomes accountability, relationships among strategic directives, accountability for results, outcomes, process flows, and performance measures that are guided by the interrogatives: input (What is invested?), output (What is achieved?), and outcome, that is, impact (What is the result and what difference are we making?).

I hope that this book will provide valuable insights to functional and executive managers (business and IT) in their search for the elusive or magical "silver-bullet" solution to performance management. To readers who may view the contents as very advanced and did not gain any immediate value, which is unlikely, I do hope you appreciate the *what, why, when, where, who,* and *how* of performance management presented in this book and that the readings at least create some revealing, "thought-provoking" ideas. In this book, the way I attempt to make clear or create objectivity from subjective or confusing performance management themes is through the use of these English language interrogatives.

I keep six honest serving-men
(They taught me all I knew)
Their names are What and Why and When
And How and Where and Who

—Rudyard Kipling

Purpose of This Book—Why

Widely published IT statistics in performance management reveal the following:

- Only 43% rated their organizational performance management systems as effective.
- There was 30% improvement in companies that chose quarterly goals in performance management over "traditional" annual reviews (2013 Bersin survey).
- "We use 2% of what we measure—the rest is CYA" (Michael Hammer).
- High performers are 44% more effective in "cascading" accountability and achieving overall strategic and operational objectives (PwC–2012).
- Two thirds (66%) of organizations are planning to evaluate new technologies for business intelligence and performance management (Ventana Research, 2013).
- On average, more than 80% of companies think their performance management processes need improvement—planning, budgeting, and forecasting processes seem to be especially problematic (BARC, BI Survey-2014).

These real-world statistics confirm the need to

- Provide accountability for achieving the results of IT services
- Optimize the allocation and utilization of IT resources
- Ensure that IT services are aligned with the goals and objectives of the business
- Improve performance, demonstrate value, and implement transformational change
- Improve decision making using evidence-based methods, measured by output and outcomes

The KPI Institute's research "Performance Management in 2014" perceives integration as a necessary and essential performance management strategy for organizational excellence.

The purpose of this book is to provide my view, from an IT industry perspective, on how to address these performance management issues and integration imperatives by providing a results-driven performance measures and accountability framework of outputs, outcomes, performance measures, processes, practices, and real-world scenarios based on my 35 years as an IT professional in Canada and the United States. I compiled these practical experiences with the hope that professionals (IT and business) involved in performance management practices will understand and use the components of this integrated performance management framework as a valuable reference guide during the management and delivery of IT services.

In this book, you will

- Learn what the key results areas of an IPMF-IT™ are and how to integrate these results areas vertically and horizontally for strategic, IT operational, and performance management alignment.
- Learn how to manage, monitor, and measure IT performance results that focus on strategic alignment with IT operational execution using accountability for results: results-based management (RBM) and results-based-budgeting (RBB), with an integrated IT performance measurement dashboard and predictive performance analytics tools and technologies.
- Learn how to improve communications and enable integration, accountability, and effective change management, both internal and external to organizational excellence, by applying simple, flexible, and consistent processes using a model that integrates strategic, IT operational, and performance management practices.

- Learn how to transform from the traditional, antiquated change management practices to a transformation change model of people, politics, process, and performance, as suggested in this performance management framework.
- Develop an appreciation for performance management best practices that I have provided by means of real-world examples of accountability for results-integrating strategic directives with outputs, outcomes, processes, and performance measures.
- Learn how strategic directives are linked with the integrated IT performance measurement dashboard, using the KPI Management Framework from The KPI Institute® and Kaplan and Norton's Balanced Scorecard (BSC)® measurement framework.
- Understand real-world issues of performance management problems that have caused stressful situations to managers and executives (business and IT), and develop an appreciation for the recommended solutions, using real-world scenarios.
- Understand the goals of accountability, transparency, and change management in enabling a results-driven performance measures and accountability framework, within the context of the entire IT service delivery life cycle, by integrating strategic, IT operational, and performance management. This understanding will provide the needed guidance in determining accountability for results—transforming toward measuring results rather than tracking resources, financials, and activities, and transforming toward measuring outcomes and outputs rather than tracking inputs and activities.
- Obtain a comprehensive set of real-world strategic directives definitions for each functional area of the IT service delivery life cycle, with practical illustrations of how these strategic directives (strategy formulation) align with the integrated IT performance measurement dashboard (IT operational execution), using outputs, outcomes, performance measures, and Microsoft® Excel spreadsheets.
- Learn the key components of specific Industry Best Practices: COBIT®—Control Objectives for Information and Related Technology, ITIL®—Information Technology Infrastructure Library, CMMI®—Capability Maturity Model Integration, Six Sigma®—Process Performance Management, PMI-PMBOK®—Project Management, The KPI Institute®, and Kaplan and Norton's Balanced Scorecard® performance measurement frameworks. You will also learn how to align and apply these frameworks with IPMF-IT during the management and delivery of the IT services using the IT delivery life cycle process.

Who Should Read This Book

First and foremost, this book is intended as a reference source for practicing managers and executives (IT and business), whose interest is toward understanding performance management from a results-driven performance measurement and accountability perspective. These practicing managers will gain an appreciation for the value of integrating strategic, operational, and performance management in implementing accountability for results to achieve organizational excellence. It is also intended to serve as a performance management reference for managers, enterprise architects, and executive managers (in IT and business) involved in making evidence-based performance management decisions. This book can serve as a reference to various performance management stakeholders: service providers, consultants, performance managers, software application developers, business analysts, and systems architects involved in performance planning and execution and who wish to expand their knowledge of integrated IT performance management processes. Finally, this book can be used by academics and researchers in information technology management courses to bridge the intellectual gap between theory and practice. The framework can be used as the fundamental structure in the design and implementation of performance management software systems or the start of a new performance management body of knowledge—Performance Excellence Body of Knowledge (PEBOK®).

How to Use This Book

Managers and executives (IT and business) who are involved or interested in understanding results-driven performance measurement and accountability practices at organizations and who have adopted the performance management integration philosophy, in whole or part, should read this book sequentially. The chapters have been organized logically based on the components of the IPMF-IT.

Executive managers and senior managers can limit their readings to Chapters 1 and 2, which provide an introduction to the output (what) and outcomes (why, impact), processes (how), and people resources (who) involved in implementing the IPMF-IT model. These chapters provide some real-world scenarios of the value of integration, accountability for results, and transformational change management for organization-wide performance management excellence, which executives and senior managers will appreciate. Some may perceive the information as being quite insightful in their elusive search for the secret of success to organizational excellence to managing and delivering IT services.

Performance managers, consultants, academics, and researchers should read this book sequentially in order to develop a complete understanding on the *what, why, how*, and *who* of implementing a results-driven performance measurement and accountability framework, by integrating strategic, IT operational, and performance management components. They may have to tailor the IPMF-IT framework model to fit the context of their existing organization. Chapter 6 and Appendices A through F will appeal to chief information officers (CIOs) and IT leaders/managers who are searching for a real-world implementation of a client-centric outsourced model that links strategic directives with IT operational execution using an integrated IT performance measurement dashboard.

Architects (IT and business), methodologists, and business analysts can limit their readings to Chapters 2, 6, and 7. Chapter 2 provides an introduction to the IPMF-IT model, Chapter 6 shows how this model can be applied during the entire IT service delivery life cycle (SDLC), and Chapter 7 provides guidelines on how this IPMF-IT framework integrates with COBIT®, ITIL®, CMMI, Six Sigma®, PMBOK®, KPI Institute and Kaplan and Norton's Balanced Scorecard to enable organizational excellence using the IPMF-IT framework.

Organization of This Book

Integrated IT Performance Management provides a results-driven performance measurement and accountability framework that is based on a specific set of strategic management, IT operational management, and performance management results areas that form the basis of the integrated (horizontal and vertical) solution. At the end of each chapter, there is a "Summary" section that highlights the key results-driven performance measurement concepts discussed in that chapter, an "Endnotes" section that further explains the meaning and context of each numbered term, and a "Questions to Think About: Performance Perspectives" section that provides some questions for the readers to objectively determine the level of performance management maturity at their company. At the end of each chapter, there are also multiple-choice questions to assist the reader in determining the basic understanding of the integrated IT performance management framework. At times, the reader may find texts or diagrams replicated throughout this book. This is intentional in order to provide the reader the necessary continuous and logical flow of information to enable a more comprehensive understanding of the foundation principles and real-world applicability.

Chapter 1, Introduction to Integrated IT Performance Management, introduces the components of integrated IT performance management, discusses real-world problems, and provides real-world solutions during the management, measurement, and delivery of IT services. Guidelines for gaining executive management support that challenge performance management myths are also presented to provide some helpful hints and useful insights for practising managers, especially those whose interests focus on achieving organizational excellence.

Chapter 2, Integrated IT Performance Management Framework, introduces the integrated IT performance management framework and discusses strategic management, IT operational management, and performance management components. The key accountabilities of the performance delivery manager are provided to demonstrate the strategic performance integration decisions required during the management, measurement, and delivery of IT services.

Chapter 3, Strategic Management Model, expands on the strategic management model introduced in Chapter 2, discusses the results areas of the model, and provides the purpose, strategic directives, accountabilities, outputs (what), outcomes (why), process flows (how), performance model, and performance measures/metrics (dashboard) for each of the results areas. The accountabilities of the performance delivery manager discussed in Chapter 2 are further expanded to include the accountabilities of the executive performance manager (sponsor), the performance delivery manager, and the performance measurement team. These roles and accountabilities demonstrate the nature of *strategic management integration* with executive sponsors, performance delivery managers, and the performance measurement team, during the management, measurement, and delivery of IT services.

Chapter 4, Performance Management Model, expands on the performance management model introduced in Chapter 2, discusses the results areas of the model, and provides the purpose, strategic directives, accountabilities, outputs (what), outcomes (why), process flows (how), performance models, and performance measures/metrics (dashboard) for each of the results areas. The accountabilities of the performance delivery manager discussed in Chapter 2 are further expanded to include the roles and accountabilities of the executive performance manager (sponsor), the performance delivery manager, and the performance measurement team. These roles and accountabilities demonstrate the nature of *performance management integration* with executive sponsors, performance delivery managers, and the performance measurement team during the management, measurement, and delivery of IT services.

Chapter 5, Information Technology Operational Management Model, expands on the IT operational management model introduced in Chapter 2, discusses the results areas of the model, and provides the purpose, strategic directives, accountabilities, outputs (what), outcomes (why), process flows (how), performance model, and performance measures/metrics (dashboard) for each of the results areas. The accountabilities of the performance delivery manager discussed in Chapter 2 are further expanded to include the roles and accountabilities of the executive performance manager (sponsor), the performance delivery manager, and the performance measurement team. These roles and accountabilities demonstrate the nature of *IT operational management integration* with executive sponsors, performance delivery managers, and the performance measurement team during the management, measurement, and delivery of IT services.

Chapter 6, Integrated IT Service Delivery Life Cycle Performance Model, expands on the IT service delivery life cycle model introduced in Chapter 2, provides the strategic directives, discusses the outputs and performance measures for each of the IT functional areas within the IT service delivery model, and provides the alignment or horizontal integration of the results areas with strategic management, performance management, and IT operational management using RACI charts. For each of the IT functional areas, the alignment of the strategic directives end results with the outputs and performance measures in the performance measurement dashboard is illustrated using matrix representations.

Chapter 7, Aligning IPMF-IT Framework with Industry Best Practices, provides insight into how IPMF-IT aligns with COBIT®, Six Sigma®, PMBOK®, ITIL®, CMMI®, The KPI Institute, and Kaplan and Norton's Balanced Scorecard to show the integrative nature of these performance measurement frameworks. The strategic, IT operational, and performance management results areas of IPMF-IT framework are integrated with the IT functional areas or stages of IT service delivery life cycle using industry best practices methods and tools. The integration of the measurement results areas with the integrated IT performance measurement dashboard is shown using a matrix representation. The functions of the performance measurement office (PMO) in providing process, standards, and technical support for integration of industry practices are discussed. Suggestions for transforming performance management in your organization, using the transformation change model—people, politics, process, and performance—will provide very useful, applicable, and sustainable real-life scenarios. Finally, suggestions for CIOs and IT leaders for transforming to a performance management culture to enable and support IT organizational excellence will provide some exciting insights, especially to those who are ready for the transformation.

The Appendices include Microsoft® Excel implementations of the integrated IT performance measurement dashboard for the six (6) functional areas of the IT service delivery life cycle in a real-life scenario. I am sure you will find the structure and analytics for evidence-based decision making practical, informative, and insightful.

Trademarks

IBM is a registered trademark of International Business Machines Corporation

Microsoft is a registered trademark of Microsoft Corporation

PMBOK is a registered trademark of the Project Management Institute-PMI

ITIL is a registered trademark of United Kingdom-Office of Government Commerce

SIX Sigma is a registered service mark and trademark of Motorola Inc.

CMMI is a registered trademark of SEI-Carnegie Mellon University

COBIT is a registered trademark of ISACA®

ISACA is a registered trademark of Information Systems Audit and Control Association

IPMF-IT is a trademark of KBAINEY Professional IT Services

The KPI Institute is a registered trademark of The KPI Institute Pty Ltd

The Balanced Scorecard (BSC) is a trademark of Kaplan and Norton

Recommended Readings

BARC, *Vendor Performance Summaries*. Germany: The BI Survey, 2014.

Bersin by Deloitte, *2013 Bersin Survey*. Oakland, CA: Deloitte University Press, 2014.

Brudan, A., *Performance Management—A Story Told Through Key Survey Figures and Statistics*. smartKPIs.com Performance Architect update, 2010.
Hammer, M., *The Agenda: What Every Business Must Do to Dominate the Decade*. New York, New York: Three Rivers Press, 2003.
Howatt, W., *9 Elements of Integrated Performance Management Elements*. McMillian Publishers India Ltd., Mumbai, India, 2010.
Kaplan, R.S. and Norton, D.P., *The Balanced Scorecard: Translating Strategy into Action*. Boston, MA: Harvard Business School Publishing, 1996.
Price Waterhouse Coopers, *Performance Management Matters: Sustaining Superior Results in a Global Economy*. Ottawa, Canada: Teller School of Management, University of Ottawa and CATA Alliance, 2012.
Ventana Research, *Optimizing Business Performance with Sales and Operations Planning*. San Francisco, CA: Ventana Research, 2012.

Acknowledgments

I wish to acknowledge the editorial assistance provided by Sami Fahmy, PhD, PMP, professor at the University of Alberta; Qing (Ching) Tan, PhD, associate professor at the School of Computing and Information Systems, Athabasca University, Alberta, Canada; Touraj Nasseri, PhD, director, Information Technology, Alberta, Canada; Jay Ramotar MEng, PEng, retired Deputy Minister, Government of Alberta, Canada; Eugene Sears, former vice-president, Information Technology Services, Ontario, Canada; Myles Diamond, senior performance manager, Edgeware Inc., Alberta, Canada; Ana Drummond, applications specialist, Servus Corporation, Alberta Canada; Deo Roopnarine, technical specialist, Government of Alberta, Canada; Navi Sunner, project control consultant, Enbridge Inc.; Kristian Bainey, project manager/business analyst, Alberta, Canada. I express my thanks and gratefully appreciate their valuable suggestions and technical support.

Finally, I acknowledge my wife, Carol Bainey, my son, Dr. Kevin Bainey, interventional cardiologist, and my younger son, Kristian Bainey, information technology project manager, as well as many executives from my previous workplaces for their encouragement. Without their support, this book would never have been written.

Author

Kenneth R. Bainey is a retired chief information officer (CIO). He is a senior information technology (IT) professional, including 10 years as a CIO with 35 years of industry experience, and 10 years as a consultant, performing leadership roles in performance management and implementation of numerous business application systems in private, public, and academic sectors in Canada and the United States. As a CIO, senior performance manager, senior project/program manager, senior systems/data architect, and IT management consultant, he has acquired excellent specialized skills in strategic management, operational management, and performance management in information technology with alignment to business management areas.

His senior-level accountabilities include 9 years as a CIO with the Government of Alberta, 10 years in telecommunications, 5 years in oil and gas, and 7 years in the transportation and utilities business, where he directed and performed "hands-on" leadership roles in the management, measurement, and delivery of IT services, using "in-sourcing" and "out-sourcing" IT service delivery models. He performed the roles of CIO, senior performance manager, enterprise/systems architect, and IT management consultant at many organizations in Canada and the United States, where he implemented various components of this "results-driven performance measurement and accountability framework"—integrated IT performance management (IPMF-IT)™.

His academic qualifications include an MBA (Edinburgh Business School), BSc (University of Alberta), and professional designations—PMP (PMI Institute), PMgr, CIM (Canadian Institute of Management), and CCP (Institute for Certification of Computer Professional). He served on the executive committee of the Institute for Certification of Computer Professionals (ICCP-USA), the academic advisory of Athabasca University, VP-Professional Development-PMINAC, and was a public member of the Alberta Government, College of Alberta Psychologists (CAP) Council.

Bainey is the owner of an IT consulting company, speaker, lecturer, researcher, and author of an IT textbook titled *Integrated IT Project Management—A Model Centric Approach*, published by Artech House Publishers (London and Boston), publishers of engineering management books. He has also published technical articles with Auerbach publishers and in the *Journal of Systems Management*.

Author

[illegible]

Chapter 1

Introduction to Integrated IT Performance Management

1.1 Introduction

> Not everything that counts can be counted, and not everything that can be counted counts.
>
> **William Bruce Cameran**
> *Sociologist*

Integrated Information Technology (IT) Performance Management as defined in this book is the process of integrating the components of strategic management, IT operational management, and performance management during the management, measurement, and delivery of IT services. The objective of this integrated process is to optimize the utilization of IT resources—people, process, financials, and technology, using a *results-driven*[1] performance measurement and accountability framework. Figure 1.1 is a conceptual representation of the three major components of this framework that are discussed in further details throughout this book. The main focus is toward measuring outcomes and results rather than only measuring efforts, financials, and activities by counting inputs and outputs. This results-driven performance management and accountability framework is a set of practical strategic directives, accountabilities, outcomes, process flows, and performance measures, which demonstrate the integrated nature of strategic, IT operational, and performance management components. The unique difference of this framework is the *model-centric*[2] approach, based on outcomes and results, rather than the traditional activity-oriented method. This model-centric approach to results-driven performance measures and accountability framework discussed in this book is a unique innovative solution that can be readily applied during the management, measurement, and delivery of IT services. It effectively addresses the root causes of performance management major challenges—integration, communications, transformational change, and accountability problems internal and external to organizational excellence.

During my 35 years of experience in IT at various large companies in the private, public, and academic sectors, across Canada and United States, I have had the opportunity of working with

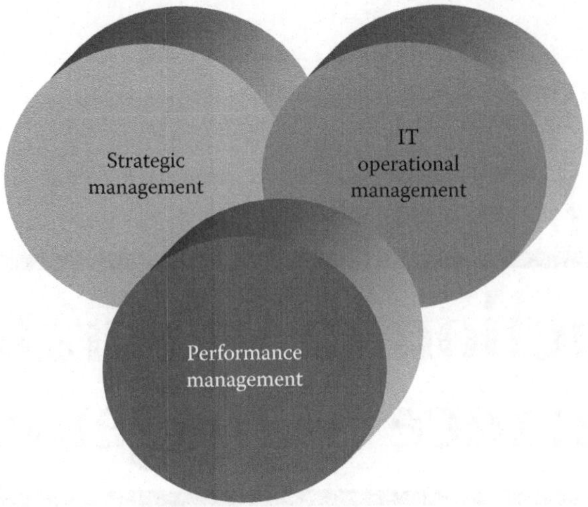

Figure 1.1 Integrated IT performance management framework—conceptual view.

senior and executive managers (IT and business) who, rightly so, stress the importance of the four famous performance management objectives:

1. Effort allocations and utilizations (effort)
2. Financial allocations and utilizations (financial)
3. Work allocations and utilizations (activity)
4. Performance measurement (KPI—Key Performance Indicators)

However, some of these senior and executive managers seem to measure performance based on these four famous performance management objectives, without any knowledge or consideration for strategic, operational, and performance management integration. In the majority of cases, these managers published performance metrics to demonstrate organizational successes, using the criteria of successfully meeting approved effort, financial, and activity objectives, with little regard for outcomes, results, and quality objectives. There was no consideration for integration, engagement, alignment, accountability, measurement, and improvement.

It is sometimes a common directive by senior and executive management who have limited exposure to the fundamental principles of integrated performance management to emphasize the human resource and personal systems aspects of performance management. They have little or no concern for what, why, or how outcomes or results are produced to support organizational excellence. Managers when confronted by executive management about the desire for consistent, integrated, and effective performance management practices across the organization, manage to recommend and convince executive management that the solution is a business process modeling or business reengineering initiative, using an activity-based performance management process. After closer assessments of this recommended solution, it is evident that some managers' perception of performance management is based on activity-driven financial measures, rather than results-driven measures. The view of integration to optimizing the utilization of IT resources while improving on performance and enabling effective transformation change seems to be limited. There was no mention for strategic, operational, and performance management integration. In my view, we have just compounded the problems rather than solving the root causes of performance management major challenges—communications, integration, accountability, and change management problems internal and external to organizational excellence.

In a majority of such cases, another business process modeling or business reengineering initiative is justified with new activity-based performance measures. There are different key performance indicators for reducing or increasing human resource capacity, to sound impressive, and promote political attractiveness. The value of performance measures to generate efficiencies for organizational excellence through alignment to strategic and operational outcomes seem to be an ignored or unfamiliar concept. The end result of these performance measurement initiatives is to either reduce or increase human resources capacity to satisfy certain senior or executive managers' ego, status, and political agenda, with the political logic to justify their decisions, using complex human resources policies. This is a typical case of illusions of efficiencies with nonproductive time, effort, and costs being applied to ineffective or wrong performance measures. The objective to optimize the utilization of people, process, financials, and technology resources for organizational excellence seems to be heading in a different direction.

The problems of the following continue to resurface, resulting in the elusive search for the magical "silver-bullet" solution:

- Accountability for Results
- Transparency
- Change Management
- Performance Improvement (Sustainability)
- Strategic Value Integration
- Redundant and Duplicated Efforts

Executive management perception of the causes for lack of meaningful performance measures, blame the rigid activity-based method—too heavy emphasis on policies and processes and too little emphasis on people and finance. This new directive from executive management to focus on people and financial aspects without alignment to outcomes or results normally evolves into a chaotic organizational environment with unclear outcomes, meaningless measures, confusing targets, and inconsistent processes. Managers having no documented accountability, transparency, and performance measures—some managers' favorite working environment. Lack of performance measurement systems encourages intuitive or emotional decision-making culture. The cycle in search for the "silver-bullet" performance solution continues, with presentations to executive management for more people and financial resources to support the existing complex policies and processes.

There is no "silver-bullet" solution. These performance management problems continue to resurface because of the lack of strategic, operational, and performance management integration framework. Structure measures organizational capability (people culture, facilities, and technology), finance measures how much services costs, process measures how services are performed, and outcomes measure results. This integration is necessary and essential to resolving the root causes of performance management challenges—integration, communications, accountability, sustainability, and transformational change problems, internal and external to organizational excellence and IT services delivery.

> There is no silver bullet.
>
> **Fred Brooks**

1.2 Performance Problems: Management of IT Services

The common performance problems that managers experience during the management, measurement, and delivery of IT services, as identified in Section 1.1, are further elaborated. The objective is to demonstrate why an integrated framework is necessary and essential to solving the root causes of performance management major challenges—integration, accountability, sustainability, and change management problems, internal and external to organizational excellence.

- Accountability for Results
  - Lack of key outcome measures, metrics, and indicators
  - Lack of reward and recognition for performance improvements
  - Activity-based not outcomes-based or results-driven culture
- Transparency
  - Complex dashboards, scorecards, and benchmarking tools
  - Lack of trust and credibility (secrecy style leadership-crisis management)
  - Lack of effective feedback and follow-up
- Change Management
  - Lack of understanding and communications of transformational change
  - Lack of clear vision of desired outcomes or disagreement of what is important
  - Lack of transformational change leadership
- Performance Improvement (Sustainability)
  - Performance measures for decision making lacks trust and credibility
  - Lack of consistent and integrated performance improvement strategies and plans
  - Inconsistent understanding of measurable targets and interpretation of results
- Strategic Value Integration
  - No alignment of performance measures to strategic and operational goals
  - Poor communications of how IT delivers value to business areas
  - Lack of adequate performance reporting for IT services delivery
- Redundant and duplicated efforts
  - Measuring resources and activities rather than measuring outcomes and results
  - Unclear accountabilities and responsibilities
  - Inconsistent use of tools, techniques, and processes among managers

The root causes of most common performance management problems presented before focus on the need for a consistent and integrated results-driven performance management framework. To drive consistency and effective performance across an organization, the best efforts and processes must come together in an integrated performance management framework. Performance management is about transforming established strategies into operational delivery of outputs, outcomes, and results. The objective is to optimize the utilization of people, process, technology, and financial resources. This will improve integration, communications, accountability, sustainability, and change management to external and internal stakeholders for organizational excellence. In order to effectively apply this framework, professional managers must execute these guiding principles during the management, measurement, and delivery of IT services, using sound *strategic value integration, performance measurement, and transformational change management skills.*[3]

There's nothing so useless as doing efficiently that which should not be done at all.

Peter Drucker

1.3 The Increasing Demand for Performance Integration

In this advancing information economy where the interactions of strategic, operational, and performance management in IT and the business areas are increasingly changing, every area of IT service delivery will require some form of integration. However, some managers manage IT services without any consideration for performance measurement integration and consistency. No wonder we have so many IT managers who operate using the sound impressive and politically attractive mentality. They lack adequate performance measurement knowledge and skills for organizational excellence, because they usually align performance management to financial and human resource management, without any consideration for integrated outcomes-based management, managing for results. In certain situations, the transformational leader gets the brunt of the blame and the reactive decision makers with crisis-style management receive praises and rewards for excellence, "excellence for the wrong and misleading results." Severe accountability and integration challenges continue to manifest itself within the organization. This ineffective performance management cycle continues, without any sound reasoning for the root causes of these performance management problems and without any real corrective action for performance improvements.

The KPI Institute™ for Performance Management has published performance management integration guidelines in their publication *Performance Management in 2013*, which is widely published internationally, within the performance management discipline. COBIT5®—Control Objectives for Information and related Technology— from ISACA®–IT Governance Institute has published a business framework for the governance and management of enterprise IT processes. Lean Six Sigma® is a set of tools and methods for process improvement, originally developed by Motorola. Carnegie Mellon University–Software Engineering Institute (SEI)[3] has published the Capability Maturity Integrated Model (CMMI®) to improve IT development process, controls, and outcomes. ITIL®—Information Technology Infrastructure Library—from the UK Government has published ITIL framework to improve IT operational processes and controls, using an IT service management life cycle. PMI®—Project Management Institute—has published PMBOK to improve project management practices. However, there is no widely accepted published performance management framework that is *integrated, results-driven, outcomes-based, model-centric*,[4] and which integrates strategic, operational, and performance management across the entire IT services delivery life cycle. This framework also provides real-world practical scenarios on what, why, and how these three major components—strategic, operational, and performance management integrate during the management, measurement, and delivery of IT services. It is based on outcomes, outputs, process flows, and accountabilities to improve strategic value alignment, evidence-based decision making, and to optimize resource utilization for organizational excellence.

Managing the delivery of IT services cannot be accomplished in isolation. It requires an integrated understanding of strategic, operational, and performance management components. We should understand how we are doing, how to measure, how to improve, and how successful we are in delivering our strategic and operational outcomes. We must provide value to internal and external stakeholders to demonstrate organizational excellence. The requirements for performance management integration in this modern technologically advancing world cannot be met, with the crude integration methods of the early days of information technology. Innovative integration methods, such as the framework presented in this book, must be effectively applied and communicated. This will significantly improve the way strategic management is aligned with IT operational management and performance management, to ensure successful delivery of IT services during the entire IT services delivery life cycle.

> Traditional Balanced Scorecard implementations often fail to deliver anticipated benefits because they are not integrated with performance management processes, particularly those executed at the strategic and operational level.
>
> **Gartner Inc.**

1.4 Role of Executive Management

Effective integrated IT performance management requires many executive level management talents and skills. Integrated IT performance management is defined in this book as: "The process of integrating strategic management, IT operational management and performance management components during the management, measurement and delivery of IT services." The objective is to optimize the utilization of IT resources—people, process, financial, and technology. Executive management will use the integrated performance measurement system for performance monitoring-optimizing the utilization of IT resources, strategic value integration, and evidence-based decisions making to improve organizational excellence. The accountabilities and decision-making structures of executive management for strategic, operational, and performance management must be established and communicated to drive integration and effective performance management using an integrated performance management framework.

- Executive Strategic Management (integrated strategic and operational programs)
  - Promote an organizational culture of results-based management
  - Define and adjust organization's goals, strategic directives, and alignment with IT
  - Establish organization's priorities, strategic value, and performance measures
  - Approve recommended performance management programs
  - Allocate performance management funding based on approved programs
  - Perform role as performance program executive sponsor and executive business sponsor, including overall accountability for performance improvement success
- Executive Operational Management (integrated strategic and operational programs)
  - Promote an IT culture of results-based management
  - Define and adjust IT goals, strategic directives, and alignment with business
  - Establish IT priorities, strategic value, and performance measures
  - Approve IT strategic directives and accountabilities for IT services delivery
  - Recommend appropriate funding levels to executive strategic management on funding allocations for delivering IT performance management program
  - Perform role as Executive IT sponsor, including accountability for optimizing the allocation of IT resources to align with business strategies

- Executive Performance Management (integrated strategic, operational, and performance management program)
  - Promote a performance culture of transparency, accountability, sustainability, improvements, and results-based management
  - Establish company's performance management (PM) objectives, strategies, priorities, and integration
  - Approve PM strategic directives, accountabilities, and performance measures
  - Recommend appropriate funding levels and program funding allocations for PM investments, to executive operational and strategic management
  - Obtain approval from executive operational and strategic management for recommended PM funding levels on approved programs
  - Perform role as executive PM sponsor to champion the performance management program, including accountability for performance management integration

> Effective leadership is not about making speeches or being liked; leadership is defined by results not attributes.
>
> **Peter Drucker**

1.5 A Real-World Problem Scenario: Measuring Major IT Program

A senior business manager at a large company mentioned:

> We seem to be experiencing several major challenges in understanding the value we are obtaining for the investments we are making towards the delivery of a major IT program. I hired a major outsourcing firm who spent extensive amount of dedicated efforts to documenting strategic and operational business process flows but cannot justify the value of such extensive documentation. They documented strategic and operational process flows, detailed plans and schedules at the activity level with measures and forecasts for financial and human resource efforts that are gradually becoming meaningless and misleading. Enormous amount of documentation was produced which looked impressive but lack integration and consistency, resulting in the demand for additional IT and business resources. We went through endless information technology performance iterations with unclear accountabilities and meaningless performance measures. The performance management process focused on counting inputs and outputs, with continuous justifications for adding more and more business and IT processes by several enthusiastic performance measurement teams. The reactive environment seems to be the normal mode of operations for this performance measurement team, with re-occurring requests for approvals appearing on my desk, for additional process managers and specialists in IT and business areas. Executive management needed proper justification on the continuous request for resources, and my frustration level seems to have reached that limiting point.
>
> My heightened frustration resulted in a decision to sign a contract with an "expert" performance management consulting firm to assist executive management in understanding the strategic value of this major business-oriented IT program. The overall

goal was to optimize the utilization of strategic and operational business and IT resources. The result was to improve the performance management communications, integration, sustainability, accountability and change management challenges, internal and external to the organization. My search was for an integrated solution, with the hope that this IT consulting company will deliver a sustained solution to this performance management challenge.

This performance management consulting firm, over-excited with this opportunity, produced more extensive documentation based on their "self-proclaimed" unique performance management methodology. This resulted in additional consulting resources, regular daily non-productive meetings, and more detail disintegrated documentation. The performance team, over-excited about the new performance management methodology, adopted the consulting firm's "fresh-start" approach with great respect and enthusiasm. The result was another set of similar financial performance measures, metrics and indicators that were activity-based rather than outcomes-based. The new performance management documentation was re-packaged with the consulting company's logo. The consulting company's confidentiality and copyrights terms appeared on the title page of each document.

The original problem of the lack of accountability, consistency and integration still prevails, with unclear linkages to understanding performance management, operational management, and strategic management integration. To add to this existing performance management chaos, the performance measures report now contain additional set of financial performance metrics and indicators at the detailed activity level, mainly to justify the need for five more senior consulting resources. This consulting firm seems to have re-packaged the inefficiencies of last year's performance measures into their report, with historical financials and employees measures incorporated in a "Victorian-novel" style documentation.

A polished report from this consulting firm recommended a solution to the problems, which required an organizational and cultural change. This change recommended the establishment of two separate performance management groups. One group to support the strategic management function and the next group to support the operational management function. This recommendation suggested the utilization of additional business and IT resources that escalated the budget to a level that was difficult to justify to executive management.

The search for the elusive integrated solution continues, and my position seems to be in more severe trouble, with valid excuses to executive management becoming non-existent. The original performance questions relative to development of this IT program of: "How we are doing?"; "Are we doing the right things?" "Are we getting the right results?"; "Are we getting the value?", still remain unanswered with more uncertainties and complexities. What should I do to get this major IT-business program back to an acceptable budget, accountability for results within the performance constraints level? What approach or technique should I apply?" These questions still remain unsolved. There are now additional resources and excessive complex performance measures, as a result of this desperate search for that elusive integrated solution.

I finally realized that there is no magical integrated solution, so decided to approach this performance management accountability, inconsistency and disintegration problems using the original internal performance team. The search for a senior program manager started. This individual must have experience with strategic management, operational management and performance management integration skills. He/she must have expertise in strategic value integration-people, process, financials, technology and transformational change-people, politics, process, and performance. I decided to search for an individual solution, after considering many risk factors. I believe that the risk impact in this case is small, and eventually hope to address these performance management challenges with this senior program manager. My expectation is that this individual has attained extensive practical integration, transformational change, performance measurement and risk management skills, on similar business-IT programs.

This problem scenario, experienced at this organization, shows some major challenges to IT performance management that often occur, internal and external to this organization.

- Committing to financial performance measures, whether or not strategic, operational, and performance measures can be effectively integrated with risks and quality objectives.
- Establishment of separate performance management groups: one for strategic management and one for operational management, with each group reporting on financial and nonfinancial measures based on historical financial results rather than understanding how nonfinancial performance measures influence financial results, using predictive analytics.
- Strategic management is accountable for establishing the financial measures with little or no integration with the operational measures—internal processes, employees, and customers. Operational management is accountable for service delivery with little or no meaningful performance measures. Human resource managers get involved during the annual employee's performance appraisals. Accountants get involved during the annual budgeting process. Integration exists in some illusionary constructs at the start and ending of the annual budgeting and employee performance appraisals processes. This approach may work well for those "self-serving and egoistic" managers who strive on subjective measures to satisfy their political agendas. In most cases, accountability for results is rarely demonstrated, which increased the need for a more integrated approach to enable effective strategic value integration and transformational change, using sound risk and quality management processes.
- Assignment of a performance manager who lacks integration, transformational change, and performance measurement skills.
- Addressing the communications issue with excessive performance management "status meetings," illusionary accountability, and secrecy style management.
- Meaningless and ambiguous measures and metrics with no baseline for improvements or how to interpret performance results.
- Disregard for the root causes of performance management challenges—communications, integration, sustainability, accountability, and transformation change.
- Performance managers disregard for measurable responsibilities and accountabilities for results, to show how the results of the performance team align with the goals and strategic directives.
- Performance measures, metrics, and indicators based on counting activities, inputs, and outputs, without regard for a *Performance Management Structure* (*PMS*).[5]
- Ineffective utilization of performance management tools such as scoreboard or dashboard, even by the "so-called" expert performance management consulting firm.

- Separation of strategic management, operational management, and performance management functions, with each group happily performing their individual responsibilities, without any overall direction or vision for integration—a recipe for chaos.
- Searching for that secret magical solution in a culture of subjective measures and reactive decision making, without sound analysis on the root causes of the problems.
- Emphasis on human resources and financial performance management with little or no consideration for integration of strategic, operational, and performance management results.

> The real secret of magic lies in the performance.
>
> **David Copperfield**

> A consultant is someone who saves his client almost enough to pay his fees.
>
> **Arnold H. Gloasow**

The solutions discussed in Section 1.6 demonstrate the value of strategic, operational, and performance management integration to solve the root cause–performance problems, resulting from the lack of accountability, communications, and integration of these major components. This real-world practical solution discussed in the next section addresses most of the critical problems presented before. It should provide some revealing and useful observations and lessons learned for those practicing performance managers, senior and executive management staff involved in measuring and improving IT programs using performance data, and whose interest is toward integration.

> We can't solve problems by using the same kind of thinking we used when we created them.
>
> **Albert Einstein**

1.6 A Real-World Solution Scenario: Measuring Major IT Program

This section highlights the performance management solution that was implemented, with a high degree of success, at this major organization, in solving the real problem scenario discussed in the earlier section. This major business-oriented IT program was managed and delivered by a newly established Business Systems Group (BSG) consisting of both IT and business resources. IT was responsible for technology infrastructure support (hardware, systems software, and network). The BSG was responsible for the business process and business applications software development and support. The key performance management principles that guided this results-driven solution are presented in this section as follows:

- Performance Management Organizational Structure
- Performance Management Accountabilities
- Performance Management Structure (PMS) model and hierarchy
- Performance Measurement Dashboard that aligns with PMS

The objective of this section is to provide the real-world solution that was successfully delivered to solve the accountability, inconsistency, and disintegration problems discussed in the problem scenario. This real-world practical solution is based on a "results-based" Performance Management Structure

(PMS). The dashboard-based solution to integrating strategic, operational, and performance management results are provided to demonstrate an example of a real-world practical and effective utilization of a performance management dashboard. Establishing order and structure to this disintegrated performance environment required the use of a Performance Measurement Dashboard by performance management professionals with strategic value integration, transformational change, and performance measurement skills.

- Performance management organizational structure presented in Figure 1.2, demonstrates the integration of strategic management, performance management, and operational management from a performance management organizational perspective. At this corporation, the newly formed Business Systems Group was responsible for performance management—measurement, delivery, and improvement of the IT program. IT operational management was responsible for technology infrastructure direction, development and support for hardware, system software including data base management system and network configuration. Strategic management was mainly responsible for providing strategic alignment and business strategies internal and external to the major IT program and also performing acceptance testing, end-users training, and transformational change management.

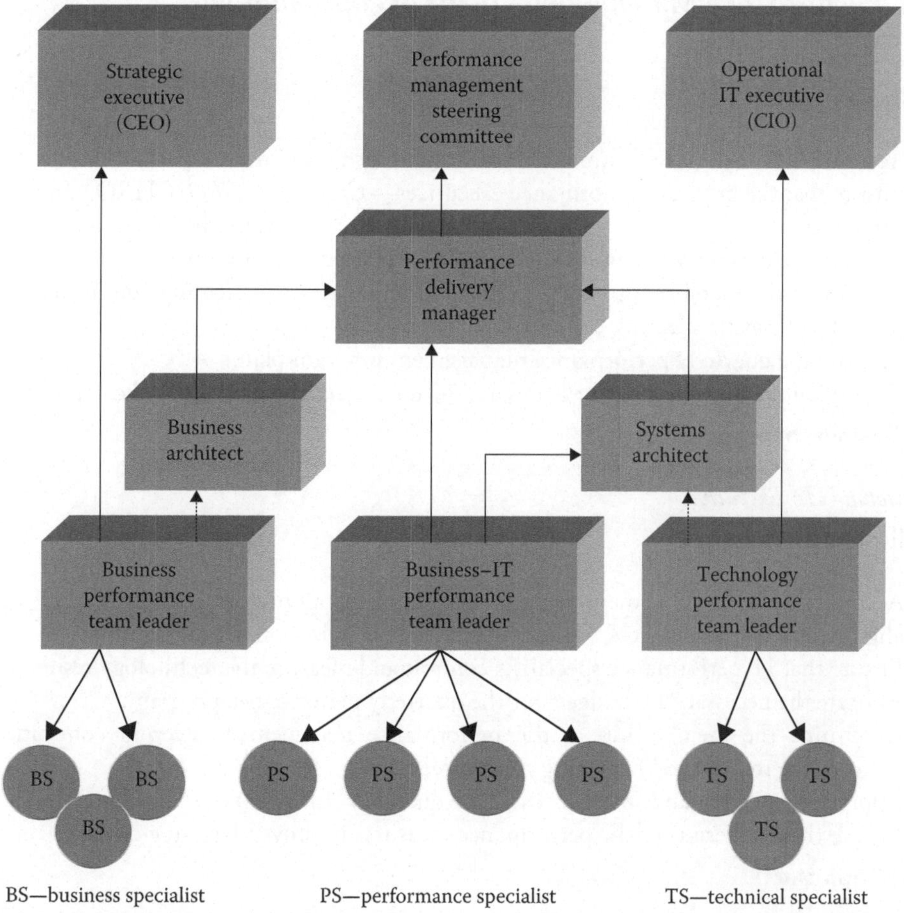

Figure 1.2 Integrated IT performance management organizational structure solution.

- Performance management accountabilities show the integration of strategic, performance, and operational management in terms of results, outcomes, processes, and people perspectives.
- PMS model and hierarchy demonstrates integration of strategic management, performance management, and operational management, in terms of performance management results, outcomes, processes, and technology perspectives.
- Performance measurement dashboard that aligns with the PMS model shows the automated implementation of the integrated PMS for a specific area—Project Portfolio Management. Appendices A through F contains the detailed performance measurement dashboards that was utilized for the IT service delivery life cycle.

1.6.1 Performance Management Organizational Structure

Please note that this organizational structure does NOT imply a new performance management structure. The intent is to identify the performance responsibilities of the existing structure to ensure accountability for results. It is also intended to resolve performance management challenges during the management, measurement, and delivery of this major IT program.

1.6.2 Performance Management Team Accountabilities

Strategic Executive
Coordination/Leadership

- Accountable for the establishment of the business goals and overall performance success.
- Ensure that the business performance executives—*CIO, CFO, CPO*, CHRO,[6] and business specialists commit to results-based culture to effectively measure the business results.
- Allocate the necessary business funding for the quarterly performance program.
- Determine the membership of the performance management steering committee and perform the role as the steering committee chairperson.
- Approve the quarterly performance management program plan.
- Champion the performance measures and its potential benefits/risks to the corporation.

Role: Business Sponsor

Operational (IT) Executive
Coordination/Leadership

- Accountable for establishment of the IT goals and overall performance success, IT strategic alignment with the business, risk strategies, and optimization of IT resources.
- Ensure that IT performance specialists commit and measure the technology results.
- Allocate the necessary IT budgets for the quarterly performance program.
- Determine the membership of the performance management steering committee and perform the role as the IT steering committee advisor.
- Approve IT performance measures and the quarterly performance management plan.
- Ensure that the results of the performance measures improve IT strategic value.

Role: IT Sponsor

Performance Management Steering Committee
Coordination/Leadership

- Provide high-level business and technical guidance, direction, and advice to performance specialists to ensure performance measures delivers optimum value to the corporation.
- Approve performance measurement output/outcomes, metrics, and indicators.
- Approve the budget for the quarterly performance program and any industry-wide benchmarking assessments and results.
- Integrate performance measures into the performance management program plan.
- Accountable for measuring and improving the effectiveness of the performance management program.
- Provide direction and approve recommendations tabled by the performance specialists on major issues, changes, and risks affecting the performance management program.

Role: Approval Committee

Performance Delivery Manager
Coordination/Leadership

- Responsible for selecting the performance team.
- Track and measure goals, targets, and achievements.
- Accountable for the quality and effectiveness of the performance program.
- Plan, organize, and coordinate the performance-related duties of the performance team.
- Coordinate the activities of the performance team within IT groups, other business groups, and external groups.
- Select and effectively apply performance measurement tools and control techniques.
- Determine resources and cost estimates for the performance program.
- Recommend a staffing plan to business, business systems group, and IT management.
- Responsible for all activities associated with performance budget and work plan for the performance program.
- Maintain working knowledge of the performance requirements, design concepts and approaches, and ensure that appropriate dashboard technologies are effectively applied.
- Critically review and be responsible for all performance-related benchmarking studies/recommendations completed by IT, business systems group, and business management.
- Responsible for the timely and accurate reporting of all performance measures, metrics, indicators, and interpretation of results.
- Administer the change management process by ensuring that the suggested changes are initiated as a result of the people, process, performance, and politics issues documented in the issues resolution log.
- Manage performance risks by analyzing risks impact on cost, schedule, and quality.
- Produce regular performance progress reports for the steering committee.
- Obtain performance funding authorization from the steering committee.

Role: Performance Delivery Manager

Systems Architect

Coordination/Leadership

- Provide leadership to performance team members on people, process, technology, and financial performance issues, goals, strategic directions, and measures.
- Communicate with IT specialists on performance measurement progress and improvement relative to Service Level Agreements (SLAs).
- Establish customer satisfaction improvement criteria to ensure that the IT products and services meet acceptable satisfaction levels.
- Communicate with performance delivery manager on performance measurement progress and improvement relative to IT services delivery.
- Responsible for ensuring that the performance team members are aware of the significant activities of other groups for the performance management program.
- Recommend resources and cost estimates to the performance delivery manager on the critical areas to be addressed in the performance management program.
- Keep the performance delivery manager, business performance team members, IT performance team members, and IT support staff informed on ongoing performance problems and their resolution.
- Ensure that IT performance standards and appropriate technologies and techniques are used during the performance delivery life cycle.
- Administer the IT performance issues resolution process by ensuring that the issues are addressed efficiently and effectively through the performance management program.
- Lead the evaluation and selection, recommend acquisition of performance measurement software tools, and coordinate the implementation of these tools.
- Maintain a single point of contact with nonbusiness system resources (internal and external suppliers and vendors).
- Evaluate, recommend, and lead the implementation of performance measurement software development methodologies and appropriate benchmarking results.
- Responsible for the overall design integrity, technical viability, documentation, and reusability of the performance measurement dashboard.

Performance Execution

- Plan, organize, control, coordinate, and maintain the performance-related duties of the assigned performance team members through the use of dashboards, balanced scorecards, and benchmarking standards.
- Define performance program charter, scope, and conceptual design of the new performance improvement system.
- Support the performance team in defining an integrated representation of the strategic, operational, and performance management measures, metrics, indicators, and benchmarking standards.
- Support the IT technical staff in establishing the SLAs and performance measures for outsourced contracts.
- Develop and publish the IT performance measures, metrics, indicators, and results.

Role: Systems Architect

Business Architect

Coordination/Leadership

- Provide leadership to performance team members on business process reengineering improvements.
- Communicate with business specialists on performance progress relative to business planning and architectural activities.
- Establish business deployment criteria (business process deployment, organizational and cultural change, and training) to ensure that the performance management program meets acceptable business changes.
- Communicate with performance delivery manager on performance measures progress and improvements relative to business–IT service delivery.
- Responsible for ensuring that the business performance team members are aware of the significant activities of other groups on the performance management program.
- Recommend business resources and provide cost estimates to the performance delivery manager on the critical areas to be addressed in the performance management program.
- Keep the business–IT performance team leader, system architect, and executive business manager informed on ongoing problems and their resolution.
- Ensure that business performance standards and appropriate business process tools and techniques are used during the performance delivery life cycle.
- Administer the business performance issues resolution process by ensuring that the issues are addressed efficiently and effectively through the performance management program.
- Administer the Issues Resolution process by ensuring that related business issues are resolved efficiently and effectively.
- Lead evaluation and selection, recommend acquisition of business process tools and techniques, and coordinate the implementation of these tools.
- Maintain a single point of contact with business system resources (internal and external suppliers and vendors).
- Evaluate, recommend, and lead implementation of business process methodologies and appropriate standards.
- Responsible for the overall business design, acceptance testing, change management viability, documentation, and reusability of the business deliverables for the Performance.

Performance Execution

- Plan, organize, control, coordinate, and maintain the business-related duties of the assigned business performance team members through the use of business process reengineering and performance management tools.
- Define performance charter, scope, and conceptual design of the new performance improvement system from a business perspective.
- Support performance team in defining an integrated representation of the strategic, operational, and performance measures.
- Support business staff in establishing the acceptance testing, change management and risk management criteria, and solution.
- Develop and publish the business performance measures, metrics, indicators, and results.

Role: Business Architect

Business–IT Performance Team Leader

The performance delivery manager is responsible for ensuring that the performance team acquires the required business process, performance measurement and technical skills set, and staffing requirements. This is done in concert with the business performance team leader, IT performance team leader, and business–IT program performance team leader. The business–IT performance team leader is assigned a lead role to ensure that the performance results are produced according to the established performance measurement standards, and that the business–IT program strategic value alignment is adequately attained. The performance specialist team consisting of the business systems group staff, IT support staff, and business support staff (Finance, Human Resource, and Business Performance Specialist) are responsible to:

- Determine the appropriate *Financial* (spending) and *Human Resource* (staffing) levels through internal assessments and external benchmarking results for business–IT program.
- Determine the essential *Internal Processes* (operating and strategic) measurement levels and adequate *Customer* (satisfying/using) satisfaction levels for this business–IT program delivery through internal assessments and external benchmarking results.
- Determine the performance measures for the essential *Internal Processes* (operating and strategic) in terms of *Service Delivery, Operational Efficiencies, Relationship Management, and Functional Management* for this business–IT program delivery through internal assessments and external benchmarking results.
- Develop the integrated IT performance measurement program consisting of performance results—measures, metrics, and indicators for financial, human resources, internal processes and customer measurements areas.
- Communicate how to interpret the performance results and to demonstrate value through progress and improvement.
- Communicate IT performance results—measures, metrics, and indicators, internally and to the business.
- Present performance results to stakeholders to highlight issues, accomplishments, and continuous improvements.

Role: Performance Team Leader—Business–IT Program

Performance Specialist

- Ensures that business and IT performance specialists understand measurement and analysis process for the business–IT program delivery.
- Collect organization level measurements and perform internal and external measurement reporting.
- Collect project level measurements and perform measurement reporting for project team.
- Maintain organization measurement repository.
- Develop monthly charts and graphs for analysis.
- Execute Performance Improvement Plans.
- Assists projects in the collection, analysis, and reporting of valid metrics.

  Four main categories of support include specific metrics identification and definition; data collection; metrics education; process improvement; and metrics analysis and reporting.

- Implement/follow measurement processes and procedures.
- Assist in identifying meaningful measures to be gathered and reported.
- Gather project and account-related measures information to be used by the project/account measurement specialists.
- Participate in the Performance Improvement activities.

Information Technology Performance Team Leader

The performance delivery manager is responsible for ensuring that the performance team acquires the required business process, performance measurement and technical skills set, and staffing requirements. This is done in concert with the business performance team leader, IT performance team leader, and business–IT program performance team leader. The IT performance team leader is assigned a lead role to ensure that the performance results are produced according to the established IT performance measurement standards, and that the business–IT program strategic value alignment is adequately attained. The IT performance team consisting of technical support staff is responsible to

- Determine the essential *Internal IT Processes* (operating and strategic) measurement levels and adequate *Customer* (using) satisfaction levels through internal assessments and external benchmarking results for delivery of the business–IT program technical areas.
- Determine the performance measures for the essential *Internal Processes* (operating and strategic) in terms of *Service Delivery, Operational Efficiencies, Relationship Management, and Functional Management.*
- Develop the IT performance measurement program consisting of performance results—measures, metrics, and indicators for financial, human resources, internal processes, and customer measurements areas.
- Communicate how to interpret the performance results and to demonstrate value through progress and improvement.
- Communicate IT performance results—measures, metrics, and indicators, internally and to the business.
- Present performance results to stakeholders to highlight issues, accomplishments, and continuous improvements.

Role: Performance Team Leader—IT

Technical Specialist (Performance)

- Perform IT performance specialists measurement and analysis process for the business–IT program delivery.
- Collect IT organization level measurements and perform internal and external measurement reporting.
- Collect project level measurements and perform measurement reporting for project team.
- Maintain organization measurement repository.
- Develop monthly charts and graphs for analysis.
- Execute Performance Improvement Plans.
- Assists projects in the collection, analysis, and reporting of valid metrics.

  Four main categories of support include specific metrics identification and definition; data collection; metrics education; process improvement; and metrics analysis and reporting.

- Implement/follow measurement processes and procedures.
- Assist in identifying meaningful measures to be gathered and reported.
- Gather project and account-related measures information to be used by the project/account measurement specialists.
- Participate in the Performance Improvement activities.

Business Performance Team Leader

The performance delivery manager is responsible for ensuring that the performance team acquires the required business process, performance measurement and technical skills set, and staffing requirements. This is done in concert with the business performance team leader, IT performance team leader, and business–IT program performance team leader. The business performance team leader is assigned a lead role to ensure that the performance results are produced according to the established business performance measurement standards, and that the business–IT program strategic value alignment is adequately attained. The business performance team consisting of business support staff is responsible for the following:

- Determine the essential *Operational* (operating and strategic) measurement levels and adequate *Customer* (using) satisfaction levels through internal assessments and external benchmarking results for delivery of the business–IT program business areas.
- Determine the performance measures for the essential *Operational* (operating and strategic) *processes* for *Service Delivery, Operational Efficiencies, Relationship Management, and Functional Management.*
- Develop the business performance measurement program consisting of performance results—measures, metrics, and indicators for financial, human resources, operational processes, and customer measurements areas.
- Communicate how to interpret the performance results and to demonstrate value through progress and improvement.
- Communicate business performance results—measures, metrics, and indicators, internally and to the business.
- Present performance results to stakeholders to highlight issues, accomplishments, and continuous improvements.

Role: Performance Team Leader—Business

Business Specialist (Performance)

- Perform business performance measurement and analysis process for the business–IT program delivery.
- Collect organization level measurements and perform internal and external measurement reporting.
- Collect project level measurements and perform measurement reporting for project team.
- Maintain organization measurement repository.
- Develop monthly charts and graphs for analysis.
- Execute Performance Improvement Plans.
- Assists projects in the collection, analysis, and reporting of valid metrics.

  Four main categories of support include specific metrics identification and definition; data collection; metrics education; process improvement; and metrics analysis and reporting.

- Implement/follow measurement processes and procedures.
- Assist in identifying meaningful measures to be gathered and reported.
- Gather project and account-related measures information to be used by the project/account measurement specialists.
- Participate in the Performance Improvement activities.

1.6.3 Performance Management Structure

The objective of this section is to present the Performance Management Structure (PMS) that was used as the key guiding principle in managing and delivering this major IT program, within the context of the overall IT service delivery life cycle. This performance management structure aligns with *Six Sigma process improvement using Deming's "PDCA" Cycle*[7] and *COBIT Governance Objectives* and supports the results-driven performance management and accountability framework, as presented in this book. The fundamental principles and guiding definition of PMS is defined in this book in accordance with *Kaplan and Norton's*[8] research as: "A results-oriented group of performance measures that aligns formulated goals and strategic directives into outcomes, outputs, performance measures and results. Each descending level represents an increasing detailed definition of the performance results."

The core measures of any performance management structure, whether or not the industry is public, private, or academic, consist of *employee—HR*, *customer*, *operational* (Internal Processes, Services, and Technology), and *financial* measures to support both business and IT processes. The key IT service areas that support the implementation of these core measures consist of *governance* and *planning*, *architecture*, *project portfolio management*, and *applications/technology services* to ensure that these measures fit within the context of the IT service delivery life cycle. Deming's PDCA performance management life cycle is used to guide the measurement of the major IT service delivery life cycle, using a more iterative and orderly performance management progression, as shown in Figure 1.3.

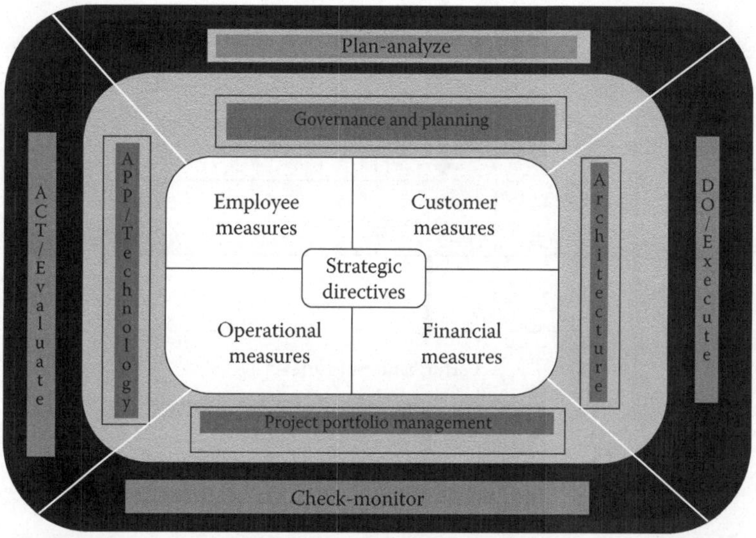

Figure 1.3 Performance Management Structure (PMS) solution.

This PMS is a key foundation principle within this manuscript that is used to demonstrate the *model-centric and results-oriented* approach to managing, measuring, and improving the delivery of IT services.

1.6.4 Performance Management Structure Hierarchy

The objective of this section is to show the PMS hierarchy, presented in Figure 1.4, which formed the basis for the development of the PMS structure. It is based on *Kaplan and Norton's*[8] foundation principles for developing a balance scorecard to ensure effective measurement of organization's goals and strategies. These principles are sound and have been applied successfully on various IT performance programs. First, specify and break down the goals and strategic directives into valuable and measurable outcomes and outputs for each performance measurement area. Second, establish performance measures, metrics and indicators to each of the outcomes and outputs. Finally, interpret the results of the graphs and charts to measure and improve how an organization is delivering its strategic and operational outcomes.

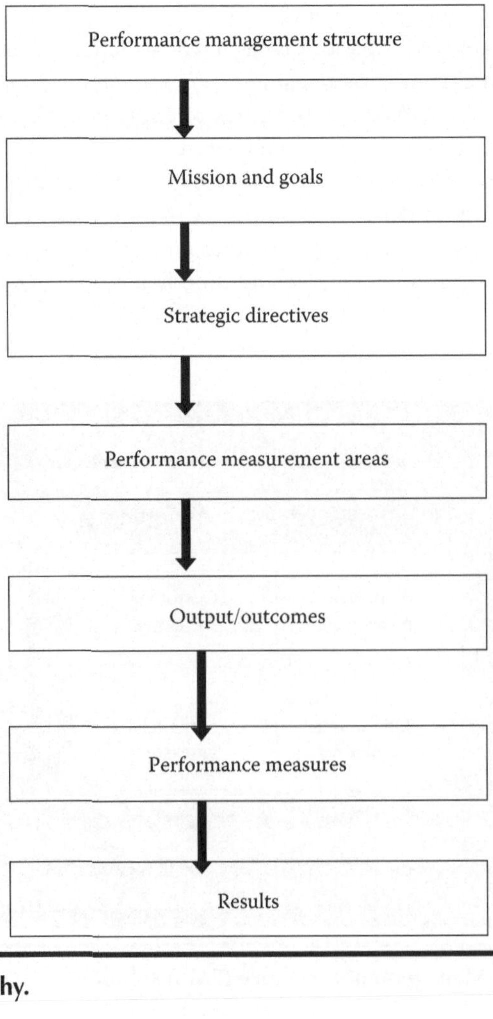

Figure 1.4 PMS hierarchy.

1.6.5 Performance Measurement Dashboard

The real-world dashboard that was used as the tool to manage, measure, and improve this major IT program is presented to demonstrate the performance management tool implementation of this performance management foundation structure. Figure 1.5a through 1.5g shows the tool-based solution to the PMS solution and the PMS hierarchy presented in Figures 1.3 and 1.4, respectively. The solution presented for project portfolio management service area shows the measures at a point in time for managing the delivery of this major IT program. Appendices A through F contain the detailed measures for the entire IT services functional areas as specified in the PMS. The strategic directives and outcomes are aligned with the performance measures and the roles and accountabilities presented in Section 1.6.2, using the performance management information system (PMIS) repository. This integrated alignment provided an effective means to optimizing: staffing—human resource, spending—financials, supporting/using—operational, and satisfying—customer through internal measures or external benchmarking. This results-based solution can be easily applied to the implementation of any major performance improvement program, as a result of the flexibility, consistency, integrity, maintainability, and reusability of this unique, simple, practical, and innovative *results-based* performance management structure.

Figure 1.5a through c shows the performance measurement areas, outputs, performance measures, and results for Project Portfolio Management outcomes/output—**Operational measures**, specified in the PMS. In this version of the performance management dashboard, the performance measurement areas were integrated with the strategic directives, outputs, performance measures, and results to show how these performance measures are integrated and aligned with the goals and strategic directives.

IT Project Portfolio Management					
Operational-FM	Start Date	End Date	Status	% Complete	Indicator
IT PPM Governance Framework	4/1/2011	12/31/2011	In progress	50%	G
IT PPM Innovative Technical Direction	4/1/2011	3/31/2012	In progress	45%	G
PPM Projects Outsourcing Framework	4/1/2011	9/30/2011	In progress	65%	Y
Operational-FM summary	4/1/2011	3/31/2012	In progress	53%	G

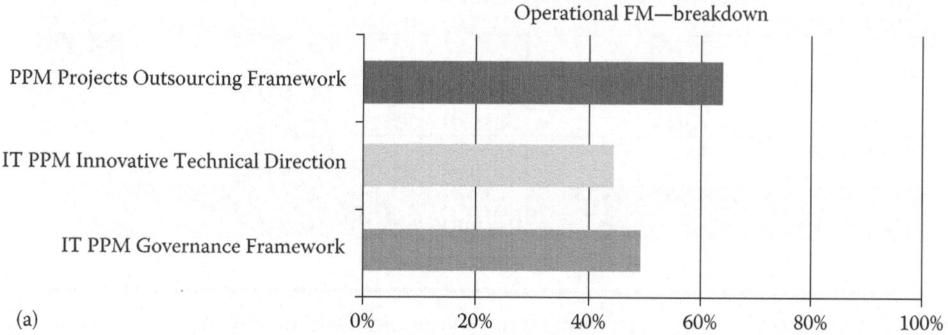

(a)

Figure 1.5 (a–g) Performance measurement dashboard-PPM. *(Continued)*

OPERATIONAL-SD	Start Date	End Date	Status	% Complete	Indicator
IT Business Projects Monitoring/Reporting	4/1/2011	3/31/2012	In-Progress	25%	Y
Innovative PMO Communications tools	4/1/2011	9/30/2011	In-Progress	75%	Y
IT PPM Productivity Tools and Processes	4/1/2011	9/30/2012	In-Progress	40%	G
PPM Systems and Regression Testing	4/1/2011	3/31/2012	In-Progress	40%	G
IT Project Management /Delivery	4/1/2011	3/31/2012	In-Progress	40%	G
IT Business Projects RFP/Contracts	4/1/2011	3/31/2012	In-Progress	40%	G
IT Business Projects Program/Projects Plan	4/1/2011	3/31/2012	In-Progress	40%	G
IT Business Project Architecture/Design	4/1/2011	3/31/2012	In-Progress	40%	G
IT PMO Support	4/1/2011	3/31/2012	In-Progress	40%	G
IT Business Project Requirements Specifications	4/1/2011	3/31/2012	In-Progress	40%	G
OPERATIONAL-SD Summary	4/1/2011	3/31/2012	In-Progress	42%	G

(b)

OPERATIONAL-SE	Start Date	End Date	Status	% Complete	Indicator
Business Projects Plan QA	4/1/2011	6/30/2011	In-Progress	75%	Past Due
IT Project Management Compliance/Approval	4/1/2011	7/31/2011	In-Progress	80%	Past Due
Business Projects Financial Measures	4/1/2011	9/30/2011	In-Progress	60%	R
PMO Compliance	4/1/2011	3/31/2012	In-Progress	35%	Y
Project Management Optimization	4/1/2011	3/31/2012	In-Progress	35%	Y
Business Projects Benchmarking Metrics	4/1/2011	9/30/2011	In-Progress	80%	G
OPERATIONAL-SE Summary	4/1/2011	3/31/2012	In-Progress	61%	G

OPERATIONAL-RM	Start Date	End Date	Status	% Complete	Indicator
PPM Client Management Relations/Feedback	4/1/2011	3/31/2012	In-Progress	100%	Black
Vendors PPM Relations/Feedback	4/1/2011	3/31/2012	In-Progress	40%	G
IT Outsourced Providers PPM Relations/Feedback	4/1/2011	3/31/2012	In-Progress	25%	Y
OPERATIONAL-RM Summary	4/1/2011	3/31/2012	In-Progress	55%	G

(c)

Figure 1.5 (*Continued*) (a–g) Performance measurement dashboard-PPM. *(Continued)*

Figure 1.5c is a continuum of the performance measurement areas, outputs, performance measures, and results for Project Portfolio Management outcomes/output—**Operational measures**, specified in the PMS. Operational measures represent Functional Management (FM), Service Delivery (SD), Service Excellence (SE) and Relationship Management (RM) measures.

Figure 1.5d through 1.5f shows the performance measurement areas, outputs, performance measures, and results for Project Portfolio Management outcomes/output—**Financial**, **Employee**, **Customer** measures, specified in the PMS.

Figure 1.5e is a continuum of the performance measurement areas, outputs, performance measures, and results for Project Portfolio Management outcomes/output—Financial, **Employee**, Customer, and Operational measures, specified in the PMS.

Figure 1.5f contains predictive analytics for summary level performance measurement areas, outputs, performance measures, and results for Project Portfolio Management outcomes/output—Financial, Employee, Customer, and **Operational** measures, specified in the PMS.

Figure 1.5g is a representation of the typical types of graphs and charts to interpret the results of the performance measurement areas, outputs, performance measures, and results for Project Portfolio Management outcomes/output—**Financial**, **Employee**, **Customer**, **and Operational**

Financial	Start Date	End Date	Status	% Complete	Indicator
IT–Business Project Costs	4/1/2011	3/31/2012	In progress	35%	Y
IT PPM Costs	4/1/2011	3/31/2012	In progress	25%	Y
Financial Summary	4/1/2011	3/31/2012	In progress	30%	Y

Customer	Start Date	End Date	Status	% Complete	Indicator
PPM Client Relationships/Satisfaction Surveys	4/1/2011	3/31/2012	In progress	30%	Y
PPM Committee Meetings	4/1/2011	3/31/2012	In progress	30%	Y
PPM Vendors Relationships/Satisfaction Surveys	4/1/2011	9/30/2011	In progress	80%	G
PPM IT Outsourced Providers Surveys	10/1/2011	3/31/2012	In progress	0%	
PPM Benchmarking Surveys/Results		6/30/2011	In progress	100%	Black
Customer Summary	4/1/2011	3/31/2012	In progress	48%	G

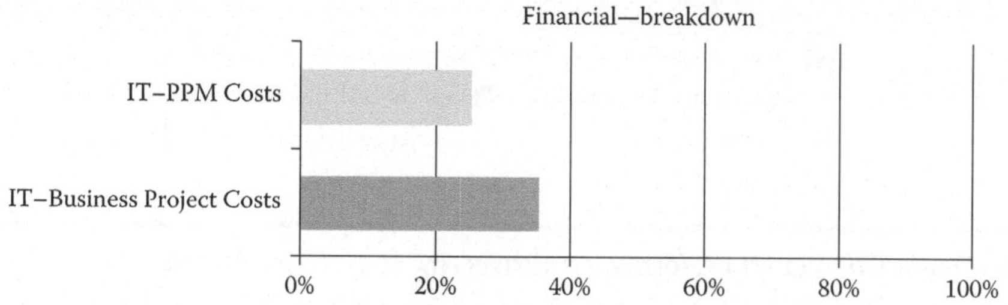

(d)

Figure 1.5 (*Continued*) (a–g) Performance measurement dashboard-PPM. *(Continued)*

Employee	Start Date	End Date	Status	% Complete	Indicator
PPM IT Progress Reporting	4/1/2011	6/30/2011	In progress	100%	Black
PPM IT Staff Performance Contract	4/1/2011	3/31/2012	In progress	35%	Y
PPM Staff Learning/Growth Reporting	4/1/2011	3/31/2012	In progress	35%	Y
PPM Staff Meetings/Communications	4/1/2011	3/31/2012	In progress	35%	Y
PPM Staff Retention/Retraining/Reward Reporting	4/1/2011	7/31/2011	In progress	100%	Black
Employee Summary	4/1/2011	3/31/2012	In progress	61%	G
IT Project Portfolio Summary	4/1/2011	3/31/2012	In progress	50%	G

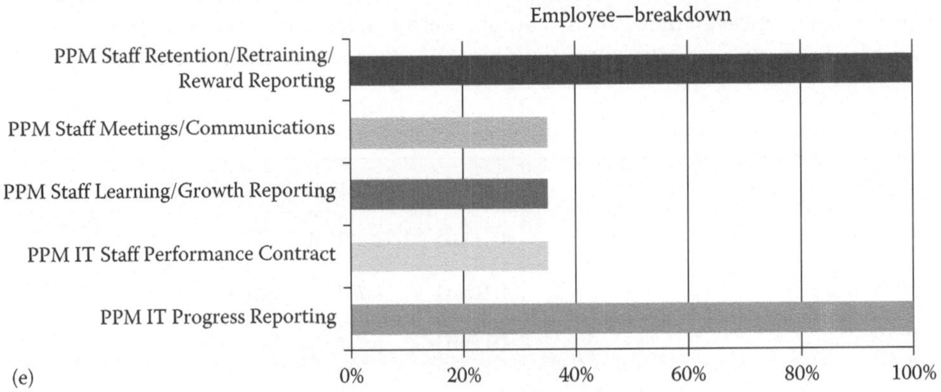

(e)

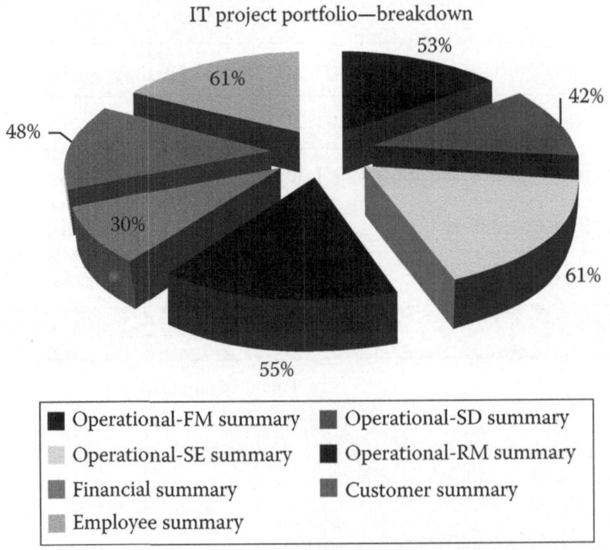

Figure 1.5 (*Continued*) (a–g) Performance measurement dashboard-PPM. *(Continued)*

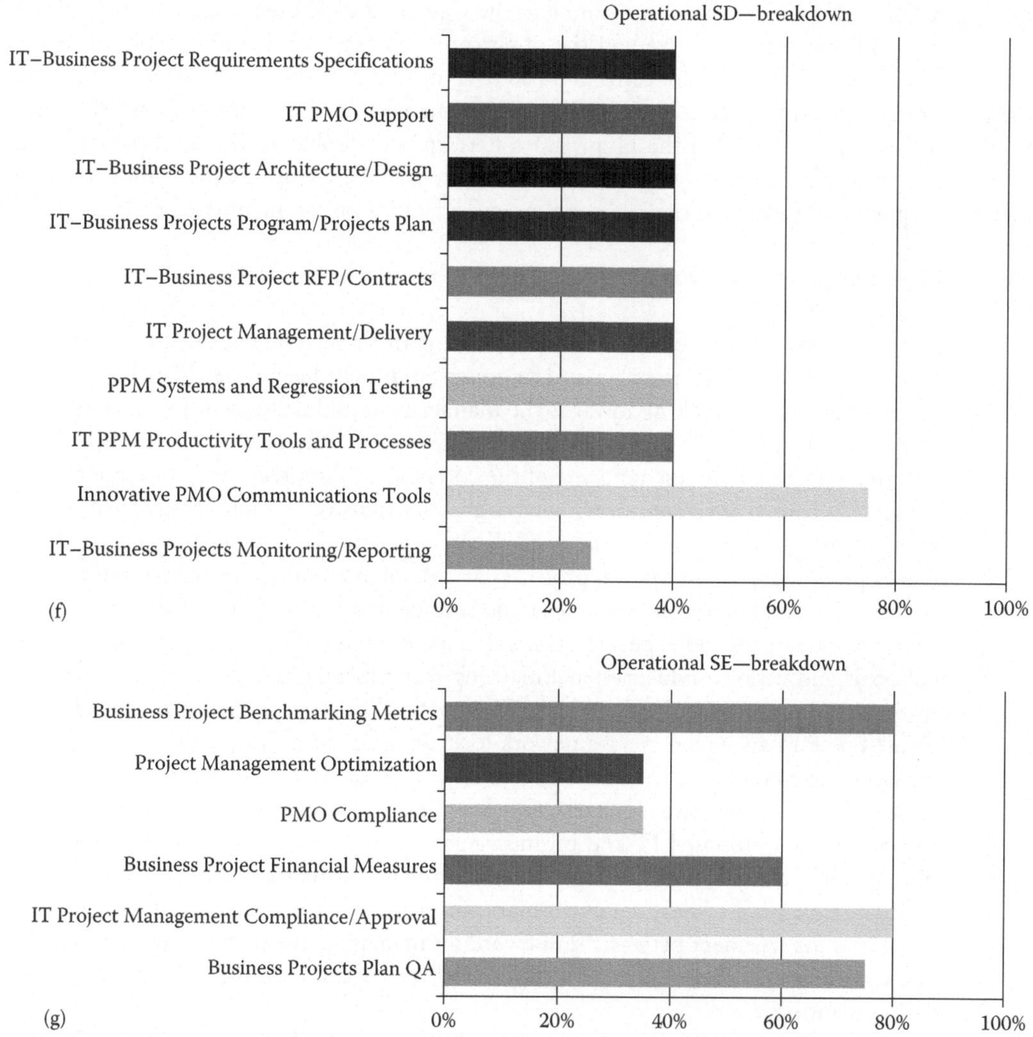

Figure 1.5 (*Continued*) (a–g) Performance measurement dashboard-PPM.

measures, specified in the PMS. These interpretations are the results of trend analysis and performance analytics that form the basis for evidence-decision making using predictive analytics.

1.7 Real-World Problem Scenario: Measuring IT Delivery Services

When a problem comes along, study it until you are completely knowledgeable. Then find that weak spot, break the problem apart, and the rest will be easy.

Norman Vincent Peale

During my 35 years in information technology in Canada and United States, in the private, public, and academic sectors, I have had the opportunity to experience similar types of performance management issues and concerns at various companies. In this case, executive management is mostly concerned with understanding how to manage, measure, and improve the entire IT delivery services, rather than the IT program performance problems discussed previously in Section 1.6. The performance management problems discussed here require a much more comprehensive integrated solution than the IT program performance solution mentioned earlier.

An Executive Manager (business and IT) from a large organization mentioned:

> We are in urgent need to establish an integrated performance management plan to measure the results against the plan and to understand the value we are obtaining for the investments we are making towards the management and delivery of IT services. How to quantify and verify investments results? Executive management made a decision to undergo a massive restructuring of the company's IT strategic and operational processes. We contracted a consulting company with extensive IT industry experience to re-engineering our current business and IT processes, perform a gap analysis, recommend proposed business and IT processes and develop an integrated performance plan. This integrated performance plan should include new business and IT processes, performance measures and expected results. It should align with strategic and operational goals and various industry benchmarking recommendations to determine the value we are obtaining for the delivery of IT services. We were planning to use this integrated performance plan as a framework for managing, measuring and delivering IT services and to optimize the utilization of IT resources. This consulting company interviewed various executive managers, and provided comprehensive documentations of the current and proposed IT and business related processes, which were approved in principle by executive management. However, the performance management plan included complex and misleading performance measures. The expectation to use this performance management plan as a framework for managing, measuring and delivering IT services and to optimize the utilization of IT resources was quite unsatisfactory and disappointing.
>
> Senior business and IT managers responsible for the deployment of the newly established processes (IT and business processes) viewed this re-engineering and performance management solution as theoretical and impractical. They decided on another approach- to deliver another reengineering and performance management plan, using in-house staff and a local consulting firm. This local consulting firm, with business process re-engineering expert knowledge, was contracted to deliver a performance management solution with support from the client's business groups. The end result was another set of voluminous documentation of the current and future business processes, in a new format and structure, with contents similar to those of the previous consulting company's recommendations. The contents of the deliverables produced were at such a detailed activity level that executive management was having great difficulties in understanding the concepts and applicability. A performance management plan was produced in the form of a performance schedule with duplicated and redundant business and IT performance measures and inconsistent tasks/activities. The performance plan emphasized the requirements for extensive business and IT resources, without any quantifiable economic justification.

> We, executive management, unsatisfied with the results produced so far, decided to hire an "expert" IT performance management consulting firm to establish yet another integrated performance management plan. The scope of this contract was modified from the previous engagement and stated, "To optimize the utilization of business and IT resources and to improve the performance management communications reporting- internal and external to the delivery of IT services." We contracted a performance management firm with "expert" knowledge of business processes, performance management and IT processes. A new set of jargon was now introduced to include Six Sigma, COBIT, ITIL, PMBOK and CMMI performance management frameworks that compounded the existing integration, communications, accountability, and transformational change problems. The desperate search for the "silver-bullet" integrated solution has started again, with the hope that this IT performance management consulting company will magically deliver the solution to this performance management problem. The expectation was that this consulting company will re-use the documentation produced so far, and this time around, we hope to make huge progress.
>
> This IT performance management consulting firm, rightly so, suggested the use of well-defined set of industry standard frameworks. The end-result was a set of extensive performance management models that aligned with various industries standard frameworks resulting in their "self-proclaimed" unique performance measurement and improvement methodology. The performance plan to implement this unique methodology required additional consulting resources, regular daily non-productive status meetings, and more detailed disintegrated performance measures. The performance team, again overly excited about the new performance measurement and improvement methodology, adopted the consulting firm "fresh-start" approach with great respect and enthusiasm. The result was another set of similar strategic, operational, and performance management processes, re-packaged with the consulting company's logo. The consulting company's confidentiality and copyrights terms appeared on the title page of each document.

The problem scenario discussed in Section 1.5, seems to be repeating itself, but to a much larger extent. This company has already spent extensive amount of efforts devoted to documenting business processes, IT strategies, and performance management measures, metrics, and indicators, but cannot justify the value of such extensive documentation. They had performance plans and schedules with financial performance measures, metrics, and indicators that were activity based rather than outcomes based, which were gradually becoming unmanageable, meaningless, and misleading measures. Enormous amounts of documentation were produced which again looked impressive. It lacked integration and consistency, resulting in the demand for additional IT, business, and performance management resources. This company seems to be going through another sort of performance measurement explosion crisis, but now to a larger extent, with unclear roles and accountabilities. Business and IT performance measures were delivered and redelivered as different versions, with performance plans and schedules managed by several enthusiastic and reactive performance management teams. The familiar headless chicken environment seems to be the performance team mode of operations, with reoccurring requests for approval appearing on the desks of executive management, for additional business and IT performance specialists and managers.

Now, a frustrating message, similar to the concerns expressed in Section 1.5, came from an IT executive, having a performance management perspective:

> The original requirement for a consistent and integrated performance management plan to measure the results against the plan is still unresolved. Also, the need to understand the value we are obtaining for the investments we are making towards the management and delivery of IT services is still non-existent. The linkages to performance management, operational management and strategic management goals and strategies are still unclear. An unexpected additional legal contracting issue as a result of the consulting firm confidentiality and copyrights terms appearing on the title page of each document needs resolution. To add to the existing performance measurement complexities, the performance management plan contains an additional set of financial performance measurement activities. The performance contract is now way over the original budget and behind schedule, with performance measures for activities, financial and human resources effort being addressed with "Victorian-novel" style documentation. A polished report from the consulting firm recommended a solution to the problems, which required organizational and cultural changes. This change recommended the establishment of two separate performance management groups. One group to support strategic management functions and the next group to support IT operational management functions. This recommendation suggested the need for additional business and IT resources that escalated the performance program budget to a level that was difficult to justify to executive management.

The search for the "silver-bullet" solution continues, and this IT executive seems to be in more severe trouble, with valid excuses to executive management becoming nonexistent. The original performance questions relative to measuring IT delivery services of "How we are doing?" "Are we doing the right things?" "Are we getting the right results?" "Are we getting the value?" still remain unanswered with more uncertainties and complexities. "What should I do to quantify, verify, and report on the value of IT investments?" "How can I ensure accountability for results and managing for outcomes?" "What approach or technique should I apply?" These questions also still remain unsolved, but now with additional resources and excessive complex performance measures, as a result of this desperate search for that elusive integrated solution.

This IT executive finally realized that there is no "silver-bullet" integrated solution, so decided to approach this "performance measurement chaos," inconsistency, disintegration, and unaccountability problems with the same IT performance management-consulting firm, and search for a senior performance manager. This individual must have experience with strategic management, operational management and performance management integration skills. He/she must have expertise in strategic value integration—people, process, financials, and technology and transformational change—people, politics, process, and performance. I decided to search for an individual solution, after considering many risk factors. I believe that the risk impact in this case is small, and eventually hope to address these performance management challenges with this senior performance manager. This individual had attained extensive practical integration, transformational change, and performance measurement skills, in managing, measuring, and improving similar IT delivery services.

This problem scenario shows some of the major performance management challenges that often occur, similar to those discussed in Section 1.5:

- Committing to financial performance measures, whether or not strategic, operational, and performance measures can be effectively integrated with risks and quality objectives.
- Establishment of separate performance management groups for strategic management and operational management. Each group reporting on financial and nonfinancial measures

based on historical financial results rather than understanding how nonfinancial performance measures influence financial results, using predictive analytics.

- Performance management is usually aligned to financials and employee measures. What about operational efficiencies/effectiveness? What about customer end-user satisfaction? What about the integration with strategic direction?
- Strategic management is accountable for establishing the financial measures with little or no integration with the operational measures—internal processes, employees, and customers. Operational management is accountable for service delivery with little or no meaningful performance measures. Human resource managers get involved during the annual employees performance appraisals and accountants get involved during the annual budgeting process. Integration exists in some illusionary constructs at the start and end of the annual budgeting and employee performance appraisals processes. This approach may work well for those "self-serving and egoistic" managers who strive on subjective measures to satisfy their political agendas. In most cases, accountability for results is rarely demonstrated, which increased the need for a more integrated approach to enable effective strategic value integration and transformational change, using sound risk and quality management processes.
- Assignment of a performance manager who lacks integration, transformational change, and performance measurement skills.
- Addressing the communications issue with excessive performance management "status meetings," illusionary accountability, and secrecy style management.
- Meaningless, ambiguous, and misleading measures and metrics with no baseline for improvements or how to interpret performance results.
- Disregard for the root causes of performance management challenges—communications, integration, accountability, sustainability, and transformation change.
- Performance managers disregard for measurable responsibilities and accountabilities for the results, to show how the results of the performance team are aligned with the goals and strategic directives to maximize the value and return of IT investments.
- Performance measures, metrics, and indicators based on counting activities, inputs, and outputs, without regard for a PMS.
- Ineffective utilization of performance management tools such as scoreboard or dashboard, even by the "so-called" expert performance management consulting firm.
- Separation of strategic management, operational management, and performance management functions, with each group happily performing their individual responsibilities, without any overall direction or vision for integration—a recipe for chaos.
- Searching for that secret magical solution in a culture of subjective measures, hierarchical positional powers, and political benchmarking, without clear understanding of the root causes of the problems.
- Emphasis on human resources and financial performance management with little or no consideration for integration of strategic, operational, and performance management results.

The solutions discussed in Section 1.8 demonstrate the value of strategic management, operational management, and performance management integration to solve the root cause–performance problems, resulting from the lack of accountability, transformational change, communications, and integration of these major components. It is worth mentioning that similar type challenges were discovered during the management, measurement, and improvement of the major business–IT program and the management and measurement of IT delivery services. However, the integrated solution to measuring IT delivery services is much more complex than measuring a major business–IT program. This will require performance managers with excellent skills in strategic value integration, specialized transformational change management, and sound performance measurement—risk/quality—to ensure successful measurement and improvement for the delivery of IT services.

1.8 Real-World Solution Scenarios: Measuring IT Delivery Services

The "how" thinker gets problems solved effectively because he wastes no time with futile "ifs" but goes right to work on the creative "how."

Norman Vincent Peale

This section introduces the recommended integrated IT performance management solution presented in this book, to solve the problems discussed in Section 1.7—Real-World Problem Scenario—managing, **measuring**, and improving IT delivery services. This recommended solution is a compilation of my extensive performance management experiences incorporated into a single volume. Various successful scenarios and lessons learned from less successful scenarios were modified accordingly to reflect modern performance management principles and applicability.

The model-centric approach to managing, measuring, and improving IT delivery services introduced in this section, represents the foundation models, detailed in this book, as follows:

- Chapter 2—Integrated IT Performance Management Framework (IPMF-IT)
- Chapter 3—Strategic Management Model
- Chapter 4—Performance Management Model
- Chapter 5—Information Technology Operational Management Model
- Chapter 6—Integrated IT Service Delivery Life Cycle Performance Model
- Chapter 7—Aligning IPMF-IT with Industry-Related Performance Frameworks

Chapter 2—Integrated IT Performance Management Framework (IPMF-IT) introduces the integrated IT Performance Management Model and discusses the strategic management, performance management, and IT operational management components of this model. It provides the roles and accountabilities of the performance delivery manager during the management, measurement, improvement, and delivery of IT services.

Chapter 3—Strategic Management Model expands on the Strategic Management Model introduced in Chapter 2, discusses the components of the model, and provides purpose, roles and accountabilities, and results—outcomes/outputs, process flows, and performance measures, for each of the components.

Chapter 4—Performance Management Model expands on the Performance Management Model introduced in Chapter 2, discusses the components of the model, and provides purpose, roles and accountabilities, and results—outcomes/outputs, process flows, and performance measures, for each of the components.

Chapter 5—Information Technology Operational Model expands on the IT Operational Management Model introduced in Chapter 2, discusses the components of the model, and provides purpose, roles, and accountabilities, and results—outcomes/outputs, process flows, and performance measures, for each of the components.

Chapter 6—Integrated IT Service Delivery Life Cycle Performance Model expands on the IT Service Delivery Life Cycle Performance Model introduced in Chapter 2 and provides the Strategic Directives for the IT functional areas and the alignment or horizontal integration with Strategic Management, IT Operational Management and Performance Management, based on the IT Service Delivery Life Cycle stages.

Chapter 7—Aligning IPMF-IT results with Industry-Related Performance Frameworks—Six Sigma, PMI-PMBOK, COBIT, ITIL, and CMMI. A revealing chapter on "Aligning IPMF-IT outcomes with industry-related performance frameworks" is provided to show the integrative nature of these outputs/outcomes and the alignment with the Integrated IT Performance Management Framework presented in this book. This framework formed the basis to understanding the alignment or horizontal integration with industry-related performance frameworks, based on the IT Service Delivery Life Cycle Performance Model.

1.9 Gaining Acceptance for Performance Integration

Misunderstandings usually occur because of differences in thinking preferences

James P. Lewis

One of the major obstacles that performance managers often have to overcome is the lack of senior management support for modern integrated performance management practices using a results-driven performance measures and accountability framework. Applications of integrated performance management practices that require a culture of accountability for results can be a challenging experience. This can be compounded when senior management fails to recognize the need for, or even worst agrees in principle to performance management integration, but questions the need for integrating financial, human resources, customer, and operational measures. The result is the classical performance managers' balancing act of standing up for what they believe is correct and risk losing their position or hesitantly supporting senior management decision. The decision is usually to maintain the "status quo" and continue with the nonintegrated, inconsistent, and command and control approach to sound impressive, increase politically attractiveness with wrong, meaningless, and misleading performance measures.

The integrated IT performance management framework discussed in this book can only be effective when properly applied with adequate support from senior management. The objective of this section is to present some guiding principles to assist performance managers in obtaining management support for execution of this integrated IT performance management framework.

Some senior business and IT management professionals resist performance integration culture and practices—accountability for results. These methods require managing for outcomes that demands consistency, standardization, and transparency, which may block the progress, ambition, and ego of individual "empire builders" who usually strive on gaining power through "single-view" management.

Often the arguments against performance management integration, as defined in this book, by senior business and IT management professionals are formulated from a number of myths, flawed assumptions, and twisted interpretations that are challenged throughout this book.

1. *Myth*: These methods are all *theoretical*; in this company things are done differently. Models, Results-Based Management (RBM) processes, and outcomes are theoretical, and best suited for the academic environment.
   Reality: Any effective method requires theory or principle, as the foundation for execution; otherwise, chaos will result. Models are abstractions of reality. Outcomes measure results.
2. *Myth*: Results-driven integrated performance management framework is NOT different than our current performance management processes. The solution is executive management commitment NOT enhanced performance management processes.
   Reality: I agree executive management commitment is necessary. However, no executive management will commit to any process that does not demonstrate explicit linkage and value to strategic, business and IT management processes. Even if commitment is gained, it has the famous quote: "Agreement in Principle." Current performance management processes, especially those for human resources and finance are activity-based (effort and account), historical results and do not align to company's goals and strategic directives. Results-driven performance measures are outcomes-based, predictive analytical results aligned to company's goals and strategic directive that enable accountability for results. Many human resource measurement cultures are controlled-based and usually result in negative judgmental measurement and accountability during performance reviews.
3. *Myth*: Senior IT Managers should NOT be Performance Managers.
   Reality: Some senior IT and business managers firmly believe that "Managing by Walking Around" is an effective approach to aligning execution with strategy. These managers normally spend 70% of their efforts on relationship management and 15%–30% on administrative efforts. They do not have time to measure results, so delegate this performance management accountability to administrative staff. The widely published quotation by Peter Drucker, "What gets measured gets managed," seems to be foreign concepts to these "walk-around" IT managers. The three key skill requirements for modern performance management are strategic value integration, transformational change, and performance measurement. It is the responsibility of senior managers to apply the integration, transformational change, and performance measurement skills necessary to manage, measure, and deliver IT services. This is one of the heresies of "old-style" IT management and that have traditionally opened the gates for people with little or no information technology training or knowledge to enter the IT field as senior managers. In my view, one of the root causes of the performance problems that companies are ignoring or failing to address is the qualifications of the "skilled" senior IT manager, probably because of political pressures from executive management with conflicting views on whom they perceived as "skilled" senior IT management resources.
   Interesting to note, some senior IT managers who have limited performance management knowledge, skills, and qualifications, based on COBIT Performance Management standards, frequently manage the delivery of IT services, without any consideration for performance measurement, strategic value integration, or transformational change. They normally express the view that human resources, finance, or business management specialists should

be accountable for measuring performance results. In my view, we have now promoted a human resource, finance, or business manager to the position of senior IT manager and have transformed the senior IT manager role to that of relationship manager "managing by walking around."

4. *Myth*: Performance management is a year-end review of the work that employees undertake, and sometimes too formalized, and strive on reward and punishment for management control in order to satisfy ego, status, and political behaviors for positional power.
   Reality: This is a true statement of traditional hierarchical human resources performance management. Performance measurement, as defined in this book is an integrated representation of employee—human resources, financial, customer, and operational measures. Traditional HR performance systems focus on accountability for effort that normally result in redundant and duplicated efforts rather than accountability for results to optimize the utilization people resources. A typical example of the subjective human resource performance measures to satisfy ego, status, and political agendas. Traditional HR performance management is usually viewed as reward for few, punishment for innovative excellence, and search for the guilty, with a focus toward sound impressive and increasing political or "hidden" agendas. Measurement should be used for the purpose of improvement rather than to make judgments or place blame.
5. *Myth*: Accountability for results is vague and political.
   Reality: This statement can be true in some areas where accountability for activities, tasks, and efforts are the preferred mode of operations, especially in the traditional human resource and finance areas. In this mode of operations, people are perceived as looking busy but may be accomplishing meaningless or invaluable results. In my view, a culture of meaningless and misleading accountability seems to be the normal mode of operations. The essence of accountability is measured responsibility where we hold people accountable for results and outcomes rather than being accountable for effort and activity utilization. COBIT and ITIL frameworks use accountability frameworks for assigning decision-making rights and improving transparency and organizational excellence. The *results-driven* performance measures and accountability framework discussed in this book provides some practical solutions to addressing this concern.
6. *Myth*: We have always managed and delivered IT projects and services without these integrated performance management framework and they have worked, so why should we use this framework now?
   Reality: The challenge here is to determine the level of success that these IT project and services have accomplished to the business and IT staff, using benchmarking or satisfaction surveys, and then demonstrate that the integrated approach to performance management is not a luxury but a necessary and essential element for organizational improvement and excellence.
7. *Myth*: Performance Management (PM) is a Human Resource responsibility.
   Reality: Interesting enough, PM is sometimes confused with HR and personal systems that are accustomed to measurement's negative side. Traditional PM is viewed as punishment and search for the guilty, and reward for few. My normal response is this statement: "The cause of most performance management problems is the inability of professionals to effectively measure and interpret results that align with strategic outcomes to improve business success and increase service excellence." The applications of performance management principles, as described in KPI Institute's publications, COBIT, Six Sigma, ITIL, and PMI-PMBOK

frameworks, are necessary to managing services and projects and in optimizing the utilization of resources to provide value and organizational success to both the business and IT environments.

8. *Myth*: These integrated IT performance management frameworks sound impressive, but our organization is not ready for such a transformation change, probably in the future.
   Reality: A typical case of a resistance to change to maintain the "status quo" and to use performance management for control purposes. The application of effective performance management processes, results, and outcomes should NOT facilitate control purposes—normally increase resistant to change, but rather should facilitate learning and improvement purposes.
9. *Myth*: None of our managers (IT and business) is familiar with these integrated frameworks. It will take too much time, effort, and costs to retrain our managers.
   Reality: This can be a valid statement, if the integrated performance management approach represents a major change in direction and culture. The best response is to determine the maturity level of performance management at the company and assess the ease of applying these new integrated methods. However, integration is one of the key requirements for modern performance management, and as such is essential for linkage with IT strategic and operating environments.
10. *Myth*: Performance management integration is only necessary for organizations with a formal performance management organizational structure.
    Reality: Nothing can be more far from the truth. In most organizations, performance management programs—people and processes—are normally integrated within the existing organizational structure and do not require any formal performance management organizational structure. However, some organizations may implement a program-based performance management organization using a matrix structure. The objective of performance integration is to ensure that performance management; however, success is measured; is a viable business investment; and provides economic, political, social, and technological value by integrating strategic and IT operational management and aligning strategy with execution for evidence-based decision making and organizational excellence. Performance management integration whether formal or informal should fit these criteria, if they do not, then we have just spent time, effort, and costs on wasted and meaningless performance measures. The application of new and effective performance management processes should be results and outcomes based that focuses on accountability for results. The foundation principles of modern performance management principles based on the essential skill requirements of strategic value integration, transformational change, and performance measurement are necessary to ensure that performance measures fully support the strategic outcomes and goals of the company.

It is important to note that these myths have persuasively swayed some professionals and senior managers whose genuine goals to strengthen the quality, consistency, integration, accountability, and applicability of performance management integration principles seem to have caused them to take an opposing viewpoint. These individuals, in particular, need examples and scenarios about the what, why, when, who, and how of integrated IT performance management, about alternatives, and about the consequences of disintegrated performance management. The integrated IT performance management framework discussed in this book provides some practical examples and scenarios to addressing these individuals concern.

1.10 Summary

A major cause of most IT performance management problems is the inability of certain IT executives/managers and senior managers to apply and interpret basic performance results during management, measurement, and delivery of IT services. Decisions are made based on emotions rather than objectivity or evidence-based decision making, because of the lack of adequate performance management knowledge and training. Senior managers, rightly so, place emphasis on financial and employee—human resource measures but lack the fundamental performance management knowledge and training to integrate operational and customers measures, results, and outcomes. The end result is disintegration, poor communications, negative accountability, and transparency and ineffective transformational change with meaningless and misleading goals because of the lack of clear alignment to the organization's strategic outcomes and goals.

Strategy is poorly executed because managers and employees do not know what the strategy means for their jobs. IT Operational performance is inappropriately managed because management decisions are based on educated guesses and managers do not know how successful their operations, people (employees and customers), and projects are performing.

To add to these set of problems and challenges, some senior managers manage the delivery of IT projects and services by demanding excessive daily performance meetings and status reporting with key performance team members supported by an executive administrative assistant. Too much emphasis is placed on reporting of efforts and financials, while ignoring the most important performance management success factors—operational and customer measures—the basic information needed to determine the effort and financial performance results. In my view, we have just promoted a glorified secretary to the position of senior performance manager to manipulate, produce, and report on financial and effort measures using various disintegrated Microsoft excel and word documents—no wonder there are so many blunders and failures in delivering meaningful performance measures and results.

The solution introduced in this chapter highlights some problems and challenges relative to performance management knowledge, skills, and experiences that surround the IT industry performance managers with specialized human resource management, financial analysts, or "glorified-secretarial" expertise, without any formal industry-recognized performance management qualifications. A recommended solution is presented in Figure 1.6, with further details included in the "Roles and Accountabilities" section of each chapter. I certainly hope that these suggested performance management skills guidelines, based on the problems discussed, will be viewed by senior managers at performance management consulting firms as informative and insightful for performance management excellence. In my view, the prerequisite to effective and efficient application of modern performance management principles demands professional qualifications in accordance with KPI Institute, COBIT, Six Sigma, PMBOK, ITIL, or similar professional guidelines. The further we deviate from this goal, the more difficult it will be to close the gap between performance management excellence and performance management inconsistency, to increase progression to SEI Capability Maturity Model (CMMI), and to improve IT development process, controls, and outcomes for performance management.

Please do not get me wrong. Skills, such as financial management and human resource management, are necessary and essential to implementing performance management key measures for effort and financial results. However, these skills cannot be effectively applied without clear, complete, and consistent understanding of the operational and customer measures and desired results and outcomes from sound IT Performance management training, education, and experiences. Executive management keeps searching for the "silver-bullet" solution to performance

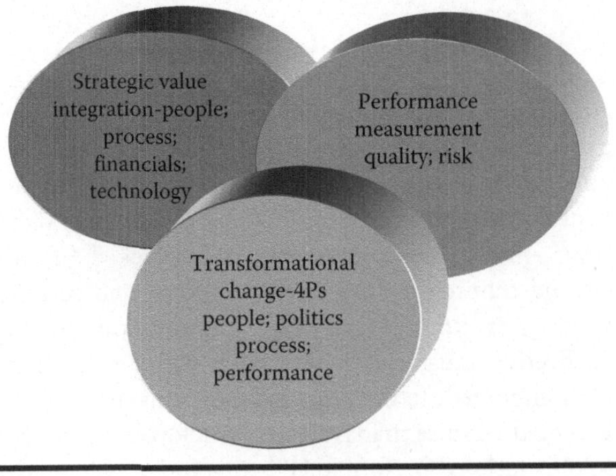

Figure 1.6 Modern IT performance management skills framework—conceptual view.

management, and the sooner they realize that there is no "silver-bullet" solution, the outcomes will be less disappointments and frustrations. Their efforts toward establishing an efficient and effective performance management environment in their elusive search for organizational improvement and excellence to optimize the utilization of IT resources, will be more realistic and practical.

I believe that in most cases, a substantial amount of IT budget is wasted on inefficient utilization, because of the dynamically advancing IT environment, complexity, and lack of understanding of IT performance measures, results, and value. In a majority of cases, the success of IT services is based on the results of financial measures—managing to budget, revenues, profits, and financial return on investments, with little or no consideration to measuring success based on eliminating operating efficiencies. My extensive experiences in addition to performance statistics from IT industry research firms, some of which is mentioned in my book, validate this belief. Why do you think there had been a recent surge in demand for benchmarking the results of IT delivery services? Investments whether IT or any other company's asset must be managed and measured based on sound performance measures and results; otherwise, illusions of efficiencies, multiplier effects of inefficiencies, continuous resource, and budget increases will be the normal mode of operations, with no accountability for "value for money." Looking busy by measuring level of effort is not the same as producing results measured by outcomes and outputs.

We need to maximize the value and return of IT investments by optimizing the utilization of IT resources—people, process, financial, and technology resources, using employee—human resources, customer, financial, and operational performance measures, as defined in this "*Integrated IT Performance Management Framework*," discussed in this book. It provides a results-driven solution that is integrated, model-driven, and outcomes-based, with strategic directives, accountabilities, outcomes, outputs, process flows, and performance measure for strategic, IT operational, and performance management, applied within the context of the entire IT service delivery life cycle.

In order to effectively implement this results-driven framework to address the integration, accountability, communications, and transformation change performance problems require managers with the right performance management, skills, training, qualifications, and experiences. The KPI Institute research in their research publications "Performance Management in 2013" mentioned that Strategic Value Integration, Transformation Change, and Performance Measurement-Quality and Risk are three major skills that will be required of managers to support modern performance management requirements. COBIT5—Control Objectives for Information and related Technology from ISACA–IT Governance Institute in their business framework shares similar skill levels for the governance and management of enterprise IT processes. Corporate performance management concepts introduced by recent Gartner research share similar skill level requirements to integrated performance management. If these observations, which I fully endorse, reflect modern performance management solution to our existing problems, industries, universities, and performance management professional institutes may have some real challenges ahead of them.

The contents of this book provide an integrated IT performance management framework that consists of results—outcomes and outputs, process models, and performance measures. It describes the purpose, strategic directives, accountabilities, outcomes—outputs, process flows, and performance measures for strategic management, IT operational management, and performance management integration. The performance measurement areas use a modified version of Kaplan and Norton's strategic measures—employee, customer, operational, and financial measures.

The overall goal is to present the components of this framework and show how the models are implemented by people having strategic value integration—people, process, financials, and technology; transformational change—people, politics, process, and performance; and performance measurement—quality and risk management skills, to solve the most common and difficult root cause of performance management problems—integration, communications, accountability, and transformational change internal and external to organizational excellence. Figure1.6 is a further elaboration of The KPI Institute and COBIT Governance Framework revealing insights to the skill requirements that are necessary and essential for modern performance management implementation.

1.11 Endnotes: Key Performance Management Terms

[1]*Results-Driven*: An approach to managing and delivering the desired result by measuring success in achieving outcomes and related outputs.

[2]*Model-Centric*: An approach to implementing this Integrated IT Performance Management Framework-IPMF-IT, using a conceptual and detailed framework consisting of strategic, IT operational, and performance management models, integrated within the management, measurement, and delivery of an IT service delivery life cycle model.

[3]*Software Engineering Institute (SEI): SEI Capability Maturity Model (CMMI) Levels*:

Levels	*CMMI Maturity Level Characteristics*
5—Optimized (Excellence)	Process improvements to performance management practices. Build a trusting relationship with business partners, suppliers, and customers.
4—Predictable	Process measured and controlled. Performance management domain integration requires discipline by the complete organization.
3—Standardized	Process characterized for the organization and is often reactive. Projects take their processes from organization's standards. Success depends on performance management competencies.
2—Managed	Process characterized for projects and is often reactive. Success depends on characteristics of management.
1—Initial (Inconsistency)	Process is poorly controlled, reactive, informal, unpredictable, and ad hoc. Success depends on characteristics of employees.

[4]*Integrated, results-driven, outcomes-based, model-centric*: An integrated model-centric approach to performance management by measuring outcomes and results for employee, customer, operational, and financial measures, rather than the traditional activity-oriented approach of measuring effort, financials, and activities, by counting inputs and outputs.

[5]*Performance Management Structure*: Based on the Balanced Scorecard concepts by Kaplan and Norton: "A results-oriented group of performance measures that aligns formulated goals and strategic directives into outcomes, outputs, performance measures and results. Each descending level represents an increasing detailed definition of the performance results."

[6]*CIO, CFO, CPO, and CHRO*: Executive Management involved in strategic decision making for performance management: Chief Information Officer—CIO; Chief Financial Officer—CFO; Chief Performance Officer—CPO; Chief Human Resource—CHRO.

[7]*Deming's "PDCA" Cycle*: Plan-Do-Check-Acts is an iterative four-step method used in business for the control and continuous improvement of processes and products.

[8]*Kaplan and Norton*: Originators of the most widely adopted performance management framework reported in the annual survey of management tools undertaken by Bain & Company.

1.12 Questions to Think About: Performance Perspectives

1. Think about how your organization measures performance. How your organization views integration? How would you align performance management processes with strategic management and IT operational management processes?
2. Think about how your organization deals with IT performance management problems. How do emotional, cultural, and political behaviors affect objectivity? Why has performance management failed? How is success or failure aligned with business value? How is strategic value aligned with business and IT key performance indicators?
3. Think about how your organization views standardization and consistency. How would you integrate human resources KPI with strategic and IT operational management KPI? What are your major performance management problems and to what extent does the integration issues cause these problems?
4. Think about how your performance management program is sponsored. What are the levels of involvement and commitment from business, IT operational, and performance management executives? How is the formal or informal structure communicated? How do you know whether or not you still have executive management support?
5. Think about how you manage performance expectations. What are your expectations of IT consulting firms? How do you manage success-magical or measurement? How do you know that your performance expectations are being met?
6. Think about how you measure, interpret, and communicate performance results. How do you structure performance organization, roles and accountabilities, PMS, and performance plan? How do you measure people, process, outcomes, outputs, and risk elements? How do you deal with integration of these elements?
7. Think about how you manage, measure, and deliver Major IT program. How do you manage and measure results—outcomes and outputs? How do you manage conflicting expectations and priorities? How do you deal with multiple consulting firms? How do you deal with

communications, integration, accountability, transparency, sustainability, transformational change issues, and IT critical success factors?

8. Think about how you manage, measure, and deliver IT services? How do you structure a performance management organization, roles and accountabilities, PMS, and measurement areas? How do you measure employee, financial, operational, and customer results? How do you deal with integration of these elements?
9. Think about how your organization addresses integration. What approach would you use to gain acceptance for performance integration? What are your skills requirements for an IT performance manager in measuring a major business–IT project? What are your skills requirements for an IT performance manager in measuring the success of the entire IT delivery services? What are the major differences?

1.13 Chapter Testing Questions

1. Performance Management Structure (PMS) consists of four measures. Three of them are employee, customer, and financials. What is the third measure?
   a. Internal Processes
   b. Operational
   c. Service Delivery
2. Integrated IT Performance Management is the process of integrating the components of strategic management, IT operational management, and performance management during the management, measurement, and delivery of IT services with the objective to optimize the utilization of IT resources. Three of these components are people, process, and financials. What is the third measure?
   a. Equipment
   b. Hardware
   c. Technology
3. Which of the following skills will NOT likely trigger a performance improvement effort?
   a. Change Management
   b. Strategic Value Integration
   c. Performance manager
4. What is the fourth level of the SEI Capability Maturity Model (CMMI)?
   a. Proactive
   b. Optimized
   c. Predictable
5. Ken is assembling a team to measure a major business–IT program. He needed someone to track performance measures, metrics, and indicators. Who do you think is missing?
   a. Technical specialist
   b. Business specialist
   c. Performance specialist
6. You are working on a performance improvement project and want to focus on operational measures to determine efficiencies of internal process. Which measure should you focus on?
   a. Operational efficiencies
   b. Financial
   c. Employee

7. What are the major skills of modern IT performance management?
   a. Integration, quality management, and risk management
   b. Transformation change, strategic integration, and performance measurement
   c. Quality Management, performance management, and risk management
8. Which one of the following common problems managers MUST address to resolve performance problems relative to accountability for results?
   a. Poor change management
   b. Ineffective integration with outcomes
   c. Lack of alignment to effort measures
9. A results-driven performance management culture should focus on
   a. Outcomes, output, and data sources
   b. Results, activities, and input
   c. Effort, financial, and activities

Recommended Readings

Performance Management

Aguinis, H., *Performance Management*. New York: Pearson Education, 2012.

Bainey, K.R., *Integrated IT Project Management: A Model-Centric Approach*. New York: Artech House, 2004.

Batshalom, B., *GreenSource ,The magazine of Sustainable Design*. Boston, MA: Sustainable Performance Institute, 2011.

Corkins, G., *Performance Management, Integrating Strategy, Execution, Methodologies, Risk, and Analytics*. Hoboken, NJ: John Wiley & Sons Inc., 2009.

Demartini, C., *Performance Management Systems: Design, Diagnosis and Use*. Berlin, Germany: Springer, 2013.

Howatt, W., *9 Elements of Integrated Performance Management Elements*. McMillian Publishers India Ltd., Mumbai, India, 2010.

Kaplan, R.S. and Norton, D.P., *The Balanced Scorecard: Translating Strategy into Action*. Boston, MA: Harvard Business School Publishing, 1996.

The KPI Institute, *The KPI Compendium: 20,000 Key Performance Indicators used in Practice*. Melbourne, Victoria, Australia: KPI Institute, 2013.

Marshall, P.W., *Improving Business Processes: Expert Solutions to Everyday Challenges*. Boston, MA: Harvard Business School Publishing, 2010.

Parmenter, D., *Key Performance Indicators, Developing Implementing, and Using Winning KPIs*. John Wiley & Sons Inc., Hoboken, New Jersey, 2010.

Spitzer, D.R., *Transforming Performance Measurement, Rethinking the Way We Measure and Drive Organizational Success*. New York: AMACOM, 2007.

Chapter 2

Integrated IT Performance Management Framework

2.1 Introduction

> Every theory is a self-fulfilling prophecy that orders experience into the framework it provides.
>
> **Ruth Hubbard**

Performance management for the measurement, management, delivery, and improvement of information technology (IT) services is a discipline that influences every aspect of a company's business. *Performance management programs*[1] that, no matter how successfully viewed, do not measure the effectiveness of management using financial, employee, customer, and operational measures to *improve* organizational excellence are not a valued investment of the company's resources. Strategic management, performance management, and IT operational management must all work together, with a consistent understanding of performance management accountabilities, outcomes, outputs, process flows, and performance measures, to successfully improve organizational performance. The components of strategic management, IT operational management, and performance management require clearly defined accountabilities using *results-driven* performance measures and accountability framework to effectively measure, manage, deliver, and improve IT services, including the quality and quantity of management. Strategic, operational, or performance management staffs that fail to fulfill their accountabilities will negatively impact the results of the performance management program.

The objectives of this chapter are to introduce the *integrated IT performance management framework* (*IPMF-IT*)[2] model, discuss the components of the conceptual and detailed models shown in Figures 2.1 and 2.2, respectively, and provide the accountabilities of the *performance delivery manager*,[3] during the measurement, management, and delivery of IT services. Further details on each of the three components are provided in succeeding chapters of this book.

Since both strategic and IT operational management integrations are vital to the success of IT performance management, accountabilities are defined within the context of the IPMF-IT. The conceptual framework is provided next.

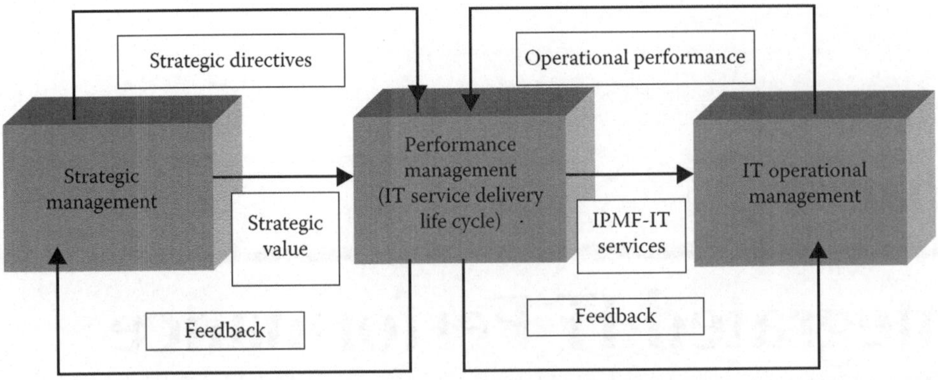

Figure 2.1 Integrated IT performance management framework (IPMF-IT) conceptual model.

Figure 2.1 is a representation of the integrated performance management model that shows a conceptual view and the linkages with strategic management, performance management, and IT operational management. Figure 2.2 is a more detailed representation of the IPMF-IT model, which shows the components of strategic management, performance management, and IT operational management, with high-level linkages. The succeeding chapters of this book provide further details on each of the three major components, with Chapter 6 focusing on the horizontal integration of these components, using the *IT service delivery life cycle performance model*[4] shown in Figure 2.2. Chapter 7 discusses the integration of IPMF-IT framework with industry performance management frameworks.

2.2 Performance Management Organizational Structure

This organizational structure does *not* imply a new performance management structure (PMS). The intent is to leverage the performance responsibilities of the existing structure to support accountability for results and to resolve performance management challenges.

2.3 Performance Organizational Structure: Rationale

During my extensive IT career experiences, I had the opportunity to evaluate, recommend, and implement performance management organizational structures at many large corporations having varying performance management maturity levels, from level 1 (Inconsistency) to level 5 (Excellence), in accordance with CMMI® performance management maturity levels. The recommendation in Figure 2.3 is based on the overwhelming need for an organizational structure to assist with the implementation of an integrated strategic management, performance management, and IT operational management solution that can be consistently applied across corporations. The goal was to optimize resource utilization and to ensure business and IT services deliver meaningful results and improve organizational performance, including the quality and quantity of management. Please note that this organizational structure does *not* imply a new PMS. The intent is to utilize the existing *resources*,[5] identify the performance accountabilities within the existing structure to ensure accountability for results—*results-based management (RBM)*,[6] improve the

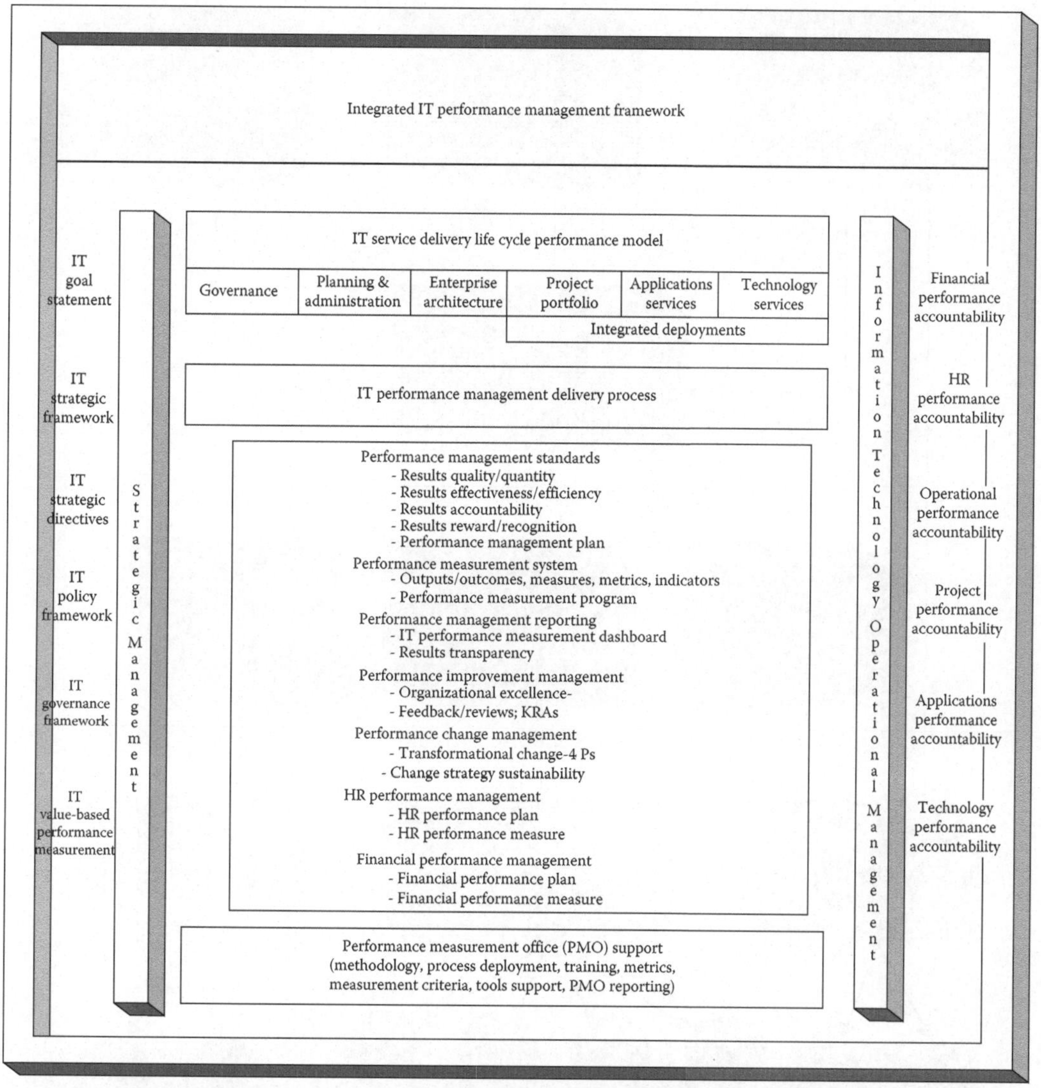

Figure 2.2 Integrated IT performance management framework (IPMF-IT) component model.

quality and quantity of management, and resolve performance management challenges during the management and delivery of IT services.

It is hoped that this recommendation will provide a more objective organizational structure, rather than some of the traditional emotional "politics-based" structures, prejudiced with certain executive management, and/or consulting company's personal interests. One of the main root causes of performance management organizational failures is the partial and prejudiced organizational structure developed by certain executive management and/or consulting company's staff with self-interest that is politically motivated. Forcing alignment of an existing organizational structure to new performance management processes or forcing alignment of existing performance management processes to new organizational structures created for political reasons, without clear accountabilities is a recipe for massive confusion and chaos. In order to address

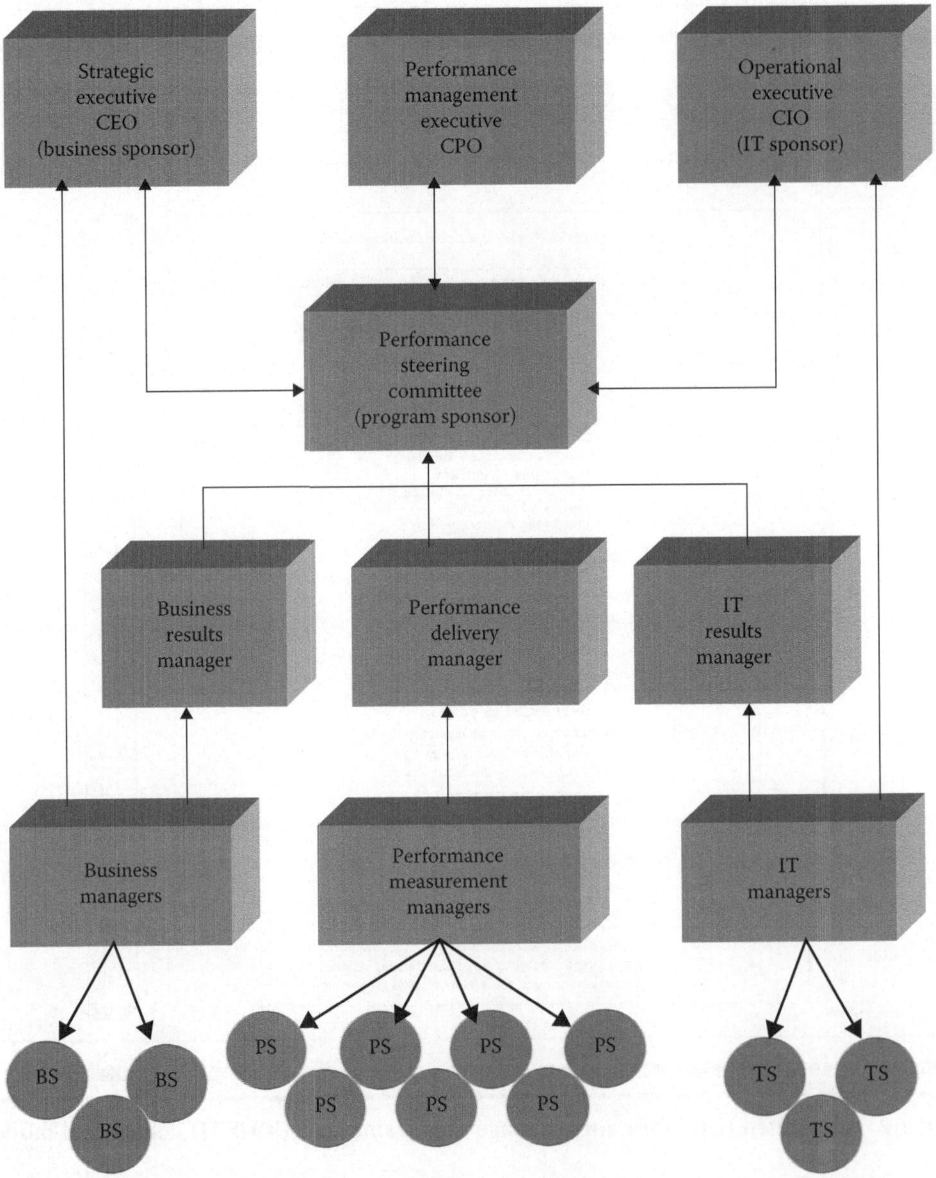

Figure 2.3 Performance management framework (IPMF-IT) organizational structure.

these organizational structural issues at a large corporation, certain senior executives endorsed the recommendation for the creation of a performance management executive position—*chief performance officer* (*CPO*).[7] This performance management executive who had the proper skills, knowledge, experiences, and professional qualifications was highly effective in implementing an integrated performance management organization structure, similar to Figure 2.3, to support the management, measurement, and delivery of IT services, based on a results-driven performance management framework. Performance management executives with the right skills, knowledge, experiences, and professional qualifications can provide the necessary integrated solution, especially to those corporations that have attained a reasonably mature cultural climate with results-driven performance management.

The integrated nature of this recommended solution is based on effective execution of accountability and evidence-based decision making by executive managers, organizational performance managers, and individual performance managers. A high-level discussion on the skills, knowledge, and qualifications of the performance management team is presented. It contains my "real-world" experiences with certain major issues, challenges, problems, and recommended solutions that may interest those involved in performance management practices.

- The role of a performance management executive (CPO)—project position was introduced, in addition to the existing strategic business executives—CEO, and the IT executive—CIO positions, to ensure that the corporate performance management results (outcomes and outputs) are effectively communicated, integrated, and consistently applied by both the business and IT staff. This CPO role, if executed, by the right person, will resolve most of the communications, integration, accountability, sustainability, and change management issues—internal and external to IT strategic services, at executive management level. This individual must demonstrate general strategic integration knowledge; specialized people, process, financials, and technology performance measurement knowledge and skills; and excellent understanding of transformational change—people, process, performance, and politics. The specialized integration skills must meet the criteria of having professional performance management expertise to ensure effective integration of performance management results with strategic directives and operational execution.

2.3.1 Real-World Observations: Performance Management Executive

It is now time to share some of my real-world observations at a certain company. This company filled this performance management executive position on many occasions with individuals having the traditional "human resource" (HR)-type performance management skills, "accounting"—type performance management skills, and "policy specialist"—type performance management skills. It is interesting to note that neither of these individuals created any impact to justify the need for a formal or informal performance management program, and as a result, the performance management program was abandoned, after some years of slow but moderately successful progress. The cause of this failure was attributed to the lack of effective performance management measures, metrics, and indicators. Senior-level executives from this company hired a management consulting firm to assess and recommend a solution to resolve this performance management issue. This consulting firm engaged various financial management consultants who had limited practical expertise in how performance management, strategic and operational management can be integrated to provide organizational excellence. These financial management consultants carefully examined this performance management deficiency problem and concluded that the existing performance management measures were ineffective, and recommended a solution based on a new set of financial performance measures, metrics, and indicators, which were more historical based rather than futuristic. The new solution failed to demonstrate how the financial measures can be used to deliver measurable results—output and outcome, to support organizational excellence. History repeated itself and executives were no further ahead in understanding how results-based budgeting can be used to improve organizational performance. In my view, the ability of executives involved in performance management programs to make evidence-based decision, affect change, and provide wisdom and vision about PMS and processes needed major improvement.

This is a typical case of the lack of understanding at the executive level on the importance for integration, accountability, sustainability, and transformational change to implementing performance management measures and results. Senior executives should understand the impact of integration, accountability, and transformational change to performance management, in order to ask the right questions and to prevent the proliferation of communications, integration, accountability, and transformational change problems internal and external to achieving organizational excellence—improving the quality and quantity of IT management.

> The productivity and competitive problems the IT industry face, result from ineffective top management, petrified in place, unwilling to accept change, and failing to provide wisdom and vision.
>
> **Harvard Business Review**

The role of the *performance steering committee (project position)*[8] consists of the following:

- Executive management (strategic executive sponsor—CEO, with support from CFO—Chief Financial Officer and CHRO—Chief Human Resource Officer, IT operational executive sponsor—CIO and performance management executive champion—CPO)
- Performance program management (business results manager, performance delivery manager, IT results manager [organizational level])
- Performance management (performance specialists from business and IT areas [individual level])

2.3.2 Real-World Observations: Performance Management Steering Committee

It's now time to share some real-world situations to emphasize the need for consistency, integration, sustainability, and accountability to implementing a results-driven performance management program. Large corporations established a performance management steering committee, consisting of executive managers, performance program managers, and performance managers whose major objective was to report and communicate on the results of the performance management program, to all members of this committee, at the annual year-end reviews. Each of the performance measurement managers produced individual measures, metrics, and indicators, in different formats, for the business process that he/she was responsible for streamlining, and submitted them to the performance delivery manager, at the annual year-end reviews. The performance delivery manager, accountable to executive management, summarized and consolidated the inconsistent and sometimes meaningless and misleading performance measures and results provided by each of the performance measurement managers. After various frustrating dialogues with the individual performance managers, this performance delivery manager managed to produce the performance measures and results, which were delivered to the performance management steering committee, business and IT executive stakeholders, at regularly planned annual year-end review status meetings.

During each of the performance steering committee meetings, the participants spent most of their time trying to explain inconsistencies, rather than reporting on the performance measures and results to improve communications—interpretation of results, accountability and integration—internal and external to organizational business processes. It's unbelievable to mention that at the end of each meeting, there were praises for everyone's efforts, with little consideration given to the administrative assistant who devoted her time nervously, making conflicting and sometimes inconsistent corrections to the performance measures and results, as suggested by the participants and/or the performance steering committee chairman. This is the result of situations that lacked consistent and integrated processes—a necessity for effective performance management reporting.

This is again a typical case of performance management reporting inconsistency at the executive and senior management level, which senior management should attempt to understand and avoid and to prevent the proliferation of communication problems and performance management complexities during performance management reporting. The need for a consistent, complete, and *integrated performance management information system* (*PMIS*),[9] to enable and support business intelligence, which is accepted and endorsed by many performance management software vendors, is essential for evidence-based analytical reporting.

The role of *performance delivery management (project positions)*[10] consists of the following:

- Business results manager—To oversee the management, measurement, and delivery of the performance program, from the perspectives of business results or outcomes.
- Performance delivery manager—To oversee management, measurement, and delivery of the integrated performance management program, by integrating strategic, performance management, and IT operational management measures, results, and processes. He or she must possess strategic value integration, performance measurement, and transformational change knowledge and skills.
- IT results manager—To oversee the management, measurement, and delivery of the performance program, from the perspectives of IT results or outcomes.

2.3.3 Real-World Observations: Performance Delivery Manager

This same organization, rightly so, appointed a senior financial manager to the perform the duties of business results manager, a senior HR manager to perform the duties of performance delivery manager, and a senior IT manager to perform the duties of IT results manager. There was no formal communications plan nor any documented accountability for results—*Accountability Assignment Matrix* (*AAM*).[11] These managers assumed his or her level of accountability, based on the level of expertise that each of the managers possess—in this case, HR, IT, and financial management skills.

The senior financial manager, being a Certified Management Accountant, developed financial performance measures and results for business areas, using various disintegrated Microsoft Excel spreadsheets. The senior HR manager, a Masters in Human Resource Management, developed HR performance measures and results and a HR resource management plan for the entire performance program, using various disintegrated tools—performance management excel charts, without any Performance Measurement Structure—so you can imagine the chaos. His style of performance management was to fill his working calendar with daily, weekly, and monthly meetings, to justify the creation of a position for the "real" performance delivery manager who must report to him.

The senior IT manager, a computer science graduate developed IT performance measures and results, using various disintegrated tools to include, Visio and Microsoft Excel spreadsheets. During the monthly reviews, these three senior managers anxiously meet to consolidate the information for the monthly steering committee meeting, celebrating with a sigh of relief and self-praise at completion. At this corporation, the delivery of IT services was viewed by senior management as a technical process, and as a result should not be integrated into the company's performance management program—an example of level-1 maturity level performance management organization, in accordance with modern performance management practices from *KPI-Institute, CMMI, COBIT, Six Sigma, PMI, Kaplan and Norton*.[12]

This is again a typical case of lack of clear understanding and expectations of performance management intended outcomes or results at the senior management level that executive management should attempt to understand, to prevent unnecessary investments in IT services delivery. The measures and results of IT operations must be integrated with those of the business areas in order to optimize business performance and realize better business results and outcomes. This culture of performance management that leverages performance measures and results based on HR staffing and finance spending is typical of organizations that lack the proper understanding of integrated IT performance management skills, knowledge, and experiences. The need for qualified performance management professionals with skills, knowledge, and experiences, similar to those recommended in this book, with strategic integration, transformational change, and performance measurement skills is necessary and essential qualifications for the practicing performance delivery managers.

The role of performance measurement managers and supporting business and IT managers is as follows:

- Business manager (functional business manager to oversee measurement, management, and delivery of business outcomes and outputs, for business performance management support).
- Performance measurement manager (functional performance measurement manager to integrate the measurement, management, and delivery of performance measures for strategic and operational management, improve productivity across business and IT operational areas, and optimize resource utilization, while meeting executive management expectations. He or she must possess conceptual strategic integration, specialized operational transformational change, and performance measurement skills).
- IT managers (functional IT manager to oversee measurement, management, and delivery of the IT results–outcomes and outputs, for IT performance management support).

2.3.4 Real-World Observations: Performance Measurement Managers

There are many obstacles that performance managers are constantly faced with, during their pursuit for strategic and operational excellence, within the constraints of the existing performance management culture, mindset, behaviors, and value system. I experienced a situation at a corporation where the major reason executive management endorsed performance management principles was to justify the dollars given to a performance management consulting firm to develop a PMS and process, with the expectation that this methodology will be the substitute for their lack of involvement. Certain functional business and IT managers resisted any change to business or technical improvements, mainly because of their level of comfort with operating the existing environments, pessimistic or regressive perspectives on the job, and fear of the unknown.

Most managers at this corporation had limited understanding of the fundamental principles of *integrated performance measurement structure—PMS*[13] or balanced scorecard, and often lacked the required expertise to apply these basic concepts on any of their previous performance management assignments. As a result of this lack of knowledge and skills, these mangers resorted to the HR and historical financial measures of performance management, with endless frustration because of the lack of executive and senior management involvement and support. Remember! These executives firmly believed that a consultant performance management methodology was the substitute for their lack of involvement.

This performance management methodology was delivered to executive and senior management by the consulting firm, in three-ring glossy binders, with "Victorian-novel" style format, suitable for the archives. The voluminous, unstructured, and meaningless performance measures, metrics, indicators, and results created an instant distaste for performance management appetite by the business and IT operational professionals at this corporation. As a result, certain senior and executive management were hesitant in enforcing the use of this methodology and adopted the nondecisive "agreement-in-principle" attitude. The bullish and emotional directive, "whatever it takes to deliver the performance management program, whether or not a formal process or performance culture was adopted," was the directive from certain senior and executive managers.

The "resistance to change" attitudes by certain functional business and IT managers were reinforced by these functional managers, as soon as they were informed of the lack of support from senior management for common, consistent, and integrated performance management measures and results. The HR manager was delegated accountability for delivering the performance management program, using any creative set of performance measures, processes, outcomes, and results, and the difficulties in obtaining business and IT operational involvement and support have reached that unresolved state. The performance delivery manager from HR is now left to deliver a performance management solution with reluctant IT and business involvement, no accepted PMS or processes, and little support from senior management. Senior management's major directive to these HR managers is to "apply their HR performance systems, knowledge and management skills." This directive is a result of their strong belief that performance management is all about "HR measures"—another typical case of the lack of integrated performance management. I agree that HR performance measurement systems and policies are one of the necessary and essential measures to implementing performance management. However, it would be rather difficult to sell a concept, idea, principle, or theory without active involvement and support from senior management and functional managers (IT and strategic business) and without sound knowledge of integrated performance management framework processes.

In the absence of an integrated performance management framework, the HR performance delivery manager, including some specialist HR consultants, adopted their "so-called" unique, proprietary methodology, and totally ignored the idea of integrated performance management—a mass confusion of political bickering and consensus—building with HR consulting resources, functional business and IT managers, and HR performance delivery manager hoping for that elusive "silver-bullet" solution. The original objective of performance management to improve the quality of management, encourage accountability for results, optimize the utilization of resources, and improve overall organizational excellence, while meeting executive management expectations, was transformed to HR performance measures and results, in line with certain senior managers view of performance management.

I never did give them hell. I just told the truth, and they thought it was hell.

Harry S. Truman

I wish to emphasize that HR and personal system aspects of performance management are absolutely essential for improvement and organizational excellence. I also believe that executives sometimes confuse performance management with HR and personal systems. Performance management is about transforming established strategies into operational services delivery consisting of output, outcomes, and results, used to manage and measure the performance of an organization.

However, application of these HR systems, without a consistent understanding of an integrated process framework driven by results—outcomes and outputs, is analogous to shooting bullets in the dark that frequently results in the managers spending unnecessary and nonproductive time and effort on looking busy with illusionary results. There exists a widespread need for a commonly accepted, consistent, and integrated understanding of results-driven IT performance management framework. This understanding of strategic and operational management integration is essential to resolve the root cause of performance management challenges—communications, integration, sustainability—sustained value creation, accountability, quality and quantity of management, and transformation change.

My view of this situation reveal that the existing HR performance management systems were based on the "Victorian-novel" procedural style processes of the 1970s by counting efforts and activities, which cannot be readily adapted to a culture of improvements and accountability for results and outcomes, using modern technology processes and tools such as business analytics, scorecards, and dashboards to support more evidence-based decision making.

The scenario discussed requires the establishment of simple, flexible, and integrated performance management framework, which is results-driven accountability and demonstrate the value and benefits of integrated performance management principles and practices and which shows the alignment with both strategic management and IT operational management.

> In an organization every employee tends to rise to his level of incompetence.
>
> **Laurence J. Peter—*The Peter Principle***

The remaining section of this chapter highlights the results-driven accountabilities of the performance delivery manager to support strategic management, performance management, and IT operational management frameworks. Managers (IT and business) and academics should find these practical guidelines very useful for the measurement, management, and delivery of IT services and projects, especially those whose interests are toward optimization and require an understanding of an integrated performance management framework solution.

2.4 Strategic Management

The strategic management framework, referenced in Figure 2.2, is introduced in this section to show the integrated nature of the performance delivery manager's accountability for results. Chapter 3 discusses the integrated nature of executives (strategic, operational, and performance management), performance delivery managers, and performance measurement managers' accountabilities for results, to improve organizational performance and quality of management and to optimize resource utilizations. The performance delivery manager measures, monitors, and reports on performance measures and results using the PMS, PMIS, and processes. The goals are to improve organizational excellence and quality of management, support evidence-based decision making using predictive analytics, and deliver IT strategic management services that support the following strategic management results areas:

- IT goal statement
- IT strategic framework
- IT strategic directives

- IT policy framework
- IT performance governance structure
- IT value-based performance measurement

These results areas are integrated using strategic, performance management, and IT operational management accountabilities, strategic directives, outcomes, process flows, and performance measures, in accordance with modified Six Sigma-PDCA cycle, Kaplan and Norton fundamental elements of performance management integration, "Balanced Scorecard" employee, customer, operational, and financial measures. Chapter 3 discusses these integrated components in greater detail, using a strategic management model as the context structure.

I have introduced the results areas (*what*) of strategic management. In the succeeding sections, I elaborated on the information contents—performance measures and results for each of the results area—and presented the accountabilities (*how*) of the performance delivery manager *who* is accountable[11] to measure, manage report, and make evidence-based decisions, using the information contents. The accountabilities of the performance delivery manager are provided using a modified Six Sigma-PDCA process cycle with highlighted results to demonstrate accountability for results and to show how integration is achieved using results to support the management, measurement, and delivery of IT strategic management services.

2.4.1 IT Goal Statement

> Obstacles are those frightful things you see when you take your eyes off your goal.
>
> **Henry Ford**

The primary objective of this results area is to highlight the major *outputs* of IT goal statement by outlining the vision, mission, goals, values, success factors, and performance areas during the management, measurement, delivery, and improvement of IT services. The IT goal statement aligns with the IT strategic framework and IT service delivery life cycle, measured using the performance management plan and implemented using IT operational plan. The integrative features of IT goal statement with IT strategic framework, integrated IT performance measurement dashboard, and IT strategic directives provide the framework to optimize the utilization of *resources* and to improve organizational performance.

Executives shall use the IT goal statement as the basis for communicating, integrating, and making evidence-based strategic and operational decisions. Strategic management decisions should be made using sound objective judgments with an understanding of operational impacts, rather than emotions based on "self-serving" political agendas. Sound objective judgments require executive management understanding of vision, mission, goals, values, and success factors, as well as an understanding of the integrated components to improve the quality of management and overall IT performance. The major *outputs* of the IT goal statements include the following:

- Vision—To achieve performance excellence by optimizing the *quality and quantity* of technology and IT labor resources while delivering innovative IT solutions to ensure economic and technical efficiencies.
- Mission—To provide IT leadership, business projects delivery and enterprise architecture services (EAS), applications and technology services, and a sound technology infrastructure

to effectively and efficiently support the goals of the business through technology innovations and performance excellence.

- Goals—Provide influential, collaborative, forward thinking, and responsive IT services to the business by providing IT governance, planning and administration, enterprise architecture and innovations, project portfolio management (PPM), applications management services (AMS), and technology operations support.
- Values—Accountability (results management accountability framework), teamwork (collaboration and coordination), integration (people, process, technology, and financials), integrity and trust (performance measures and accountability reporting), service and quality (IT resource optimization), service excellence and innovation (continuous improvement), and treat people with dignity and respect (attitude, positive thinking).
- Success factors—The success of the IT department is contingent upon its ability to act as a catalyst for innovatively leveraging technology to advance the IT strategic and operational plans, in accordance with the performance measurement areas. This will guide and support the management and delivery of applications and technology services and enable the integration of IT services into the business area to improve and transform the quality of services provided in the business areas.
- Performance measurement areas: *Employee (*to increase learning, innovations and to sustain our capacity and capabilities to change, transform, and improve), *customer* (to increase customer satisfaction and service excellence), *financial* (to optimize the utilization of financial resources and provide financial transparency), and *operational* (to improve service delivery, operational efficiencies, relationship management, and functional management).

2.4.1.1 Performance Delivery Manager Accountabilities

- Manage and define the context and contents of the IT goal statement and areas of improvements.
- Measure the progress of the established IT goal statement to ensure integration with IT strategic plan, alignment to company's business plan, and understanding the benefits and linkages with desired outcomes.
- Monitor and analyze performance trends in the performance scorecard or dashboard to understand the following: (a) "How we are doing?" (b) "Are we doing/measuring the right things?" (c) "Are we getting the right results?" (d) "Are we getting the value?"
- Deliver and evaluate stakeholders' satisfaction levels for strategic and IT operational management to understand the value of IT goal statement and to improve service delivery through stakeholders satisfaction surveys.
- Improve IT goal statement and increase understanding of benefits and intended outcomes statement within the overall IT strategic framework by recommending areas of improvements for customer, employee, financial, and operational performance measures and results.
- Report on performance measures and results to performance steering committee, with direct accountability to performance management executive.

2.4.2 IT Strategic Framework

If you don't know where you are going, you are certain to end up somewhere else.

Yogi Berra

The primary objective of this results area is to highlight the major *outputs* of IT strategic framework by outlining the outcomes, goals, strategies, programs, benefits, costs, and performance measurement areas during the management, measurement, delivery, and improvement of IT services. The IT strategic framework aligns with IT strategic directives and IT service delivery life cycle, measured using the performance management plan and implemented using IT operational plan. The integrative features of IT strategic framework include the development or reengineering of business processes and the integration of strategic initiatives with operational initiatives to optimize *resource* allocations and to improve organizational performance and quality of management.

Executives shall use the IT strategic framework as the basis for communicating, integrating, and making strategic and operational decisions. It represents the strategic framework for organizational performance. Sound objective decisions require executive management understanding of the management and delivery of the company's IT products and services, within the context of the IT service delivery life cycle. For each of the six functional areas of the IT service delivery life cycle—governance, planning and administration, enterprise architecture and innovations, PPM, AMS, and IT operational support—the major *outputs* of the IT strategic framework include the following:

- Outcomes—Intended to cover the results of IT services, within the context of the IT services delivery life cycle. Outcomes are the results that express benefits, accomplishments, goals, and impacts/changes—what difference are we making? For each of the IT functional areas, providing "what, how, when, and to whom" IT services should be delivered.
- Goals—Provide the result (what) to achieving the outcomes and realizing the benefits for each of the functional areas of the IT service delivery life cycle.
- Strategies—Provide the actions (how) to achieving the goals for each of the functional areas of the IT service delivery life cycle.
- Programs/initiatives—Provide the programs (capital project expenditures) and initiatives operating expenditures for each functional area of the IT service delivery life cycle.
- Benefits—Provide the favorable result (what) to successfully delivering the programs and initiatives from results or outcomes perspectives for each of the functional areas of the IT service delivery life cycle.
- Cost—Provide a cost estimate for delivering the services for each of the functional areas of the IT service delivery life cycle.
- Performance measures—Provide performance measures and results (targets) for each of the functional areas of the IT service delivery life cycle.
- Linkage to IT strategic plan, IT operational plan, and IT performance management plan to ensure that the technology solution is aligned with business goals, objectives, and strategies and measured using the *integrated IT performance measurement dashboard.*[13]
- Program delivery plan—Projects, priorities, implementation sequences, performance measures, and results that support the programs/initiatives.

2.4.2.1 Performance Delivery Manager Accountabilities

- Manage and define the context and contents of the IT strategic framework and areas of improvement.
- Measure the progress of the established IT strategic framework to ensure integration with IT operational plan and alignment to company's business plan by assessing strengths, weaknesses, opportunities, and threats.

- Monitor and analyze performance trends in the performance scorecard or dashboard to understand the following: (a) "How we are doing?" (b) "Are we doing/measuring the right things?" (c) "Are we getting the right results?" (d) "Are we getting the value?"
- Deliver and communicate stakeholders' satisfaction levels for strategic and IT operational management staff to understanding the benefits of the IT strategic framework to improve service delivery, using stakeholders satisfaction surveys.
- Improve IT strategic framework and IT strategic processes by recommending areas of performance improvements for customer, employee, financial, and operational measures and results.
- Report on performance measures and results to performance steering committee, with direct accountability to performance management executive.

2.4.3 IT Strategic Directives

> The result of planning should be effective, efficient, and economical ... that is, suitable for the intended purpose, capable of producing the desired results, and involving the least investment of resources.
>
> **Clark Crouch**

The primary objective of this results area is to highlight the major *outputs* of the six (6) IT functional areas: executive leadership; planning and administration; enterprise architecture; PPM; applications management; and technology operations services (TOS) for management, measurement, delivery, and improvement of IT services. The IT strategic directives align with IT service delivery life cycle and the *performance measurement area or balanced scorecard*,[13] measured by the performance management plan and implemented by IT operational plan. The integrative features of IT strategic directive include the development or reengineering of IT policy framework and the integration of the performance measurement areas with operational initiatives to optimize resource allocations and to improve organizational excellence and quality of management.

Executives shall use the IT strategic directives as the basis for communicating, integrating, and making strategic and operational decisions. These IT strategic directives, which are aligned with the performance measurement areas or *balance scorecard*, formed the basis for the identification of outputs, outcomes, and performance measures. Sound objective judgments require executive management understanding of the management and delivery of the company's IT products and services, within the context of the IT service delivery life cycle. For each of the six functional areas of the IT service delivery life cycle—governance, planning and administration, enterprise architecture and innovations, PPM, AMS, and IT operational support—the major *outputs* of IT strategic directives include the following:

- Executive Leadership Services (ELS)—Provides ELS strategic directives for leadership, contract administration, management policies, capital and operating expenses reviews, employee performance, client and vendor relationships, and quality assurance compliance.
- Planning and Administration Services (PAS)—Provides PAS strategic directives for leadership, strategic/operational plans, invoice processing, capital and operating expenses, employee performance, client and vendor relationships, and quality assurance compliance.
- Enterprise architecture services—Provides EAS architecture strategic directives for leadership, contract management, project management (IT infrastructure), EAS management

policies, capital and operating expenses, employee performance, client and vendor relationships, and quality assurance compliance.

- Project portfolio management—Provides PPM strategic directives for leadership, contract administration, project management (business projects), performance measurement office (PMO) management policies, capital and operating expenses reviews, employee performance, client and vendor relationships, and quality assurance compliance.
- Applications management services—Provides AMS strategic directives for leadership, contract administration, AMS management policies, capital and operating expenses reviews, employee performance, client and vendor relationships, and quality assurance compliance.
- Technology operations services—Provides TOS strategic directives for leadership, contract administration, TOS management policies, capital and operating expenses reviews, employee performance, client and vendor relationships, and quality assurance compliance.

2.4.3.1 Performance Delivery Manager Accountabilities

- Manage and define the context and contents of IT strategic directives and areas of improvement.
- Measure the progress of the established IT strategic directives to ensure integration with IT operational plan and alignment to company's business plan by assessing strengths, weaknesses, opportunities, and threats.
- Monitor and analyze performance trends in the performance scorecard or dashboard to understand the following: (a) "How we are doing?" (b) "Are we doing/measuring the right things?" (c) "Are we getting the right results?" (d) "Are we getting the value?"
- Deliver and communicate stakeholders' satisfaction levels for strategic and IT operational management staff to understanding the benefits of the IT strategic directives to improve service delivery, using stakeholders satisfaction surveys.
- Improve IT strategic directives and overall IT strategic processes by recommending areas of performance improvements for customer, employee, financial, and operational measures and results.
- Report on performance measures and results to performance steering committee, with direct accountability to performance management executive.

2.4.4 IT Policy Framework

> High achievement always takes place in the framework of high expectation.
>
> **Charles Kettering**

The primary objective of this results area is to highlight the major *outputs* of IT policy framework by outlining the policy, purpose, scope, responsibilities, definitions, references, and related policies for each of the IT strategic directives, during the management, measurement, delivery, and improvement of IT services. The IT policy framework aligns with IT strategic directives and the performance measurement areas or *balanced scorecard*, measured by the performance management plan and implemented by IT operational plan. The integrative features of IT policy framework include the development or reengineering of IT operational procedures and the integration of the performance measurement areas with operational initiatives to optimize resource allocations and to improve organizational performance and quality of management.

Executives shall use the IT policy framework to managing IT assets and services, selecting appropriate IT delivery model, and contracting for IT services. This policy framework provides an extensive set of policies, which allows for associated standards to be adopted and best practices or guidelines to be developed, to support more objective-based decisions. Sound objective judgments require executive management understanding of the management and delivery of IT assets and services, within the context of the IT service delivery life cycle and the IT strategic directives. For the IT strategic directives within each of the six functional areas of the IT service delivery life cycle—governance, planning and administration, enterprise architecture and innovations, PPM, AMS, and IT operational support—the major *outputs* of the IT policy framework include the following:

- Policy—A statement of outcomes of the policy itself for each of the strategic directive within the functional areas and the IT services delivery life cycle.
- Purpose—The reason or result (what) to achieving the outcomes and realizing the benefits of the policy.
- Principles—Provide the actions (how) to achieving the goals of the policy.
- Roles and responsibilities—Provide roles and responsibilities (who does what) to executing the policy using the *RACI-Responsible, Approval, Consulting and Informed-RACI* Chart.
- Definitions—Provide supporting definitions relevant to the policy.
- References and related policies—Provide references and related policies to support the policy statement.

2.4.4.1 Performance Delivery Manager Accountabilities

- Manage and define the context and contents of the IT policy framework and areas of improvement.
- Measure the progress of the established IT policy framework to ensure integration with IT operational plan and alignment to performance measurement areas by assessing strengths, weaknesses, opportunities, and threats.
- Monitor and analyze performance trends in the performance scorecard or dashboard to understand the following: (a) "How we are doing?" (b) "Are we doing/measuring the right things?" (c) "Are we getting the right results?" (d) "Are we getting the value?"
- Deliver and communicate stakeholders' satisfaction levels for strategic and IT operational management staff to understanding the benefits of the IT policy framework and to improve service delivery, using stakeholders satisfaction surveys.
- Improve IT policy framework and IT strategic processes by recommending areas of performance improvements for customer, employee, financial, and operational measures and results.
- Report on performance measures and results to performance steering committee, with direct accountability to performance management executive.

2.4.5 IT Performance Governance Structure

> Governance is the process whereby people in power make decisions that create, destroy or maintain social systems.
>
> **Maria Ramos (CEO, Transnet)**

The primary objective of this results area is to highlight the major *outputs* of IT performance governance structure by outlining the structure and process during the management, measurement, delivery, and improvements of IT services. The *IT performance governance structure*[14] aligns with the IT strategic framework and IT service delivery life cycle, measured using the performance management plan and implemented using IT operational plan. The integrative features of IT performance governance structure align with IT policy framework, *IT performance measurement dashboard*[15], and IT strategic directives, which provide the framework to optimize the utilization of *resources* and to improve organizational performance and quality of management. This IT performance governance structure aligns with IT policy framework and ensures that associated standards are adopted and best practices or guidelines are developed. It is based on KPI Institute-Performance Management and COBIT industry-wide guidelines.

Executives shall use the IT performance governance structure as the basis for communicating, integrating, and making evidence-based strategic and operational decisions. This decision-making structure shows how decisions are made, who makes the decision, who is held accountable, and how the results of the decisions are measured, monitored, and managed to ensure effective and efficient utilization of IT resources. Sound objective judgments require executive management understanding of IT performance structure, as well as an understanding of the integrated components to improve the quality of management and overall IT performance. The major *outputs* of the IT performance governance structure include the following:

- Structure—Answers "who" and "what" question of IT governance. Who are they governing and what are they governing. Decision-making structure in several layers of governance (executive level), program/business process (IT business council/steering committee), technical operational level (change advisory council).
- Process—Answers "how" an organization is governed. Performs measurement and communications of performance results. How did we do? Decision-making processes associated with IT as well as the practices (balanced scorecard) and policies used to measure and control the way IT decisions are made and delivered within the organization.

2.4.5.1 Performance Delivery Manager Accountabilities

- Manage and define the context and contents of the IT performance governance structure areas for improvements—reducing quantity of governance and increasing quality of governance.
- Measure the progress of the established IT performance governance structure to ensure integration with IT strategic plan, alignment to company's business plan, and understanding the benefits and linkages with desired outcomes.
- Monitor and analyze performance trends in the performance scorecard or dashboard to understand the following: (a) "How we are doing?" (b) "Are we doing/measuring the right things?" (c) "Are we getting the right results?" (d) "Are we getting the value?"
- Deliver and evaluate stakeholders' satisfaction levels of strategic and IT operational management to understand the value of IT performance governance structure to improve service delivery through stakeholders satisfaction surveys.
- Improve IT performance governance structure and increase understanding of benefits and intended outcomes statement within the overall IT strategic framework by recommending

areas of improvements for customer, employee, financial, and operational performance measures and results.
- Report on performance measures and results to performance steering committee, with direct accountability to performance management executive.

2.4.6 IT Value-Based Performance Measurements

Most individuals and organizations don't get what they want because they don't measure what they really want.

W. Edwards Deming

The primary objective of this results area is to highlight the major *outputs* of IT value-based performance measurement by outlining process improvement, organizational alignment, technology enablement, performance culture, financial performance and accountability for results, during the management, measurement, delivery, and improvement of IT services. Value-based measurements are aligned with operational performance and IT strategic framework performance, measured using the performance measurement dashboard, and implemented using IT operational plan. The integrative features of IT value-based performance measurements with IT strategic framework, IT performance management dashboard, and IT strategic directives provide the framework to optimize the utilization of *resources* and to improve organizational performance and quality of management.

In a results-based accountability environment, executives shall use the IT value-based performance measurement as the basis for getting the right performance measurement in place for organizational success. In order to drive performance, executive decisions need to be based on measurements that are clearly linked with business value to obtain an accurate indication of what is working and what is not working. The major *outputs* of the IT value-based performance measurement include the following:

- Process improvement—To achieve process performance excellence by simplifying and streamlining IT processes and related business processes to managing, measuring, delivering, and improving IT services.
- Organizational alignment—To achieve organizational excellence by demonstrating alignment of IT organizational structures and processes to business structures and processes, using a RBM structure (accountability for results).
- Technology enablement—To achieve operational excellence by enabling innovative technology solutions, such as integrated IT performance measurement dashboard, to enable operational excellence, optimize resource utilizations, and improve quality of management.
- Performance culture—Transforms your company's culture through collaboration and transparency by moving from counting services or activities to measuring meaningful *RBM culture.*[16]
- Financial performance—Optimize the utilization of financial resources through *results-based budgeting (RBB)*[17] by measuring and monitoring financial expenditures, using financial trend and analytics.
- Accountability for results—An RBM approach focused in achieving results. A broad-based strategy aimed at changing the way organization operates, with improving performance (achieving results) as the central orientation.

2.4.6.1 Real-World Observations: Performance Measurement Dashboard

It's worth mentioning a real-world scenario at a company, which established a value-based performance measurement dashboard to manage, monitor, measure, and improve the delivery of IT services. Business and IT resources were approved, budget allocated and the performance measurement dashboard were implemented according to the established schedule. During the performance measurement dashboard implementation, there was a certain level of frustration or "political power struggles," which resulted in the strategic management group identifying and delivering various strategic outputs and performance measures, managed by an appointed business results manager. At the same time, IT operational group also identified and delivered various IT outputs and performance measures, managed by an appointed IT results manager.

However, neither of these IT operational nor strategic management outputs and performance measures were integrated or aligned with the approved performance management program, and as such there was an overwhelming demand for integrated strategic, IT operational, and performance management outputs and performance measures. This is a typical case of inefficient use of the company's most vital resources (people), because of the lack of the basic knowledge, skills, and application for performance measurement integration. One of the recommended solutions presented in this book is based on the foundation principles of integrating strategic, IT operational, and performance management as outlined in the performance management plan—an integrated PMS and process, for implementing the performance management program. Since the focus of this section is on IT value-based performance measurements using an integrated IT performance measurement dashboard, an overview of the main contents is provided, with a highlight of the major accountabilities of the performance delivery manager who was involved in delivering this integrated IT performance measurement dashboard.

Integrated IT performance measurements dashboard includes

- Dashboard structure—operations, employee, customer, financial outputs; outputs start and target dates
- Dashboard change—organizational, cultural, trend analysis, analytics
- Dashboard resource—% complete, # improvements; progress indicator

If you have a desire to increase reporting value and enable clear understanding of where the performance of your business can be improved, then value-based measurements can be suitable for your purpose. The integrated IT performance measurement dashboard is the basis for determining areas of improvements and understanding what's working and what is not working. The performance delivery manager will have accountabilities for the overall accuracy, completeness, timeliness, relevancy, and consistency of the integrated IT performance measurement dashboard. These accountabilities and performance measurement characteristics will make the dashboard desirable for evidence-based decision making, using predictive analytics.

2.4.6.1.1 Performance Delivery Manager Accountabilities

- Manage and define the context and contents of IT value-based performance measurement and areas for improvements.
- Measure the progress of the established IT value-based performance measurement areas to ensure integration with IT strategic plan, alignment to company's business plan, and understanding the benefits and linkages with desired outcomes.

- Monitor and analyze performance trends in the performance scorecard or dashboard to understand the following: (a) "How we are doing?" (b) "Are we doing/measuring the right things?" (c) "Are we getting the right results?" (d) "Are we getting the value?"
- Deliver and evaluate stakeholders' satisfaction levels for strategic and IT operational management to understand the value of IT performance measurement and to improve service delivery through stakeholders satisfaction surveys.
- Improve IT performance measurements and increase understanding of benefits and intended outcomes statement within the overall IT strategic framework by recommending areas of improvements for customer, employee, financial, and operations performance measures and results.
- Report on performance measures, results, and trends to performance steering committee, with direct accountability to performance management executive.

2.5 Performance Management

The performance management framework, referenced in Figure 2.2, is introduced in this section to show the integrated nature of the performance delivery manager's accountabilities. Chapter 4 discusses the integrated nature of strategic, IT operational, and performance management executives, performance delivery managers, and performance measurement managers' accountabilities to ensure optimum resource utilization and improve organizational performance. The performance delivery manager measures, manages, delivers, and improves IT performance management services to effectively support the following IT performance management results areas:

- IT service delivery life cycle performance model
- IT performance management delivery processes
  - Performance management standard
  - Performance measurement systems
  - Performance management reporting
  - Performance improvement management
  - Performance change management
  - HR performance management
  - Financial performance management
- Performance measurement office support

These performance management results areas are integrated through execution of strategic management, performance management and IT operational management accountabilities, outputs/outcomes, processes, and performance measures, in accordance with KPI Institute Performance Management fundamental elements of IT resources integration (people, process, technology, and financials). Chapter 4 of this book discusses these integrated components in greater detail, using a performance management model, as the communications medium.

I introduced the results areas (*what*) of performance management. In the succeeding sections, I elaborated on the results—outputs/outcomes for each of the results areas and presented the accountabilities (*how*) of the performance delivery manager *who* is accountable to manage, measure, communicate, and make decisions, based on the results. The accountabilities of the performance delivery manager show the integrated nature of the performance management results areas, to support the management, measurement, delivery, and improvement of the overall performance management program.

2.5.1 *IT Service Delivery Life Cycle Performance Model*

> The result of planning should be effective, efficient, and economical ... that is, suitable for the intended purpose, capable of producing the desired results, and involving the least investment of resources.
>
> **Clark Crouch**

The primary objective is to ensure that IT services are managed, measured, delivered, and improved in compliance with the six (6) functional area of the IT service delivery life cycle. Each of the six (6) functional areas establishes outcomes, goals, strategies, programs and initiatives, benefits, costs, and performance measures as the framework to ensure optimum utilization of IT resources and to improve organizational performance and quality of management.

The IT service delivery life cycle discussed in this book focuses on a RBM approach, with alignment to the six (6) functional areas. The six (6) functional areas of IT service delivery life cycle, which aligns with IT performance measurement dashboard and IT products/service life cycle, are as follows:

- IT ELS—The primary result from this functional area is executive leadership/governance outputs and outcomes, which consist of the following:
  - IT leadership
  - IT contract administration
  - IT management policies and procedures
  - IT capital and operating expenses review
  - Employee performance
  - Client and vendor relationship management
  - Quality assurance compliance
- PAS—The primary result from this functional area is planning and administration output and outcomes, which consist of the following:
  - PAS leadership
  - IT strategic/operational plans
  - Invoice processing
  - IT capital and operating expenses
  - Employee performance
  - Client and vendor relationship management
  - Quality assurance compliance
- EAS—The primary result from this functional area is enterprise architecture/innovations outputs and outcomes, which consist of the following:
  - EAS leadership
  - Project and contract management (IT infrastructure projects)
  - EAS management policies and procedures
  - EAS capital and operating expenses review
  - Employee performance
  - Client and vendor relationship management
  - Quality assurance compliance

- PPM—The primary result from this functional area is project portfolio management outputs and outcomes, which consist of the following:
  - PPM leadership
  - Project and contract management (business projects)
  - PPM management policies and procedures
  - PPM capital and operating expenses review
  - Employee performance
  - Client and vendor relationship management
  - Quality assurance compliance
- AMS—The primary result from this functional area is applications management outputs and outcomes, which consist of the following:
  - AMS leadership
  - AMS outsourced contract management
  - AMS management policies and procedures
  - AMS capital and operating expenses review
  - Employee performance
  - Client and vendor relationship management
  - Quality assurance compliance
- TOS—The primary result from this functional area is IT operating services outputs and outcomes, which consist of the following:
  - AMS leadership
  - AMS outsourced contract management
  - AMS management policies and procedures
  - AMS capital and operating expenses review
  - Employee performance
  - Client and vendor relationship management
  - Quality assurance compliance

2.5.1.1 Performance Delivery Manager Accountabilities

- Manage and define the context and contents of the IT service delivery life cycle and areas for improvements.
- Measure the progress of the established IT service delivery life cycle to ensure integration with IT strategic plan, alignment to company's business plan, and understanding the benefits and linkages with desired outcomes.
- Monitor and analyze performance trends in the performance scorecard or dashboard to understand the following: (a) "How we are doing?" (b) "Are we doing/measuring the right things?" (c) "Are we getting the right results?" (d) "Are we getting the value?"
- Deliver and evaluate stakeholders' satisfaction levels for strategic and IT operational management to understand the value of IT service delivery life cycle and to improve service delivery through stakeholders satisfaction surveys.
- Improve IT service delivery life cycle and increase understanding of benefits and intended outcomes statement within the overall IT strategic framework by recommending areas of improvements for customer, employee, financial, and operational performance measures and results.
- Report on performance measures and results to performance steering committee, with direct accountability to performance management executive.

2.5.2 *IT Performance Management Delivery Processes*

Leadership is getting the right people to do the right thing for the right reason in the right way at the right time at the right use of resources (costs).

Clark Crouch

The primary objective is to ensure that performance results are managed, measured, delivered, and improved using a set of consistent and integrated strategic and IT operational performance management outcomes, processes, and performance measures. Performance management of IT products and services require accurate, complete, timely, consistent, and effective performance measurement processes within the overall *performance management plan*.[18] Every performance management plan, whether strategic or IT oriented, aligns with the balanced scorecard or performance measurement dashboard and a clear understanding of these alignment permit performance managers to better control the performance results to ensure integration with strategic and IT operational processes.

The major responsibilities of the performance delivery manager are highlighted to show why this individual requires the essential skills (strategic value integration [people, process, financials, technology]), transformational change (people/culture, politics, process, performance), and performance measurement (quality, risk management). These are skills needed to resolve the most common and complex root causes of performance management problems (integration, communications, accountability, and transformational change for organizational excellence).

The IT performance management delivery processes, which can also apply to the business, as discussed in this book, are based on the guidelines published by KPI Performance Management Institute. The seven (7) Key Results Areas (KRAs)[19] mentioned in this book, which formed the basis in defining the IT performance management delivery processes, are as follows:

1. Performance management standards: Key results are results quality/quantity, results effectiveness/efficiencies, results accountability, results rewards/recognition, and performance management program.
2. Performance measurement systems: Key results are output/outcomes, measures, metrics, indicators; performance measurement program.
3. Performance management reporting: Key results are integrated performance measurement dashboard analytics, results transparency.
4. Performance management improvements: Key results are organizational excellence, feedback/reviews, KRAs.
5. Performance change management: Key results are transformational change (people/culture, politics, process, and performance) and change sustainability.
6. HR performance management: Key results are HR performance plan and HR performance measures.
7. Financial performance management: Key results are financial performance plan and financial performance measures.

2.5.2.1 *Performance Management Standards*

Without a standard there is no logical basis for making a decision or taking action.

Joseph M. Juran

Performance management standards as presented in this book focus on four (4) major key results—results quality/quantity, results effectiveness/efficiencies, results accountability, results rewards/recognition, and performance management plan. The performance management standards results area establishes a common understanding of expectations and results for employee, customer, financial, and operations performance measures, as outlined in the performance management program.

2.5.2.1.1 Results Quality/Quantity

The purpose of results quality/quantity is

- To clearly and concisely define the quality/quantity for the expected results to ensure compliance with performance management standards for employee, customer, financial, and operations performance measures
- To document the quality/quantity of the performance results and to ensure that results are reviewed to align expectations with results, for the *performance measurement areas*[20]

2.5.2.1.2 Results Effectiveness/Efficiency

The purpose of results effectiveness/efficiency is

- To clearly and concisely define the effectiveness/efficiency for the expected results to ensure compliance with performance management standards for employee, customer, financial, and operations performance measurement areas
- To document the effectiveness/efficiency of the performance results and to ensure the results are reviewed to verify expectations meet results, for the performance measurement areas

2.5.2.1.3 Results Accountability

The purpose of results accountability is

- To clearly and concisely define the accountability for the expected results to ensure compliance with performance management standards for employee, customer, financial, and operations performance measurement areas
- To document the accountability of the performance results and to ensure that results are reviewed to align expectations with results, for the performance measurement areas

2.5.2.1.4 Results Rewards/Recognition

The purpose of results rewards/recognition is

- To clearly and concisely define the rewards/recognition for the expected results to ensure compliance with performance management standards for employee, customer, financial, and operations performance measurement areas

- To document the rewards/recognition of the performance results and to ensure that results are reviewed to align expectations with results, for the performance measurement areas

2.5.2.1.5 Performance Management Plan

The purpose of performance management plan is

- To clearly and concisely define the performance management program to ensure compliance with performance management standards for employee, customer, financial, and operations performance measurement areas
- To document the performance management program and to ensure that results are reviewed to align expectations with results, for the performance measurement areas

2.5.2.1.6 Performance Delivery Manager Accountabilities

- Manage and define the context and contents of the performance management standards and areas for improvements.
- Measure the progress of the established performance management standards to ensure integration with IT strategic plan, alignment to company's business plan, and understanding the benefits and linkages with desired outcomes.
- Monitor and analyze performance trends in the performance scorecard or dashboard to understand the following: (a) "How we are doing?" (b) "Are we doing/measuring the right things?" (c) "Are we getting the right results?" (d) "Are we getting the value?"
- Deliver and evaluate stakeholders' satisfaction levels for strategic and IT operational management to understand the value of IT performance management standards and to improve service delivery through stakeholders satisfaction surveys.
- Improve performance management standards and increase understanding of benefits and intended outcomes statement within the overall IT strategic framework by recommending areas of improvements for customer, employee, financial, and operations performance measures and results.
- Report on performance measures and results to performance steering committee, with direct accountability to performance management executive.

2.5.2.2 Performance Measurement System

> Measurement systems create the basis for effective management.
>
> **Dean R. Spitzer**

Performance measurement system as presented in this book focuses on two (2) major key results—outputs/outcomes measures, metrics, indicators, and performance measurement plan. Performance measurement system results area establishes a common framework of measurement for employee, customer, financial, and operations performance measures, as outlined in the integrated performance measurement dashboard. It establishes the framework for effective performance management and measurement processes. Outputs represent internal and external products and services produced, also identified as deliverables: outcomes represent purpose, direction, and effects of output on clients.

2.5.2.2.1 Outputs/Outcomes, Measures, Metrics, Indicators

The purpose of outputs/outcomes, measures, metrics, indicators is

- To clearly and concisely define the outputs/outcomes, measures, metrics, indicators for the expected results to ensure compliance with performance management standards for employee, customer, financial, and operational performance measures
- To document the outputs/outcomes, measures, metrics, indicators for the expected results and to ensure that results are reviewed to align expectations with results, for the performance measurement areas

2.5.2.2.2 Performance Measurement Plan

The purpose of performance measurement plan is

- To clearly and concisely define the performance measurement plan to ensure compliance with performance management standards for employee, customer, financial, and operational performance measures
- To document the performance measurement plan and to ensure that results are reviewed to align expectations with results, for the performance measurement areas

2.5.2.2.3 Performance Delivery Manager Accountabilities

- Manage and define the context and contents of the performance measurement system and areas for improvements.
- Measure the progress of the established performance measurement system to ensure integration with IT strategic plan, alignment to company's business plan, and understanding the benefits and linkages with desired outcomes.
- Monitor and analyze performance trends in the performance scorecard or dashboard to understand the following: (a) "How we are doing?" (b) "Are we doing/measuring the right things?" (c) "Are we getting the right results?" (d) "Are we getting the value?"
- Deliver and evaluate satisfaction levels of stakeholders' strategic and IT operational management to understand the value of performance measurement system and to improve service delivery through stakeholders' satisfaction surveys.
- Improve performance management system and increase understanding of benefits and intended outcomes statement within the overall IT strategic framework by recommending areas of improvements for customer, employee, financial, and operational performance measures and results.
- Report on performance measures and results to performance steering committee, with direct accountability to performance management executive.

2.5.2.3 Performance Management Reporting

> The more time you spend on reporting, the less time you have to do anything. Stability is achieved when you spend all your time reporting on nothing you are doing—Murphy's law.

Performance management reporting as presented in this book focuses on two (2) major key results—integrated IT performance measurement dashboard and results transparency. Performance management reporting results area establishes a common framework for reporting of employee, customer, financial, and operations performance measures, as presented in the performance measurement dashboard. It establishes the basis to ensure transparency of performance results. Results transparency provides the visibility for results-based accountability, a RBM approach focused on achieving results.

2.5.2.3.1 Integrated IT Performance Measurement Dashboard

The purpose of integrated IT performance measurement dashboard is

- To clearly and concisely define the Integrated IT performance measurement dashboard to ensure compliance with performance management standards for employee, customer, financial, and operations performance measures
- To document the Integrated IT performance measurement dashboard and to ensure that results are reviewed to align expectations with results, for the performance measurement areas

2.5.2.3.2 Results Transparency

The purpose of results transparency is

- To clearly and concisely define results transparency for the expected performance results to ensure compliance with performance management standards for employee, customer, financial, and process performance measures
- To document results transparency and to ensure that results are reviewed to align expectations with results, for the performance measurement areas

The integrated IT performance measurement dashboard or balanced scorecard was developed based on the integrated IT performance management results breakdown structure,[21] in accordance with PMO guidelines to ensure that the performance management teams understand and follow guidelines. The integrated IT performance management results-breakdown structure (RBS) provides a uniform structure for measuring, monitoring, improving, and reporting performance results in a consistent manner across the IT service delivery life cycle. The use of this balanced scorecard provides quantifiable evidence of the consequences of a decision or action, using predictive analytics.

Figure 2.4 shows a graphical representation.

2.5.2.3.3 Performance Delivery Manager Accountabilities

- Manage and define the context and contents of performance management reporting and areas of improvements.
- Measure the progress of the established performance management reporting to ensure integration with IT strategic plan, alignment to company's business plan, and understanding the benefits and linkages with desired outcomes.
- Monitor and analyze performance trends in the performance scorecard or dashboard to understand the following: (a) "How we are doing?" (b) "Are we doing the right things?" (c) "Are we getting the right results?" (d) "Are we getting the value?"

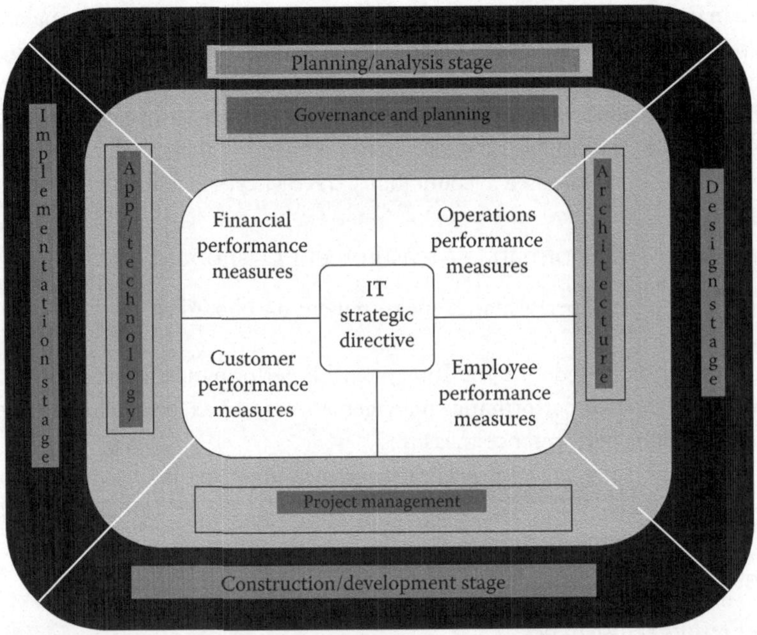

Figure 2.4 Integrated IT performance management results breakdown structure (RBS).

- Deliver and evaluate stakeholders' satisfaction levels of strategic and IT operational management to understand the value of performance management reporting and to improve service delivery through stakeholders satisfaction surveys.
- Improve performance management reporting and increase understanding of benefits and intended outcomes statement within the overall IT strategic framework by recommending areas of improvements for customer, employee, financial, and operational performance measures and results.
- Report on performance measures and results to performance steering committee, with direct accountability to performance management executive.

Figure 2.4 is an integrated performance management RBS to support the financial, operations, employee, and customer performance measures, for IT functional areas and stages of the IT service delivery life cycle performance model.

> To map out a course of action and follow it to an end requires some of the same courage that a soldier needs.
>
> **Ralph Waldo Emerson**

2.5.2.4 Performance Improvement Management

> Measurement is the first step that leads to control and eventually to improvement. If you can't understand it, you can't control it. If you can't control it, you can't improve it.
>
> **H. James Harrington**

Performance improvement management results area, as presented in this book focuses on three (3) major key results: organizational excellence, feedback/reviews, KRAs. Performance improvement management results area establishes a common framework for improving employee, customer, financial, and operations performance measures, as presented in the integrated IT performance measurement dashboard. It is the practice of using performance data to improve the management and delivery of IT services. This involves the strategic use of performance standards, measures (integrated IT performance measurement dashboard), progress reporting, and quality improvements, which should be integrated into the IT service delivery life cycle. It establishes the basis to ensure effective feedback/reviews of performance results. KRAs provide data on how you have done from the perspective of the critical success factors.

2.5.2.4.1 Organizational Excellence

The purpose of organizational excellence is

- To clearly and concisely define organizational excellence for the expected performance results to ensure compliance with performance management standards for employee, customer, financial, and operations performance measures
- To document the organizational excellence for the performance results and to ensure that results are reviewed to align expectations with results, for the performance measurement areas

2.5.2.4.2 Feedback/Reviews

The purpose of feedback/reviews is

- To clearly and concisely define the feedback/reviews for the expected performance results to ensure compliance with performance management standards for employee, customer, financial, and operations performance measures
- To document the feedback/reviews for the performance results and to ensure that results are reviewed to align expectations with results, for the performance measurement areas

2.5.2.4.3 Key Results Areas

The purpose of KRAs is

- To clearly and concisely define KRAs for the expected performance results to ensure compliance with performance management standards for employee, customer, financial, and operations performance measures
- To document the KRAs for the performance results and to ensure that results are reviewed to align expectations with results, for the performance measurement areas

2.5.2.4.4 Performance Delivery Manager Accountabilities

- Manage and define the context and contents of the performance improvement management areas: employee, customer, operations, and financials.

- Measure the progress of the established performance improvement management area to ensure integration with IT strategic plan, alignment to IT strategic directives, and integrated IT performance measurement dashboard and understanding the benefits and linkages with desired outcomes.
- Monitor and analyze performance trends in the performance scorecard or dashboard to understand the following: (a) "How we are doing?" (b) "Are we doing/measuring the right things?" (c) "Are we getting the right results?" (d) "Are we getting the value?"
- Deliver and evaluate stakeholders' satisfaction levels of strategic and IT operational management to understand the value of performance improvement management areas and to improve service delivery through stakeholders satisfaction surveys.
- Improve performance management areas and increase understanding of benefits and intended outcomes statement within the overall IT strategic framework by recommending areas of improvements for customer, employee, financial, and operational performance measures and results.
- Report on performance measures and results to performance steering committee, with direct accountability to performance management executive.

2.5.2.5 Performance Change Management

> In order to improve something you have to able to change it. In order to change it, you have to be able to understand it. In order to understand it, you have to be able to measure it.
>
> **The Author**

Performance change management as presented in this book focuses on two (2) major outputs: transformational change and change strategy sustainability. Performance change management results area establishes a common framework for sustaining change for employee, customer, financial, and operations performance measures, as presented in the performance measurement dashboard. It establishes the basis to ensure transformation change from the perspectives of 4Ps—people/culture, politics, process, and performance results. Culture is the result of mindset, shared values/beliefs, attitudes/behaviors, and informal rules. You need to use the power of culture to effect transformational change. Politics is the manifested result of self-interest, conflicting goals, hidden agenda, and loss of power. Process is the result of strategy, standards, policy, plans, and structures.

Sustainable change strategy as defined by Harvard business guru John Kotter's eight (8) stages of organizational transformation are as follows:

1. Establishing a sense of urgency
2. Forming a powerful guiding coalition
3. Creating a vision
4. Communicating the vision
5. Removing obstacles and empowering others
6. Planning for and creating short-term wins
7. Consolidating improvements
8. Institutionalizing new approaches

2.5.2.5.1 Transformational Change

The purpose of transformational change is

- To clearly and concisely define transformational change for the expected performance results to ensure compliance with performance management standards for employee, customer, financial, and operations performance measures
- To document the transformational change for the performance results and to ensure that results are reviewed to align expectations with results, for the performance measurement areas

2.5.2.5.2 Change Strategy Sustainability

The purpose of change strategy sustainability is

- To clearly and concisely define change strategy sustainability for the expected performance results to ensure compliance with performance management standards for employee, customer, financial, and process performance measures
- To document change strategy sustainability for the performance results and to ensure that results are reviewed to align expectations with results, for the performance measurement areas

2.5.2.5.3 Performance Delivery Manager Accountabilities

- Manage and define the context and contents of change management areas of improvements—people/culture, process, politics, and performance.
- Measure the progress of the established change management improvements areas to ensure integration with IT strategic plan, alignment to company's business plan, and understanding the benefits and linkages with desired outcomes.
- Monitor and analyze performance trends in the performance scorecard or dashboard to understand the following: (a) "How we are doing?" (b) "Are we doing/measuring the right things?" (c) "Are we getting the right results?" (d) "Are we getting the value?"
- Deliver and evaluate satisfaction levels of strategic and IT operational management to understand the value of change management to improve service delivery through stakeholders satisfaction surveys.
- Improve change management and increase understanding of benefits and intended outcomes statement within the overall IT strategic framework by recommending areas of improvements for customer, employee, financial, and operations performance measures and results.
- Report on performance measures and results to performance steering committee, with direct accountability to performance management executive.

2.5.2.6 Human Resource Performance Management

> Before you are a leader, success is all about growing yourself. When you become a leader, success is all about growing others.
>
> **Jack Welch**

HR performance management as presented in this book focuses on two (2) major outputs: staff–employees/customer performance plan and staff–employee/customer performance measures. HR performance management results area establishes a common framework for managing, measuring, delivering, and transforming employee and customer performance measures, as presented in the *performance management plan, performance measurement plan, and performance improvement plan.*[22] It establishes the basis for defining HR performance outcomes/outputs, monitoring progress, and evaluating accomplishments. Staff performance plan consists of progress, accomplishments, and comments for each of the employees' and customers outcomes/outputs. Staff performance measures identify how results will be measured using the performance measurement plan and the integrated IT performance management dashboard.

2.5.2.6.1 Staff (Employee/Customer) Performance Plan

The purpose of staff performance plan is

- To clearly and concisely define the staff performance plan to ensure compliance with performance management standards for employee, customer, financial, and operations performance measures
- To document the staff performance plan and to ensure that results are reviewed to align expectations with results, for the performance measurement areas

2.5.2.6.2 Staff (Employee/Customer) Performance Measures

The purpose of staff performance measures is

- To clearly and concisely define the staff performance measures to ensure compliance with performance measurement systems for employee, customer, financial, and operations performance measures
- To document the staff performance measures and to ensure that results are reviewed to align expectations with results, for the performance measurement areas

2.5.2.6.3 Performance Delivery Manager Accountabilities

- Manage and define the context and contents of the HR performance management and areas of improvements.
- Measure the progress of the established HR performance management to ensure integration with IT strategic plan, alignment to company's business plan, and understanding the benefits and linkages with desired outcomes.
- Monitor and analyze performance trends in the performance scorecard or dashboard to understand the following: (a) "How we are doing?" (b) "Are we doing/measuring the right things?" (c) "Are we getting the right results?" (d) "Are we getting the value?"
- Deliver and evaluate stakeholders' satisfaction levels of strategic and IT operational management to understand the value of HR performance management and to improve service delivery through stakeholders satisfaction surveys.
- Improve HR performance management and increase understanding of benefits and intended outcomes statement within the overall IT strategic framework by recommending areas of

improvements for customer, employee, financial, and operational performance measures and results.

- Report on performance measures and results to performance steering committee, with direct accountability to performance management executive.

2.5.2.7 Financial Performance Management

> Operating plans and budgets must be consistent with the performance measurement baseline.
>
> **Three Sigma Inc.**

Financial performance management as presented in this book focuses on two (2) major outputs: financial performance plan and financial performance measures. Financial performance management results area establishes a common framework for managing, measuring, delivering, and transforming financial performance measures, as presented in the performance management plan, performance measurement plan, and performance improvement plan. It establishes the basis for planning, monitoring progress, and evaluating expenditures. Financial performance plan consists of budget, YTD actual expenses, forecast expenses, and comments for each of the financial operating item, outlined in the IT budget plan. Financial performance measures identify how expenses will be measured and monitored using the performance measurement plan, IT budget plan, and the financial performance area in the integrated IT performance management dashboard.

2.5.2.7.1 Financial Performance Plan

The purpose of financial performance Plan is

- To clearly and concisely define the financial performance plan to ensure compliance with performance management standards for employee, customer, financial, and operations performance measures
- To document the financial performance plan and to ensure that results are reviewed to align expectations with results, for the performance measurement areas

2.5.2.7.2 Financial Performance Measures

The purpose of financial performance measures is

- To clearly and concisely define the financial performance measures to ensure compliance with performance measurement systems for employee, customer, financial, and operations performance measures
- To document the financial performance measures and to ensure that results are reviewed to align expectations with results, for the performance measurement areas

2.5.2.7.3 Performance Delivery Manager Accountabilities

- Manage and define the context and contents of the financial performance management and areas for improvements.

- Measure the progress of the established financial performance management to ensure integration with IT strategic plan, alignment to company's business plan, and understanding the benefits and linkages with desired outcomes.
- Monitor and analyze performance trends in the performance scorecard or dashboard to understand the following: (a) "How we are doing?" (b) "Are we doing/measuring the right things?" (c) "Are we getting the right results?" (d) "Are we getting the value?"
- Deliver and evaluate stakeholders' satisfaction levels for strategic and IT operational management to understand the value of the financial performance management and to improve service delivery through stakeholders' satisfaction surveys.
- Improve financial performance management and increase understanding of benefits and intended outcomes statement within the overall IT strategic framework by recommending areas of improvements for customer, employee, financial, and operations performance measures and results.
- Report on performance measures and results to performance steering committee, with direct accountability to performance management executive.

2.5.3 Performance Measurement Office Processes

> Measurement is not something that should be reserved for the select few; in a high-performing organization, measurement is everybody's job.
>
> **Charles Kettering**

Many IT consultants are providing leadership in helping organizations establish formal performance measurement processes to support the delivery of IT services by optimizing the utilization of IT resources, improving organizational excellence, reducing quantity of management, and increasing quality of management. These leadership roles are the result of urgent requests from stakeholders to optimize the utilization of the company's IT resource assets. The ability to effectively deliver IT services more effectively and efficiently requires the implementation of common measurement processes and practices across the entire organization. The result normally is very little learning curve for the performance delivery manager, performance measurement managers, and performance specialists as they progress throughout the IT service delivery life cycle.

The larger an organization gets, and the more demand for IT performance measures, the more difficult it becomes to enforce this organizational performance consistency. Without this consistency, the full value of implementing a common performance measurement methodology cannot be realized. Some IT consulting firms recognize this and usually provide a common framework or a full methodology that most of their consultants execute in their consulting practices. However, this practice of common, integrated, and consistent performance measurement processes is highly dependent on the maturity level of the client companies. This is where consulting firms—with the right skills level and experience in applying performance measurement processes—can offer tremendous useful support to their clients.

The right consultant can help to establish a centralized organization that is responsible for varying aspects of performance measurement methodologies. This group can be called performance office, enterprise performance office, performance measurement center of excellence, or the performance measurement resource team. Here, I will use the term PMO. A PMO can offer many potential performance-related products and services, depending on the performance needs of the organization and the vision of the PMO sponsor (the person who is generally responsible for the PMO funding). Before the PMO can be successful, agreement must be obtained from the management team on the overall role and general expectations of the PMO. A typical PMO is responsible for deploying a consistent performance measurement methodology within the organization, including people-performance specialists, processes-templates and best practices, and technology-automated dashboard/scorecard. This is not a one-time event but a culture of improvement mindset. While a PMO requires performance specialist type of resources, the hope is that investments in the PMO will be justified by implementing common practices and ensuring a results-based accountability culture. This establishes the performance structure and process to enable IT services within IT service delivery life cycle to be managed and delivered with reduced quantity of management and increased quality of management, in meeting stakeholders' expectations.

Certain IT consultants tend to be further along in their adoption of common and consistent performance measurement processes that utilize outcomes-driven or results-based accountability orientation. Many companies use these IT consulting services to assist them in their desperate search for a more effective and efficient integrated solution. Here is a list that shows the major accountabilities that the PMO will normally execute within an organization. It presents the accountabilities to show how the PMO can influence the client's business. The PMO value proposition can be established to provide a narrow or broad set of measurement and/or assessment services. This list includes many of the common accountabilities that a PMO would normally perform. In general, in a PMO:

2.5.3.1 Performance Delivery Manager Accountabilities

(Accountable for the delivery of result)

- Performance measurement processes, outputs/outcomes, and inputs templates, defined in the performance measurement plan
- Performance improvement processes, outputs/outcomes, and inputs templates, defined in the performance improvement plan
- Integrated IT performance measurement dashboard: employee, financial, customer, and operations
- Benchmarking and assessment results: Six (6) functional areas of IT services delivery life cycle

PMO staff is accountable for the execution of the following processes:

- Establishes and deploys a common set of performance measurement processes and templates, which saves each performance specialist or manager from having to recreate these performance measurement constructs. These reusable performance measurement processes and structures help in the execution of performance management program.
- Provides a methodology and the necessary updates to maintain improvements and best practices. For example, as new or revised processes and templates are made available, the PMO deploys them consistently across the organization.
- Facilitates improved performance specialists communications by having common processes, outputs/outcomes, and terminology. Less misunderstanding and confusion occurs within the organization if everyone uses the same performance measurement language and terminology for results-based accountability.

- Provides training (internal or outsourced) to build core performance measurement competencies and a common set of experiences. If the training is delivered by the PMO, there is a further reduction in overall training costs paid to outside vendors.
- Delivers performance measurement coaching services to prevent performance management resistivity. Performance change management—people/culture, politics, process, and performance—can also experience smoother transition.
- Tracks basic information on the current status of all performance results–outputs/outcomes and provides performance trends and analytics to management in a common and consistent manner.
- Tracks organization-wide metrics on the state of performance management, integrated IT performance measurement dashboard, and the value being provided to the business. The PMO also assesses the general IT services management and delivery environment on an ongoing basis to monitor the improvements.
- Acts as the overall advocate for performance management to the organization. This includes actively educating, selling executives, managers, and team members on the value gained through the use of consistent performance measurement processes.

In summary, companies are finding that they need to standardize on how IT performance measurement processes are delivered. They are recognizing that the process takes much more than just training the staff. It requires a holistic approach, covering many aspects of work and the company culture. However, in their search for this process solution, certain companies have experienced endless frustration, and lack of professional integrity, resulting in the expensive lesson-learned scenarios. Here is a real-world situation that executive management should avoid in their search for that ultimate performance measurement process solution.

> Processes or methodologies can be SMART—Specific, Measurable, Achievable, Realistic, and Timely, or DUMB—Doubtful, Unrealistic, Massive, and Boring
>
> **The Author**

2.5.3.2 Real-World Observations: PMO Processes

A large corporation employed an IT consulting firm to develop and deploy a performance measurement methodology with the expectation that this process framework will solve most of the communications and accountability problems previously recommended during a recent assessment of IT services. The expectation is that this process solution will ensure a more evidence-based decision-making process, using predictive analytics. This consulting firm proudly produced a set of performance measurement processes that had the characteristics of a "DUMB" methodology, with volumes of disjointed processes, outputs/outcomes, measures, and indicators.

Senior management at this corporation, overwhelmed and confused with the voluminous contents of the "DUMB" methodology, decided to establish an innovative performance measurement methodology, similar to KPI Institute, CMMI, and Six Sigma process framework. Another IT management consulting firm was contracted to deliver this solution. This consulting firm, and the lead consultant, believed that performance measurement is a distinct and isolated discipline. The final deliverable from this consulting firm was a set of performance measurement processes, with no alignment to the previously developed performance measurement methodology. In my assessment, this consulting firm produced an integrated subset of

Six Sigma, KPI Institute, and CMMI processes with their company's logo, with no reference to how these processes can be applied.

The IT operations group, whose mandate was to deliver IT services, adopted the outsourced vendor's performance measurement process solutions, for all outsourced services, and totally ignored the recommendations from the PMO. One of their main reasons for nonacceptance of the PMO recommendation was the lack of strategic management integration with the methodology and the performance measurement processes.

Senior management decided to addresses the IT operations group's concerns by employing yet another consulting firm with strategic management expertise, to deliver a strategic management methodology.

This consulting firm, and the lead consultant, believed that enterprise architecture was the process solution for this corporation. They convinced senior management on the establishment of an Enterprise Architecture Office (EAO). The resulting product was an enterprise architecture methodology and recommended EAO structure, with no clear alignment to performance measurement processes and the IT services delivery life cycle performance model. The client company is now left with three useless methodologies that can be characterized as DUMB.

This is a real-world scenario, where these IT consulting firms have "secretly turned client's problems to their personal gold treasures," a common practice in the IT industry that senior executive management must be aware of and take proactive actions to avoid. PMO processes cannot be developed and deployed in isolation of strategic management and IT operational management processes. The need for PMO process integration is a necessary and essential requirement for success, to deliver value to the corporation, and to ensure IT services are delivered to optimize the utilization of IT resource and improve operational performance and quality of management, to effectively meet stakeholders' expectations.

I have introduced the component processes (*what*) of the PMO. I will now present the accountabilities/responsibilities (*how*) of the performance delivery manager *who* is responsible to manage, communicate, and make decisions, based on the information contents. The accountabilities/responsibilities of the performance delivery manager show the integrated nature of the PMO component processes, to support the management and delivery of the overall performance management program.

2.5.3.3 Performance Delivery Manager Accountabilities

- Manage and define the context and contents of the PMO to ensure consistency. Manage the PMO processes by reporting on the contents and recommend solutions to the appropriate management team and update PMO processes to keep it effective.
- Measure the progress of the established PMO to ensure consistency and integration with strategic management, IT operational management and performance management, alignment to IT strategic directives, and understanding the benefits and linkages with desired outcomes. Ensure that performance specialists adhere to the guideline processes, output/outcomes, tools, and techniques established by the PMO to ensure performance management consistency, completeness, and integration. Communicate PMO policies and ensure performance teams adhere to IT PMO methodology, processes, tools, and techniques.
- Monitor and analyze performance trends in the integrated IT performance measurement dashboard to understand the following: (a) "How we are doing?" (b) "Are we doing/measuring the right things?" (c) "Are we getting the right results?" (d) "Are we getting the value?"

Maintain the *performance management information repository* (*PMIR*)[23] and integrated IT performance measurement dashboard.

- Deliver and evaluate stakeholders' satisfaction levels for strategic and IT operational performance management to understand the value of the PMO and to improve service delivery through the use of stakeholders satisfaction surveys. Provide policies, guidelines, best practices, and templates to enable cost-effective and -efficient measurement and assessment of IT services. Lead and coordinate the integration of all IT performance standards, templates, and measures into a single consolidated repository for access by performance measurement teams. Provide performance guidance and counsel to the various performance roles. Provide guidelines in defining acceptable levels of measures for assessment and measurement of IT services. Provide standard templates and tools for performance measurement activities and guidelines for reporting frequency.
- Improve PMO process and increase understanding of benefits and intended outcomes statement within the overall IT operational framework by recommending areas of improvements for customer, employee, financial, and operations performance measures and results. Assist project teams in the use of performance measurement templates and provide the necessary training on the use of performance measurement standards, practices, and templates. Provide information on past performance initiatives relevant to current initiatives. Conduct or arrange for externally conducted steering committee directed performance reviews. Ensure that post-performance reviews are completed and findings are executed. Identify to the steering committee, appropriate trend analysis of the key indicators for performance monitoring in terms of customer, employee, financial, and operations.
- Report on performance measures and results to performance steering committee, with direct accountability to performance management executive. Keep performance managers and stakeholders informed on the effectiveness of the PMO processes.

2.6 IT Operational Management

The components of IT operational management, referenced in Figure 2.2, are introduced in this section to identify and define the major IT results areas and to show how the performance delivery manager manages, measures, delivers, and improves these results areas. Chapter 5 elaborates on these results areas, including details on the integrated nature of the performance delivery manager with accountabilities of the executive performance manager and performance measurement team. The performance delivery manager measures, delivers, and improves on IT service delivery life cycle performance model and IT operational management major results areas of

- Financial performance accountability
- HR performance accountability
- Operational performance accountability
- AMS performance accountability
- Project management performance accountability
- TOS performance accountability

These major results area are integrated through execution of strategic management, performance management, and IT operational management accountabilities, outputs/outcomes, process flows, and performance measures, in accordance with KPI Institute Performance Management and Nolan and Kaplan Balanced Scorecard fundamental elements of integration: people, process, technology, and financials. Chapter 5 of this book discusses these components in greater details, using an IT operational management model as the communications medium.

I have introduced the major results areas (*what*) of IT operational management. In the succeeding sections, I elaborated on the results/outputs/outcomes for each of the results areas and presented the accountabilities (*how*) of the performance delivery manager *who* is accountable to manage, communicate, and make decisions, based on the results. The accountabilities of the performance delivery manager show the integrated nature of IT operational management results areas, to support the management, measurement, and delivery of the overall performance management program.

2.6.1 Financial Accountability

> The budget process is in shambles, devoid of accountability, transparency and enforcement measures.
>
> **Tom Schatz**

The primary objective is to improve financial accountability by committing to managing, *measuring*, delivering, and improving *capital costs* and *operating costs* by optimizing budget allocations, actual expenses, and forecasted expenses. Financial accountability is a measured financial commitment that delivers transparent, credible, and effective capital, and operating costs. It formed the basis for sound financial management, improved organizational performance, and optimized resource utilizations. Decisions regarding IT investments must be evidenced based, driven from the IT budget plan and the integrated IT performance measurement dashboard. IT investment costs for projects—capital and operational services—operating, include the following:

- Capital cost (business projects)
  - Business project-1
  - Business project-2
  - Business project-n
- Capital costs (technology projects)
  - IT infrastructure project-1
  - IT infrastructure project-2
  - IT infrastructure project-n
- Operating costs (technology)
  - Technology upgrades
  - Licensing agreements
  - Operating agreements
- Operating costs (operational)
  - AMS (outsourced)
  - TOS (outsourced)
  - IT staff

Financial accountability refers to the commitment an individual, team, or organization assumes for the delivery of the financial results/output/outcomes and accountabilities. This commitment includes

- Answering—providing an explanation or justification—for delivery of the financial results/output/outcomes and accountabilities
- Measuring and reporting on the performance results
- Demonstrating and ensuring accountability for the credibility, integrity, and reliability of the financial results

2.6.1.1 Performance Delivery Manager Accountabilities

(Accountable for delivery of results and execution of processes)

- Performance measures, metrics, variances (capital costs for business and technology programs/projects).
- Performance measures, metrics, indicators, variances (operating costs for technology upgrades and operational services).
- IT investments value for capital and operating costs
- Benchmarking performance results for IT budget plan (capital and operating expenditures).
- Performance delivery manager is accountable for execution of processes:
- Manage and define the performance, context and contents of IT financial accountability (capital and operating costs), and areas of improvements.
- Measure the performance of IT financial accountability areas to ensure integration with IT budget plan, alignment to IT strategic directives, and understanding the benefits and linkages with desired outcomes.
- Monitor and analyze financial performance trends in the integrated IT performance measurement dashboard to understand the following: (a) "How we are doing?" (b) "Are we doing/measuring the right things?" (c) "Are we getting the right results?" (d) "Are we getting the value?"
- Deliver and evaluate stakeholders' satisfaction levels for strategic and performance management to understand the value of IT financial accountability and to improve service delivery through the use of stakeholders satisfaction surveys.
- Improve on IT financial accountability and increase understanding of benefits and intended outcomes statement within the overall IT operational framework by recommending areas of improvements for customer, employee, financial, and operations performance measures and results.
- Report on financial accountability performance measures and results to performance steering committee, with direct accountability to performance management executive.

2.6.2 Human Resource Accountability

> Delegating responsibility does not relinquish personal accountability.
>
> **Jeffrey Benjamin**

The primary objective is to improve accountability among all stakeholders–customers (IT service providers, vendors) and employees and to ensure business value; operational excellence and IT resource optimization are obtained during the IT service delivery life cycle stages, using a RBM approach. HR accountability is a measured commitment that delivers engaged, motivated to learn and improve, accountable for results, mutual trust, ethical, and credible HR capital investments. It formed the basis for sound people management, improved organizational performance, and optimized HR utilizations. Decisions regarding HR capital investments must be evidence based, driven from the IT performance management contract/plan, strategic directives, and the integrated IT performance measurement dashboard.

Proper resource allocations begin with an understanding of the organization's IT labor resource utilization and skills inventory, documented in the *IT Resource Plan*.[24] IT resource capacity and staff planning enables organizations to optimize skills usage to ensure that all high-quality critical resources are productively aligned with high priority technology services.

HR accountability for outsourced, contract and in-house IT services delivery, include

- Outsourced-services
  - AMS-operating
  - TOS-operating
  - Special business program
- Contract services-business
  - Business program/project-1
  - Business program/project-2
  - Business program/project-n
- Contract services-technology
  - IT infrastructure program-1
  - IT infrastructure program-2
  - IT infrastructure program-n
- In-house services
  - IT governance/management
  - IT planning and administration
  - IT architecture

HR accountability refers to the commitment an individual, team, or organization assumes for delivery of HR results/output/outcomes and accountabilities. This commitment includes

- Answering—providing an explanation or justification—for delivery of labor results/output/outcomes and accountabilities
- Measuring and reporting on the performance results
- Demonstrating and ensuring accountability for the credibility, integrity, and reliability of HR results

2.6.2.1 Performance Delivery Manager Accountabilities

(Accountable for delivery of results and execution of processes)

- Performance measures, metrics, and variances (HR performance for outsourced services [AMS, TOS, and major business program/projects]).
- Performance measures, metrics, and variances (HR performance for contract services [business programs/projects]).
- Performance measures, metrics, and variances (HR performance for contract services [IT infrastructure program/projects]).

- Performance measures, metrics, and variances (HR performance for in-house services [IT governance and management, planning and administrative, and IT architecture staff]).
- IT staff performance for outsourced, contract, and in-house services.
- Benchmarking performance results for outsourced, contract, and in-house services.
- Performance delivery manager is accountable for execution of processes:
- Manage and define the performance, context and contents of IT HR accountability (outsourced), contract, in-house services, and areas of improvements.
- Measure the performance of the established IT HR accountability areas to ensure integration with IT HR plan, alignment to IT strategic directives, and understanding the benefits and linkages with desired outcomes.
- Monitor and analyze employees and customers performance trends in the integrated IT performance measurement dashboard to understand the following: (a) "How we are doing?" (b) "Are we doing the right things?" (c) "Are we getting the right results?" (d) "Are we getting the value?"
- Deliver and evaluate stakeholder's satisfaction levels for strategic and performance management to understand the value of IT HR accountability and to improve service delivery through the use of stakeholders satisfaction surveys.
- Improve IT HR accountability and increase understanding of benefits and intended outcomes statement within the overall IT operational framework by recommending areas of improvements for customer, employee, financial, and operational performance measures and results.
- Report on HR accountability measures and results to performance steering committee, with direct accountability to performance management executive.

2.6.3 Operational Process Accountability

Accountability breeds response-ability.

Stephen R. Covey

The primary objective is to improve operational process accountability by committing to managing, *measuring*, delivering, and improving business processes and IT processes by streamlining processes and/or performing reengineering initiatives. Operational process accountability is a process measure that delivers management (functional and relationship) and delivery services (service delivery and service excellence). It formed the basis for simple and streamlined processes management, improved organizational performance, and optimized process utilizations. Decisions regarding operational process accountability must be results based, driven from IT strategic plan, IT operating plan, and the integrated IT performance management dashboard. Operational process accountability—business and IT processes, includes

- Business process (management)
  - Functional management
  - Relationship management
- Business process (delivery)
  - Service delivery
  - Service excellence
- IT process (management)
  - Functional management
  - Relationship management

- IT process (delivery)
  - Service delivery
  - Service excellence

Operational process accountability refers to the commitment an individual, team, or organization assumes for the delivery of the operational process results/output/outcomes and accountabilities for business and IT processes. This commitment includes

- Answering—providing an explanation or justification—for the delivery of the operational process results/output/outcomes and accountabilities
- Measuring and reporting on the operational process results
- Demonstrating and ensuring accountability for the credibility, integrity, and reliability of the operational performance results

2.6.3.1 Performance Delivery Manager Accountabilities

(Accountable for delivery of results and execution of processes)

- Performance measures, metrics, variances for business processes (management and delivery).
- Performance measures, metrics, indicators, and variances for IT processes (management and delivery).
- Value of operational performance results for business and IT process simplification.
- Benchmarking performance results for operational performance plan (business and IT processes).

Performance delivery manager is accountable for execution of the following processes:

- Manage and define the performance, context and contents of IT operational process accountability (business and IT processes), and areas of improvements.
- Measure the progress of the established IT operational process accountability to ensure integration with IT operational plan, alignment to IT strategic directives, and understanding the benefits and linkages with desired outcomes.
- Monitor and analyze operational performance trends in the integrated IT performance measurement dashboard to understand the following: (a) "How we are doing?" (b) "Are we doing/measuring the right things?" (c) "Are we getting the right results?" (d) "Are we getting the value?"
- Deliver and evaluate stakeholders' satisfaction levels for strategic and performance management to understand the value of IT operational process accountability and to improve service delivery through the use of stakeholders satisfaction surveys.
- Improve IT operational process accountability and increase understanding of benefits and intended outcomes statement within the overall IT operational framework by recommending areas of improvements for customer, employee, financial, and operational performance measures and results.
- Report on operational process accountability measures and results to performance steering committee, with direct accountability to performance management executive.

2.6.4 Project Management Accountability

> The process of preparing programs for a digital computer is especially attractive, not only because it can be economically and scientifically rewarding, but also because it can be an aesthetic experience much like composing poetry or music.
>
> **Donald E. Knuth**

The primary objective is to improve accountability of project management by committing to managing, *measuring*, delivering, and improving project management accountability by streamlining processes, improving operational performance, and optimizing resource utilizations. Project management accountability is a measure that delivers project management *core and supporting knowledge areas*[25] for the effective and efficient delivery of business and IT infrastructure projects. It formed the basis for effective and efficient project management, improved organizational performance, and optimized project resource utilizations. Decisions regarding project management performance must be results based, driven from the IT strategic plan, IT operating plan, and the integrated IT performance management dashboard. Project management performance accountability—business and IT infrastructure projects—include the following:

- Business projects (strategic)
  - Core knowledge areas
  - Supporting knowledge areas
- Business projects (operational)
  - Core knowledge areas
  - Supporting knowledge areas
- IT infrastructure projects (strategic)
  - Core knowledge areas
  - Supporting knowledge areas
- IT infrastructure projects/operations
  - Core knowledge areas
  - Supporting knowledge areas

Project management accountability refers to the commitment an individual, team, or organization assumes for the delivery of the project performance results/output/outcomes and accountabilities for business and IT infrastructure projects. This commitment includes

- Answering—providing an explanation or justification—for the delivery of the project performance results/output/outcomes and accountabilities
- Measuring and reporting on the project performance results
- Demonstrating and ensuring accountability for the credibility, integrity, and reliability of the project performance results

2.6.4.1 Performance Delivery Manager Accountabilities

(Accountable for delivery of results and execution of processes)

- Performance measures, metrics, variances for business projects (strategic and operational).
- Performance measures, metrics, indicators, and variances for IT infrastructure projects (strategic and operational).

- Project performance value (results for IT infrastructure projects [strategic and operational]).
- Benchmarking results (IT infrastructure projects [strategic and operational]).

Performance delivery manager is accountable for execution of the following processes:

- Manage and define the performance, context and contents of IT project management accountability (business and IT infrastructure projects), and areas of improvements.
- Measure the performance of IT project management accountability areas to ensure integration with IT budget plan, alignment to IT strategic directives, and understanding the benefits and linkages with desired outcomes.
- Monitor and analyze project performance trends in the integrated IT performance management dashboard to understand the following: (a) "How we are doing?" (b) "Are we doing/ measuring the right things?" (c) "Are we getting the right results?" (d) "Are we getting the value?"
- Deliver and evaluate satisfaction levels for strategic and performance management to understand the value of IT project management accountability to improve service delivery through the use of stakeholders satisfaction surveys.
- Improve IT project management accountability and increase understanding of benefits and intended outcomes statement within the overall IT operational framework by recommending areas of improvements for customer, employee, financial, and operational performance measures and results.
- Report on project management accountability performance measures and results to performance steering committee, with direct accountability to performance management executive.

2.6.5 Applications Management Services Accountability

> Of everyone else who was running, and there were some very talented people, none of them had anywhere near the experience I had in hiring people, holding them accountable, creating systems for accountability.
>
> **John Hickenlooper**

The primary objective is to improve accountability for AMS[26] by committing to managing, *measuring*, delivering, and improving AMS services by streamlining processes, improving organizational performance, and optimizing resource utilizations. AMS accountability is a measured commitment that delivers contracted services, AMS performance measures, accountability reporting, and outsourced governance model for the effective and efficient delivery of AMS outsourced services. It formed the basis for effective and efficient AMS management, improved organizational performance, and optimized resource utilizations. Decisions regarding AMS accountability must be results based, driven from a results-based accountability management culture, IT strategic plan, IT operating plan, and the integrated IT performance management dashboard. AMS accountability—contract services, AMS performance measures, accountability reporting, and governance model consists of the following:

- Contract services
  - SD, SE, RM
  - Output/outcomes

- AMS performance measures
  - SD, SE, RM
  - Output/outcomes, KPI
- Accountability reporting
  - SD, SE, RM costs
  - Performance reports
- Governance model
  - Oversight/decisions
  - Outsourced strategy

AMS accountability refers to the commitment an individual, team, or organization assumes for the delivery of the AMS performance results/output/outcomes and accountabilities. This commitment includes

- Answering—providing an explanation or justification—for delivery of AMS performance results/output/outcomes and accountabilities
- Measuring and reporting on the AMS performance results
- Demonstrating and ensuring accountability for the credibility, integrity, and reliability of the AMS performance results

2.6.5.1 Performance Delivery Manager Accountabilities

(Accountable for delivery of results and execution of processes)

- Performance measures, metrics, variances (measurement criteria) for contract/outsourced services.
- Performance tracking, corrective action, analytics for AMS performance measures and results.
- Accountability reporting for AMS performance measures and results by contract/outsourced services
- Governance structure for AMS performance measures and results, contract/outsourced services and accountability reporting to support evidence-based decision making.
- Value of AMS performance results for improved operational efficiencies, resource optimization, and quality of management.
- Benchmarking results on AMS performance—contracted/outsourced services.

Performance delivery manager is accountable for the execution of the following processes:

- Manage and define the performance, context and contents of AMS accountability, and areas for improvements.
- Measure the progress of the established AMS accountability areas to ensure integration with AMS Outsourced Contract, alignment to IT strategic directives, and understanding the benefits and linkages with desired outcomes.
- Monitor and analyze AMS performance trends in the integrated IT performance measurement dashboard to understand the following: (a) "How we are doing?" (b) "Are we doing/measuring the right things?" (c) "Are we getting the right results?" (d) "Are we getting the value?"

- Deliver and evaluate stakeholders' satisfaction levels for strategic and performance management to understand the value of AMS accountability and to improve service delivery through the use of stakeholders satisfaction surveys.
- Improve AMS accountability and increase understanding of benefits and intended outcomes statement within the overall IT operational framework by recommending areas of improvements for customer, employee, financial, and operational performance measures and results.
- Report on AMS accountability performance measures and results to performance steering committee, with direct accountability to performance management executive.

2.6.6 Technology Operations Support Accountability

Employers should not focus on employee accountability alone.

Helen Darling

The primary objective is to improve accountability for *Technology Operations Support* (*TOS*)[27] by committing to managing, *measuring,* delivering, and improving TOS services by streamlining support processes, improving performance, and optimizing resources. Technology operations support is a measure that delivers contracted services, performance measures, accountability reporting, and outsourced governance model for the effective and efficient delivery of TOS outsourced services. It formed the basis for effective and efficient TOS management, improved organizational performance, and optimized TOS resource utilizations. Decisions regarding TOS performance must be results based, driven from a results-based accountability management culture, IT strategic plan, TOS outsourced contract, and the integrated IT performance management dashboard. TOS performance accountability—contract services, TOS performance measures, accountability reporting, and governance model consists of the following:

- Contracted services
  - SD, SE, RM
  - Output/outcomes
- AMS performance measures
  - SD, SE,RM
  - Output/outcomes, KPI
- Accountability reporting
  - SD, SE,RM Costs
  - Performance reports
- Governance model
  - Oversight/decisions
  - Outsourced strategy

TOS accountability refers to the commitment an individual, team, or organization assumes for the delivery of the TOS performance results/output/outcomes and accountabilities for technology operations outsourced services. This commitment includes

- Answering—providing an explanation or justification—for the delivery of the TOS performance results/output/outcomes and accountabilities

- Measuring and reporting on the TOS performance results
- Demonstrating and ensuring accountability for the credibility, integrity, and reliability of the TOS performance results

2.6.6.1 Performance Delivery Manager Accountabilities

(Accountable for delivery of results and execution of processes)

- Performance measures, metrics, variances (measurement criteria) for contract/outsourced services
- Performance tracking, corrective action, analytics for TOS performance measures and results.
- Accountability reporting for TOS performance measures and results by contract/outsourced services
- Governance structure for TOS performance measures and results, contract/outsourced services and accountability reporting to support evidence-based decision making.
- Value of TOS performance results for improved operational efficiencies, resource optimization, and quality of management.
- Benchmarking results on TOS performance—contracted/outsourced services.

Performance Delivery Manager is accountable for execution of processes:

- Manage and define the performance, context and contents of TOS accountability, and areas for improvements.
- Measure the performance of the TOS accountability areas to ensure integration with TOS outsourced contract, alignment to IT strategic directives, and understanding the benefits and linkages with desired outcomes.
- Monitor and analyze TOS performance trends in the integrated IT performance measurement dashboard to understand the following: (a) "How we are doing?" (b) "Are we doing/measuring the right things?" (c) "Are we getting the right results?" (d) "Are we getting the value?"
- Deliver and evaluate satisfaction levels for strategic and performance management to understand the value of TOS accountability and to improve service delivery through the use of stakeholders satisfaction surveys.
- Improve TOS accountability and increase understanding of benefits and intended outcomes statement within the overall IT operational framework by recommending areas of improvements for customer, employee, financial, and operational performance measures and results.
- Report on TOS accountability performance measures and results to performance steering committee, with direct accountability to performance management executive.

2.7 Performance Delivery Manager Key Accountabilities

> Accept responsibility for your actions, be accountable for your results, take ownership for your mistakes.
>
> **The Author**

Generalized strategic value integration (people, process, financials, technology), specialized transformational change (people, politics, process, performance), and excellent performance measurement (quality, risk management skills) are the major HR competencies needed to effectively manage, measure, improve, and assess the delivery of IT services. The major accountabilities of the performance delivery manager are highlighted in Tables 2.1 through 2.3, to show the strategic level knowledge and skills requirements of this individual.

Table 2.1 Performance Delivery Manager Accountabilities—Strategic Management

Performance Delivery Manager Results Areas	*Performance Delivery Manager Accountabilities*	*Skills*
Strategic Management: Who	*How*	*What*
IT goal statement	Manage, monitor, measure, and report on the performance of IT services using IT goal statement—outputs/outcomes and analytics from the integrated IT performance measurement dashboard.	Strategic value integration
IT strategic framework	Manage, monitor, measure, and report on the performance of IT services using IT strategic framework—outputs/outcomes and analytics from the integrated IT performance measurement dashboard.	Strategic value integration
IT strategic directives	Manage, monitor, measure, and report on the performance of IT services using IT strategic directives—outputs/outcomes and analytics from the integrated IT performance measurement dashboard.	Strategic value integration
IT policy framework	Manage, monitor, measure, and report on the performance of IT services using IT policy framework—outputs/outcomes and analytics from the integrated IT performance measurement dashboard.	Strategic value integration
IT performance governance structure	Manage, monitor, measure, and report on the performance of IT services using IT performance governance structure—outputs/outcomes and analytics from the integrated IT performance measurement dashboard.	Strategic value integration
IT value-based performance measurement	Manage, monitor, measure, and report on the performance of IT services using IT value-based performance measurement—outputs/outcomes and analytics from the integrated IT performance measurement dashboard.	Strategic value integration

Table 2.2 Performance Delivery Manager Accountabilities—Performance Management

Performance Delivery Manager Results Areas	*Performance Delivery Manager Accountabilities*	*Skills*
Performance Management: Who	*How*	*What*
IT service delivery life cycle performance model	Advise performance measurement staff on applying performance measures to IT service delivery life cycle stages.	Performance management
IT performance management delivery processes		
Performance standard results • Quality and quantity • Efficiency and Effectiveness • Accountability • Rewards and Recognition • Performance management plan	Define performance standards for the expected results to ensure compliance with performance management standards for employee, customer, financial, and operations performance measures, defined in the integrated IT performance measurement dashboard.	Strategic value integration Performance measurement
Performance measurement systems results • Outputs/outcomes measures, metrics, indicators • Performance measurement plan	Define performance measurement systems for the expected results to ensure compliance with performance management standards for employee, customer, financial, and operations performance measures, defined in the integrated IT performance measurement dashboard.	Strategic value integration Performance measurement
Performance management reporting results • IT performance measurement dashboard • Results transparency	Define performance management reporting for the expected results to ensure compliance with performance management standards for employee, customer, financial, and operations performance measures, defined in the integrated IT performance measurement dashboard.	Strategic value integration Performance measurement
Performance improvement management results • Organizational excellence • Feedback/reviews • KRAs	Define performance improvement management for the expected results to ensure compliance with performance management standards for employee, customer, financial, and operations performance measures, defined in the integrated IT performance measurement dashboard.	Transformational change Performance measurement

(*Continued*)

Table 2.2 (*Continued*) Performance Delivery Manager Accountabilities—Performance Management

Performance Delivery Manager Results Areas	*Performance Delivery Manager Accountabilities*	*Skills*
Performance Management: Who	*How*	*What*
Performance change management results • Transformational change (4 Ps) • Change strategy sustainability	Define performance change management for the expected results to ensure compliance with performance management standards for employee, customer, financial, and operations performance measures, defined in the integrated IT performance measurement dashboard	Transformational change Performance measurement
HR performance management results • Staff performance plan • Staff performance measures	Define HR performance management for the expected results to ensure compliance with performance management standards for employee, customer, financial, and operations performance measures, defined in the integrated IT performance measurement dashboard.	Strategic value integration Performance measurement
Financial performance management results • Financial performance plan • Financial performance measures	Define financial performance management for the expected results to ensure compliance with performance management standards for employee, customer, financial, and operations performance measures, defined in the integrated IT performance measurement dashboard.	Strategic value integration Performance measurement
PMO processes results • Performance measurement methodology • Measurement process deployment • Training • Metrics, measurement • Tools support • PMO reporting	Performance measurement processes, outputs/outcomes, and inputs templates, defined in the performance measurement plan. Performance improvement processes, outputs/outcomes, inputs, and templates, defined in the performance improvement plan. Integrated IT performance measurement dashboard—employee, financial, customer, and operations. Benchmarking and assessment results—six (6) functional areas of IT services delivery life cycle.	Strategic value integration Performance measurement Transformational change

Table 2.3 Performance Delivery Manager Accountabilities—IT Operational Management

Performance Delivery Manager Results Areas	*Performance Delivery Manager Accountabilities*	*Skills*
IT Operational Management: Who	*How*	*What*
HR accountability results • Capital costs, business projects • Capital costs, technology projects • Operating costs, technology • Operating costs, operational	Performance measures, metrics, variances, capital costs for business and technology programs/projects Performance measures, metrics, indicators, and variances, operating costs for technology upgrades and operational services IT investments value for capital and operating costs Benchmarking results for IT budget plan, capital and operating expenditures	Performance measurement Transformational change
Financial accountability results • Outsourced services • Contract services • In-house services • Staff performance • Benchmarking	Performance measures, matrics, variances, HR performance for outsourced services Performance measures, metrics, and variances, HR performance for contract services Performance measures, metrics, and variances, HR performance for in-house services IT staff performance for outsourced, contract, and in-house services Benchmarking results for outsourced, contract, and in-house services	Performance measurement Transformational change
Operational process accountability results • Business processes • IT processes • Value • Benchmarking	Performance measures, metrics, and variances for business processes—management and delivery Performance, measures, metrics, indicators, and variances for IT processes—management and delivery Value of operational performance results for business and IT process simplification Benchmarking results for operational performance plan—business and IT processes	Performance measurement Transformational change

(Continued)

Table 2.3 (*Continued*) Performance Delivery Manager Accountabilities—IT Operational Management

Performance Delivery Manager Results Areas	*Performance Delivery Manager Accountabilities*	*Skills*
IT Operational Management: Who	*How*	*What*
Project management accountability results • Business projects • IT infrastructure projects • Value • Benchmarking	Performance measures, metrics, and variances for business projects—strategic and operational Performance measures, metrics, indicators, and variances for IT infrastructure projects—strategic and operational Project performance value, results for IT infrastructure projects—strategic and operational Benchmarking results, IT infrastructure projects—strategic and operational	Performance measurement Transformational change
AMS accountability results • Contract/outsourced services • AMS performance measures • Governance • Value • Benchmarking	Performance measures, metrics, and variances (measurement criteria) for AMS contract/outsourced services Performance tracking, corrective action, and analytics for AMS performance measures and results Accountability reporting for AMS performance measures and results Governance structure for AMS performance measures and results Value of AMS performance results Benchmarking results on AMS performance—contracted/outsourced	Performance measurement Transformational change
TOS accountability results • Contract/outsourced services • AMS performance measures • Governance • Value • Benchmarking	Performance measures, metrics, and variances (measurement criteria) for TOS contract/outsourced services Performance tracking, corrective action, and analytics for TOS performance measures and results Accountability reporting for TOS performance measures and results Governance structure for TOS performance measures and results Value of TOS performance results Benchmarking results on TOS performance—contracted/outsourced	Performance measurement Transformational change

The major accountabilities of the performance delivery manager in performing *strategic management* duties are highlighted in Table 2.1 to show the integrated performance management knowledge and skills requirements of this individual.

The major responsibilities of the performance delivery manager in performing *performance management* duties are highlighted in Table 2.2 to show the necessary integrated performance management knowledge and skills requirements.

The major accountabilities of the performance delivery manager in performing *IT operational management* duties are highlighted in Table 2.3 to show the necessary integrated performance management knowledge and skills requirements.

2.7.1 Real-World Observations: Performance Delivery Manager Accountabilities

Many performance managers and senior managers, especially those without the basic IT qualifications and skills, strongly express their views that IT professionals with technology qualifications, skills, and knowledge are not suitable to perform the role of IT performance delivery manager. They make statements to the effect that these "techies" should be IT architects not IT performance managers. These senior managers firmly believe that the *only* skill required of IT performance delivery managers is relationship management. I firmly support this necessary communications skills requirement. However, lesson learned, as a result of my extensive experiences in technologically advancing industry, is that performance measures and results reported by managers without the necessary IT qualifications, skills, and knowledge normally result in being misunderstood, misrepresented, and poorly communicated-twisted logic.

I will end this real-world observation with two simple and powerful quotations:

> A stupid man's report of what a clever man says can never be accurate, because he unconsciously translates what he hears into something he can understand.
>
> **Bertrand Russell**

> Misunderstandings usually occur because of differences in thinking preferences.
>
> **James P. Lewis**

2.8 Applying Integrated Framework to Other Disciplines

> Customers require the effective integration of technologies to simplify their workflow and boost efficiency.
>
> **Anne M. Mulcahy**

Although this book is based on an integrated IT performance management model (framework) represented in Figure 2.2, this framework can be adapted to fit within the performance management context of other business discipline, such as engineering, manufacturing, and accounting. The basic functional components of performance management may not change drastically. However, the strategic and operational components of the industry business discipline will change

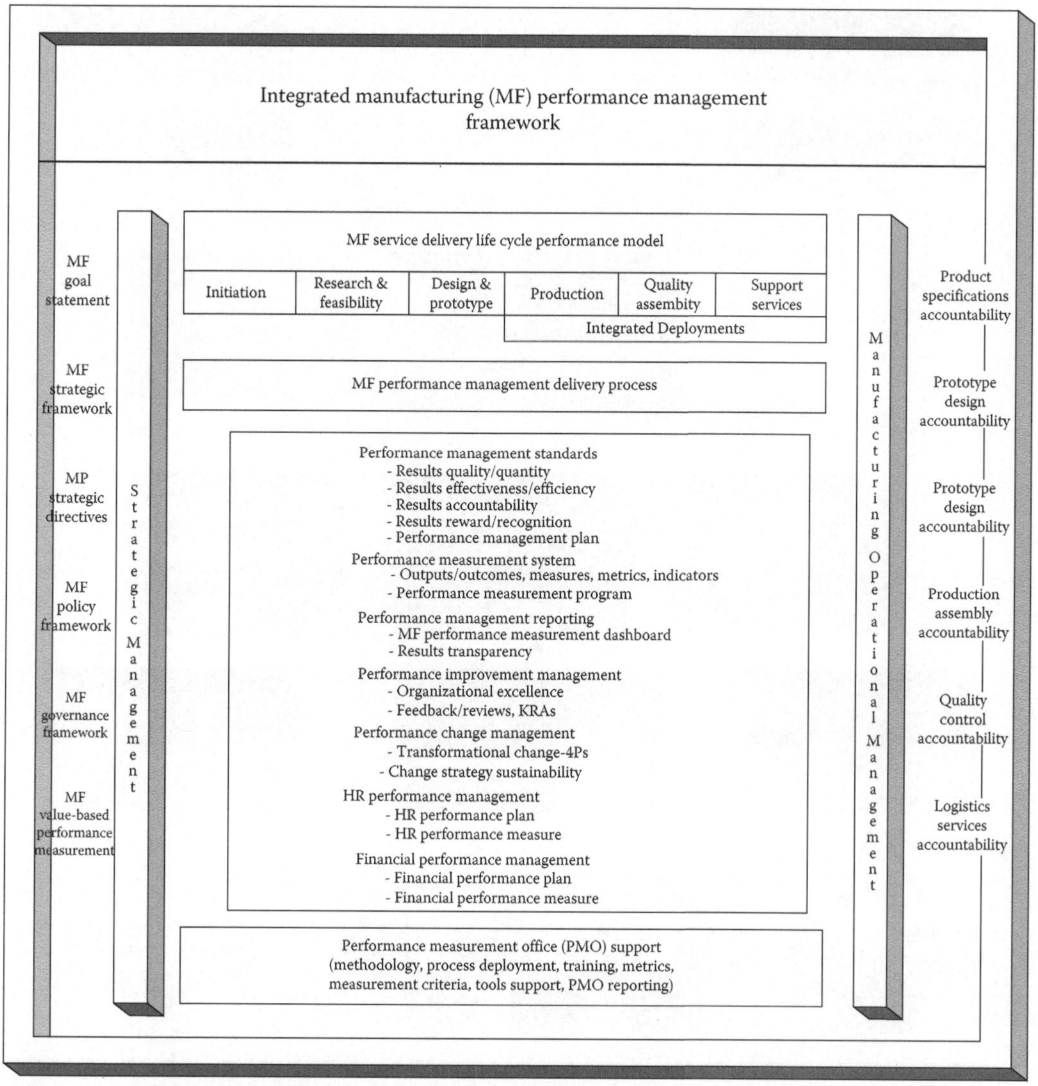

Figure 2.5 Integrated MF performance management component model.

based on the product/service life cycle of the industry business. Figure 2.5 shows a framework to measure performance in the manufacturing (MF) industry.

2.9 Alternate Project-Based Organizational Structure

The more alternatives, the more difficult the choice.

Abbe' D'Allanival

There are certain companies where performance management culture and maturity is not widely accepted by corporate executives to justify the need for a performance management executive at

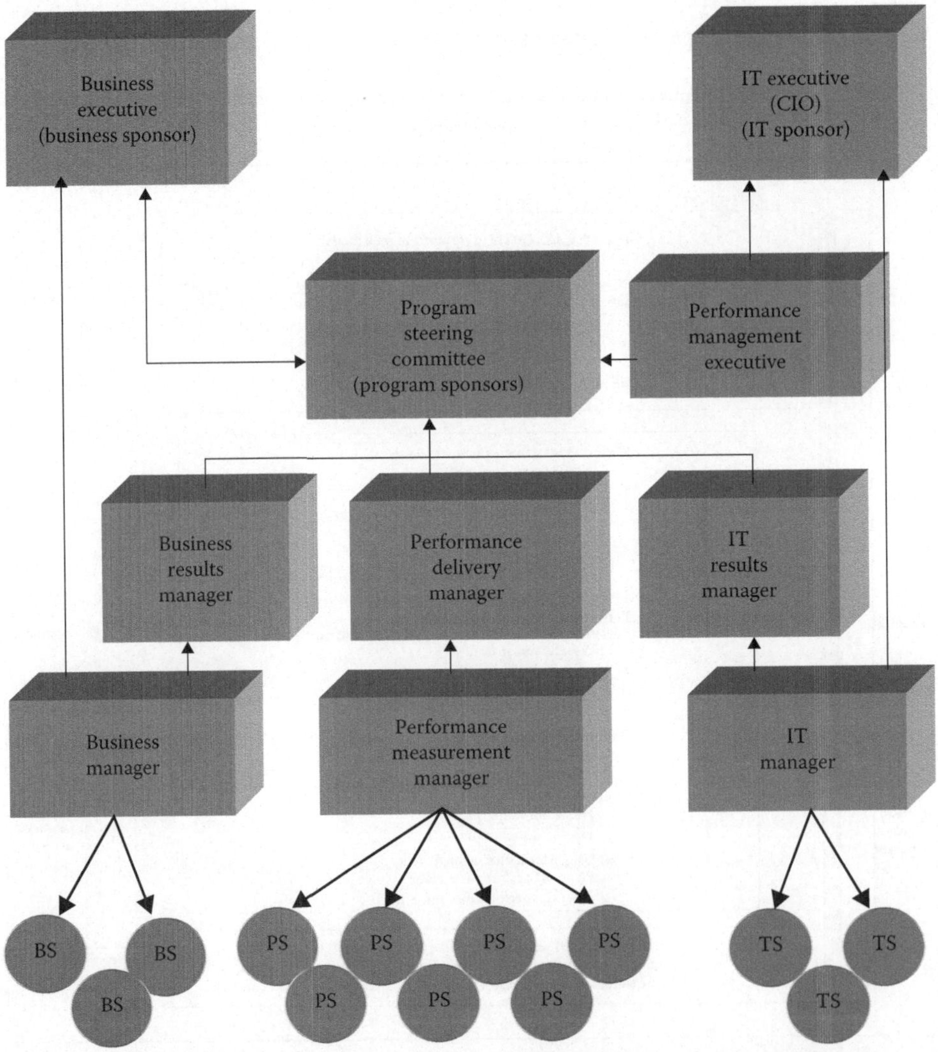

Figure 2.6 Alternate performance management organizational structure solution.

the vice-president level. As a result of this perspective, I decided to show a typical organization structure, represented in Figure 2.6, which these types of companies normally deploy.

2.10 Summary

The integrated IT performance management (framework) presented in this chapter shows the component results areas of this framework. It also discusses the accountabilities of the performance delivery manager to demonstrate the integrated nature in managing, measuring, and delivering IT services. RBM processes integrated with traditionally managed organizations in a regressive culture—"It's a matter of survival not efficiency," sound impressive but in reality is not likely to make an improved difference. To make a difference for success requires a culture that values the necessity for accountability, integrity, and ethics.

These organizations should consider the following recommendations, as a framework, to guide them toward successful management, measurement, and delivery of IT services.

- Develop goal statement, strategic framework, strategic directives, performance governance, and value-based performance measurement for IT strategic management that shows the alignment of IT strategic directives with IT operational management, IT service delivery life cycle, and performance measurement dashboard. The end result is a performance measurement dashboard with outputs and outcomes that directly align with the IT strategic directives. The performance measures, metrics, and analytics are descriptive properties of the output/outcomes, which demonstrate the integrative components of the three major results areas: strategic management, performance management, and IT operational management.
- Define the IT service delivery life cycle and measure, manage, and monitor the results/outcomes/outputs of these IT services, using an integrated IT performance dashboard for evidence-based decision making, using predictive analytics.
- Establish and communicate PMO processes, tools, and techniques to business and IT staff.
- Define clear accountabilities for executive management, performance program management, and performance measurement, for strategic, performance, and IT operational management.
- Obtain approval and support from executive managers on the goal statement, strategic framework, strategic directives, policy framework, performance governance, and value-based performance measurement. Also, the integrated IT performance measurement dashboard and IPMF-IT.
- Communicate and ensure performance managers adhere to performance management policies, processes, standards/guidelines, and RBM.
- Ensure that the performance delivery manager is a performance management professional, with strategic integration, transformational change, and performance management skills.
- Ensure that the performance delivery manager understands the linkage between operational, strategic, and performance management, as presented in this chapter, and detailed in the remaining chapters of book.

In this foundation chapter, I introduced an IPMF-IT model, discussed the applications of this framework in terms of the three functional components of strategic, IT operational, and performance management, and highlighted the key accountabilities of the performance delivery manager. Chapters 3 through 5 elaborate on each of these three functional components; Chapter 6 shows the horizontal integration of these three functional components with the IT service delivery life cycle performance model and the strategic directives. Chapter 7 discusses the implementation of this IPMF-IT model, using various industry-wide guidelines.

2.11 Endnotes: Key Performance Management Terms

[1]*Performance management program*: A program that enables accountability for results to improve operational excellence by measuring success, using a results-driven performance measurement and accountability framework, based on outcomes measures and results.

[2]*Integrated IT performance management framework* (*IPMF-IT*): An integrated representation of strategic management, performance management, and IT operational management component processes to manage, measure, deliver, and improve IT services, using a results-driven performance measurement and accountability framework that is based on outcomes and outputs measures and results, rather than the traditional effort and activity-oriented measures.

[3]*Performance delivery manager*: A manager who is accountable for the delivery of an integrated performance management program that ensures effective transition to a culture of "accountability for results" within both business and IT areas.

[4]*IT service delivery life cycle performance model*: A results-based representation that provides performance measures for the outputs/outcomes of the six functional areas within the IT service delivery life cycle.

[5]*Resources*: The IT and business assets of a company represented as people, process, technology/materials, and financial resources. People represent employees, customers, vendors, service providers–stakeholders; process represents organizational structures, IT and business process flows, and information contents; technology represents hardware, software, network, facilities, and applications; materials represent raw and processed products; financial represent financial assets.

[6]*Results-based management* (*RBM*): An approach focused on achieving results-broad management strategy aimed at changing the way organization operates, with improving performance and achieving results as the central orientation.

[7]*Chief Performance Officer* (*CPO*): An executive who is accountable for the strategic and operational direction to ensure effective measurement of IT and business services and to improve operational excellence and increase value and alignment to organizational goals and strategic directives.

[8]*Performance program steering committee–project position*: A senior management committee position held by executive and senior business, IT, and performance management staff with performance management oversight and approval accountabilities.

[9]*Integrated performance management information system* (*PMIS*): An integrated performance management information system and associated data and processes that provide automated support to gather, integrate, and distribute the output, outcomes, performance measures, and process flows of performance management processes.

[10]*Performance delivery management–project positions*: Organizational or program-level management positions held by senior business, IT, and performance management staff with results-based accountabilities (responsibilities + authorities).

[11]*Accountability assignment matrix* (*AAM*): A structure used to assign accountabilities to particular people to produce specific results/outputs/outcomes. An AAM defines who is accountable for the delivery of each RBS measures and result.

[12]*KPI Institute, CMMI, COBIT, Six Sigma, PMI, Kaplan and Norton*: These companies provide training and consulting services in the areas of performance management and measurement.

[13]*Performance measurement structure* (*PMS*): A performance measurement structure based on Kaplan and Norton's-Balanced Scorecard; synonymous with integrated IT performance measurement dashboard, results breakdown structure (RBS) and performance management structure.

[14]*IT performance governance structure*: A results-driven governance structure that focuses on accountability performance measures in support of evidence-based decision making, using processes and structures.

[15]*Integrated IT performance measurement dashboard*: A performance measurement structure based on Kaplan and Norton's-Balanced Scorecard; synonymous with performance measurement structure.

[16]*Results-based management (RBM) culture*: A culture that promotes high performance to achieving results, accountability, engaged managers (setting and accomplishing pragmatic goals).

[17]*Results-based budgeting (RBB)*: A financial budgeting approach focused on achieving results-broad management budgeting strategy aimed at changing the way organization managed budgets, with improving performance and achieving results as the central orientation.

[18]*Performance management plan*: A plan that provides the procedures (how) and organizational structure (who) to manage the performance of IT services, as defined in the performance management program.

[19]*Key results area*: General areas of outputs or outcomes for the IT performance management delivery process.

[20]*Performance measurement areas*: Areas of outputs, outcomes, and performance measures, as defined in the integrated IT performance measurement dashboard for employee, customer, financial, and operational process.

[21]*Integrated IT performance management results breakdown structure (RBS)*: A results-based performance structure that formed the foundation in the development of the integrated IT performance measurement dashboard to managing and measuring the results of IT services.

[22]*Performance management plan, performance measurement plan, performance improvement plan*: Plans that provide the procedures (how) and organizational structure (who) to manage, measure, and improve on the performance of IT services, as defined in the performance management program.

[23]*PMIR*: The repository of all performance documentation. It is the database that the PMIS uses to generate performance management reports.

[24]*IT resource plan*: A formal approved document consisting of labor, technology/facilities, process and financial resources, used as the baseline to allocate resources, estimate costs, and develop staffing plans to support the performance management program.

[25]*Core and supporting knowledge areas*: Knowledge areas as defined in PMI to support project performance management accountability during the management and measurement of business and IT infrastructure projects.

[26]*Applications management services (AMS)*: Performance accountability for outsourced AMS using service level agreements and performance measures framework to support results-based accountability.

[27]*Technology operations services (TOS)*: Performance accountability for outsourced technology operations services using service-level agreements and performance measures framework to support results-based accountability.

2.12 Questions to Think About: Management Perspectives

1. Think about how your organization manages and measures IT services. How is the cultural of RBM and RBB being transformed? How does your organization view integration, accountability, and change management? How are IT services structured? What is the key

rationale for the organizational structure? How does individual greed for power, politics, performance, and personal financial interests affect the organization structure? What are the major results areas of integrated IT performance management? How do these results areas relate to your IT structures and processes? What is the mindset of senior management for results-based management and performance improvement?

2. Think about how your organization involves executives and business staff during performance management strategy formulation and execution. What are the performance management delivery processes that align operational management with strategic management during IT services delivery life cycle? How are these performance management delivery processes communicated?
3. Think about how your organization involves performance measurement staff during project initiation and execution. What are the performance measurement outcomes/outputs and performance measures that align IT operational management with strategic management during IT services delivery life cycle? How are these processes communicated? How does your organization integrate IT service delivery life cycle with performance measurement processes? What is senior managements' perception on the responsibilities, needs, and benefits of an integrated IT performance measurement dashboard? How does senior management in your organization promote Six Sigma certification? What is the level of professional qualifications, skills, and experience of the performance delivery manager? What is the level of professional qualifications, skills, and experience of the performance measurement manager? What are the differences in thinking preferences?
4. Think about how your organization involves business managers and IT managers during performance management strategy formulation and IT operational execution. What are the outputs/outcomes that align IT operational management and PMO with strategic management during IT services delivery life cycle? How are these outputs/outcomes communicated?
5. Think about how your organization involves PMO during performance management strategy formulation and execution. What is the level of involvement and commitment from business and IT management executives? How is the formal or informal PMO processes communicated? How do you know that you no longer have executive management support for the PMO? RBM? RBB? Integrated IT performance measurement dashboard?
6. Think about your organization culture—mindset, values, and beliefs—toward performance management? What are staff attitudes toward measurement? How is your measurement system being used? For improvements or for judgments and blame? How does your financial, HR, IT operational, and business operational staff measure performance? How do you measure the performance of your customers, service providers, and vendors?

2.13 Chapter Testing Questions

1. Integrated IT performance measurement dashboard consists of four operational process measures. Three of them are service delivery, functional management, and service excellence. What is the fourth measure?
   a. Account management
   b. Operational efficiencies
   c. Relationship management

2. Integrated IT performance management results breakdown structure (RBS) is a results-based structure that measures IT resource assets. Three of these components are people, process, and financials. What is the fourth measure?
   a. Equipment
   b. Hardware
   c. Technology
3. Which of the following accountability will *most* likely fit the definition of "A framework for measuring progress and results"?
   a. Performance accountability
   b. Strategic accountability
   c. Policy accountability
4. Which of the following IT assets will *not* likely fit the goal of "optimizing the utilization of IT resources"?
   a. Structure
   b. Processes
   c. People
5. Which of the following will *not* likely trigger a performance improvement for operational processes?
   a. Transformational change
   b. Relationship management
   c. New employee
6. At one stage of a performance measurement effort, you decided to use the dashboard to understand the progress, trends, and performance results for measuring the results of new enterprise architecture processes. What would you *most* likely examine?
   a. Improvements analytics of new processes
   b. Performance progress indicator of new process
   c. Change strategy sustainability of the new process
7. What are the major outputs of IT performance governance structure?
   a. Structure and processes
   b. People, process, technology, financials
   c. People, politics, process, performance
8. Which one of the following results areas is *best* input for the performance dashboard?
   a. IT strategic framework
   b. IT performance governance structure
   c. IT strategic directives
9. Results-based accountability should *most* likely focus on
   a. Outcomes, output, results
   b. Results, activities, input
   c. Effort, financial, results

Recommended Readings

Performance Management

Aguinis, H., *Performance Management*. New York: Pearson Education, 2012.

Bainey, K.R., *Integrated IT Project Management: A Model-Centric Approach*. New York: Artech House, 2004.

Batshalom, B., *The Green Source, The Magazine of Sustainable Design*. Boston, MA: Sustainable Performance Institute, 2011.

Corkins, G., *Performance Management, Integrating Strategy, Execution, Methodologies, Risk, and Analytics*. Hoboken, NJ: John Wiley & Sons Inc., 2009.

Davenport, T., Jeanne, H., Robert, H., *Analytics at work, Smarter Decisions, Better Results*. Boston, MA: Harvard Business School Publishing, 2010.

Demartini, C., *Performance Management Systems: Design, Diagnosis and Use*. Berlin, Germany: Springer, 2013.

Harvard Business Review, *Improving Business Processes, Expert Solutions to Everyday Challenges*, Boston, MA: Harvard Business School Publishing, 2010.

Kaplan, R.S. and Norton, D.P., *The Balanced Scorecard: Translating Strategy into Action*. Boston, MA: Harvard Business School Publishing, 1996.

KPI Institute, *The KPI Compendium: 20,000 Key Performance Indicators used in Practice*. Melbourne, Victoria, Australia: KPI Institute, 2013.

Parmenter, D., *Key Performance Indicators, Developing Implementing, and Using Winning KPIs*. Hoboken, NJ: John Wiley & Sons Inc., 2010.

Spitzer, D.R., *Transforming Performance Measurement, Rethinking the Way We Measure and Drive Organizational Success*. New York: AMACOM, 2007.

Chapter 3

Strategic Management Model

3.1 Strategic Management

The function of strategic management XE "business management" is to ensure that IT services are effectively measured, managed, delivered, reported, and improved using a results-based accountability framework. It consists of the following results areas:

- IT goal statements
- IT strategic framework
- IT strategic directives
- IT policy framework
- IT governance framework
- IT value-based performance measurement (VBPM)

Figure 3.1 is a graphical representation of the modeling concepts that demonstrates the structure and relationships of the definitions or processing components of strategic management, from a performance management perspective.

The intent of this chapter is *not* to provide detailed processes or procedures on the implementation of the strategic management processes or similar strategic improvement processes. There are many excellent books on strategic management processes, concepts, theory, and applicability, some of which are mentioned in the "Recommended Readings" section provided at the end of each chapter. The main objective of this chapter is to provide an overview of the contents (what), purpose (why), accountabilities (who is accountable for what), and results (what, how, why) of strategic management and to demonstrate how it fits within the context of the overall integrated IT performance management framework. The "accountability" section provides results-based accountability for the executive performance manager, the performance delivery manager, and the performance measurement team—performance measurement manager and performance specialists. The results sections for each of the IT strategic management results areas provide the outputs/outcomes (what), process flow (how), and performance measures (why) to support the measurement, management, delivery, improvement, and integration of the strategic management results areas. The performance measures from the performance measurement dashboard mainly

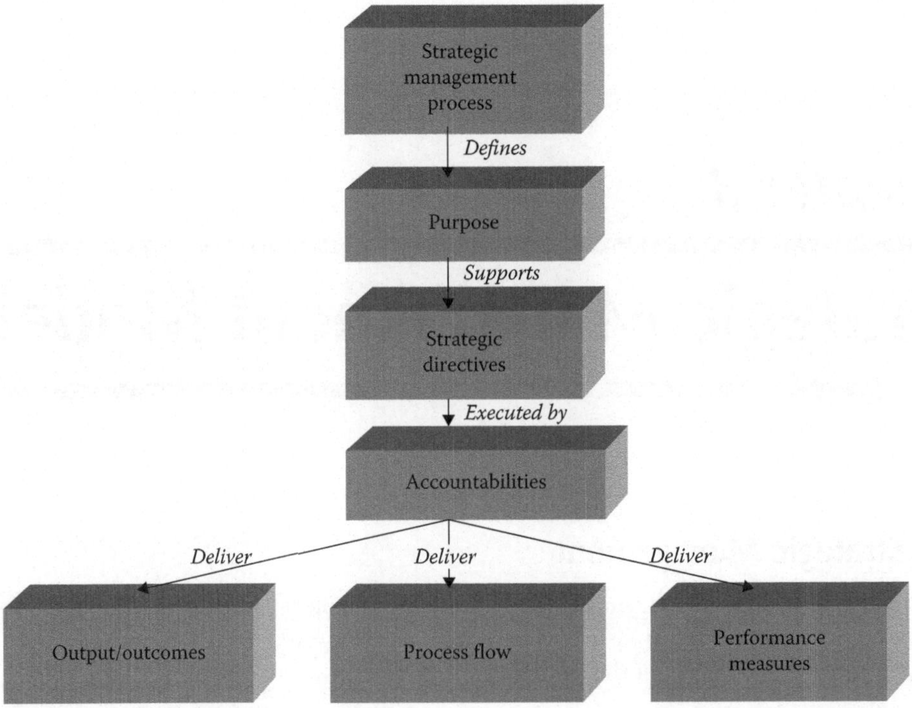

Figure 3.1 Strategic management model.

show staff input metrics for demonstration purposes. In reality, the dashboard contains many combinations of results for input, process, and output/outcomes measures.

> Don't measure your performance by what you have accomplished, but by what you should have accomplished within your capabilities.
>
> **Jeroen De Flander**

The material presented in the following sections is organized to support the structure represented in Figure 3.1. This structure will provide the readers with a logical and consistent flow of information to enable them to gain a better understanding and better appreciate the integrated nature of IT performance management.

3.2 IT Goal Statement

Executives shall use the *IT goal statement*[1] as the basis for communicating, integrating, and making evidence-based strategic and operational decisions. Strategic management decisions should be made using sound objective judgments with an understanding of operational impacts, rather than emotions-based with "self-serving" political agendas. Sound objective judgments require executive management understanding of vision, mission, goals, values, success factors, performance measurement areas, as well as an understanding of the integrated components to improve the quality of management and overall IT performance. The major *outputs* of the IT goal statements include the following:

- *Vision*: To achieve performance excellence by optimizing the *quality and quantity* of technology and IT labor resources while delivering innovative information technology solutions to ensure economic and technical efficiencies.
- *Mission*: To provide information technology leadership, business projects delivery and enterprise architecture services, applications and technology services, and a sound technology infrastructure to effectively and efficiently support the goals of the business through improved technology innovations and performance excellence.
- *Goals*: To provide influential, collaborative, forward thinking, and responsive IT-integrated services through IT governance, planning and administration, enterprise architecture and innovations, project portfolio management, applications and technology services, and IT operations support, in collaboration with the business.
- *Values*: Accountability-results management accountability framework: (1) teamwork—collaboration/coordination; (2) integration—people, process, technology, and financials; (3) integrity and trust—performance measures and accountability reporting; (4) service and quality—IT resource optimization; (5) service excellence and innovation—continuous improvement; and (6) treat people with dignity and respect—attitude, positive thinking.
- *Success factors*: The success of the IT department is contingent upon its ability to act as a catalyst for innovatively leveraging technology to advance the IT strategic and operational plans, in accordance with the performance measurement areas. This will guide and support the management and delivery of applications and technology services and enable the integration of IT services into the business area to improve and transform the quality of services provided in the business areas.
- *Performance measurement areas*: (1) *employee*—to increase learning and innovations and to sustain our capacity and capabilities to change, transform, and improve; (2) *customer*—to increase customer satisfaction and service excellence; (3) *financial*—to optimize the utilization of financial resources and provide financial transparency; and (5) *operational*—to improve service delivery, service/operational efficiencies, relationship management, and functional management/leadership.

3.2.1 Purpose

The purpose of this result area is to provide influential, collaborative, and forward-thinking *leadership* for the measurement and delivery of IT services, using a *result-based accountability framework*.[2] This framework will form the baseline to measure and monitor the results of the delivered IT services, within the context of the established performance measurement areas. The performance steering committee will have approval accountabilities for both the business and IT program or organizational performance. This committee will also have accountability with the performance measurement managers, for the operational performance using the IT goals measurement areas defined in the performance management plan and the integrated IT performance measurement dashboard.

3.2.2 Strategic Directives

- IT services will be directed and measured by a performance steering committee using an IT goal statement that specifies the outputs—vision, mission, goals, values, success factors, and performance measurement areas—to direct and measure the success and value of IT. This IT goal statement includes transformational performance leadership strategies with the objective toward integration of IT services into the business.

- The performance steering committee will provide performance approval accountabilities for the measurement, management, and delivery of the IT goal statement, represented in the performance measurement dashboard as IT goals leadership/functional management output.
- All changes to the IT goal statement outputs must be approved by the performance steering committee. The performance delivery manager will document and present all changes to the performance steering committee for approval.
- The performance steering committee will meet, at a minimum, on a monthly basis to review the performance indicators, trends, and analytics for IT goals outputs and outcomes, represented in the performance measurement dashboard as *Operational-FM and Performance Metrics.*[3] If the overall progress of this output is *red* or *yellow*, more frequent meetings may be required.

3.2.3 Accountabilities

3.2.3.1 Executive Performance Manager

This person is accountable for *approval* of performance results.

- Strengths, weaknesses, opportunities, and threats (*SWOT*)[4] analysis for IT goals statement outputs—vision, mission, goals, values, success factors, and performance measurement areas
- Linkages of IT goals statement outputs and outcomes with performance measures and performance measurement dashboard
- Performance measurement dashboard results—performance measures, metrics and variances for IT goal leadership/functional management measures
- Stakeholders' satisfaction survey results for IT goal statement measures—effectiveness/quality
- Integrated IT goals performance measurement results—areas for improvements
- *Performance measurement/management program*[5] sponsorship and champion

3.2.3.2 Performance Delivery Manager

This person is accountable for *management* of performance results.

- SWOT analysis for IT goals statement outputs—vision, mission, goals, values, success factors, and performance measurement areas—areas of improvements
- Linkages of IT goals statement outputs and outcomes with performance measures and performance measurement dashboard
- Performance measurement dashboard results—performance measures, metrics, and variances for IT goal leadership/functional management measures
- Stakeholders' satisfaction surveys for IT goal statement results—effectiveness/quality
- Integrated IT goals performance measurement results—areas for improvements
- Accountability reports to performance steering committee on IT goal statement outputs/outcomes, performance measures, and results

3.2.3.3 Performance Measurement Team

This team is accountable for the *delivery* of performance results.

- Meaningful and credible input data for SWOT analysis for IT goals statement outputs—vision, mission, goals, values, success factors, and performance measurement areas—areas of improvements.

- Clear alignment data to demonstrate linkages of IT goals statement outputs and outcomes with performance measures and performance measurement dashboard.
- Integrated IT goal performance measurement data for performance measurement results—areas for improvements.
- Stakeholders' satisfaction survey data for IT goal measures—effectiveness and quality.
- Performance improvement data for IT goal performance measurement results—areas for improvements.
- Result-based accountability data for accountability reports to performance steering committee on IT goal statement outputs/outcomes, performance measures, and results.

3.2.4 Results: IT Goal Statement

Accountabilities[6] discussed earlier are brief because they are intended to serve as a reference for *who is accountable* for *what* during the delivery of the IT goals statement outputs/outcomes. Results are now introduced to highlight the outputs of this IT goal statement results area and respective outcomes (what), process flow (how), and performance measures (why). It is intended to serve as a reference based on the English language interrogatives: Who *is accountable for what, how, and why.* The outputs/outcomes, process flow, and performance measures, based on real-world practical implementation, will serve as excellent references for the practicing performance managers during measurement, delivery, and reporting of IT goal statement outputs and outcomes.

The outputs/outcomes highlight the key results the performance managers are accountable to manage, measure, and report during the delivery of the IT goal statement results area. The process flow, based on real-world practical implementations, is a graphical representation of the inputs, process, outputs, and relationships. The goal statement performance model diagram shows a representation to communicate the integrated components of IT goal statement with strategic, IT operational, and performance management staff.

The performance measures from the integrated IT performance measurement dashboard for IT goal statement outputs/outcomes are illustrated for "IT Executive Leadership: Operational-FM" measures. Appendices A through F provide further details. Performance metrics, indicators, progress, trends, and analytics formed the basis for evidence-based decision making to enable improved organizational excellence.

3.2.4.1 Outputs/Outcomes—IT Goal Statement

The outputs and outcomes of the IT goal statement are given in Table 3.1.

3.2.4.2 Process Flows—IT Goal Statement

The process flows of the IT goal statement are shown in Figure 3.2.

3.2.4.3 Performance Model—IT Goal Statement

The performance model of the IT goal statement is shown in Figure 3.3.

3.2.4.4 Performance Measures—IT Goal Statement

The performance measures of the IT goal statement are shown in Figure 3.4.

Table 3.1 IT Goal Statement Output/Outcomes

Results Area	*Output*	*Outcome*
IT goal statement	Vision—Innovative IT Solutions	• Optimized *quality and quantity* of technology and labor resources
	Mission—leadership, IT services, IT infrastructure	• Improved technology innovations and operational performance excellence • Increased *quality* of management and decrease *quantity* of management
	Goals—integrated IT services	• Increased collaborations with business
	Values—results-based Management (RBM)	• Improved results-based accountability
	Success factors—strategic, operating plans and performance measures integration	• Increased integration of IT services into business areas • Improved transformation of quality services provided to business areas
	Performance measurement areas—operations, financials, employee, customer	• Increased transformation to performance measurement culture • Increased value of performance measurement dashboard analytics

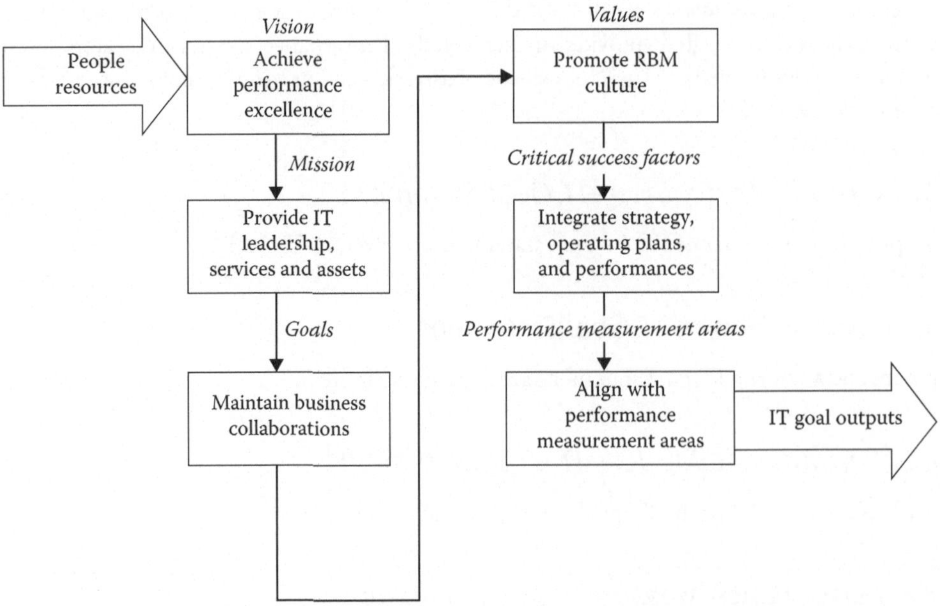

Figure 3.2 IT goal statement process flow.

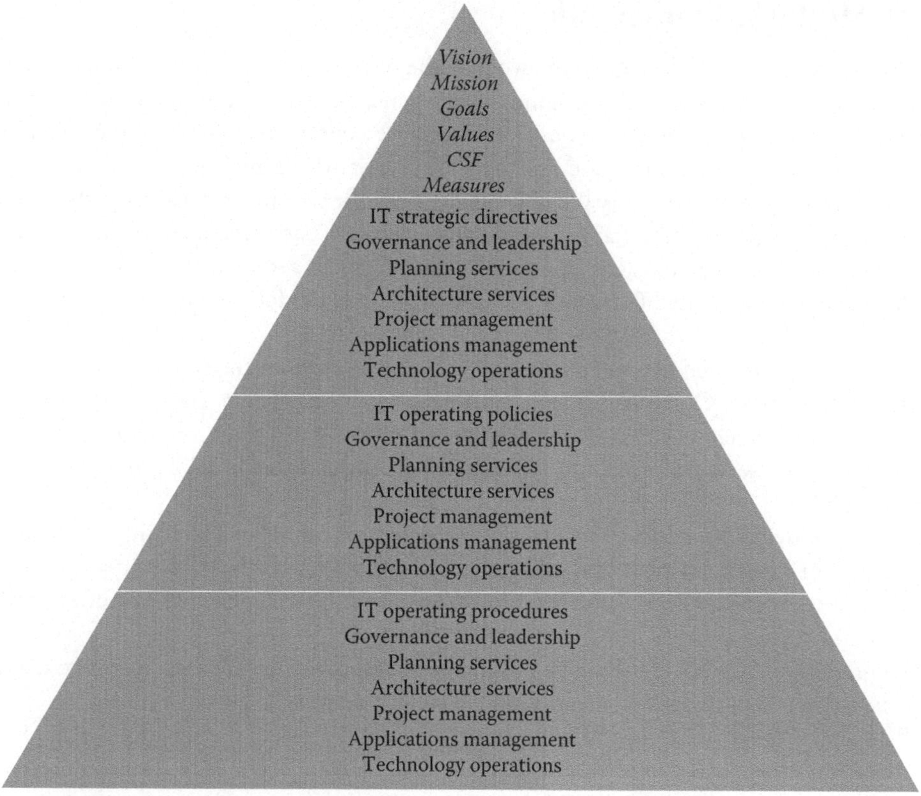

Figure 3.3 IT goal statement performance model.

IT PERFORMANCE MANAGEMENT DASHBOARD (2011–2012) ANALYTICS August 31/2011

IT EXECUTIVE LEADERSHIP

OPERATIONAL-FM	Start Date	End Date	Status	% Complete	Indicator
IT Governance Accountability Framework	4/1/2011	12/31/2011	In-Progress	60%	G
HR Performance Contract Alignment	4/1/2011	9/30/2011	In-Progress	80%	G
Executive Management (EM) Progress Status	4/1/2011	3/31/2012	In-Progress	40%	G
Executive Management Presentation/Approvals	4/1/2011	3/31/2012	In-Progress	60%	G
IT Policies and Procedures	4/1/2011	3/31/2012	In-Progress	60%	G
IT Operational Accountability Framework	4/1/2011	3/31/2012	In-Progress	40%	G
OPERATIONAL-FM Summary	4/1/2011	3/31/2012	In-Progress	57%	G

Performance Metrics

% IT staff performing IT Governance; # Improvements completed
% IT staff performing HR Alignment; # Improvements completed
% IT staff performing EM Communications; # Improvements completed
% IT staff performing EM Presentation; # Improvements completed
% IT staff performing IT Policies; # Improvements completed
%Stakeholders satisfaction levels with IT Policies: # unsatisfied stakeholders
% IT staff performing IT Operations; # Improvements completed

Figure 3.4 IT goal statement performance measures.

3.3 IT Strategic Framework

Executives shall use the IT strategic framework as the basis for communicating, integrating, and making strategic and operational decisions. It represents the strategic framework for organizational performance. Sound objective decisions require executive management understanding of the measurement, management, and delivery of the company's IT products and services, within the context of the IT service delivery life cycle. For each of the six functional areas of the IT service delivery life cycle—governance, planning and administration, enterprise architecture and innovations, project portfolio management, applications management services, and IT operational support, the major *outputs* of the IT strategic framework include the following:

- Outcomes—Intended to cover the results of IT services within the context of the IT services delivery life cycle. Outcomes are the results that express benefits, accomplishments, goals, and impacts/changes—what difference are we making? For each of the functional areas within the IT services, providing "what, how, when, and to whom" IT services should be delivered.
- Goals—Provide the result (what) to achieving the outcomes and realizing the benefits for each of the functional areas of the IT service delivery life cycle.
- Strategies—Provide the actions (how) to achieving the goals for each of the functional areas of the IT service delivery life cycle.
- Programs and Initiatives—Provide programs-capital projects expenses; initiative-operating expenses for each functional areas of the IT service delivery life cycle.
- Benefits—Provide the benefits (what) to successfully delivering the programs and initiatives that align with the outcomes for each of the functional areas of the IT service delivery life cycle.
- Cost—Provide cost estimates for delivering the services for each of the functional areas of the IT service delivery life cycle.
- Performance measures—Provide performance measures and results (targets) for each of the functional areas of the IT service delivery life cycle.
- Linkages to business strategic plan, IT operational plan and IT performance management plan to ensure that the technology solution is aligned with business goals, objectives, and strategies, and measured using the *integrated IT performance measurement dashboard.*
- *Program delivery plan*—Projects, priorities, implementation sequences, *performance measures and results* that support the programs initiatives.

3.3.1 Purpose

The purpose of this result area is to provide a sound and forward-thinking *framework* for the planning, delivery, and measurement of IT services, using a *results-based accountability framework.*[2] This framework will form the baseline to measure and monitor the results of the delivered IT services within the context of the functional areas of the IT services delivery life cycle and the established performance measurement areas. The performance steering committee will have approval accountabilities for organizational performance—business and IT performance program. This committee will also have accountability with the performance measurement managers for the operational performance using the IT strategy measurement areas defined in the performance management plan and the integrated IT performance measurement dashboard.

3.3.2 Strategic Directives

- IT services will be planned, delivered, and measured by a performance steering committee using an IT strategic framework that specifies the outputs/outcomes, goals, strategies, programs/initiatives, benefits, costs, performance measures, linkages to business strategic plan, and program delivery plan. This IT strategic framework will be used to direct and measure the success and value of delivered IT services using transformational performance leadership strategies, with the goal toward integration of IT services into the business.
- The performance steering committee will provide performance approval accountabilities for the measurement, management, and delivery of the IT strategic framework, represented in the performance measurement dashboard as leadership/functional management and operational service delivery output.
- All changes to the IT strategic framework outputs must be approved by the performance steering committee. The performance delivery manager will document and present all changes to the performance steering committee for approval.
- The performance steering committee will meet, at a minimum, on a monthly basis to review the performance indicators, trends, and analytics for the IT strategic framework outputs and outcomes, represented in the performance measurement dashboard as *Operational-FM, SD, and Performance Metrics.*[3] If the overall progress of this output is *red* or *yellow*, more frequent meetings will be required.
- Program initiatives will be identified, justified, and assessed for each of the six functional areas based on the goals, strategies, and benefits outlined in the IT strategic framework.
- Senior managers will be thoroughly familiar with the IT strategic framework to ensure consistency in delivery across the business areas.

3.3.3 Accountabilities

3.3.3.1 Executive Performance Manager

This person is accountable for *approval* of performance results.

- SWOT analysis for IT strategic framework outputs—outputs/outcomes, goals, strategies, programs/initiatives, benefits, costs, performance measures, linkages to business strategic plan, and program delivery plan
- Linkages of IT strategic framework outputs and outcomes with performance measures and performance measurement dashboard
- Performance measurement dashboard results—performance measures, metrics, and variances—for IT strategic framework leadership/functional management measures
- Stakeholders' satisfaction surveys results for IT strategic framework measures—effectiveness/quality
- Integrated IT strategic framework performance measurement results—areas for improvements
- Performance measurement/management program sponsorship and champion

3.3.3.2 Performance Delivery Manager

This person is accountable for *management* of performance results.

- SWOT analysis for IT strategic framework outputs—outputs/outcomes, goals, strategies, programs/initiatives, benefits, costs, performance measures, linkages to business strategic plan, and program delivery plan

- Linkages of IT strategic framework outputs and outcomes with performance measures and performance measurement dashboard
- Performance measurement dashboard results—performance measures, metrics, and variances for IT strategic framework leadership/functional management measures
- Stakeholders' satisfaction surveys results for IT strategic framework measures—effectiveness/quality
- Integrated IT strategy performance measurement results—areas for improvements
- Accountability reports to performance steering committee for IT strategic framework outputs/outcomes, performance measures, and results

3.3.3.3 Performance Measurement Team

This team is accountable for the *delivery* of performance results.

- Meaningful and credible input data for SWOT analysis for IT strategic framework outputs—outputs/outcomes, goals, strategies, programs/initiatives, benefits, costs, performance measures, linkages to business strategic plan, and program delivery plan
- Clear alignment data to demonstrate linkages of IT strategic framework outputs and outcomes with performance measures and performance measurement dashboard
- Performance measurement data for IT strategic framework performance measurement dashboard results—areas for improvements
- Stakeholders' satisfaction surveys data for IT strategic framework performance measures—effectiveness/quality
- Integrated IT strategy improvement data for performance measurement results—areas for improvements
- Result-based accountability data for accountability reports to performance steering committee on IT strategic framework outputs/outcomes, performance measures, and results

3.3.4 Results: IT Strategic Framework

Accountabilities discussed earlier are brief because they are intended to serve as a reference for *who is accountable* for *what* during the delivery of the IT Strategic Framework. Results are now introduced to highlight the outputs of this IT strategic framework results area and associated outcomes (what), process flow (how), and performance measures (why). It is intended to serve as a reference based on the English language interrogatives: Who *is accountable for what, how, and why*. The outputs/outcomes, process flow, and performance measures, based on real-world practical implementation, will serve as excellent references for practicing performance managers during measurement, delivery, and reporting of IT strategic framework outputs and outcomes.

The outputs/outcomes highlight the key results for IT strategic framework that the performance managers measure and report during the delivery of the IT strategic framework results area. The process flow, based on real-world practical implementations, is a graphical representation of the inputs, process, outputs, and relationships. The IT strategic framework performance model diagram shows the foundation representation to effectively communicate the integrated components of this IT strategic framework to strategic, IT operational, and performance management staff.

The performance measures from the integrated IT performance measurement dashboard for IT strategic framework outputs/outcomes are illustrated for "IT Planning & Administration Services: Operational-FM and SD" measures. Appendices A through F provide further details. Performance metrics, indicators, progress, trends, and analytics formed the basis for evidence-based decision making to enable improved organizational excellence.

3.3.4.1 Outputs/Outcomes—IT Strategic Framework

The outputs and outcomes of the IT strategic framework are given in Table 3.2.

3.3.4.2 Process Flows—IT Strategic Framework

The process flows of the IT strategic framework are shown in Figure 3.5.

Table 3.2 IT Strategic Framework Output/Outcomes

Results Area	*Output*	*Outcome*
IT strategic framework	Outcomes—IT resources/assets	• Optimized utilization of IT resources • Increased accountability and transparency of IT resources • Increased collaborations with business • Improved results-based accountability • Increased transformation to performance measurement culture • Increased value of performance measurement dashboard analytics • Increased accountability and transparency of program directives
	Goals—IT governance services; Integrated IT services into business	
	Strategies—Results-driven accountability—RBM; performance measurement dashboard	
	Program initiatives—Directives on IT technology assets consolidations and optimizations; emerging technologies; staff retention and retraining; IT transformation	
	Benefits—Optimized utilization of IT resources	
	Costs—Capital and operating costs	
	Linkages to operations—Strategic plan, operating plan, and performance measures alignment	
	Program delivery plan • IT technology assets consolidations and optimizations directives; • Emerging technologies directives; • staff retention and retraining directives; • IT transformation directives	

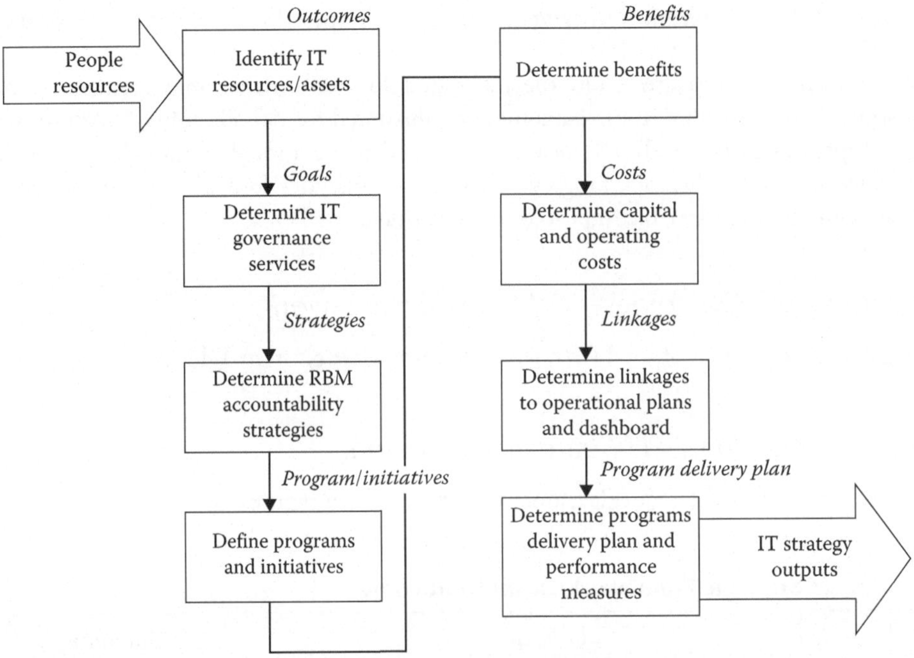

Figure 3.5 IT strategic framework process flow.

3.3.4.3 Performance Model—IT Strategic Framework

The performance model of the IT strategic framework is shown in Figure 3.6.

3.3.4.4 Performance Measures—IT Strategic Framework

The performance measures of the IT strategic framework are shown in Figure 3.7.

3.4 IT Strategic Directives

Executives shall use the IT strategic directives as the basis for communicating, integrating, and making strategic and operational decisions. These IT strategic directives, which are aligned with the performance measurement areas or *Balance Scorecard*, formed the basis for the identification of outputs, outcomes, and performance measures. Sound objective judgments require executive management understanding of the measurement, management, and delivery of the company's IT products and services, within the context of the IT service delivery life cycle. For each of the six functional areas of the IT service delivery life cycle—governance, planning and administration, enterprise architecture and innovations, project portfolio management, applications management services, and IT operational support, the major *outputs* of IT strategic directive include the following:

- Executive leadership services (ELS)—Provides ELS strategic directives for leadership, contract administration, management policies, capital and operating expenses reviews, employee performance, client and vendor relationships, and quality assurance compliance.
- Planning and administration services (PAS)—Provides PAS strategic directives for leadership, strategic/operational plans, invoice processing, capital and operating

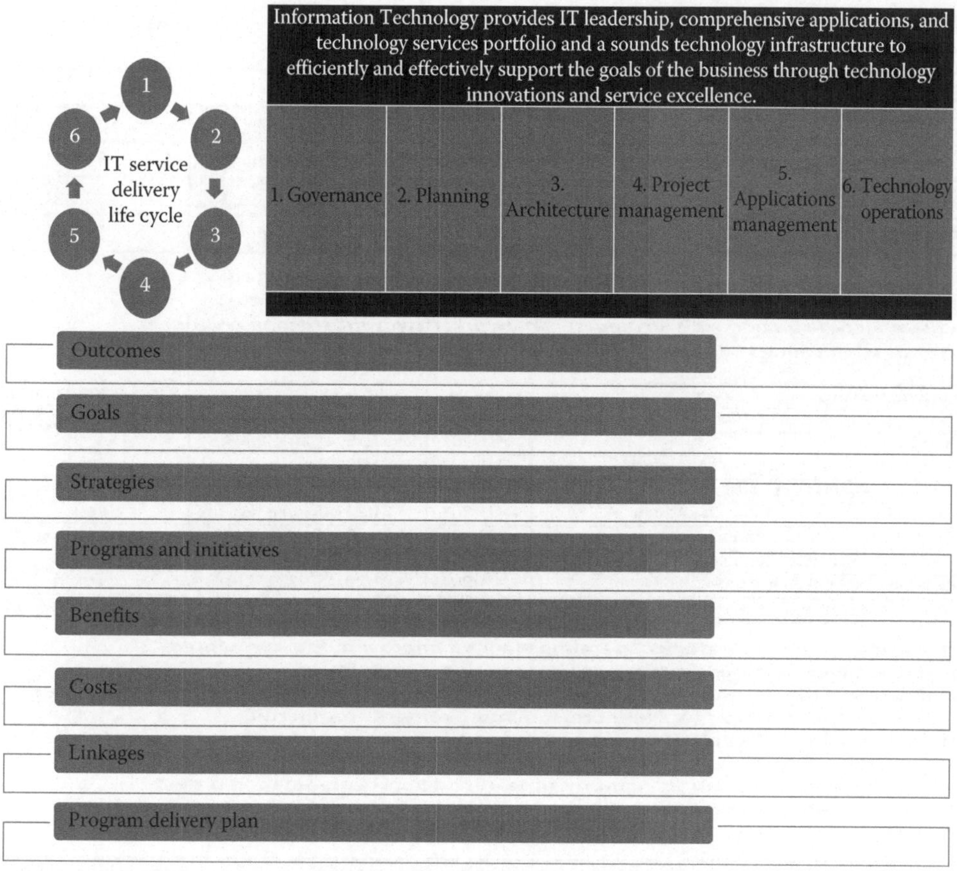

Figure 3.6 IT strategic framework performance model.

expenses, employee performance, client and vendor relationships, and quality assurance compliance.

- Enterprise architecture services (EAS)—Provides EAS architecture strategic directives for leadership, contract management, EAS services, project management—IT infrastructure, EAS management policies, capital and operating expenses, employee performance, client and vendor relationships, and quality assurance compliance.
- Project portfolio management (PPM)—Provides PPM strategic directives for leadership, contract administration, project management—business projects, PMO management policies, capital and operating expenses reviews, employee performance, client and vendor relationships, and quality assurance compliance.
- Applications management services (AMS)—Provides AMS strategic directives for leadership, contract administration, AMS services, AMS management policies, capital and operating expenses reviews, employee performance, client and vendor relationships, and quality assurance compliance.
- Technology operations services (TOS)—Provides TOS strategic directives for leadership, contract administration, TOS services, TOS management policies, capital and operating expenses reviews, employee performance, client and vendor relationships, and quality assurance compliance.

IT PERFORMANCE MANAGEMENT DASHBOARD (2011-2012) ANALYTICS			August 31/2011		
IT PLANNING & ADMINISTRATION SERVICES (PAS)					
OPERATIONAL-FM	Start Date	End Date	Status	% Complete	Indicator
IT Strategic Planning Framework	4/1/2011	9/30/2011	In-Progress	100%	Black
IT Operating Planning Framework	4/1/2011	3/31/2012	In-Progress	35%	Y
IT Budgeting Planning Framework	4/1/2011	12/31/2011	In-Progress	30%	R
OPERATIONAL-FM Summary	4/1/2011	3/31/2012	In-Progress	55%	G

% IT staff performing IT Strategic Planning ; # Improvements completed
% IT staff performing IT Operating Planning ; # Improvements completed
% Customer Satisfaction with Strategic Framework; # high satisfaction responses
% IT staff performing IT Budget Planning ; # Improvements completed

OPERATIONAL-SD	Start Date	End Date	Status	% Complete	Indicator
IT Strategic and Operating Plan	4/1/2011	4/30/2011	In-Progress	100%	Black
IT Budget Plan	4/1/2011	12/31/2011	In-Progress	50%	G
IT Budget Plan status/ progress/forecasts	1/1/2012	3/31/2012	Not-Started	0%	
IT Capital/Operating Expenditures Coding	4/1/2011	3/31/2012	In-Progress	45%	G
IT Invoice Processing & Financial Admin	4/1/2011	3/31/2012	In-Progress	45%	G
IT Contract Agreement Status	4/1/2011	6/30/2011	In-Progress	55%	Past Due
Stakeholders Financial Support	4/1/2011	3/31/2012	In-Progress	45%	G
Finance and HR collaborations	4/1/2011	3/31/2012	In-Progress	45%	G
OPERATIONAL-SD Summary	4/1/2011	3/31/2012	In-Progress	48%	G

% IT staff delivering IT Strategic/Operating Plans ; # Improvements completed
% IT staff delivering IT Budget Plans ; # Improvements completed
% stakeholders satisfaction with IT Budget Plan; #stakeholders with unacceptable responses
% IT staff delivering IT Budget Plan status ; # Improvements completed
% IT staff delivering IT Capital/Operating Expenditures ; # Improvements completed
% IT staff delivering IT Invoicing ; # Improvements completed
% IT staff delivering IT Contract Agreement Status ; # Improvements completed
% IT staff delivering Stakeholders Financial Support ; # Improvements completed
% IT staff delivering Finance and HR Collaborations ; # Improvements completed

Figure 3.7 IT strategic framework performance measures.

3.4.1 Purpose

The purpose of this results area is to provide clear, consistent, and complete *strategic direction* for the planning, delivery, and measurement of the six functional areas of the IT service life cycles, using a *result-based accountability framework*.[2] The contents of the strategic directives established the foundation to identifying the outputs and outcomes for each of the functional areas. The outputs and outcomes formed the major input data source to the integrated IT performance measurement dashboard, which was utilized to measure and monitor the results of the delivered IT services. The performance metrics, indicators, variances, trends, and predictive analytics formed the basis for sound evidence-based decision-making process, using the established performance measurement areas—operational, financial, employee, and customer. The performance steering committee will have approval accountabilities for organizational performance—business and IT performance program. This committee will have accountability with the performance measurement managers for the operational performance using the IT strategic directives measurement areas defined in the performance management plan and the integrated IT performance measurement dashboard.

3.4.2 Strategic Directives

- IT services will be planned, delivered, and measured by a performance steering committee using IT strategic directives for each of the six IT services, structured to align with operational, financial, employee, and customer performance measures. These IT strategic directives will be used to direct and measure the success and value of delivered IT services using transformational performance leadership strategies, with the goal toward aligning the outputs of IT strategic directives within the structure of the integrated IT performance measurement dashboard.
- The performance steering committee will provide performance approval accountabilities for the measurement, management, and delivery of the IT strategic directives. These directives are structured as *Operations*—leadership, strategic/operating plans, architecture services, contract management, project management, applications services, technology services, management policies, and quality assurance; *Financial*—capital and operating expenses; *Employee*—Employee Performance; *Customer*—client and vendor relationships.
- All changes to the IT strategic directives outputs must be approved by the performance steering committee. The performance delivery manager will document and present all changes to the performance steering committee for approval.
- The performance steering committee will meet, at a minimum, on a monthly basis to review the performance indicators, trends, and analytics for the IT strategic directives output in the performance measurement dashboard. If the overall progress of this output is *red* or *yellow*, more frequent meetings will be required.
- IT strategic directives will be described and assessed for each of the six functional areas based on the operations, financial, customer, and employee measures outlined in the *IT operational plan with alignment to strategic directives.*[7]
- Senior managers will be thoroughly familiar with the IT strategic directives to ensure consistency in delivery across the IT services functional areas.

3.4.3 Accountabilities

3.4.3.1 Executive Performance Manager

This person is accountable for *approval* of performance results.

- SWOT analysis for IT strategic directives outputs—operations, financial, customer, and employee
- Linkages of IT strategic directives outputs and outcomes with performance measures and performance measurement dashboard
- Performance measurement dashboard results—performance measures, metrics, and variances—for IT strategic directives strategic and operational measures
- Stakeholders' satisfaction surveys results for IT strategic directives measures—effectiveness/quality
- Integrated IT strategic directives performance measurement results—areas for improvements
- Performance measurement/management program sponsorship and champion

3.4.3.2 Performance Delivery Manager

This person is accountable for *management* of performance results.

- SWOT analysis for IT strategic directives outputs—operations, financial, customer, and employee
- Linkages of IT strategic directives outputs and outcomes with performance measures and performance measurement dashboard
- Performance measurement dashboard results—performance measures, metrics, and variances for IT strategic directives strategic and operational measures
- Stakeholders' satisfaction surveys results for IT strategic directives measures—effectiveness/quality
- Integrated IT Strategy Directives performance measurement results—areas for improvements
- Accountability reports to performance steering committee for IT strategic directives outputs/outcomes, performance measures, and results

3.4.3.3 Performance Measurement Team

This team is accountable for the *delivery* of performance results.

- Meaningful and credible input data for SWOT analysis for IT strategic directives outputs—operations, financial, customer, and employee
- Clear alignment data to demonstrate linkages of IT strategic directives outputs and outcomes with performance measures and performance measurement dashboard
- Performance measurement data for IT strategic directives performance measurement dashboard results—areas for improvements
- Stakeholders' satisfaction surveys data for IT strategic directives performance measures—effectiveness/quality
- Integrated IT Strategy improvement data for performance measurement results—areas for improvements
- Result-based accountability data for accountability reports to performance steering committee on IT strategic directives outputs/outcomes, performance measures, and results

3.4.4 Results: IT Strategic Directives

Accountabilities discussed earlier are brief because they are intended to serve as a reference for *who is accountable* for *what* during the delivery of the IT strategic directives. Results are now introduced to highlight the outputs of this IT strategic directives results area and related outcomes (what), process flow (how), and performance measures (why). It is intended to serve as a reference based on the English language interrogatives: Who *is accountable for what, how, and why*. The outputs/outcomes, process flow and performance measures, based on real-world practical implementation, will serve as excellent references for the practicing performance managers during measurement, delivery, and reporting of IT strategic directives outputs and outcomes.

The outputs/outcomes highlight the key outputs/outcomes for *IT strategic directives*[8] that the performance managers measure and report during the delivery of the IT services performance results. The outcomes provide impact answers—what difference does the IT strategic directives make? The process flow, based on real-world practical implementations, is a graphical representation of the inputs, process, outputs, and relationships. The IT strategic directives performance model shows the foundation representation to effectively communicate the integrated components of the IT strategic directives to strategic, IT operational, and performance management staff.

The performance measures from the integrated IT performance measurement dashboard for IT strategic directives outputs/outcomes are illustrated for "IT Enterprise Architecture: Operational, Financial, Employee and Customer measures." Appendices A through F provide further details. Performance metrics, indicators, progress, trends, and analytics formed the basis for evidence-based decision making to enable improved organizational excellence.

3.4.4.1 Outputs/Outcomes—IT Strategic Directives

The outputs and outcomes of the IT strategic directives are given in Table 3.3.

3.4.4.2 Process Flows—IT Strategic Directives

The process flows of the IT strategic directives are shown in Figure 3.8.

3.4.4.3 Performance Model—IT Strategic Directives

The performance model of the IT strategic directives is shown in Figure 3.9.

3.4.4.4 Performance Measures—IT Strategic Directives

The performance measures of the IT strategic directives are shown in Figure 3.10a–c.

Table 3.3 IT Strategic Directives Output/Outcomes

Results Area	*Output*	*Outcome*
IT strategic directives	Leadership/ governance—ELS	• Improved accountability • Improved quality of management
	Planning & administration services—PAS	• Improved IT planning services
	Enterprise architecture services—EAS	• Improved IT architecture services
	Project portfolio management—PPM	• Improved project management services
	Applications management services—AMS	• Improved applications management services
	Technology operations services—TOS	• Improved technology operations services

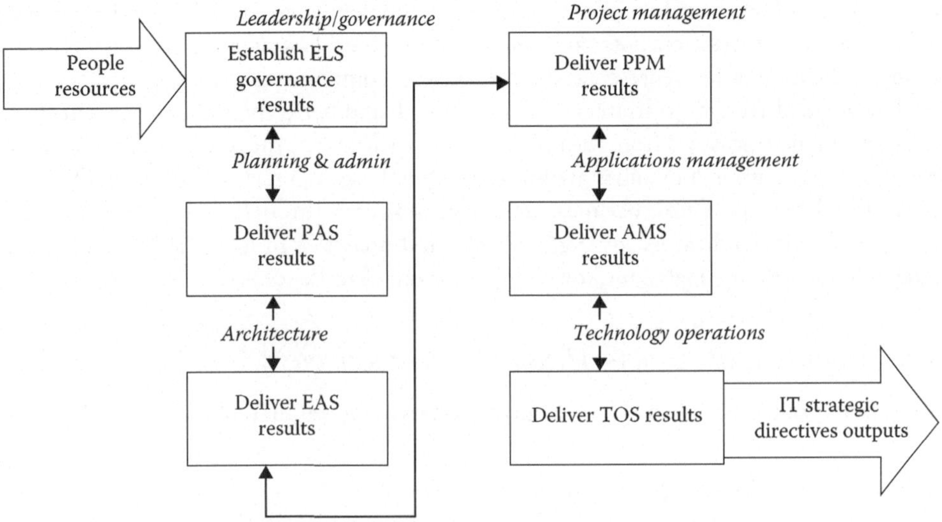

Figure 3.8 IT strategic directives process flow.

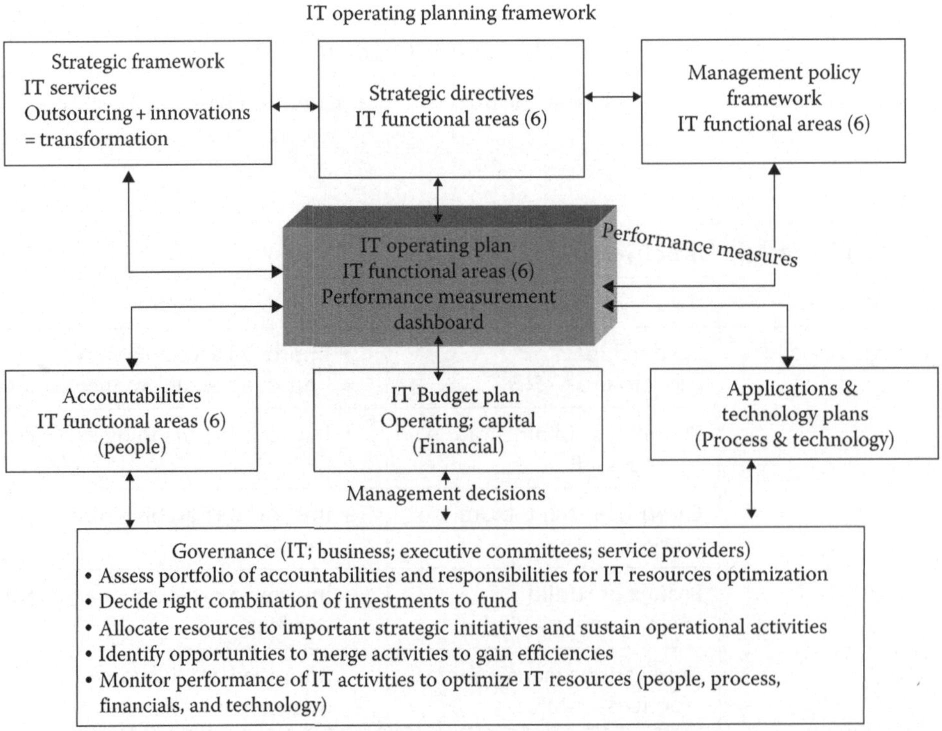

Figure 3.9 IT strategic directives performance model.

3.5 IT Policy Framework

Executives shall use the IT policy framework to managing information technology assets and services, selecting appropriate IT delivery model, and contracting information technology services. This policy framework provides an extensive set of policies, which allows for associated standards to be adopted and best practices or guidelines to be developed, to support more objective-based decisions. Sound objective judgments require executive management understanding of the measurement, management, and delivery of information technology assets and services, within the context of the IT service delivery life cycle and the IT strategic directives. For each of the IT strategic directives for the six functional areas of the IT service delivery life cycle—governance, planning and administration, enterprise architecture and innovations, project portfolio management, applications management services and IT operational support, the major *outputs* of the IT policy framework include the following:

- Policy—A statement of outcomes of the policy itself for each of the strategic directive within the functional areas and the IT services delivery life cycle.
- Purpose—The reason or result (what) to achieving the outcomes and realizing the benefits of the policy.
- Principles—Provide the actions (how) to achieving the goals of the policy.

IT PERFORMANCE MANAGEMENT DASHBOARD (2011-2012) ANALYTICS			August 31/2011		
OPERATIONAL-SD	Budget	YTD Actual	Status	% Complete	Indicator
Business Systems Planning Support	4/1/2011	3/31/2012	In-Progress	25%	Y
Business Case/Architecture Support	4/1/2011	3/31/2012	In-Progress	25%	Y
IT Enterprise Architectures	4/1/2011	3/31/2012	In-Progress	35%	Y
IT Enterprise Architecture Standards	4/1/2011	3/31/2012	In-Progress	30%	Y
IT Security Plans	4/1/2011	9/30/2011	In-Progress	80%	G
IT Security Implementation	4/1/2011	3/31/2012	In-Progress	30%	Y
Innovative Communications tools	4/1/2011	3/31/2012	In-Progress	35%	Y
Technology Projects Contract Management	4/1/2011	3/31/2012	In-Progress	35%	Y
Technology Program/Project Management	4/1/2011	9/30/2011	In-Progress	90%	G
IT Productivity Tools and Framework	4/1/2011	9/30/2011	In-Progress	40%	R
Technology Infrastructure Delivery/Support	4/1/2011	9/30/2011	In-Progress	35%	R
Technology Research/Trends	4/1/2011	3/31/2012	In-Progress	35%	Y
OPERATIONAL-SD Summary	4/1/2011	3/31/2012	In-Progress	41%	G

% IT staff delivering Business Systems Planning; # Improvements completed
% IT staff delivering Architecture Business Case; # Improvements completed
% IT staff delivering IT Enterprise Architecture ; # Improvements completed
%stakeholders satisfaction with EAS services; #stakeholders with unacceptable responses
% IT staff delivering IT Enterprise Architecture Stds ; # Improvements completed
% IT staff delivering IT Security Plans ; # Improvements completed
% IT staff delivering IT Security ; # Improvements completed
%security initiatives implemented;# security initiatives "on-hold"
% IT staff delivering Communications Tools ; # Improvements completed
% IT staff delivering Technology Projects CM; # Improvements completed
% IT staff delivering Technology Projects PM ; # Improvements completed
% IT staff delivering IT Productivity Tools ; # Improvements completed
% IT staff delivering Technology Infrastructure ; # Improvements completed
% IT staff delivering Technology Research ; # Improvements completed

(a)

Figure 3.10 (a–c) IT strategic directives (EAS) performance measures. *(Continued)*

OPERATIONAL-SE	Start Date	End Date	Status	% Complete	Indicator
Technology Infrastructure Project Plan QA	4/1/2011	6/30/2011	In-Progress	75%	Past Due
IT Security and Privacy Compliance/Approval	4/1/2011	7/31/2011	In-Progress	80%	Past Due
Infrastructure Projects Financial Measures	4/1/2011	9/30/2011	In-Progress	60%	
Technology Infrastructure Compliance	4/1/2011	3/31/2012	In-Progress	35%	Y
Technology Infrastructure Optimization	4/1/2011	3/31/2012	In-Progress	35%	Y
Technology Infrastructure Benchmarking Metrics	4/1/2011	9/30/2011	In-Progress	80%	G
OPERATIONAL-SE Summary	4/1/2011	3/31/2012	In-Progress	61%	G

% IT staff performing Technology Projects QA ; # Improvements completed
% IT staff performing Technology Projects Compliance # Improvements completed
% IT staff performing Infrastructure Projects Measures; # Improvements completed
% IT staff performing IT Infrastructure Compliance; # Improvements completed
% IT staff performing IT Infrastructure Optimization; # Improvements completed
% IT staff performing IT Infrastructure Benchmarking; # Improvements completed

OPERATIONAL-RM	Start Date	End Date	Status	% Complete	Indicator
EAI Client Management Relations/Feedback	4/1/2011	3/31/2012	In-Progress	100%	Black
Vendors EAI Relations/Feedback	4/1/2011	3/31/2012	In-Progress	40%	G
IT Outsourced Providers EAI Relations/Feedback	4/1/2011	3/31/2012	In-Progress	25%	Y
OPERATIONAL-RM Summary	4/1/2011	3/31/2012	In-Progress	55%	G

% IT staff performing Client Feedback; # Improvements completed
% IT staff performing Vendors Feedback; # Improvements completed
% IT staff performing IT Service Providers Feedback; # Improvements completed

FINANCIAL	Start Date	End Date	Status	% Complete	Indicator
IT Infrastructure Project Costs	4/1/2011	3/31/2012	In-Progress	35%	Y
IT Enterprise Architecture Costs	4/1/2011	3/31/2012	In-Progress	25%	Y
FINANCIAL Summary	4/1/2011	3/31/2012	In-Progress	30%	Y

(b)

CUSTOMER	Date	End Date	Status	Complete	Indicator
EAS Client Relationships/Satisfaction Surveys	4/1/2011	3/31/2012	In-Progress	40%	G
EAS Committee Meetings	4/1/2011	3/31/2012	In-Progress	40%	G
EAS Vendors Relationships/Satisfaction Surveys	4/1/2011	3/31/2012	In-Progress	40%	G
EAS IT Outsourced Providers Surveys	4/1/2011	3/31/2012	In-Progress	40%	G
EAS Benchmarking Surveys/Results	4/1/2011	3/31/2012	In-Progress	40%	G
CUSTOMER Summary	4/1/2011	3/31/2012	In-Progress	40%	G

% IT staff performing Client Satisfaction Surveys ; # Improvements completed
% IT staff performing EAS Committee Meetings; # Improvements completed
% IT staff performing Vendors Satisfaction Surveys; # Improvements completed
% IT staff performing IT Service Providers Surveys; # Improvements completed
% IT staff performing EAS Benchmarking Surveys ; # Improvements completed

EMPLOYEE	Start Date	End Date	Status	% Complete	Indicator
EAS IT Progress Reporting	4/1/2011	6/30/2011	Complete	100%	Black
EAS IT Staff Performance Contract	4/1/2011	3/31/2012	In-Progress	35%	Y
EAS Staff Learning/Growth Reporting	4/1/2011	3/31/2012	In-Progress	35%	Y
EAS Staff Meetings/Communications	4/1/2011	3/31/2012	In-Progress	35%	Y
EAS Staff Retention/Retraining/Reward Reporting	4/1/2011	7/31/2011	In-Progress	100%	Black
EMPLOYEE Summary	4/1/2011	3/31/2012	In-Progress	61%	G
[illegible]	[illegible]	[illegible]	[illegible]	[illegible]	G

% IT staff performing Progress Reporting ; # Improvements completed
% IT Staff performing Staff Performance Contract ; # Improvements completed
% IT staff performing Learning/Growth sessions; # Improvements completed
% IT staff performing staff communications/meetings ; # Improvements completed
% IT staff performing IT Benchmarking ; # Improvements completed

(c)

Figure 3.10 (*Continued*) (a–c) IT strategic directives (EAS) performance measures.

- Roles and responsibilities—Provide roles and responsibilities (who does what) to executing the policy using the *RACI—Responsible, Approval, Consulting and Informed—RACI C*hart.
- Definitions—Provide supporting definitions relevant to the policy.
- References and related policies—Provide references and related policies to support the policy statement.

3.5.1 Purpose

The purpose of this results area is to provide an extensive set of policies that allow for associated standards to be adopted and best practices or procedures to be developed to ensure that information technology assets and services are planned, delivered, and measured. The *policy management framework*[9] integrates the policy statement with strategic directives for each of the six function areas of the IT service delivery life cycle. The "principles" heading of the policy framework contain the associated strategic directives for that policy to ensure integration with IT strategic directives and result-based accountability. The clear, concise, and complete policy framework expands upon the strategic directives to improve the productivity of employees and *service providers.*[10] The performance steering committee will have approval accountabilities for organizational performance—business and IT performance program. This committee will also have accountability with the performance measurement managers for the operational performance using the IT policy framework measurement areas, as defined in the performance management plan and the integrated IT performance measurement dashboard.

3.5.2 Strategic Directives

- IT services will be planned, delivered, and measured by a performance steering committee using an IT policy framework that specifies the policy, purpose, principles, roles and responsibilities, definition, references, and related policies. IT policies for each of the six IT services are structured to integrate with IT strategic directives and operational–functional management and service excellence performance measures. This IT policy framework will be used to direct and measure the success and value of delivered IT services using transformational performance leadership strategies, with the goal toward aligning IT policy framework outputs with the structure of the integrated IT performance measurement dashboard.
- The performance steering committee will provide performance approval accountabilities for the measurement, management, and delivery of the IT policy framework. These policies management output incorporated under *Operations*—leadership/functional management and service excellence in the performance measurement dashboard.
- All changes to the IT policy framework outputs must be approved by the performance steering committee. The performance delivery manager will document and present all changes to the performance steering committee for approval.
- The performance steering committee will meet, at a minimum, on a monthly basis to review the performance indicators, trends, and analytics for the IT policy framework output in the performance measurement dashboard. If the overall progress of this output is *red* or *yellow*, more frequent meetings will be required.

- IT policy framework will be described and assessed for each of the six functional areas and integration with IT strategic directives and measured using the performance measurement dashboard.
- Senior managers will be thoroughly familiar with the IT policy framework to ensure consistency in delivery across the IT services functional areas.

3.5.3 Accountabilities

3.5.3.1 Executive Performance Manager

This person is accountable for *approval* of performance results.

- SWOT analysis for IT policy framework outputs—policy, purpose, principles, roles and responsibilities, definition, references, and related policies
- Linkages of IT Policy Framework outputs and outcomes with performance measures and performance measurement dashboard
- Performance measurement dashboard results—performance measures, metrics, and variances—for IT policy framework operational measures
- Stakeholders' satisfaction surveys results for IT policy framework measures—effectiveness/quality
- Integrated IT policy framework performance measurement results—areas for improvements
- Performance measurement/management program sponsorship and champion

3.5.3.2 Performance Delivery Manager

This person is accountable for *management* of performance results.

- SWOT analysis for IT policy framework outputs—policy, purpose, principles, roles and responsibilities, definition, references, and related policies
- Linkages of IT policy framework outputs and outcomes with performance measures and performance measurement dashboard
- Performance measurement dashboard results—performance measures, metrics, and variances—for IT policy framework operational measures
- Stakeholders' satisfaction surveys results for IT policy framework measures—effectiveness/quality
- Integrated IT policy framework performance measurement results—areas for improvements
- Accountability reports to performance steering committee for IT policy framework outputs/outcomes, performance measures, and results

3.5.3.3 Performance Measurement Team

This team is accountable for the *delivery* of performance results.

- Meaningful and credible input data for SWOT analysis for IT policy framework outputs—policy, purpose, principles, roles and responsibilities, definition, references, and related policies
- Clear alignment data to demonstrate linkages of IT policy framework outputs and outcomes with IT strategic directives and performance measurement dashboard
- Performance measurement data for IT policy framework performance measurement dashboard results—areas for improvements

- Stakeholders' satisfaction surveys data for IT policy framework performance measures—effectiveness/quality
- Integrated IT policy framework improvement data for performance measurement results—areas for improvements
- Result-based accountability data for accountability reports to performance steering committee on IT policy framework outputs/outcomes and performance measures

3.5.4 Results: IT Policy Framework

Accountabilities discussed earlier are brief because they are intended to serve as a reference for *who is accountable* for *what* during the delivery of the IT policy framework. Results are now introduced to highlight the outputs of this IT policy framework results area and related outcomes (what), process flow (how), and performance measures (why). It is intended to serve as a reference based on the English language interrogatives: Who *is accountable for what, how, and why.* The outputs/outcomes, process flow, and performance measures, based on real-world practical implementation, will serve as excellent references for the practicing performance managers during measurement, delivery, and reporting of IT policy framework outputs and outcomes.

The outputs/outcomes highlight the key outputs/outcomes for IT policy framework that the performance managers use to measure and report progress, during the delivery of the IT policy framework results. The outcomes provide impact answers—what difference does the IT policy framework make? The process flow, based on real-world practical implementations, is a graphical representation of the inputs, process, outputs, and relationships. This IT policy framework performance model shows the foundation representation to effectively communicate the integrated components of this IT policy framework with strategic, IT operational, and performance management staff.

The performance measures from the integrated IT performance measurement dashboard for IT policy framework outputs/outcomes are illustrated for "IT Executive Leadership: Operational-FM and SE measures." Appendices A through F provide further details. Performance metrics, indicators, progress, trends, and analytics formed the basis for evidence-based decision making to enable improved organizational excellence.

3.5.4.1 Outputs/Outcomes—IT Policy Framework

The outputs and outcomes of the IT policy framework are given in Table 3.4.

Table 3.4 IT Policy Framework Output/Outcomes

Results Area	*Output*	*Outcome*
IT policy framework	Policy—outcomes	• Improved accountability • Improved quality of process, standards, and procedures
	Purpose—reason	
	Principles-actions, strategic directives	
	Roles and responsibilities—RACI standards	
	Definitions	
	Related policies—references, policies	

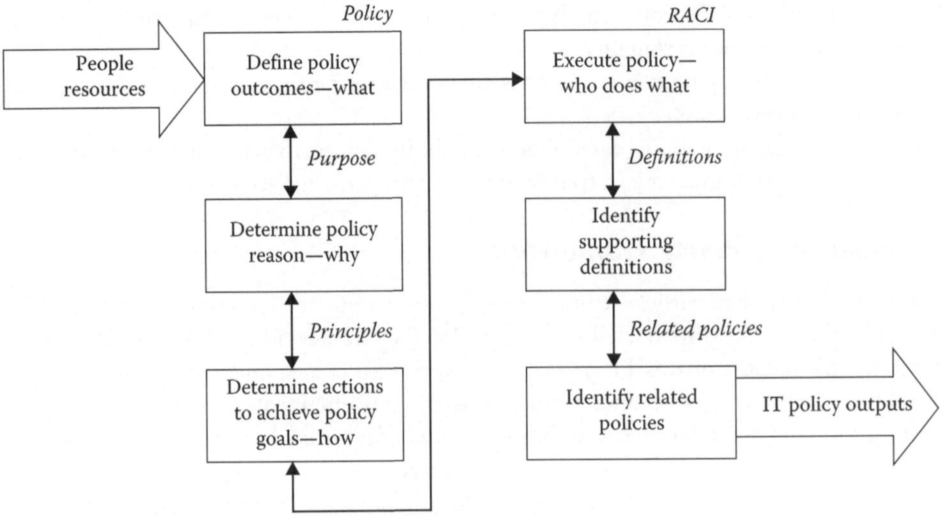

Figure 3.11 IT policy framework process flow.

3.5.4.2 Process Flows—IT Policy Framework (Figure 3.11)

The process flows of the IT policy framework are shown in Figure 3.11.

3.5.4.3 Performance Model—IT Policy Framework

The performance model of the IT policy framework is shown in Figure 3.12.

3.5.4.4 Performance Measures—IT Policy Framework

The performance measures of the IT policy framework are shown in Figure 3.13.

3.6 IT Governance Framework

Executives shall use the three pillars of IT governance—culture, structure, and process as the basis for communicating, integrating, and making evidence-based strategic and operational decisions. This decision-making structure shows how decisions are made, who makes the decision, who is held accountable, and how the results of the decisions are measured, monitored, and managed to ensure effective and efficient utilization of IT resources. Sound objective judgments require executive management understanding of IT governance performance, as well as an understanding of the integrated components to improve the quality of management and overall IT decision-making performances. The major *outputs* of the IT governance framework include the following:

- *Culture*: Answers the questions of corporate mindset, shared values, beliefs, attitudes, behaviors, and informal rules of the organization. Decision-making culture, feedback, and responses will be misinterpreted with flawed assumptions as a result of the lack of proper

Policy Title	Client and Vendor Relationship Management	
Policy Number	EXEC-006	
Department	Information Technology (IT) Department	
Version Number	003	May 1, 2012
Purpose	The purpose of Client and Vendor Relationship Management is to establish principles, rules or processes by which the interaction with Vendor is carried out. Decisions are made about events and forms of interactions between organization's staff and vendors. How these interactions are made, who does the interaction, who is held accountable, and how the results of the interactions are measured, monitored, and managed are all part of Client and Vendor Relationship Management.	
Principles Aligned with Strategic Directives	• ITS will maintain effective client relationships on a regular basis, through client satisfation surverys. • ITS will continuously communicate progress on IT directives and issues to the business areas by participating at section head meetings and chairing the IT Business Council meetings • ITS will maintain effective vendor relationships on a regular basis, through vendor client satisfaction surverys. • ITS will continuously communicate progress of IT Service Providers by monitoring and measuring performance measurement and accountability.	
RACI	• Responsibility; Authority; Consulting; Informed for the stated policy.	
Related Policy	ITS STAFF PROGRESS PERFORMANCE	
	• ITS will comply with the processes and procedures in the Master Services Contractual Agreement with the Vendors when applicable. • ITS will collaboratively work with the organization's operational business staffs, who deal with the Vendors on a day-to-day basis.	
Definitions	IT—Information Technology Services ITS—Information Technology Services Branch CIO—Chief Information Officer Vendor—IT Service Providers and Suppliers	

Figure 3.12 IT policy framework performance model.

understanding of the corporate culture. Culture influences IT governance performance with regard to structure and process in understanding how IT decisions are made and delivered within the organization. Performance excellence culture must be viewed as an attitude and behavior to maintain sustainability.

- *Structure*: Answers "who" and "what" question of IT governance. Who are they governing and what are they governing. Decision-making structure in several layers of governance—executive level, program/business process (IT business council/steering committee), technical operational level (change advisory council).
- *Process*: Answers "how" an organization is governed. Performs measurement and communications of performance results. How did we do? Decision-making processes associated with IT as well as the practices (balanced scorecard) and policies used to measure and control the way IT decisions are made and delivered within the organization.

IT PERFORMANCE MANAGEMENT DASHBOARD (2011-2012) ANALYTICS			August 31/2011		
IT EXECUTIVE LEADERSHIP					
OPERATIONAL-FM	Start Date	End Date	Status	% Complete	Indicator
IT Governance Accountability Framework	4/1/2011	12/31/2011	In-Progress	60%	G
HR Performance Contract Alignment	4/1/2011	9/30/2011	In-Progress	80%	G
Executive Management (EM) Progress Status	4/1/2011	3/31/2012	In-Progress	40%	G
Executive Management Presentation/Approvals	4/1/2011	3/31/2012	In-Progress	60%	G
IT Policies and Procedures	4/1/2011	3/31/2012	In-Progress	60%	G
IT Operational Accountability Framework	4/1/2011	3/31/2012	In-Progress	40%	G
OPERATIONAL-FM Summary	4/1/2011	3/31/2012	In-Progress	57%	G
% IT staff performing IT Governance; # Improvements completed					
% IT staff performing HR Alignment; # Improvements completed					
% IT staff performing EM Communications; # Improvements completed					
% IT staff performing EM Presentation; # Improvements completed					
% IT staff performing IT Policies; # Improvements completed					
% IT Policies and Procedures established; # outstanding					
% IT staff performing IT Operations; # Improvements completed					

OPERATIONAL-SE	Start Date	End Date	Status	% Complete	Indicator
IT Management Policies Framework	4/1/2011	3/31/2012	In-Progress	30%	Y
IT Management Procedures	4/1/2011	3/31/2012	In-Progress	30%	Y
IT Business Council Accountability Framework	4/1/2011	9/30/2011	In-Progress	80%	G
IT Compliance - Industry Performance Measures	4/1/2011	3/31/2012	Not-Started	30%	Y
IT Benchmarking Metrics	4/1/2011	6/30/2011	Complete	100%	Black
OPERATIONAL-SE Summary	4/1/2011	3/31/2012	In-Progress	54%	G
% IT staff performing IT Mgnt Policies; # Improvements completed					
% IT staff performing IT Mgnt Procedures; # Improvements completed					
% IT management policies delivered; #outstanding					
% IT staff performing IT Business Council Accountability; # Improvements completed					
% IT staff performing IT Compliance-Industry; # Improvements completed					
% IT staff performing IT Benchmarking Metrics; # Improvements completed					

Figure 3.13 IT policy framework performance measures.

3.6.1 Purpose

The purpose of this results area is to provide an *IT governance framework*[11] for decision making that uses the three pillars to ensure effective performance measurement, management, delivery, and improvement of IT decision-making structure. The IT governance framework (decision-making structure) shows how decisions are made, who makes the decision, who is held accountable, and how the results are measured, monitored, and managed. This goal of this decision-making framework is to ensure effective and efficient utilization of IT resources—people, process, technology, and financials—and improved organizational performance and quality of management.

This IT governance framework integrates with the six functional areas of the IT service delivery life cycle and the performance measurement dashboard. It is based on *ITIL*[12] and COBIT industry—wide guidelines to ensure results-based accountability.

3.6.2 Strategic Directives

- IT decision making will be delivered and measured by a performance steering committee using an IT governance framework that specifies the culture, structure, and processes of decision making. IT decision-making structure integrates with the six IT functional areas, IT strategic directives, and operational–functional management outputs in the performance measurement dashboard. This IT governance framework will be used to direct and measure the success and value of decision making using transformational performance leadership strategies, with the goal toward aligning IT governance framework outputs with the structure of the integrated IT performance measurement dashboard.
- The performance steering committee will provide performance approval accountabilities for the measurement, management, and delivery of the IT governance framework. These decision-making management outputs are incorporated under *operations–leadership/functional* management measures.
- All changes to the IT governance framework outputs must be approved by the performance steering committee. The performance delivery manager will document and present all changes to the performance steering committee for approval.
- The performance steering committee will meet, at a minimum, on a monthly basis to review the performance indicators, trends, and analytics for the IT governance output in the performance measurement dashboard. If the overall progress of this output is *red* or *yellow*, more frequent meetings will be required.
- IT governance framework will be described and assessed for each of the six functional areas and integration with IT strategic directives and measured using the performance measurement dashboard.
- Senior managers will be thoroughly familiar with the IT governance framework to ensure consistency in delivery across the IT services functional areas.

3.6.3 Accountabilities

3.6.3.1 Executive Performance Manager

This person is accountable for *approval* of performance results.

- SWOT analysis for IT governance framework outputs—culture, structure, and process
- Linkages of IT governance framework outputs and outcomes with performance measures and performance measurement dashboard
- Performance measurement dashboard results—performance measures, metrics, and variances—for IT governance framework operational measures
- Stakeholders' satisfaction surveys results for IT governance framework measures—effectiveness/quality
- Integrated IT governance framework performance measurement results—areas for improvements
- Performance measurement and management program sponsorship and champion

3.6.3.2 Performance Delivery Manager

This person is accountable for *management* of performance results.

- SWOT analysis for IT governance framework outputs—culture, structure, and process

- Linkages of IT governance framework outputs and outcomes with performance measures and performance measurement dashboard
- Performance measurement dashboard results—performance measures, metrics, and variances—for IT governance framework operational measures
- Stakeholders' satisfaction surveys results for IT governance framework measures—effectiveness/quality
- Integrated IT governance framework performance measurement results—areas for improvements
- Accountability reports to performance steering committee for IT governance framework outputs/outcomes, performance measures, and results

3.6.3.3 Performance Measurement Team

This team is accountable for the *delivery* of performance results.

- Meaningful and credible input data for SWOT analysis for IT governance framework outputs—culture, structure, and process
- Clear alignment data to demonstrate linkages of IT governance framework outputs and outcomes with IT strategic directives and performance measurement dashboard
- Performance measurement data for IT governance framework performance measurement dashboard results—areas for improvements
- Stakeholders' satisfaction surveys data for IT governance framework performance measures—effectiveness/quality
- Integrated IT governance framework improvement data for performance measurement results—areas for improvements
- Result-based accountability data for accountability reports to performance steering committee on IT governance framework outputs/outcomes, and performance measures

3.6.4 Results: IT Governance Framework

Accountabilities discussed earlier are brief because they are intended to serve as a reference for *who is accountable* for *what* during the delivery of the IT governance framework. Results are now introduced to highlight the outputs of this IT governance framework results area and related outcomes (what), process flow (how), and performance measures (why). It is intended to serve as a reference based on the English language interrogatives: Who *is accountable for what, how, and why*. The outputs/outcomes, process flow, and performance measures, based on real-world practical implementation, will serve as excellent references for the practicing performance managers during measurement, delivery, and reporting of IT governance framework outputs and outcomes.

The outputs/outcomes highlight the key outputs/outcomes for IT governance framework that the performance managers use to measure and report progress, during the delivery of the IT governance framework results. The outcomes provide impact answers—what difference does the IT governance framework make? The process flow, based on real-world practical implementations, is a graphical representation of the inputs, process, outputs, and relationships. This IT governance framework performance model shows the foundation representation to effectively communicate the integrated components of this IT governance framework with strategic, IT operational, and performance management staff.

The performance measures from the integrated IT performance measurement dashboard for IT governance framework outputs/outcomes are illustrated for "IT Executive Leadership and Planning & Administration: Operational-FM measures." Appendices A through F provide further details. Performance metrics, indicators, progress, trends, and analytics formed the basis for evidence-based decision making to enable improved organizational excellence.

3.6.4.1 Outputs/Outcomes—IT Governance Framework

The outputs and outcomes of the IT governance framework are given in Table 3.5.

3.6.4.2 Process Flows—IT Governance Framework

The process flows of the IT governance framework are shown in Figure 3.14.

3.6.4.3 Performance Model—IT Governance Framework

The performance model of the IT governance framework is shown in Figure 3.15.

3.6.4.4 Performance Measures—IT Governance Framework

The performance measures of the IT governance framework are shown in Figure 3.16.

3.7 IT Value-Based Performance Measurement

In a result-based accountability environment, executives shall use the IT VBPM as the basis for getting the right IT performance measurement in place for organizational success. In order to drive performance, executive decisions should be based on measurements that are clearly linked with business value to obtain an accurate indication of what is working and what is not working. The major *outputs* of the IT VBPM include the following:

Table 3.5 IT Governance Framework Output/Outcomes

Results Area	*Output*	*Outcome*
IT governance framework	Culture—corporate mindset, shared values, beliefs, attitudes, behaviors, informal rules Structure—executive, organizational, operational Process—performance measures/results	• Improved accountability • Increased performance culture • Improved quality of decision making • Optimized resource utilization • Increased IT services value • Increased quality of IT governance • Decreased quantity of IT governance

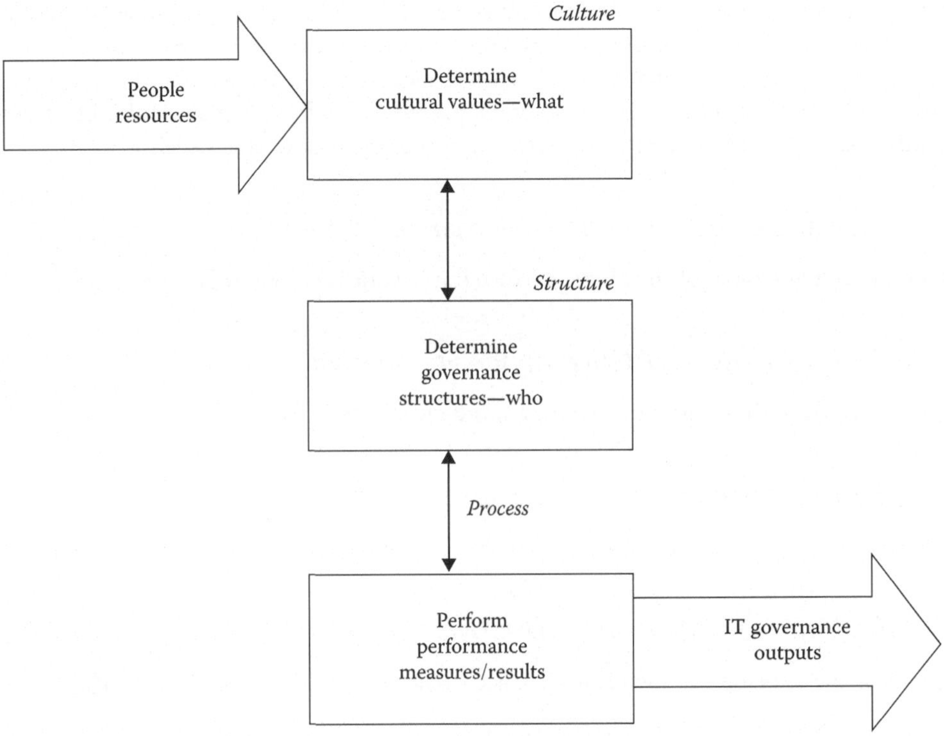

Figure 3.14 IT governance structure process flow.

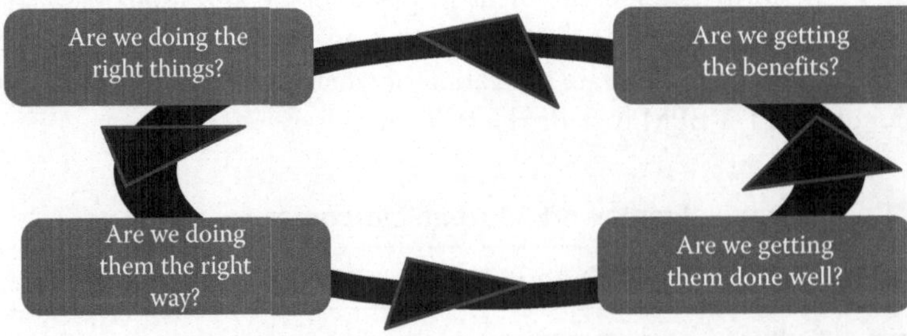

Figure 3.15 IT governance structure performance model.

- Process improvement—To achieve process performance excellence by simplifying and streamlining IT processes and related business processes to managing, measuring, delivering, and improving IT services.
- Organizational alignment—To achieve organizational excellence by demonstrating alignment of IT organizational structures and processes to business structures and processes, using a result-based management structure accountability for results.

IT PERFORMANCE MANAGEMENT DASHBOARD (2011-2012) ANALYTICS				August 31/2011	
IT EXECUTIVE LEADERSHIP					
OPERATIONAL-FM	Start Date	End Date	Status	% Complete	Indicator
IT Governance Accountability Framework	4/1/2011	12/31/2011	In-Progress	60%	G
HR Performance Contract Alignment	4/1/2011	9/30/2011	In-Progress	80%	G
Executive Management (EM) Progress Status	4/1/2011	3/31/2012	In-Progress	40%	G
Executive Management Presentation/Approvals	4/1/2011	3/31/2012	In-Progress	60%	G
IT Policies and Procedures	4/1/2011	3/31/2012	In-Progress	60%	G
IT Operational Accountability Framework	4/1/2011	3/31/2012	In-Progress	40%	G
OPERATIONAL-FM Summary	4/1/2011	3/31/2012	In-Progress	57%	G
% IT staff performing IT Governance; # Improvements completed					
% stakeholders satisfied with IT Governance Framework; # unsatisfied					
% IT staff performing HR Alignment; # Improvements completed					
% IT staff performing EM Communications; # Improvements completed					
% IT staff performing EM Presentation; # Improvements completed					
% IT staff performing IT Policies; # Improvements completed					
% IT staff performing IT Operations; # Improvements completed					

IT PLANNING & ADMINISTRATION SERVICES (PAS)					
OPERATIONAL-FM	Start Date	End Date	Status	% Complete	Indicator
IT Strategic Planning Framework	4/1/2011	9/30/2011	In-Progress	100%	Black
IT Operating Planning Framework	4/1/2011	3/31/2012	In-Progress	35%	Y
IT Budgeting Planning Framework	4/1/2011	12/31/2011	In-Progress	30%	R
OPERATIONAL-FM Summary	4/1/2011	3/31/2012	In-Progress	55%	G
% IT staff performing IT Strategic Planning; # Improvements completed					
% IT staff performing IT Operating Planning; # Improvements completed					
% IT budget spent on IT operational plans; # revisions completed					
% IT staff performing IT Budget Planning; # Improvements completed					

Figure 3.16 IT governance structure performance measures.

- Technology enablement—To achieve operational excellence by enabling innovative technology solutions, such as integrated IT performance measurement dashboard, to enable operational excellence, optimize resource utilizations, and improve quality of management.
- Performance culture—Transforms your company's culture through collaboration and transparency by moving from counting services or activities to measuring meaningful outcomes—*results-based management (RBM) culture.*[13]
- Financial performance—Optimize the utilization of financial resources through *results-based budgeting—RBB*[14] by measuring and monitoring financial expenditures, using financial trend and analytics.
- Accountability for results—An RBM approach focused on achieving results. A broad-based strategy aimed at changing the way organization operates, with improving performance (achieving results) as the central orientation.

3.7.1 Purpose

The purpose of this results area is to provide an *IT VBPM*[15] to clearly align operational performance with goals and strategic directives while measuring the performance of IT services. This performance measurement approach enables increased reporting value in understanding what, where, and how the performance of IT organization can be improved. Value-based metrics are developed to fit the IT organizational culture, processes, and structures to determine what needs to be measured now? What needs to be measured in future? IT VBPM is more advanced than traditional measures in determining areas of improvements. The integration of the six outputs of IT VBPM with the four measurement areas of IT performance measurement dashboard facilitates an understanding of improvement areas that have achieved success and areas that need further improvements. The overall goal of IT VBPM is to ensure effective and efficient utilization of IT resources—people, process, technology, and financials—and improved organizational performance and improved quality of management.

3.7.2 Strategic Directives

- IT performance measures will be managed by the IT delivery performance manager and delivered by the performance measurement team using value-based IT performance measures for process improvement, organizational alignment, technology enablement, performance culture, financial performance, and accountability for results. IT value-based performance measures integrate with the six IT functional areas, IT strategic directives, and operational–functional management outputs in the performance measurement dashboard. This IT VBPM will be used to understand measurements that are clearly linked with business value to obtain an accurate indication of what is working and what is not working.
- The performance steering committee will provide performance approval accountabilities for the management and delivery of IT VBPM. These VBPM outputs are represented as *operations-leadership/functional* management measures in the performance measurement dashboard.
- All changes to the IT VBPM outputs must be approved by the performance steering committee. The performance delivery manager will document and present all changes to the performance steering committee for approval.
- The performance steering committee will meet, at a minimum, on a monthly basis to review the performance indicators, trends, and analytics for the IT VBPM outputs in the performance measurement dashboard. If the overall progress of this output is *red* or *yellow*, more frequent meetings will be required.
- IT VBPM will be defined and assessed for each of the six functional areas, integrated with IT strategic directives, and delivered using the performance measurement dashboard.
- Senior managers will be thoroughly familiar with the IT VBPM to ensure consistency in delivery across the IT services functional areas.

3.7.3 Accountabilities

3.7.3.1 Executive Performance Manager

This person is accountable for *approval* of performance results.

- SWOT analysis for IT VBPM outputs—process improvement, organizational alignment, technology enablement, performance culture, financial performance, and accountability for results

- Linkages of IT VBPM outputs and outcomes with performance measurement dashboard
- Performance measurement dashboard results—performance measures, metrics, and variances—for IT VBPM operational measures
- Stakeholders' satisfaction surveys results for IT VBPM—effectiveness/quality
- Integrated IT VBPM areas for improvements
- Performance measurement/management program sponsorship and champion

3.7.3.2 Performance Delivery Manager

This person is accountable for *management* of performance results.

- SWOT analysis for IT VBPM outputs—process improvement, organizational alignment, technology enablement, performance culture, financial performance, and accountability for results
- Linkages of IT VBPM outputs and outcomes with performance measurement dashboard
- Performance measurement dashboard results—performance measures, metrics, and variances—for IT VBPM operational measures
- Stakeholders' satisfaction surveys results for IT VBPM metrics—effectiveness/quality
- Integrated IT VBPM areas for improvements
- Accountability reports to performance steering committee for IT VBPM outputs/outcomes, performance metrics, and results

3.7.3.3 Performance Measurement Team

The team is accountable for the *delivery* of performance results.

- Meaningful and credible input data for SWOT analysis for IT VBPM outputs—process improvement, organizational alignment, technology enablement, performance culture, financial performance, and accountability for results
- Clear alignment data to demonstrate linkages of IT VBPM outputs and outcomes with IT strategic directives and performance measurement dashboard
- Performance measurement data for IT VBPM metrics—areas for improvements
- Stakeholders' satisfaction surveys data for Value-Based IT Performance metrics—effectiveness/quality
- Integrated IT VBPM improvement data for areas for improvements
- Result-based accountability data for accountability reports to performance steering committee on IT VBPM outputs/outcomes, and performance metrics

3.7.4 Results: IT Value-Based Performance Measurement

Accountabilities discussed earlier are brief because they are intended to serve as a reference for *who is accountable* for *what* during the delivery of IT VBPM. Results are now introduced to highlight the outputs of this IT VBPM results area and related outcomes (what), process flow (how), and performance measures (why). It is intended to serve as a reference based on the English language interrogatives: Who *is accountable for what, how, and why.* The outputs/outcomes, process flow and performance measures, based on real-world practical implementation, will serve as excellent references for the practicing performance managers during measurement, delivery, and reporting of IT VBPM outputs and outcomes.

The outputs/outcomes highlight the key outputs/outcomes for IT VBPM that the performance managers use to measure and report progress, during the delivery of the IT VBPM results. The outcomes provide impact answers—what difference does the IT VBPM make? The process flow, based on real-world practical implementations, is a graphical representation of the inputs, process, outputs, and relationships. *The IT VBPM model*[16] shows the foundation measures to assess IT and business areas for organizational excellence and communicate the areas of improvements with strategic, IT operational, and performance management staff.

The performance measures from the integrated IT performance measurement dashboard for IT value-based performance measures outputs/outcomes are illustrated for "IT Enterprise Architecture and IT Planning and Administration Services: Operational-FM measures". Appendices A through F provide further details. Performance metrics, indicators, progress, trends, and analytics formed the basis for measurements that are clearly aligned with business value to obtain an accurate indication of what is working and what is not working to enable improved organizational excellence.

3.7.4.1 Outputs/Outcomes—IT Value-Based Performance Measurement

The outputs and outcomes of the IT value-based performance measurement are given in Table 3.6.

3.7.4.2 Process Flows—IT Value-Based Performance Measurement

The process flows of the IT value-based performance measurement are shown in Figure 3.17.

3.7.4.3 Performance Model—IT Value-Based Performance Measurement

The performance model of the IT value-based performance measurement is shown in Figure 3.18.

3.7.4.4 Performance Measures—IT Value-Based Performance Measurement

The performance measures of the IT value-based performance measurement are shown in Figure 3.19.

Table 3.6 IT Value-Based Performance Measurement Output/Outcomes

Results Area	*Output*	*Outcome*
IT value-based performance measurement	Process—IT and business	• Improved quality of IT performance measures • Increased alignment of IT with business structures and processes • Increased transformation to RBM and RBB culture • Optimized financial resource utilization • Increased understanding of improvement areas effectiveness
	Organizational structure—IT and business	
	Technology solutions—dashboard	
	Performance culture—RBM	
	Financial trends, analytics—RBB	
	Accountability for results—RBM	

Figure 3.17 IT value-based performance measurement process flow.

Degree of Value/Risk	Process Improve ment	Organization al Alignment	Technology Enablement	Performance Culture	Financial Performance RBB	RBM
Value-H	□	□	□	□	□	□
Value-L	□	□	□	□	□	□
Risk-H	□	□	□	□	□	□
Risk-L	□	□	□	□	□	□

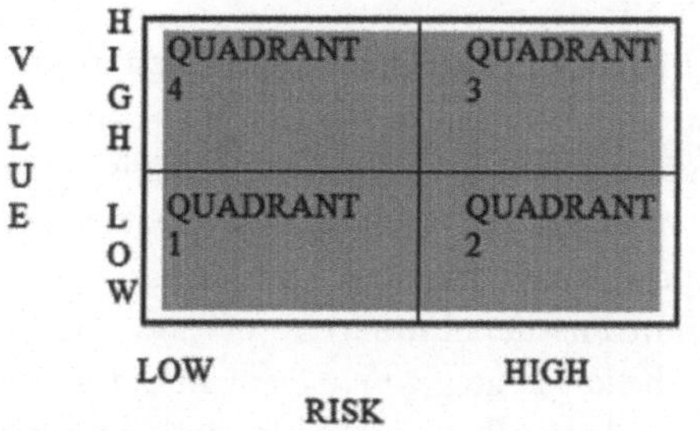

QUADRANT 1: Low Value and Low Risk- Minor Impact
QUADRANT 2: Low Value and High Risk- Definitely Avoid
QUADRANT 3: High Value and High Risk- Major Impact
QUADRANT 4: High Value and Low Risk- Accept

Figure 3.18 IT value-based performance measurement model.

IT PERFORMANCE MANAGEMENT DASHBOARD (2011-2012) ANALYTICS				August 31/2011	
IT EXECUTIVE LEADERSHIP					
OPERATIONAL-FM	Start Date	End Date	Status	% Complete	Indicator
IT Governance Accountability Framework	4/1/2011	12/31/2011	In-Progress	60%	G
HR Performance Contract Alignment	4/1/2011	9/30/2011	In-Progress	80%	G
Executive Management (EM) Progress Status	4/1/2011	3/31/2012	In-Progress	40%	G
Executive Management Presentation/Approvals	4/1/2011	3/31/2012	In-Progress	60%	G
IT Policies and Procedures	4/1/2011	3/31/2012	In-Progress	60%	G
IT Operational Accountability Framework	4/1/2011	3/31/2012	In-Progress	40%	G
OPERATIONAL-FM Summary	4/1/2011	3/31/2012	In-Progress	57%	G
% IT staff performing IT Governance; # Improvements completed					
% IT staff performing HR Alignment; # Improvements completed					
% IT staff performing EM Communications; # Improvements completed					
% IT staff performing EM Presentation; # Improvements completed					
% IT staff performing IT Policies; # Improvements completed					
% IT staff performing IT Operations; # Improvements completed					
% customers support IT operational accountability framework; # dis-satisfied					

IT PLANNING & ADMINISTRATION SERVICES (PAS)					
OPERATIONAL-FM	Start Date	End Date	Status	% Complete	Indicator
IT Strategic Planning Framework	4/1/2011	9/30/2011	In-Progress	100%	Black
IT Operating Planning Framework	4/1/2011	3/31/2012	In-Progress	35%	Y
IT Budgeting Planning Framework	4/1/2011	12/31/2011	In-Progress	30%	R
OPERATIONAL-FM Summary	4/1/2011	3/31/2012	In-Progress	55%	G
% IT staff performing IT Strategic Planning; # Improvements completed					
% IT staff performing IT Operating Planning; # Improvements completed					
% IT staff performing IT Budget Planning; # Improvements completed					
% Value (EVA) of IT budget; # budget updates					

Figure 3.19 IT value-based performance measures.

3.8 Summary

The strategic management model presented in this chapter describes the results areas of strategic management. The "purpose" section provides a statement of the derived result, and the "strategic directives" section provides various guiding principles and major directives to achieving the purpose statement, for each of the strategic management results areas. The accountabilities of the executive performance manager, performance delivery manager, and performance measurement team are presented to demonstrate the integrated nature of these outputs and outcomes in measuring, managing, and delivering IT services. The key strategic management outputs and outcomes, process flows, and performance measures provide excellent real-world implementation guidelines, which can be referenced and applied to IT strategic management processes.

Information technology staff who are in the process of measuring, managing, and delivering IT services with the goal toward integrated performance management should consider the following strategic management recommendations, as a framework, to guide them toward successful measurement, management, and delivery of IT services:

- Establish an IT strategic directives framework that will guide the measurement, management, and delivery of performance measurement program, to improve organizational performance and quality of management, and to optimize the utilization of IT resources.
- Determine the value of performance measurement to IT and the business based on the six areas of performance measurement and the integrated IT performance measurement dashboard.
- Establish a governance model that embraces the characteristics of performance culture, process, and structure.
- Obtain commitments or non-commitments from executive and senior management for enforcing the integration of the IT performance measurement dashboard, using Norton and Kaplan measures—employee, customer, financials, and operations—leadership, service excellence, service delivery, and relationship management.
- Establish a performance steering committee to provide performance approval responsibilities and accountability for the input, process and output measures, and overall results as determined from the integrated IT performance measurement dashboard.
- Manage and track the integrated IT performance measurement dashboard, determine the value of input, process and output performance measures, trends and analytics, and align with IT strategic directive and IT policy framework.

The main focus of this chapter is to provide the readers with further details on the strategic management results areas of the integrated IT performance management framework (IPMF-IT). By now, the readers should have gained a fairly good understanding of the integrated nature of these results areas. Chapter 6 includes further discussions to show the horizontal integration of these strategic management results areas using the IT Service Delivery Life Cycle Performance Model. Business and IT managers, and academics, especially those with a passion for improvements, measurements, and assessments will be able to appreciate the value of this horizontal and vertical integration, to better prepare them in understanding performance measurement and management in this dynamically changing IT industry.

3.9 Endnotes: Key Performance Management Terms

[1]*IT goal statement*: A representation of vision, mission, goals, values, success factors, and performance measures, which are used to guide the identification outputs, outcomes, and performance and align with IT strategic framework and IT strategic directives.

[2]*Results based accountability framework*: A framework that is results driven not activity driven. Result driven specifies outputs and outcomes to measure and manage organizational performance.

[3]*Operational-FM and performance metrics*: Performance measures that focuses on internal operational processes for executive leadership and senior functional management, as defined in the integrated IT performance measurement dashboard.

[4]*SWOT*: A method or process used to access the current and future state of a company's business by analyzing the strengths, weaknesses, opportunities, and threats of the business.

[5]*Performance measurement/management program*: A program that that describes who, when, and how the performance results will be measured, managed, delivered, and improved. It is synonymous with performance improvement plan.

[6]*Accountabilities*: Accountability refers to holding others accountable for results rather than activities. Shifting from measurement is primarily designed to provide accountability for effort, activities, and tasks to accountability for results/outputs/outcomes.

Accountability = Responsibility + Authority.

[7]*IT operational plan with alignment to strategic directives*: A document that describes IT operational plan with clear alignment to strategic directives using COBIT framework and accountability for results leadership strategies.

[8]*IT strategic directives*: A framework document that describes the strategic directives for the six IT functional areas with direct alignment to the operational, financial, employee, and customer performance measures and the IT-integrated performance measurement dashboard.

[9]*Policy management framework*: A framework of policies that aligns with strategic directives to support accountability for results.

[10]*Service providers*: In this book, service providers are more generally used to refer to third party or outsourced suppliers, who provide consulting services to organizations.

[11]*IT governance framework*: A framework that uses accountability for results to decision making, which focuses on culture, process, and structure.

[12]*ITIL*: A framework for Information Technology Infrastructure Library that strives for predictable and consistent service management services to support accountability for results with COBIT framework.

[13]*Results-based management (RBM) culture*: A culture that supports results-based management (RBM). Meaningful measures aligned with outcomes.

[14]*Resluts-based budgeting (RBB)*: An RBM approach to measuring and managing budgets.

[15]*IT value-based performance measurement (VBPM)*: A value-based measurement approach to results-based management accountability for results.

[16]*The IT value-based performance measurement (VBPM) model*: A model that represents value-based performance measures accountability for results.

3.10 Questions to Think About: Management Perspectives

1. Think about how your organization measures, manages, and delivers IT services. How does your organization measure and manage conflicting business and IT priorities? What are the key rationales for determining the value of IT performance measurement? What are the major results areas of strategic management? How do these results areas relate to your IT environment? What is the perception of senior management on the need for an integrated IT performance measurement dashboard to guide the measurement, management, and delivery of IT services?
2. Think about how your organization evaluates the effectiveness of performance measurement programs, initiatives, and organizational areas? What are the six value areas for performance measurement? How do these six value areas relate to your performance measurement assessment approach?
3. Think about how your organization establishes an integrated performance measurement dashboard? How are outputs/outcomes and performance measures determined? How does this performance measurement dashboard align your IT strategic directives and IT policy framework?

4. Think about how your organization approves performance measurement program? How does your organization approve the results—input, process, and output measures? What are the performance measurement areas discussed in this book? How does this measurement approach relate to your performance measurement approach?
5. Think about how your organization establishes IT strategic directives? How do these strategic directives align with results/outputs/outcomes and performance measures? How do these strategic directives align with IT goals, strategic framework, and IT policy framework? How do these strategic directives align with IT operational management?
6. Think about how your organization establishes IT performance governance structure? How does personal greed for power and politics affect performance and decision-making structures? What is the IT performance governance structure recommended in this book? How does this recommendation relate to your approach?
7. Think about how your organization promotes the value of performance measurement? What are the outputs/outcomes of IT value-based performance measurement? What do you think is the maturity of performance culture in your organization? Identify areas of improvements?
8. Think about how your organization measures and manages business and IT results/outputs/outcomes. How do these business results impact IT services? How are these business results integrated with IT results, as discussed in this book? How does this process relate to your approach to measuring, managing, and delivering integrated business and IT results?
9. Think about how your organization enables and supports results-based budgeting (RBB) and results-based management (RBM)? What is the difference? What is your critical success factor for IT services delivery in your organization?

3.11 Chapter Testing Questions

1. Which one of the integrated IT performance measurement dashboard measures is used to measure IT services performance?
   a. Employee, customer, operations, financials measures
   b. Input, process, output measures
   c. Operational processes measures
2. Executives shall use the integrated IT performance measurement dashboard to
   a. Understand the performance scope
   b. Make sound objective decisions on IT performance
   c. Determine performance results trends and analytics
3. Who is the appropriate person accountable for delivering performance measurement results for projects?
   a. Performance Delivery Manager
   b. Project Manager
   c. Performance Specialist
4. The components of strategic management model MUST include
   a. Process, purpose, strategic directives, accountabilities
   b. Strategic management, performance management, IT operational management
   c. Output/outcome, process flows, performance measures
5. Strategic management result areas do NOT include
   a. Goals, strategic framework, policy framework
   b. Performance governance, transformational change, strategic directives
   c. Strategic directives, value-based performance measurement, policy framework

6. At one stage of a performance measurement effort, you decided to use the IT performance governance structure to understand the areas of governance. What would you *most* likely examine?
   a. Process, culture, structure
   b. Are we doing the right things? Right way? Getting benefits? How well?
   c. Transformational change, sustainability, performance culture
7. What are the major outputs of IT performance governance structure?
   a. Structure, culture, processes
   b. People, process, technology, financials
   c. People, politics, process, performance
8. Which one of the following results areas is *best* input for the performance dashboard?
   a. IT strategic framework
   b. IT performance governance structure
   c. IT strategic directives
9. Which one of the following is *most* effective in assessing the value of performance measurement programs, initiatives, and organizational areas to executives?
   a. Performance culture, process improvement, RBB, technology enablement, RBM
   b. ROI, RBB, RBM, organizational alignment, VBPM
   c. Business case, VBPM, earned Value, performance culture, governance

Recommended Readings

Strategic Management

Aguinis, H., *Performance Management.* New York: Pearson Education, 2012.

Bainey, K.R., *Integrated IT Project Management: A Model-Centric Approach.* New York: Artech House, 2004.

Batshalom, B., *The Green Source, The Magazine of Sustainable Design.* Boston, MA, Sustainable Performance Institute, 2011.

Corkins, G., *Performance Management, Integrating Strategy, Execution, Methodologies, Risk, and Analytics.* Hoboken, NJ: John Wiley & Sons Inc., 2009.

Demartini, C., *Performance Management Systems: Design, Diagnosis and Use.* Berlin, Germany: Springer, 2013.

Hall, D., *Corporate Governance: Ensuring Propriety for Performance: A Contemporary Themes in Strategic People Management.* New York: Palgrave Macmillan, 2013.

Kaplan, R.S. and Norton, D.P., *The Balanced Scorecard: Translating Strategy into Action.* Boston, MA: Harvard Business School Publishing, 1996.

KPI Institute Performance Management in 2013. Melbourne, Victoria, Australia: KPI Institute Melbourne, 2013.

Marr, B., *Strategic Performance Management, Leveraging and Measuring Your Intangible Value Driver.* Burlington, MA: Elsevier Ltd., 2006.

Spitzer, D.R., *Transforming Performance Measurement, Rethinking the Way We Measure and Drive Organizational Success.* New York: AMACOM, 2007.

Waal, A.D., *Strategic Performance Management: A Managerial and Behavioral Approach.* New York: Palgrave Macmillan, 2013.

Chapter 4

Performance Management Model

4.1 Performance Management

The function of performance management is to help managers integrate strategic and operational performance to ensure that IT Services are managed, monitored, measured, and delivered using an outcomes-based performance measurement and accountability framework with continuous integrated governance. IT services are managed and delivered using six functional areas during the IT service delivery life cycle, and a clear understanding of these functional areas will enable managers to effectively measure the results, outputs, outcomes, and services, with the goal to optimize utilization of resources and improve organizational performance. It consists of the following results areas:

- IT service delivery life cycle performance model
- IT performance management delivery processes
  - Performance management standards (PMSD)
  - Performance measurement system (PMS)
  - Performance management reporting (PMR)
  - Financial performance management (FPM)
  - Performance improvement management (PIM)
  - Performance change management (PCM)
  - Human resource performance management (HRPM)
- Performance measurement office (PMO) support

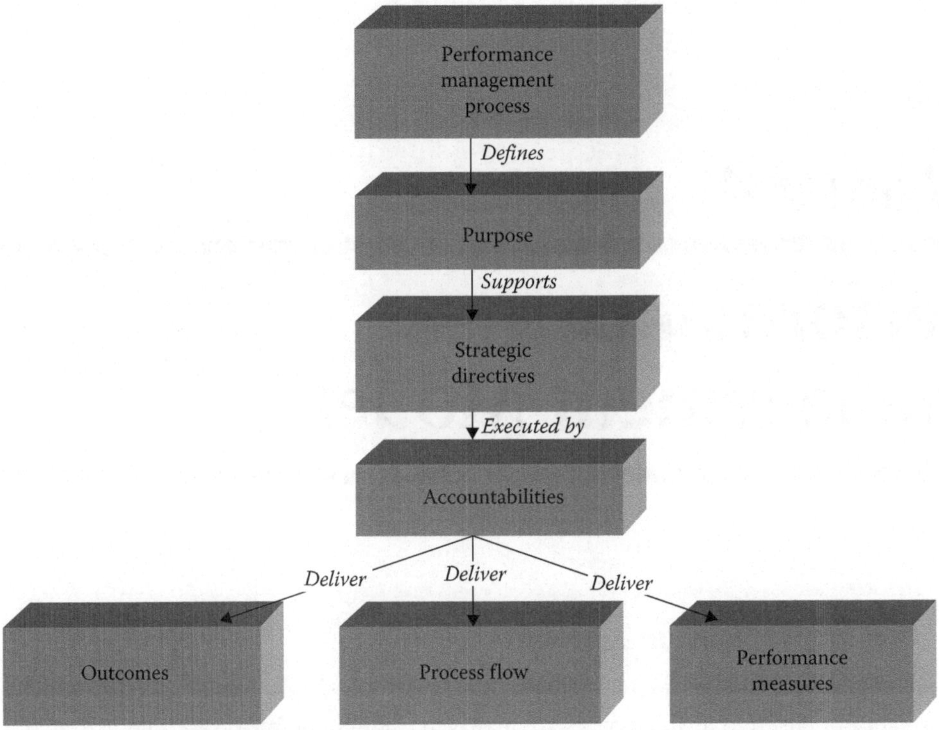

Figure 4.1 Performance management model.

Figure 4.1 is a graphical representation of the modeling concepts that is used to demonstrate the structure and relationships or processing components of performance management, from *accountability for results*[1] perspectives.

4.2 IT SDLC Performance Model

Executive management shall use the six functional areas of the IT service delivery life cycle performance model to guide the implementation of the PMS in alignment with IT strategic directives. Outputs, outcomes, goals, strategies, and performance measures are developed for each functional area, which formed the basis for developments of IT strategic directives and IT strategic framework. IT service delivery life cycle performance model presented in this book focuses on an integrated governance approach accountability for results, consisting of the following results:

- Governance—The primary result is *executive leadership/governance services* (*ELS*)[2] outputs and outcomes, which include the governance structure and IT strategic directives.
- Planning and administration—The primary result is *planning and administration services* (*PAS*)[3] outputs and outcomes, which include strategic and operational plans.
- Enterprise architecture and innovations—The primary result is *enterprise architecture services* (*EAS*)[4] outputs and outcomes, which include EAS project management and contract management for IT Infrastructure projects and enterprise architectures.

- Project portfolio management—The primary result is *project portfolio management* (*PPM*)[5] outputs and outcomes, which include project management and contract management for business projects.
- Applications management services—The primary result is *applications management services* (*AMS*)[6] outputs and outcomes, which include AMS outsourced contract management.
- Technology operations services—The primary result is *technology operations services* (*TOS*)[7] outputs and outcomes, which include TOS outsourced contract management.

Accountability breeds responsibility.
Begin with the end in mind.

Stephen Covey

The intent of this section is *not* to provide detailed processes or procedures on the implementation of any specific IT service delivery life cycle performance model. There are many excellent books on IT service delivery life cycle processes, concepts, theory, and applicability, some of which are mentioned in the "Recommended Readings" section provided at the end of this chapter. The main objective of this chapter is to provide an overview of the contents (what), purpose (why), accountabilities (who is accountable for what), and results (what, how, why) of performance management and to demonstrate how it fits within the context of the overall integrated IT performance management framework. The "accountability" section provides results-based accountability for the executive performance manager, performance delivery manager, and performance measurement team—performance measurement manager and performance specialists. The results sections for each of the IT performance management results areas provide the outputs/outcomes (what), process flow (how), and performance measures (why) to support the measurement, management, delivery, improvement, and integration of the performance management results areas. The performance measures from the performance measurement dashboard mainly show staff input metrics/measures for demonstration purposes. In reality, the dashboard contains results for input, process, and output/outcomes measures.

The materials presented in the following sections are organized to support the structure represented in Figure 4.1. This structure provides a logical and consistent flow of information to enable the readers to gain a better understanding and appreciation for the integrated nature of IT performance management, as presented in this book.

4.2.1 Purpose

The purpose of this results area is to present an IT service delivery life cycle performance model, consisting of well-established functional areas, to support the integrated governance approach to accountability for results. This model will form the baseline to managing, measuring, delivering, and improving IT services, using the IT strategic directives document and the integrated IT performance measurement dashboard, within the context of the performance measurement areas. The performance steering committee shall have approval accountabilities for both the business and IT program for organizational performance. This committee will also have accountability with the performance measurement managers, for the operational performance of the six functional areas, using the measurement areas defined in the performance management plan and the integrated IT performance measurement dashboard.

4.2.2 Strategic Directives

IT services will be directed and measured by a performance steering committee for each of the functional areas that specify the outputs, outcomes, and performance metrics in the performance measurement dashboard. These established functional areas formed the six pillars to measuring, managing, delivering, and improving IT services, using the six stages of the IT service delivery life cycle: (1) strategy, (2) plan, (3) design, (4) deliver, (5) deliver/support applications, and (6) deliver/support technology. The transformational performance leadership strategies for the six functional areas are based on the following principles:

Outsourcing + innovations = transformation.[8]

- The performance steering committee will provide performance approval accountabilities for the measurement, management, and delivery of the functional areas, represented as measurement areas in the performance measurement dashboard.
- All changes to outputs, outcomes, and performance metrics for each functional area must be approved by the performance steering committee. The performance delivery manager will document and present changes to the performance steering committee for approval.
- The performance steering committee will meet, at a minimum, on a monthly basis to review the performance indicators, trends, and analytics for each function area outputs, outcomes, and performance metrics as represented in the performance measurement dashboard. If the overall progress of the output is *red* or *yellow*, more frequent meetings may be required.
- The outputs and outcomes for each of the six functional areas will be measured and managed based on operations, financial, customer, and employee measures, identified in the performance measurement dashboard and outlined in the *IT operational plan with alignment to strategic directives.*
- Senior managers will be thoroughly familiar with the outputs, outcomes, performance metrics, and indicators for each functional area to ensure consistency and integration in measurement, management, and delivery of IT services.

4.2.3 Accountabilities

4.2.3.1 Executive Performance Manager

This person is accountable for *approval* of the results.

- Executive support and approval for the *context and contents* of the functional areas and areas for improvements within the IT service delivery life cycle performance model
- Executive support and approval for the *progress results* on the established functional areas within the IT service delivery life cycle performance model to ensure integration with IT strategic plan, alignment to company's business plan, and understanding the benefits and linkages with desired outcomes
- Executive support and approval for *performance trend results* in the performance scorecard or dashboard to understand the following: (a) "How we are doing?" (b) "Are we doing/measuring the right things?" (c) "Are we getting the right results?" (d) "Are we getting the value?"

- Executive support for stakeholders' *survey satisfaction results* for strategic and IT operational management assessments to understand the value of the functional areas with the IT service delivery life cycle performance model and to improve service delivery through stakeholders' satisfaction surveys
- Executive support and approval for *delivery services improvements* on the functional areas with the IT service delivery life cycle performance model and increased understanding of benefits and intended outcomes statement within the overall IT strategic framework as well as recommending areas of improvements for *customer, employee, financial,* and *operational performance measures and results*
- Executive support and approval for *performance measures and benchmarking results* on reporting to performance steering committee, with direct accountability to performance management executive

4.2.3.2 Performance Delivery Manager

This person is accountable for *management* of the results.

- Manage and define the *context and contents* of the functional areas for improvements, within the IT service delivery life cycle performance model.
- Measure the *progress results* of the established functional areas within the IT service delivery life cycle to ensure integration with IT strategic plan, alignment to company's business plan, and understanding the benefits and linkages with desired outcomes.
- Monitor and analyze *performance trend results* in the performance scorecard or dashboard to understand the following: (a) "How we are doing?" (b) "Are we doing/measuring the right things?" (c) "Are we getting the right results?" (d) "Are we getting the value?"
- Deliver and evaluate stakeholders' *survey satisfaction results* for strategic and IT operational management to understand the value of the functional areas with the IT service delivery life cycle performance model and to improve service delivery through stakeholders' satisfaction surveys.
- Improve *delivery services* for the functional areas with the IT service delivery life cycle model and increase understanding of benefits and intended outcomes statement within the overall IT strategic framework by recommending areas of improvements for *customer, employee, financial,* and *operational performance measures and results.*
- Report on *performance measures and benchmarking results* to performance steering committee, with direct accountability to performance management executive.

4.2.3.3 Performance Measurement Team

This team is accountable for *delivery* of performance results.

- Provide meaningful and credible data for defining the *context and contents* of the functional areas for improvements, within the IT service delivery life cycle model.
- Provide meaningful and credible data for measuring the *progress results* of the established functional areas within the IT service delivery life cycle performance model to ensure integration with IT strategic plan, alignment to company's business plan, and understanding the benefits and linkages with desired outcomes.

- Provide meaningful and credible data for monitoring and analyzing *performance trend results* in the performance scorecard or dashboard to understand the following: (a) "How we are doing?" (b) "Are we doing/measuring the right things?" (c) "Are we getting the right results?" (d) "Are we getting the value?"
- Provide meaningful and credible survey data for delivering and evaluating stakeholders' *satisfaction results* for strategic and IT operational management to understand the value of the functional areas with the IT service delivery life cycle performance model and to improve service delivery through stakeholders' satisfaction surveys.
- Provide meaningful and credible data for improving *delivery services* for the functional areas with the IT service delivery life cycle performance model and increase understanding of benefits and intended outcomes statement within the overall IT strategic framework by recommending areas of improvements for *customer, employee, financial,* and *operational performance measures and results.*
- Provide meaningful and credible data on *benchmarking data results* for reporting on *performance measures and results* to performance steering committee, with direct accountability to performance management executive.

4.2.4 Results: IT SDLC Performance Model

Accountabilities discussed earlier are brief because they are intended to serve as a reference for *who is accountable* for *what* during the delivery of the six functional areas within the IT service delivery life cycle performance model . Results are now introduced to highlight the outputs of this IT service delivery life cycle model results area and associated outcomes (what), process flow (how), and performance measures (why). It is intended to serve as a reference based on the English language interrogatives: Who *is accountable for what, how,* and *why.* The outputs/outcomes, process flow, and performance measures, based on real-world practical implementation, will serve as excellent references for practicing performance managers during measurement, delivery, and reporting of the six functional areas outputs and outcomes.

The outputs/outcomes highlight the key results for IT service delivery life cycle performance model that the performance managers measure and report during the delivery of the functional results area . The process flows, based on real-world practical implementations, is a graphical representation of the inputs, process, outputs, and relationships. The IT service delivery life cycle performance model shows the foundation representation to effectively communicate the integrated components of the six functional areas to strategic, IT operational, and performance management staff.

The performance measures from the integrated IT performance measurement dashboard for IT service delivery life cycle performance model outputs/outcomes are illustrated for the six IT functional areas, using operational functional management measures. Appendices A through F provide further details. Performance metrics, indicators, progress, trends, and analytics formed the basis for evidence-based decision making to enable improved organizational excellence.

> However beautiful the strategy, you should occasionally look at the results.
>
> **Winston Churchill**

4.2.4.1 Outputs/Outcomes: IT SDLC Performance Model

The outputs and outcomes of the IT SDLC performance model are given in Table 4.1.

Table 4.1 IT Service Delivery Life Cycle Performance Model Output/Outcomes

Results Area	*Output*	*Outcome*
IT service delivery life cycle	IT executive leadership/ governance services (ELS)	• Optimized utilization of IT resources • Increased accountability and transparency of IT resources • Increased quality of governance and management staff and decreased quantity of governance and management staff • Improved results-based accountability • Increased transformation to performance measurement culture • Increased value of performance measurement dashboard-analytics • Increased accountability and transparency of program directives
	Planning and administration services (PAS)	• Increased quality and alignment of strategic with operational plans • Optimized utilization of capital and operating budgets • Decreased administrative overhead and meaningless meetings
	Enterprise architecture services (EAS)	• Increased understanding and value of IT infrastructure assets
	Project portfolio management (PPM)	• Increased value justifications and risks of IT business projects • Increased collaborations with business
	Applications management services (AMS)	• Increased stability, sustainability, and reliability of business applications services
	Technology operations services (TOS)	• Increased stability, sustainability, and reliability of technology operations services

4.2.4.2 Process Flows: IT SDLC Performance Model

The process flows of the IT SDLC performance model are shown in Figure 4.2.

4.2.4.3 Performance Model: IT SDLC

The performance model of the IT SDLC performance model is shown in Figure 4.3.

4.2.4.4 Performance Measures: IT SDLC Model

The performance measures of the IT SDLC performance model are shown in Figure 4.4.

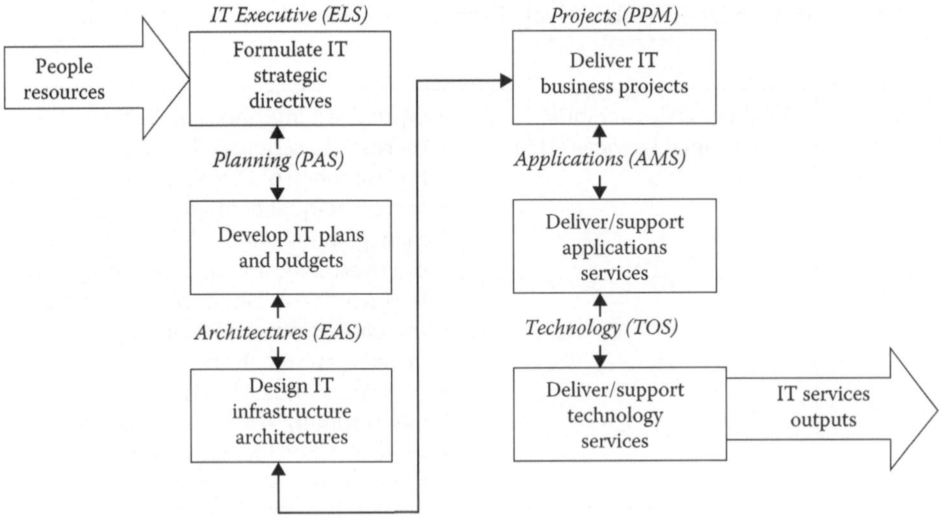

Figure 4.2 IT service delivery life cycle performance model process flow.

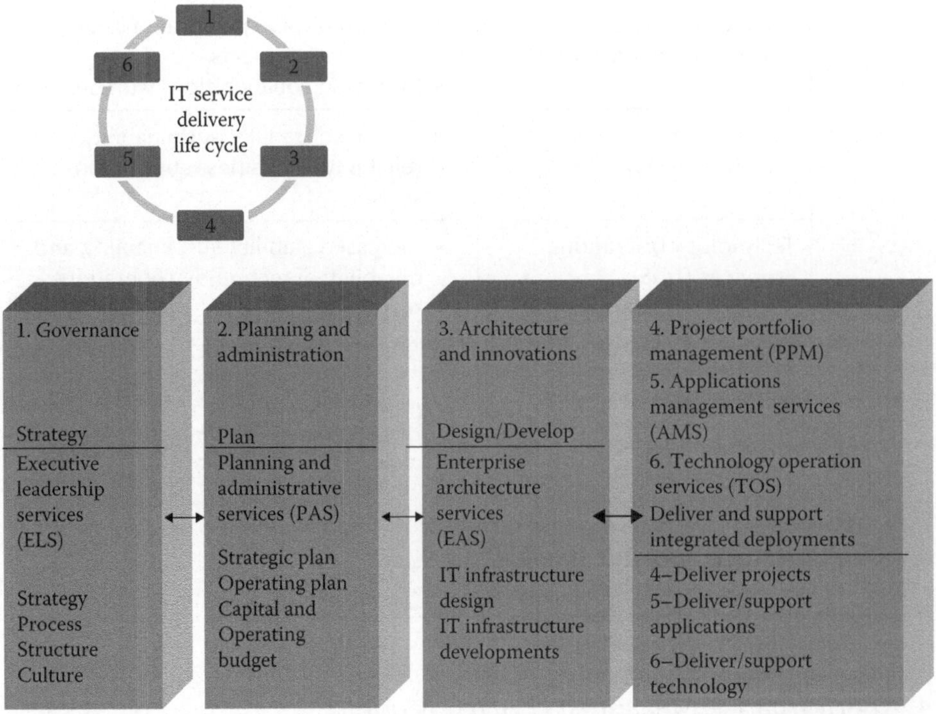

Figure 4.3 IT service delivery life cycle performance model.

IT PERFORMANCE MANAGEMENT DASHBOARD (2011-2012) ANALYTICS					August 31/2011
IT EXECUTIVE LEADERSHIP					
OPERATIONAL-FM	Start Date	End Date	Status	% Complete	Indicator
IT Governance Accountability Framework	4/1/2011	12/31/2011	In-Progress	60%	G
HR Performance Contract Alignment	4/1/2011	9/30/2011	In-Progress	80%	G
Executive Management (EM) Progress Status	4/1/2011	3/31/2012	In-Progress	40%	G
Executive Management Presentation/Approvals	4/1/2011	3/31/2012	In-Progress	60%	G
IT Policies and Procedures	4/1/2011	3/31/2012	In-Progress	60%	G
IT Operational Accountability Framework	4/1/2011	3/31/2012	In-Progress	40%	G
OPERATIONAL-FM Summary	4/1/2011	3/31/2012	In-Progress	57%	G

Performance Metrics
% IT staff performing IT Governance; # Improvements completed
% IT staff performing HR Alignment; # Improvements completed
% IT staff performing EM Communications; # Improvements completed
% IT staff performing EM Presentation; # Improvements completed
% IT staff performing IT Policies; # Improvements completed
% IT staff performing IT Operations; # Improvements completed

IT PLANNING & ADMINISTRATION SERVICES (PAS)					
OPERATIONAL-FM	Start Date	End Date	Status	% Complete	Indicator
IT Strategic Planning Framework	4/1/2011	9/30/2011	In-Progress	100%	Black
IT Operating Planning Framework	4/1/2011	3/31/2012	In-Progress	35%	Y
IT Budgeting Planning Framework	4/1/2011	12/31/2011	In-Progress	30%	R
OPERATIONAL-FM Summary	4/1/2011	3/31/2012	In-Progress	55%	G

Performance Metrics
% IT staff performing IT Strategic Planning ; # Improvements completed
% IT staff performing IT Operating Planning ; # Improvements completed
% IT staff performing IT Budget Planning ; # Improvements completed

(a)

IT ENTERPRISE ARCHITECTURE SERVICES (EAS)					
OPERATIONAL-FM	Start Date	End Date	Status	% Complete	Indicator
IT Enterprise Architecture Framework	4/1/2011	9/30/2011	In-Progress	25%	R
Information Management Framework	4/1/2011	9/30/2011	In-Progress	25%	R
Technology Project Management Governance	4/1/2011	3/31/2012	In-Progress	25%	Y
OPERATIONAL-FM Summary	4/1/2011	3/31/2012	In-Progress	25%	Y

Performance Metrics
% IT staff performing IT Enterprise Architecture; # Improvements completed
% IT staff performing IM Framework; # Improvements completed
% IT staff performing Technology PM Governance; # Improvements completed

IT PROJECT PORTFOLIO MANAGEMENT (PPM)					
OPERATIONAL-FM	Start Date	End Date	Status	% Complete	Indicator
IT PPM Governance Framework	4/1/2011	12/31/2011	In-Progress	50%	G
IT PPM Innovative Technical Direction	4/1/2011	3/31/2012	In-Progress	45%	G
PPM Projects Outsourcing Framework	4/1/2011	9/30/2011	In-Progress	65%	Y
OPERATIONAL-FM Summary	4/1/2011	3/31/2012	In-Progress	53%	G

Performance Metrics
% IT staff performing PPM Governance ; # Improvements completed
% IT staff performing PPM Innovations ; # Improvements completed
% IT staff performing PPM Outsourcing Strategies ; # Improvements completed

(b)

Figure 4.4 (a–c) IT service delivery life cycle performance model measures. *(Continued)*

IT APPLICATIONS MANAGEMENT SERVICES (AMS)					
OPERATIONAL-FM	Start Date	End Date	Status	% Complete	Indicator
IT AMS Governance Framework	4/1/2011	12/31/2011	In-Progress	50%	G
IT AMS Innovative Technical Direction	4/1/2011	3/31/2012	In-Progress	45%	G
AMS Outsourcing Framework	4/1/2011	9/30/2011	In-Progress	65%	Y
OPERATIONAL-FM Summary	4/1/2011	3/31/2012	In-Progress	53%	G

Performance Metrics
% IT staff performing AMS Governance ; # Improvements completed
% IT staff performing AMS Innovations ; # Improvements completed
% IT staff performing AMS Outsourcing Strategies ; # Improvements completed

IT OPERATIONS SERVICES (TOS)					
OPERATIONAL-FM	Start Date	End Date	Status	% Complete	Indicator
TOS Governance Framework	4/1/2011	12/31/2011	In-Progress	50%	G
TOS Innovative Technical Direction	4/1/2011	3/31/2012	In-Progress	45%	G
TOS Outsourcing Framework	4/1/2011	9/30/2011	In-Progress	65%	Y
TOS Data Centre Technology Direction	4/1/2011	3/31/2012	In-Progress	45%	G
OPERATIONAL-FM Summary	4/1/2011	3/31/2012	In-Progress	51%	G

Performance Metrics
% IT staff performing TOS Governance ; # Improvements completed
% IT staff performing TOS Innovations ; # Improvements completed
% IT staff performing TOS Outsourcing Strategies ; # Improvements completed
% IT staff performing TOS Data Centre Technology Direction ; # Improvements completed

(c)

Figure 4.4 (*Continued*) (a–c) IT service delivery life cycle performance model measures.

4.3 IT Performance Management Delivery Processes

The IT performance management delivery processes discussed in this section represent the fundamentals to establishing an integrated performance management body of knowledge. These fundamentals consist of the culture, structure, and processes and outputs, outcomes, and performance measures for standards, measurement systems, reporting, improvements, change management, human resources (HR), and FPM key results areas (KRAs). The lack of standards and integrated body of knowledge on performance management and measurement leaves room for interpretations, false assumptions, and confusion. PMBOK® Guide 5th Edition does not sufficiently address performance management for project management. The purpose of this book is to provide that integrated body of knowledge from a strategic, operational, and performance management perspective. The focus is toward enabling a culture of accountability for results—results-based management (RBM). An accountability culture that transforms from creating and carrying out activities to a culture of being accountable for achieving results, meeting goals, affecting change, and improving quality of services. An accountability culture toward measuring results rather than only measuring resources and activities, toward measuring outputs and outcomes, rather than merely counting inputs and outputs. The performance management body of knowledge presented here should enhance the materials presented in this book to provide a clearer understanding of the integrated IT performance management process, presented as the theme of this book. The IT performance management delivery processes presented in this section outline the fundamental performance standards, measurement systems, and reporting processes to integrate employee, customer, financial, and operational performance measures with the structure of the integrated IT performance measurement dashboard.

> All organizations are perfectly designed to get the results they are now getting. If we want different results, we must change the way we do things.
>
> **Tom Northup**

The intent of this section is *not* to provide detailed processes or procedures on the implementation of *PMI-PMBOK* performance management process or similar performance management processes. There are many excellent books on performance management processes, concepts, theory, and applicability, some of which are mentioned in the "Recommended Readings" section provided at the end of this chapter. The main objective of this chapter is to provide an overview of the contents (what), purpose (why), accountabilities (who is accountable for what), and results (what, how, why) of performance management and to demonstrate how it fits within the context of the overall integrated IT performance management framework. This framework forms the foundation for the integrated performance management body of knowledge as presented in this book. The "accountability" section provides results-based accountability for the executive performance manager, performance delivery manager, and performance measurement team—performance measurement manager and performance specialists. The results sections for each of the IT performance management results areas provide the outputs/outcomes (what), process flow (how), and performance measures (why) to support the measurement, management, delivery, improvement, and integration of the performance management results areas. The performance measures from the performance measurement dashboard mainly show staff input metrics/measures for demonstration purposes. In reality, the dashboard contains many combinations of results for input, process, and output/outcomes measures.

The materials presented in the following sections are organized to support the structure represented in Figure 4.1. This structure provides a logical and consistent flow of information to enable the readers to gain a better understanding and appreciation for the integrated nature of IT performance management, as presented in this book.

4.3.1 Performance Management Standards

Managers and performance specialists shall use the *PMSD*[9] results area to determine the major key results and to establish a common understanding of expectations and results for employee, customer, financial, and operations performance measures, as outlined in the performance management program. Executives shall use the PMSD to ensure that an appropriate level of quality, effectiveness, accountability, and rewards have been effectively applied to the management and delivery of IT services and that performance results has not been reduced to inappropriate levels due to political or other performance pressures. Performance management is when an organization uses performance measures and standards to achieve desired result. The PMSD presented in this book focuses more on managing the quality, effectiveness, accountability, and rewards of the results and measuring these results in accordance with customer, employee, financial, and operational performance measures. PMS ensures that an appropriate level of performance is attained that adheres to the company's IT strategic and operational framework to ensure

- Compliance to organizational policies
- Compliance to guidelines and requirements imposed by the service delivery life cycle guidelines
- Compliance to PMO guidelines, appropriate for use by the performance management and measurement plan/program

The major key results of PMS area are

- Results quality/quantity
- Results effectiveness/efficiencies
- Results accountability
- Results rewards/recognition
- Performance management plan

There is never enough time to do it right, but there is always time to do it over.

Murphy's Law

4.3.1.1 Purpose

The purpose of this results area is to communicate expected results in terms of quality/quantity, effectiveness/efficiencies, accountability, and rewards/recognition for management and delivery of IT services. The purpose of standards is to communicate expectations—you always expect certain behaviors and actions—accountability, integrity, ethics, quality, effectiveness, and efficiencies. Accountability improves the effectiveness/efficiencies and quality/quantity of management. PMSD ensure that appropriate levels of quality/quantity, effectiveness/efficiency, accountability, and rewards/recognition have been effectively applied to the delivery of IT services and that performance has not been reduced to some inappropriate levels because of political or other performance pressures. This information will form the baseline to measure and integrate the performance objectives of IT service delivery. The performance steering committee will use these performance standards as a baseline in assessing the quality of the performance results and the overall performance management program.

4.3.1.2 Strategic Directives

- The PMSD will be maintained at the level that is appropriate for the management and delivery of IT services. Adherence to PMO guidelines and policies will be objectively verified.
- The minimum level of performance standards will be established by PMO policies, guidelines, and procedures. Specific IT services that require higher performance results will be documented in the *integrated performance management plan*.[10]
- The company's PMSD will be published and readily available. Performance delivery managers will develop specific variances based upon the results of the IT products and services. Variances shall be documented in the integrated performance management plan.
- Performance metrics will be developed and available as guidelines in delivering results on major products and services for each functional area of the IT service delivery life cycle. PMO metrics and indicators will also be made available during the development of the integrated performance management plan.

- Performance metrics reviews, with the appropriate management approval, will be conducted for each functional area of the IT service delivery life.
- The performance measurement team will provide recommendations and corrective actions for each assessment of the performance results.

4.3.1.3 Accountabilities

4.3.1.3.1 Executive Performance Manager

This person is accountable for *approval* of the results.

- Executive support and approval for the *context and contents* of the PMS and areas for improvements on the *established performance results criteria*[11]
- Executive support and approval for the progress of the *established performance results* against the PMSD to ensure alignment with IT strategic and operational management framework and to understand the benefits and linkages with desired outcomes
- Executive support and approval for the *trends analysis of established performance results* in the performance scorecard or dashboard to understand the following: (a) "How we are doing?" (b) "Are we doing/measuring the right things?" (c) "Are we getting the right results?" (d) "Are we getting the value?"
- Executive support and approval for *results of stakeholders' satisfaction survey* on strategic and IT operational management assessments to understanding the value of the PMSD, and to improve service delivery through stakeholders' satisfaction surveys
- Executive support and approval for *delivery* services improvements on *established performance results* and increased understanding of benefits and intended outcomes statement within the constraints of the PMSD by recommending areas of improvements for *customer, employee, financial,* and *operational performance measures and results*
- Executive support and approval for *performance measures, benchmarking results,* and *established performance results* to performance steering committee, with direct accountability to performance management executive

4.3.1.3.2 Performance Delivery Manager

This person is accountable for *management* of the results.

- Manage and define the *context and contents* of the PMSD and areas for improvements, for the *established performance results.*
- Measure the progress of the *established performance results* against the PMSD to ensure alignment with IT strategic and operational management framework and to understand the benefits and linkages with desired outcomes.
- Monitor and analyze *trends of established performance results* in the performance scorecard or dashboard to understand the following: (a) "How we are doing?" (b) "Are we doing/measuring the right things?" (c) "Are we getting the right results?" (d) "Are we getting the value?"
- Deliver and evaluate *results of stakeholders' satisfaction survey* on strategic and IT operational management assessments to understand the value of PMSD, and improve service delivery using satisfaction surveys.

- Improve *delivery services for established performance results* and increased understanding of benefits and intended outcomes statement within the constraints of the PMS by recommending areas of improvements for *customer, employee, financial,* and *operational performance measures and results.*
- Report on *performance measures, benchmarking results,* and *established performance results* to performance steering committee, with direct accountability to performance management executive.

4.3.1.3.3 Performance Measurement Team

This team is accountable for *delivery* of performance results.

- Provide meaningful and credible data for defining the *context and contents* of the PMS and areas for improvements, on the *established performance results criteria.*
- Provide meaningful and credible data for measuring the progress of the *established performance results* against the PMSD to ensure alignment with IT strategic and operational management framework and to understand the benefits and linkages with desired outcomes.
- Provide meaningful and credible data for monitoring and analyzing *trends of established performance results* in the performance scorecard or dashboard to understand the following: (a) "How we are doing?" (b) "Are we doing/measuring the right things?" (c) "Are we getting the right results?" (d) "Are we getting the value?"
- Provide meaningful and credible *results of stakeholders' satisfaction survey* on strategic and IT operational management assessments to understand the value of the PMS, and to improve service delivery through satisfaction surveys.
- Provide meaningful and credible data for improving *delivery services for established performance results* and increased understanding of benefits and intended outcomes statement within the constraints of the PMSD by recommending areas of improvements for *customer, employee, financial,* and *operational performance measures and results.*
- Provide meaningful and credible data on *performance measures, benchmarking results,* and *established performance results* to performance steering committee, with direct accountability to performance management executive.

4.3.1.4 Results: Performance Management Standards

Accountabilities discussed earlier are brief because they are intended to serve as a reference for *who is accountable* for *what* during the delivery of the established performance results against PMSD. Results are now introduced to highlight the outputs of this PMSD results area and associated outcomes (what), process flow (how), and performance measures (why). It is intended to serve as a reference based on the English language interrogatives: Who *is accountable for what, how,* and *why.* The outputs/outcomes, process flow, and performance measures, based on real-world practical implementation, will serve as excellent references for practicing performance managers during measurement, delivery, and reporting of the outputs and outcomes for the established performance results.

The outputs/outcomes highlight the key results for PMSD that the performance managers measure and report during the delivery of the established performance results. The process flows, based on real-world practical implementations, is a graphical representation of the inputs, process, outputs, and relationships. The PMSD model shows the foundation representation to effectively communicate the integrated components of the established performance results to strategic, IT operational, and performance management staff.

The performance measures from the integrated IT performance measurement dashboard for PMS outputs/outcomes are illustrated for "executive leadership" functional areas, using operational service excellence measures. Appendices A through F provide further details. Performance metrics, indicators, progress, trends, and analytics formed the basis for evidence-based decision making to enable improved organizational excellence.

> Setting a goal is not the main thing. It is deciding how you will go about achieving it and staying with that plan.
>
> **Tom Landry**

4.3.1.4.1 Output/Outcomes: Performance Management Standards

The output and outcomes of the performance management standards are given in Table 4.2.

4.3.1.4.2 Process Flows: Performance Management Standards

The process flows of the performance management standards are shown in Figure 4.5.

Table 4.2 Performance Management Standards Output/Outcomes

Results Area	*Output*	*Outcome*
Performance management standards	Results quality/ quantity	• Increased quality of IT services • Optimized utilization of IT resources • Increased accountability and transparency of IT resources • Increased quality of governance and management staff and decreased quantity of governance and management staff • Improved results-based accountability • Increased transformation to performance measurement culture • Increased value of performance measurement dashboard-analytics • Increased accountability and transparency of program directives
	Results effectiveness/ efficiency	• Increased quality and alignment of strategic with operational plans • Optimized utilization of capital and operating budgets • Decreased administrative overhead and meaningless meetings
	Results accountability	• Increased understanding and value of IT infrastructure assets
	Results reward/ recognition	• Increased value justifications and risks of IT business projects • Increased collaborations with business
	Performance management plan	• Increased stability, sustainability, and reliability of IT service delivery

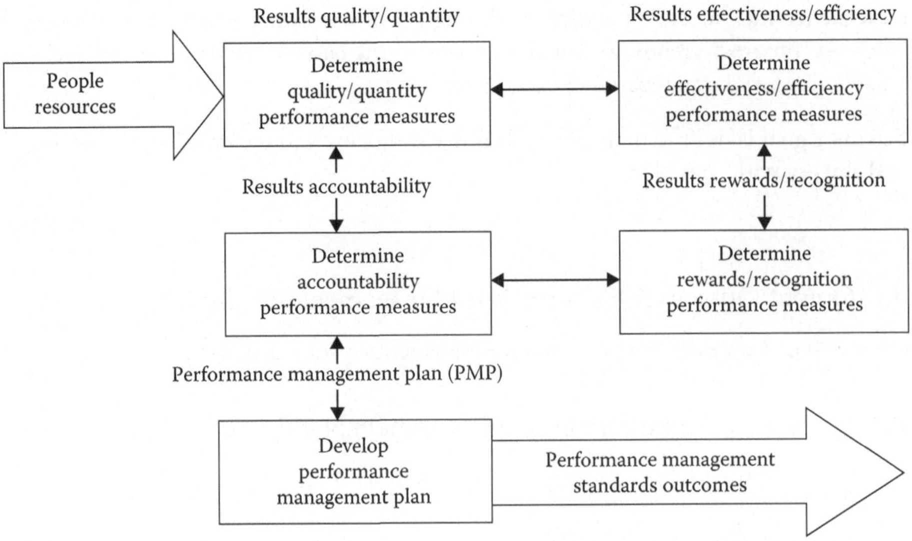

Figure 4.5 Performance management standards process flows.

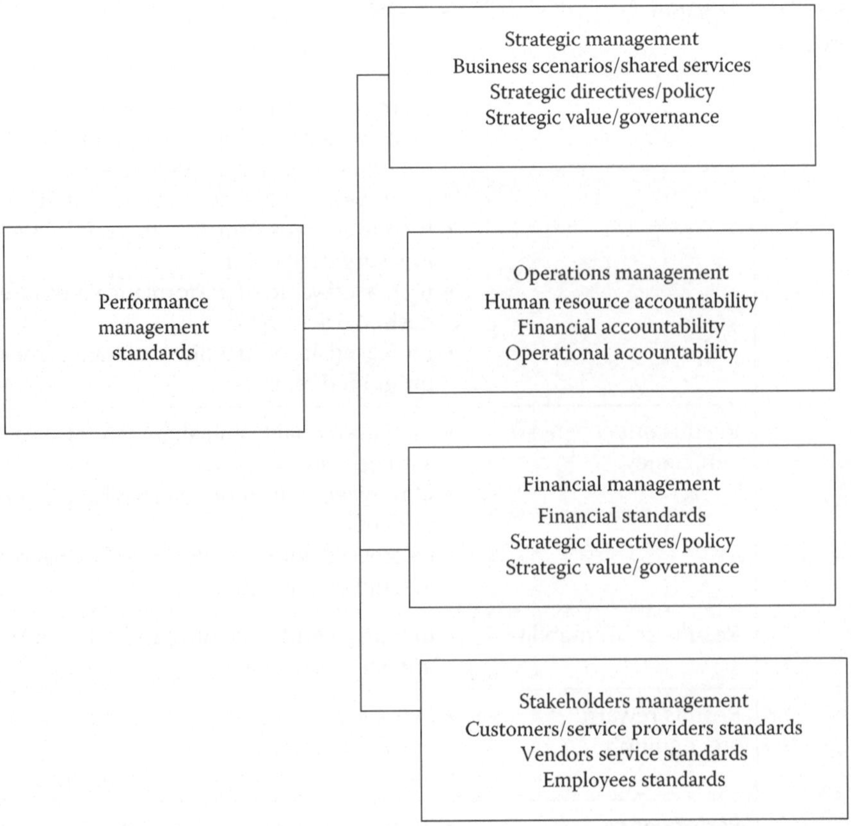

Figure 4.6 Performance management standards model.

IT EXECUTIVE LEADERSHIP					
OPERATIONAL-SE	Start Date	End Date	Status	% Complete	Indicator
IT Management Policies Framework	4/1/2011	3/31/2012	In-Progress	30%	Y
IT Management Procedures	4/1/2011	3/31/2012	In-Progress	30%	Y
IT Business Council Accountability Framework	4/1/2011	9/30/2011	In-Progress	80%	G
IT Compliance - Industry Performance Measures	4/1/2011	3/31/2012	Not-Started	30%	Y
IT Benchmarking Metrics	4/1/2011	6/30/2011	Complete	100%	Black
OPERATIONAL-SE Summary	4/1/2011	3/31/2012	In-Progress	54%	G

Performance Metrics
% IT staff performing IT Mgnt Policies; # Improvements completed
% IT staff performing IT Mgnt Procedures; # Improvements completed
-% IT services delivering - high quality ratings; # Improvements completed
-%IT services delivering-high efficiency/effectiveness ratings; # Improvements completed
-%IT staff achieving –high accountability ratings; # Improvements completed
-%IT staff achieving-high rewards/recognition ratings; # Improvements completed
% IT staff performing IT Business Council Accountability; # Improvements completed
% IT staff performing IT Compliance-Industry; # Improvements completed
% IT staff performing IT Benchmarking Metrics; # Improvements completed

Figure 4.7 Performance management standards performance measures.

4.3.1.4.3 Performance Model: Performance Management Standards

The performance model of the performance management standards is shown in Figure 4.6.

4.3.1.4.4 Performance Measures: Performance Management Standards

The performance measures of the performance management standards are shown in Figure 4.7.

4.3.2 Performance Measurement System

Managers and performance specialists shall use the *PMS*[12] results area to determine the major key results and to establish a common understanding of expectations and results for employee, customer, financial, and operations performance measures, as outlined in the performance measurement plan. Executives shall use the PMS to ensure that an appropriate level of clarity, consistency, and completeness has been applied in determining outputs/outcomes measures, metrics, and indicators and that performance results have not been reduced to inappropriate levels due to political or other performance pressures. The PMS presented in this book focuses more on how to identify, determine, and verify completeness of outputs, outcomes, metrics, and indicators in accordance with customer, employee, financial, and operational performance measures, as defined in the performance measurement dashboard. It is similar to the processes outlined in KPI[*] Institute. However, the performance processes presented here demonstrate a more outcomes/outputs/results-based approach, rather than the traditional activity/procedural-oriented approach. The results-based focus on performance measurement, presented in this section, is better suited to implementing integrated performance management for management and delivery of IT services, because of the dynamic and changing nature of the information technology industry. PMS is based on accountability for results approach to ensure that an appropriate level of correctness is attained that adheres to the PMO standards, policies, and procedures:

- Compliance to PMO policies
- Compliance to PMO guidelines and requirements imposed by the PMS
- Compliance to PMO guidelines, appropriate for use by the performance management and measurement plan/program

The major key results of PMS area are

- Inputs–resources measures
- Output/outcomes measures
- Performance metrics
- Performance indicators

4.3.2.1 Purpose

The purpose of this results area is to develop an *integrated performance measurement plan*[13] for managing, measuring, and integrating the context and contents of the integrated IT performance measurement dashboard. It includes the start date, end date, status, % complete, performance indicator, performance metrics, and outcomes, for the outputs/results/deliverables, aligned with operational, financial, customer, and employee performance measures, and the functional areas within the IT services life cycle. The performance steering committee will use these performance results as a baseline in managing, measuring, and improving performance results for the management and delivery of IT products and services.

4.3.2.2 Strategic Directives

- Integrated performance measurement plan will establish a baseline for measuring progress and reporting status of operational, financial, customer, and employee performance results. The contents of this plan will be updated on a regular basis and reflected in the integrated performance measurement dashboard.
- Every performance measurement area will be integrated for each functional area of the IT service delivery life cycle. The IT performance measurement dashboard will include sufficient details to provide reactive, proactive, and predictive decision-making capabilities for improving organizational performances and quality of management.
  - Outputs and outcomes.
  - End date; start date; % complete; performance indicator.
  - Performance metrics.
  - Predictive analytics (trends data).
  - Performance measurement areas and IT functional areas.
- Trend analysis and analytics from the performance measurement dashboard will form the basis for proactive and predictive performance results. The integrated performance measurement plan and the performance dashboard will be integrated with the outputs, outcomes, metrics, and indicators and will form the basis for established performance measurement areas—operations, financial, customer, and employee.

4.3.2.3 Accountabilities

4.3.2.3.1 Executive Performance Manager

This person is accountable for *approval* of the results.

- Executive support and approval for the *context and contents* of the established PMS and areas for improvements
- Executive support and approval for the *progress results* of the established PMS to ensure integration with IT performance measurement dashboard, IT performance measurement plan, and understanding the benefits and linkages with desired outcomes
- Executive support and approval for *performance trend results* in the performance scorecard or dashboard to understand the following: (a) "How we are doing?" (b) "Are we doing/measuring the right things?" (c) "Are we getting the right results?" (d) "Are we getting the value?"
- Executive support for *levels of survey satisfaction results* for strategic and IT operational management to understand the value of the PMS and to improve service delivery through stakeholders' satisfaction surveys
- Executive support and approval for *delivery services improvements* for the PMS and increased understanding of benefits and intended outcomes statement within the performance measurement dashboard as well as the recommended areas of improvements for *customer, employee, financial,* and *operational performance measures and results*
- Executive support and approval for PMS/*processes, performance measures,* and *benchmarking results* for reporting to performance steering committee, with direct accountability to performance management executive

4.3.2.3.2 Performance Delivery Manager

This person is accountable for *management* of the results.

- Manage and define the *context and contents* of the established PMS and areas for improvements.
- Measure the *progress results* of the established PMS to ensure integration with IT performance measurement dashboard, IT performance measurement plan, and understanding the benefits and linkages with desired outcomes.
- Monitor and analyze *performance trend results* in the performance scorecard or dashboard to understand the following: (a) "How we are doing?" (b) "Are we doing/measuring the right things?" (c) "Are we getting the right results?" (d) "Are we getting the value?"
- Deliver and evaluate *levels of survey satisfaction results* for strategic and IT operational management to understand the value of the PMS and to improve service delivery through stakeholders' satisfaction surveys.
- Improve *delivery services* for the PMS and increase understanding of benefits and intended outcomes statement within the IT performance measurement dashboard by recommending areas of improvements for *customer, employee, financial,* and *operational performance measures and results.*
- Report on PMS, *performance measures,* and *benchmarking results* to performance steering committee, with direct accountability to performance management executive.

4.3.2.3.3 Performance Measurement Team

This team is accountable for *delivery* of performance results.

- Provide meaningful and credible data for defining the *context and contents* of the PMS and areas for improvements.
- Provide meaningful and credible data for measuring the *progress results* of the established PMS to ensure integration with IT performance measurement dashboard, IT performance measurement plan, and understanding the benefits and linkages with desired outcomes.
- Provide meaningful and credible data for monitoring and analyzing *performance trend results* in the performance scorecard or dashboard to understand the following: (a) "How we are doing?" (b) "Are we doing/measuring the right things?" (c) "Are we getting the right results?" (d) "Are we getting the value?"
- Provide meaningful and credible survey data for delivering and evaluating *levels of satisfaction results* for strategic and IT operational management to understand the value of the established PMS and to improve service delivery through stakeholders' satisfaction surveys.
- Provide meaningful and credible data for improving *delivery services* for the PMS and increase understanding of benefits and intended outcomes statement within the overall IT performance measurement dashboard by recommending areas of improvements for *customer, employee, financial,* and *operational performance measures and results.*
- Provide meaningful and credible data on PMS, *performance measures and results,* and *benchmarking results* for reporting to performance steering committee, with direct accountability to performance management executive.

4.3.2.4 Results: Performance Measurement Systems

Accountabilities discussed earlier are brief because they are intended to serve as a reference for *who is accountable* for *what* during the delivery of the performance results in support of the performance management system. Results are now introduced to highlight the outputs of this PMS results area and associated outcomes (what), process flow (how), and performance measures (why). It is intended to serve as a reference based on the English language interrogatives: Who *is accountable for what, how,* and *why.* The outputs/outcomes, process flow, and performance measures, based on real-world practical implementation, will serve as excellent references for practicing performance managers during measurement, delivery, and reporting of the outputs and outcomes for the performance results.

The outputs/outcomes highlight the key results for PMS that the performance managers measure and report during the delivery of the established performance results. The process flows, based on real-world practical implementations, is a graphical representation of the inputs, process, outputs, and relationships. The PMS model shows the foundation representation to effectively communicate the integrated components of the established performance results to strategic, IT operational, and performance management staff.

The performance measures from the integrated IT performance measurement dashboard show the performance results outputs/outcomes for operational service excellence. Appendices A through F provide further details. Performance metrics, indicators, progress, trends, and analytics formed the basis for evidence-based decision making to enable improved organizational excellence.

Never measure in more detail than you can control.

The more important the performance deadline, the more important the result becomes.–

The Author

4.3.2.4.1 Output/Outcomes: Performance Measurement System (Table 4.3)

The output and outcomes of the performance measurement system are given in Table 4.3.

4.3.2.4.2 Process Flows: Performance Measurement System

The process flows of the performance measurement system are shown in Figure 4.8.

Table 4.3 Performance Measurement System Output/Outcomes

Results Area	*Output*	*Outcome*
Performance measurement system	Inputs—resources • People • Financials • Technology/materials • Information/process/structures	• Optimized utilization of IT resources
	Outputs	• Increased results—products/ services produced internally and externally • Improved results-based accountability
	Outcomes	• Increased impact of managing and delivering products and services (outputs) • Increased effects of outputs on customers/stakeholders
	Performance metrics • % resources performing services • # improvements completed	• Increased value of performance measurement dashboard-analytics
	Performance indicators • % completes (progress status) • Indicator—Black, Red, Green, Yellow)	• Increased value of performance measurement dashboard-analytics
	Performance measurement plan	• Increased accountability and transparency of IT resources • Increased transformation to performance measurement culture

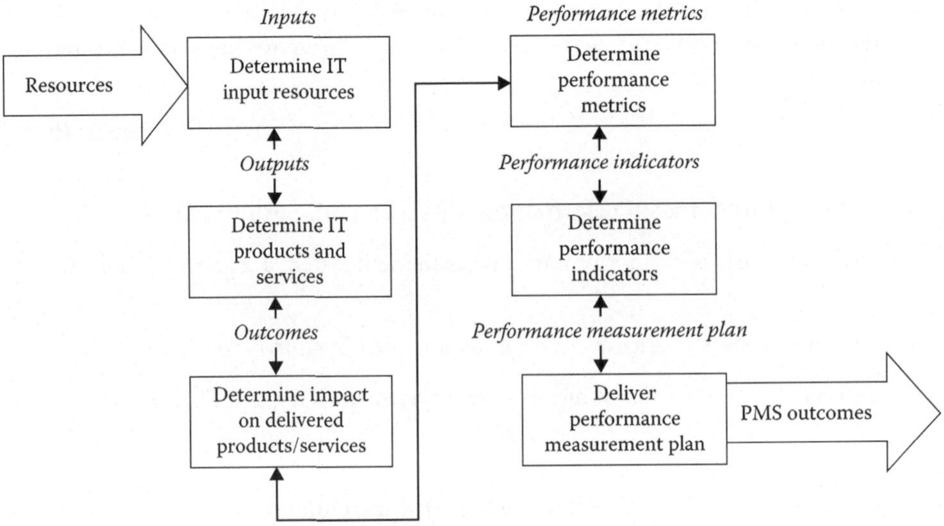

Figure 4.8 Performance measurement system flow.

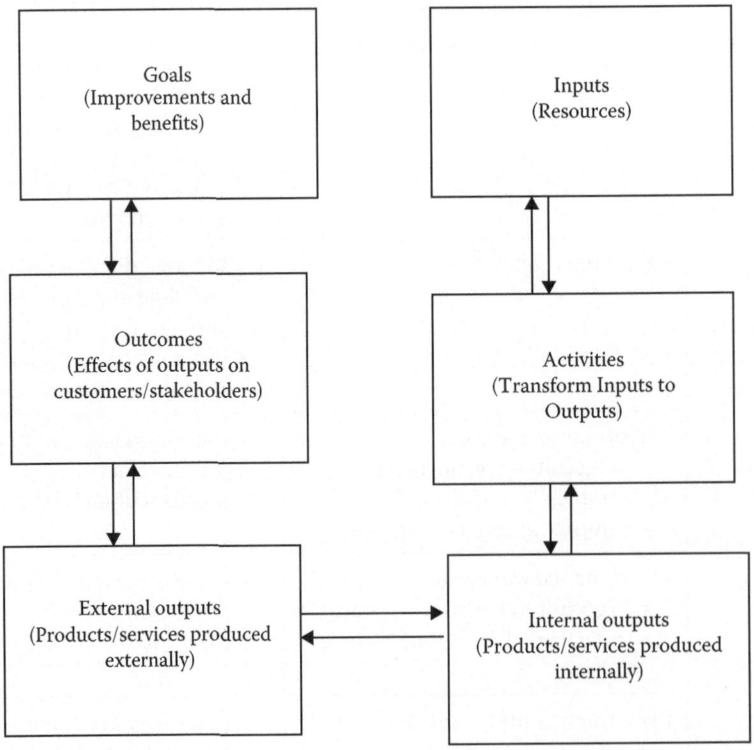

Figure 4.9 Performance measurement system performance model.

4.3.2.4.3 Performance Model: Performance Measurement System

The performance model of the performance measurement system is shown in Figure 4.9.

4.3.2.4.4 Performance Measures: Performance Measurement System

The performance measures of the performance measurement system are shown in Figure 4.10.

It Exec Leadership and Relationship Mgmt

Operational-SE	Start Date	End Date	Status	% Complete	Indicator
IT management policies framework	4/1/2011	3/31/2012	In progress	30%	Y
IT management processes and procedures	4/1/2011	3/31/2012	In progress	30%	Y
IT business council accountability framework	4/1/2011	9/30/2011	In progress	80%	G
IT compliance—industry performance measures	4/1/2011	3/31/2012	Not started	30%	Y
IT benchmarking metrics	4/1/2011	6/30/2011	Completed	100%	Black
Operational-SE Summary	4/1/2011	3/31/2012	In progress	54%	G

Performance Metrics

% IT staff performing IT Mgnt Policies; # Improvements completed

% IT staff performing IT Mgnt Procedures; # Improvements completed

% IT staff performing IT Business Council Accountability; # Improvements completed

% IT staff performing IT Compliance-Industry; # Improvements completed

% IT staff performing IT Benchmarking Metrics; # Improvements completed

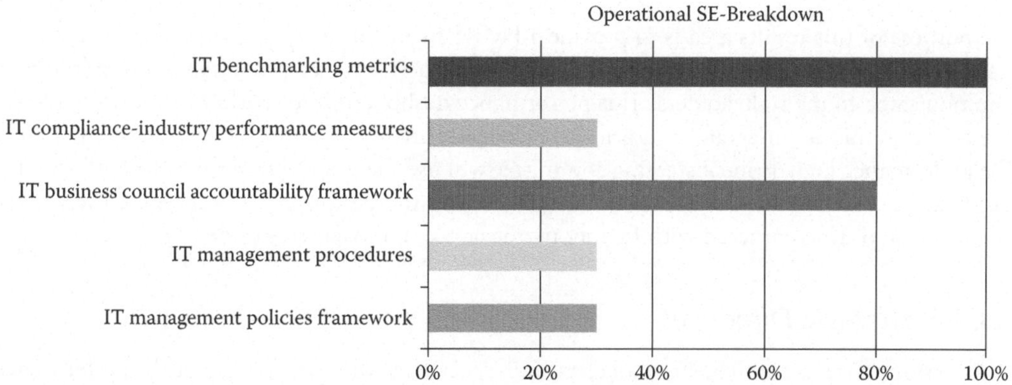

Figure 4.10 Performance measurement system performance measures.

4.3.3 Performance Management Reporting

Managers and performance specialists shall use *PMR*[14] results area to determine the major key results and to establish a common understanding of PMR for employee, customer, financial, and operations performance measures, as defined in the integrated performance measurement dashboard. Executives shall use the *performance management reporting system* (*PMRS*) to ensure transparency of performance results. PMR presented in this book focuses more on results transparency that provides visibility for results-based accountability, an RBM approach, focused on achieving results for employees, customers, internal process operations, and financials, as defined in the integrated performance measurement dashboard. It is based on the performance measures, similar to the balanced scorecard framework, published by Norton and Kaplan. PMR is based on organizational excellence for reporting measured results using integrated performance management dashboard and results transparency for KRAs to ensure that performance reporting results are credible, consistent, and effectively communicated to stakeholders. It establishes the basis to ensure effective transparency of performance results. Results transparency provides data on how you are progressing from the perspective of the performance results. Performance reporting results provide formal written communications between the performance measurement team and senior managers. The performance measurement team and performance delivery manager will compile the performance reporting results for each functional area, using the metrics and analytics from the integrated performance measurement dashboard. The performance reporting results for each functional area will be integrated by the PMO into a PMRS and will be distributed each month to the performance steering committee and to other stakeholders, as appropriate.

The major key results of PMR results area are

- Integrated performance measurement dashboard
- Results transparency

> When performance is measured, performance improves. When performance is measured and reported, the rate of performance is accelerated.
>
> **Thomas S. Honson**

4.3.3.1 Purpose

The purpose of this results area is to provide a PMRS using an integrated performance management dashboard to ensure that the appropriate level of performance progress reporting has been communicated to the stakeholders. This performance dashboard information will form the baseline to communicate, integrate, and prioritize the performance progress for each functional area. The performance management steering committee will use the information from the performance dashboard as the baseline for approvals in determining the performance progress of each functional area in order to proceed with further performance improvements or deployments.

4.3.3.2 Strategic Directives

- Performance measurement managers and specialists will provide monthly performance progress reports for each functional area in accordance with the performance measurement dashboard results, in the format provided by the PMO.
- Performance measurement team and performance delivery manager will develop a PMRS that will form an integral component of the performance management plan.

- An integrated performance measurement dashboard and PMRS will be used to produce performance status and progress reports to ensure completeness, consistency, and integrity of IT services.
- Performance management progress reports will be used to communicate the impact of the outputs or products/services on the customers, defined as outcomes.

4.3.3.3 Accountabilities

4.3.3.3.1 Executive Performance Manager

This person is accountable for *approval* of the results.

- Executive support and approval for the *context and contents* of the established PMRS and areas for improvements
- Executive support and approval for the *progress results* of the established PMRS to ensure integration with IT performance measurement dashboard, IT performance measurement plan, and understanding the benefits and linkages with desired outcomes
- Executive support and approval for *performance trend results* in the performance scorecard or dashboard to understand the following: (a) "How we are doing?" (b) "Are we doing/measuring the right things?" (c) "Are we getting the right results?" (d) "Are we getting the value?"
- Executive support for *stakeholders' survey satisfaction results* on strategic and IT operational management to understand the value of the PMRS and to improve service delivery through stakeholders' satisfaction surveys
- Executive support and approval for *delivery services improvements* on the PMRS and increased understanding of benefits and intended outcomes statement within the performance measurement dashboard as well as the recommended areas of improvements for *customer, employee, financial,* and *operational performance measures and results*
- Executive support and approval for PMRS, *performance measures,* and *benchmarking results* on reporting to performance steering committee, with direct accountability to performance management executive

4.3.3.3.2 Performance Delivery Manager

This person is accountable for *management* of the results.

- Manage and define the *context and contents* of the established PMRS and areas for improvements.
- Measure the *progress results* of the established PMRS to ensure integration with IT performance measurement dashboard, IT performance measurement plan, and understanding the benefits and linkages with desired outcomes.
- Monitor and analyze *performance trend results* in the performance scorecard or dashboard to understand the following: (a) "How we are doing?" (b) "Are we doing/measuring the right things?" (c) "Are we getting the right results?" (d) "Are we getting the value?"
- Deliver and evaluate *levels of survey satisfaction results* for strategic and IT operational management to understand the value of the PMRS and to improve service delivery through stakeholders satisfaction surveys.

- Improve *delivery services* for the PMRS and increase understanding of benefits and intended outcomes statement within the IT performance measurement dashboard by recommending areas of improvements for *customer, employee, financial,* and *operational performance measures and results.*
- Report on PMRS, *performance measures,* and *benchmarking results* to performance steering committee, with direct accountability to performance management executive.

4.3.3.3.3 Performance Measurement Team

This team is accountable for *delivery* of performance results.

- Provide meaningful and credible data for defining the *context and contents* of the PMRS for improvements.
- Provide meaningful and credible data for measuring the *progress results* of the established PMRS to ensure integration with IT performance measurement dashboard, IT performance measurement plan, and understanding the benefits and linkages with desired outcomes.
- Provide meaningful and credible data for monitoring and analyzing *performance trend results* in the performance scorecard or dashboard to understand the following: (a) "How we are doing?" (b) "Are we doing/measuring the right things?" (c) "Are we getting the right results?" (d) "Are we getting the value?"
- Provide meaningful and credible survey data for delivering and evaluating *levels of satisfaction results* for strategic and IT operational management to understand the value of the established PMRS and to improve service delivery through stakeholders' satisfaction surveys.
- Provide meaningful and credible data for improving *delivery services* for the PMRS and increase understanding of benefits and intended outcomes statement within the overall IT performance measurement dashboard by recommending areas of improvements for *customer, employee, financial,* and *operational performance measures and results.*
- Provide meaningful and credible data on PMRS, *performance measures, and results,* and *benchmarking results* for reporting to performance steering committee, with direct accountability to performance management executive.

4.3.3.4 Results: Performance Management Reporting

Accountabilities discussed earlier are brief because they are intended to serve as a reference for *who is accountable* for *what* during the delivery of the performance results in support of the performance management process. Results are now introduced to highlight the outputs of this PMR results area and associated outcomes (what), process flow (how), and performance measures (why). It is intended to serve as a reference based on the English language interrogatives: Who *is accountable for what, how,* and *why.* The outputs/outcomes, process flow, and performance measures, based on real-world practical implementation, will serve as excellent references for practicing performance managers during measurement, delivery, and reporting of the outputs and outcomes for the performance results.

The outputs/outcomes highlight the key results for PMR that the performance managers measure and report during the delivery of the established performance results. The process flows, based on real-world practical implementations, is a graphical representation of the inputs, process, outputs, and relationships. The PMR performance model shows the foundation representation to effectively communicate the integrated components of the established performance results to strategic, IT operational, and performance management staff.

The performance measures from the integrated IT performance measurement dashboard show performance results analytics for IT service delivery. Appendices A through F provide further details. Performance metrics, indicators, progress, trends, and analytics formed the basis for evidence-based decision making to enable improved organizational excellence.

4.3.3.4.1 Output/Outcomes: Performance Management Reporting

The output and outcomes of the performance management reporting system are given in Table 4.4.

4.3.3.4.2 Process Flows: Performance Management Reporting

The output and outcomes of the performance management reporting system are shown in Figure 4.11.

Table 4.4 Performance Management Reporting Output/Outcomes

Results Area	*Output*	*Outcome*
Performance management reporting	Employee—resources • People • Financials • Technology/materials • Information/process/structures	• Optimized utilization of IT resources
	Customer—vendors; IT service providers	• Increased results—products/services produced internally and externally • Improved results-based accountability
	Financial	• Increased financial impact of managing and delivering products and services (outputs) • Optimized utilization of financial resources
	Operations • Internal processes	• Increased streamlining of internal processes
	IT strategic directives	• Increased alignment of performance measures with IT strategic directives and performance measurement dashboard-analytics
	Performance results transparency	• Increased accountability and transparency of IT resource utilizations • Increased transformation to performance transparency culture

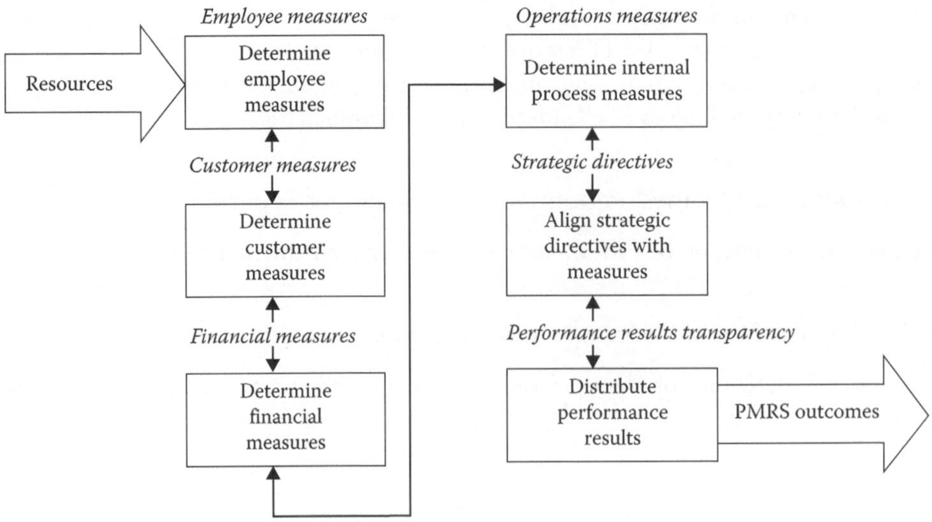

Figure 4.11 Performance management reporting process flow.

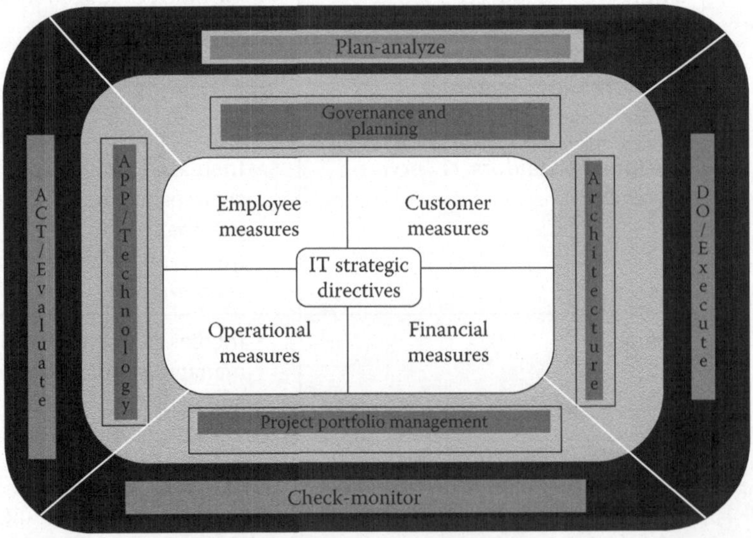

Figure 4.12 Performance management reporting system model.

4.3.3.4.3 Performance Model: Performance Management Reporting System (PMRS)

The performance model of the performance management reporting system is shown in Figure 4.12.

4.3.3.4.4 Performance Measures: Performance Management Reporting System

The performance measures of the performance management reporting system are shown in Figure 4.13.

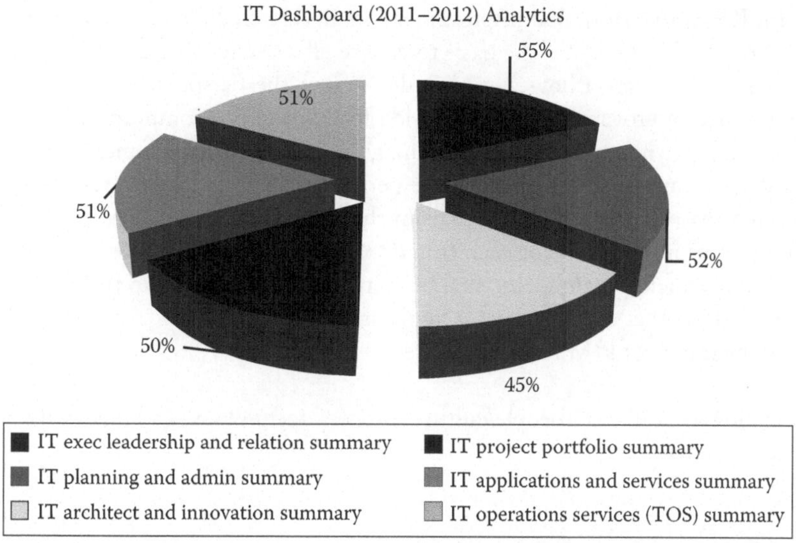

IT Dashboard (2011–2012) Analytics	Start Date	End Date	Status	% Complete	Indicator
IT exec leadership and relation summary	4/1/2011	3/31/2012	In Progress	55%	Green
IT planning and admin relation summary	4/1/2011	3/31/2012	In Progress	52%	Green
IT architect and innovation relation summary	4/1/2011	3/31/2012	In Progress	45%	Yellow
IT project portfolio summary	4/1/2011	3/31/2012	In Progress	50%	Green
IT applications and services summary	4/1/2011	3/31/2012	In Progress	51%	Green
IT operations services (TOS) summary	4/1/2011	3/31/2012	In Progress	51%	Green
Total % Complete	4/1/2011	3/31/2012	In Progress	51%	Green
					Green

Figure 4.13 Performance management reporting system performance measures.

4.3.4 Performance Improvement Management

Managers and performance specialists shall use *PIM*[15] results area to determine the major key results and to establish a common understanding of performance improvements for employee, customer, financial, and operations performance measures, as defined in the performance measurement dashboard. Executives shall use the PIM areas to improve organizational excellence while reducing costs and ensuring the appropriate level of performance improvement results have been communicated to the stakeholders. PIM presented in this book focuses more on measurement results to improve organizational excellence for employees, customers, internal process operations, and financials, as defined in the performance measurement dashboard. It is based on the performance measures, similar to the balanced scorecard framework, published by Norton and Kaplan. PIM is based on organizational excellence for measured results using verified feedback and reviews for KRAs to ensure that improvement results are credible, consistent, and communicated to stakeholders. It establishes the basis to ensure effective feedback/reviews of performance results. KRAs provide data on how you have done from the perspective of the critical success factors. Performance improvement results provide formal written communications between the performance measurement team and senior managers. The performance measurement team and performance delivery manager will compile the performance improvement results for each functional area, using the metrics and analytics from the performance measurement dashboard. The performance improvement results for each functional area will be integrated by the PMO into a performance improvement portfolio and will be distributed each month to the performance steering committee and to other stakeholders, as appropriate.

The major key results of PIM results area are

- Organizational excellence (people/culture, process, technology, and financials)
- Feedback/reviews
- *KRAs*

> The business improvement strategy is not to just perform excellent but to perform excellent consistently
>
> I am constantly amazed how many leaders pursue the wrong things- and it always comes down to performance measures.
>
> **The Author**

4.3.4.1 Purpose

The purpose of this results area is to provide PIM to ensure that appropriate levels of organizational excellence, feedback/reviews, and KRA have been effectively applied to the delivery of IT services and that performance has not been reduced to some inappropriate levels because of political or other performance pressures. This information will form the baseline to measure, integrate, and improve the performance objectives of IT service delivery and to ensure effective feedback/reviews of performance results. The performance steering committee will use these performance standards as a baseline in assessing the quality of the performance results and the overall performance management program.

4.3.4.2 Strategic Directives

- Performance measurement managers and specialists will provide monthly performance improvement reports for each functional area in accordance with the performance measurement dashboard results, in the format provided by the PMO.
- Performance measurement team and performance delivery manager will develop PIM results that will form an integral component of the performance management plan.
- An integrated performance measurement dashboard and PIM results will be used to produce performance status, progress, and improvement reports to ensure completeness, credibility, and improvement of IT services.
- Performance improvement progress reports will be used to communicate the improvements of the outputs or products/services on the customers, defined as outcomes.

4.3.4.3 Accountabilities

4.3.4.3.1 Executive Performance Manager

This person is accountable for *approval* of the results.

- Executive support and approval for the *context and contents* of the established PIM results and areas for priority improvements
- Executive support and approval for the *progress results* of the established PIM results to ensure integration with IT performance measurement dashboard, IT performance measurement plan, and understanding the benefits and linkages with desired outcomes
- Executive support and approval for *performance trend results* in the performance scorecard or dashboard to understand the following: (a) "How we are improving?" (b) "Are we measuring the right things?" (c) "Are we getting the right results?" (d) "Are we getting the value?"
- Executive support on *stakeholders' survey satisfaction results* for strategic and IT operational management to understand the value of the PIM results and to communicate service delivery improvements through stakeholders' satisfaction surveys
- Executive support and approval for *delivery services improvements* of the PIM results and increased understanding of benefits and intended outcomes statement within the performance measurement dashboard as well as the recommended areas of improvements for *customer, employee, financial,* and *operational performance measures and results*
- Executive support and approval for *PIM portfolio, performance measures,* and *benchmarking results* on reporting to performance steering committee, with direct accountability to performance management executive

4.3.4.3.2 Performance Delivery Manager

This person is accountable for *management* of the results.

- Manage and define the *context and contents* of the established PIM results and areas for priority improvements.
- Measure the *progress results* of the established PIM results to ensure integration with IT performance measurement dashboard, IT performance measurement plan, and understanding the benefits and linkages with desired outcomes.
- Monitor and analyze *performance trend results* in the performance scorecard or dashboard to understand the following: (a) "How we are improving?" (b) "Are we measuring the right things?" (c) "Are we getting the right results?" (d) "Are we getting the value?"
- Deliver and evaluate *stakeholders' survey satisfaction results* for strategic and IT operational management to understand the value of the PIM results to improve service delivery through stakeholders' satisfaction surveys.
- Improve *delivery services* for the PIM results and increase understanding of benefits and intended outcomes statement within the IT performance measurement dashboard by recommending areas of improvements for *customer, employee, financial,* and *operational performance measures and results.*
- Report on *PIM results, performance measures,* and *benchmarking results* to performance steering committee, with direct accountability to performance management executive.

4.3.4.3.3 Performance Measurement Team

This team is accountable for *delivery* of performance results.

- Provide meaningful and credible data for defining the *context and contents* of the *PIM* results and areas for priority improvements.
- Provide meaningful and credible data for measuring the *progress results* of the established PIM results to ensure integration with IT performance measurement dashboard, IT performance measurement plan, and understanding the benefits and linkages with desired outcomes.
- Provide meaningful and credible data for monitoring and analyzing *performance trend results* in the performance scorecard or dashboard to understand the following: (a) "How we are improving?" (b) "Are we measuring the right things?" (c) "Are we getting the right results?" (d) "Are we getting the value?"
- Provide meaningful and credible survey data for delivering and evaluating stakeholders' *survey satisfaction results* for strategic and IT operational management to understand the value of the established PIM results and to improve service delivery through stakeholders' satisfaction surveys.
- Provide meaningful and credible data for improving *delivery services* for the PIM results and increase understanding of benefits and intended outcomes statement within the overall IT performance measurement dashboard by recommending areas of improvements for *customer, employee, financial,* and *operational performance measures and results.*
- Provide meaningful and credible data on *PIM results, performance measures and results,* and *benchmarking results* for reporting to performance steering committee, with direct accountability to performance management executive.

4.3.4.4 Results: Performance Improvement Management

Accountabilities discussed earlier are brief because they are intended to serve as a reference for *who is accountable* for *what* during the delivery of the performance results in support of the performance management process. Results are now introduced to highlight the outputs of this PIM results area and associated outcomes (what), process flow (how), and performance measures (why). It is intended to serve as a reference based on the English language interrogatives: Who *is accountable for what, how,* and *why.* The outputs/outcomes, process flow, and performance measures, based on real-world practical implementation, will serve as excellent references for practicing performance managers during measurement, delivery, and reporting of the outputs and outcomes for the performance results.

The outputs/outcomes highlight the key results for PIM results that the performance managers measure and report during the delivery of the established performance results. The process flows, based on real-world practical implementations, is a graphical representation of the inputs, process, outputs, and relationships. The PIM results model shows the foundation representation to effectively communicate the integrated components of the established performance results to strategic, IT operational, and performance management staff.

The performance measures from the integrated IT performance measurement dashboard show the performance results outputs/outcomes for "executive leadership" functional area. Appendices A through F provide further details. Performance metrics, indicators, progress, trends, and analytics formed the basis for evidence-based decision making to enable improved organizational excellence.

4.3.4.4.1 Output/Outcomes: Performance Improvement Management

The output and outcomes of performance improvement management are given in Table 4.5.

4.3.4.4.2 Process Flows: Performance Improvement Management (PIM)

The process flows of performance improvement management are shown in Figure 4.14.

4.3.4.4.3 Performance Model: Performance Improvement Management (PIM)

The performance model of performance improvement management is shown in Figure 4.15.

4.3.4.4.4 Performance Measures: Performance Improvement Management

The performance measures of performance improvement management are shown in Figure 4.16a and b.

Table 4.5 Performance Improvement Management Output/Outcomes

Results Area	*Output*	*Outcome*
Performance improvement management	Employee—resources • People/culture • Financials • Technology/materials • Information/process/structures	• Improved utilization of IT resources
	Customer—vendors; IT service providers	• Improved results—products/services produced internally and externally • Improved results-based accountability
	Financial	• Improved financial impact of managing and delivering products and services (outputs) • Improved utilization of financial resources
	Operations • Internal processes	• Improved streamlining of internal processes
	Organizational excellence	• Improved alignment of performance measures with organizational excellence and performance measurement dashboard-analytics
	Review/feedback key results areas—KRAs	• Improved reviews/feedback of IT services delivery • Improved communications and understanding of KRAs and critical success factors.

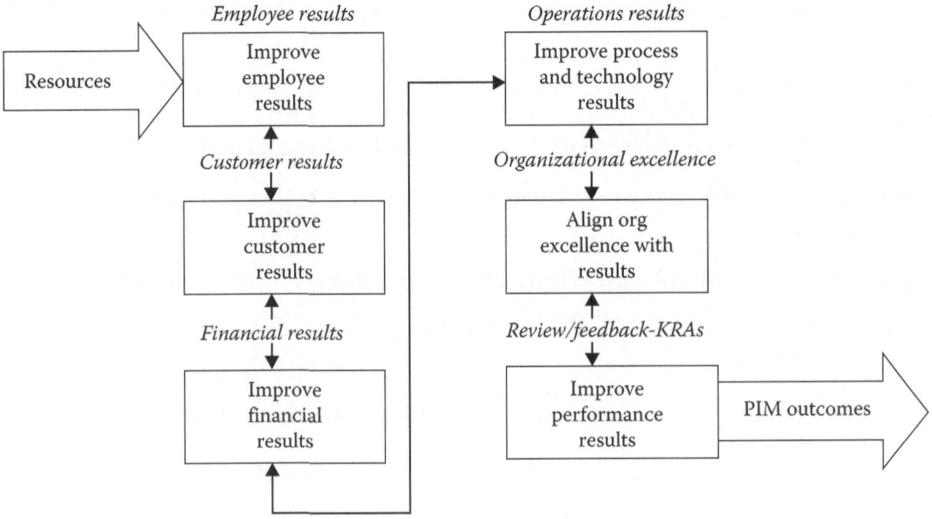

Figure 4.14 Performance improvement management process flow.

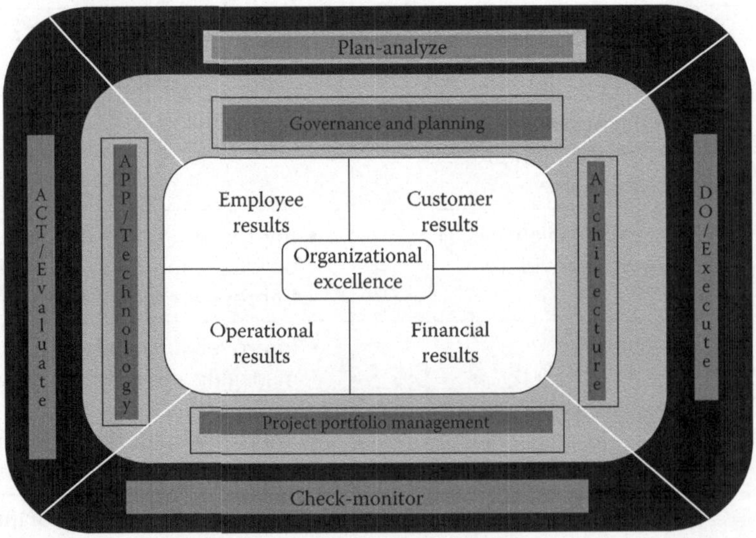

Figure 4.15 Performance improvement management model.

4.3.5 Performance Change Management

Managers and performance specialists shall use the *PCM*[15] results area to determine the major key results and to establish a common framework for sustaining change for employee, customer, financial, and operations performance measures, as presented in the performance measurement dashboard. It establishes the basis to ensure transformation change from the perspectives of 4Ps (people/culture, politics, process, and performance results). Executives shall use the PCM areas to establish the basis to ensure transformation change from the perspectives of 4Ps (people/culture, politics, process, and performance results) while maintaining sustainable change strategy. PCM presented in this book focuses more on measurement results to improve organizational excellence for employees, customers, internal process operations, and financials, as defined in the performance measurement dashboard. It is based on the performance measures, similar to the balanced scorecard framework, published by Norton and Kaplan. PCM must be sustained using transformation change and change strategy to effectively enable performance management. PCM results provide formal written communications between the performance measurement team and senior managers. The performance measurement team and performance delivery manager will compile the PCM results for each functional area, using the metrics and analytics from the performance measurement dashboard. The performance changes will form the basis to ensure performance improvement results for each functional area will be integrated by the PMO into a PCM portfolio and distributed each month to the performance steering committee and to other stakeholders, as appropriate.

IT EXECUTIVE LEADERSHIP

OPERATIONAL-SE	Start Date	End Date	Status	% Complete	Indicator
IT Management Policies Framework	4/1/2011	3/31/2012	In-Progress	30%	Y
IT Management Procedures	4/1/2011	3/31/2012	In-Progress	30%	Y
IT Business Council Accountability Framework	4/1/2011	9/30/2011	In-Progress	80%	G
IT Compliance—Industry Performance Measures	4/1/2011	3/31/2012	Not-Started	30%	Y
IT Benchmarking Metrics	4/1/2011	6/30/2011	Complete	100%	Black
OPERATIONAL-SE Summary	4/1/2011	3/31/2012	In-Progress	54%	G

Performance Metrics
% IT staff performing IT Mgnt Policies; # Improvements completed
% IT staff performing IT Mgnt Procedures; # Improvements completed
% IT staff performing IT Business Council Accountability; # Improvements completed
% IT staff performing IT Compliance-Industry; # Improvements completed
% IT staff performing IT Benchmarking Metrics; # Improvements completed

FINANCIAL	Start Date	End Date	Status	% Complete	Indicator
IT Capital Costs	4/1/2011	3/31/2012	In-Progress	30%	Y
IT Operational Costs	4/1/2011	3/31/2012	In-Progress	30%	Y
IT Outsourced/Consulting Costs	4/1/2011	9/30/2011	In-Progress	80%	G
IT Staff Costs	10/1/2011	3/31/2012	Not-Started	0%	
Major Business Projects Costs	4/1/2011	6/30/2011	Complete	100%	Black
Major Technology Infrastructure Project Costs	4/1/2011	6/30/2011	Complete	100%	Black
FINANCIAL Summary	4/1/2011	3/31/2012	In-Progress	57%	G

Performance Metrics
% IT staff managing IT Capital Costs; # Improvements completed
% IT staff managing IT Operational Costs Mgnt; # Improvements completed
% IT staff managing IT Outsourced Costs Mgnt; # Improvements completed
% IT staff managing IT Staff Costs Mgnt; # Improvements completed
% IT staff managing IT Business Projects Costs Mgnt; # Improvements completed
% IT staff managing IT Technology Costs Mgnt; # Improvements completed

(a)

Figure 4.16 (a and b) Performance improvement management performance measures.

(Continued)

CUSTOMER	Start Date	End Date	Status	% Complete	Indicator
Client Relationships/Satisfaction Surveys	4/1/2011	3/31/2012	In-Progress	30%	Y
IT Business Council Meetings	4/1/2011	3/31/2012	In-Progress	30%	Y
Vendor Relationships/Satisfaction Surveys	4/1/2011	9/30/2011	In-Progress	80%	G
IT Outsourced Providers Performance Measures	10/1/2011	3/31/2012	Not-Started	0%	
IT Benchmarking Surveys/Results	4/1/2011	6/30/2011	Complete	100%	Black
CUSTOMER Summary	4/1/2011	3/31/2012	In-Progress	48%	G

Performance Metrics
% IT staff performing Client Satisfaction Surveys; # Improvements completed
% IT staff attending IT Business Council Meetings; # Improvements completed
% IT staff performing Vendor Satisfaction Surveys; # Improvements completed
% IT staff performing IT Vendors Performance Measures; # Improvements completed
% IT staff performing IT Benchmarking surveys ; # Improvements completed

EMPLOYEE	Start Date	End Date	Status	% Complete	Indicator
IT Progress Reporting	4/1/2011	6/30/2011	Complete	100%	Black
IT Staff Performance Contract	4/1/2011	3/31/2012	In-Progress	35%	Y
Staff Learning/Growth	4/1/2011	3/31/2012	In-Progress	35%	Y
Staff Meetings/Communications	4/1/2011	3/31/2012	In-Progress	35%	Y
Staff Retention/Retraining/Reward Reporting	4/1/2011	7/31/2011	In-Progress	100%	Black
EMPLOYEE Summary	4/1/2011	3/31/2012	In-Progress	61%	G
IT EXECUTIVE LEADERSHIP SUMMARY	4/1/2011	3/31/2012	In-Progress	55%	G

Performance Metrics
% IT staff performing Progress Reporting ; # Improvements completed
% IT Staff performing Staff Performance Contract ; # Improvements completed
% IT staff performing Learning/Growth sessions; # Improvements completed
% IT staff performing staff communications/meetings ; # Improvements completed
% IT staff performing staff retention/retraining, etc.; # Improvements completed

(b)

Figure 4.16 (*Continued*) (a and b) Performance improvement management performance measures.

The major key results of PCM results area are

- Transformational change (people/culture, politics, process, and performance results)
- Change strategy sustainability

4.3.5.1 Purpose

The purpose of this results area is to provide PCM to ensure that appropriate levels of transformational change and change strategy sustainability results have been effectively applied to the delivery of IT services and that performance improvements have not been reduced to some inappropriate levels because of political or other performance pressures. This information will form the baseline to measure, integrate, and improve the performance objectives of IT service delivery and to ensure effective transformational change using sustained change strategy. The performance steering committee will use these performance transformation change strategy as a baseline in assessing the quality of the performance results and the overall *integrated performance management program.*

4.3.5.2 Strategic Directives

- Performance measurement managers and specialists will provide monthly performance transformational change reports for each functional area in accordance with the performance measurement dashboard results, in the format provided by the PMO.
- Performance measurement team and performance delivery manager will develop PCM results that will form an integral component of the performance management plan.
- An integrated performance measurement dashboard and PCM results will be used to produce performance status, progress, and change reports to ensure effective transformation and improvement of IT services.
- Performance change progress reports will be used to communicate the transformational changes of the outputs or products/services on the customers, defined as outcomes.

4.3.5.3 Accountabilities

4.3.5.3.1 Executive Performance Manager

This person is accountable for *approval* of the results.

- Executive support and approval for the *context and contents* of the established PCM results and areas for priority improvements
- Executive support and approval for the *progress results* of the established PCM results to ensure integration with IT performance measurement dashboard, IT performance measurement plan, and understanding the benefits and linkages with desired outcomes
- Executive support and approval for *performance trend results* in the performance scorecard or dashboard to understand the following: (a) "How we are improving?" (b) "Are we measuring/changing the right things?" (c) "Are we getting the right results?" (d) "Are we getting the value?"
- Executive support and approval on *stakeholders' survey satisfaction results* on strategic and IT operational management to understand the value of the PCM results and to communicate service delivery improvements through stakeholders' satisfaction surveys
- Executive support and approval for *delivery services improvements* of the PCM results and increased understanding of benefits and intended outcomes statement within the performance measurement dashboard as well as the recommended areas of improvements for *customer, employee, financial,* and *operational performance measures and results*
- Executive support and approval for *PCM results, performance measures,* and *benchmarking results* for reporting to performance steering committee, with direct accountability to performance management executive

4.3.5.3.2 Performance Delivery Manager

This person is accountable for *management* of the results.

- Manage and define the *context and contents* of the established PCM results and areas for priority improvements.

- Measure the *progress results* of the established PCM results to ensure integration with IT performance measurement dashboard, IT performance measurement plan, and understanding the benefits and linkages with desired outcomes.
- Monitor and analyze *performance trend results* in the performance scorecard or dashboard to understand the following: (a) "How we are improving?" (b) "Are we measuring/changing the right things?" (c) "Are we getting the right results?" (d) "Are we getting the value?"
- Deliver and evaluate *stakeholders' survey satisfaction results* for strategic and IT operational management to understand the value of the PCM results and to improve service delivery through stakeholders' satisfaction surveys.
- Improve *delivery services* for the PCM results and increase understanding of benefits and intended outcomes statement within the IT performance measurement dashboard by recommending areas of improvements for *customer, employee, financial,* and *operational performance measures and results.*
- Report on PCM *results, performance measures,* and *benchmarking results* to performance steering committee, with direct accountability to performance management executive.

4.3.5.3.3 Performance Measurement Team

This team is accountable for *delivery* of performance results.

- Provide meaningful and credible data for defining the *context and contents* of the PCM results and areas for priority improvements.
- Provide meaningful and credible data for measuring the *progress results* of the established PCM results to ensure integration with IT performance measurement dashboard, IT performance measurement plan, and understanding the benefits and linkages with desired outcomes.
- Provide meaningful and credible data for monitoring and analyzing *performance trend results* in the performance scorecard or dashboard to understand the following: (a) "How we are improving?" (b) "Are we measuring/changing the right things?" (c) "Are we getting the right results?" (d) "Are we getting the value?"
- Provide meaningful and credible survey data for delivering and evaluating *stakeholders' survey satisfaction results* for strategic and IT operational management to understand the value of the established PCM results and to improve service delivery through stakeholders' satisfaction surveys.
- Provide meaningful and credible data for improving *delivery services* on the PCM results and increase understanding of benefits and intended outcomes statement within the overall IT performance measurement dashboard by recommending areas of improvements for *customer, employee, financial,* and *operational performance measures and results.*
- Provide meaningful and credible data on *PCM results, performance measures,* and *benchmarking results* for reporting to performance steering committee, with direct accountability to performance management executive.

4.3.5.4 Results: Performance Change Management

Accountabilities discussed earlier are brief because they are intended to serve as a reference for *who is accountable* for *what* during the delivery of the performance results in support of the performance management process. Results are now introduced to highlight the outputs of this PCM results area and associated outcomes (what), process flow (how), and performance measures (why). It is intended to serve as a reference based on the English language interrogatives: Who *is accountable for what, how,* and *why.* The outputs/outcomes, process flow, and performance measures, based on real-world practical implementation, will serve as excellent references for practicing performance managers during measurement, delivery, and reporting of the outputs and outcomes for the performance results.

The outputs/outcomes highlight the key results for PCM that the performance managers measure and report during the delivery of the established performance results. The process flows, based on real-world practical implementations, is a graphical representation of the inputs, process, outputs, and relationships. The PCM model shows the foundation representation to effectively communicate the integrated components of the established performance results to strategic, IT operational, and performance management staff.

The performance measures from the integrated IT performance measurement dashboard show the performance results outputs/outcomes for "executive leadership" functional area. Appendices A through F provide further details. Performance metrics, indicators, progress, trends, and analytics formed the basis for evidence-based decision making to enable improved organizational excellence.

4.3.5.4.1 Output/Outcomes: Performance Change Management

The outputs and outcomes of performance change management are given in Table 4.6.

Table 4.6 Performance Change Management Output/Outcomes

Results Area	*Output*	*Outcome*
Performance change management	Change strategy sustainability	• Improved sustainability of change strategy
	People/culture	• Increased social behaviors towards performance improvements • Improved results-based accountability mindset
	Politics	• Reduced political interferences in managing and delivering results • Reduced resistance to change
	Process	• Improved engagement and implementation of performance policies, processes and standards
	Performance	• Improved alignment of performance measures with organizational excellence and performance measurement dashboard-analytics
	Transformation change	• Improved people/culture, politics, process, and performance results of IT services delivery • Improved communications and understanding of change strategy sustainability

4.3.5.4.2 Process Flows: Performance Change Management (PCM)

The process flows of the performance measurement system are shown in Figure 4.17.

4.3.5.4.3 Performance Model: Performance Change Management (PCM)

The performance model of the performance change management is shown in Figure 4.18.

4.3.5.4.4 Performance Measures: Performance Change Management

The performance measures of the performance change management are shown in Figure 4.19a and b.

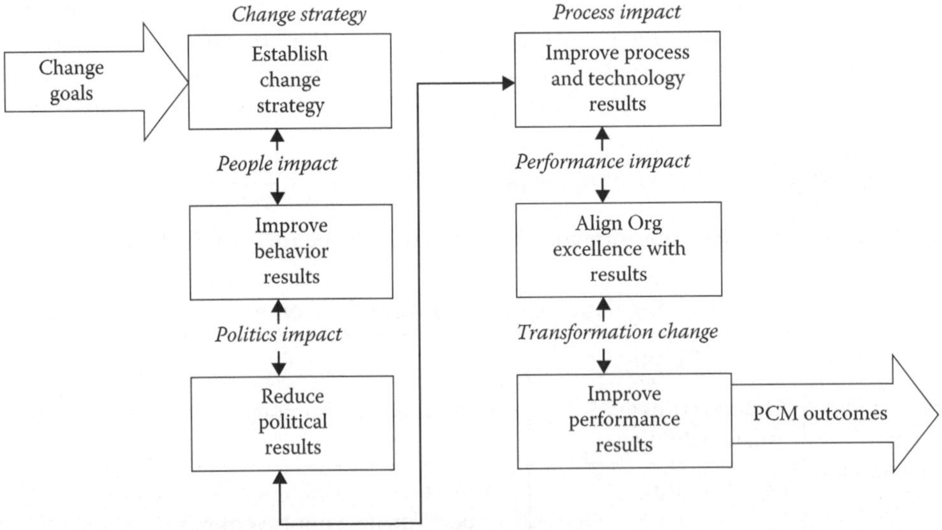

Figure 4.17 Performance change management process flow.

Figure 4.18 Performance change management model.

4.3.6 Human Resource Performance Management

Managers and performance specialists shall use *HRPM*[17] results area to determine the major key results and to establish a common framework for managing, measuring, delivering, and improving employee and customer performance measures, as presented in the *performance management plan, performance measurement plan,* and *performance improvement plan.* It establishes the basis for defining HR performance outcomes/outputs, monitoring progress, and evaluating accomplishments. Executives shall use the HRPM results areas as the framework to ensure clear, concise, consistent, complete, credible, and reliable staff performance plan, and staff performance measures are determined during employees' performance appraisals. Measurement should be used for the purpose of improvement rather than to make judgments or place blame.

HRPM results area focuses on the outputs/outcomes of employees, guides them to achieving organizational goals, and assists them in aligning to strategic and operational plans. Appraisal without these objectives is a mistake that provides little value to the employees, managers, and the organization. HRPM should be integrated into every employee's and manager's value system. Progressive organizations embrace performance management as a tool to include and link every employee and manager to the strategic and operational imperatives of the organization.

IT APPLICATIONS MANAGEMENT SERVICES (AMS)

OPERATIONAL-SD	Budget	YTD Actual	Status	% Complete	Indicator
AMS Services & SLA mgmt	4/1/2011	3/31/2012	In-Progress	45%	G
AMS SLA Support	4/1/2011	3/31/2012	In-Progress	45%	G
Web-Services Policy/Strategy Development	4/1/2011	6/30/2011	In-Progress	50%	Past Due
Innovative Communications tools	4/1/2011	3/31/2012	In-Progress	45%	G
AMS RFP/Contract Mgnt	4/1/2011	3/31/2012	In-Progress	45%	G
AMS Committee Meetings	4/1/2011	3/31/2012	In-Progress	45%	G
AMS Migrations	4/1/2011	3/31/2012	In-Progress	45%	G
AMS Change Management	4/1/2011	3/31/2012	In-Progress	45%	G
OPERATIONAL-SD Summary	4/1/2011	3/31/2012	In-Progress	46%	G

% IT staff delivering IT AMS Services & SLA Mgnt ; # Improvements completed
% IT staff delivering AMS SLA Support; # Improvements completed
% IT staff delivering Web-Services Strategy; # Improvements Completed
% IT staff delivering AMS Communications Tools; # Improvements completed
% IT staff delivering AMS RFP/Contract Mgnt; # Improvements completed
% IT staff delivering AMS Committee Meetings; # Improvements completed
% IT staff delivering AMS Migrations; # Improvements completed
% IT staff delivering AMS Change Mgnt; # Improvements completed

OPERATIONAL-SE	Start Date	End Date	Status	% Complete	Indicator
AMS QA	4/1/2011	6/30/2011	In-Progress	75%	Past Due
AMS Compliance/Approval	4/1/2011	7/31/2011	In-Progress	80%	Past Due
AMS Financial Measures	4/1/2011	9/30/2011	In-Progress	60%	R
AMS SLA Compliance	4/1/2011	3/31/2012	In-Progress	35%	Y
AMS Optimization	4/1/2011	3/31/2012	In-Progress	35%	Y
AMS Benchmarking Metrics	4/1/2011	9/30/2011	In-Progress	80%	G
OPERATIONAL-SE Summary	4/1/2011	3/31/2012	In-Progress	61%	G

% IT staff performing AMS QA ; # Improvements completed
% IT staff performing AMS Compliance; # Improvements completed
% IT staff performing AMS Financial Measures; # Improvements completed
% IT staff performing AMS SLA Compliance ; # Improvements completed
% IT staff performing AMS Optimization ; # Improvements completed
% IT staff performing AMS Benchmarking ; # Improvements completed

(a)

Figure 4.19 (a and b) Performance change management performance measures. *(Continued)*

FINANCIAL	Start Date	End Date	Status	% Complete	Indicator
IT AMS Innovative Initiative Costs-Capital	4/1/2011	12/31/2011	In-Progress	50%	G
IT AMS Operating Costs	4/1/2011	3/31/2012	In-Progress	15%	R
FINANCIAL Summary	4/1/2011	3/31/2012	In-Progress	33%	Y

% IT staff managing AMS Capital Costs; # Improvements completed
% IT staff managing AMS Operating Costs; # Improvements completed

CUSTOMER	Start Date	End Date	Status	% Complete	Indicator
AMS Client Relationships/Satisfaction Surveys	4/1/2011	3/31/2012	In-Progress	30%	Y
AMS Committee Meetings	4/1/2011	3/31/2012	In-Progress	30%	Y
AMS Vendors Relationships/Satisfaction Surveys	4/1/2011	9/30/2011	In-Progress	80%	G
AMS IT Outsourced Providers Surveys	10/1/2011	3/31/2012	Not-Started	0%	
AMS Benchmarking Surveys/Results	4/1/2011	6/30/2011	Complete	100%	Black
CUSTOMER Summary	4/1/2011	3/31/2012	In-Progress	48%	G

% IT staff performing Client Satisfaction Surveys; # Improvements completed
% IT staff attending AMS Committee Meetings; # Improvements completed
% IT staff performing Vendor Satisfaction Surveys; # Improvements completed
% IT staff performing IT Vendors Performance Measures; # Improvements completed
% IT staff performing IT Benchmarking surveys ; # Improvements completed

EMPLOYEE	Start Date	End Date	Status	% Complete	Indicator
AMS Progress Reporting	4/1/2011	6/30/2011	Complete	100%	Black
AMS Staff Performance Contract	4/1/2011	3/31/2012	In-Progress	35%	Y
AMS Staff Learning/Growth Reporting	4/1/2011	3/31/2012	In-Progress	35%	Y
AMS Staff Meetings/Communications	4/1/2011	3/31/2012	In-Progress	35%	Y
AMS Staff Retention/Retraining/Reward Reporting	4/1/2011	7/31/2011	In-Progress	100%	Black
EMPLOYEE Summary	4/1/2011	3/31/2012	In-Progress	61%	G
IT APPLICATIONS SERVICES SUMMARY	4/1/2011	3/31/2012	In-Progress	51%	G

% IT staff performing Progress Reporting ; # Improvements completed
% IT Staff managing Staff Performance Contract ; # Improvements completed
% IT staff attending Learning/Growth sessions; # Improvements completed
% IT staff performing staff communications/meetings ; # Improvements completed
% IT staff performing AMS retention/retraining ; # Improvements completed

(b)

Figure 4.19 (*Continued*) (a and b) Performance change management performance measures.

HRPM is sometimes confused with employee appraisal where the employee is rated against a set of competencies. The appraisal process does not achieve alignment as there is no objective or goal setting at the start of the process. Goal setting is critical to communicating objectives to the employee and, therefore, achieving alignment to the strategic directives and operational execution. In my experience, many managers and executives do not understand the linkages between performance management and the strategy to communicate how the strategy cascades down to each staff member. I believe a skill gap exist with most IT managers and executives. Some of these managers and executives are only familiar with appraisal systems and believe that HRPM is all about appraisals. These managers and executives need a solid foundation in HRPM, strategy alignment, and objective setting.

And yet, we still find that many organizations persist with once-per-year appraisals. HRPM differs from appraisal in many ways. The predominant disadvantage of appraisals is that employees and managers are *not* linked with the organizational strategy, and this issue makes appraisal a waste of time in tighter economic times.

The method of implementation of the HRPM initiatives need to consider the elements of employee engagement, retention, and innovations to ensure that the initiatives will achieve the desired engagement and retention outcomes sought by the business, in a culture of innovations. The method of transforming your organizational culture is through collaborations and transparency. It is constant improvement with a team who can translate innovations into added value for stakeholders. Innovations are trending in business. How can organizations derive optimum benefit through innovations?

HRPM presented in this book focuses more on HR measurement results to improve organizational excellence for employees, as defined in the performance measurement dashboard. It is based on the employee performance measures, similar to the balanced scorecard framework, published by Norton and Kaplan. HRPM must be maintained using consistent, credible, and reliable staff performance plan and staff performance measures for effective implementation. HRPM results provide formal written communications between the performance measurement team and senior managers. The performance measurement team and performance delivery manager will compile the HRPM results for each functional area, using the metrics and analytics from the performance measurement dashboard. The HR performance results will form the basis to ensure HR performance improvement for each functional area will be integrated by the PMO into a HRPM system and distributed each month to the performance steering committee and to other stakeholders, as appropriate.

The major key results of HRPM are

- Staff (employee/customer) performance plan
- Staff (employee/customer) performance measures

> Human Resource systems, designed to provide clear objectives for employees do not typically align to Strategy. Only 7% of U.S. Line Employees (and 3% in the U.K.) had their personal goals linked to Strategy
>
> **Robert S. Kaplan and David P. Norton**
> *The Strategy Focused Organization, Harvard Business School Press*

> In my experience, 70-80% of managers don't know how to set Objectives aligned to the plan
>
> **Peter Vlant**
> *Vice President of the Performance Management Institute of Australia, 2007*

4.3.6.1 Purpose

The purpose of this results area is to provide HRPM results to ensure that HR PMS are appropriately applied to the developments of staff performance plan and staff performance measures. The HRPM results must be aligned to the delivery of IT services and that performance improvements have not been reduced to some inappropriate levels because of political or other performance pressures. This HRPM information will form the baseline to measure, integrate, and improve the HR performance objectives of IT service delivery and to ensure effective staff performance plan and staff performance measures. The performance steering committee will use these HR performance plans and measures as a baseline in assessing the quality of the HR performance results and the overall *integrated performance management program.*

4.3.6.2 Strategic Directives

- Performance measurement managers and specialists will provide monthly HRPM reports for each functional area in accordance with the performance measurement dashboard results, in the format provided by the PMO.
- Performance measurement team and performance delivery manager will develop HRPM results that will form an integral component of the performance management plan.
- An integrated performance measurement dashboard and HRPM results will be used to produce performance status, progress, and accomplishments to ensure effective transformation and improvement of IT services.
- HRPM progress reports will be used to communicate the accomplishments of the outputs or products/services on the customers, defined as outcomes.

4.3.6.3 Accountabilities

4.3.6.3.1 Executive Performance Manager

This person is accountable for *approval* of the results.

- Executive support and approval for the *context and contents* of the established HRPM results and areas for priority improvements
- Executive support and approval for the *progress results* of the established HRPM results to ensure integration with IT performance measurement dashboard, IT performance measurement plan, and understanding the benefits and linkages with desired outcomes
- Executive support and approval for *performance trend results* in the performance scorecard or dashboard to understand the following: (a) "How we are improving?" (b) "Are we measuring/changing the right things?" (c) "Are we getting the right results?" (d) "Are we getting the value?"
- Executive support and approval on *stakeholders' survey satisfaction results* on strategic and IT operational management to understand the value of the HRPM results and to communicate service delivery improvements through stakeholders' satisfaction surveys
- Executive support and approval for *delivery services improvements* of the HRPM results and increased understanding of benefits and intended outcomes statement within the performance measurement dashboard as well as the recommended areas of improvements for *customer, employee, financial,* and *operational performance measures and results*
- Executive support and approval for HR *performance management results, performance measures,* and *benchmarking results* for reporting to performance steering committee, with direct accountability to performance management executive

4.3.6.3.2 Performance Delivery Manager

This person is accountable for *management* of the results.

- Manage and define the *context and contents* of the established HRPM results and areas for priority improvements.
- Measure the *progress results* of the established HRPM results to ensure integration with IT performance measurement dashboard, IT performance measurement plan, and understanding the benefits and linkages with desired outcomes.

- Monitor and analyze *performance trend results* in the performance scorecard or dashboard to understand the following: (a) "How we are improving?" (b) "Are we measuring/changing the right things?" (c) "Are we getting the right results?" (d) "Are we getting the value?"
- Deliver and evaluate *stakeholders' survey satisfaction results* for strategic and IT operational management to understand the value of the HRPM results and to improve service delivery through stakeholders' satisfaction surveys.
- Improve *delivery services* for the HRPM results and increase understanding of benefits and intended outcomes statement within the IT performance measurement dashboard by recommending areas of improvements for *customer, employee, financial,* and *operational performance measures and results.*
- Report on HRPM *results, performance measures,* and *benchmarking results* to performance steering committee, with direct accountability to performance management executive.

4.3.6.3.3 Performance Measurement Team

This team is accountable for *delivery* of performance results.

- Provide meaningful and credible data for defining the *context and contents* of the HRPM results and areas for priority improvements.
- Provide meaningful and credible data for measuring the *progress results* of the established HRPM results to ensure integration with IT performance measurement dashboard, IT performance measurement plan, and understanding the benefits and linkages with desired outcomes.
- Provide meaningful and credible data for monitoring and analyzing *performance trend results* in the performance scorecard or dashboard to understand the following: (a) "How we are improving?" (b) "Are we measuring/changing the right things?" (c) "Are we getting the right results?" (d) "Are we getting the value?"
- Provide meaningful and credible survey data for delivering and evaluating stakeholders' *satisfaction results* for strategic and IT operational management to understand the value of the established HRPM results and to improve service delivery through stakeholders' satisfaction surveys.
- Provide meaningful and credible data for improving *delivery services* for the HRPM results and increase understanding of benefits and intended outcomes statement within the overall IT performance measurement dashboard by recommending areas of improvements for *customer, employee, financial,* and *operational performance measures and results.*
- Provide meaningful and credible data on HRPM *results, performance measures,* and *benchmarking results* for reporting to performance steering committee, with direct accountability to performance management executive.

4.3.6.4 Results: Human Resource Performance Management

Accountabilities discussed earlier are brief because they are intended to serve as a reference for *who is accountable* for *what* during the delivery of the performance results in support of the performance management process. Results are now introduced to highlight the outputs of this HRPM results area and associated outcomes (what), process flow (how), and performance measures (why). It is intended to serve as a reference based on the English language interrogatives: Who *is accountable for what, how,* and *why.* The outputs/outcomes, process flow, and performance measures, based on real-world practical implementation, will serve as excellent references for practicing performance managers during measurement, delivery, and reporting of the outputs and outcomes for the performance results.

The outputs/outcomes highlight the key results for HRPM that the performance managers measure and report during the delivery of the established performance results. The process flows, based on real-world practical implementations, is a graphical representation of the inputs, process, outputs, and relationships. The HRPM model shows the foundation representation to effectively communicate the integrated components of the established performance results to strategic, IT operational, and performance management staff.

The performance measures from the integrated IT performance measurement dashboard only show the performance results outputs/outcomes for employee measures. Appendices A through F provide further details. Performance metrics, indicators, progress, trends, and analytics formed the basis for evidence-based decision making to enable improved organizational excellence.

4.3.6.4.1 Output/Outcomes: Human Resource Performance Management

The outputs and outcomes of human resource performance management are given in Table 4.7.

4.3.6.4.2 Process Flows: Human Resource Performance Management

The process flows of human resource performance management are shown in Figure 4.20.

Table 4.7 HR Performance Management Output/Outcomes

Results Area	*Output*	*Outcome*
HR performance management	HR strategic directives (Goals)	• Increased alignment of HR strategic directives with staff performance plan
	HR performance management standards	• Increased HR performance management standards compliance • Improved results-based accountability mindset
	HR progress	• Improved satisfaction of HR progress • Improved alignment of HR progress with accountability for results
	HR accomplishments	• Improved value of HR performance measurement dashboard-analytics
	HR performance plan	• Improved alignment of performance measures with organizational excellence and performance measurement dashboard-analytics
	HR performance measure	• Improved employee engagement, retention, competency assessments, innovations, reviews/feedback for IT services delivery • Improved communications and understanding of HR performance measures and critical success factors

4.3.6.4.3 Performance Model: Human Resource Performance Management

The performance model of human resource performance management is shown in Figure 4.21.

4.3.6.4.4 Performance Measures: Human Resource Performance Management

The performance measures of human resource performance management are shown in Figure 4.22a and b.

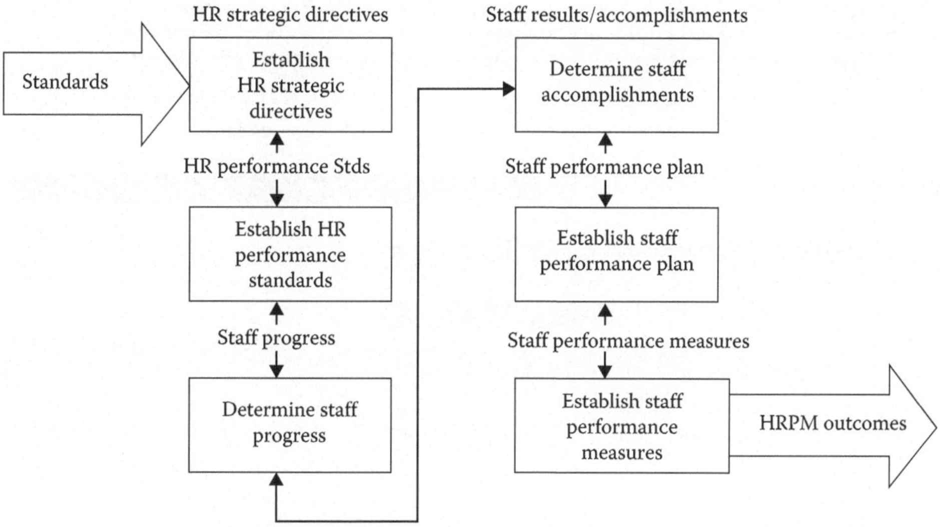

Figure 4.20 HR performance management process flow.

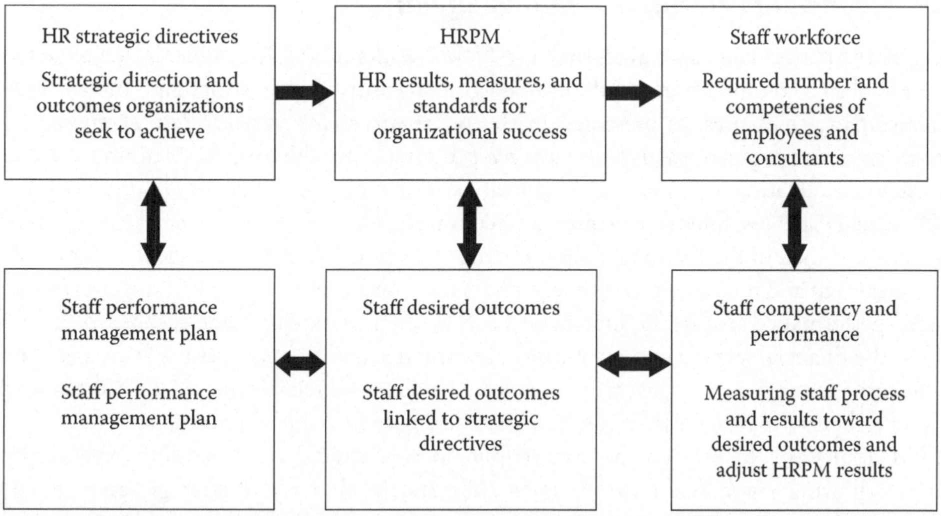

Figure 4.21 HR performance management model.

IT EXECUTIVE LEADERSHIP					
EMPLOYEE	Start Date	End Date	Status	% Complete	Indicator
IT Progress Reporting	4/1/2011	6/30/2011	Complete	100%	Black
IT Staff Performance Contract	4/1/2011	3/31/2012	In-Progress	35%	Y
Staff Learning/Growth	4/1/2011	3/31/2012	In-Progress	35%	Y
Staff Meetings/Communications	4/1/2011	3/31/2012	In-Progress	35%	Y
Staff Retention/Retraining/Reward Reporting	4/1/2011	7/31/2011	In-Progress	100%	Black
EMPLOYEE Summary	4/1/2011	3/31/2012	In-Progress	61%	G

Performance Metrics
% IT staff performing Progress Reporting ; # Improvements completed
% IT Staff performing Staff Performance Contract ; # Improvements completed
% IT staff performing Learning/Growth sessions; # Improvements completed
% IT staff performing staff communications/meetings ; # Improvements completed
% IT staff performing staff retention/retraining, etc.; # Improvements completed

(a)

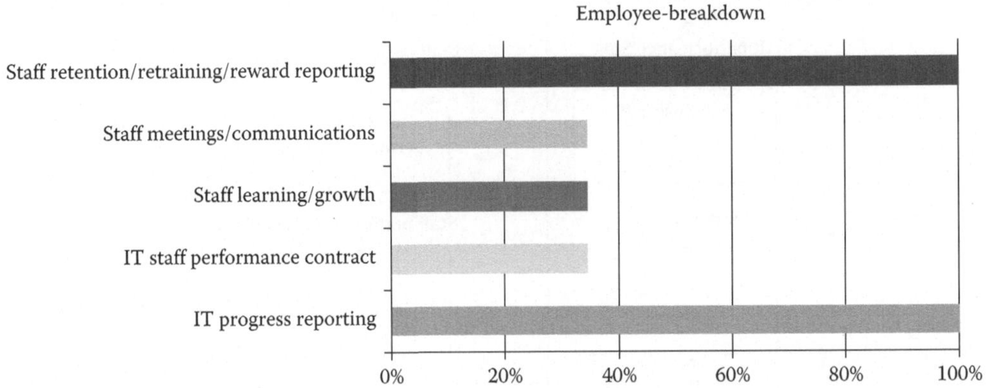

(b)

Figure 4.22 (a and b) HR performance management performance measures.

4.3.7 Financial Performance Management

Managers and performance specialists shall use *FPM*[18] results area to determine the major key results and to establish a common framework for managing, measuring, delivering, and improving financial performance measures, as presented in the *performance management plan, performance measurement plan,* and *performance improvement plan.* It establishes the basis for planning, monitoring progress, and evaluating expenditures. Financial performance plan consists of budget, year-to-date (YTD), actual expenses, forecast expenses, and comments for each of the financial capital and operating item, outlined in the IT budget plan. Financial performance measures identify how expenses will be measured and monitored using the performance measurement plan, IT budget plan, and the financial performance area in the integrated IT performance management dashboard. Executives shall use the financial (capital and operating) performance management results areas as the framework to ensure clear, concise, consistent, complete, credible, and reliable financial performance plan, and financial performance measures are provided during financial performance reviews.

FPM results area focuses on the outputs/outcomes of capital and operating expenses framework to achieving *results-based budgeting* (*RBB*)[19] and in aligning to strategic and operational initiatives and projects. Financial assessments and reviews without these objectives provide little economic value to the organization. FPM should be aligned and integrated with every strategic and operational initiatives and projects. Progressive organizations embrace FPM as a tool to include and link every capital and operating expenses to the strategic and operational imperatives of the organization.

FPM is sometimes confused with financial tracking where the financials are tracked against a budget, using financial coding structures. The financial tracking processes do not demonstrate alignment to strategic and operating initiatives—there is no objective or goal setting at the start of the financial allocation process. Goal setting is critical to communicating results achieved for expenses incurred and, therefore, achieving alignment to the strategic directives and operational execution. In my experiences, many managers and executives do not understand the linkages between performance management and the financial strategy to communicate how the strategy cascades down to capital and operating expenses. I believe a skill gap exist with most finance staff, IT managers, and executives. Some of these financial staff, managers, and executives are only familiar with financial tracking system using financial coding structures, with no alignment to results. They firmly believe that FPM is all about this method of financial tracking. These financial staff, IT managers, and executives need a solid foundation in FPM, strategic and operating alignment, and RBB.

And yet, we still find that many organizations persist with financial tracking reviews, independent of results. Some deploy *activity-based budgeting* (*ABB*)[20] with an accounting coding structure that has little or no alignment to planned or achievement results, outcomes, or outputs. A nonproductive and useless exercise based on the traditional financial model that most financial executives endorsed. FPM differs from financial tracking in many ways. The predominant disadvantage of financial tracking is that capital and operating expenses are *not* linked with the organizational strategic and operating initiatives/projects, and this issue makes traditional financial tracking a waste of time in tighter economic times.

The method of implementing FPM needs to outline the *elements and killers of IT budget*[21] that affect IT financial resource optimization (people, process/project/information, and technology resources) to ensure that IT financial resources will achieve the desired optimization outcomes sought by the business, in an RBB culture. The method of transforming your organizational from *traditional ABB*[20] to an RBB culture is through IT resource optimization, accountability, and transparency. It is huge financial improvements of a team who can translate RBB into added value for stakeholders. RBB is the financial outcomes of IT resource optimization. How can organizations derive optimum benefit through RBB?

FPM presented in this book focuses more on financial measurement results to improve organizational financial excellence for results accomplished, as defined in the performance measurement dashboard. It is based on the financial performance measures, similar to the balanced scorecard framework, published by Norton and Kaplan. FPM must be maintained using consistent, credible, and reliable financial performance plan and results-based financial performance measures to effectively implement FPM. FPM results provide formal written communications between the performance measurement team and senior managers. The performance measurement team and performance delivery manager will compile the FPM results for each functional area, using the metrics and analytics from the performance measurement dashboard. The financial performance results will form the basis to ensure financial performance improvement for each functional area will be integrated by the PMO into a FPM system and distributed each month to the performance steering committee and to other stakeholders, as appropriate.

The major key results of FPM area are

- Financial performance plan
- Financial performance measures

It is an immutable law in business that words are words, explanations are explanations, promises are promises but only performance is reality.

Harold S. Geneen

Fixed cost structure remains a barrier to acceptable financial performance.

Ralph Hake

Cutting costs without improvements in performance is futile.

W. Edwards Deming

4.3.7.1 Purpose

The purpose of this results area is to provide FPM to ensure that financial performance standards are appropriately applied to the developments of financial performance plan and financial performance measures. The FPM must be aligned to the results of IT-delivered services and RBB, and that performance improvements have not been reduced to some inappropriate levels because of political or other performance pressures. This financial information will form the baseline to measure, integrate, and improve the financial performance objectives of IT service delivery and to ensure effective financial performance plan and financial performance measures. The performance steering committee will use these financial performance plans and measures as a baseline in assessing the quality of the financial performance results and the overall *integrated performance management program.*

4.3.7.2 Strategic Directives

- Performance measurement managers and specialists will provide monthly FPM reports for each functional area in accordance with the performance measurement dashboard results, in the format provided by the PMO.
- Performance measurement team and performance delivery manager will develop a *financial performance management system* (*FPMS*)[22] that will form an integral component of the performance management plan.
- An integrated performance measurement dashboard and FPMS will be used to produce performance status, budget, YTD actual expenses, and forecast expenses to ensure effective transformation and improvement of IT services.
- FPM progress reports will be used to communicate the accomplishments of the outputs or products/services on the customers, with alignment to outcomes.

4.3.7.3 Accountabilities

4.3.7.3.1 Executive Performance Manager

This person is accountable for *approval* of the results.

- Executive support and approval for the *context and contents* of the established FPM results and areas for priority improvements
- Executive support and approval for the *progress results* of the established FPM results to ensure integration with IT performance measurement dashboard, IT performance measurement plan, and understanding the benefits and linkages with desired outcomes

- Executive support and approval for *performance trend results* in the performance scorecard or dashboard to understand the following: (a) "How we are improving?" (b) "Are we measuring/changing the right things?" (c) "Are we getting the right results?" (d) "Are we getting the value?"
- Executive support and approval on *stakeholders' survey satisfaction results* for strategic and IT operational management to understand the value of the FPM results and to communicate service delivery improvements through stakeholders' satisfaction surveys
- Executive support and approval for *delivery services improvements* of the FPM results and increased understanding of benefits and intended outcomes statement within the performance measurement dashboard as well as the recommended areas of improvements for *customer, employee, financial,* and *operational performance measures and results*
- Executive support and approval for *FPM results, performance measures,* and *benchmarking results* for reporting to performance steering committee, with direct accountability to performance management executive

4.3.7.3.2 Performance Delivery Manager

This person is accountable for *management* of the results.

- Manage and define the *context and contents* of the established FPM results and areas for priority improvements.
- Measure the *progress results* of the established FPM results to ensure integration with IT performance measurement dashboard, IT performance measurement plan, and understanding the benefits and linkages with desired outcomes.
- Monitor and analyze *performance trend results* in the performance scorecard or dashboard to understand the following: (a) "How we are improving?" (b) "Are we measuring/changing the right things?" (c) "Are we getting the right results?" (d) "Are we getting the value?"
- Deliver and evaluate stakeholders' *survey satisfaction results* for strategic and IT operational management to understand the value of the FPM results and to improve service delivery to financial stakeholders' satisfaction surveys.
- Improve *delivery services* for the financial management results and increase understanding of benefits and intended outcomes statement within the IT performance measurement dashboard by recommending areas of improvements for *customer, employee, financial,* and *operational performance measures and results.*
- Report on *FPM results, performance measures,* and *benchmarking results* to performance steering committee, with direct accountability to performance management executive.

4.3.7.3.3 Performance Measurement Team

This team is accountable for *delivery* of performance results.

- Provide meaningful and credible data for defining the *context and contents* of the FPM results and areas for priority improvements.
- Provide meaningful and credible data for measuring the *progress results* of the established FPM results to ensure integration with IT performance measurement dashboard, IT performance measurement plan, and understanding the benefits and linkages with desired outcomes.

- Provide meaningful and credible data for monitoring and analyzing *performance trend results* in the performance scorecard or dashboard to understand the following: (a) "How we are improving?" (b) "Are we measuring/changing the right things?" (c) "Are we getting the right results?" (d) "Are we getting the value?"
- Provide meaningful and credible survey data for delivering and evaluating *stakeholders' satisfaction results* for strategic and IT operational management to understand the value of the established FPM results and to improve service delivery through stakeholders' satisfaction surveys.
- Provide meaningful and credible data for improving *delivery services* for the FPMS and increase understanding of benefits and intended outcomes statement within the overall IT performance measurement dashboard by recommending areas of improvements for *customer, employee, financial,* and *operational performance measures and results.*
- Provide meaningful and credible data on FPM *results, performance measures,* and *benchmarking results* for reporting to performance steering committee, with direct accountability to performance management executive.

4.3.7.4 Results: Financial Performance Management

Accountabilities discussed earlier are brief because they are intended to serve as a reference for *who is accountable* for *what* during the delivery of the performance results in support of the performance management process. Results are now introduced to highlight the outputs of this FPM results and associated outcomes (what), process flow (how), and performance measures (why). It is intended to serve as a reference based on the English language interrogatives: Who *is accountable for what, how,* and *why.* The outputs/outcomes, process flow, and performance measures, based on real-world practical implementation, will serve as excellent references for practicing performance managers during measurement, delivery, and reporting of the outputs and outcomes for the performance results.

The outputs/outcomes highlight the key results for FPMS that the performance managers measure and report during the delivery of the established performance results. The process flows, based on real-world practical implementations, is a graphical representation of the inputs, process, outputs, and relationships. The FPM results show the foundation representation to effectively communicate the integrated components of the established performance results to strategic, IT operational, and performance management staff.

The performance measures from the integrated IT performance measurement dashboard show the performance results outputs/outcomes for "financial" measures. Appendices A through F provide further details. Performance metrics, indicators, progress, trends, and analytics formed the basis for evidence-based decision making to enable improved organizational excellence.

4.3.7.4.1 Output/Outcomes: Financial Performance Management (Table 4.8)

The outputs and outcomes of financial performance management are given in Table 4.8.

4.3.7.4.2 Process Flows: Financial Performance Management (FPM)

The process flows of financial performance management are shown in Figure 4.23.

Table 4.8 Financial Performance Management Output/Outcomes

Results Area	*Output*	*Outcome*
Financial performance management	Financial strategic directives (goals)	• Improved financial utilization of IT resources
	Financial budget	• Improved financial results—products/services produced internally and externally • Improved results-based budgeting (RBB)
	Financial actual expenses	• Improved actual financial expenses in managing and delivering products and services (outputs) • Improved financial impacts of outputs on customers/stakeholders
	Financial forecast	• Improved forecasting of financial performance in performance measurement dashboard-analytical trends for financial forecasting
	Financial performance plan	• Improved alignment of performance measures with RBB financial excellence and performance measurement dashboard-analytics
	Financial performance measure	• Improved financial (capital and operating) variances for IT services delivery • Improved communications and understanding of financials for RBB and critical success factors.

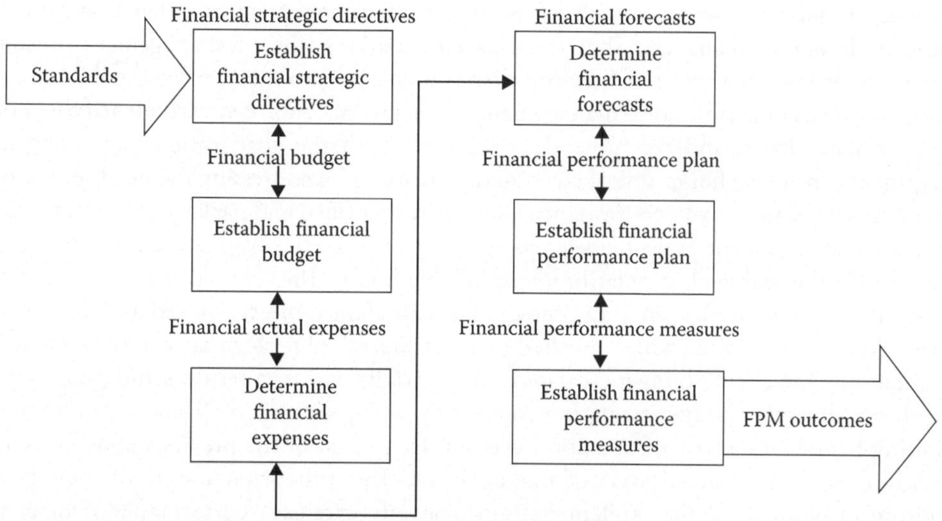

Figure 4.23 Financial performance management process flow.

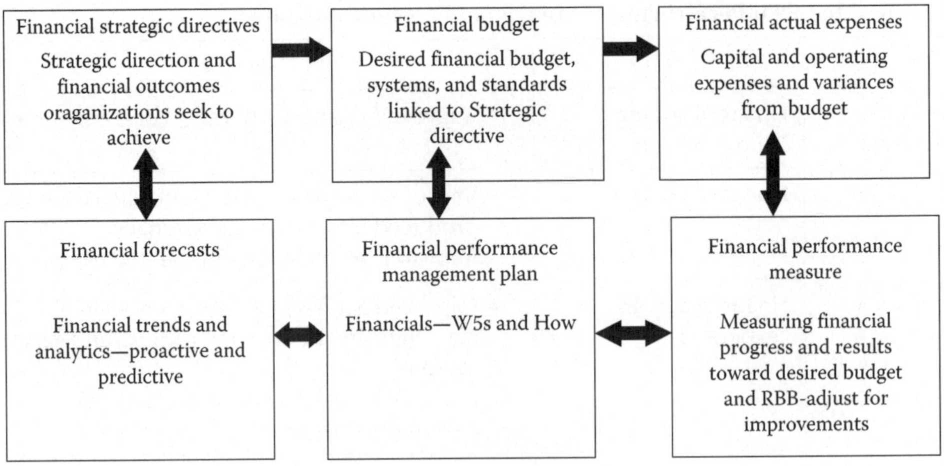

Figure 4.24 Financial performance management model.

4.3.7.4.3 Performance Model: Financial Performance Management (FPM)

The performance model of financial performance management is shown in Figure 4.24.

4.3.7.4.4 Performance Measures: Financial Performance Management (FPM)

The performance measures of financial performance management are shown in Figure 4.25a and b.

4.3.7.4.5 Real-World Scenario

Situation: A major organization that favored the "outsourcing" mode of operations for all IT services decided to contract most performance management services rather than using the services of "in-house" managers. They experienced situations where a management consulting firm seem to operate in a mode of "turning client's problems into their personal gold treasures." The primary focus of performance management seemed to be concerned with identifying potential performance issues and recommending solutions with the goal toward generating more management consulting hours and, then secondly, focusing on addressing the needs of the organization. In some cases, many performance issues were identified and packaged into unnecessary performance management project labeled as "phase 1 to n" of the original performance project name, to hide the real goal, generating more billable hours. The original performance project evolved into multiple overlapping, disjointed, and redundant projects, labeled as "phase 1 to n" of the original project name, which resulted in an uncontrolled performance management contract situation. The client's budget escalated exponentially and, as a result, senior management decided to address this budget escalation concern by hiring another performance management consulting firm whose mode of operation was similar to that of the previous consulting firm, but with a more professional style of management. This professional style of management consulting recommended the implementation of overly extensive performance management processes, including the management consulting hidden agenda. The uncontrolled budget environment, which resulted in the identification of performance management projects to address the so-called uncontrolled performance issues, continued to manifest itself, and this

IT EXECUTIVE LEADERSHIP

FINANCIAL	Start Date	End Date	Status	% Complete	Indicator
IT Capital Costs	4/1/2011	3/31/2012	In-Progress	30%	Y
IT Operational Costs	4/1/2011	3/31/2012	In-Progress	30%	Y
IT Outsourced/Consulting Costs	4/1/2011	9/30/2011	In-Progress	80%	G
IT Staff Costs	10/1/2011	3/31/2012	Not-Started	0%	
Major Business Projects Costs	4/1/2011	6/30/2011	Complete	100%	Black
Major Technology Infrastructure Project Costs	4/1/2011	6/30/2011	Complete	100%	Black
FINANCIAL Summary	4/1/2011	3/31/2012	In-Progress	57%	G

Performance Metrics
% IT staff managing IT Capital Costs; # Improvements completed
% IT staff managing IT Operational Costs Mgnt; # Improvements completed
% IT staff managing IT Outsourced Costs Mgnt; # Improvements completed
% IT staff managing IT Staff Costs Mgnt; # Improvements completed
% IT staff managing IT Business Projects Costs Mgnt; # Improvements completed
% IT staff managing IT Technology Costs Mgnt; # Improvements completed

(a)

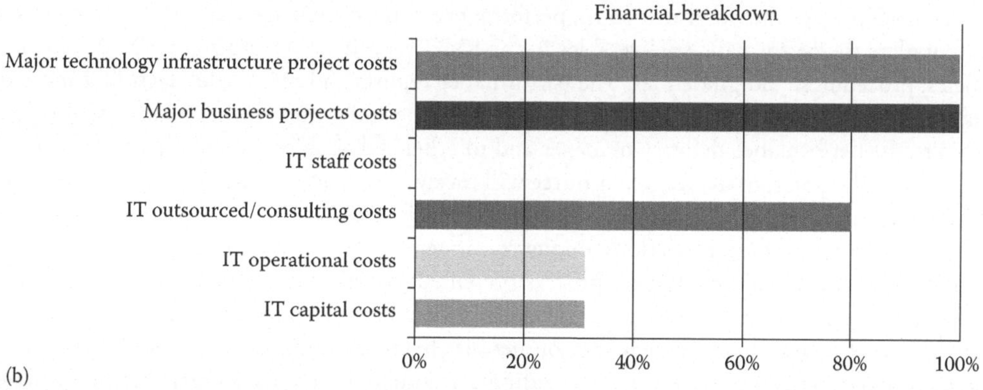

(b)

Figure 4.25 (a and b) Financial performance management performance measures.

organization's performance management environment evolved to a series of "performance issues fire-fighting" reactive mode of operations.

> Nothing is less productive than to make more efficient what should not be done at all.
>
> **Peter Drucker**

Root cause of problem: In this situation, I believed that the root cause of these identified performance problems is the lack of applicable performance culture, structure, accountability, and performance management process, to assess, prioritize, integrate, and align these issues with the organization's strategic and operational goals. Management must be aware of the subtle professional qualities of some consulting firms, whose "hidden" objective may evolve to "turning clients' problems into their personal gold treasures." These types of management consulting firms usually provide "labor-intensive" performance management services, with the main focus toward identifying vague performance issues with justifications for more detailed analysis, rather than providing results-based performance management services.

Solution: The solution to this type of situation is the establishment and application of a performance management culture, structure, and processes, similar in content and structure, as presented in this chapter. Senior management involvement, approval, and understanding of the integrated performance management dashboard are absolutely necessary for successful implementation. Evidence-based decision using predictive analytics is often the key to managing, measuring, and improving organizational performance.

4.4 Performance Measurement Office

Executive management shall use the PMO report to ensure that all performance deliverables, plans, reports, and processes are documented consistently in the PMO repository.[23] Managing, measuring, and improving performance outputs, outcomes, measures, and reports in the performance repository is often the key to ensuring the IT services deliver complete, consistent, and integrated deliverables. This process will enhance the communications among the stakeholders, internal, and external to the organization.

The performance measurement team, performance delivery manager, and PMO support staff will populate the performance deliverables in the PMO repository, according to PMO standards, policies, procedures, and guidelines. The performance reports and metrics for each IT functional area will be compiled by the PMO using the PMO repository, and inconsistencies will be presented to the performance delivery manager and to other stakeholders, as appropriate, for corrective actions. The program steering committee will review the structure and contents of the reports and will suggest changes to improve completeness, consistency, and integration of the reports, in order to enhance the communications among team members and stakeholders.

The PMO infrastructure support process presented in this chapter emphasizes the need for consistency and standardization of processes, deliverables, tools, and techniques to ensure an integrated IT performance management environment is effectively implemented. The PMO supports the performance measurement team by providing methodology, process deployment, performance management training, performance metrics, performance measurement criteria, tools, and PMR support, to increase performance measurement team productivity and reusability.

The major key results of the PMO discussed in this chapter are

- PMO infrastructure support strategy
- PMO processes and structure
- PMO management plan[24]
- PMO repository (performance management information repository [PMIR][23] and performance management information system [PMIS])
- PMO metrics and performance reporting
- PMO predictive analytics and informed decision making

The processing components of the PMO, which focuses on common responsibilities, are as follows:

1. Establishes and deploys a common set of *performance measurement processes, metrics, results, and templates*, which saves effort for each performance measurement staff, or each performance manager, from having to create these on their own time. These reusable performance

measurement components help performance initiatives/projects start up more quickly and with less effort.

2. Builds the *methodology* and updates it to account for improvements and best practices. For example, as new or revised performance measures, metrics, results, processes, and templates are made available, the PMO deploys them consistently throughout the organization.
3. Facilitates improved performance measurement team *communications* by having common measures, metrics, processes, outputs/outcomes, and terminology. Less misunderstanding and confusion occurs, if everyone uses the same language and terminology for performance-related work.
4. Provides *training* (internal or outsourced) to build core performance measurement competencies and a common set of experiences. If the training is delivered by the PMO, there is a further reduction in overall training costs paid to outside vendors.
5. Delivers performance measurement *coaching* services to keep IT services from getting into trouble. IT results at risk can also be coached to ensure they don't become more risky.
6. Tracks basic information on the current status of IT services in the organization and provides performance visibility and analytics to management in a common and consistent manner.
7. Tracks organization-wide *metrics* on the state of performance measurement and management, IT service delivery, and the value being provided to the business. The PMO also assesses the general IT service delivery environment on an ongoing basis to determine the improvements that have been made.
8. Acts as the overall advocate for performance measurement and management to the organization. This includes actively educating, selling managers, and performance team members on the value gained though the use of consistent and integrated performance measurement processes.

In summary, companies are finding that they need to standardize on how performance are managed, measured, and improved by utilizing consistent and integrated processes. They are recognizing that the process takes much more than just training the staff. It requires a holistic approach, covering many aspects of work and the company culture.

> Whoever admits that he is too busy to improve his methods has acknowledged himself to be at the end of his rope.
>
> **J. Ogden Armour (via Information Week)**

The intent of this section is *not* to provide detailed processes or procedures on the implementation of any specific PMO model or similar IT PMO process. There are many excellent books on PMO processes, concepts, theory, and applicability, some of which are mentioned in the "Recommended Readings" section provided at the end of this chapter. The main objective of this chapter is to provide an overview of the contents (what), purpose (why), accountabilities (who is accountable for what), and results (what, how, why) of PMO and to demonstrate how it fits within the context of the overall integrated IT performance management framework. The "accountability" section provides results-based accountability for the executive performance manager, performance delivery manager, and performance measurement team—performance measurement manager and performance specialists. The results sections for each of the IT performance management results areas provide the outputs/outcomes (what), process flow (how), and performance measures (why) to support the measurement, management, delivery, improvement, and integration of the performance management results areas. The performance measures from the performance measurement dashboard mainly show staff input metrics for demonstration purposes. In reality, the dashboard contained many combinations of results for input, process, and output/outcomes measures.

4.4.1 Purpose

The purpose of this PMO support process is to support the performance measurement team with methodology, templates, process deployment, performance measurement training, performance metrics, performance measurement criteria, performance measurement tools, and performance measurement reporting, to increase the performance measurement team productivity and reusability. The PMO staffs advocate the need for consistency, standardization, and integration of results/output/outcomes, tools, and techniques to ensure that the integrated IT performance management environment is effectively implemented.

4.4.2 Strategic Directives

- PMO methodology and processes shall be results based-rather than procedure oriented. The "processes or methodologies shall be SMART (*S*pecific, *M*easurable, *A*chievable, *R*ealistic, and *T*imely) rather than DUMB (*D*oubtful, *U*nrealistic, *M*assive, and *B*oring)." It must be flexible enough, not rigid, so that it can be easily adapted to different performance development approaches.
- Executive and senior management shall commit to using the company's approved performance measurement methodology and processes during IT service delivery.
- Performance delivery managers shall ensure that all PMO outputs, outcomes, and measures are included in the integrated performance measurement dashboard.
- Performance measurement teams shall adhere to PMO policies, standards, guidelines, and procedures.

4.4.3 Accountabilities

4.4.3.1 Executive Performance Manager

This person is accountable for *approval* of the results.

- Executive support and approval for the *context and contents* of the PMO to ensure consistency. Manage the PMO processes by reporting on the contents, recommend solutions to the appropriate management team, and update PMO processes to keep it effective.
- Executive support and approval for the *progress* of the established PMO results to ensure consistency and integration with strategic management, IT operational management and performance management, alignment to IT strategic directives, and understanding the benefits and linkages with desired outcomes. Ensure that performance specialists adhere to the guideline processes, output/outcomes, tools, and techniques established by the PMO to ensure performance measurement and management consistency, completeness, and integration. Communicate PMO policies and ensure performance teams adhere to IT PMO output/outcomes, methodology, processes, tools, and techniques.
- Executive support and approval for the *performance trend results* in the integrated IT performance measurement dashboard to understand the following: (a) "How we are doing?" (b) "Are we doing/measuring the right things?" (c) "Are we getting the right results?" (d) "Are we getting the value?" Maintain the *PMIR*[23] and integrated IT performance measurement dashboard.

- Executive support and approval on *stakeholders' survey satisfaction results* for strategic and IT operational performance management to understand the value of the PMO to improve service delivery through the use of *stakeholders' satisfaction surveys*. Provide policies, guidelines, best practices, and templates to enable cost-effective and cost-efficient measurement and assessment of IT services. Lead and coordinate the integration of all IT performance standards, templates, and measures into a single consolidated repository for access by performance measurement teams. Provide performance guidance and counsel to the various performance roles. Provide guidelines in defining acceptable levels of measures for assessment and measurement of IT services. Provide standard templates and tools for performance measurement activities and guidelines for reporting frequency.
- Executive support and approval for *improvements* to PMO process and increase understanding of benefits and intended outcomes statement within the overall IT operational framework by recommending areas of improvements for customer, employee, financial, and operations performance measures and results. Assist project teams in the use of performance measurement templates and provide the necessary training on the use of performance measurement standards, practices, and templates. Provide information on past performance initiatives relevant to current initiatives. Conduct or arrange for externally conducted steering committee-directed performance reviews. Ensure that postperformance reviews are completed and findings are executed. Identify to the steering committee, appropriate trend analysis of the key indicators for performance monitoring in terms of customer, employee, financial, and operations.
- Executive support and approval for *PMO results*, *performance measures*, and *benchmarking results*. Report on performance measures and results to performance steering committee, with direct accountability to performance management executive. Keep performance managers and stakeholders informed on the effectiveness of the PMO processes.

4.4.3.2 Performance Delivery Manager

This person is accountable for *management* of the results.

- Manage and define the *context and contents* of the PMO to ensure consistency. Manage the PMO processes by reporting on the contents, recommend solutions to the appropriate management team, and update PMO processes to keep it effective.
- Measure the *progress* of the established PMO to ensure consistency and integration with strategic management, IT operational management and performance management, alignment to IT strategic directives, and understanding the benefits and linkages with desired outcomes. Ensure that performance specialists adhere to the guideline processes, output/outcomes, tools, and techniques established by the PMO to ensure performance management consistency, completeness, and integration. Communicate PMO policies and ensure performance teams adhere to IT PMO methodology, processes, tools, and techniques.
- Monitor and analyze *performance trends results* in the integrated IT performance measurement dashboard to understand the following: (a) "How we are doing?" (b) "Are we doing/measuring the right things?" (c) "Are we getting the right results?" (d) "Are we getting the value?" Maintain the *PMIR*[23] and integrated IT performance measurement dashboard.
- Deliver and evaluate *stakeholders' survey satisfaction results* for strategic and IT operational performance management to understand the value of the PMO to improve service delivery through the use of *stakeholders satisfaction surveys*. Provide policies, guidelines, best practices,

and templates to enable cost-effective and cost-efficient measurement and assessment of IT services. Lead and coordinate the integration of all IT performance standards, templates, and measures into a single consolidated repository for access by performance measurement teams. Provide performance guidance and counsel to the various performance roles. Provide guidelines in defining acceptable levels of measures for assessment and measurement of IT services. Provide standard templates and tools for performance measurement activities and guidelines for reporting frequency.

- Improve *PMO process* and increase understanding of benefits and intended outcomes statement within the overall IT operational framework by recommending areas of improvements for customer, employee, financial, and operations performance measures and results. Assist project teams in the use of performance measurement templates and provide the necessary training on the use of performance measurement standards, practices, and templates. Provide information on past performance initiatives relevant to current initiatives. Conduct or arrange for externally conducted steering committee-directed performance reviews. Ensure that postperformance reviews are completed and findings are executed. Identify to the steering committee, appropriate trend analysis of the key indicators for performance monitoring in terms of customer, employee, financial, and operations.
- Report on *performance measures and results* to performance steering committee, with direct accountability to performance management executive. Keep performance managers and stakeholders informed on the effectiveness of the PMO processes.

4.4.3.3 Performance Measurement Team

This team is accountable for *delivery* of performance results.

- Provide the *context and contents* of the PMO to ensure consistency. Manage the PMO processes by reporting on the contents, recommend solutions to the appropriate management team, and update PMO processes to keep it effective.
- Provide the *progress* of the established PMO to ensure consistency and integration with strategic management, IT operational management and performance management, alignment to IT strategic directives, and understanding the benefits and linkages with desired outcomes. Ensure that performance specialists adhere to the guideline processes, output/outcomes, tools, and techniques established by the PMO to ensure performance management consistency, completeness, and integration. Communicate PMO policies and ensure performance teams adhere to IT PMO methodology, processes, tools, and techniques.
- Provide *performance trends* in the integrated IT performance measurement dashboard to understand the following: (a) "How we are doing?" (b) "Are we doing/measuring the right things?" (c) "Are we getting the right results?" (d) "Are we getting the value?" Maintain the *PMIR*[23] and integrated IT performance measurement dashboard.
- Provide *stakeholders' survey satisfaction results* for strategic and IT operational performance management to understand the value of the PMO to improve service delivery through the use of *stakeholders' satisfaction surveys*. Provide policies, guidelines, best practices, and templates to enable cost-effective and cost-efficient measurement and assessment of IT services. Lead and coordinate the integration of all IT performance standards, templates, and measures into a single consolidated repository for access by performance measurement teams. Provide performance guidance and counsel to the various performance

roles. Provide guidelines in defining acceptable levels of measures for assessment and measurement of IT services. Provide standard templates and tools for performance measurement activities and guidelines for reporting frequency.

- Provide *PMO process* and increase understanding of benefits and intended outcomes statement within the overall IT operational framework by recommending areas of improvements for customer, employee, financial, and operations performance measures and results. Assist project teams in the use of performance measurement templates and provide the necessary training on the use of performance measurement standards, practices, and templates. Provide information on past performance initiatives relevant to current initiatives. Conduct or arrange for externally conducted steering committee-directed performance reviews. Ensure that postperformance reviews are completed and findings are executed. Identify to the steering committee, appropriate trend analysis of the key indicators for performance monitoring in terms of customer, employee, financial, and operations.
- Provide report on *performance measures and results* to performance steering committee, with direct accountability to performance management executive. Keep performance managers and stakeholders informed on the effectiveness of the PMO processes.

4.4.4 Results: Performance Measurement Office

Accountabilities discussed earlier are brief because they are intended to serve as a reference for *who is accountable* for *what* during the delivery of the performance results in support of the PMO processes. Results are now introduced to highlight the outputs of this PMO results and associated outcomes (what), process flow (how), and performance measures (why). It is intended to serve as a reference based on the English language interrogatives: Who *is accountable for what, how,* and *why*. The outputs/outcomes, process flow, and performance measures, based on real-world practical implementation, will serve as excellent references for practicing performance managers during measurement, delivery, and reporting of the outputs and outcomes for the performance results.

The outputs/outcomes highlight the key results for the PMO that the performance managers measure and report during the delivery of the established performance results. The process flows, based on real-world practical implementations, is a graphical representation of the inputs, process, outputs, and relationships. The PMO results show the foundation representation to effectively communicate the integrated components of the established performance results to strategic, IT operational, and performance management staff.

The performance measures from the integrated IT performance measurement dashboard show performance results outputs/outcomes for project portfolio management Operational (FM, SD, SE and RM) measures, for applicability purposes. Appendices A through F provide further details. Performance metrics, indicators, progress, trends, and analytics formed the basis for evidence-based decision making to enable improved organizational excellence.

4.4.4.1 Outputs/Outcomes: Performance Measurement Office (Table 4.9)

The outputs and outcomes of a performance measurement office are given in Table 4.9.

4.4.4.2 Process Flows: Performance Measurement Office

The process flows of a performance measurement office are shown in Figure 4.26.

Table 4.9 Performance Measurement Office Output/Outcomes

Results Area	*Output*	*Outcome*
Performance measurement office (PMO)	PMO infrastructure support strategy	• Improved utilization of PMO resources
	PMO processes, standards and structure	• Improved PMO results—products/services produced internally and externally • Improved results-based consistency
	PMO management plan	• Improved PMO effectiveness of managing, measuring, and delivering products and services (outputs) • Improved PMO effects of outputs on customers/stakeholders
	PMO repository PMIR and PMIS	• Improved value of performance measurement dashboard-analytics
	PMO metrics and reporting	• Improved alignment of performance measures with organizational excellence and performance measurement dashboard-analytics
	PMO predictive analytics and informed decision making	• Improved predictive and prescriptive analytics • Improved informed decision making and understanding of PMO value and critical success factors.

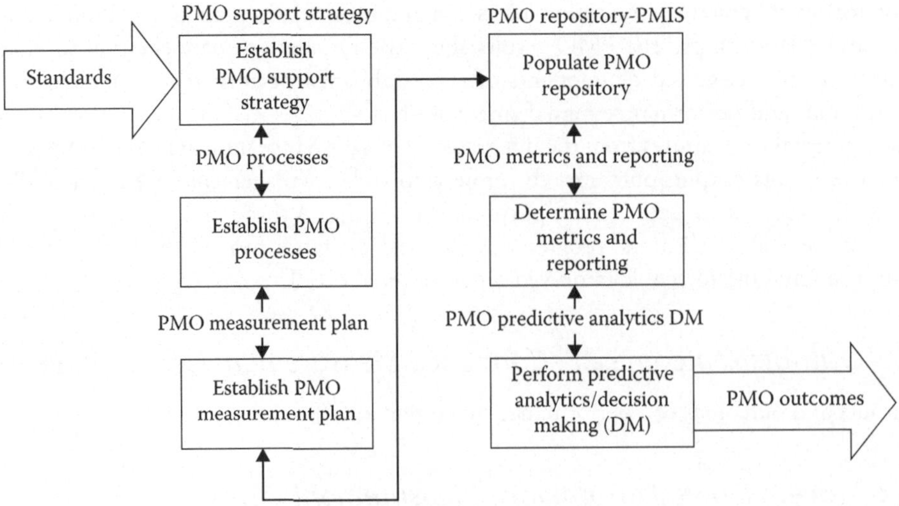

Figure 4.26 Performance measurement office process flow.

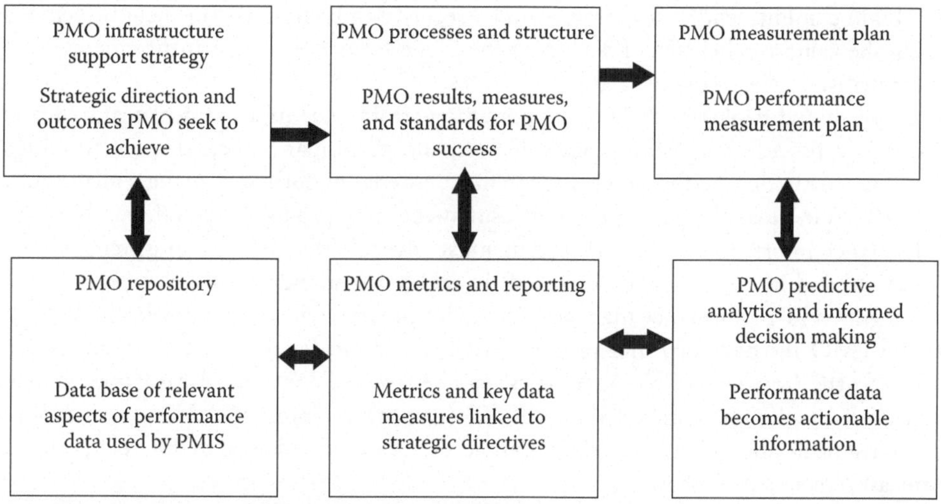

Figure 4.27 Performance measurement office model.

4.4.4.3 Performance Model: Performance Measurement Office

The performance model of a performance measurement office is shown in Figure 4.27.

4.4.4.4 Performance Measures: Performance Measurement Office

The performance measures of a performance measurement office are shown in Figure 4.28.

4.5 Summary

The performance management model presented in this chapter describes the results areas of performance management. The "purpose" section provides a statement of the derived result, and the "strategic directives" section provides various guiding principles and major directives to achieving the purpose statement, for each of the performance management results areas. The accountabilities of the executive performance manager, performance delivery manager, and performance measurement team are presented to demonstrate the integrated nature of these outputs and outcomes in measuring, managing, and delivering IT services. The key performance management outputs and outcomes, process flows, and performance measures provide excellent real-world implementation guidelines, which can be referenced and applied to performance management processes.

Business organizations that are in the process of measuring, managing, delivering, and improving IT services with the goal toward integrated or enterprise performance management should consider the following performance management recommendations, as a framework, to guide them toward successful measuring, management, delivery, and improvement of IT services.

- Establish an IT service delivery life cycle performance model that supports an iterative and incremental approach, which consists of well-defined IT functional areas to ensure orderly management, approval, control, and delivery of IT services.
- Conform to IPMF-IT performance management processes and modify the guidelines based on your existing IT project environment and the framework presented in this chapter.

- Obtain commitments and approvals from executive and senior management by demonstrating the value and benefits of deploying the IT performance management processes in your company, on one or many IT functional areas.
- Establish and deploy a PMO to support the performance measurement team with methodology, process, templates, process deployment, performance measurement training, performance metrics, performance measurement criteria, performance management tools, and PMR, to increase the performance measurement team productivity and reusability of performance information. The PMO staffs must advocate the need for consistency, standardization, and integration of processes, deliverables, tools, and techniques to ensure that the integrated IT performance management environment is effectively implemented.
- The PMO methodology and processes shall be results-based rather than procedure oriented. The "processes or methodologies shall be SMART (*S*pecific, *M*easurable, *A*chievable, *R*ealistic, and *T*imely) rather than DUMB (*D*oubtful, *U*nrealistic, *M*assive, and *B*oring)." It must be flexible enough, not rigid, so that it can be easily adapted to different performance measurement approaches.

IT PROJECT PORTFOLIO mgmt					
OPERATIONAL-FM	**Start Date**	**End Date**	**Status**	**% Complete**	**Indicator**
IT PPM Governance Framework	4/1/2011	12/31/2011	In-Progress	50%	G
IT PPM Innovative Technical Direction	4/1/2011	3/31/2012	In-Progress	45%	G
PPM Projects Outsourcing Framework	4/1/2011	9/30/2011	In-Progress	65%	Y
OPERATIONAL-FM Summary	4/1/2011	3/31/2012	In-Progress	53%	G

OPERATIONAL-SD	Start Date	End Date	Status	% Complete	Indicator
IT Business Projects Monitoring/Reporting	4/1/2011	3/31/2012	In-Progress	25%	Y
Innovative PMO Communications tools	4/1/2011	9/30/2011	In-Progress	75%	Y
IT PPM Productivity Tools and Processes	4/1/2011	9/30/2012	In-Progress	40%	G
PPM Systems and Regression Testing	4/1/2011	3/31/2012	In-Progress	40%	G
IT Project Management/Delivery	4/1/2011	3/31/2012	In-Progress	40%	G
IT Business Projects RFP/Contracts	4/1/2011	3/31/2012	In-Progress	40%	G
IT Business Projects Program/Projects Plan	4/1/2011	3/31/2012	In-Progress	40%	G
IT Business Project Architecture/Design	4/1/2011	3/31/2012	In-Progress	40%	G
IT PMO Support	4/1/2011	3/31/2012	In-Progress	40%	G
IT Business Project Requirements Specifications	4/1/2011	3/31/2012	In-Progress	40%	G
OPERATIONAL-SD Summary	4/1/2011	3/31/2012	In-Progress	42%	G

(a)

Figure 4.28 (a–d) Performance measurement office performance measure. *(Continued)*

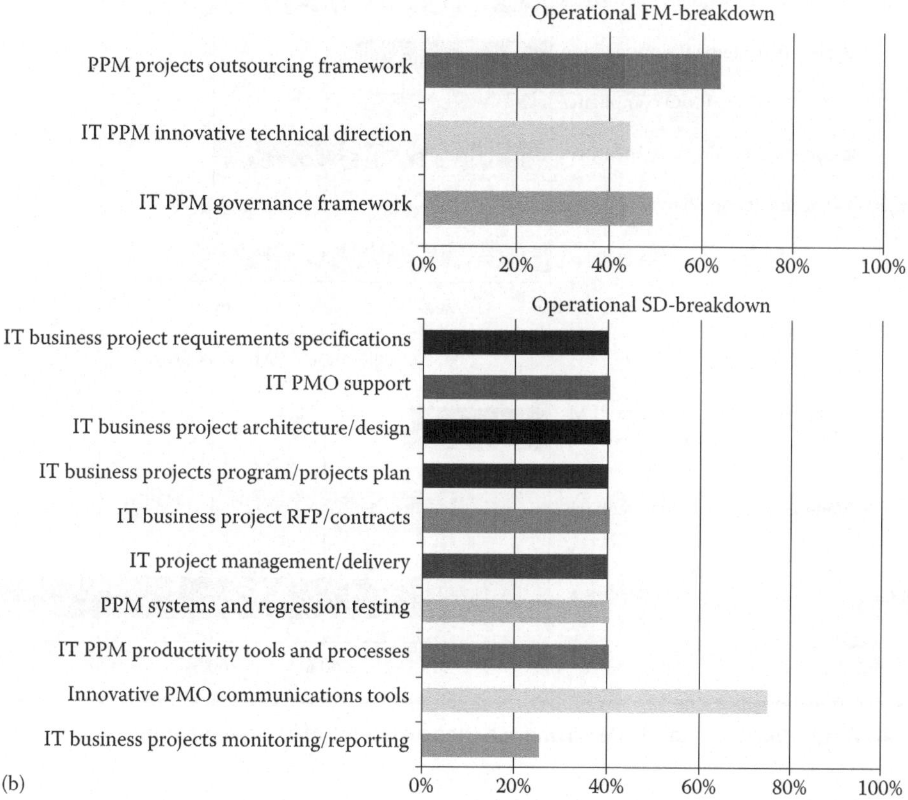

(b)

OPERATIONAL-SE	Start Date	End Date	Status	% Complete	Indicator
Business Projects Plan QA	4/1/2011	6/30/2011	In-Progress	75%	Past Due
IT Project Management Compliance/Approval	4/1/2011	7/31/2011	In-Progress	80%	Past Due
Business Projects Financial Measures	4/1/2011	9/30/2011	In-Progress	60%	R
PMO Compliance	4/1/2011	3/31/2012	In-Progress	35%	Y
Project Management Optimization	4/1/2011	3/31/2012	In-Progress	35%	Y
Business Projects Benchmarking Metrics	4/1/2011	9/30/2011	In-Progress	80%	G
OPERATIONAL-SE Summary	4/1/2011	3/31/2012	In-Progress	61%	G

OPERATIONAL-RM	Start Date	End Date	Status	% Complete	Indicator
PPM Client Management Relations/Feedback	4/1/2011	3/31/2012	In-Progress	100%	Black
Vendors PPM Relations/Feedback	4/1/2011	3/31/2012	In-Progress	40%	G
IT Outsourced Providers PPM Relations/Feedback	4/1/2011	3/31/2012	In-Progress	25%	Y
OPERATIONAL-RM Summary	4/1/2011	3/31/2012	In-Progress	55%	G

(c)

Figure 4.28 (*Continued*) (a–d) Performance measurement office performance measure.

(Continued)

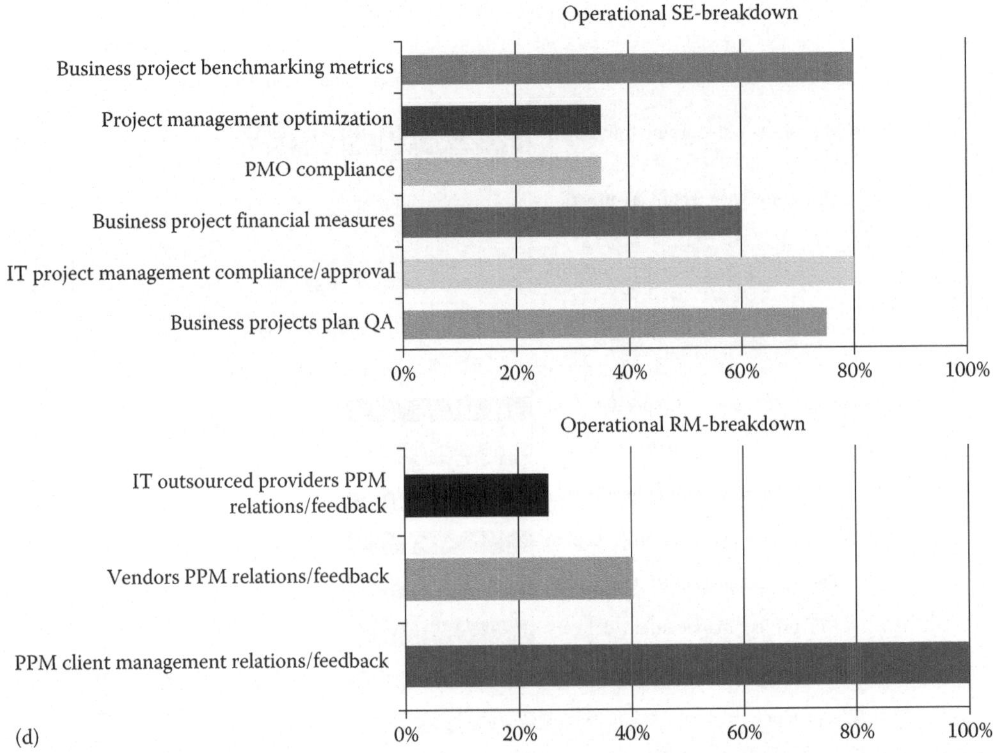

Figure 4.28 (*Continued*) (a–d) Performance measurement office performance measure.

The main focus of this chapter is to provide the readers with further details on the performance management component processes of the integrated performance management framework model. By now, the readers should have gained a fairly good understanding of the integrated nature of these processes. Chapter 6 includes further discussions to show the horizontal integration of these performance management processes based on an iterative and incremental IT service delivery life cycle performance model. Performance delivery managers and performance measurement staff, especially those with keen interests toward integrated performance management processes, will be able to appreciate the value of these horizontal and vertical integration processes, to better prepare them for measuring, managing, and delivering successful IT services, in this dynamically changing IT industry.

4.6 Endnotes: Key Performance Management Terms

[1]*Accountability for results*: A shift in culture from being accountable for creating and carrying out activities to being accountable for achieving results, meeting goals, affecting change, and improving quality of products and services using output (efficiency) and outcomes (effectiveness) metrics and measures.

[2]*Executive leadership/governance services* (*ELS*): The primary results achieved from the governance functional area of the IT service delivery life cycle performance model. It is represented in the performance measurement dashboard using output and outcomes metrics and measures.

[3]*Planning and administration services* (*PAS*): The primary results achieved from the planning and administration functional area of the IT service delivery life cycle performance model. It is represented in the performance measurement dashboard using output and outcomes metrics and measures.

[4]*Enterprise architecture services* (*EAS*): The primary results achieved from the enterprise architecture functional area of the IT service delivery life cycle performance model. It is represented in the performance measurement dashboard using output and outcomes metrics and measures.

[5]*Project portfolio management* (*PPM*): The primary results achieved from the project portfolio management functional area of the IT service delivery life cycle performance model. It is represented in the performance measurement dashboard using output and outcomes metrics and measures.

[6]*Applications management services* (*AMS*): The primary results achieved from the applications management functional area of the IT service delivery life cycle performance model. It is represented in the performance measurement dashboard using output and outcomes metrics and measures.

[7]*Technology operations services* (*TOS*): The primary results achieved from the technology operations functional area of the IT service delivery life cycle performance model. It is represented in the performance measurement dashboard using output and outcomes metrics and measures.

[8]*Outsourcing + innovations = transformation*: The transformational performance leadership strategy for the six functional areas of the IT service delivery life cycle performance model that promotes "client-driven" outsourcing using innovative processes and technologies.

[9]*Performance management standards* (*PMSD*): The results area of the integrated performance management knowledge areas that establish standards for measuring and managing results based on the elements of quality/quantity, efficiency/effectiveness, accountability, and rewards/recognition, described in the performance management plan.

[10]*Integrated performance management plan*: An integrated document that describes who, when, and how the results of IT management and delivery services will be measured, managed, delivered, and improved. It consists of the performance measurement plan, performance improvement plan, and various performance management plans for each of the IT functions areas, within the IT service delivery life cycle performance model.

[11]*Performance results criteria*: The criteria used to measure and manage the results of the IT management and delivery services for each of the IT functional areas.

[12]*Performance measurement system* (*PMS*): The results area of the integrated performance management knowledge areas that establish the system for measuring the results of IT services based on the elements of input resource measures, output/outcomes measures, processes (analytics), tools (dashboard), performance metrics, and performance indicators.

[13]*Integrated performance measurement plan*: An integrated document that describes who, when, and how the results of IT management and delivery services will be monitored, measured, and managed. It is a subset of the performance management plan.

[14]*Performance management repository system* (*PMRS*): An automated system that is used to access, manipulate, integrate, and update performance repository. The results area that store, retrieve, and make transparent the results of IT services documented in the integrated performance measurement dashboard and various performance repositories.

[15]*Performance improvement management* (*PIM*): The results area of the integrated performance management knowledge areas that analyzes performances and improves results of IT services based on the elements of organizational excellence (people/culture, process, technology and

financials, feedback/reviews, and KRAs). PIM is a method of analyzing performance problems and setting up systems to ensure good performance.

[16]*Performance change management* (*PCM*): The results area of the integrated performance management knowledge areas that focuses on transformational change of IT services based on the elements of 4Ps (people/culture, politics, process, and performance), as well as maintaining change strategy sustainability.

[17]*Human resource performance management* (*HRPM*): The results area of the integrated performance management knowledge areas that focuses on human resource performances of IT services based on the elements of staff performance plan and staff performance measures.

[18]*Financial performance management* (*FPM*): The results area of the integrated performance management knowledge areas that focuses on financial performances of IT services based on the elements of financial performance plan and financial performance measures (RBB).

[19]*Results-based budgeting* (*RBB*): An approach to financial management that focuses on achieving results that align with strategic and operational goals. A broad financial management strategy aimed at changing the way organizations manage financials by aligning financial budget with the achievement of results as the central orientation.

[20]*Activity-based budgeting*: An approach to financial management that aligns with financial activity coding structures with no alignment to strategic and operational goals. Traditional financial management strategy aimed at aligning financial budget with predefined activity codes, using an activity-based coding structure.

[21]*Elements and killers of IT budget*: An approach to assessing IT budget using the financial elements of people (management overhead), process (heavy layered structures), and technology complexities (hardware, software, facilities), using results-based budgeting.

[22]*Financial performance management system* (*FPMS*): An automated system that is used to access, manipulate, integrate, and update financial performance repository. It integrates with various subsystems such as financial performance forecasting system and financial performance tracking system , results-based budgeting , and various financial performance repositories.

[23]*PMO repository* (*PMIR and PMIS*): A database containing performance deliverables, reports, and plans that PMIR and PMIS uses as the database.

[24]*PMO management plan*: A document that describes who, when, and how PMO processes will be deployed.

4.7 Questions to Think About: Management Perspectives

1. Think about how your organization measures, manages, monitors, delivers, and improves IT performance results/outputs/outcomes. How does your organization manage, measure, and control the results of IT services? What are the key rationales in determining the value of an integrated and incremental approach to IT performance management? What are the major results areas of performance management? How do these results areas relate to your performance environment? What is the perception of senior management on the need for consistent, standard, and integrated performance management results/outputs/outcomes and processes to guide the delivery of IT services results?
2. Think about how your organization applies performance management processes. What are the 10 results areas of performance management? What are the integrated performance

management IT results areas? How do these results areas relate to your performance management processes?

3. Think about how your organization manages and measures IT services from the perspectives of efficiency, effectiveness, quality, and accountability. How is accountability and transparency defined? What are the components of the performance RBS? How are operational results measured? What are the core performance management measures? How do the core IT performance management measures discussed in this chapter relate to your organization approach?
4. Think about how your organization reports performance results? What are the four major results criteria of the performance measurement dashboard? How does your organization communicate performance status? How does your organization manage staff utilization for IT services? How does your organization manage and control improvements and changes to the results of IT service? How does your organization administer IT financials? What are the performance management results areas? How do the performance management results area discussed in this book relate to your organization performance management approaches?
5. Think about how your organization deploys performance measurement methodologies, templates, training, etc., to performance measurement teams? What are your management perspectives of the value of PMO? What are consultants' views of the PMO? How does personal greed for power, politics, and personal financial interests affect the PMO office? What are the major responsibilities or process components of the PMO? How do these responsibilities or process components relate to those of your PMO staff?
6. Think about how your organization manages the results of IT services? What are your management perspectives on results-based versus procedural-based methodologies? What are the components of a SMART methodology versus DUMB methodology? How does your methodology support different development approaches? How does the performance management methodology or process discussed in this book relate to your approach to managing the delivery of IT services?

4.8 Chapter Testing Questions

1. Which one of the integrated IT performance measurement dashboard measures is used to measure IT services performance?
   a. Employee, customer, operations, and financials measures
   b. Input, process, output measures
   c. Operational processes measures
2. Executives shall use the integrated IT performance measurement dashboard to
   a. Understand the performance scope.
   b. Make sound objective decisions on IT performance.
   c. Determine performance results trends and analytics.
3. Who is the appropriate person accountable for delivering performance measurement results for performance initiatives?
   a. Performance delivery manager
   b. Project manager
   c. Performance measurement specialist
4. The results area for performance management model MUST include
   a. Process, purpose, strategic directives, accountabilities
   b. Strategic management, performance management, IT operational management
   c. Output/outcome, process flows, performance measures

5. Performance management results areas do *not* include
   a. Goals, strategic framework, policy framework
   b. Performance governance, transformational change, strategic directives
   c. Strategic directives, value-based performance measurement, policy framework
6. At one stage of a performance measurement effort, you decided to use the IT performance governance structure to understand the areas of governance. What would you *most* likely examine?
   a. Process, culture, structure
   b. Are we doing the right things? Right way? Getting benefits? How well?
   c. Transformational change, sustainability, performance culture
7. What are the major outputs of IT performance governance structure?
   a. Structure, culture, processes
   b. People, process, technology, financials
   c. People, politics, process, performance
8. Which one of the following results areas is *best* input for the performance dashboard?
   a. IT strategic framework
   b. IT performance governance structure
   c. IT strategic directives
9. Which one of the following is *most* effective in assessing the value of performance measurement programs, initiatives, and organizational areas to executives?
   a. Performance culture, process improvement, RBB, technology enablement, RBM
   b. ROI, RBB, RBM, organizational alignment, VBPM
   c. Business case, VBPM, earned value, performance culture, governance

Recommended Readings

Performance Management

Aguinis, H., *Performance Management*. New York: Pearson Education, 2012.

Bainey, K.R., *Integrated IT Project Management, A Model-Centric Approach*. Boston, MA: Artech House, 2004.

Batshalom, B., *Green Source, The Magazine of Sustainable Design*. Boston, MA: Sustainable Performance Institute, 2011.

Corkins, G., *Performance Management, Integrating Strategy, Execution, Methodologies, Risk, and Analytics*. Hoboken, NJ: John Wiley & Sons Inc., 2009.

De Waal, A., *Strategic Performance Management: A Managerial and Behavioral Approach*. New York: Palgrave Macmillan, 2013.

Demartini, C., *Performance Management Systems: Design, Diagnosis and Use*. Berlin, Germany: Springer, 2013.

Hall, D., *Corporate Governance: Ensuring Propriety for Performance: A Contemporary themes in Strategic People Management*. New York: Palgrave Macmillan, 2013.

Kaplan, R.S. and Norton, D.P., *The Balanced Scorecard: Translating Strategy into Action*. Boston, MA: Harvard Business School Publishing, 1996.

KPI Institute, *The KPI Compendium:20,000 Key Performance Indicators used in Practice*. Melbourne, Victoria, Australia: KPI Institute, 2013.

Marr, B., *Strategic Performance Management, Leveraging and Measuring Your Intangible Value Driver*. Burlington, MA: Elsevier Ltd., 2006.

Spitzer, D.R., *Transforming Performance Measurement, Rethinking the Way We Measure and Drive Organizational Success*. New York: AMACOM, 2007.

Chapter 5

Information Technology Operational Management Model

5.1 Information Technology Operational Management

The component of information technology (IT) operational management is to ensure that IT services are effectively measured, managed, delivered, reported, and improved, using a results-based performance accountability framework. It consists of the following results areas:

- Financial accountability
- Human resource (HR) accountability
- Operational process accountability
- Project management accountability
- Applications management accountability
- Technology operations accountability

Figure 5.1 is a graphical representation of the modeling concept that is used to demonstrate the structure and relationships of the processing components for IT operational management, from a performance management perspective.

The intent of this chapter is *not* to provide detailed outcomes and processes on the implementation of IT operational management or similar IT operational management services. There are many excellent books on IT operational management outcomes, processes, concepts, theory, and applicability, some of which are mentioned in the "Recommended Readings" section provided at the end of this chapter. The main objective of this chapter is to provide an overview of the contents (what), purpose (why), accountabilities (who is accountable for what), and results (what, how, why) of IT operational management and to demonstrate how it fits within the context of the overall integrated IT performance management framework. The "accountability" section

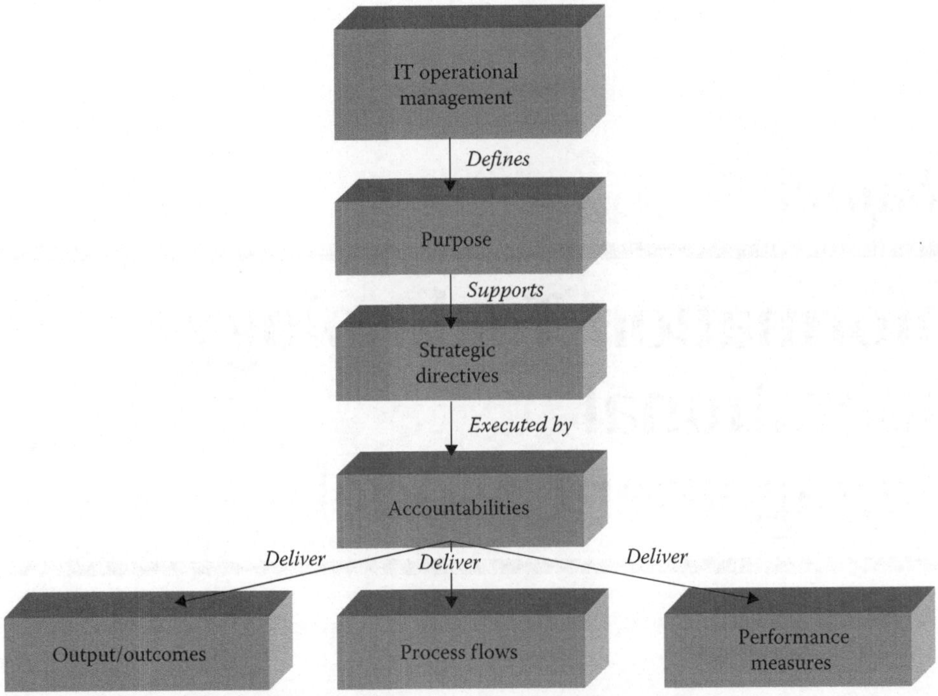

Figure 5.1 Information technology operational management model.

provides results-based accountability for the executive performance manager, performance delivery manager, and performance measurement team—performance measurement manager and performance specialists. The results sections for each of the IT operational management results areas provide the outputs/outcomes (what), process flow (how), and performance measures (why) to support the measurement, management, delivery, improvement, and integration of the IT operational management results areas. The performance measures from the performance measurement dashboard mainly show staff input metrics for demonstration purposes. In reality, the dashboard contains many combinations of results for input, process, and output/outcomes measures.

The materials presented in these following sections are organized to support the structure represented in Figure 5.1. The contents will provide the readers with a logical and consistent flow of information to enable them to gain a better understanding and appreciation for the integrated nature of IT performance management, as presented in this book. IT performance managers should measure success based on financial, HR, process, projects, applications, and technology accountability, to optimize resource utilizations and to enable organizational excellence.

> The first rule of any technology used in a business is that automation applied to an efficient operation will magnify the efficiency. The second is that automation applied to an inefficient operation will magnify the inefficiency.
>
> **Bill Gates**

5.2 Financial Accountability

Executives shall use the *financial accountability framework*[1] as the basis for ensuring the commitment that an individual, team, or organization assumes for the delivery of financial results/output/outcomes and accountabilities. This commitment includes

- Answering—providing an explanation or justification—for delivery of the financial results/output/outcomes and accountabilities
- Measuring and reporting on the performance results
- Demonstrating and ensuring accountability for the transparency, credibility, integrity, and reliability of the financial results

Many organizations overinvest in IT because they don't have a clear understanding and expectations as to the intended outcomes and results. Financial performance accountability is a measured financial commitment that delivers transparent, credible, accurate, and reliable *capital and operating costs*.[2] It formed the basis for sound financial management, improved organizational performance, and optimized financial utilizations. Decisions regarding IT investments must be results based, driven from the IT budget plan and the integrated IT performance measurement dashboard, as well as an understanding of the components of IT *capital and operating costs*. IT should not only measure success based on revenue and profits generated but also by means of reducing expense or cost inefficiencies, to measure financial performance results.

The major *outputs* of financial accountability include

- Capital costs (business projects)—To improve financial accountability by committing to managing, *measuring*, delivering, and improving *capital costs* for *IT business projects* by optimizing budget allocations, actual expenses, and forecasted expenses.
- Capital costs (IT infrastructure projects)—To improve financial accountability by committing to managing, *measuring*, delivering, and improving *capital costs* for *IT infrastructure projects* by optimizing budget allocations, actual expenses, and forecasted expenses.
- Operating costs (technology services)—To improve financial accountability by committing to managing, *measuring*, delivering, and improving *operating costs* for *IT technology upgrades*, *IT licensing agreements*, and *IT operating agreements* by optimizing budget allocations, actual expenses, and forecasted expenses.
- Operating costs (operations services)—To improve financial accountability by committing to managing, *measuring*, delivering, and improving *operating costs* for *outsourced IT applications management services* (*AMS*), *outsourced IT technology operations services* (*TOS*), and *in-house IT staff* by optimizing budget allocations, actual expenses, and forecasted expenses.

As a team we ask ourselves, how do we measure accountability.

Dennis Welch

Financial accountability is the same as educational accountability.

Randy Daniels

5.2.1 Purpose

The purpose of this results area is to demonstrate and ensure accountability for the transparency, credibility, integrity, and reliability of the financial results, using a *results-based financial accountability framework— results-based budgeting (RBB)*.[3] This RBB framework will form the baseline to measure and monitor the financial results of the delivered IT services for each of the IT functional areas, within the context of the financial performance measurement areas. The performance steering committee shall have approval accountabilities for both the capital and operating budget to ensure financial accountability. This committee will also have accountability with the performance measurement managers, for the financial performance using the financial measurement areas defined in the performance management plan and the integrated IT performance measurement dashboard.

5.2.2 Strategic Directive

- IT capital and operating costs will be reviewed by the performance steering committee on a monthly basis, using a *financial accountability framework* that describes *RBB*. The *RBB capital framework*[4] specifies planned value (IT budget), actual costs (YTD), earned value, forecasted costs, variances, % complete, and progress indicator for business and IT infrastructure projects. The *RBB operating framework*[5] also specifies planned value (IT budget), actual costs (YTD), earned value, forecasted costs, variances, % complete, and progress indicator for technology and operations services to include outsourcing/consultant, staff costs, and IT operating costs.
- The performance steering committee will provide performance approval accountabilities for the transparency, sustainability, and results-based delivery of the *financial accountability framework*, represented in the performance measurement dashboard as the finance measurement area.
- All changes to the *financial accountability framework* must be approved by the performance steering committee. The performance delivery manager will document and present all changes to the performance steering committee for approval.
- The performance steering committee will meet, at a minimum, on a monthly basis to review the performance indicators, trends, and analytics for *financial accountability framework*, represented in the performance measurement dashboard as *finance* output and outcomes and *finance performance metrics*.[6] If the overall progress of this output is *red* or *yellow*, more frequent meetings may be required for financial accountability improvements.

5.2.3 Accountabilities

5.2.3.1 Executive Performance Manager

This person is accountable for the *approval* of the results.

- Executive support and approval for the performance, *context and contents* of IT financial accountability (capital and operating costs), and areas of improvements
- Executive support and approval for the *progress results* on IT financial accountability areas to ensure integration with IT budget plan, alignment to IT strategic directives, and understanding the benefits and linkages with desired outcomes

- Executive support and approval for *financial performance trend results* in the integrated IT performance measurement dashboard to understand the following: (a) "How we are doing?" (b) "Are we doing/measuring the right things?" (c) "Are we getting the right results?" (d) "Are we getting the value?"
- Executive support and approval for *stakeholders' survey satisfaction results* on strategic and operational performance to understand the value of IT financial accountability and to improve service delivery
- Executive support and approval for *improvements results* on IT financial accountability and increased understanding of benefits and intended outcomes within IT operational management framework by recommending areas of improvements for customer, employee, financial, and operational performance measures and results
- Executive support and approval for *performance measures* and *benchmarking results* during IT financial reporting to performance steering committee, with direct accountability to performance management executive

5.2.3.2 Performance Delivery Manager

This person is accountable for the *management* of the results.

- Manage and define the performance, *context and contents* of IT financial accountability (capital and operating costs), and areas of improvements.
- Measure *progress results* on IT financial accountability areas to ensure integration with IT budget plan, alignment to IT strategic directives, and understanding the benefits and linkages with desired outcomes.
- Monitor and analyze *financial performance trend results* in the integrated IT performance measurement dashboard to understand the following: (a) "How we are doing?" (b) "Are we doing/measuring the right things?" (c) "Are we getting the right results?" (d) "Are we getting the value?"
- Deliver *stakeholders' survey satisfaction results* on strategic and operational performance to understand the value of IT financial accountability and to improve service delivery.
- Improve on *IT financial accountability results* and increased understanding of benefits and intended outcomes of IT operational management framework by recommending areas of *improvements* for *financial* performance measures and results.
- Report on *performance measures* and *benchmarking results* during IT financial reporting to performance steering committee, with direct accountability to performance management executive.

5.2.3.3 Performance Measurement Team

This team is accountable for the *delivery* of performance results.

- Provide performance, *context and contents* of IT financial accountability (capital and operating costs), and areas of improvements.
- Provide *progress results* on IT financial accountability areas to ensure integration with IT budget plan, alignment to IT strategic directives, and understanding the benefits and linkages with desired outcomes.

- Provide *financial performance trend results* in the integrated IT performance measurement dashboard to understand the following: (a) "How we are doing?" (b) "Are we doing/measuring the right things?" (c) "Are we getting the right results?" (d) "Are we getting the value?"
- Provide *stakeholders' survey satisfaction results* on strategic and operational performance to understand the value of IT financial accountability and to improve service delivery.
- Provide *improvements results* on IT financial accountability and increased understanding of benefits and intended outcomes of IT operational management framework by recommending areas of improvements for financial performance measures and results.
- Provide report on *performance measures and benchmarking results* during IT financial reporting to performance delivery manager and performance steering committee.

5.2.4 Results: Financial Accountability

Accountabilities discussed earlier are brief because they are intended to serve as a reference for *who is accountable* for *what* during the delivery of IT financial services within the six functional areas of the IT service delivery life cycle (SDLC) . Results are now introduced to highlight the outputs of this IT financial accountability results area and associated outcomes (what), process flow (how), and performance measures (why). It is intended to serve as a reference based on the English language interrogatives: Who *is accountable for what, how, and why.* The outputs/outcomes, process flow, and performance measures, based on real-world practical implementation, will serve as excellent references for practicing performance managers during measurement, delivery, and reporting of IT financial accountability outputs and outcomes. The outputs/outcomes highlight the key results on IT finance accountability that performance managers measure and report during the management and delivery of IT financials. The process flows, based on real-world practical implementations, are graphical representation of the inputs, process, outputs, and relationships. The IT financial accountability performance model shows the foundation representation to effectively communicate the integrated components of IT financials to strategic, IT operational, and performance management staff. The performance measures from the integrated IT performance measurement dashboard show "IT finance" measures for the six functional areas. Appendices A through F provide further details. Performance metrics, indicators, progress, trends, and analytics for financial analysis formed the basis for evidence-based decision making to enable improved organizational excellence.

5.2.4.1 Outputs/Outcomes: Financial Accountability

The outputs and outcomes of the financial accountability are given in Table 5.1.

5.2.4.2 Process Flows: Financial Accountability

The process flows of the financial accountability are shown in Figure 5.2.

5.2.4.3 Performance Model: Financial Accountability

The performance model of the financial accountability is shown in Table 5.2.

Table 5.1 Financial Accountability Output/Outcomes

Results Area	*Output*	*Outcome*
IT financial accountability	Commitment • RBB • Transparency • Reliability • Integrity, credibility • IT financial results	• Optimized utilization of IT financial resources • Improved RBB • Increased value of financial performance measurement dashboard-analytics
	Capital costs—business projects	• Improved results—IT financial products/services produced for business projects • Improved RBB for business projects
	Capital costs—IT infrastructure projects • Data center (hardware, software, network, facilities)	• Improved results—IT financial products/services produced for IT infrastructure projects • Improved RBB for IT infrastructure projects
	Operating costs technology services • IT asset upgrades • IT asset licenses • IT operating agreements	• Improved results—IT financial products/services supported for technology operating services • Improved RBB for IT operating services
	Operating costs operational services • Outsourcing • In-house Staff	• Improved results—IT financial products/services supported for operational services • Improved RBB for IT operating services
	IT financial accountability framework	• Increased accountability and transparency of IT financial resources • Increased transformation to RBB performance measurement culture

IT financial accountability performance model: guiding principles

- Results (outputs/outcomes) delivered in the company or organization IT SDLC guidelines, within the six IT functional areas, as defined in the integrated IT performance management dashboard are as follows:
  - Executive governance/leadership services (ELS) include executive leadership and oversight for operational/strategic directives, financials, customers, and employee results.
  - Planning and administration services (PAS) include management, administration, and delivery for operational/strategic plans, financials, customers, and employee results.
  - Enterprise architecture services (EAS) include management and delivery for IT infrastructure projects and contracts, financials, customers, and employee results.

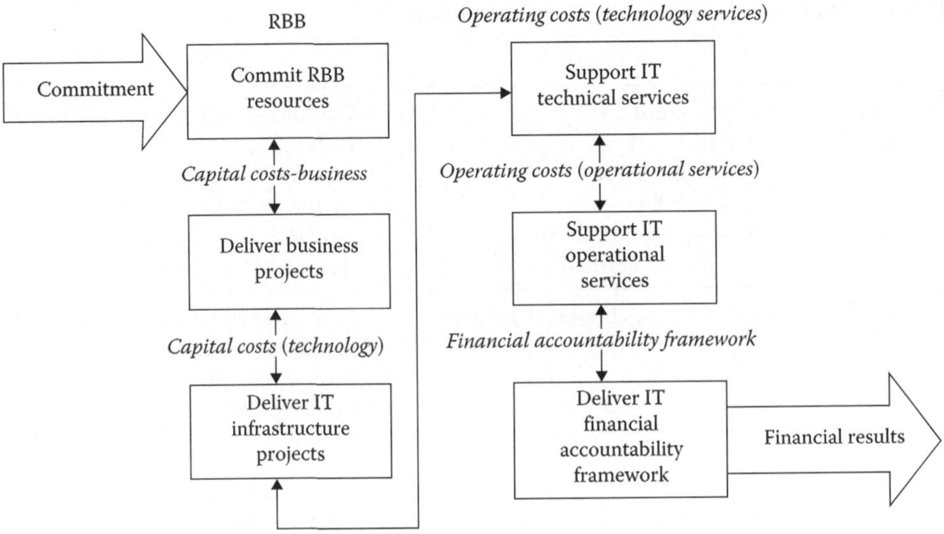

Figure 5.2 Financial accountability process flow.

Table 5.2 Financial Accountability Performance Model

IT Service Delivery Functional Areas	*% IT Budget Capital Costs—Business Projects*	*% IT Budget Capital Costs—Infrastructure Projects*	*% IT Budget Operating Costs—Technical Services*	*% IT Budget Operating Costs—Operational Services*	*IT SDLC Guidelines*
Executive governance—ELS	1%	1%	1%	1%	4%
Planning and administration services—PAS	1%	1%	1%	1%	4%
Enterprise architecture services—EAS	2%	10%	2%	2%	16%
Project portfolio management—PPM	30%	2%	0%	0%	32%
Applications management services—AMS	2%	1%	4%	15%	22%
Technology operational services—TOS	1%	2%	4%	15%	22%
PM % Guidelines	**37%**	**17%**	**12%**	**34%**	**100%**

  - Project portfolio management (PPM) includes management and delivery for business project and contracts, financials, customers, and employee results.
  - AMS include management and delivery for AMS outsourced contracts, financials, customers, and employee results.
  - TOS include management and delivery for TOS outsourced contracts, financials, customers, and employee results.
- According to standard IT performance management guidelines, in an organization with at least Capability Maturity Model Integration (CMMI) level 2 for IT cultural maturity
  - 37% of IT Budget should be invested on IT Capital Costs for business project delivery.
  - 17% of IT budget should be invested on IT capital costs for IT infrastructure project delivery.
  - 12% of IT budget should be expensed on IT operating costs for IT technical support services.
  - 34% of IT budget should be expensed on IT operating costs for IT operational support services.
- According to the company's IT SDLC performance guidelines
  - 4% of IT budget should be utilized by the ELS functional area.
  - 4% of IT budget should be utilized by the PAS functional area.
  - 16% of IT budget should be utilized by the EAS functional area.
  - 32% of IT budget should be utilized by the PPM functional area.
  - 22% of IT budget should be utilized by the AMS functional area.
  - 22% of IT budget should be utilized by the TOS functional area.
- RBB guidelines for IT services defined in the company's IT budget planning guidelines formed the basis for IT budget distribution or allocation within each of the six IT functional areas.

5.2.4.4 Performance Measures: Financial Accountability

The performance measures of the financial accountability are shown in Figure 5.3.

5.3 Human Resource Accountability

Executives shall use the *HR accountability framework*[7] as the basis for ensuring the commitment that an individual, team, or organization assumes for the delivery of human capital resource/output/outcomes and accountabilities. This commitment includes

- Answering—providing an explanation or justification—for delivery of human capital resource/output/outcomes and accountabilities
- Measuring and reporting on HR performance results
- Demonstrating and ensuring accountability for engaged, motivated to learn and improve, accountable for results, mutual trust, ethical, and credible HR

Performance management improves compliance, sustainability, accountability, and transparency. These functions are critically important to business progress in good economic times and essential to survival of business in tough economic times. HR performance accountability is a measured commitment among stakeholders, customers (IT service providers, vendors), and employees that delivers engaged, committed, credible, trustworthy, and ethical human capital resources, documented in the *IT resource plan*.[8] It formed the basis for sound people management, improved organizational performance, and optimized HR utilizations. Decisions regarding HR capital investments must be evidence based, driven from the IT performance management plan, strategic directives, and the integrated IT performance management dashboard.

The major *outputs* of HR accountability include

- Outsourced services—To improve HR accountability by committing to managing, *measuring,* delivering, and improving *outsourced services* for *AMS operating services, TOS operating services,* and *special business program* by optimizing HR resource utilization (current and planned), using results-based management.

IT EXECUTIVE LEADERSHIP (ELS)

FINANCIAL	Start Date	End Date	Status	% Complete	Indicator
IT Capital Costs	4/1/2011	3/31/2012	In-Progress	30%	Y
IT Operational Costs	4/1/2011	3/31/2012	In-Progress	30%	Y
IT Outsourced/Consulting Costs	4/1/2011	9/30/2011	In-Progress	80%	G
IT Staff Costs	10/1/2011	3/31/2012	Not-Started	0%	
Major Business Projects Costs	4/1/2011	6/30/2011	Complete	100%	Black
Major Technology Infrastructure Project Costs	4/1/2011	6/30/2011	Complete	100%	Black
FINANCIAL Summary	4/1/2011	3/31/2012	In-Progress	57%	G

Performance Metrics
% IT staff managing IT Capital Costs; # Improvements completed
% IT staff managing IT Operational Costs Mgnt; # Improvements completed
% IT staff managing IT Outsourced Costs Mgnt; # Improvements completed
% IT staff managing IT Staff Costs Mgnt; # Improvements completed
% IT staff managing IT Business Projects Costs Mgnt; # Improvements completed
% IT staff managing IT Technology Costs Mgnt; # Improvements completed

IT PLANNING & ADMINISTRATION SERVICES (PAS)

FINANCIAL	Start Date	End Date	Status	% Complete	Indicator
IT Planning Costs	4/1/2011	3/31/2012	In-Progress	30%	Y
IT Administration Costs	4/1/2011	3/31/2012	In-Progress	30%	Y
FINANCIAL Summary	4/1/2011	3/31/2012	In-Progress	30%	Y

Performance Metrics
% IT staff managing IT Capital Costs; # Improvements completed
% IT staff managing IT Operational Costs Mgnt; # Improvements completed

IT ENTERPRISE ARCHITECTURE SERVICES (EAS)

FINANCIAL	Start Date	End Date	Status	% Complete	Indicator
IT Infrastructure Project Costs	4/1/2011	3/31/2012	In-Progress	35%	Y
IT Enterprise Architecture Costs	4/1/2011	3/31/2012	In-Progress	25%	Y
FINANCIAL Summary	4/1/2011	3/31/2012	In-Progress	30%	Y

Performance Metrics
% IT staff managing IT Infrastructure Project Costs; # Improvements completed
% IT staff managing IT Enterprise Architecture Costs; # Improvements completed

(a)

Figure 5.3 (a and b) Financial accountability performance measures. *(Continued)*

IT PROJECT PORTFOLIO MANAGEMENT (PPM)

FINANCIAL	Start Date	End Date	Status	% Complete	Indicator
IT Business Project Costs	4/1/2011	3/31/2012	In-Progress	35%	Y
IT PPM Costs	4/1/2011	3/31/2012	In-Progress	25%	Y
FINANCIAL Summary	4/1/2011	3/31/2012	In-Progress	30%	Y

Performance Metrics
% IT staff managing Business Project Costs; # Improvements completed
% IT staff managing IT PPM Costs; # Improvements completed

IT APPLICATIONS MANAGEMENT SERVICES (AMS)

FINANCIAL	Start Date	End Date	Status	% Complete	Indicator
IT AMS Innovative Initiative Costs-Capital	4/1/2011	12/31/2011	In-Progress	50%	G
IT AMS Operating Costs	4/1/2011	3/31/2012	In-Progress	15%	R
FINANCIAL Summary	4/1/2011	3/31/2012	In-Progress	33%	Y

Performance Metrics
% IT staff managing AMS Capital Costs; # Improvements completed
% IT staff managing AMS Operating Costs; # Improvements completed

IT OPERATIONS SERVICES (TOS)

FINANCIAL	Start Date	End Date	Status	% Complete	Indicator
IT TOS Innovative Initiative Costs-Capital	4/1/2011	12/31/2011	In-Progress	50%	G
IT TOS Operating Costs	4/1/2011	3/31/2012	In-Progress	15%	R
FINANCIAL Summary	4/1/2011	3/31/2012	In-Progress	33%	Y

Performance Metrics
% IT staff managing TOS Capital Costs; # Improvements completed
% IT staff managing TOS Operating Costs; # Improvements completed

(b)

Figure 5.3 (*Continued*) (a and b) Financial accountability performance measures.

- Contracted services (business projects)—To improve HR accountability by committing to managing, *measuring,* delivering, and improving *contracted services* for *business projects* by optimizing HR resource utilization (current and planned), using results-based management.
- Contracted services (technology projects)—To improve HR accountability by committing to managing, *measuring,* delivering, and improving *contracted services* for *IT infrastructure programs/projects* by optimizing HR resource utilization (current and planned), using results-based management.
- In-house services—To improve HR accountability by committing to managing, *measuring,* delivering, and improving *in-house services* for *IT ELS, IT PAS,* and *IT EAS* by optimizing HR resource utilization (current and planned), using results-based management.

Accountability is a glue that ties Commitment to Results.

Beachbody Challenge

Accountability is not only what we do, but what we do not do, for what we are accountable.

Moliere

5.3.1 Purpose

The purpose of this results area is to demonstrate and ensure accountability from stakeholders, customers (IT service providers, vendors), and employees to deliver engaged, committed, credible, trustworthy, and ethical human capital resources, as documented in the *IT HR plan*,[8] using *HR results-based management and accountability framework* (*HR-RBM*).[9] This HR-RBM framework will form the baseline to monitor and measure the HR performance of the delivered IT services for each of the IT functional areas, for customers and employees' performance measurement areas. The performance steering committee will have approval accountabilities for the *outsourced, contracted,* and *in-house*[10] services to ensure HR accountability. This committee will also have accountability with the performance measurement managers, for the HR performance using customer and employee measurement areas, defined in the performance management plan and the integrated IT performance measurement dashboard.

5.3.2 Strategic Directives

- IT HR resource plan for *outsourced, contracted,* and *in-house*[10] labor utilizations will be reviewed by the performance steering committee on a monthly basis, using the *HR accountability framework* that describes HR-RBM. The *HR Results-Based Management framework* specifies planned resources, IT resource plan (full time employee), actual resource utilizations, competencies, competencies gap, % complete, and progress indicator for customer and employee performance measurement areas.
- The performance steering committee will provide performance approval accountabilities for the competencies, commitment, conformance, sustainability, and results-based delivery of the *HR accountability framework*, represented in the performance measurement dashboard as customer and employee measurement areas.
- All changes to the *HR accountability framework* must be approved by the performance steering committee. The performance delivery manager will document and present all changes to the performance steering committee for approval.
- The performance steering committee will meet, at a minimum, on a monthly basis to review the performance indicators, trends, and analytics for *HR accountability framework*, represented in the performance measurement dashboard as customer and employee output and outcomes *and customer and employee performance metrics*.[11] If the overall progress of the output is *red* or *yellow*, more frequent meetings may be required for HR improvements.

5.3.3 Accountabilities

5.3.3.1 Executive Performance Manager

This person is accountable for the *approval* of the results.

- Executive support and approval for the performance; *context and contents* of IT HR accountability on *outsourced, contracted,* and *in-house* staff utilizations; and areas of improvements
- Executive support and approval for *progress results* of IT HR accountability areas to ensure integration with IT resource plan, alignment to IT strategic directives, and understanding the benefits and linkages with desired outcomes

- Executive support and approval for *HR performance trend results* in the integrated IT performance measurement dashboard to understand the following: (a) "How we are doing?" (b) "Are we doing/measuring the right things?" (c) "Are we getting the right results?" (d) "Are we getting the value?"
- Executive support and approval for *stakeholders' survey satisfaction results* on strategic and operational performance to understand the value of IT HR accountability and to improve service delivery
- Executive support and approval for *improvements results* on IT HR accountability and increase understanding of benefits and intended outcomes within the overall IT operational management framework by recommending areas of improvements for customer and employee measures and results
- Executive support and approval for *performance measures* and *benchmarking results* during IT HR reporting to performance steering committee, with direct accountability to performance management executive

5.3.3.2 Performance Delivery Manager

This person is accountable for the *managemen*t of the results.

- Manage and define the performance; *context and contents* of IT HR accountability on o*utsourced, contracted,* and *in-house* staff utilizations; and areas of improvements.
- Monitor *progress results* of IT HR accountability areas to ensure integration with IT resource plan, alignment to IT strategic directives, and understanding the benefits and linkages with desired outcomes.
- Measure and analyze *HR performance trend results* in the integrated IT performance measurement dashboard to understand the following: (a) "How we are doing?" (b) "Are we doing/measuring the right things?" (c) "Are we getting the right results?" (d) "Are we getting the value?"
- Deliver and evaluate *stakeholders' survey satisfaction results* on strategic and operational performance to understand the value of IT HR accountability and to improve service delivery.
- Improve *IT HR accountability results* and increase understanding of benefits and intended outcomes of IT operational management framework by recommending areas of *improvements* for customer and employee measures and results.
- Report on *performance measures and benchmarking results* during IT HR reporting to performance delivery manager and performance steering committee.

5.3.3.3 Performance Measurement Team

This team is accountable for the *delivery* of performance results.

- Provide the performance; *context and contents* of IT HR accountability for o*utsourced, contracted,* and *in-house* staff utilizations; and areas of improvements.
- Provide *progress results* of IT HR accountability areas to ensure integration with IT resource plan, alignment to IT strategic directives, and understanding the benefits and linkages with desired outcomes.

- Provide *HR performance trend results* in the integrated IT performance measurement dashboard to understand the following: (a) "How we are doing?" (b) "Are we doing/measuring the right things?" (c) "Are we getting the right results?" (d) "Are we getting the value?"
- Provide *stakeholders' survey satisfaction results* on strategic and operation performance to understand the value of IT HR accountability and to improve service delivery.
- Provide *improvement results on IT HR accountability* and increase understanding of benefits and intended outcomes of the IT operational framework by recommending areas of improvements for customer and employee performance measures and results.
- Provide report on *performance measures and benchmarking results* to performance steering committee and with direct accountability to performance management executive.

5.3.4 Results: Human Resource Accountability

Accountabilities discussed earlier are brief because they are intended to serve as a reference for *who is accountable* for *what* during the delivery of IT HR services within the six functional areas of the IT SDLC . Results are now introduced to highlight the outputs of this HR (customer and employee) accountability results area and associated outcomes (what), process flow (how), and performance measures (why). It is intended to serve as a reference based on the English language interrogatives: Who *is accountable for what, how, and why.* The outputs/outcomes, process flow, and performance measures, based on real-world practical implementation, will serve as excellent references for practicing performance managers during the measurement, delivery, and reporting of HR accountability outputs and outcomes. The outputs/outcomes highlight the key results for HR accountability that performance managers measure and report during the management and delivery of human capital resource utilizations. The process flows, based on real-world practical implementations, are graphical representations of the inputs, process, outputs, and relationships. The HR accountability model shows the foundation representation to effectively communicate the integrated components of HR staff utilizations to strategic, IT operational, and performance management staff.

The performance measures from the integrated IT performance measurement dashboard show staff outputs for IT executive leadership functional area using customer and employee performance measures. Appendices A through F provide further details. Performance metrics, indicators, progress, trends, and analytics for staffing analysis formed the basis for evidence-based decision making to enable improved organizational excellence.

5.3.4.1 Outputs/Outcomes: Human Resource Accountability

The outputs and outcomes of the human resource accountability are given in Table 5.3.

5.3.4.2 Process Flows: Human Resource Accountability

The process flows of the human resource accountability are shown in Figure 5.4.

5.3.4.3 Performance Model: Human Resource Accountability

The performance model of the human resource accountability is shown in Figure 5.5.

5.3.4.4 Performance Measures: Human Resource Accountability

The performance measures of the operational process accountability are shown in Figure 5.6.

Table 5.3 Human Resource Accountability Output/Outcomes

Results Area	*Output*	*Outcome*
IT human resource (HR) accountability	Commitment • RBM • Competency • Commitment • Conformance • Ethics and integrity • IT HR results	• Optimized utilization of IT HR resources • Improved HR-RBM • Increased value of customer and employee performance measurement dashboard-analytics
	Outsourced services • Special business projects • AMS and TOS	• Improved results—IT HR results delivered for outsourced services • Improved HR-RBM for outsourced services
	Contracted services—IT infrastructure projects • Data center (hardware, software, network, facilities)	• Improved results—IT HR results delivered for contract services—IT infrastructure projects • Improved HR-RBM for contract services—IT infrastructure projects
	Contracted services • Business projects	• Improved results—IT HR results delivered for contract services-business projects • Improved HR-RBM for contract services—business projects
	In-house services • Governance (ELS) • Planning and admin (PAS) • IT architecture (EAS)	• Improved results—IT HR results delivered for in-house services • Improved HR-RBM for in-house services
	IT HR accountability framework	• Increased accountability and transparency of IT HR-RBM • Increased transformation to HR-RBM performance measurement culture

5.4 Operational Process Accountability

Executives shall use the *operational process accountability framework*[12] as the basis for ensuring the commitment that an individual, team, or organization assumes for the reengineering/streamlining of the operational processes (business and IT), output/outcomes, and accountabilities. This commitment includes

- Answering—providing an explanation or justification—for streamlining/reengineering the operational processes; functional management (FM), service delivery (SD), service excellence (SE), and relationship management (RM)
- Measuring and reporting on the operational process performance results

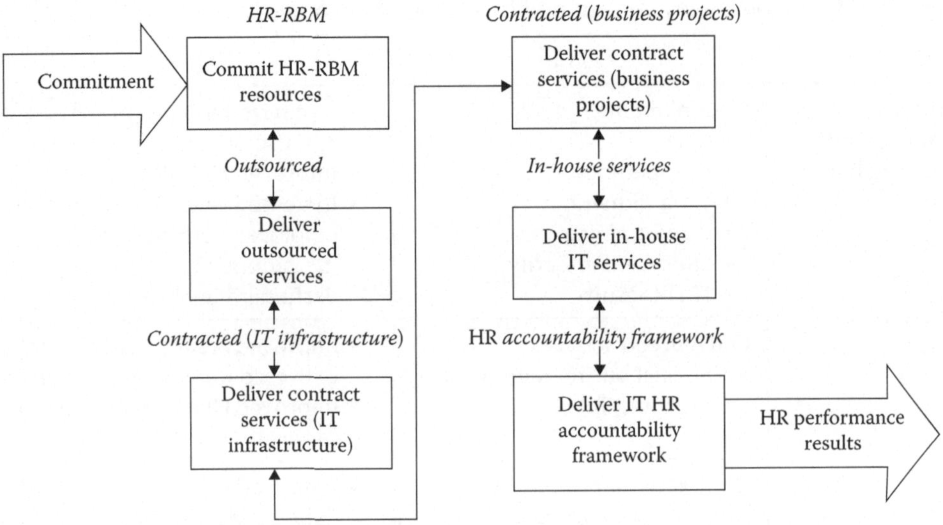

Figure 5.4 Human resource accountability process flow.

- Demonstrating and ensuring accountability for business and IT process reengineering, accountable for streamlined results, business value, efficiencies, and organizational excellence

Operational process performance accountability is a measured commitment between business and IT management and business and IT delivery, documented in the *business/IT* process *reengineering plan.*[13] It formed the basis for simple and streamlined processes management, improved organizational performance, and optimized process utilizations. Decisions regarding operational process accountability must be results-based, driven from IT strategic plan, IT operating plan, and the integrated IT performance management dashboard.

The major *outputs* of operational process accountability include

- Business process (management)—To improve operational process accountability by committing to managing, *measuring,* delivering, and improving *business process management* services for functional and relationship management measurement areas by reengineering the management of business process, using results-based management.
- IT process (management)—To improve operational process accountability by committing to managing, *measuring,* delivering, and improving *IT process management* services for functional and relationship management measurement areas by reengineering the management of IT process, using results-based management.
- Business process (delivery)—To improve operational process accountability by committing to managing, *measuring,* delivering, and improving *business process delivery* services for service delivery and service excellence measurement areas by reengineering the delivery of business process, using results-based management.
- IT process (delivery)—To improve operational process accountability by committing to managing, *measuring,* delivering, and improving *IT process delivery* services for service delivery and service excellence measurement areas by reengineering the delivery of IT process, using results-based management.

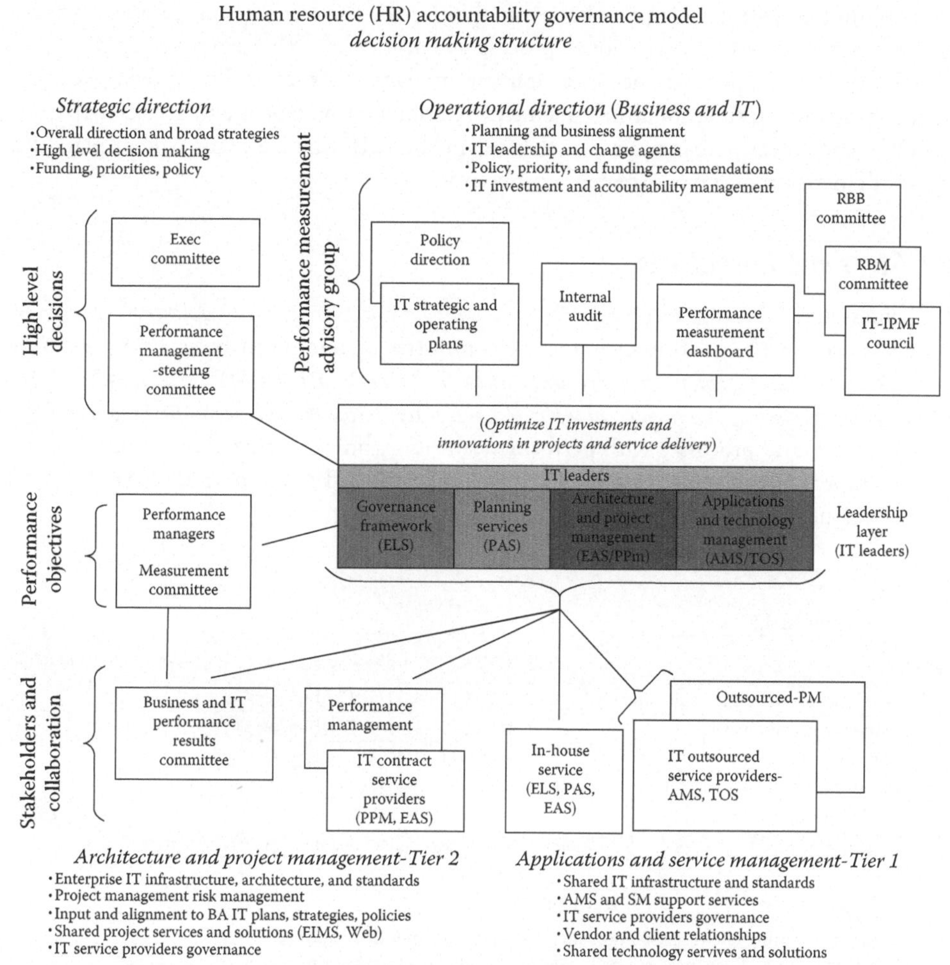

Figure 5.5 Human resource accountability performance model.

> Accountability is the obligation of an individual or organization to account for its activities, accept responsibilities for them, and to disclose the results in a transparent manner.
>
> **Wendy Myers**

5.4.1 Purpose

The purpose of this results area is to demonstrate and ensure accountability from the business and IT staff to deliver simple and streamlined processes, improved organizational performance, and optimized process utilizations, as documented in the *business/IT reengineering plan*,[13] using *reengineering results-based management and accountability framework* (*RE-RBM*).[14] This RE-RBM framework will form the baseline to monitor and measure the performance results of the delivered IT services for each of the six IT functional areas, on functional management, relationship management, service delivery, and service excellence performance measurement areas. The performance steering committee will have approval accountabilities for the *business and IT management and delivery processes*[15] to ensure operational process accountability. This committee will also have accountability with the performance measurement managers, for streamlining/reengineering performance results using functional management, relationship management, service delivery, and service excellence measurement areas, as defined in the performance management plan and the integrated IT performance measurement dashboard.

5.4.2 Strategic Directives

- Business and IT reengineering for *business and IT management and delivery*[15] processes will be reviewed by the performance steering committee on a monthly basis, using *reengineering results-based management and accountability framework (RE-RBM)*[14] that describes *results-based reengineering management (RE-RBM)*. The *results-based reengineering management* aligns goals and processes with performance results, process utilizations, process inefficiencies, improvement areas, % complete, and progress indicator for FM, RM, SD, and SE performance measurement areas.

IT executive leadership

Customer	Start date	End date	Status	% Complete	Indicator
Client relationships/satisfaction surveys	4/1/2011	3/31/2012	In progress	30%	Y
IT business council meetings	4/1/2011	3/31/2012	In progress	30%	Y
Vendor relationships/satisfaction surveys	4/1/2011	9/30/2011	In progress	80%	G
IT outsourced providers performance measures	10/1/2011	3/31/2012	Not-started	0%	
IT Benchmarking surveys/results	4/1/2011	6/30/2011	Complete	100%	Black
Customer summary	4/1/2011	3/31/2012	In progress	48%	G

Performance Metrics

% IT staff performing client satisfaction surveys; # Improvements completed
% IT staff attending IT business council meetings; # Improvements completed
% IT staff performing vendor satisfaction surveys; # Improvements completed
% IT staff performing IT vendors performance measures; # Improvements completed
% IT staff performing IT benchmarking; # Improvements completed

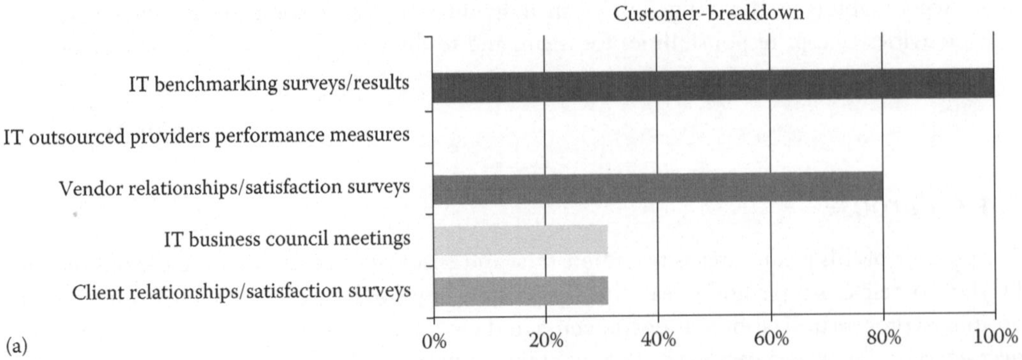

(a)

Figure 5.6 (a and b) Human resource accountability performance measures. *(Continued)*

Employee	Start date	End date	Status	% Complete	Indicator
IT progress reporting	4/1/2011	6/30/2011	Complete	100%	Black
IT staff performance contract	4/1/2011	3/31/2012	In progress	35%	Y
Staff learning/growth	4/1/2011	3/31/2012	In progress	35%	Y
Staff meeting/communications	4/1/2011	3/31/2012	In progress	35%	Y
Staff retention/retraining/reward reporting	4/1/2011	7/31/2011	In progress	100%	Black
Employee summary	4/1/2011	3/31/2012	In progress	61%	G
IT Executive leadership summary	4/1/2011	3/31/2012	In progress	55%	G

Performance metrics

% IT staff performing progress reporting; # Improvements completed
% IT staff performing staff performance contract; # Improvements completed
% IT staff performing learning/growth sessions; # Improvements completed
% IT staff performing staff communications/meetings; # Improvements completed
% IT staff performing staff retraining, etc.; # Improvements completed

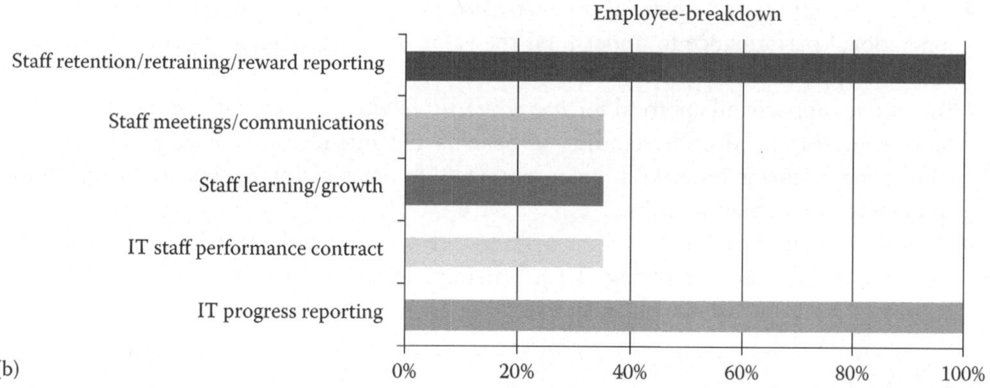

(b)

Figure 5.6 (*Continued*) (a and b) Human resource accountability performance measures.

- The performance steering committee will provide performance approval accountabilities for the competencies, commitment, conformance, sustainability, and results-based delivery of the *reengineering results-based management and accountability framework* (*RE-RBM*), represented in the performance measurement dashboard as FM, RM, SD, and SE performance measurement areas.
- All changes to the *reengineering results-based management and accountability framework* must be approved by the performance steering committee. The performance delivery manager will document and present all changes to the performance steering committee for approval.
- The performance steering committee will meet, at a minimum, on a monthly basis to review the performance indicators, trends, and analytics for *reengineering results-based management and accountability framework*, represented in the performance measurement dashboard as FM, RM, SD, and SE output/outcomes and *performance metrics*. If the overall progress of the output is *red* or *yellow*, more frequent meetings may be required for reengineering operational processes.

5.4.3 Accountabilities

5.4.3.1 Executive Performance Manager

This person is accountable for the *approval* of the results.

- Executive support and approval for the performance, *context and contents* of operational process accountability on business and IT process reengineering, and areas of improvements
- Executive support and approval for *progress results* of operational process accountability to ensure integration with IT reengineering plan, alignment to IT strategic directives, and understanding the benefits and linkages with desired outcomes
- Executive support and approval for operational process *performance trend results* in the integrated IT performance measurement dashboard to understand the following: (a) "How we are doing?" (b) "Are we doing/measuring the right things?" (c) "Are we getting the right results?" (d) "Are we getting the value?"
- Executive support and approval for *stakeholders' survey satisfaction results* on strategic and operational performance to understand the value of IT operational process accountability and to improve service delivery
- Executive support and approval for *improvements results* on IT operational process accountability and increased understanding of benefits and intended outcomes within IT operational management framework by recommending areas of improvements for operational processes measures and results
- Executive support and approval for *performance measures* and *benchmarking results* on IT operational processes, reporting to performance steering committee, with direct accountability to performance management executive

5.4.3.2 Performance Delivery Manager

This person is accountable for the *management* of the results.

- Manage and define the performance, *context and contents* of IT operational process accountability for reengineering of *business and IT management and delivery processes*, and areas of improvements.
- Measure *progress results* of *IT operational process accountability areas* to ensure integration with business/IT process reengineering plan, alignment to IT strategic directives, and understanding the benefits and linkages with desired outcomes.
- Monitor and analyze *IT operational process performance trends* in the integrated IT performance measurement dashboard to understand the following: (a) "How we are doing?" (b) "Are we doing/measuring the right things?" (c) "Are we getting the right results?" (d) "Are we getting the value?"
- Deliver and evaluate *stakeholders' survey satisfaction results* on strategic and operational performance to understand the value of IT operational process accountability and to improve service delivery.
- Improve on *IT operational process accountability results* and increase understanding of benefits and intended outcomes within IT operational process framework by recommending areas of improvements for IT operational process performance measures and results.

- Report on *performance measures* and *benchmarking results* for IT operational processes, reporting to performance steering committee, with direct accountability to performance management executive.

5.4.3.3 Performance Measurement Team

This team is accountable for the *delivery* of performance results.

- Provide the performance, *context and contents* of IT operational process accountability for reengineering *business and IT management and delivery processes*, and areas of improvements.
- Provide *IT operational process accountability results* to ensure integration with business/IT process reengineering plan, alignment to IT strategic directives, and understanding the benefits and linkages with desired outcomes.
- Provide *IT operational process performance trends* in the integrated IT performance measurement dashboard to understand the following: (a) "How we are doing?" (b) "Are we doing/measuring the right things?" (c) "Are we getting the right results?" (d) "Are we getting the value?"
- Provide *stakeholders' survey satisfaction results* for strategic and operational performance to understand the value of IT operational process accountability and to improve service delivery.
- Provide *improvement results* on IT operational process accountability and increase understanding of benefits and intended outcomes within IT operational management framework by recommending areas of improvements for operational performance measures and results.
- Provide report on IT operational process accountability *performance measures and benchmarking results*, reporting to performance steering committee, with direct accountability to performance delivery manager.

5.4.4 Results: Operational Process Accountability

Accountabilities discussed earlier are brief because they are intended to serve as a reference for *who is accountable* for *what* during the management and delivery of IT operational processes within the six functional areas of the IT service delivery life cycle. Results are now introduced to highlight the outputs of this operational process (FM, RM, SD, SE) accountability results and associated outcomes (what), process flow (how), and performance measures (why). It is intended to serve as a reference based on the English language interrogatives: Who *is accountable for what, how, and why.* The outputs/outcomes, process flow, and performance measures, based on real-world practical implementation, will serve as excellent references for practicing performance managers during measurement, delivery, and reporting of operational process accountability outputs and outcomes. The outputs/outcomes highlight the key results for IT operational process accountability that performance managers measure and report during the delivery of the business/IT process reengineering program. The process flows, based on real-world practical implementations, are a graphical representation of the inputs, process, outputs, and relationships. The operational process accountability model shows the foundation representation to effectively communicate the integrated components of process reengineering alignment to strategic, IT operational, and performance management processes. The performance measures from the integrated IT performance measurement dashboard show operational process outputs for IT executive leadership using operational performance measures. Appendix A provides further details. Performance metrics, indicators, progress, trends, and analytics for operational process analysis formed the basis for evidence-based decision on process reengineering to enable improved organizational excellence.

5.4.4.1 Outputs/Outcomes: Operational Process Accountability

The outputs and outcomes of the operational process accountability are given in Table 5.4.

5.4.4.2 Process Flows: Operational Process Accountability

The process flows of the operational process accountability are shown in Figure 5.7.

5.4.4.3 Performance Model: Operational Process Accountability

The performance model of the operational process accountability is shown in Figure 5.8.

5.4.4.4 Performance Measures: Operational Process Accountability

The performance measures of the operational process accountability are shown in Figure 5.9.

5.5 Project Management Accountability

Executives shall use the *project management accountability framework*[16] as the basis for ensuring the commitment that an individual, team, or organization assumes for the delivery of business and IT infrastructure projects, output/outcomes, and accountabilities. This commitment includes

- Answering—providing an explanation or justification—for delivery of strategic and operational projects (business and IT infrastructure), using the performance results for PPM functional area, obtained from the IT performance measurement dashboard
- Measuring and reporting on the project management performance results
- Demonstrating and ensuring accountability for the credibility, integrity, and reliability of the performance results for business and IT infrastructure projects

Project management performance accountability is a measured commitment between strategic business and IT infrastructure projects and operational business and IT infrastructure projects, documented in the *PPM plan*.[17] It formed the basis for effective and efficient project management, improved organizational performance, and optimized project resource utilizations. Decisions regarding project management performance must be results based, driven from the IT strategic plan, IT operating plan, and the integrated IT performance management dashboard.

The major *outputs* of project management accountability include

- Business projects (strategic)—To improve project management accountability by committing to managing, *measuring*, delivering, and improving *strategic business project delivery* for *PPM* measurement areas, as defined in the IT performance measurement dashboard, using results-based management.

Table 5.4 Operational Process Accountability Output/Outcomes

Results Area	*Output*	*Outcome*
IT operational process accountability	Commitment • RE-RBM • Streamlined/simplified • Business value • Strategic alignment • Results-based • IT operational process results	• Optimized utilization of IT operational processes • Improved RE-RBM • Increased value of operational performance measurement dashboard-analytics
	Business process management • FM, RM	• Improved results—operational business process results delivered for management services • Improved RE-RBM for management of business processes
	IT process management • FM, RM	• Improved results—operational IT process results delivered for IT management services • Improved RE-RBM for management of IT processes
	Business process delivery • SD, SE	• Improved results—operational business process results delivered for delivery services • Improved RE-RBM for delivery of business processes
	IT process delivery • SD, SE	• Improved results—operational IT process results for IT delivery services • Improved RE-RBM for delivery of IT processes
	IT operational process accountability framework	• Increased accountability and transparency of IT RE-RBM • Increased transformation to RE-RBM performance measurement culture

- IT infrastructure projects (strategic)—To improve project management accountability by committing to managing, *measuring*, delivering, and improving *strategic IT infrastructure project* delivery for *PPM* measurement areas, as defined in the IT performance measurement dashboard, using results-based management.
- Business projects (operational)—To improve project management accountability by committing to managing, *measuring*, delivering, and improving *operational business project* delivery for PPM measurement areas, as defined in the IT performance measurement dashboard, using results-based management.

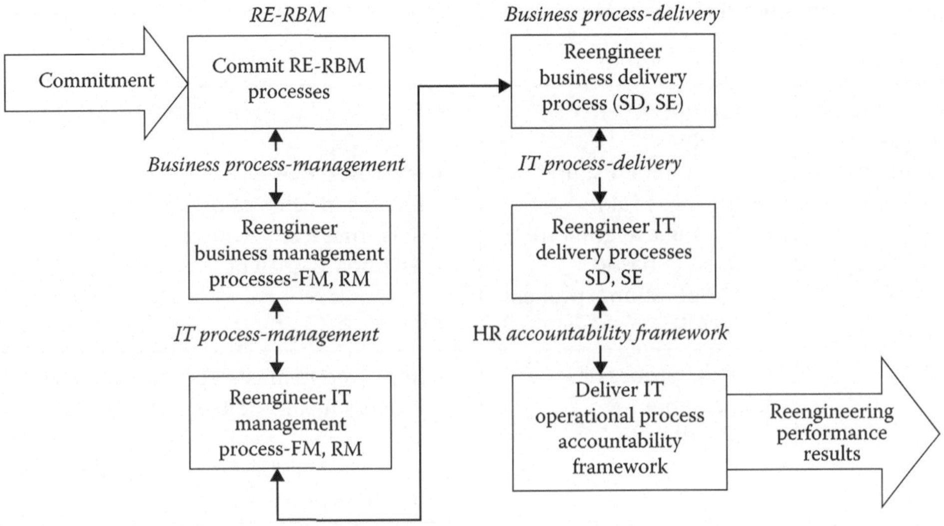

Figure 5.7 Operational process accountability process flow.

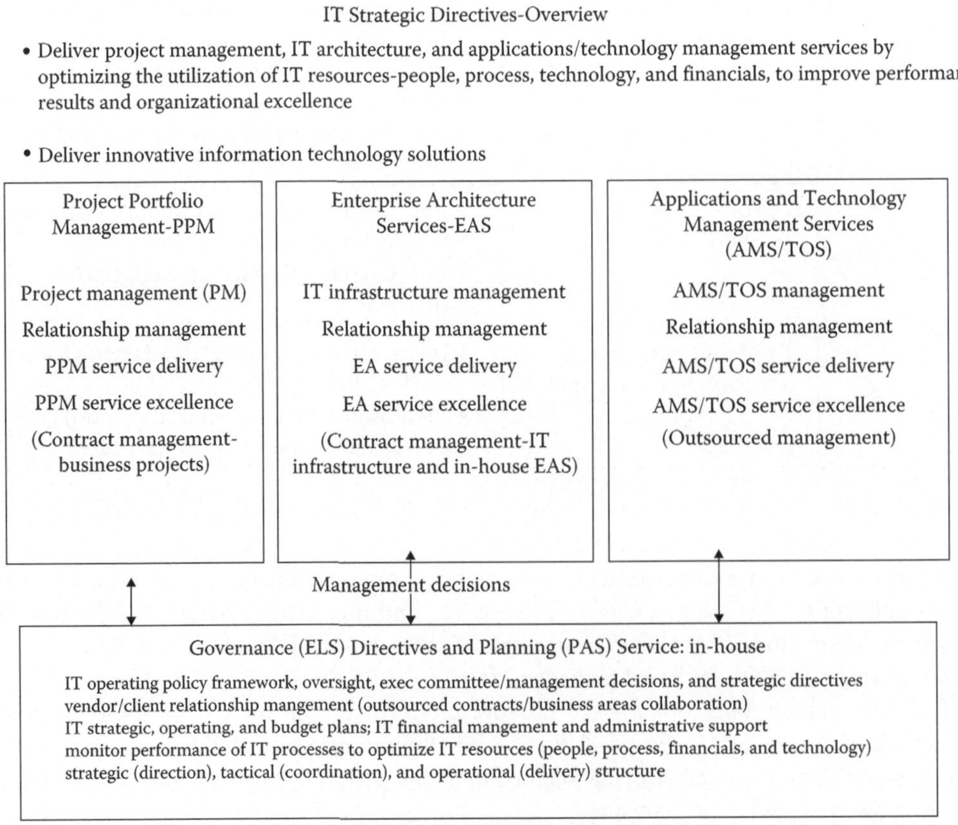

Figure 5.8 Operational process accountability performance model.

- IT infrastructure projects (operational)—To improve project management accountability by committing to managing, *measuring*, delivering, and improving *operational IT infrastructure project* delivery for PPM measurement areas, as defined in the IT performance measurement dashboard, using results-based management.

When a system becomes completely defined, some damn fool discovers something which either abolishes the system or expands it beyond recognition

Murphy's Law

5.5.1 Purpose

The purpose of this results area is to demonstrate and ensure accountability from business and IT staff to deliver *strategic and operational business and IT infrastructure projects.* This accountability result in simple and streamlined project management, improved organizational performance, and

IT EXECUTIVE LEADERSHIP

OPERATIONAL-FM	Start Date	End Date	Status	% Complete	Indicator
IT Governance Accountability Framework	4/1/2011	12/31/2011	In-Progress	60%	G
HR Performance Contract Alignment	4/1/2011	9/30/2011	In-Progress	80%	G
Executive Management (EM) Progress Status	4/1/2011	3/31/2012	In-Progress	40%	G
Executive Management Presentation/Approvals	4/1/2011	3/31/2012	In-Progress	60%	G
IT Policies and Procedures	4/1/2011	3/31/2012	In-Progress	60%	G
IT Operational Accountability Framework	4/1/2011	3/31/2012	In-Progress	40%	G
OPERATIONAL-FM Summary	4/1/2011	3/31/2012	In-Progress	57%	G

Performance Metrics

% IT staff performing IT Governance; # Improvements completed
% IT staff performing HR Alignment; # Improvements completed
% IT staff performing EM Communications; # Improvements completed
% IT staff performing EM Presentation; # Improvements completed
% IT staff performing IT Policies; # Improvements completed
% IT staff performing IT Operations; # Improvements completed

OPERATIONAL-RM	Start Date	End Date	Status	% Complete	Indicator
Executive Management Relations/Feedback	4/1/2011	3/31/2012	In-Progress	30%	Y
Business Areas Relations/Feedback	4/1/2011	3/31/2012	In-Progress	30%	Y
Vendors Relations/Feedback	4/1/2011	9/30/2011	In-Progress	80%	G
IT Outsourced Providers Relations/Feedback	10/1/2011	3/31/2012	Not-Started	0%	
Other Stakeholders Relations/Feedback	4/1/2011	6/30/2011	Complete	100%	Black
OPERATIONAL-RM Summary	4/1/2011	3/31/2012	In-Progress	48%	G

Performance Metrics

% IT staff performing IT Mgnt Policies; # Improvements completed
% IT staff performing IT Mgnt Procedures; # Improvements completed
% IT staff performing IT Business Council Accountability; # Improvements completed
% IT staff performing IT Compliance-Industry; # Improvements completed
% IT staff performing IT Benchmarking Metrics; # Improvements completed

(a)

Figure 5.9 (a and b) Operational process accountability performance measures. *(Continued)*

OPERATIONAL-SD	StartDate	End Date	Status	% Complete	Indicator
IT Contract Accountability Framework	4/1/2011	9/30/2011	In-Progress	80%	G
IT Consultants NDA	4/1/2011	9/30/2011	In-Progress	70%	Y
CIO Approvals-RFP	4/1/2011	3/31/2012	In-Progress	35%	Y
CIO Approvals-IT Infrastructure Impact	4/1/2011	9/30/2011	In-Progress	80%	G
IT Equipment Purchases Records	4/1/2011	12/31/2011	In-Progress	50%	G
CIO Approvals-Business Projects	4/1/2011	9/30/2011	In-Progress	90%	G
CIO Approvals-Technology Infrastructure Projects	4/1/2011	3/31/2012	Not-Started	40%	G
CIO Approvals-IT Equipment Expenditures	4/1/2011	3/31/2012	In-Progress	40%	G
CIO Approvals-IT Outsourced/Consulting Services	4/1/2011	8/31/2011	In-Progress	80%	R
CIO/CEO Approvals-Special Business Projects	4/1/2011	9/30/2011	In-Progress	80%	G
CIO/CEO Approvals-Special Technology Projects	4/1/2011	12/31/2011	In-Progress	50%	G
OPERATIONAL-SD Summary	4/1/2011	3/31/2012	In-Progress	63%	G

Performance Metrics
%IT staff delivering Contract Management; # Improvements completed
%IT staff delivering Consultants NDA; # Improvements completed
%IT staff delivering RFP Approvals; # Improvements completed
%IT staff delivering IT Infrastructure Impacts; # Improvements completed
%IT staff delivering IT Equipment Purchases; # Improvements completed
%IT staff delivering Business Projects Approvals; # Improvements completed
%IT staff delivering IT Infrastructure Project Approvals; # Improvements completed
%IT staff delivering IT Equipment Expenses Approvals; # Improvements completed
%IT staff delivering IT Contracting Approvals; # Improvements completed
%IT staff delivering Special Business Projects Approvals; # Improvements completed
%IT staff delivering Special Technology Projects Approvals; # Improvements completed

OPERATIONAL-SE	Start Date	End Date	Status	% Complete	Indicator
IT Management Policies Framework	4/1/2011	3/31/2012	In-Progress	30%	Y
IT Management Procedures	4/1/2011	3/31/2012	In-Progress	30%	Y
IT Business Council Accountability Framework	4/1/2011	9/30/2011	In-Progress	80%	G
IT Compliance - Industry Performance Measures	4/1/2011	3/31/2012	Not-Started	30%	Y
IT Benchmarking Metrics	4/1/2011	6/30/2011	Complete	100%	Black
OPERATIONAL-SE Summary	4/1/2011	3/31/2012	In-Progress	54%	G

Performance Metrics
% IT staff performing IT Mgnt Policies; # Improvements completed
% IT staff performing IT Mgnt Procedures; # Improvements completed
% IT staff performing IT Business Council Accountability; # Improvements completed
% IT staff performing IT Compliance-Industry; # Improvements completed
% IT staff performing IT Benchmarking Metrics; # Improvements completed

(b)

Figure 5.9 (*Continued*) (a and b) Operational process accountability performance measures.

optimized project management utilizations, as documented in the *PPM plan*,[17] using a *results-based project management and accountability framework* (*PM-RBM*).[18] This PM-RBM framework will form the baseline to monitor and measure the performance results for project delivery and to ensure that the output/outcomes and performance goals of PPM functional areas are effectively achieved. The performance steering committee will have approval accountabilities for the *strategic and operational business and IT infrastructure projects*[19] to ensure project management accountability. This committee will also have joint accountability with the performance measurement managers for the project management performance results using the PPM measurement areas defined in the performance management plan and the integrated IT performance measurement dashboard.

5.5.2 Strategic Directives

- Business and IT infrastructure projects for strategic and operational processes will be reviewed by the performance steering committee on a monthly basis, using the *project results-based management and accountability framework* (*PM-RBM*),[18] which describes results-based project management. *Results-based project management* aligns goals and processes with performance results, project resource utilizations, project management inefficiencies and improvement areas, % complete, and progress indicator for PPM performance measurement areas.
- The performance steering committee will provide performance approval accountabilities for the credibility, integrity, and reliability of the performance results for business and IT Infrastructure projects, using the PPM results area, as represented in the performance measurement dashboard as PPM performance measures.
- All changes to the *project results-based management and accountability framework* must be approved by the performance steering committee. The performance delivery manager will document and present all changes to the performance steering committee for approval.
- The performance steering committee will meet, at a minimum, on a monthly basis to review the performance indicators, trends, and analytics for project *results-based management and accountability framework*, represented in the performance measurement dashboard as PPM output/outcomes *and performance metrics*. If the overall progress of the output is *red* or *yellow*, more frequent meetings may be required for improvement to project performance results.

5.5.3 Accountabilities

5.5.3.1 Executive Performance Manager

This person is accountable for the *approval* of the results.

- Executive support and approval for the performance, *context and contents* of project management accountability on strategic business and IT infrastructure projects and operational business and IT infrastructure projects, and areas of improvements
- Executive support and approval for the *progress results* of project management accountability to ensure integration with PPM plan, alignment to IT strategic directives, and understanding the benefits and linkages with desired outcomes
- Executive support and approval for project management *performance trend results* in the integrated IT performance measurement dashboard to understand the following: (a) "How we are doing?" (b) "Are we doing/measuring the right things?" (c) "Are we getting the right results?" (d) "Are we getting the value?"
- Executive support and approval for *stakeholders' survey satisfaction results* for strategic and operational performance to understand the value of project management accountability and to improve service delivery
- Executive support and approval for *improvements results* to project management accountability and increased understanding of benefits and intended outcomes within IT operational management by recommending areas of improvements to PPM measures and results
- Executive support and approval for *performance measures and benchmarking results* on project management accountability, reporting to performance steering committee, with direct accountability to performance management executive

5.5.3.2 Performance Delivery Manager

This person is accountable for the *management* of the results.

- Manage and define the performance, *context and contents* of project management accountability for *strategic business and IT infrastructure projects and operational business and IT infrastructure projects*, and areas of improvements.
- Measure *progress results* of *project management accountability areas* to ensure integration with PPM Plan, alignment to IT strategic directives, and understanding the benefits and linkages with desired outcomes.
- Monitor and analyze *project management performance trends* in the integrated IT performance measurement dashboard to understand the following: (a) "How we are doing?" (b) "Are we doing/measuring the right things?" (c) "Are we getting the right results?" (d) "Are we getting the value?"
- Deliver and evaluate *stakeholders' survey satisfaction results* for strategic and operational performance to understand the value of project management accountability and to improve service delivery.
- Improve on *project management accountability results* and increase understanding of benefits and intended outcomes within IT operational management framework by recommending areas of improvements for PPM performance measures and results.
- Report on project management accountability for *performance measures and benchmarking results* to performance steering committee, with direct accountability to performance management executive.

5.5.3.3 Performance Measurement Team

This team is accountable for the *delivery* of performance results.

- Provide the performance, *context and contents* of project management accountability for strategic business and IT infrastructure projects and operational business and IT infrastructure projects, and areas of improvements.
- Provide *progress results* of project management accountability areas to ensure integration with PPM plan, alignment to IT strategic directives, and understanding the benefits and linkages with desired outcomes.
- Provide project management *performance trends* in the integrated IT performance measurement dashboard to understand the following: (a) "How we are doing?" (b) "Are we doing/measuring the right things?" (c) "Are we getting the right results?" (d) "Are we getting the value?"
- Provide stakeholders' survey satisfaction results for strategic and performance management to understand the value of project management accountability to improve service delivery through the use of stakeholders' satisfaction surveys.
- Provide *improvement results* on project management accountability and increase understanding of benefits and intended outcomes statement within the overall IT operational management framework by recommending areas of improvements for PPM performance measures and results.
- Provide report on project management accountability *performance measures and benchmarking results* to performance steering committee, with direct accountability to performance delivery manager.

5.5.4 Results: Project Management Accountability

Accountabilities discussed earlier are brief because they are intended to serve as a reference for *who is accountable* for *what* during the management and delivery of PPM within the six functional areas of the IT SDLC. Results are now introduced to highlight the outputs of project management accountability results and associated outcomes (what), process flow (how), and performance measures (why). It is intended to serve as a reference based on the English language interrogatives: Who *is accountable for what, how, and why.* The outputs/outcomes, process flow, and performance measures, based on real-world practical implementation, will serve as excellent references for practicing performance managers during measurement, delivery, and reporting of the project management accountability outputs and outcomes. The outputs/outcomes highlight the key results for project management accountability that the performance managers measure and report during the delivery of the business/IT infrastructure program. The process flows, based on real-world practical implementations, are a graphical representation of the inputs, process, outputs, and relationships. The project management accountability performance model shows the foundation representation to effectively communicate the integrated components of process reengineering alignment to strategic, IT operational, and performance management processes.

The performance measures from the integrated IT performance measurement dashboard show project management outputs for PPM functional areas using operational, financial, customer, and employee performance measures. Appendix D provides further details. Performance metrics, indicators, progress, trends, and analytics on project analysis formed the basis for evidence-based decision on project management to enable improved organizational excellence.

5.5.4.1 Outputs/Outcomes: Project Management Accountability

The outputs and outcomes of the project management accountability are given in Table 5.5.

5.5.4.2 Process Flows: Project Management Accountability

The process flows of the project management accountability are shown in Figure 5.10.

5.5.4.3 Performance Model: Project Management Accountability

The performance model of the project management accountability is shown in Figure 5.11.

5.5.4.4 Performance Measures: Project Management Accountability

The performance measures of the project management accountability are shown in Figure 5.12.

5.6 Applications Management Accountability

Executives shall use the *applications management accountability framework*[20] as the basis for ensuring the commitment that an individual, team, or organization assumes for the delivery of applications management outsourced services, output/outcomes, and accountabilities. This commitment includes

Table 5.5 Project Management Accountability Output/Outcomes

Results Area	*Output*	*Outcome*
Project management accountability	Commitment • PM-RBM • Credibility, integrity • Business value • Strategic alignment • Results-based • Project management accountability results	• Optimized utilization of PM resource • Improved PM-RBM • Increased value of PPM results area performance measurement dashboard-analytics
	Business projects strategic • PPM results area	• Improved results—business projects results delivered to support strategic processes • Improved PM-RBM for delivery of strategic business projects
	IT infrastructure projects strategic • PPM results area	• Improved results—IT infrastructure projects results delivered to support strategic processes • Improved PM-RBM for delivery of strategic IT infrastructure projects
	Business projects operational • PPM results area	• Improved results—business projects results delivered to support operating processes • Improved PM-RBM for delivery of operating business projects
	IT infrastructure projects operational • PPM results area	• Improved results—IT infrastructure projects results delivered to support operating processes • Improved PM-RBM for delivery of operating IT infrastructure projects
	Project management process accountability framework	• Increased accountability and transparency of PM-RBM • Increased transformation to PM-RBM performance measurement culture

- Answering—providing an explanation or justification—for delivery of applications management outsourced services, using the performance results for AMS functional area, obtained from the IT performance measurement dashboard
- Measuring and reporting on the AMS performance results
- Demonstrating and ensuring accountability for the credibility, integrity, and reliability of the performance results for AMS

Applications management performance accountability is a measured commitment that delivers outsourced services, performance measures, accountability reporting, and governance model for the effective and efficient delivery of AMS outsourced services, documented in the *AMS plan*.[21]

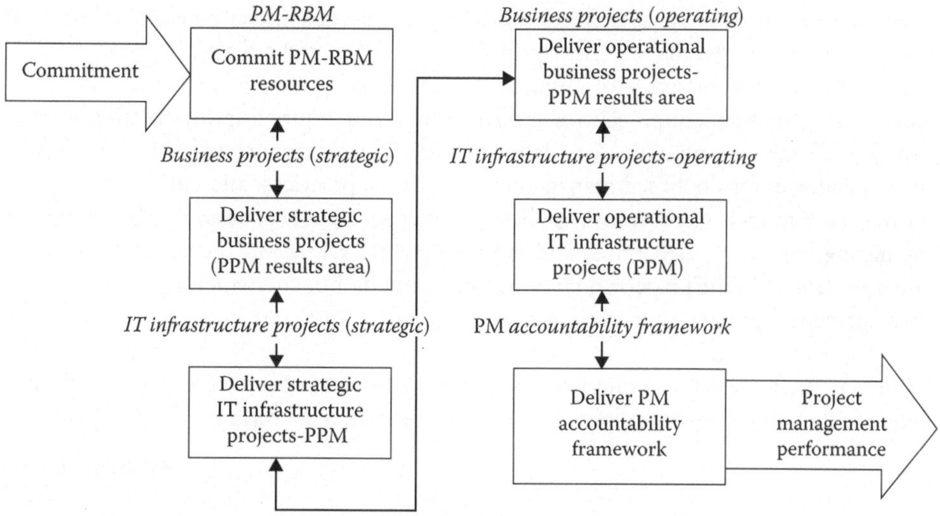

Figure 5.10 Project management accountability process flow.

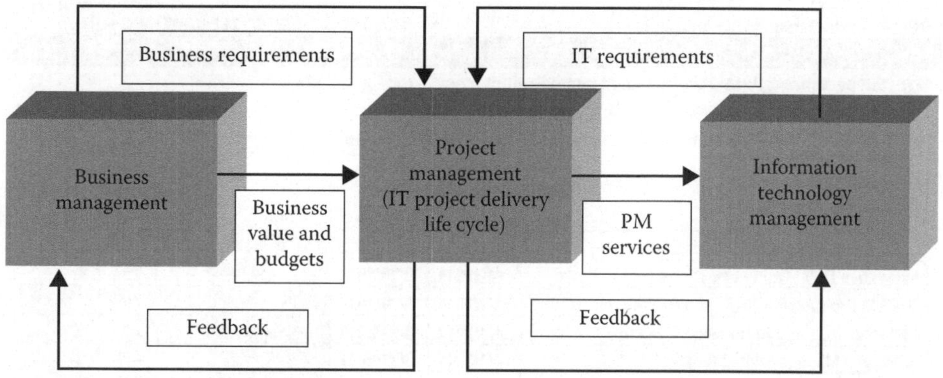

Figure 5.11 Project management accountability-performance model.

It formed the basis for effective and efficient AMS, improved organizational performance, and optimized AMS resource utilizations. Decisions regarding AMS accountability must be results based, driven from a results-based accountability management culture, IT strategic plan, IT operating plan, and the integrated IT performance management dashboard.

The major *outputs* of applications management accountability include

- Outsourced contracted services—To improve applications management accountability by committing to managing, *measuring*, delivering, and improving *AMS outsourced delivery*, using AMS measurement areas, as defined in the IT performance measurement dashboard, which endorses results-based management principles, practices, and culture.
- Performance measures—To improve applications management accountability by committing to managing, *measuring*, delivering, and improving *AMS performance measures*, using

AMS measurement areas, as defined in the IT performance measurement dashboard, which endorses results-based management principles, practices, and culture.

- Accountability reporting—To improve applications management accountability by committing to managing, *measuring*, delivering, and improving *accountability reporting*, using AMS measurement areas, as defined in the IT performance measurement dashboard, which endorses results-based management principles, practices, and culture.
- Governance model—To improve applications management accountability by committing to managing, *measuring*, delivering, and improving *AMS governance*, using AMS measurement areas, as defined in the IT performance measurement dashboard, which endorses results-based management principles, practices, and culture (Figure 5.13).

When a system becomes completely defined, some damn fool discovers something which either abolishes the system or expands it beyond recognition.

Murphy's Law

IT PROJECT PORTIFOLIO MANAGEMENT (PPM)

OPERATIONAL-FM	Start Date	End Date	Status	% Co
IT PPM Governance Framework	4/1/2011	12/31/2011	In-Progress	
IT PPM Innovative Technical Direction	4/1/2011	3/31/2012	In-Progress	
PPM Projects Outsourcing Framework	4/1/2011	9/30/2011	In-Progress	
OPERATIONAL-FM Summary	4/1/2011	3/31/2012	In-Progress	

% IT staff performing PPM Governance ; # Improvements completed
% IT staff performing PPM Innovations ; # Improvements completed
% IT staff performing PPM Outsourcing Strategies ; # Improvements completed

OPERATIONAL-SD	Start Date	End Date	Status	% Complete	Indicator
IT Business Projects Monitoring/Reporting	4/1/2011	3/31/2012	In-Progress	25%	Y
Innovative PMO Communications tools	4/1/2011	9/30/2011	In-Progress	75%	Y
IT PPM Productivity Tools and Processes	4/1/2011	9/30/2012	In-Progress	40%	G
PPM Systems and Regression Testing	4/1/2011	3/31/2012	In-Progress	40%	G
IT Project Management/Delivery	4/1/2011	3/31/2012	In-Progress	40%	G
IT Business Projects RFP/Contracts	4/1/2011	3/31/2012	In-Progress	40%	G
IT Business Projects Program/Projects Plan	4/1/2011	3/31/2012	In-Progress	40%	G
IT Business Project Architecture/Design	4/1/2011	3/31/2012	In-Progress	40%	G
IT PMO Support	4/1/2011	3/31/2012	In-Progress	40%	G
IT Business Project Requirements Specifications	4/1/2011	3/31/2012	In-Progress	40%	G
OPERATIONAL-SD Summary	4/1/2011	3/31/2012	In-Progress	42%	G

% IT staff delivering IT Business Projects Progress; # Improvements completed
% IT staff delivering PMO Tools ; # Improvements completed
% IT staff delivering IT productivity Processes ; # Improvements completed
% IT staff delivering System Testing; # Improvements completed
% IT staff delivering IT Project Management ; # Improvements completed
% IT staff delivering Business Projects RFPs; # Improvements completed
% IT staff delivering Business Projects Program/Project Plans ; # Improvements completed
% IT staff delivering Business Projects Architecture ; # Improvements completed
% IT PMO Support; # Improvements completed
% IT staff delivering Business Projects Specifications ; # Improvements completed

(a)

Figure 5.12 (a–d) Project management accountability performance measures. *(Continued)*

OPERATIONAL-SE	Start Date	End Date	Status	% Complete	Indicator
Business Projects Plan QA	4/1/2011	6/30/2011	In-Progress	75%	Past Due
IT Project Management Compliance/Approval	4/1/2011	7/31/2011	In-Progress	80%	Past Due
Business Projects Financial Measures	4/1/2011	9/30/2011	In-Progress	60%	R
PMO Compliance	4/1/2011	3/31/2012	In-Progress	35%	Y
Project Management Optimization	4/1/2011	3/31/2012	In-Progress	35%	Y
Business Projects Benchmarking Metrics	4/1/2011	9/30/2011	In-Progress	80%	G
OPERATIONAL-SE Summary	4/1/2011	3/31/2012	In-Progress	61%	G

% IT staff performing Business Projects Plan QA ; # Improvements completed
% IT staff performing PM Compliance; # Improvements completed
% IT staff performing Business Projects Financial Measures; # Improvements completed
% IT staff performing PMO Compliance ; # Improvements completed
% IT staff performing PM Optimization ; # Improvements completed
% IT staff performing Business Projects Benchmarking ; # Improvements completed

OPERATIONAL-RM	Start Date	End Date	Status	% Complete	Indicator
PPM Client Management Relations/Feedback	4/1/2011	3/31/2012	In-Progress	100%	Black
Vendors PPM Relations/Feedback	4/1/2011	3/31/2012	In-Progress	40%	G
IT Outsourced Providers PPM Relations/Feedback	4/1/2011	3/31/2012	In-Progress	25%	Y
OPERATIONAL-RM Summary	4/1/2011	3/31/2012	In-Progress	55%	G

% IT staff performing Client Feedback ; # Improvements completed
% IT staff performing Vendors Innovations ; # Improvements completed
% IT staff performing Service Providers Feedback ; # Improvements completed

(b)

CUSTOMER	Start Date	End Date	Status	% Complete	Indicator
PPM Client Relationships/Satisfaction Surveys	4/1/2011	3/31/2012	In-Progress	30%	Y
PPM Committee Meetings	4/1/2011	3/31/2012	In-Progress	30%	Y
PPM Vendors Relationships/Satisfaction Surveys	4/1/2011	9/30/2011	In-Progress	80%	G
PPM IT Outsourced Providers Surveys	10/1/2011	3/31/2012	Not-Started	0%	
PPM Benchmarking Surveys/Results	4/1/2011	6/30/2011	Complete	100%	Black
CUSTOMER Summary	4/1/2011	3/31/2012	In-Progress	48%	G

% IT staff performing Client Satisfaction Surveys; # Improvements completed
% IT staff attending PPM Committee Meetings; # Improvements completed
% IT staff performing Vendor Satisfaction Surveys; # Improvements completed
% IT staff performing IT Vendors Performance Measures; # Improvements completed
% IT staff performing PPM Benchmarking surveys; # Improvements completed

(c)

EMPLOYEE	Start Date	End Date	Status	% Complete	Indicator
PPM IT Progress Reporting	4/1/2011	6/30/2011	Complete	100%	Black
PPM IT Staff Performance Contract	4/1/2011	3/31/2012	In-Progress	35%	Y
PPM Staff Learning/Growth Reporting	4/1/2011	3/31/2012	In-Progress	35%	Y
PPM Staff Meetings/Communications	4/1/2011	3/31/2012	In-Progress	35%	Y
PPM Staff Retention/Retraining/Reward Reporting	4/1/2011	7/31/2011	In-Progress	100%	Black
EMPLOYEE Summary	4/1/2011	3/31/2012	In-Progress	61%	G
IT PROJECT PORTFOLIO SUMMARY	4/1/2011	3/31/2012	In-Progress	50%	G

% IT staff performing Progress Reporting ; # Improvements completed
% IT Staff performing Staff Performance Contract ; # Improvements completed
% IT staff performing Learning/Growth sessions; # Improvements completed
% IT staff performing staff communications/meetings ; # Improvements completed
% IT staff performing PPM Benchmarking/retention/retraining ; # Improvements completed

(d)

Figure 5.12 (*Continued*) (a–d) Project management accountability performance measures.

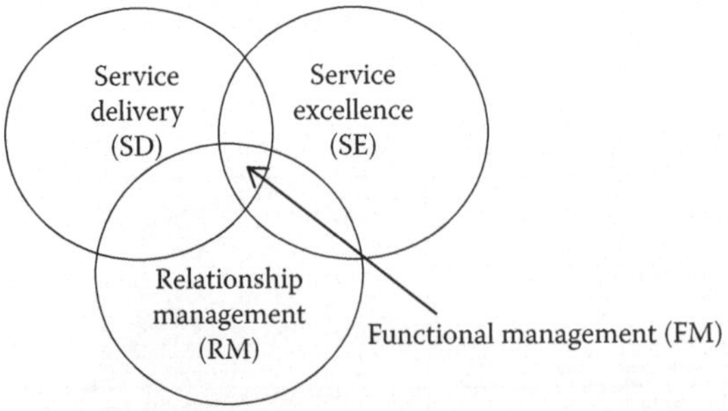

Figure 5.13 Applications management services measurement (operational).

5.6.1 Purpose

The purpose of this results area is to demonstrate and ensure accountability for delivery of *AMS*. This accountability will result in effective and efficient AMS management, improved organizational performance, and optimized AMS resource utilizations, documented in the *AMS plan*[21] using *applications results-based management and accountability framework* (*AM-RBM*).[22] This AM-RBM framework will form the baseline to monitor and measure the performance results for applications management and to ensure that the output/outcomes and performance goals of applications management functional areas are effectively achieved. The performance steering committee shall have approval accountabilities for the *outsourced AMS*[23] to ensure applications management accountability. This committee will have accountability with the performance measurement managers, for the applications management performance results using the AMS measurement areas, defined in the performance management plan and the integrated IT performance measurement dashboard.

5.6.2 Strategic Directives

- Applications management accountability for outsourced AMS will be reviewed by the performance steering committee on a monthly basis, using the applications *results-based management and accountability framework* (*AM-RBM*)[22] that describes results-based applications management. The *results-based applications management* aligns goals and processes with performance results, AMS resource utilizations, applications management inefficiencies and improvement areas, % complete, and progress indicator for AMS performance measurement areas.
- The performance steering committee will provide performance approval accountabilities for the credibility, integrity, and reliability of the performance results for applications management, using the AMS results area, as represented in the performance measurement dashboard as operational process, financial, customer, and employee performance measures.
- All changes to *applications results-based management and accountability framework* must be approved by the performance steering committee. The performance delivery manager will document and present all changes to the performance steering committee for approval.
- The performance steering committee will meet, at a minimum, on a monthly basis to review the performance indicators, trends, and analytics for *results-based applications management*, represented in the performance measurement dashboard as operational process, financial, customer, and employee output/outcomes and *performance metrics*. If the overall progress of the output is *red* or *yellow*, more frequent meetings may be required for improvement to applications management performance results.

5.6.3 Accountabilities

5.6.3.1 Executive Performance Manager

This person is accountable for the *approval* of the results.

- Executive support and approval for the performance, *context and contents* of applications management accountability for outsourced AMS, and areas of improvements
- Executive support and approval for *progress results* of applications management accountability to ensure integration with AMS plan, alignment to IT strategic directives, and understanding the benefits and linkages with desired outcomes
- Executive support and approval for applications management *performance trend results* in the integrated IT performance measurement dashboard to understand the following: (a) "How we are doing?" (b) "Are we doing/measuring the right things?" (c) "Are we getting the right results?" (d) "Are we getting the value?"
- Executive support and approval for *stakeholders' survey satisfaction results* for strategic and operational performance to understand the value of applications management accountability and to improve service delivery
- Executive support and approval for *improvements results* to applications management accountability and increased understanding of benefits and intended outcomes within IT operational management by recommending areas of improvements to AMS measures and results
- Executive support and approval for *performance measures and benchmarking results* on applications management accountability, reporting to performance steering committee, with direct accountability to performance management executive

5.6.3.2 Performance Delivery Manager

This person is accountable for the *management* of the results.

- Manage and define the performance, *context and contents* of applications management accountability for *outsourced AMS*, and areas of improvements.
- Measure *progress results* of *applications management accountability areas* to ensure integration with AMS plan, alignment to IT strategic directives, and understanding the benefits and linkages with desired outcomes.
- Monitor and analyze applications management *performance trends* in the integrated IT performance measurement dashboard to understand the following: (a) "How we are doing?" (b) "Are we doing/measuring the right things?" (c) "Are we getting the right results?" (d) "Are we getting the value?"
- Deliver and evaluate *stakeholders' survey satisfaction results* for strategic and operational performance to understand the value of applications management accountability and to improve service delivery.
- Improve *on applications management accountability results* and increased understanding of benefits and intended outcomes within IT operational management framework by recommending areas of improvements for AMS performance measures and results.
- Report on applications management accountability *performance measures and benchmarking results* to performance steering committee, with direct accountability to performance management executive.

5.6.3.3 Performance Measurement Team

This team is accountable for the *delivery* of performance results.

- Provide the performance, *context and contents* of applications management accountability for outsourced AMS, and areas of improvements.
- Provide *progress results* on applications management accountability areas to ensure integration with AMS plan, alignment to IT strategic directives, and understanding the benefits and linkages with desired outcomes.
- Provide applications management *performance trends* in the integrated IT performance measurement dashboard to understand the following: (a) "How we are doing?" (b) "Are we doing/measuring the right things?" (c) "Are we getting the right results?" (d) "Are we getting the value?"
- Provide *stakeholders' survey satisfaction results* for strategic and operational performance to understand the value of applications management accountability and to improve service delivery.
- Provide *improvement results* on accountability *improvement results* and increase understanding of benefits and intended outcomes within IT operational management framework by recommending areas of improvements for AMS performance measures and results.
- Provide report on applications management accountability *performance measures and benchmarking results* to performance steering committee, with direct accountability to performance delivery manager.

5.6.4 Results: Applications Management Accountability

Accountabilities discussed earlier are brief because they are intended to serve as a reference for *who is accountable* for *what* during the management and delivery of AMS within the six functional areas of the IT SDLC. Results are now introduced to highlight the outputs of applications management accountability results and associated outcomes (what), process flow (how), and performance measures (why). It is intended to serve as a reference based on the English language interrogatives: Who *is accountable for what, how, and why.* The outputs/outcomes, process flow, and performance measures, based on real-world practical implementation, will serve as excellent references for practicing performance managers during measurement, delivery, and reporting of the applications management accountability outputs and outcomes. The outputs/outcomes highlight the key results for applications management accountability that the performance managers measure and report during the delivery of the outsourced AMS contractual agreements. The process flows, based on real-world practical implementations, are graphical representations of the inputs, process, outputs, and relationships. The applications management accountability performance model shows the foundation representation to effectively communicate the integrated components of AMS alignment to strategic, IT operational, and performance management processes.

The performance measures from the integrated IT performance measurement dashboard show applications management outputs for AMS functional areas, using operational, finance, customer, and employee performance measures. Appendix E provides further details. Performance metrics, indicators, progress, trends, and analytics for AMS analysis formed the basis for evidence-based decision making to enable improved organizational excellence.

5.6.4.1 Outputs/Outcomes: Applications Management Accountability

The outputs and outcomes of the applications management accountability are given in Table 5.6.

5.6.4.2 Process Flows: Applications Management Accountability

The process flows of the applications management accountability are shown in Figure 5.14.

Table 5.6 Applications Management Accountability Output/Outcomes

Results Area	*Output*	*Outcome*
Applications management accountability	Commitment • AM-RBM • Credibility, integrity, reliability • Business value • Strategic alignment • Applications management accountability results	• Optimized utilization of AM resource • Improved AM-RBM • Increased value of AMS results area performance measurement dashboard-analytics
	Outsourced AMS • AMS results area	• Improved results—AMS results delivered to support outsourced contractual agreements • Improved AM-RBM for delivery of AMS output/outcomes
	Performance measures-(SD, OE, RM) • AMS results area	• Improved results—AMS performance measures for SD, OE, RM • Improved AM-RBM for delivery of AMS performance measures
	Accountability reporting-(SD, OE, RM) • AMS results area	• Improved results—AMS accountability reporting for SD, OE, RM • Improved AM-RBM for delivery of AMS accountability reporting
	AMS governance • AMS results area	• Improved results—AMS governance for oversight and strategy • Improved AM-RBM for delivery of AMS governance
	Applications management accountability framework	• Increased accountability and transparency of AM-RBM • Increased transformation to AM-RBM performance measurement culture

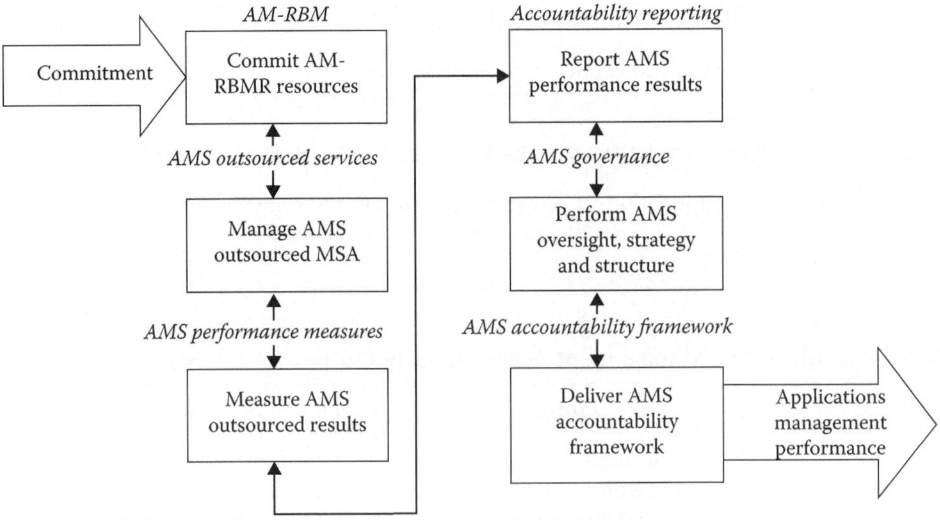

Figure 5.14 Applications management accountability process flow.

5.6.4.3 Performance Model: Applications Management Accountability

The performance model of the applications management accountability is shown in Figure 5.15.

5.6.4.4 Performance Measures: Applications Management Accountability

The performance measures of the applications management accountability are shown in Figure 5.16.

5.7 Technology Operations Accountability

Executives shall use the *technology operations accountability framework*[24] as the basis for ensuring the commitment that an individual, team, or organization assumes for the delivery of technology operations outsourced services, output/outcomes, and accountabilities. This commitment includes

- Answering—providing an explanation or justification—for delivery of technology operations outsourced services, using the performance results for TOS functional area, obtained from the IT performance measurement dashboard
- Measuring and reporting on the TOS performance results
- Demonstrating and ensuring accountability for the credibility, integrity, and reliability of the performance results for TOS

Technology operations performance accountability is a measured commitment that delivers outsourced services, performance measures, accountability reporting, and governance model for the effective and efficient delivery of TOS outsourced services, documented in the *TOS plan.*[25] It formed the basis for effective and efficient TOS, improved organizational performance, and optimized TOS resource utilizations. Decisions regarding TOS accountability must be results based,

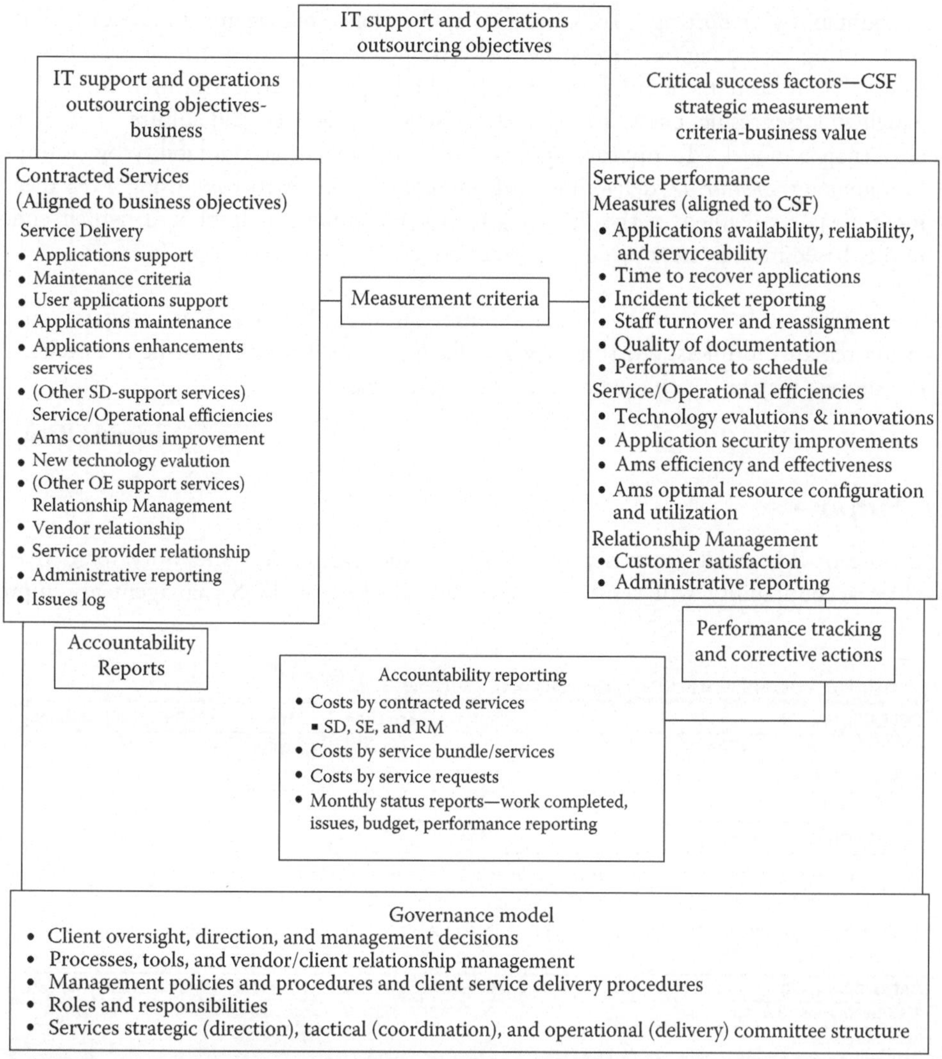

Figure 5.15 Applications management accountability performance model.

driven from a results-based accountability management culture, IT strategic plan, IT operating plan, and the integrated IT performance management dashboard.

The major *outputs* of technology operations accountability include

- Outsourced contracted services—To improve technology operations accountability by committing to managing, *measuring,* delivering, and improving *TOS outsourced delivery,* using TOS measurement areas, as defined in the IT performance measurement dashboard, which endorses results-based management principles, practices, and culture.
- Performance measures—To improve applications management accountability by committing to managing, *measuring,* delivering, and improving *TOS performance measures,* using TOS measurement areas, as defined in the IT performance measurement dashboard, which endorses results-based management principles, practices, and culture.

- Accountability reporting—To improve applications management accountability by committing to managing, *measuring*, delivering, and improving *accountability reporting*, using TOS measurement areas, as defined in the IT performance measurement dashboard, which endorses results-based management principles, practices, and culture.
- Governance model—To improve applications management accountability by committing to managing, *measuring*, delivering, and improving *TOS governance*, using TOS measurement areas, as defined in the IT performance measurement dashboard, which endorses results-based management principles, practices, and culture (Figure 5.17).

> We might possess every technological resource but if our language is inadequate, our vision remains formless, our thinking and feeling are still running in the old cycles, our process may be 'revolutionary' but not transformative.
>
> **Adrienne Rich**

5.7.1 Purpose

The purpose of this results area is to demonstrate and ensure accountability for delivery of *TOS*. This accountability will result in effective and efficient TOS management, improved

IT APPLICATIONS MANAGEMENT SERVICES (AMS)

OPERATIONAL-FM	Start Date	End Date	Status	% Complete	Indicator
IT AMS Governance Framework	4/1/2011	12/31/2011	In-Progress	50%	G
IT AMS Innovative Technical Direction	4/1/2011	3/31/2012	In-Progress	45%	G
AMS Outsourcing Framework	4/1/2011	9/30/2011	In-Progress	65%	Y
OPERATIONAL-FM Summary	4/1/2011	3/31/2012	In-Progress	53%	G

% IT staff performing AMS Governance ; # Improvements completed
% IT staff performing AMS Innovations ; # Improvements completed
% IT staff performing AMS Outsourcing Strategies ; # Improvements completed

OPERATIONAL-SD	Budget	YTD Actual	Status	% Complete	Indicator
AMS Services & SLA mgmt	4/1/2011	3/31/2012	In-Progress	45%	G
AMS SLA Support	4/1/2011	3/31/2012	In-Progress	45%	G
Web-Services Policy/Strategy Development	4/1/2011	6/30/2011	In-Progress	50%	Past Due
Innovative Communications tools	4/1/2011	3/31/2012	In-Progress	45%	G
AMS RFP/Contract Mgnt	4/1/2011	3/31/2012	In-Progress	45%	G
AMS Committee Meetings	4/1/2011	3/31/2012	In-Progress	45%	G
AMS Migrations	4/1/2011	3/31/2012	In-Progress	45%	G
AMS Change Management	4/1/2011	3/31/2012	In-Progress	45%	G
OPERATIONAL-SD Summary	4/1/2011	3/31/2012	In-Progress	46%	G

% IT staff delivering IT AMS Services & SLA Mgnt ; # Improvements completed
% IT staff delivering AMS SLA Support; # Improvements completed
% IT staff delivering Web-Services Strategy; # Improvements Completed
% IT staff delivering AMS Communications Tools; # Improvements completed
% IT staff delivering AMS RFP/Contract Mgnt; # Improvements completed
% IT staff delivering AMS Committee Meetings; # Improvements completed
% IT staff delivering AMS Migrations; # Improvements completed
% IT staff delivering AMS Change Mgnt; # Improvements completed

(a)

Figure 5.16 (a–d) Applications management accountability performance measures. *(Continued)*

OPERATIONAL-SE	Start Date	End Date	Status	% Complete	Indicator
AMS QA	4/1/2011	6/30/2011	In-Progress	75%	Past Due
AMS Compliance/Approval	4/1/2011	7/31/2011	In-Progress	80%	Past Due
AMS Financial Measures	4/1/2011	9/30/2011	In-Progress	60%	R
AMS SLA Compliance	4/1/2011	3/31/2012	In-Progress	35%	Y
AMS Optimization	4/1/2011	3/31/2012	In-Progress	35%	Y
AMS Benchmarking Metrics	4/1/2011	9/30/2011	In-Progress	80%	G
OPERATIONAL-SE Summary	4/1/2011	3/31/2012	In-Progress	61%	G

% IT staff performing AMS QA ; # Improvements completed
% IT staff performing AMS Compliance; # Improvements completed
% IT staff performing AMS Financial Measures; # Improvements completed
% IT staff performing AMS SLA Compliance ; # Improvements completed
% IT staff performing AMS Optimization ; # Improvements completed
% IT staff performing AMS Benchmarking ; # Improvements completed

OPERATIONAL-RM	Start Date	End Date	Status	% Complete	Indicator
AMS Client Management Relations/Feedback	4/1/2011	3/31/2012	In-Progress	100%	Black
Vendors AMS Relations/Feedback	4/1/2011	3/31/2012	In-Progress	40%	G
IT Outsourced Providers AMS Relations/Feedback	4/1/2011	3/31/2012	In-Progress	25%	Y
OPERATIONAL-RM Summary	4/1/2011	3/31/2012	In-Progress	55%	G

% IT staff performing Client Feedback ; # Improvements completed
% IT staff performing Vendors Innovations ; # Improvements completed
% IT staff performing Service Providers Feedback ; # Improvements completed

(b)

CUSTOMER	Start Date	End Date	Status	% Complete	Indicator
AMS Client Relationships/Satisfaction Surveys	4/1/2011	3/31/2012	In-Progress	30%	Y
AMS Committee Meetings	4/1/2011	3/31/2012	In-Progress	30%	Y
AMS Vendors Relationships/Satisfaction Surveys	4/1/2011	9/30/2011	In-Progress	80%	G
AMS IT Outsourced Providers Surveys	10/1/2011	3/31/2012	Not-Started	0%	
AMS Benchmarking Surveys/Results	4/1/2011	6/30/2011	Complete	100%	Black
CUSTOMER Summary	4/1/2011	3/31/2012	In-Progress	48%	G

% IT staff performing Client Satisfaction Surveys; # Improvements completed
% IT staff attending AMS Committee Meetings; # Improvements completed
% IT staff performing Vendor Satisfaction Surveys; # Improvements completed
% IT staff performing IT Vendors Performance Measures; # Improvements completed
% IT staff performing AMS Benchmarking surveys ; # Improvements completed

(c)

EMPLOYEE	Start Date	End Date	Status	% Complete	Indicator
AMS Progress Reporting	4/1/2011	6/30/2011	Complete	100%	Black
AMS Staff Performance Contract	4/1/2011	3/31/2012	In-Progress	35%	Y
AMS Staff Learning/Growth Reporting	4/1/2011	3/31/2012	In-Progress	35%	Y
AMS Staff Meetings/Communications	4/1/2011	3/31/2012	In-Progress	35%	Y
AMS Staff Retention/Retraining/Reward Reporting	4/1/2011	7/31/2011	In-Progress	100%	Black
EMPLOYEE Summary	4/1/2011	3/31/2012	In-Progress	61%	G
IT APPLICATIONS SERVICES SUMMARY	4/1/2011	3/31/2012	In-Progress	51%	G

% IT staff performing Progress Reporting ; # Improvements completed
% IT Staff managing Staff Performance Contract ; # Improvements completed
% IT staff attending Learning/Growth sessions; # Improvements completed
% IT staff performing staff communications/meetings ; # Improvements completed
% IT staff performing AMS retention/retraining ; # Improvements completed

(d)

Figure 5.16 (*Continued*) (a–d) Applications management accountability performance measures.

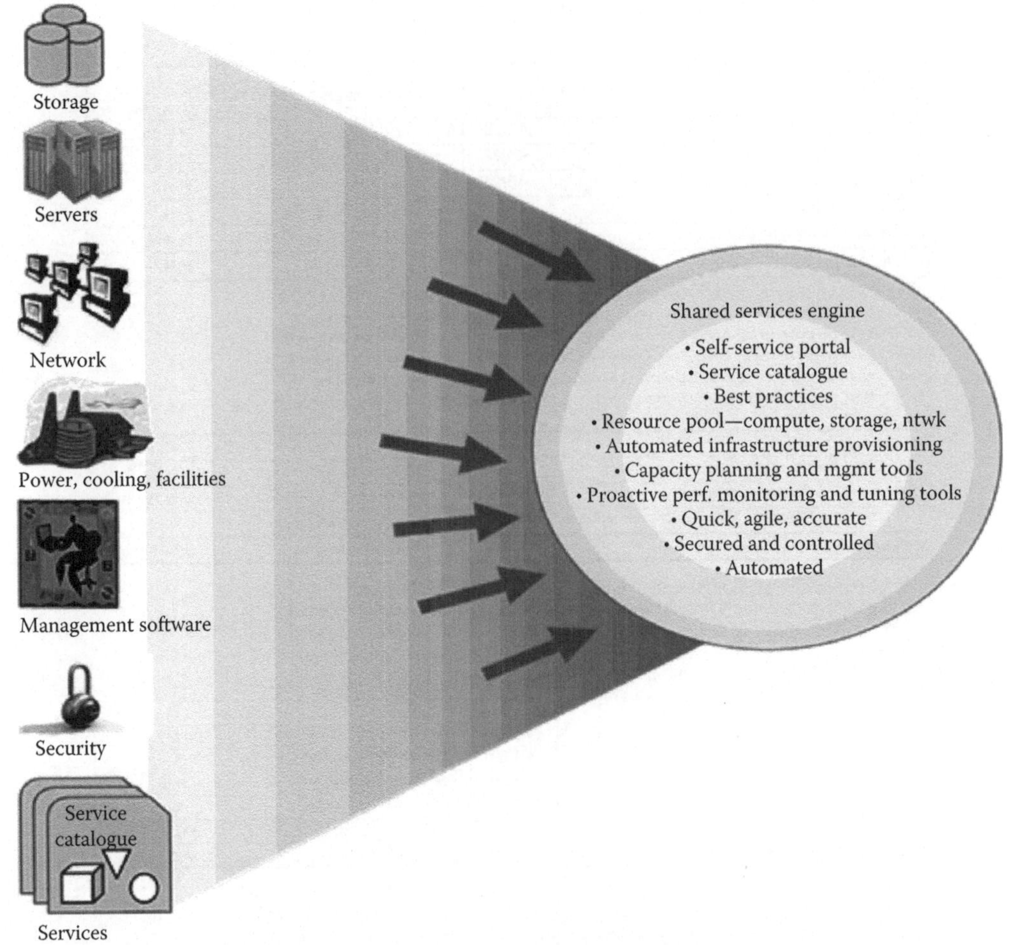

Figure 5.17 Integrated information technology operations service.

organizational performance, and optimized TOS resource utilizations, documented in the *TOS plan*[25] *using technology results-based management and accountability framework* (*TM-RBM*).[18] This TM-RBM framework will form the baseline to monitor and measure the performance results for technology operations management and to ensure that the output/outcomes and performance goals of TOS functional areas are effectively achieved. The performance steering committee shall have approval accountabilities for the *outsourced TOS*[26] to ensure technology operations accountability. This committee will also have accountability with the performance measurement managers, for the technology operations performance results using the TOS measurement areas defined in the performance management plan and the integrated IT performance measurement dashboard.

5.7.2 Strategic Directives

- Technology operations accountability for outsourced TOS will be reviewed by the performance steering committee on a monthly basis, using the *technology results-based management and accountability framework* (*TM-RBM*)[27] that describes results-based technology operations management. The *results-based technology operations management* aligns goals and processes with performance results, TOS resource utilizations, technology operations inefficiencies and improvement areas, % complete, and progress indicator for TOS performance measurement areas.

- The performance steering committee will provide performance approval accountabilities for the credibility, integrity, and reliability of the performance results for technology operations management, using the TOS results area, as represented in the performance measurement dashboard as operational process, financial, customer, and employee performance measures.
- All changes to the *results-based technology operations management and accountability framework* must be approved by the performance steering committee. The performance delivery manager will document and present all changes to the performance steering committee for approval.
- The performance steering committee will meet, at a minimum, on a monthly basis to review the performance indicators, trends, and analytics for *results-based technology operations management and accountability framework*, represented in the performance measurement dashboard as operational process, financial, customer, and employee output/outcomes and *performance metrics*. If the overall progress of the output is *red* or *yellow*, more frequent meetings may be required for improvement to technology operations management performance results.

5.7.3 Accountabilities

5.7.3.1 Executive Performance Manager

This person is accountable for the *approval* of the results.

- Executive support and approval for the performance, *context and contents* of technology operations accountability for outsourced AMS, and areas of improvements
- Executive support and approval for the *progress results* of technology operations accountability to ensure integration with TOS plan, alignment to IT strategic directives, and understanding the benefits and linkages with desired outcomes
- Executive support and approval for technology operations *performance trend results* in the integrated IT performance measurement dashboard to understand the following: (a) "How we are doing?" (b) "Are we doing/measuring the right things?" (c) "Are we getting the right results?" (d) "Are we getting the value?"
- Executive support and approval for *stakeholders' satisfaction results* for strategic and performance management to understand the value of technology operations accountability to improve service delivery through the use of stakeholders' satisfaction surveys
- Executive support and approval for *improvements results* to technology operations accountability and increase understanding of benefits and intended outcomes statement within the overall IT operational management by recommending areas of improvements to TOS measures and results
- Executive support and approval for *performance measures and benchmarking results* on technology operations accountability reporting to performance steering committee, with direct accountability to performance management executive

5.7.3.2 Performance Delivery Manager

This person is accountable for the *management* of the results.

- Manage and define the performance, *context and contents* of technology operations accountability for *outsourced TOS*, and areas of improvements.
- Measure *progress results* of technology operations accountability areas to ensure integration with TOS Plan, alignment to IT strategic directives, and understanding the benefits and linkages with desired outcomes.
- Monitor and analyze technology operations *performance trends* in the integrated IT performance measurement dashboard to understand the following: (a) "How we are doing?" (b) "Are we doing/measuring the right things?" (c) "Are we getting the right results?" (d) "Are we getting the value?"
- Deliver and evaluate *stakeholders' survey satisfaction results* for strategic and performance management to understand the value of technology operations accountability to improve service delivery through the use of *stakeholders' satisfaction surveys.*
- Improve on *technology operations accountability results* and increase understanding of benefits and intended outcomes statement within the overall IT operational management framework by recommending areas of improvements for TOS performance measures and results.
- Report on technology operations accountability *performance measures and benchmarking* results to performance steering committee, with direct accountability to performance management executive.

5.7.3.3 Performance Measurement Team

This team is accountable for the *delivery* of performance results.

- Provide the performance, *context and contents* of technology operations accountability for outsourced TOS, and areas of improvements.
- Provide *progress results* of technology operations accountability areas to ensure integration with TOS Plan, alignment to IT strategic directives, and understanding the benefits and linkages with desired outcomes.
- Provide technology operations *performance trends* in the integrated IT performance measurement dashboard to understand the following: (a) "How we are doing?" (b) "Are we doing/measuring the right things?" (c) "Are we getting the right results?" (d) "Are we getting the value?"
- Provide *stakeholders' survey satisfaction results* for strategic and performance management to understand the value of technology operations accountability to improve service delivery through the use of *stakeholders' satisfaction surveys.*
- Provide *improvement results* on technology operations accountability and increase understanding of benefits and intended outcomes statement within the overall IT operational management framework by recommending areas of improvements for TOS performance measures and results.
- Report on technology operations accountability *performance measures and benchmarking* results to performance steering committee, with direct accountability to performance management executive.

5.7.4 Results: Technology Operations Accountability

Accountabilities discussed earlier are brief because they are intended to serve as a reference for *who is accountable* for *what* during the management and delivery of TOS within the six functional areas of the IT SDLC . Results are now introduced to highlight the outputs of technology operations accountability results and associated outcomes (what), process flow (how), and performance measures (why). It is intended to serve as a reference based on the English language interrogatives: Who *is accountable for what, how, and why.* The outputs/outcomes, process flow, and performance measures, based on real-world practical implementation, will serve as excellent references for practicing performance managers during measurement, delivery, and reporting of the technology operations accountability outputs and outcomes. The outputs/outcomes highlight the key results for technology operations management accountability that the performance managers measure and report during the delivery of the outsourced AMS contractual agreements. The process flows, based on real-world practical implementations, are a graphical representation of the inputs, process, outputs, and relationships. The technology operations accountability shows the foundation representation to effectively communicate the integrated components of AMS alignment to strategic, IT operational, and performance management processes.

The performance measures from the integrated IT performance measurement dashboard show TOS outputs for TOS using operational, financial customer, and employee performance measures. Appendix A provides further details. Performance metrics, indicators, progress, trends, and analytics formed the basis for technology operations evidence-based decision making to enable improved organizational excellence.

5.7.4.1 Outputs/Outcomes: Technology Operations Accountability

The outputs and outcomes of the technology operations accountability are given in Table 5.7.

5.7.4.2 Process Flows: Technology Operations Accountability

The process flows of the technology operations accountability are shown in Figure 5.18.

5.7.4.3 Performance Measures Model: Technology Operations Accountability

The performance model of the technology operations accountability is shown in Figure 5.19.

5.7.4.4 Performance Measures: Technology Operations Accountability

The performance measures of the technology operations accountability are shown in Figure 5.20.

5.8 Summary

The IT operational management model presented in this chapter describes the results areas of IT operational management. The "purpose" section provides a statement of the derived result, and the "strategic directives" section provides various guiding principles and major directives to achieving the purpose statement, for each of the IT operational management results areas. The accountabilities

Table 5.7 Technology Operations Accountability Output/Outcomes

Results Area	*Output*	*Outcome*
Technology operations accountability	Commitment • TM-RBM • Credibility, integrity, reliability • Business value • Strategic alignment • Applications management accountability results	• Optimized utilization of TM resource • Improved TM-RBM • Increased value of TOS results area performance measurement dashboard-analytics
	Outsourced TOS • TOS results area	• Improved results—TOS results delivered to support outsourced contractual agreements • Improved TM-RBM for delivery of TOS output/outcomes
	Performance measures—SD, OE, RM • TOS results area	• Improved results—TOS performance measures for SD, OE, RM • Improved TM-RBM for delivery of TOS performance measures
	Accountability reporting—SD, OE, RM • TOS results area	• Improved results—AMS accountability reporting for SD, OE, RM • Improved TM-RBM for delivery of TOS accountability reporting
	TOS governance • TOS results area	• Improved results—TMS governance for oversight and strategy • Improved TM-RBM for delivery of TOS governance
	Technology operations accountability framework	• Increased accountability and transparency of TM-RBM • Increased transformation to TM-RBM performance measurement culture

of the executive performance manager, performance delivery manager, and performance measurement team are presented to demonstrate the integrated nature of these outputs and outcomes in measuring, managing, and delivering IT services. The key IT operational management outputs and outcomes, process flows, and performance measures provide excellent real-world implementation guidelines, which can be referenced and applied to IT operational management processes.

IT staff who are in the process of measuring, managing, and delivering IT operations services with the goal toward integrated performance management should consider the following IT operational management recommendations, as a framework, to guide them toward successful measurement, management, and delivery of IT services:

- Establish IT operational direction and accountabilities that will guide the measurement, management, and delivery of IT operational management results areas, to improve

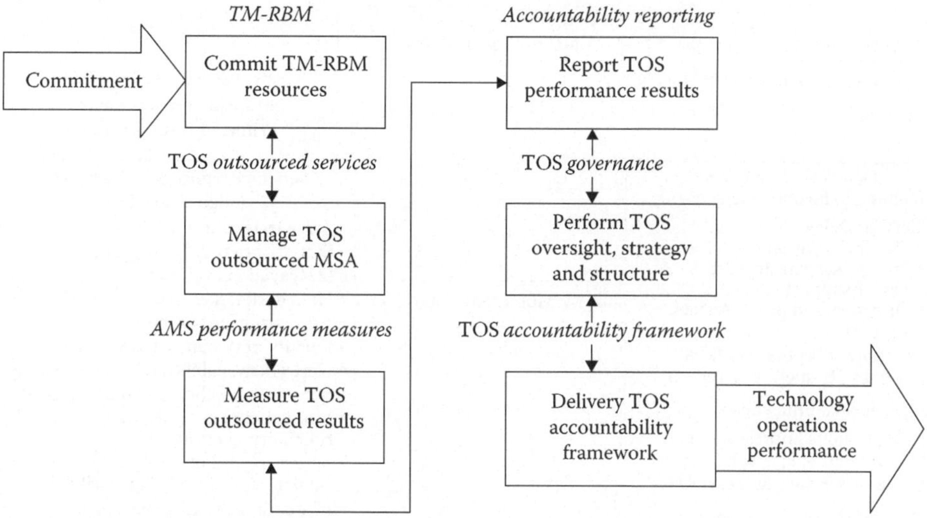

Figure 5.18 Technology operations accountability process flow.

organizational performance, quality of management, and to optimize the utilization of IT resources.

- Define performance measures and accountability models to demonstrate alignment with the integrated IT performance measurement dashboard and IT operational management results area.
- Establish accountability frameworks for financial, HR, operational processes, project management, applications management, and technology operations to better communicate how outputs, outcomes, and processes are used to ensure results-based management and to provide that balance with stability, applicability, and consistency.
- Obtain commitments or noncommitments from executive and senior management for enforcing the integration of the IT performance measurement dashboard, using Norton and Kaplan measures (employee, customer, financials, and operations), leadership, service excellence, service delivery, and relationship management.
- Identify the roles of the performance steering committee to provide performance approval responsibilities and accountability for the input, process, and output measures and overall results as determined from the integrated IT performance measurement dashboard.
- Manage and track the performance results in the integrated IT performance measurement dashboard, determine the input, process and output performance measures, trends, and analytics, and align with IT operational management strategic directive.

The main focus of this chapter is to provide readers with further details on IT operational management results areas of the integrated IT performance management framework (IPMF-IT). By now, the readers should have gained a fairly good understanding of the integrated nature of these results areas. Chapter 6 includes further discussions to show the horizontal integration of these IT operational management results areas using IT SDLC performance model. Business, IT managers, and academics, with a passion for improvements, measurements, and assessments, will be able to appreciate the value of the horizontal and vertical integration, to better prepare

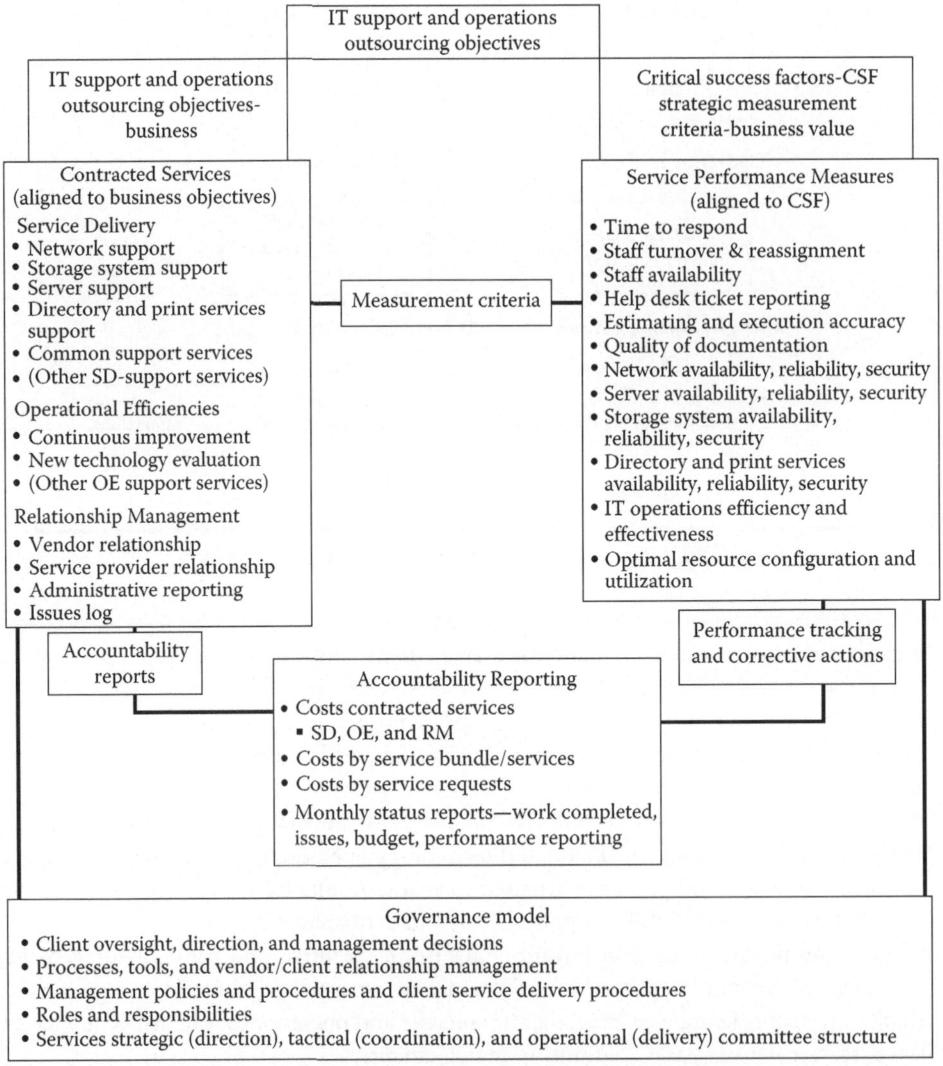

Figure 5.19 Technology operations accountability performance model.

them in understanding performance measurement and management in this dynamically changing IT industry.

5.9 Endnotes: Key Project Management Terms

[1]*Financial performance accountability*: The commitment that an organization assumes for the delivery of financial services, accepts responsibilities for actions, and accounts for financial results, using open and transparent communications.

[2]*Capital and operating costs*: Funds utilized in the results-based budgeting structure for development/acquisition of fixed assets (business and IT infrastructure projects) and funds utilized for daily ongoing expenses (technology and operations services).

[3]*Results-based financial accountability framework* (*RBB*): A results-based budgeting structure that an organization uses for the management and delivery of financial results/output/outcomes, accepts responsibilities, and accounts for results that align with the goals and strategies of the organization.

[4]*RBB capital framework*: A results-based budgeting structure that an organization uses for the management of capital investments for business and IT infrastructure projects that align with the goals and strategies of the organization.

[5]*RBB operating framework*: A results-based budgeting structure that an organization uses for the management of operating expenses for technology and operations services that align with the goals and strategies of the organization.

IT OPERATIONS SERVICES (TOS)

OPERATIONAL-FM	Start Date	End Date	Status	% Complete	Indicator
TOS Governance Framework	4/1/2011	12/31/2011	In-Progress	50%	G
TOS Innovative Technical Direction	4/1/2011	3/31/2012	In-Progress	45%	G
TOS Outsourcing Framework	4/1/2011	9/30/2011	In-Progress	65%	Y
TOS Data Centre Technology Direction	4/1/2011	3/31/2012	In-Progress	45%	G
OPERATIONAL-FM Summary	4/1/2011	3/31/2012	In-Progress	51%	G

% IT staff performing TOS Governance ; # Improvements completed
% IT staff performing TOS Innovations ; # Improvements completed
% IT staff performing TOS Outsourcing Strategies ; # Improvements completed
% IT staff performing TOS Data Centre Technology Direction ; # Improvements completed

OPERATIONAL-SD	Budget	YTD Actual	Status	% Complete	Indicator
TOS Services & SLA Management	4/1/2011	3/31/2012	In-Progress	45%	G
TOS SLA Support	4/1/2011	3/31/2012	In-Progress	45%	G
Data Centre Policy/Strategy Development	4/1/2011	6/30/2011	In-Progress	50%	Past Due
Innovative Communications tools	4/1/2011	3/31/2012	In-Progress	45%	G
TOS RFP/Contract Mgnt	4/1/2011	3/31/2012	In-Progress	45%	G
TOS Committee Meetings	4/1/2011	3/31/2012	In-Progress	45%	G
TOS Migrations	4/1/2011	3/31/2012	In-Progress	45%	G
TOS Change Management	4/1/2011	3/31/2012	In-Progress	45%	G
Managed Operations Support	4/1/2011	3/31/2012	In-Progress	45%	G
Technology Infrastructure Delivery	4/1/2011	6/30/2011	In-Progress	50%	**Past Due**
TOS Innovative Productivity tools	4/1/2011	3/31/2012	In-Progress	45%	G
OPERATIONAL-SD Summary	4/1/2011	3/31/2012	In-Progress	46%	G

% IT staff delivering IT TOS Services & SLA Mgnt ; # Improvements completed
% IT staff delivering TOS SLA Support; # Improvements completed
% IT staff delivering Data Centre Strategy; # Improvements Completed
% IT staff delivering TOS Communications Tools; # Improvements completed
% IT staff delivering AMS RFP/Contract Mgnt; # Improvements completed
% IT staff delivering TOS Committee Meetings; # Improvements completed
% IT staff delivering TOS Migrations; # Improvements completed
% IT staff delivering TOS Change Mgnt; # Improvements completed
% IT staff delivering TOS Managed Operations; # Improvements completed
% IT staff delivering Technology Infrastructure Delivery; # Improvements completed
% IT staff delivering productivity tools; # Improvements completed

(a)

Figure 5.20 (a–d) Technology operations accountability performance measures. *(Continued)*

OPERATIONAL-SE	Start Date	End Date	Status	% Complete	Indicator
TOS QA	4/1/2011	6/30/2011	In-Progress	75%	Past Due
TOS Compliance/Approval	4/1/2011	7/31/2011	In-Progress	80%	Past Due
TOS Financial Measures	4/1/2011	9/30/2011	In-Progress	60%	R
TOS SLA Compliance	4/1/2011	3/31/2012	In-Progress	35%	Y
TOS Asset Optimization	4/1/2011	3/31/2012	In-Progress	35%	Y
TOS Benchmarking Metrics	4/1/2011	9/30/2011	In-Progress	80%	G
IT Infrastructure Purchases Approvals	4/1/2011	5/31/2011	In-Progress	75%	Past Due
OPERATIONAL-SE Summary	4/1/2011	3/31/2012	In-Progress	63%	G

% IT staff performing Business Projects Plan QA ; # Improvements completed
% IT staff performing PM Compliance; # Improvements completed
% IT staff performing Business Projects Financial Measures; # Improvements completed
% IT staff performing PMO Compliance ; # Improvements completed
% IT staff performing PM Optimization ; # Improvements completed
% IT staff performing Business Projects Benchmarking ; # Improvements completed
% IT staff performing IT Infrastructure Purchases Approvals ; # Improvements completed

OPERATIONAL-RM	Start Date	End Date	Status	% Complete	Indicator
TOS Client Management Relations/Feedback	4/1/2011	3/31/2012	In-Progress	100%	Black
Vendors TOS Relations/Feedback	4/1/2011	3/31/2012	In-Progress	40%	G
IT Outsourced Providers TOS Relations/Feedback	4/1/2011	3/31/2012	In-Progress	25%	Y
OPERATIONAL-RM Summary	4/1/2011	3/31/2012	In-Progress	55%	G

% IT staff performing Client Feedback ; # Improvements completed
% IT staff performing Vendors Feedback ; # Improvements completed
% IT staff performing Service Providers Feedback ; # Improvements completed

(b)

FINANCIAL	Start Date	End Date	Status	% Complete	Indicator
IT TOS Innovative Initiative Costs-Capital	4/1/2011	12/31/2011	In-Progress	50%	G
IT TOS Operating Costs	4/1/2011	3/31/2012	In-Progress	15%	R
FINANCIAL Summary	4/1/2011	3/31/2012	In-Progress	33%	Y

% IT staff managing TOS Capital Costs; # Improvements completed
% IT staff managing TOS Operating Costs; # Improvements completed

(c)

Figure 5.20 (*Continued*) (a–d) Technology operations accountability performance measures.
(*Continued*)

[6]*Finance performance metrics*: A measure of an organization's financial output/outcomes/results, using financial performance measures.

[7]*HR accountability framework*: A structure that an organization uses for the management and delivery of HR services, accepts responsibilities for actions, and accounts for results that align with HR goals and strategies of the organization.

[8]*IT human resource plan*: A plan that states how IT staff (employees and customers) performance will be managed, monitored, and measured.

[9]*HR results-based management and accountability framework*: A results-based management structure that an organization uses for the management and delivery of HR results/output/outcomes, accepts responsibilities for actions, and accounts for results that align with the goals and strategies of the organization. Synonymous with HR accountability framework.

CUSTOMER	Start Date	End Date	Status	% Complete	Indicator
TOS Client Relationships/Satisfaction Surveys	4/1/2011	3/31/2012	In-Progress	30%	Y
TOS Committee Meetings	4/1/2011	3/31/2012	In-Progress	30%	Y
TOS Vendors Relationships/Satisfaction Surveys	4/1/2011	9/30/2011	In-Progress	80%	G
TOS IT Outsourced Providers Surveys	10/1/2011	3/31/2012	Not-Started	0%	
TOS Benchmarking Surveys/Results	4/1/2011	6/30/2011	Complete	100%	Black
CUSTOMER Summary	4/1/2011	3/31/2012	In-Progress	48%	G

% IT staff performing Client Satisfaction Surveys; # Improvements completed
% IT staff attending PPM Committee Meetings; # Improvements completed
% IT staff performing Vendor Satisfaction Surveys; # Improvements completed
% IT staff performing IT Vendors Performance Measures; # Improvements completed
% IT staff performing TOS Benchmarking surveys; # Improvements completed

EMPLOYEE	Start Date	End Date	Status	% Complete	Indicator
TOS Staff Progress Reporting	4/1/2011	6/30/2011	Complete	100%	Black
TOS Staff Performance Contract	4/1/2011	3/31/2012	In-Progress	35%	Y
TOS Staff Learning/Growth Reporting	4/1/2011	3/31/2012	In-Progress	35%	Y
TOS Staff Meetings/Communications	4/1/2011	3/31/2012	In-Progress	35%	Y
TOS Staff Retention/Retraining/Reward Reporting	4/1/2011	7/31/2011	In-Progress	100%	Black
EMPLOYEE Summary	4/1/2011	3/31/2012	In-Progress	61%	G
IT OPERATIONS SERVICES SUMMARY	4/1/2011	3/31/2012	In-Progress	51%	G

% IT staff performing Progress Reporting ; # Improvements completed
% IT Staff managing Staff Performance Contract ; # Improvements completed
% IT staff attending Learning/Growth sessions; # Improvements completed
% IT staff performing staff communications/meetings ; # Improvements completed
% IT staff performing TOS retention/retraining ; # Improvements completed

(d)

Figure 5.20 (*Continued*) (a–d) Technology operations accountability performance measures.

[10]*Outsourced, contracted, and in-house*: An approach used to manage and deliver IT services, using outsourced service providers (external management and delivery), contract resources (internal management and external delivery), and in-house (in house management and delivery) resources.

[11]*Customer and employee performance metrics*: A measure of an organization's financial output/outcomes/results, using customer and employee performance measures.

[12]*Operational process accountability framework*: A structure that an organization utilizes uses for the management, reengineering, and delivery of operational processes, accepts responsibilities for actions, and accounts for results that align with operational processes goals and strategies of the organization.

[13]*Business/IT reengineering plan*: A plan that states how business/IT reengineering services will be executed and deployed.

[14]*Reengineering results-based management and accountability framework*: A results-based management structure that an organization utilizes for the management and delivery of reengineering results/output/outcomes, accepts responsibilities for actions, and accounts for results that align with the goals and strategies of the organization. It is synonymous with operational process accountability framework.

[15]*Business/IT management and delivery process*: An integrated representation of business management and delivery process and IT management and delivery processes, used in streamlining or reengineering organization's processes.

[16]*Project portfolio management (PPM) accountability framework*: A structure that an organization utilizes for the management and delivery of PPM services, accepts responsibilities for actions, and accounts for results that align with project management resource goals and strategies of the organization.

[17]*Project portfolio management plan*: A plan that states how project management services will be executed and deployed.

[18]*Project management results-based management and accountability framework*: A results-based management structure that an organization utilizes for the management and delivery of project results/output/outcomes, accepts responsibilities for actions, and accounts for results that align with the goals and strategies of the organization. It is synonymous with project portfolio management accountability framework.

[19]*Strategic and operational business and IT infrastructure projects*: An integrated representation of strategic and operational business projects and strategic and operational IT infrastructure (technical) projects, used in optimizing the delivery of IT projects.

[20]*Applications management accountability framework*: A structure that an organization uses for the management and delivery of applications management services, accepts responsibilities for actions, and accounts for results that align with applications management goals and strategies of the organization.

[21]*Applications management services (AMS) plan*: A plan that states how applications management services will be executed and deployed.

[22]*Applications management results-based management and accountability framework*: A results-based management structure that an organization uses for the management and delivery of applications management results/output/outcomes, accepts responsibilities for actions, and accounts for results that align with AMS goals and strategies of the organization. It is synonymous with applications management accountability framework.

[23]*Outsourced applications management services*: A plan that states how applications management services will be outsourced.

[24]*Technology operational accountability framework*: A structure that an organization uses for the management and delivery of technology operations services, accepts responsibilities for actions, and accounts for results that align with technology operations goals and strategies of the organization.

[25]*Technology operations services plan*: A plan that states how to execute technology operations services.

[26]*Technology operations services (TOS)*: Technology operations services as defined in the outsourced contractual agreements.

[27]*Technology operational results-based management and accountability framework*: A results-based management structure an organization uses for the management and delivery of technology operations services results/output/outcomes, accepts responsibilities for actions, and accounts for results that align with TOS goals and strategies of the organization. It is synonymous with technology operational management accountability framework.

5.10 Questions to Think About: Management Perspectives

1. Think about how your organization demonstrates accountability (people, process, projects, technology, and financials) using results-based culture, process, and structure. How does your organization measure and manage performance results of IT operations services? What

are the key rationales for ensuring accountability for results? What are the major results areas of IT operational management? How do these results areas relate to your IT environment? What is your perception of senior management on the need for an integrated IT performance measurement dashboard to guide evidence-based decision making using predictive analytics?

2. Think about how your organization demonstrates financial accountability for IT operational management services. What is your senior management commitment on RBB? How does RBB as presented in this chapter relate to your IT financial accountability framework? How does the financial accountability model presented in this chapter compare to your organization's financial structure?
3. Think about how your organization demonstrates HR accountability for IT operations services. What is your organization culture toward RBM? How does RBM as presented in this chapter relate to your HR accountability framework? How does the HR governance model presented in this chapter compare to your organization IT accountability model?
4. Think about how your organization demonstrates project management accountability. What is your organization culture toward integrated project management? How does your project management performance measures align with PPM performance measures, described in this chapter? What are the major output and outcomes for project management accountability?
5. Think about how your organization demonstrates AMS accountability for IT operations services. What is your organization culture toward results-based management for AMS? How does your applications management performance measures align with AMS performance measures, described in this chapter? What are the major output and outcomes for applications management accountability?
6. Think about how your organization demonstrates TOS accountability for IT operations services? What is your organization culture toward results-based management for TOS? How does your technology operations performance measures align with TOS performance measures, described in this chapter? What are the major outputs and outcomes for technology operations accountability?

5.11 Chapter Testing Questions

1. Which one of the IT financial accountability results areas delivers the outcome: "optimize the utilization of IT financial resources"?
   a. RBB
   b. Capital costs
   c. Operational costs
2. Executives shall use the HR accountability governance performance model to
   a. Understand the decision-making process
   b. Make sound objective decisions on IT performance
   c. Determine culture, process, and structure of HR accountability results
3. What is the end result of operational process accountability process flows?
   a. Reengineering performance results
   b. Business process management
   c. Business process delivery

4. The major outputs of project management accountability *must* include
   a. Strategic business projects, strategic IT infrastructure projects
   b. Results-based management (RBM)
   c. Operational business projects, operational IT infrastructure projects
5. IT operational management results areas do *not* include
   a. Financial accountability, RBM
   b. Performance measurement office (PMO), transformational change
   c. AMS accountability, TOS accountability, PPM accountability
6. At one stage of a performance measurement effort, you decided to use the applications management accountability performance model to understand the areas of AMS performance measures. What would you *most* likely examine?
   a. Contract services, service performance measures, accountability reporting, AMS governance
   b. Are we doing the right things? Right way? Getting benefits? How well?
   c. Transformational change, sustainability, performance culture
7. What are the major outputs of outsourced IT operations services?
   a. Contract services, outsourced services, performance measures
   b. People, process, technology, financials
   c. People, politics, process, performance
8. Which one of the following results areas is *best* input for TOS performance dashboard?
   a. IT strategic framework
   b. IT performance governance structure
   c. IT strategic directives
9. Which one of the following is *most* effective in demonstrating accountability for results for IT operational management results area to executives?
   a. Performance culture, process improvement, RBB, technology enablement, RBM
   b. Commitment, RBB, RBM, transformational change, culture, TOS governance
   c. Financial, HR, performance culture, governance

Recommended Readings

Operational Management

Aguinis, H., *Performance Management*, New York: Pearson Education, 2012.

Bainey, K.R., *Integrated IT Project Management, A Model-Centric Approach*. New York: Artech House, 2004.

Batshalom, B., *GreenSource, The Magazine of Sustainable Design*. Boston, MA: Sustainable Performance Institute, 2011.

Corkins, G., *Performance Management, Integrating Strategy, Execution, Methodologies, Risk, and Analytics*. Hoboken, NJ: John Wiley & Sons Inc., 2009.

De Waal, A., *Strategic Performance Management: A Managerial and Behavioral Approach*. New York: Palgrave Macmillan, 2013.

Demartini, C., *Performance Management Systems: Design, Diagnosis and Use*. Berlin, Germany: Springer, 2013.

Hall, D., *Corporate Governance: Ensuring Propriety for Performance: A Contemporary Themes in Strategic People Management*. New York: Palgrave Macmillan, 2013.

Kaplan, R.S. and Norton, D.P., *The Balanced Scorecard: Translating Strategy into Action*. Boston, MA: Harvard Business School Publishing, 1996.

KPI Institute, *The KPI Compendium: 20,000 Key Performance Indicators used in Practice*. Melbourne, Victoria, Australia: KPI Institute, 2013.

Marr, B., Strategic *Performance Management, Leveraging and Measuring Your Intangible Value Driver*. Burlington, MA: Elsevier Ltd., 2006.

Spitzer, D.R., *Transforming Performance Measurement, Rethinking the Way We Measure and Drive Organizational Success*. New York: AMACOM, 2007.

Chapter 6

Integrated IT Service Delivery Life Cycle Performance Model

It is not a question of how well each process works, the question is how well they all work together.

Lloyd Dobens and Clare Crawford-Mason, *Thinking About Quality*

6.1 Introduction

In this technologically advancing world of information technology (IT), we should have the capability to adapt using performance management processes with proactive and predictive analytical cultures that value *results-based management* (*RBM*). A more *results-driven model-centric*[1] process, with a culture of performance *analytics-rational evidence-based decision making*, must replace the traditional negative, judgmental, regressive, and reactive approach to performance management. The objective of this chapter is to provide the strategic directives and associated outputs, outcomes, and performance measures to support the IT service delivery life cycle (SDLC) performance model and to show the alignment with the integrated IT performance measurement dashboard.

The functional areas of the integrated IT SDLC performance model connect the end results of the strategic directives with outputs, outcomes, and performance measures represented in the integrated IT performance measurement dashboard. This integrated IT performance measurement dashboard is structured based on a modified version of *Kaplan and Norton's Balanced Scorecard* that supports operational, financial, customer, and employee performance measures. The IT SDLC performance model, presented in this chapter, also shows how strategic management, performance management, and IT operational management results areas are integrated. The more practical, flexible, and innovative approach to effectively manage the delivery of information technology services (ITS) is to classify ITS into logical functional areas, using the logical stages of the IT SDLC.

The integrated SDLC performance model presented in this chapter represents further elaboration of the integrated IT performance management framework (IPMF-IT) shown in Figure 6.1. This framework is a graphical representation that shows the integration of IT functional areas with strategic management, performance management, and IT operational management results areas. The integrated

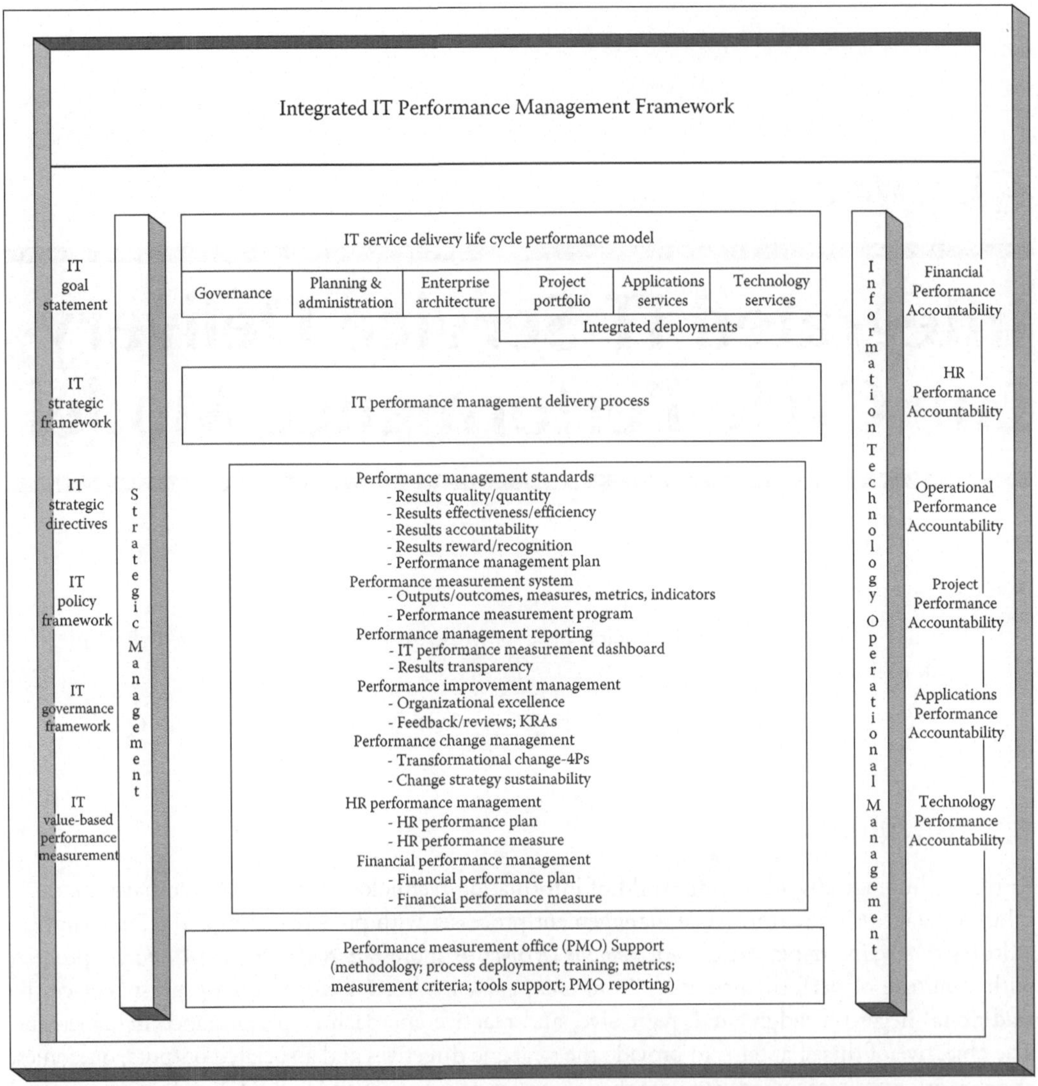

Figure 6.1 Integrated information technology performance management model.

IT performance management results breakdown structure (RBS), shown in Figure 6.2, is the logical performance management structure that represents the associations of strategic directive end results with the outputs, outcomes, and performance measures in the integrated IT performance measurement dashboard, using operational, financial, customer, and employee performance measures. Appendices A through F show a software tool implementation of this IPMF-IT RBS, using Microsoft Excel.

6.1.1 Integrated IT Performance Management Framework

This IPMF-IT represents the foundation principle to integrating strategic management, performance management, and IT operational management results areas, using the functional areas of the IT SDLC performance model.

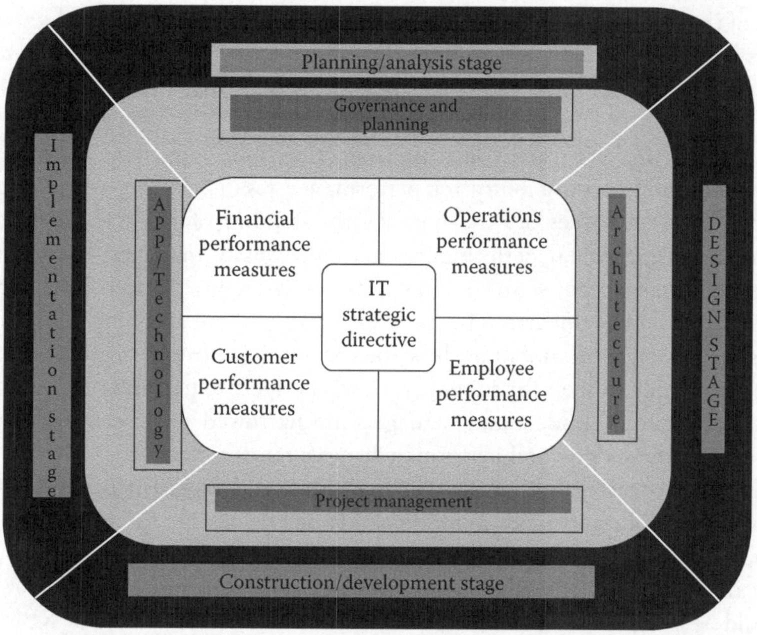

Figure 6.2 Integrated information technology performance management results breakdown structure.

6.1.2 Master RBS

This *master RBS* shows a results-driven model-centric approach to managing ITS that supports the IPMF-IT and *Kaplan and Norton's Balanced Scorecard* guiding performance measures.

My guiding definition of RBS: "A results-driven model-centric framework of IT strategic directives that describes the end-results of ITS for IT functional areas, and aligns with the established organizational performance measures. Each descending level provides an increasingly detailed definition of the performance results, represented in the performance measurement dashboard." The end result and associated outputs, outcomes, and performance measures of the IPMF-IT have four distinguishing characteristics: *results driven, model centric, analytical, and integrated.*[2] IPMF-IT provides the integration between financial (budget, investments, expenses), customer (external stakeholders), operations (process, technology), and employee (internal stakeholders) performance results, for the IT functional areas. Integrated performance management is when an organization uses performance measures and standards to achieve desired results, which is implemented and integrated at the strategic and operational levels. ITS are managed, measured, and monitored based on the performance results of the six IT functional areas: leadership/governance, planning and administration, enterprise architecture, project portfolio, applications services, and technology services.

6.1.3 Real-World Scenarios: RBS

As a result of my 35 years of practical industry experiences as an IT professional in the public, private, and academic sectors, I finally concluded that one of the major reasons for the failure of ITS delivery in either *in-house, contracted, or outsourced*[3] environments was the result of ineffective measurement of the delivered ITS. Many IT leaders and managers have limited knowledge of the critical factors that contribute to their success. They have contributed to these failures because of their inability to apply a performance management process during the management and delivery of ITS.

These IT decision makers usually lack understanding and agreement of what is important and lack ownership and accountability for performance results. Strategies are poorly executed because managers and employees lack the mutual understanding of how the strategy fits with their job responsibilities. Operational performances are emotionally managed because management decision-making powers of ego, status, and politics are based on educated guesses and best-case scenarios. Employees do not understand what is expected of them and how results meet expectations. Leaders and managers do not know how their employees, customer, processes, and projects/initiatives are performing in their functional areas, with respect to performance results. The thinking preferences of these IT leaders and managers are narrowed to procedural or task-oriented focus, with negative and judgmental performance measurement mentality.

They lack real strategic value integration, performance measurement, and transformation change management skills and place more emphasis on the efforts, financials, and activities by counting inputs and outputs, with little or no regard for the results—outputs and outcomes. In most cases, a rigid methodology is applied, with little consideration for "why" or "how" these activities should be integrated to producing the results. The concept of RBS or RBM is unknown and treated as theoretical, and in cases where this RBS technique is applied, the focus is usually task oriented not results based. This is a typical example of misuse of the RBS or RBM guidelines, in accordance with the integrated performance management framework defined in this book, which is central to organizational excellence, accountability for results, and sustained value creation. We must hold others accountable for results rather than effort and activities. People look busy and accomplish little—being busy is not the same as producing results. The main trust of performance management is to make better decisions that will be evidence based and ultimately measured by outputs and outcomes. We need to shift from measurement that is primarily designed for effort, activities, and tasks to accountability for results (RBM), with meaningful outcome metrics that demonstrate the value of these transformational change—people, politics, process, and performance.

6.1.4 IT SDLC Performance Model

The IT SDLC process, represented in Figure 6.3, is a model-centric approach that provides a structure for integrating IT SDLC stages, IT functional areas, results areas, and processes. This structure integrates IPMF-IT, integrated IT performance management RBS, and IT performance measurement dashboard, using the IT strategic directives as the foundation. The alignment of the IT strategic directives with the performance measures, and the integration of strategic management, IT operational management, and performance management components for each of the six IT functional areas, is presented to show the horizontal integration of this performance management framework. The flexibility of this framework makes it applicable for "in-house," contracted, and outsourced IT environments because of the sound logical and sustainable IT functional areas.

The objective of this performance model is to establish a framework that will assist strategic, IT operational, and performance management staff to consistently use performance measurement information to manage, monitor, and measure your organization asset capacity—people, process, financials, and technology—during the management and delivery of ITS.

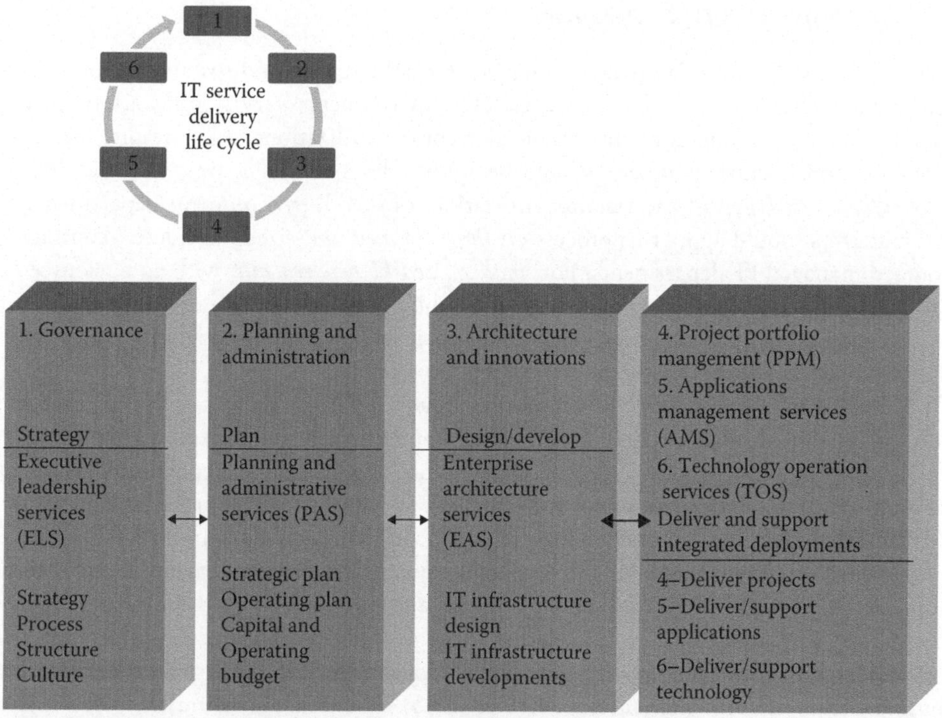

Figure 6.3 Information technology service delivery life cycle process.

Specific objectives when applying this process are to

- Foster ongoing accountability, transparency, and communications among the strategic, IT operational, and performance management staff, to improve performance of IT management and delivery services, and to enable a culture of rational evidence-based decision making, instead of judgmental or intuitive decision making
- Provide consistency in determining fundamental performance characteristics of efficiencies (outputs), effectiveness (outcomes), and service delivery (quality/quantity), during the management, measurement, improvement, and delivery of ITS
- Provide strategic, IT operational, and performance managers with an RBM framework based on strategic directives, outputs, outcomes, and performance measurement information, to guide in establishing performance goals, optimize IT resource utilization, improve or confirm current processes, and report successes on the management and delivery of ITS
- Provide a framework of strategic directives, outputs, outcomes, and performance measurement information, which can be refined and applied to meet the performance measurement characteristics of a particular IT department

> If you can't describe what you are doing as a process, you don't know what you're doing.
>
> **W. Edwards Deming**

6.1.5 Applying IT SDLC Process

IT SDLC process (Figure 6.3) provides a flexible, logically sound, and sustained approach to the management and delivery of ITS. However, ITS environments vary significantly with respect to people, process, technology, and financial resource utilizations. As a result, implementation of this model-centric approach should be applicable to the objectives, strategic directions, *outsourced/in-sourced model*,[4] and resource utilizations of the IT environments/departments.

IT managers should apply this process on *large- to medium*[5]-sized "in-house," contracted, or outsourced managed IT departments. For *smaller-sized IT departments*[6] with an outsourced and/or in-sourced model, IT decision makers may combine the life cycle stages or functional areas, outputs/outcomes, performance measures, and associated strategic directives to reflect the most applicable approach for the management and delivery of ITS.

The demand for a *client-centric outsourced*[7] approach to ITS delivery is becoming increasingly important, to support this evidence-based decision-making process, measured by outputs and outcomes. Implementing a *client-centric outsourced* model provides the opportunity for clients to collaborate with the outsourced service providers and/or contracted resources (*staff augmentation model*)[8] and to maintain a sustained culture of trust, credibility, transparency, and accountability. The *client-centric outsourced* model delivers applications management services (AMS), technology operations services (TOS), and special business and/or technology infrastructure projects by an outsourced ITS provider, usually awarded through a *fixed-priced request for proposal* (*RFP*)[9] process. This model also includes the delivery of project portfolio management (PPM) services for business and enterprise architecture services (EAS) for technology infrastructure projects by contracted resource-staff augmentation model, awarded through a *time and materials RFP*[10] process. The IT industry has struggled to balance innovations with applicability, consistency, and stability. *Client-centric outsourced* model is the framework that provides innovative, cost-effective, adaptable, and practical implementation of the IT SDLC process, discussed in this chapter.

In-house or in-sourced model delivers leadership/governance services (executive leadership services [ELS]), planning and administration services (PAS), and enterprise architecture/innovations services (excluding technology projects—EAS), which have been classified as having *strategic value* to IT and the business areas. The decision to *manage and deliver* these ITS (functional areas), using "in-house," resources was based on the "strategic value" policy. *In-house or in-sourced* model requires that accountability for results, ownership, transparency, integrity, sustainability, ethics, and performance management reside with the ITS departments.

In the *client-centric outsourced model, client centric* can be defined from the perspectives of outsourced and *contracted-resource*-staff augmentation managed services. *Client-centric outsourced model* for outsourced services is usually *managed and delivered* by *outsourced* ITS *providers*[11] in #3 (special technology projects—EAS), #4 (special business projects—PPM), #5 (AMS), and #6 (TOS), as represented in Figure 6.3, IT SDLC process. *Client-centric outsourced model* for contracted resources services is usually *delivered* by staff augmentation resources in #3 (technology projects—EAS) and #4 (business projects—PPM), as represented in Figure 6.3, IT SDLC process.

Successful outsourced managed services require regular oversight and measurement of performance results for output and outcomes by the clients, based on the performance measurement model outlined in the outsourced contractual agreement. Many IT leaders and managers do not know how their outsourced services are performing with respect to performance results. We must hold our ITS providers and contracted resources accountable for results rather than effort and activities. We need to shift from measurement that is traditionally designed for effort, activities, and tasks to *accountability for results* (*RBM*)[12] with meaningful outcome metrics that demonstrate the value of *outsourcing*. It is not only about communications as many traditional IT decision makers tend to believe. It is about building win–win alliance and trust while improving performance using accountability for results (RBM).

6.1.6 Real-World Scenarios: SDLC Outsourced Model

Several IT leaders prefer to use their "in-house"-managed services to gain control of their entire ITS delivery. Several other IT leaders prefer to use an outsourced approach to transfer control of their entire ITS management and delivery to an outsourced service provider. Some IT leaders prefer to use a hybrid approach to manage and deliver ITS by gaining control of "strategic value" services and transferring control to outsourced ITS providers and contracted resources for project delivery and IT operational services, similar to the *client-centric outsourced model* discussed in this chapter.

Many consulting firms that specialize in IT outsourcing prefer to sign contractual agreements to manage and deliver IT outsourced services for the entire IT department, similar to the second scenario earlier. This usually means transferring ownership and accountability to an IT consulting firm–ITS provider. In many cases, these consulting firms usually convince their clients to use their (consulting firm) propriety rigid "process-control" SDLC methodologies to manage and deliver ITS, with little or no performance measures for any delivered services. Accountability for result is nonexistent. Accountability for results is not normally in the best interest of many IT outsourced service providers. In many cases, their main interest is to generate revenue, even if this means using their propriety methodology to justify excessive management overhead, "change request" and "billable hours." In many cases, this lack of accountability for results is never realized by the client–owner, and the contractual agreements usually result in mistrust, "blame" game, and judgmental and negative performance measurements.

The major reason for this lack of trust, transparency, and accountability is because of the lack of required skills, experience, and knowledge of the IT leaders to convert formulated strategies into execution, output, outcomes, and result, to effectively manage, monitor, and measure performance results. Leadership + transparency + accountability = trust; trust and transparency and accountability are always linked.

The remaining sections of this chapter provide a real-world implementation of the *client-centric outsourced model* using a results-based, model-centric, and integrated approach that aligns strategic directives with IT operational execution, output, outcomes and results, and performance measures. Modern performance management approaches require a more *results-driven model-centric*[1] process with a culture of *performance analytics*[13]*-rational evidence-based decision making, and trustful relationships*, which must replace the traditional negative, judgmental, and reactive approach to performance management. The *client-centric outsourced model* provides a practical, flexible, and sustainable framework that supports this modern performance management model.

For *client-centric outsourced model* solution to be deployed or transitioned effectively into the entire ITS environment, the following major results must be produced, for each IT functional area, as illustrated in Figure 6.3, *IT SDLC process:*

- ELS
  - ELS leadership, contract administration, IT management policies and procedures, financial management (capital and operating expenses reviews), client and vendor relationships, employee progress performance, and customer satisfaction surveys

- PAS
  - PAS leadership, strategic/operational plans, invoice processing, financial management (capital and operating expenses), employee performance, client and vendor relationships, and customer satisfaction surveys
- Enterprise architecture/innovations services (EAS)
  - EAS leadership, contract management, EAS, project management (IT infrastructure), EAS management policies, financial management (capital and operating expenses), employee performance, client and vendor relationships, and customer satisfaction surveys
- PPM
  - PPM leadership, contract administration, project management (business projects), project management office (PMO) policies, financial management (capital and operating expenses reviews), employee performance, client and vendor relationships, and customer satisfaction surveys
- AMS
  - AMS leadership, contract administration, AMS, AMS management policies, financial management (capital and operating expenses reviews), employee performance, client and vendor relationships, and customer satisfaction surveys
- TOS
  - TOS leadership, contract administration, TOS, TOS management policies, financial management (capital and operating expenses reviews), employee performance, client and vendor relationships, and customer satisfaction surveys

Transformation to this *client-centric outsourced model* solution must include

- *Results-driven model-centric*[1] process (RBM)
- Culture of *performance analytics-rational evidence-based decision making*
- Trustful relationships (leadership + transparency + accountability = trust)
- Integrated IT performance measurement dashboard (intelligent dashboard)
- Innovative IT performance management framework (flexible and integrated)
- Strategic directives integration with IT operational execution, output, outcomes and results, and performance measures (It is not only about communications, it is about improving performance results by measuring and monitoring outputs and outcomes.)
- Next-generation performance management

Next-generation performance management is gaining widespread acceptance in this advancing technological world, because of the technological advancements toward performance management software. The transformation to the culture of performance analytics with proactive alert tools, predictive performance reports, and automated root cause analysis is also the result of technology advancements. The increasing demands to build win–win alliances and trust relationships between clients and ITS providers and vendors, and between employees and managers, require collaborative and delayered organizational structures, with reduced administrative and bureaucratic overhead. Modern performance management practices from KPI Institute, Capability Maturity Model Integrated (CMMI), COBIT, Six Sigma, Information Technology Infrastructure Library (ITIL), Project Management Institute (PMI), Kaplan and Norton[14] seem to be gaining wide acceptance in the IT industry.

Chapter 7 of this book provides foundation principles and processes on "aligning IPMF-IT processes with these industry practices." I hope this introduction will provide an understanding for IT decision makers and professionals and prevent the types of IT decision-making disasters that normally cause chaos, confusion, mistrust, and bureaucratic reorganization. IT leaders, who lack the understanding of the fundamental principles of client-centric outsourced model, usually try to create new alignments/structures to satisfy their ego, status, and politics. This decision normally ends up generating bureaucracy and negativity impacting staff morale and productivity-degrading performance rather than improving performance.

In order to effectively apply the SDLC performance model presented in this chapter, the strategic directives, results, outputs, outcomes, and performance measures that support this client-centric outsourced model must be carefully managed, monitored, and measured using this IPMF-IT. The functional areas or stages of the SDLC performance model are discussed to show how the strategic directives integrate with the performance measurement dashboard and strategic, IT operational, and performance management results areas. The major results of the strategic directives are highlighted to show the linkage with the outputs in the performance measurement dashboard. The matrices, "alignment to performance measures," provide graphical representation of how the IT strategic directives are aligned with the performance measurement dashboard, using the results (outputs and outcomes).

6.2 IT Executive Leadership Services (ELS)

> Management is efficiency in climbing the ladder of success; leadership determines whether the ladder is leaning against the right wall.
>
> **Stephen R. Covey**

The IT SDLC performance model, also referred to as the *IT service delivery life cycle* process, consists of six (6) IT functional areas, as shown in Figure 6.3, IT SDLC process. The *chief information officer* (*CIO*)[15] is accountable for the delivery of IT ELS and associated outputs, outcomes, and performance measures.

IT ELS provides

- Strategic directives for executive leadership, contract administration, IT management policies and procedures, financial management (capital and operating expenses reviews), client and vendor relationships, employee progress performance, and customer satisfaction surveys

This functional area produces the following major results, based on the IPMF-IT (Figure 6.1), and the IT SDLC process (Figure 6.3), aligned with the integrated IT performance dashboard (Appendices A through F). These strategic directives for ELS are updated as ITS are managed, measured, and monitored throughout the IT SDLC.

IT ELS consists of

- Operational (functional management) outputs
  - IT governance accountability framework
  - Human resource (HR) performance contract alignment
  - Executive management (EM) progress status
  - EM presentation/approvals
  - IT policies and procedures
  - IT operational accountability framework
- Operational (service delivery) outputs
  - IT contract accountability framework

  - IT consultant nondisclosure agreement (NDA)
  - CIO approvals—RFP
  - CIO approvals—IT infrastructure impact
  - IT equipment purchases records
  - CIO approvals—business projects
  - CIO approvals—technology infrastructure projects
  - CIO approvals—IT equipment expenditures
  - CIO approvals—IT outsourced/consulting services
  - CIO/CEO approvals—special business projects
  - CIO/CEO approvals—special technology projects
- Operational (service/operational excellence) outputs
  - IT management policy framework
  - IT management procedures
  - IT business council accountability framework
  - IT compliance—industry performance measures
  - IT benchmarking metrics
- Operational (relationship management) outputs
  - EM relations/feedback
  - Business areas' relations/feedback
  - Vendors' relations/feedback
  - IT outsourced providers' relations/feedback
  - IT contracted resources' relations/feedback
- Financial outputs
  - IT capital costs
  - IT operational costs
  - IT outsourced/consulting costs
  - IT staff costs
  - Major business projects costs
  - Major technology infrastructure project costs
- Customer outputs
  - Client relationships/satisfaction surveys
  - IT business council meetings
  - Vendor relationships/satisfaction surveys
  - IT outsourced providers performance measures
  - IT benchmarking surveys/results
- Employee outputs
  - IT progress reporting
  - IT staff performance contract
  - Staff learning/growth
  - Staff meetings/communications
  - Staff retention/retraining/reward reporting

6.2.1 Strategic Directives: Executive Governance

Many IT executives manage the utilization of their resources—people, process, technology, and financials—using intuitional and emotional judgmental guesses, which sounds impressive and politically attractive, and decision-making powers, with illusions of real efficiencies. In most cases, there are neither strategic directives nor performance measures to measure success of IT governance and the entire ITS. The performance culture of improvement is usually foreign to many IT executives. They are usually not aware that performance measurement culture adopted by their organization with regard to strategy, process, and structure contribute to the success or failures of IT governance. Their IT executive's style of governance/leadership normally focuses on communications to satisfy their ego, status, and political agendas.

This is clearly the result of lack of understanding of accountability for results culture (RBM). There are ineffective communications of the required results (outputs and outcomes) (what), processes to produce the results (how), processes to measure the results (why), and people resources (who) required to manage and deliver the results. In reality, an atmosphere of confusion, disagreements, and conflicting views prevail among the people resources internal and external to the ITS departments. Effective delivery of accountability for results starts with an understanding of *strategic directives* and alignment to IT operational execution, using output, outcomes, and performance measures.

Executive Leadership

- ITS will be directed by an IT steering committee using an *IT governance accountability framework* that specifies the mission, goals, objectives, critical success factors, performance measures, and *accountability for results (RBM)*, to direct and measure the success and business value of ITS. This governance framework includes transformation leadership strategies (strategic directives), modeling the way (*measuring performance results*), empowerment and collaboration, and inspiring shared vision, with the objective toward integrating ITS into business areas.
- *HR performance contract* for IT staff will be *aligned* to this "ITS strategic directive" to ensure that IT efforts are directed toward the stated goals and objectives. Provide an environment that encourages young graduates with competent, committed, and confidence characteristics, to enter the IT workforce.
- The CIO with IT outsourced service providers will present the *progress status* to the *EM* on a quarterly or "as-required" basis.
- IT operational plan (budget) and *contractual agreements* with the outsourced ITS providers, as well as major change requests, will be *presented* to the *EM* for approval.
- The CIO and IT directors will establish and ensure *compliance* with the *IT policies and procedures*, which include IT project management processes, ITS governance strategies, and signed contractual agreements with ITS providers, to ensure consistency in the delivery across the business areas.
- Everyday management of ITS will be managed by the IT directors, using an *IT operational accountability framework* that specifies the *strategic directives*, critical success factors, performance measures, and *accountability for results* (*RBM*) for IT planning and architecture services, IT PPM, and IT applications and technology management services.

Contract Administration

- IT *contracts* (outsourced and contracted) will be administered by IT contract services group (CSG), using IT contract accountability framework that specifies the contractual accountability guidelines.
- *Contractors/consultants will sign an NDA* and a conflict of interest clause managed under the nonemployee security policy and selected through the RFP competitive process. Any exception will seek approval from the CIO and CSG.

- *RFPs and contract agreements* from ITS providers and consultants will be reviewed and approved by the CIO and CSG, prior to execution. *RFPs and contract agreements* that can have major IT infrastructure implications will also be reviewed and approved by the CIO and IT *infrastructure/architecture standards committee*, prior to execution.
- *Records for IT equipment purchases* (hardware, software, network, storage, and data center facilities) will be documented, monitored, and maintained, using the purchasing order system and IT equipment purchasing policies. These records will be used to monitor IT equipment expenditures during each fiscal year.
- Change requests for *business projects and technology infrastructure projects* will be reviewed and approved by the CIO, prior to execution.
- *IT equipment expenditures* will be reviewed and *approved by the CIO*, prior to purchase.
- *IT outsourced/contracted agreements* will be reviewed and *approved by the CIO*, prior to execution.
- Change requests for *special business projects and technology infrastructure projects* will be reviewed and *approved by the CIO and CEO*, prior to execution.
- For documents and change requests requiring CIO approval, staff work and business approvals will be completed, prior to seeking *CIO approval.*

IT Management Policies and Procedures

- The ITS department will update and communicate *IT management policy framework*, integrated with the IT governance framework, to ensure accountability for results, operational consistency, and integrity during the management and delivery of ITS.
- The ITS department will update and communicate *IT management procedures*, integrated with the IT governance framework and aligned with IT management policy framework, to ensure operational consistency and integrity during the management and delivery of ITS.
- The ITS department will update and communicate *IT business council accountability framework*, integrated with IT governance framework, to better understand the terms of reference for IT business council and associated IT committees, address and resolve issues, communicate and monitor the progress, measure the performance results and value of ITS, and take necessary corrective actions for improvements.
- *IT industry performance measures* will be determined from IT research firms and reviewed by the CIO and IT leaders to ensure *compliance* with IT industry best practices.
- *IT benchmarking metrics* will be obtained from IT research firms to measure performance results of ITS and to compare with IT industry best practices.

Client and Vendor Relationship Management

- The ITS department will maintain *effective relationships* with the *EM* on a regular basis, by communicating and ensuring feedback of executive expectations and follow-up of client satisfaction surveys (EM).
- The ITS department will maintain *effective relationships* with *business areas* on a regular basis, by communicating and ensuring feedback of business areas' staff expectations and follow-up of client satisfaction surveys (business areas).
- The ITS department will maintain *effective relationships* with *vendors* on a regular basis, by communicating and ensuring feedback of vendors' services and follow-up of client satisfaction surveys (vendor).

- The ITS department will continuously communicate *progress of IT outsourced service providers* by monitoring and measuring *performance results and accountability*, based on contractual agreements, and follow-up of client satisfaction surveys (ITS provider), and chairing regular meetings to discuss directives, issues, and corrective actions.
- The ITS department will continuously communicate *progress of IT contracted resources by* monitoring and measuring *performance results and accountability*, based on contractual agreements, and follow-up of client satisfaction surveys (IT contracted resources).

Financial Management

- *IT operational plan* (*budget*) will be structured to support results-based budgeting (RBB), in accordance with capital and operating guidelines from the finance department, and will be *presented* to *EM and chief financial officer* for approval.
- *IT capital costs* for business projects and IT infrastructure projects will be determined using RBB. Expenses will be managed, monitored, and measured using earned value technique and financial tracking system (FTS) that tracks and forecasts progress of financial performance results, using financial predictive analytics.
- *IT operational costs* for ongoing hardware, software, network, storage, data center facilities, telecommunications, staff, and other operating costs will be determined using RBB. Expenses will be managed, monitored, and measured using earned value technique and FTS that tracks and forecasts progress of financial performance results, using financial predictive analytics.
- *IT outsourced/consulting costs* for AMS, TOS, and *major business and IT infrastructure projects* will be determined using the outsourced contractual agreements. Expenses will be managed, monitored, and measured using service-level agreements (SLAs) and performance measurement framework, earned value technique, and FTS that tracks and forecasts progress of financial performance results, using financial predictive analytics.
- *IT staff costs* for IT management and technical and administrative staff will be determined using salary budget. Expenses will be managed, monitored, and measured using an integrated HR/FTS that tracks and forecasts progress of HR/financial performance results, using HR/financial predictive analytics.
- *Major business and IT infrastructure projects* (*total costs > $500,000*) will be submitted with business case to the EM for approval.

Customer Satisfaction Surveys

- The ITS department will review results of *client satisfaction surveys* (*internal stakeholders*) (*business areas and EM*) and initiate follow-up for the execution of action items.
- The ITS department will review expectations and results of *IT business council meetings* and initiate follow-up for execution of action items.
- The ITS department will review results of *client satisfaction surveys* (*vendor* external stakeholders) and initiate follow-up for execution of action items.
- The ITS department will review results of *client satisfaction surveys* (*external stakeholders*) (*IT outsourced ITS providers*) for contractual performance measures and initiate follow-up for execution of action items.
- The ITS department will review results of *benchmarking survey/results* to assess and compare IT performance results with similar IT industries and to initiate follow-up for compliance to industry best practices.

Employee Progress Performance

- *ITS staff time progress reporting* will be entered every month into the *ITS time reporting system*, which is aligned with HR job description and HR performance contract.
- The ITS department *staff performance contracts and training plans* will be established at the beginning of the fiscal year and performance appraisals completed at the end of the fiscal year. Intermediate performance appraisals will be completed on an "as-required" basis.
- The ITS department staff will *have regular monthly staff meetings* (*1 h*) to discuss major issues and directives and to assign corrective action plans. CIO and ITS managers will *have regular biweekly staff meetings* (*1 h*) to discuss major issues and directives and to assign a corrective action plan.
- The CIO and HR staff will assess IT *staff retention/retraining/reward/reporting* requirements and ensure corrective action plan.

6.2.2 Alignment with Performance Measures

Table 6.1 is an integrated representation illustrating how the results of the strategic directives relate to the outputs, outcomes, and performance measures in the IT performance measurement dashboard. Appendix A provides a real-world implementation of the integrated IT performance measurement dashboard.

6.2.3 Integration with Strategic, IT Operational, and Performance Management

In Figure 6.4a through c, strategic, IT operational, and performance management accountability matrices are shown illustrating how the results areas from ELS integrate with the results areas from strategic management, IT operational management, and performance management. The acronyms on the matrices are abbreviations for executive manager's (business, performance, and IT), performance steering committee's (PSC's), performance delivery manager's (PDM's), performance measurement manager's (PMM's), and performance specialist team (PST) accountabilities/responsibilities.

6.2.3.1 Accountability Matrix: Executive Leadership/Governance Services

The accountability matrix of the executive leadership/governance services is shown in Figure 6.4.

6.3 Planning and Administration Services (PAS)

Proper Planning, Preparation, and Practice Prevent Poor Performance.

British Army adage

The PAS, as shown in Figure 6.3, IT SDLC process, is managed by the director of PAS. The director is accountable for the delivery of IT PAS and associated outputs, outcomes, and performance measures:

- Strategic directives for PAS leadership, strategic and operational planning, financial administration, client and vendor relationships, financial management (PAS expenses), customer satisfaction surveys, and employee progress performance

Table 6.1 Executive Leadership Services Strategic Directives Alignment with Performance Measures

Strategic Directives	*Outputs/Deliverables*	*Performance Measures*
Executive leadership	IT governance accountability framework HR performance contract alignment Executive management (EM) progress status Executive management presentation/approvals IT policies and procedures IT operational accountability framework	Operational FM
Contract administration	IT contract accountability framework IT consultants NDA CIO approvals—RFP CIO approvals—IT infrastructure impact IT equipment purchases records CIO approvals—business projects CIO approvals—technology infrastructure project CIO approvals—IT equipment expenditures CIO approvals—IT outsourced/consulting services CIO/CEO approvals—special business/Tec projects	Operational SD
IT management policies and procedures	IT management policies framework IT management procedures IT business council accountability framework IT compliance—industry performance measures IT benchmarking metrics	Operational SE
Client and vendor relationship management	Executive management relations/feedback Business areas relations/feedback Vendors relations/feedback IT outsourced providers relations/feedback IT contracted resources relations/feedback	Operational RM
Financial management	IT capital costs IT operational costs IT outsourced/consulting costs IT staff costs Major business projects costs Major technology infrastructure project costs	Financial

(Continued)

Table 6.1 (*Continued*) Executive Leadership Services Strategic Directives Alignment with Performance Measures

Strategic Directives	*Outputs/Deliverables*	*Performance Measures*
Customer satisfaction surveys	Client relationships/satisfaction surveys IT business council meetings Vendor relationships/satisfaction surveys IT outsourced providers performance measures IT benchmarking surveys/results	Customer
Employee progress performance	IT progress reporting IT staff performance contract Staff learning/growth Staff meetings/communications Staff retention/retraining/reward reporting	Employee

This functional area produces the following major results, based on the IPMF-IT (Figure 6.1), and the IT SDLC process (Figure 6.3), aligned with the integrated IT performance dashboard (Appendix B). These strategic directives for PAS are updated as ITS are managed, measured, and monitored throughout the IT SDLC.

IT PAS consists of

- Operational (functional management) outputs
  - IT strategic planning framework
  - IT operating planning framework
  - IT budgeting planning framework

Roles → *Results Areas* ↓	*EBM* *CEO*	*EPM* *CPO*	*EITM* *CIO*	*PSC* *Sponsor*	*PDM*	*PMM*	*PST*
Strategic Management							
IT goal statement	I	C	A	C	R	R	R
IT strategic framework	I	C	A	C	R	R	R
IT strategic directives	I	C	A	C	R	R	R
IT policy framework	I	C	A	C	R	R	R
IT governance framework	I	C	A	C	R	R	R
IT value-based performance measurements	I	C	A	C	R	R	R

(a)

Figure 6.4 (a) Strategic management accountability matrix: executive leadership service (ELS). *Legend*: R, responsible; A, accountable; C, consulted; I, informed. *(Continued)*

Roles → *Results Areas* ↓	*EBM* *CEO*	*EPM* *CPO*	*EITM* *CIO*	*PSC* *Sponsor*	*PDM*	*PMM*	*PST*
Performance Management							
Performance management standards	I	A	C	C	R	R	R
Performance measurement systems	I	A	C	C	R	R	R
Performance management reporting	I	A	C	C	R	R	R
Performance improvement management	I	A	C	C	R	R	R
Performance change management	I	A	C	C	R	R	R
HR performance management	I	A	R	C	R	R	R
Financial performance management	I	A	C	C	R	R	R

(b)

Roles → *Results Areas* ↓	*EBM* *CEO*	*EPM* *CPO*	*EITM* *CIO*	*PSC* *Sponsor*	*PDM*	*PMM*	*PST*
IT Operations Management							
Financial accountability	I	C	A	C	C	R	R
HR accountability	I	C	A	C	C	R	R
Operational accountability	I	C	C	C	A	R	R
Project accountability	I	C	C	C	A	R	R
Applications accountability	I	C	C	C	A	R	R
Technology accountability	I	C	C	C	A	R	R

(c)

Figure 6.4 (*Continued*) (b) Performance management accountability: ELS. (c) Information technology operations management accountability matrix: ELS. *Legend*: R, responsible; A, accountable; C, consulted; I, informed.

- Operational (service delivery) outputs
  - IT strategic and operating plan
  - IT budget plan
  - IT budget plan status/progress/forecasts
  - IT capital/operating expenditures coding

  - IT invoice processing and financial administration
  - IT contract agreement status
  - Stakeholders' financial support
  - Finance and HR collaborations
- Operational (service/operational excellence) outputs
  - IT strategic/operating plan—guidelines
  - IT financial accountability framework
  - IT financial guidelines
  - IT financial compliance—financial measures
  - IT financial benchmarking metrics
- Operational (relationship management) outputs
  - Financial management relations/feedback
  - Vendors' PAS relations/feedback
  - IT outsourced providers' PAS relations/feedback
- Financial outputs
  - IT planning costs
  - IT administration costs
- Customer outputs
  - PAS client relationships/satisfaction surveys
  - PAS committee meetings
  - PAS vendors' relationships/satisfaction surveys
  - PAS IT outsourced providers' surveys
  - PAS benchmarking surveys/results
- Employee outputs
  - PAS progress reporting
  - PAS staff performance contract
  - PAS staff learning/growth reporting
  - PAS staff meetings/communications
  - PAS staff retention/retraining/reward reporting

6.3.1 Strategic Directives: Planning and Administration

Many IT directors manage the delivery of PAS by spending their efforts on strategic planning, IT operational planning, and IT budget planning, with overly excessive administrative overhead. Strategic plan, IT operational plan, and IT budget plan are normally disjoined, with no linkages to show how strategic plan is executed by IT operational plan and IT budget plan. The concepts of RBB are normally ignored. Activity-based budgeting (ABB) using financial accounting coding structures, without any alignment to strategic or IT operational plan, is the mind-set that is understood and accepted. Excessive administrative overhead normally results from frequent ineffective planning meetings to satisfy an egoistic manager. In most cases, there are neither strategic directives nor performance measures to measure success of IT planning and administration. The performance culture of accountability for results is normally ignored or treated as theoretical. They do not understand the difference between developing a strategic plan and executing it using an IT operation plan and an IT budget plan, with output, outcomes, and performance—accountability for results.

This is clearly the result of a lack of understanding or resistance to accountability for results culture–RBM and RBB. In reality, an atmosphere of excessive planning and administrative overhead, as a result of disjointed strategic and operational plan, with manual FTS (disjoined spreadsheets), is the preferred mode of operations. Effective delivery of accountability for results starts with an understanding of *strategic directives* and alignment to IT operational execution, using output, outcomes, and performance measures.

PAS Leadership

- PAS will be directed by a PAS working committee, using an *IT operational framework* that specifies the strategic directives, critical success factors, and performance measures for IT planning and administration in order to direct and measure the success and value of PAS. The everyday management of this IT functional area will be managed by an IT director, using an *IT operational framework*, which consists of *IT strategic planning framework, IT operating planning framework, and IT budgeting planning framework.*
- IT directors will ensure *compliance* with the *IT policies and procedures*, during the management and delivery of strategic plans, IT operating plans, and IT budget plans, using an automated *FTS*[16] to ensure consistency and integration with plans and RBB.

Strategic and Operational Planning

- The ITS department will have a documented *IT strategic plan* that adheres to IT policy and procedure guidelines and aligns with the organization's business plan. The *IT strategic plan* will include the outcomes, goals, strategies, programs and initiatives, benefits, costs, critical success factors and performance measures, and linkages to business strategic plan and program delivery plan.
- The ITS department will have an *IT operating plan* and an *IT budget plan* that will be approved by *executive steering committee.*[17] It must align with the IT strategic plan and will be used to guide the budgeting process during each fiscal year.
- IT costs will not exceed IT budget plan, as represented in the approved budget, unless explicit approval is granted through an *approved change management process*, by executive steering committee.
- The ITS department will provide monthly *progress* to business areas on the *status* and *forecast* for cost and schedule *of the IT budget plan* and recommend improvements to support additional IT initiatives.
- The ITS department will *code capital and operating expenditures*, using finance department coding structures, implemented in the FTS.
- The ITS department will monitor and maintain documented records of all *processed invoice and approvals*, as well as *specified financial reports* to manage the expenditures during each fiscal year (*financial administration*).
- The ITS department will provide progress to business areas and IT staff on the status of cost and schedule for *contract agreements* and recommend improvements to support additional IT initiatives.
- IT budget plan will be presented to *stakeholders* (internal and external), at the beginning of each fiscal year, for *approval and support.*
- *Finance and HR* will *collaborate* to ensure accuracy of IT staff utilizations in financial and HR records for "in-house"-managed services.

Financial Administration

- The PAS section will update and communicate *IT strategic/operating planning guidelines*, integrated with IT management policies and procedures, to ensure operational consistency and integrity during the management and delivery of PAS.
- The PAS section will update and communicate *IT financial accountability management framework*, integrated with the IT governance framework and aligned with IT management policy framework, to ensure accountability for results, operational consistency, and integrity.
- The PAS section and the finance department will update and communicate *IT financial guidelines*, integrated with IT management policies and procedures, to ensure operational consistency and integrity during the management and delivery of PAS.
- *IT industry performance measures* will be determined from IT research firms and reviewed by the CIO and IT leaders to ensure *compliance* with IT industry best practices for *IT financial expenditures*.
- *IT benchmarking metrics* will be obtained from IT research firms to measure performance results of *IT financials* and to compare with IT industry best practices.

Client and Vendor Relationship Management

- The PAS section will maintain effective *relationships with finance, vendors, service providers, and clients* in resolving IT PAS management and delivery issues through regular feedback and follow-up communications to improve performance results.

Financial Management: PAS

- The PAS section will *review IT planning and administration expenses on a monthly basis* to maintain accuracy in the IT budget plan and FTS and to ensure compliance to financial policies and recommend improvements to expenses for proper realization of business value.

Customer Satisfaction Surveys

- The PAS section will review PAS results of *client satisfaction surveys* (*internal stakeholders*) (*business areas and EM*) and initiate follow-up for execution of action items.
- The PAS section will review expectations and results of *PAS section meetings* and initiate follow-up for execution of action items.
- The PAS section will review PAS results of *client satisfaction surveys* (*vendor* external stakeholders) and initiate follow-up for execution of action items.
- The PAS section will review PAS results of *client satisfaction surveys* (*external stakeholders*) (*IT outsourced ITS providers*) for contractual performance measures and initiate follow-up for execution of action items.
- The PAS section will review PAS results of *benchmarking survey/results* to assess and compare IT performance results with similar IT industries and to initiate follow-up for compliance to industry best practices.

Employee Progress Performance

- *PAS staff time progress reporting* will be entered every month into the *ITS time reporting system*, which aligns with HR job description and HR performance contract.

- PAS *staff performance contracts and training plans* will be established at the beginning of the fiscal year and performance appraisals completed at the end of the fiscal year. Intermediate performance appraisals will be completed on an "as-required" basis.
- The PAS staff will *have regular monthly staff meetings* (*1 h*) to discuss major issues and directives and to assign corrective action plans. CIO and PAS managers will *have regular biweekly staff meetings* (*1 h*) to discuss major issues and directives and to assign corrective action plan.
- The PAS director, CIO, and HR staff will assess *retention/retraining/reward/reporting* requirements for PAS staff and ensure corrective action plan.

6.3.2 Alignment with Performance Measures

Table 6.2 is an integrated representation illustrating how the results of the strategic directives relate to the outputs, outcomes, and performance measures in the IT performance measurement dashboard. Appendix B provides a real-world implementation of the integrated IT performance measurement dashboard.

6.3.3 Integration with Strategic, IT Operational, and Performance Management

In Figure 6.5a through c, strategic, IT operational and performance management accountability matrices are presented illustrating how the results areas from PAS integrate with the results areas from strategic management, IT operational management, and performance management. The acronyms on the matrices are abbreviations for executive manager's (business, performance, and IT), PSC's, PDM's, PMM's, and PST accountabilities/responsibilities.

6.3.3.1 Accountability Matrix: PAS

The accountability matrix of PAS is shown in Figure 6.5.

6.4 Enterprise Architecture Services (EAS)

> A model is an abstraction of reality constructed to explore particular aspects or properties of a system.
>
> **NAAIDT Computer Conference—2003**

The enterprise architecture and innovations services (EAS), as shown in Figure 6.3, IT SDLC process, can be managed by the director of enterprise architecture and innovations services, who will be accountable for the delivery of IT enterprise architecture services, outputs, outcomes, and performance measures:

- Strategic directives for EAS leadership, enterprise architectures, EAS quality assurance (QA), client and vendor relationships, financial management (EAS expenses), customer satisfaction surveys, and employee progress performance

This EAS functional area produces the following major results, based on the IPMF-IT (Figure 6.1) and the IT SDLC process (Figure 6.3), aligned with the integrated IT performance measurement dashboard (Appendix C). These strategic directives for enterprise architecture services are updated as ITS are managed, measured, and monitored throughout the IT SDLC.

Table 6.2 Planning and Administration Services Strategic Directives Alignment with Performance Measures

Strategic Directives	*Outputs/Deliverables*	*Performance Measures*
PAS leadership	IT strategic planning framework IT operating planning framework IT budgeting planning framework	Operational FM
Strategic and operational plans	IT strategic and operating plan IT budget plan IT budget plan status/progress/forecasts IT capital/operating expenditures coding IT invoice processing and financial admin IT contract agreement status Stakeholders financial support Finance and HR collaborations	Operational SD
Financial administration	IT strategic/operating plan—guidelines IT financial accountability framework IT financial guidelines IT financial compliance—financial measures IT financial benchmarking metrics	Operational SE
Client/vendor relationships	Financial management relations/feedback Vendors PAS relations/feedback IT outsourced providers PAS relations/feedback	Operational RM
Financial management	IT planning costs IT administration costs	Financial
Customer satisfaction surveys	PAS client relationships/satisfaction surveys PAS committee meetings PAS vendors relationships/satisfaction surveys PAS IT outsourced providers surveys PAS benchmarking surveys/results	Customer
Employee performance	PAS progress reporting PAS staff performance contract PAS staff learning/growth reporting PAS staff meetings/communications PAS staff retention/retraining/reward reporting	Employee

Roles → *Results Areas* ↓	*EBM* *CEO*	*EPM* *CPO*	*EITM* *CIO*	*PSC* *Sponsor*	*PDM*	*PMM*	*PST*
Strategic Management							
IT goal statement	I	C	A	C	R	R	R
IT strategic framework	I	C	A	C	R	R	R
IT strategic directives	I	C	A	C	R	R	R
IT policy framework	I	C	A	C	R	R	R
IT governance framework	I	C	A	C	R	R	R
IT value-based performance measurements	I	C	A	C	R	R	R

(a)

Roles → *Results Areas* ↓	*EBM* *CEO*	*EPM* *CPO*	*EITM* *CIO*	*PSC* *Sponsor*	*PDM*	*PMM*	*PST*
Performance Management							
Performance management standards	I	A	C	C	R	R	R
Performance measurement systems	I	A	C	C	R	R	R
Performance management reporting	I	A	C	C	R	R	R
Performance improvement management	I	A	C	C	R	R	R
Performance change management	I	A	C	C	R	R	R
HR performance management	I	A	C	C	R	R	R
Financial performance management	I	A	R	C	R	R	R

(b)

Figure 6.5 (a) Strategic management accountability matrix: planning and administration services (PAS). (b) Performance management accountability: PAS. *Legend*: R, responsible; A, accountable; C, consulted; I, informed. *(Continued)*

Roles → *Results Areas* *↓*	*EBM* *CEO*	*EPM* *CPO*	*EITM* *CIO*	*PSC* *Sponsor*	*PDM*	*PMM*	*PST*
IT Operations Management							
Financial accountability	I	C	A	C	R	R	R
HR accountability	I	C	A	C	C	R	R
Operational accountability	I	C	C	C	A	R	R
Project accountability	I	C	C	C	A	R	R
Applications accountability	I	C	C	C	A	R	R
Technology accountability	I	C	C	C	A	R	R

(c)

Figure 6.5 (*Continued*) (c) Information technology operations management accountability matrix: PAS. *Legend*: R, responsible; A, accountable; C, consulted; I, informed.

IT enterprise architecture services (EAS) consists of

- Operational (functional management) outputs
  - IT enterprise architecture framework
  - Information management framework
  - Technology project management governance
- Operational (service delivery) outputs
  - Business systems planning support
  - Business case/architecture support
  - IT enterprise architectures
  - IT enterprise architecture standards
  - IT security plans
  - IT security implementation
  - Innovative communications tools
  - Technology projects contract management
  - Technology program/project management
  - IT productivity tools and framework
  - Technology infrastructure delivery/support
  - Technology research/trends
- Operational (service/operational excellence) outputs
  - Technology infrastructure project plan QA
  - IT security and privacy compliance/approval
  - Infrastructure project financial measures
  - Technology infrastructure compliance
  - Technology infrastructure optimization
  - Technology infrastructure benchmarking
- Operational (relationship management) outputs
  - EAS client management relations/feedback

  - Vendors' EAI relations/feedback
  - IT outsourced providers' EAI relations/feedback
- Financial outputs
  - IT infrastructure project costs
  - IT enterprise architecture costs
- Customer outputs
  - EAS client relationships/satisfaction surveys
  - EAS committee meetings
  - EAS vendors' relationships/satisfaction surveys
  - EAS IT outsourced providers' surveys
  - EAS benchmarking surveys/results
- Employee outputs
  - EAS progress reporting
  - EAS staff performance contract
  - EAS staff learning/growth reporting
  - EAS staff meetings/communications
  - EAS staff retention/retraining/reward reporting

6.4.1 Strategic Directives: Enterprise Architecture Services

Many IT directors manage the delivery of enterprise architecture services (EAS) by spending their efforts on architectures (data, applications, technology, and security), and technology infrastructure projects, with overly complex diagrams and documentations. Architectures and project plans are normally disjoined, with no linkages to show how architectures are mapped to IT project plans and IT operational plans. The concept of model-based architectures or model-based software developments are normally ignored or treated as theoretical. Huge colorful diagrams are normally posted on the walls of the ITS departments; to look impressive, without any alignment to strategic or IT operational plans, is the mind-set that is understood and accepted. Excessive administrative overhead and rework normally result from frequent ineffective planning meetings to satisfy an egoistic manager. In most cases, there are neither strategic directives nor performance measures to measure success of IT architectures. The performance culture of accountability for results with predictive analytics, using *big data and analytics*[18] for insights on decision making and predictions, is normally ignored or treated as theoretical. They do not understand the difference between architecture development, aligning it with strategic plan and executing it using IT operational plan, output, outcomes, and performance—accountability for results.

This is clearly the result of a lack of understanding or resistance to accountability for results culture–RBM and predictive analytics. In reality, an atmosphere of excessive analysis, architecture rework, and administrative overhead prevails, as a result of disjointed architectures, strategic and operational plan, and IT infrastructure projects. Effective delivery of accountability for results starts with an understanding of *strategic directives* and alignment to IT operational execution, using output, outcomes, and performance measures.

EAS Leadership

- Enterprise architecture services (EAS) will be directed by an EAS working committee, using an *IT enterprise architecture framework* that specifies the strategic directives, decision structure (accountability for results), processes and communications, critical success factors, and performance measures for enterprise architectures and *IT infrastructure projects*[19] in order to direct and measure the success and value of EAS. The everyday management of this IT functional area will be managed by an IT director, using an *IT enterprise architecture framework*, which consists of data architecture, applications architecture, and technology architecture (security and privacy), with alignment to business architecture.

- The EAS director will ensure *compliance* with the *information management framework and IT project management governance*, during the management and delivery of information management and IT infrastructure projects, using automated model-based service-oriented architecture software tools to ensure consistency, reusability, and integration with architectures, strategic plans, IT operational plans, and IT projects.
- The EAS director will chair the *technology architecture committee* by using the terms of reference as the framework to guide the identification and resolution of IT architecture and business issues.

Enterprise Architecture

- The EAS section will deliver *business planning support* to the business areas, including *information management framework* for data management (big data), social computing, and web service initiatives/projects that align with information management strategy and standards.
- The EAS section will ensure that the *business systems plans/architectures* are consistent and integrated across the business areas and comply with the guidelines from the enterprise architecture, strategic plan, IT operational plan, and the organization's business plans.
- EAS will provide *business case/architecture support* to the business areas during the identification, definition, and justification of IT initiatives to support the development of architectures, information management, and IT infrastructure initiatives/projects.
- The EAS section will deliver a documented *enterprise architecture* (business, data, applications, and technology [security and privacy]) for project delivery, applications, and TOS, which aligns with the business area architectures.
- The EAS section will develop and deliver *enterprise architecture* and *information management standards, policies, and processes* for project delivery, applications, and TOS that align with strategic and IT operational plans.
- The EAS section will develop *IT security plan* and ensure compliance with the IT information security and privacy policy during *implementation of IT security projects/initiatives.*
- The EAS section will deliver enhanced *innovative communications tools* and processes (website, SharePoint sites, newsletter, and data management [big data]) to maintain effective relationships and communications with vendors and clients and to ensure that expectations and results are clearly communicated.
- The EAS section will develop and deliver *IT productivity processes and tools* (dashboards, time reporting, etc.) to streamline the management and administrative processes of the IT department and to optimize the utilization of IT management and technical staff. This includes outsourcing/contracting decisions for special IT Infrastructure projects.
- *Technology infrastructure, information management, and business projects* will adhere to IT infrastructure standards or seek exception approval. Technology infrastructure projects over $250,000 in total cost must be approved through the early look architecture assessment process, prior to IT operating plan submission for approval.

- The EAS section will direct the initiation and execution of *technology infrastructure and information management projects*, by developing high-level project statement of work (SOW) documentation. The IT infrastructure support staff will be directly involved during project initiation, giving the infrastructure staff an opportunity to directly participate in the initial design of systems solutions.
- The EAS section will perform overall program delivery for *technology infrastructure and information management projects* by developing and maintaining a *technology infrastructure program plan*, reviewing overall project deliverables and progress, and providing status to PMO.
- EAS will review capital and operating expenses for *technology infrastructure projects and information management projects* and ensure value is realized.
- EAS will monitor existing storage, network, servers, and power/cooling capacity and implement *IT productivity tools*, for proactive monitoring and alert, to enable and support proactive and predictive decision making for the IT data center. Enhancements will be made based on projected growth and new business needs.
- The EAS section will *research* and implement solutions to meet business and technology needs. EAS staff will assess *technology trends* and keep current with new technology solutions that support business needs.

Quality Assurance: EAS

- The EAS section will ensure that *IT infrastructure project plans and information management project plans* comply with IT project management and architecture standards, during the management and delivery of these projects.
- *Information security and privacy* approval must be secured prior to implementing new technology or making major enhancements to existing technology. This review and approval will take place before any informal or formal obligations are made between the organization and an ITS provider and vendor. All credential and access management to the organization's sensitive applications will be managed and controlled through the information security and privacy policies.
- The EAS section will monitor financial progress of *IT infrastructure projects, using financial measures* and earned value performance results, in the FTS.
- The EAS section will ensure *IT infrastructure compliance* to standards and industry practices through active participations at specified technology committees.
- The EAS section will *optimize* the *utilization IT infrastructure resources* through delivery of IT productivity tools and processes for proactive and predictive alerts in managing operating software, hardware, network, storage, servers, and data center power/cooling technical performance.
- IT industry performance measures will be determined from IT research firms and reviewed by the CIO and EAS staff to ensure compliance with IT industry best practices for *IT infrastructure–data center performance.*
- *IT benchmarking metrics* will be obtained from IT research firms to measure performance results of *IT infrastructure–data center*, and to compare with IT industry best practices.

Client and Vendor Relationship Management

- The EAS section will maintain effective *relationships with finance, vendors, service providers, and clients* in resolving enterprise architecture services (EAS) management and delivery issues through regular feedback and follow-up communications to improve performance results.

Financial Management

- The EAS section will *review IT architecture expenses on a monthly basis* to maintain accuracy in the IT budget plan and FTS and to ensure compliance to financial policies and recommend improvements to expenses for proper realization of business value.

Customer Satisfaction Surveys

- The EAS section will review EAS results of *client satisfaction surveys* (*internal stakeholders*) (*business areas and EM*) and initiate follow-up for execution of action items.
- The EAS section will review expectations and results of *EAS section meetings* and initiate follow-up for execution of action items.
- The EAS section will review EAS results of *client satisfaction surveys* (*vendor* external stakeholders) and initiate follow-up for execution of action items.
- The EAS section will review EAS results of *client satisfaction surveys* (*external stakeholders*) (*IT outsourced ITS providers*) for contractual performance measures and initiate follow-up for execution of action items.
- The EAS section will review EAS results of *benchmarking survey/results* to assess and compare IT performance results with similar IT industries and to initiate follow-up for compliance to industry best practices.

Employee Progress Performance

- *EAS staff time progress reporting* will be entered every month into the *ITS time reporting system*, which aligns with HR job description and HR performance contract.
- EAS *staff performance contracts and training plans* will be established at the beginning of the fiscal year and performance appraisals completed at the end of the fiscal year. Intermediate performance appraisals will be completed on an "as-required" basis.
- The EAS staff will *have regular monthly staff meetings* (*1 h*) to discuss major issues and directives and to assign corrective action plans. CIO and EAS managers will *have regular biweekly staff meetings* (*1 h*) to discuss major issues and directives and to assign corrective action plan.
- The EAS director, CIO, and HR staff will assess *retention, retraining, reward, and reporting* requirements for EAS staff and ensure corrective action plan.

6.4.2 Alignment with Performance Measures

Table 6.3 is an integrated representation illustrating how the results of the strategic directives relate to the outputs, outcomes, and performance measures in the IT performance measurement dashboard. Appendix C provides a real-world implementation of the integrated IT performance dashboard.

6.4.3 Integration with Strategic, IT Operational, and Performance Management

In Figure 6.6a through c, strategic, IT operational, and performance management accountability matrices are presented illustrating how the results areas from EAS integrate with the results areas from strategic management, IT operational management, and performance management.

Table 6.3 EAS Strategic Directives Alignment with Performance Measures

Strategic Directives	*Outputs/Deliverables*	*Performance Measures*
EAS leadership	IT enterprise architecture framework Information management framework Technology project management governance	Operational FM
Enterprise architectures	Business systems planning support Business case/architecture support IT enterprise architectures IT enterprise architecture standards IT security plans IT security implementation Innovative communications tools Technology projects contract management Technology program/project management IT productivity tools and framework Technology infrastructure delivery/support Technology research/trends	Operational SD
Quality assurance-EAS	Technology infrastructure project plan QA IT security and privacy compliance/approval Infrastructure projects financial measures Technology infrastructure compliance Technology infrastructure optimization Technology infrastructure benchmarking metrics	Operational SE
Vendor/client relationships	EAS client management relations/feedback Vendors EAS relations/feedback IT outsourced providers EAS relations/ feedback	Operational RM
Financial	IT infrastructure project costs IT enterprise architecture costs	Financial
Customer satisfaction surveys	EAS client relationships/satisfaction surveys EAS committee meetings EAS vendors relationships/satisfaction surveys EAS IT outsourced providers surveys EAS benchmarking surveys/results	Customer
Employee performance	EAS IT progress reporting EAS IT staff performance contract EAS staff learning/growth reporting EAS staff meetings/communications EAS staff retention/retraining/reward reporting	Employee

The acronyms on the matrices are abbreviations for executive manager's, PDM's, PMM's, and PST accountabilities/responsibilities.

6.4.3.1 Accountability Matrix: Executive Enterprise Architecture Services

The accountability matrix of EAS is shown in Figure 6.6.

6.5 Project Portfolio Management (PPM)

To improve is to change; to be perfect is to change often.

Sir Winston Churchill

The PPM, as shown in Figure 6.3, IT SDLC process, is managed by the director of PPM, who is accountable for the delivery of PPM outputs, outcomes, and performance measures:

- Strategic directives for PPM leadership, project management, PPM QA, client and vendor relationships, financial management (PPM expenses), customer satisfaction surveys, and employee progress performance

This PPM functional area produces the following major results, based on the IPMF-IT (Figure 6.1) and the IT SDLC process (Figure 6.3), aligned with the integrated IT performance measurement dashboard (Appendix D). These strategic directives for PPM are updated as ITS are managed, measured, and monitored throughout the IT SDLC.

IT PPM consists of

- Operational (functional management) outputs
  - IT PPM governance framework
  - IT PPM innovative technical direction
  - PPM projects outsourcing framework

Roles → *Results Areas* *↓*	*EBM* *CEO*	*EPM* *CPO*	*EITM* *CIO*	*PSC* *Sponsor*	*PDM*	*PMM*	*PST*
Strategic Management							
IT goal statement	I	C	A	C	R	R	R
IT strategic framework	I	C	A	C	R	R	R
IT strategic directives	I	C	A	C	R	R	R
IT policy framework	I	C	A	C	R	R	R
IT governance framework	I	C	A	C	R	R	R
IT value-based performance measurements	I	C	A	C	R	R	R

(a)

Figure 6.6 (a) Strategic management accountability matrix: enterprise architecture services. ***Legend*: R, responsible; A, accountable; C, consulted; I, informed.** *(Continued)*

Roles → *Results Areas* ↓	*EBM* *CEO*	*EPM* *CPO*	*EITM* *CIO*	*PSC* *Sponsor*	*PDM*	*PMM*	*PST*
Performance Management							
Performance management standards	I	A	C	C	R	R	R
Performance measurement systems	I	A	C	C	R	R	R
Performance management reporting	I	A	C	C	R	R	R
Performance improvement management	I	A	C	C	R	R	R
Performance change management	I	A	C	C	R	R	R
HR performance management	I	A	C	C	R	R	R
Financial performance management	I	A	C	C	R	R	R

(b)

Roles → *Results Areas* ↓	*EBM* *CEO*	*EPM* *CPO*	*EITM* *CIO*	*PSC* *Sponsor*	*PDM*	*PMM*	*PST*
IT Operations Management							
Financial accountability	I	C	A	C	C	R	R
HR accountability	I	C	A	C	C	R	R
Operational accountability	I	C	A	C	R	R	R
Project accountability	I	C	C	C	A	R	R
Applications accountability	I	C	C	C	A	R	R
Technology accountability	I	C	C	C	A	R	R

(c)

Figure 6.6 (*Continued*) (b) Performance management accountability: enterprise architecture services. (c) Information technology operations management accountability matrix: enterprise architecture services. *Legend*: R, responsible; A, accountable; C, consulted; I, informed.

- Operational (service delivery) outputs
  - IT business projects monitoring/reporting
  - Innovative PMO communications tools
  - IT PPM productivity tools and processes
  - PPM systems and regression testing

- IT project management/delivery
- IT business projects' RFP/contracts
- IT business projects' program/projects plan
- IT business project architecture/design
- IT PMO support
- IT business project requirements specifications

- Operational (service/operational excellence) outputs
  - Business project plan QA
  - IT project management compliance/approval
  - Business project financial measures
  - PMO compliance
  - Project management optimization
  - Business project benchmarking metrics
- Operational (relationship management) outputs
  - PPM client management relations/feedback
  - Vendors' PPM relations/feedback
  - IT outsourced providers' PPM relations/feedback financial outputs
- Financial outputs
  - IT business project costs
  - IT PPM costs
- Customer outputs
  - PPM client relationships/satisfaction surveys
  - PPM committee meetings
  - PPM vendors' relationships/satisfaction surveys
  - PPM IT outsourced providers' surveys
  - PPM benchmarking surveys/results
- Employee outputs
  - PPM IT progress reporting
  - PPM IT staff performance contract
  - PPM staff learning/growth reporting
  - PPM staff meetings/communications
  - PPM staff retention/retraining/reward reporting

6.5.1 Strategic Directives: PPM

Many IT directors manage the delivery of projects by spending their efforts on business projects, with overly complex PMO processes and documentations that require heavy administrative overhead. Project plans and architectures are normally disjoined, with no linkages to show how architectures are mapped to IT project plans and IT operational plans. The concept of model-based software developments is normally ignored or treated as theoretical. Massive unstructured project documentation, which normally requires many management approval signatures, in accordance with PMO standards is usually the project management mind-set of this IT director. In most cases, there are unclear references as to what, why, and how these deliverables/outputs and outcomes are produced and measured. Excessive administrative overhead and rework normally result from frequent ineffective meetings to satisfy an egoistic manager. In most cases, strategic directives, critical success factors, or performance measures are not available in order to measure success of IT projects. The performance culture of accountability for results with proactive and predictive analytics, using earned value and trend analysis for insights on decision making and predictions for projects cost, schedule, scope, quality, and risk, is normally ignored or treated as theoretical. They do not understand model-based iterative software development methods, aligning it with architecture, strategic plan, and IT operational plan, using deliverables/output, outcomes, and performance success factors—accountability for results.

This is clearly the result of a lack of understanding or resistance to accountability for results culture–RBM with predictive analytics. In reality, an environment of excessive analysis paralysis, project documentation rework, and administrative overhead prevails, as a result of disjointed architectures and strategic and operational plans, for the delivery of IT business projects. Effective delivery of accountability for results starts with an understanding of strategic directives with alignment to IT operational execution, using output, outcomes, and performance measures.

PPM Leadership

- PPM will be directed by a PPM working committee, using an *IT PPM governance framework* that specifies the strategic directives, decision structure (accountability for results), processes and communications, critical success factors, and performance measures for *IT project management* (*business projects*) in order to direct and measure the success and value of PPM services. The everyday management of this IT functional area will be managed by an IT director, using an *IT PPM outsourcing framework* and *integrated IT project management framework*, which consists of the IT outsourcing strategy and IT project management integration processes—business management, project management, and IT management.
- The PPM director will establish and ensure *compliance* with the *IT PPM governance framework and IT project delivery outsourcing framework*, during the management and delivery of business projects, using *innovative project management processes and tools* (model based, dashboard, integrated/agile, etc.) to ensure consistency, reusability, and integration with strategic plans, IT operational plans, and architectures (business and technical).
- The PPM director will chair the *project management committee* by using the terms of reference as the framework to guide the identification and resolution of business and technical issues for IT business projects.

Project Management

- The PPM section will publish progress of business projects on a monthly basis via PMO dashboard/innovative *PMO productivity tools* that support PMO project management processes. This group will also deliver enhanced *innovative communications tools and processes* (website, SharePoint sites, newsletter, project management analytics, etc.) to maintain effective relationships and communications with internal and external stakeholders and to ensure that expectations and results are clearly communicated.
- The PPM section will produce *RFP and contract agreements* and obtain required professional services, business, and CIO approvals for the management and delivery of *business projects*, using an outsourced/contracted delivery model.
- The PPM section will develop *high-level program/project plan* with the business, during project initiations, prior to engaging into outsourced/contract negotiations.

- The PPM section will deliver documented *project management* and *software product deliverables* for the management and delivery of IT business projects that support applications and TOS, which aligns with the business area architectures.
- The PPM section will develop and deliver *integrated IT project management framework, standards, policies, and processes* for project delivery and migration to applications management and TOS that align with strategic and IT operational plans.
- The PPM section will perform overall *program delivery for business projects* by managing outsourced/contracted contract agreements, reviewing project deliverables and progress, and providing status to *PMO*. This group will maintain a *log of project-related issues*, documented in the Project Management Information System (PMIS). This log will be used as the basis for project and nonproject-related decisions.
- The PPM section will continuously communicate progress of project directives and issues to the business by participating at business areas' *project/program steering committee meetings*.[20]
- The PPM section will perform overall IT program delivery for *business projects*, by chairing the program/project committees, developing and maintaining the project/program plans, managing vendor/client relations, and *monitoring, measuring, and reporting project progress* based on output/outcome-driven performance measures.
- The PPM section will work with outsourced/contracted resources to develop scripts to manage and monitor defects, system, and *regression tests*, execute them, and record results using an automated testing tool for predictive and proactive decision making, during *testing phase of project delivery*.
- The PPM section will direct the initiation and definition of all business projects, by assisting the business during the development of *IT business requirements specifications*, master project plan, project expenditure approval, and SOW, *prior to engaging consulting resources*. The business support staff will be directly involved during project initiation, giving the business staff an opportunity to directly participate in the initial business design of the system solution.
- The PPM section will deliver *project architecture designs* to ensure compliance to IT project architecture guidelines by developing *conceptual system flow solutions and project architecture specifications*.
- Development projects will have specifically *identified business sponsor, business project manager, and specifically identified IT project manager/leader* prior to project execution.
- Projects are required to have appropriate *business case and business requirements statement approval signatures* prior to submission to the annual IT budget plan. Projects will adhere to *project expenditure authorization*[21] processes.
- Development projects will involve *technology operations support staff* during project initiation, giving the technical operations staff an opportunity to directly participate in the initial design of business systems solutions.
- *Business sponsors are 100% accountable for the success* of all business projects, in support of the business areas they support, with compliance to IT PMO standards, policies and procedures, and cost/value performance measures.

Quality Assurance: PPM

- The PPM section will ensure that *IT business project plans* comply with IT project management and architecture standards, during the management and delivery of IT business projects. This group will ensure that the *project management plans and deliverables* are consistent and integrated across the business areas and comply with the guidelines from the PMO, enterprise architecture, strategic plan, IT operational plan, and the organization's business plans.

- The PPM section will ensure *IT project management and PMO delivery compliance* to standards and industry practices through active participations at specified project management committees.
- The PPM section will monitor financial progress of *IT business projects, using financial measures* and earned value performance results, in the FTS.
- The PPM section will streamline/optimize the *utilization IT project management and PMO processes/resources* through the use of IT productivity tools and processes, to reduce administrative and coordination overhead.
- IT industry performance measures will be determined from IT research firms and reviewed by the CIO and PPM director to ensure *compliance* with IT industry best practices for *IT project management and PMO performance.*
- *IT benchmarking metrics* will be obtained from IT research firms to measure performance results of *IT business projects* and to compare with IT industry best practices.

Client and Vendor Relationship Management

- The PPM section will maintain effective *relationships with finance, vendors, service providers, and clients* in resolving PPM management and delivery issues through regular feedback and follow-up communications to improve performance results.

Financial Management: PPM Expenses

- The PPM section will *review PPM expenses, business projects costs* (*capital and operating expenses* for IT projects), and *PPM costs, on a monthly basis* to maintain accuracy in the IT budget plan and FTS, and to ensure compliance to financial policies and recommend improvements to expenses for proper realization of business value.

Customer Satisfaction Surveys

- The PPM director will review PPM results of *client satisfaction surveys* (*internal stakeholders*) (*business areas and EM*) and initiate follow-up for execution of action items.
- The PPM director will review expectations and results of *PPM section meetings* and initiate follow-up for execution of action items.
- The PPM director will review PPM results of *client satisfaction surveys* (*vendor* external stakeholders) and initiate follow-up for execution of action items.
- The PPM director will review PPM results of *client satisfaction surveys* (*external stakeholders*) (*IT outsourced ITS providers*) for contractual performance measures and initiate follow-up for execution of action items.
- The PPM director will review PPM results of *benchmarking survey/results* to assess and compare IT performance results with similar IT industries and to initiate follow-up for compliance to industry best practices.

Employee Progress Performance

- *PPM staff time progress reporting* will be entered every month into the *ITS time reporting system*, which aligns with HR job description and HR performance contract.
- PPM *staff performance contracts and training plans* will be established at the beginning of the fiscal year and performance appraisals completed at the end of the fiscal year. Intermediate performance appraisals will be completed on an "as-required" basis.
- The PPM staff will *have regular monthly staff meetings* (*1 h*) to discuss major issues and directives and to assign corrective action plans. CIO and EAS managers will *have regular biweekly staff meetings* (*1 h*) to discuss major issues and directives and to assign corrective action plan.
- The EAS director, CIO, and HR staff will assess *retention/retraining/reward/reporting* requirements for EAS staff and ensure corrective action plan.

6.5.2 Alignment with Performance Measures

Table 6.4 is an integrated representation illustrating how the results of the strategic directives relate to the outputs, outcomes, and performance measures in the IT performance measurement dashboard. Appendix D provides a real-world implementation of the integrated IT performance dashboard.

6.5.3 Integration with Strategic, IT Operational, and Performance Management

In Figure 6.7a through c, strategic, IT operational, and performance management accountability matrices are presented illustrating how the results areas from PPM integrate with the results areas from strategic management, IT operational management, and performance management. The acronyms on the matrices are abbreviations for executive manager's, PDM's, PMM's, and PST accountabilities/responsibilities.

6.5.3.1 Accountability Matrix: PPM

The accountability matrix of PPM is shown in Figure 6.7.

6.6 Applications Management Services (AMS)

> Trust gives you the permission to give people direction, get everyone aligned, and give them the energy to go get the job done. Trust enables you to execute with excellence and produce extraordinary results. As you execute with excellence and deliver on your commitments, trust becomes easier to inspire, creating a flywheel of performance.
>
> **Douglas Conant**

The AMS, as shown in Figure 6.3, IT SDLC process, is managed by the director of AMS, who is accountable for the delivery of AMS, outputs, outcomes, and performance measures.

- Strategic directives for AMS leadership, applications management, AMS QA, client and vendor relationships, financial management (AMS expenses), customer satisfaction surveys, and employee progress performance.

Table 6.4 Project Portfolio Management Strategic Directives Alignment with Performance Measures

Strategic Directives	*Outputs/Deliverables*	*Performance Measures*
PPM leadership	IT PPM governance framework IT PPM innovative technical direction PPM projects outsourcing framework	Operational FM
Project management	IT business projects monitoring/reporting Innovative PMO communications tools IT PPM productivity tools and processes PPM systems and regression testing IT project management/delivery IT business projects RFP/contracts IT business projects program/projects plan IT business project architecture/design IT PMO support IT business project requirements specifications	Operational SD
Quality assurance-PPM	Business projects plan QA IT project management compliance/approval Business projects financial measures PMO compliance Project management optimization Business projects benchmarking metrics	Operational SE
Vendor/client relationships	PPM client management relations/feedback Vendors PPM relations/feedback IT outsourced providers PPM relations/feedback	Operational RM
Financial	IT business project costs IT PPM costs	Financial
Customer satisfaction surveys	PPM client relationships/satisfaction surveys PPM committee meetings PPM vendors relationships/satisfaction surveys PPM IT outsourced providers surveys PPM benchmarking surveys/results	Customer
Employee performance	PPM IT progress reporting PPM IT staff performance contract PPM staff learning/growth reporting PPM staff meetings/communications PPM staff retention/retraining/reward reporting	Employee

Roles → *Results Areas* ↓	*EBM* *CEO*	*EPM* *CPO*	*EITM* *CIO*	*PSC* *Sponsor*	*PDM*	*PMM*	*PST*
Strategic Management							
IT goal statement	I	C	A	C	R	R	R
IT strategic framework	I	C	A	C	R	R	R
IT strategic directives	I	C	A	C	R	R	R
IT policy framework	I	C	A	C	R	R	R
IT governance framework	I	C	A	C	R	R	R
IT value-based performance measurements	I	C	A	C	R	R	R

(a)

Roles → *Results Areas* ↓	*EBM* *CEO*	*EPM* *CPO*	*EITM* *CIO*	*PSC* *Sponsor*	*PDM*	*PMM*	*PST*
Performance Management							
Performance management standards	I	A	C	C	R	R	R
Performance measurement systems	I	A	C	C	R	R	R
Performance management reporting	I	A	C	C	R	R	R
Performance improvement management	I	A	C	C	R	R	R
Performance change management	I	A	C	C	R	R	R
HR performance management	I	A	C	C	R	R	R
Financial performance management	I	A	C	C	R	R	R

(b)

Figure 6.7 (a) Strategic management accountability matrix: project portfolio management (PPM). (b) Performance management accountability: PPM. *Legend*: R, responsible; A, accountable; C, consulted; I, informed. *(Continued)*

Roles → *Results Areas* ↓	*EBM* *CEO*	*EPM* *CPO*	*EITM* *CIO*	*PSC* *Sponsor*	*PDM*	*PMM*	*PST*
IT Operations Management							
Financial accountability	I	C	A	C	C	R	R
HR accountability	I	C	A	C	C	R	R
Operational accountability	I	C	C	C	A	R	R
Project accountability	I	C	A	C	R	R	R
Applications accountability	I	C	C	C	A	R	R
Technology accountability	I	C	C	C	A	R	R

(c)

Figure 6.7 (*Continued*) (c) Information technology operations management accountability matrix: PPM. *Legend*: R, responsible; A, accountable; C, consulted; I, informed.

This AMS functional area produces the following major results, based on the IPMF-IT (Figure 6.1) and the IT SDLC process (Figure 6.3), aligned with the integrated IT performance measurement dashboard (Appendix E). These strategic directives for AMS are updated as ITS are managed, measured, and monitored throughout the IT SDLC.

IT AMS consists of

- Operational (functional management) outputs
  - IT AMS governance framework
  - IT AMS innovative technical direction
  - AMS outsourcing framework
- Operational (service delivery) outputs
  - AMS and SLA management
  - AMS SLA support
  - Web service policy/strategy development
  - Innovative communications tools
  - AMS RFP/contract management
  - AMS committee meetings
  - AMS migrations
  - AMS change management
- Operational (service/operational excellence) outputs
  - AMS QA
  - AMS compliance/approval
  - AMS financial measures
  - AMS SLA compliance
  - AMS optimization
  - AMS benchmarking metrics
- Operational (relationship management) outputs
  - AMS client management relations/feedback

  - Vendors' AMS relations/feedback
  - IT outsourced providers' AMS relations/feedback
- Financial outputs
  - IT AMS innovative initiative costs (capital)
  - IT AMS operating costs
- Customer outputs
  - AMS client relationships/satisfaction surveys
  - AMS committee meetings
  - AMS vendors' relationships/satisfaction surveys
  - AMS IT outsourced providers' surveys
  - AMS benchmarking surveys/results
- Employee outputs
  - AMS progress reporting
  - AMS staff performance contract
  - AMS staff learning/growth reporting
  - AMS staff meetings/communications
  - AMS staff retention/retraining/reward reporting

6.6.1 Strategic Directives: AMS

Many IT directors manage the delivery of AMS by spending their efforts on coordinating applications maintenance and enhancement issues log, with overly complex change management processes, procedures, and priority ranking system, with little or no understanding of the impact of the change to the business and technical environment. Proactive alerts, predictive reports, and accurate and automated root cause analysis using software tools are normally ignored or treated as too costly and time-consuming. AMS management culture, in most cases, has been reactive-extensive data analysis. Issue logs are normally posted on the walls of the ITS departments; to look impressive is the mind-set of the AMS director that is understood and accepted. There is no understanding of alignment to strategic and urgent IT operational applications. Excessive administrative overhead and rework normally result from frequent ineffective change management meetings to satisfy an egoistic manager. In most cases, there are neither strategic directives nor performance measures to measure success of applications maintenance and enhancement. The performance culture of accountability for results with accurate automated root cause analysis, proactive alerts, and predictive reports, using dashboard analytics for insights on decision making and predictions, is normally ignored or treated as too costly and time-consuming. Effective measures of efficiency and effectiveness include innovations and technologies. The IT industry has struggled to balance innovation with stability and applicability. These IT directors do not understand the difference between change and configuration management, applications maintenance and enhancements, and alignment with strategic applications and key IT operational application output, outcomes, and performance—accountability for results. IT decision makers usually reject the idea of client-centric outsourced model, because of perceived lack of power and control and status, even in cases where the model-centric outsourced model is evaluated as being cost-effective, sustainable, and applicable to the IT environment.

This is clearly the result of lack of understanding of trust, preference to hierarchical command and control, and resistance to accountability for results (management culture) with predictive analytics. An environment of analysis paralysis, applications maintenance and enhancements rework with excessive administrative overhead, in a hierarchical management culture of command and control, seem to be evolving. Effective delivery of accountability for results starts with an understanding of *strategic directives* and alignment to IT operational execution, using output, outcomes, and performance measures.

AMS Leadership

- AMS will be directed by an AMS working committee, using an *IT applications management governance framework* that specifies the strategic directives, decision structure (accountability for results), processes and communications, critical success factors, and performance measures for *IT AMS* in order to direct and measure the success and value of AMS. The everyday management of this IT functional area will be managed by an IT director, using an *IT AMS outsourcing framework and AMS innovative technical direction*, which consists of the IT outsourcing strategy and IT applications management innovative processes and tools strategy.
- The AMS director will ensure *compliance* with the *IT AMS governance framework and IT AMS outsourcing framework*, during the management and delivery of applications support and enhancement services, using *innovative applications management processes and tools* (model based, dashboard, predictive analytics, etc.) to ensure consistency, reusability, transition and integration with strategic applications, IT operational applications, and project delivery migrations (business and technical).
- The AMS director will chair the *applications management committee* by using the terms of reference as the framework to guide the identification and resolution of business and technical issues for IT AMS.

Applications Management

- The AMS section will provide the following *outsourced applications services*:
  - Applications maintenance—corrective, adaptive, and proactive
  - Applications support—user and ongoing operational support
  - Applications documentation—problem management and archiving
  - Applications environment administration—production quality control, software configuration/change management, repository software, DBMS, backup and recovery, special software services, and DBMS batch processing
  - Applications enhancement—development, integration, migration, upgrades, retirements, and technology infrastructure deployments
  - Applications improvements—AMS processes, new technology innovations, policies and processes, disaster recovery, security, control audit, transition, and transformation
  - Relationship management—outsourced ITS provider, vendor, competitive outsourced pricing, and quality benchmarking
- The AMS section will monitor and maintain record of ITS providers' *AMS deliverables for applications maintenance and enhancements*, using the *contracted SLAs*, performance management model, and AMS governance model.
- The AMS section will work with outsourced ITS providers to develop *effort usage trends* for deliverables produced and suggest corrective actions for optimization.
- The AMS section will ensure that *business approvals* are obtained for *applications production service requests (PSRs)*[22] *and innovative service requests*[23] (*ISRs*), for migration of applications changes to production status.

- *SLAs* will support all production applications, with measurable penalty and incentive clauses and reasonable exit clauses. *Application services contracts* will be managed, monitored, and measured, based on reporting requirements documented in the contract agreements.
- The AMS section will develop and deliver *web service policy, strategy, and standards,* including security for mobile technology applications maintenance and enhancements.
- The AMS section will deliver enhanced *innovative AMS communications tools* and processes (website, SharePoint sites, newsletter, and AMS data management [big data]) to maintain effective relationships and communications with vendors and clients and to ensure that expectations and results are clearly communicated.
- The AMS section will deliver *productivity processes and tools* (dashboards, change/configuration management, etc.) to streamline the management and administrative processes of the AMS department and to optimize the utilization of AMS management and technical staff. This includes outsourcing decisions for AMS delivery.
- The AMS will be delivered using an *RFP outsourced contractual agreement* that is model based, client centric, with outputs, outcomes, and performance measures—accountability for results.
- The AMS section will hold regular *committee meetings* to make decisions on applications migration and applications change and configuration management processes.
- The AMS section will develop and deliver *applications management policies, strategy, standards, and procedures* for applications migration and change management using proactive performance-based tools in managing AMS support services.

Quality Assurance: AMS

- The AMS section will ensure that *IT applications management plans* comply with IT *applications management policy, standards, and procedures,* including application *disaster recovery.*
- *Applications security and privacy* approval must be secured prior to implementing new applications or making major enhancements to existing applications. This review and approval will take place before any informal or formal obligations are made between the organization and an ITS provider and vendor. All credential and access management to the organization's sensitive applications will be managed and controlled through the applications security and privacy policies.
- The AMS section will monitor financial progress of *IT AMS, using financial measures* and outsourced performance management model results, in the FTS.
- The AMS section will ensure *AMS SLA* compliance to standards and industry practices through active participations at specified applications management and technology committees.
- The AMS section will optimize the *utilization IT applications resources*—through the delivery of IT productivity tools and processes for proactive and predictive alerts in managing applications (software, systems software, data base management software, and technological environments [cloud computing, virtualization, software productivity tools]).
- IT industry performance measures will be determined from IT research firms and reviewed by the CIO and AMS staff to ensure compliance with IT industry best practices for *IT AMS (applications performance).*
- *IT benchmarking metrics* will be obtained from IT research firms to measure performance results of *IT AMS* (*applications performance*) and to compare with IT industry best practices.

Client and Vendor Relationship Management

- The AMS section will maintain effective *relationships with finance, vendors, service providers, and clients* in resolving AMS management and delivery issues through regular feedback and follow-up communications to improve performance results.

Financial Management

- The AMS section will *review AMS expenses* (*capital and operating expenses*) for *AMS innovations and operating costs, on a monthly basis* to maintain accuracy in the IT budget plan and FTS and to ensure compliance to financial policies and recommend improvements to expenses for proper realization of business value.

Customer Satisfaction Surveys

- The AMS section will review AMS results of *client satisfaction surveys* (*internal stakeholders*) (*business areas and EM*) and initiate follow-up for execution of action items.
- The AMS section will review expectations and results of *AMS group meetings* and initiate follow-up for execution of action items.
- The AMS section will review AMS results of *client satisfaction surveys* (*vendor* external stakeholders) and initiate follow-up for execution of action items.
- The AMS section will review AMS results of *client satisfaction surveys* (*external stakeholders*) (*IT outsourced ITS providers*) for contractual performance measures and initiate follow-up for execution of action items.
- AMS section will review AMS results of *benchmarking survey/results* to assess and compare IT performance results with similar IT industries and to initiate follow-up for compliance to industry best practices.

Employee Progress Performance

- *AMS staff time progress reporting* will be entered every month into the *ITS time reporting system*, which aligns with HR job description and HR performance contract.
- AMS *staff performance contracts and training plans* will be established at the beginning of the fiscal year and performance appraisals completed at the end of the fiscal year. Intermediate performance appraisals will be completed on an "as-required" basis.
- AMS section staff will *have regular monthly staff meetings* (*1 h*) to discuss major issues and directives and to assign corrective action plans. The CIO and AMS managers will *have regular biweekly staff meetings* (*1 h*) to discuss major issues and directives and to assign corrective action plan.
- The AMS director, CIO, and HR staff will assess *retention, retraining, reward, and reporting* requirements for the AMS staff and ensure corrective action plan.

6.6.2 Alignment with Performance Measures

Table 6.5 is an integrated representation illustrating how the results of the strategic directives relate to the outputs, outcomes, and performance measures in the IT performance measurement dashboard. Appendix E provides a real-world implementation of the integrated IT performance dashboard.

Table 6.5 Applications Management Services Strategic Directives Alignment with Performance Measures

Strategic Directives	*Outputs/Deliverables*	*Performance Measures*
AMS leadership	IT AMS Governance Framework IT AMS Innovative Technical Direction AMS Outsourcing Framework	Operational FM
Project management	AMS Services and SLA mgmt AMS SLA Support Web-Services Policy/Strategy Development Innovative Communications tools AMS RFP/Contract management AMS committee meetings AMS migrations AMS change management	Operational SD
Quality assurance-AMS	AMS QA AMS compliance/approval AMS financial measures AMS SLA compliance AMS optimization AMS benchmarking metrics	Operational SE
Vendor/client relationships	AMS client management relations/ feedback Vendors AMS relations/feedback IT outsourced providers AMS relations/feedback	Operational RM
Financial	IT AMS innovative initiative costs-capital IT AMS operating costs	Financial
Customer satisfaction surveys	AMS client relationships/satisfaction surveys AMS committee meetings AMS vendors relationships/ satisfaction surveys AMS IT outsourced providers surveys AMS benchmarking surveys/results	Customer
Employee performance	AMS progress reporting AMS staff performance contract AMS staff learning/growth reporting AMS staff meetings/communications AMS staff retention/retraining/ reward reporting	Employee

6.6.3 Integration with Strategic, IT Operational, and Performance Management

In Figure 6.8a through c, strategic, IT operational, and performance management accountability matrices are presented illustrating how the results areas from AMS integrate with the results areas from strategic management, IT operational management, and performance management. The acronyms on the matrices are abbreviations for executive manager's, performance manager's, PMM's, and performance team accountabilities/responsibilities.

6.6.3.1 Accountability Matrix: AMS

The accountability matrix of AMS is shown in Figure 6.8.

6.7 Technology Management Services (TOS)

> Technology is dominated by two types of people: those who understand what they do not manage, and those who manage what they do not understand.
>
> **Archibald Putt**

The TOS, as shown in Figure 6.3, IT SDLC process, can be managed by the director of enterprise architecture and innovations services, who will be accountable for the delivery of IT enterprise architecture services, outputs, outcomes, and performance measures:

- Strategic directives for TOS leadership, technology operations, TOS QA, client and vendor relationships, financial management (TOS expenses), customer satisfaction surveys, and employee performance

Roles → *Results Areas* ↓	*EBM* *CEO*	*EPM* *CPO*	*EITM* *CIO*	*PSC* *Sponsor*	*PDM*	*PMM*	*PST*
Strategic Management							
IT goal statement	I	C	A	C	R	R	R
IT strategic framework	I	C	A	C	R	R	R
IT strategic directives	I	C	A	C	R	R	R
IT policy framework	I	C	A	C	R	R	R
IT governance framework	I	C	A	C	R	R	R
IT value-based performance measurements	I	C	A	C	R	R	R

(a)

Figure 6.8 (a) Strategic management accountability matrix: applications management services. *Legend*: R, responsible; A, accountable; C, consulted; I, informed. *(Continued)*

Roles → *Results Areas* ↓	*EBM* *CEO*	*EPM* *CPO*	*EITM* *CIO*	*PSC* *Sponsor*	*PDM*	*PMM*	*PST*
Performance Management							
Performance management standards	I	A	C	C	R	R	R
Performance measurement systems	I	A	C	C	R	R	R
Performance management reporting	I	A	C	C	R	R	R
Performance improvement management	I	A	C	C	R	R	R
Performance change management	I	A	C	C	R	R	R
HR performance management	I	A	C	C	R	R	R
Financial performance management	I	A	C	C	R	R	R

(b)

Roles → *Results Areas* ↓	*EBM* *CEO*	*EPM* *CPO*	*EITM* *CIO*	*PSC* *Sponsor*	*PDM*	*PMM*	*PST*
IT Operations Management							
Financial accountability	I	C	A	C	C	R	R
HR accountability	I	C	A	C	C	R	R
Operational accountability	I	C	C	C	A	R	R
Project accountability	I	C	C	C	A	R	R
Applications accountability	I	C	A	C	C	R	R
Technology accountability	I	C	C	C	A	R	R

(c)

Figure 6.8 (*Continued*) (b) Performance management accountability: applications management. (c) Information Technology operations management accountability matrix: applications management. *Legend*: R, responsible; A, accountable; C, consulted; I, informed.

This TOS functional area produces the following major results, based on the IPMF-IT (Figure 6.1) and the IT SDLC process (Figure 6.3), aligned with the integrated IT performance dashboard (Appendix F). These strategic directives for TOS are updated as ITS are managed, measured, and monitored throughout the IT SDLC.

IT TOS consists of

- Operational (functional management) outputs
  - TOS governance framework
  - TOS innovative technical direction
  - TOS outsourcing framework
  - TOS data center technology direction
- Operational (service delivery) outputs
  - TOS and SLA management
  - TOS SLA support
  - Data center policy/strategy development
  - Innovative communications tools
  - TOS RFP/contract management
  - TOS committee meetings
  - TOS migrations
  - TOS change management
  - Managed operations support
  - Technology infrastructure delivery
  - TOS innovative productivity tools
- Operational (service/operational excellence) outputs
  - TOS QA
  - TOS compliance/approval
  - TOS financial measures
  - TOS SLA compliance
  - TOS asset optimization
  - TOS benchmarking metrics
  - IT infrastructure purchases approvals
- Operational (relationship management) outputs
  - TOS client management relations/feedback
  - Vendors' TOS relations/feedback
  - IT outsourced providers' TOS relations/feedback
- Financial outputs
  - IT TOS innovative initiative costs (capital)
  - IT TOS operating
- Customer outputs
  - TOS client relationships/satisfaction surveys
  - TOS committee meetings
  - TOS vendors' relationships/satisfaction surveys
  - TOS IT outsourced providers' surveys
  - TOS benchmarking surveys/results
- Employee outputs
  - TOS staff progress reporting
  - TOS staff performance contract

- TOS staff learning/growth reporting
- TOS staff meetings/communications
- TOS staff retention/retraining/reward reporting

6.7.1 Strategic Directives: TOS

Many IT directors manage the delivery of TOS by spending their efforts on technical coordination services (technical asset coordination services, problem, incident, change, and release management log), with little or no understanding of the impact of change to the business and technical environment. Proactive alerts, predictive reports, and accurate and automated root cause analysis using software tools are normally ignored or treated as too costly and time-consuming. TOS management culture, in most cases, has been reactive-extensive data analysis. Issue logs are normally posted on the walls of the data center of the ITS department; to look impressive is the mind-set of the TOS director that is understood and accepted. There is no understanding of alignment to strategic and urgent IT operational applications and technologies. Excessive administrative overhead and rework normally result from frequent ineffective change management meetings to satisfy an egoistic manager. In most cases, there are neither strategic directives nor performance measures to measure success of technology asset performance, utilization, and optimization, with respect to service delivery, operational efficiencies, and relationship management. The performance culture of accountability for results with accurate automated root cause analysis, proactive alerts, and predictive reports, using dashboard analytics for insights on decision making and predictions, is normally ignored or treated as too costly and time-consuming. Effective measures of efficiency and effectiveness include innovations—technologies. The IT industry has struggled to balance innovation with stability and applicability. These IT directors do not understand the difference between service catalog and client hardware support and integration with hardware, network, storage, servers, power and cooling and management software output, outcomes, and performance—accountability for results. IT decision makers usually reject the idea of client-centric outsourced model, because of perceived loss of power and control status, even in cases where the model-centric outsourced model is evaluated as being cost-effective, sustainable, and applicable to the IT environment.

This is clearly the result of a lack of understanding of technology, preference to hierarchical command and control and resistance to accountability for results (management culture) with predictive analytics. An environment of analysis paralysis, technology support, and upgrades rework and excessive administrative overhead, in a hierarchical management culture of command and control seem to be evolving. Effective delivery of accountability for results starts with an understanding of strategic directives and alignment to IT operational execution, using output, outcomes, and performance measures.

TOS Leadership

- TOS will be directed by a TOS working committee, using an *IT operations services governance framework* that specifies the strategic directives, decision structure (accountability for results), processes and communications, critical success factors, and performance measures for *TOS* in order to direct and measure the success and value of TOS. The everyday management of this IT functional area will be managed by an IT director, using a *TOS outsourcing framework and TOS data center technical direction,* which consists of the IT outsourcing strategy and IT operations innovative processes and tools strategy.

- The TOS director will ensure *compliance* with the *TOS governance framework and TOS outsourcing framework*, during the management and delivery of technology support and innovations services, using *innovative technology processes and tools* (model based, dashboard, proactive alerts, predictive analytics, etc.) to ensure consistency, reusability, migration, and integration with strategic, IT operational, and project applications and technology migration (business and technical).
- The TOS director will chair the *TOS management committee* by using the terms of reference as the framework to guide the identification and resolution of IT infrastructure support business and technical issues.

Technology Operations

- TOS will provide the following *outsourced operational support services*:
  - Help desk and desk side support—directory/print and technical coordination
  - Network support—performance, security, software/hardware, equipment changes, maintenance, monitoring, automated proactive alert tools, LAN, WAN/Internet, and documentation
  - Server support—monitoring, fault management, software/hardware, performance, virtualization, backup, and technical coordination
  - Storage support—system, performance, security, hardware/software, backup/restore, DBMS, and technical coordination
  - Data center support—performance, cabling, power, cooling, security, technical coordination, and hardware/software asset inventory maintenance
- The TOS section will monitor and maintain records of ITS providers' *TOS* deliverables for *technology operations support and innovations services*, using the *contracted SLAs*, performance management model, and TOS governance model.
- *SLAs* will support TOS, with measurable penalty and incentive clauses and reasonable exit clauses. TOS contracts will be managed, monitored, and measured, based on reporting requirements documented in the *contract agreements*.
- TOS will be delivered using and an *RFP outsourced contractual agreement* that is model based and client centric, with outputs, outcomes, and performance measures—accountability for results.
- The TOS section will work with outsourced ITS providers to develop *effort usage trends* for deliverables produced and suggest corrective actions for optimization.
- The TOS section will ensure *business approvals are obtained for Technology PSRs and ISRs*, for migration of technology changes to production status.
- The TOS section will develop and deliver *data center policy, strategy, and standards, including security* for technology infrastructure support and upgrades.
- The TOS section will deliver enhanced *innovative communications tools and processes* (website, SharePoint sites, newsletter, TOS data management [big data]) to maintain effective relationships and communications with vendors and clients and to ensure that expectations and results are clearly communicated.
- The TOS section will deliver *productivity processes and tools* (dashboards, change/configuration management, network, storage, servers, etc.) to streamline the management and administrative processes of the AMS department and to optimize the utilization of AMS management and technical staff. This includes *outsourcing decisions for AMS delivery.*

- The TOS section will hold regular *committee meetings* to make decisions on technology support and coordination services, data center changes, and configuration management processes.
- The TOS section will deliver *applications management policies, strategy, standards, and procedures* for applications migration and change management using proactive performance-based tools in managing AMS support services.
- TOS will maintain a *log of technology operation–related issues*, documented in the operations management system. This log will be used as the basis for service/operations management–related decisions.
- The TOS section will analyze the *monthly operating reports*[24] from the ITS provider to ensure that all *SLAs* are maintained and suggest corrective actions for improvements.
- The TOS section will analyze and compare the services provided with the *SLAs* for service/operations management and recommend corrective actions, where necessary.
- *Severity One production problems* will take resource precedent. The ITS provider staff will work on Severity One problems immediately and continually until resolved.
- The TOS section will be accountable for the *upgrade of the organization's infrastructure* (*hardware, servers, storage, system software, network, and data center—power, cooling, cabling, and security*), in compliance with the procurement guidelines.
- The TOS section will make *IT infrastructure decisions* for deployment of new hardware, servers, system software, storage, and network components.
- The TOS section will support *IT infrastructure initiatives* such as technology domain migration, help desk, desktop/mobile technologies, e-business (web services), cloud computing, virtualization, and security.
- The TOS section will own and direct *IT infrastructure capital asset*, in compliance with the organization procurement guidelines.
- TOS will approve *managed operations initiatives*[25] and will suggest corrective actions to optimize the utilization of technology resources.
- The TOS section will review the *purchase order requests for IT equipment* (workstations, printers and laptop, software) after approval is obtained from the appropriate head of the business area.
- The TOS section will manage the *purchase order requests and purchases* for IT expenditures and suggest corrective actions.
- The TOS section will track and report *IT assets*, based on the contractual reporting agreements with outsourced ITS provider.
- TOS will deliver the *Internet, intranet, and extranet operational services and provide web service support* to the business areas.
- TOS will deliver *electronic document management system* operational services and provide *electronic information management* support services to the business areas, in support of information/data management strategic directives.

Quality Assurance: TOS

- The TOS section will ensure that *IT operations services plan comply* with IT *technology operations policy, standards, and procedures*, including application *disaster recovery*.
- *Technology security and privacy* approval must be secured prior to implementing new technology or making major enhancements to existing technology. This review and approval will

take place before any informal or formal obligations are made between the organization and an ITS provider and vendor. All credential and access management to the organization's sensitive applications will be managed and controlled through the technology security and privacy policies.

- The TOS section will monitor financial progress of *IT operations services, using financial measures* and outsourced performance management model results, in the FTS.
- The TOS section will ensure TOS *SLA* compliance to standards and industry practices through active participations at specified technology operations committees.
- The TOS section will optimize the *utilization IT technology operations* resources—through the delivery of *IT productivity tools and processes* for proactive and predictive alerts in managing technology operations (system operating software, hardware, network, storage, servers, Data center [power, cooling, and security]).
- IT industry performance measures will be determined from IT research firms and reviewed by the CIO and TOS staff to ensure compliance with IT industry best practices for *IT operations performance.*
- *IT benchmarking metrics* will be obtained from IT research firms to measure performance results of *IT operations performance* and to compare with IT industry best practices.

Client and Vendor Relationship Management

- The TOS section will maintain effective *relationships with finance, vendors, service providers, and clients* in resolving TOS management and delivery issues through regular feedback and follow-up communications to improve performance results.

Financial Management

- The TOS section will review *AMS expenses* (*capital and operating expenses*) for *innovations and operating costs*, on a monthly basis to maintain accuracy in the IT budget plan and FTS and to ensure compliance to financial policies and recommend improvements to expenses for proper realization of business value.

Customer Satisfaction Surveys

- The TOS section will review EAS results of *client satisfaction surveys* (*internal stakeholders*) (*business areas and EM*) and initiate follow-up for execution of action items.
- The TOS section will review expectations and results of *EAS section meetings* and initiate follow-up for execution of action items.
- The TOS section will review EAS results of *client satisfaction surveys* (*vendor* external stakeholders) and initiate follow-up for execution of action items.
- The TOS section will review EAS results of *client satisfaction surveys* (*external stakeholders*) (*IT outsourced ITS providers*) for contractual performance measures, and initiate follow-up for execution of action items.
- The TOS section will review EAS results of *benchmarking survey/results* to assess and compare IT performance results with similar IT industries and to initiate follow-up for compliance to industry best practices.

Employee Progress Performance

- *TOS staff time progress reporting* will be entered every month into the *ITS time reporting system*, which aligns with HR job description and HR performance contract.
- TOS *staff performance contracts and training plans* will be established at the beginning of the fiscal year and performance appraisals completed at the end of the fiscal year. Intermediate performance appraisals will be completed on an "as-required" basis.
- TOS section staff will *have regular monthly staff meetings* (*1 h*) to discuss major issues and directives and to assign corrective action plans. The CIO and EAS managers will *have regular biweekly staff meetings* (*1 h*) to discuss major issues and directives and to assign corrective action plan.
- The TOS director, CIO, and HR staff will assess *retention/retraining/reward/reporting* requirements for the EAS staff and ensure corrective action plan.

6.7.2 Alignment with Performance Measures

Table 6.6 is an integrated representation illustrating how the results of the strategic directives relate to the outputs, outcomes, and performance measures in the IT performance measurement dashboard. Appendix F provides a real-world implementation of the integrated IT performance dashboard.

6.7.3 Integration with Strategic, IT Operational, and Performance Management

In Figure 6.9a through c, strategic, IT operational, and performance management accountability matrices are presented illustrating how the results areas from TOS integrate with the results areas from strategic management, IT operational management, and performance management. The acronyms on the matrices are abbreviations for executive manager's, performance manager's, PMM's, and performance team accountabilities/responsibilities.

6.7.3.1 Accountability Matrix: TOS

The accountability matrix of TOS is shown in Figure 6.9.

6.8 Summary

The integrated IT SDLC performance model presented in this chapter provides the strategic directives and associated outputs, outcomes, and performance measures to support the IT SDLC process (accountability for results) and to show the alignment with the integrated IT performance measurement dashboard. The end results of the strategic directives align with the outputs, outcomes, and performance measures represented in the integrated IT performance measurement dashboard. This integrated IT performance measurement dashboard is structured based on a modified version of *Kaplan and Norton's Balanced Scorecard* that supports operational, financial, customer, and employee performance measures. It also describes how the results areas of strategic management, performance management, and IT operational management are horizontally integrated, in accordance with the stages or functional areas of the IT SDLC process.

Table 6.6 Technology Operations Services Strategic Directives Alignment with Performance Measures

Strategic Directives	*Outputs/Deliverables*	*Performance Measures*
TOS leadership	TOS governance framework TOS innovative technical direction TOS outsourcing framework TOS data center technology direction	Operational FM
Technology operations	TOS services and SLA mgmt TOS SLA support Data center policy/strategy development Innovative communications tools TOS RFP/contract management TOS committee meetings TOS migrations TOS change management Managed operations support Technology infrastructure delivery TOS innovative productivity tools	Operational SD
Quality assurance-TOS	TOS QA TOS compliance/approval TOS financial measures TOS SLA compliance TOS asset optimization TOS benchmarking metrics IT infrastructure purchases approvals	Operational SE
Vendor/client relationships	TOS client management relations/ feedback Vendors TOS relations/feedback IT outsourced providers TOS relations/ feedback	Operational RM
Financial	IT TOS innovative initiative costs-capital IT TOS operating costs	Financial
Customer satisfaction surveys	TOS client relationships/satisfaction surveys TOS committee meetings TOS vendors relationships/satisfaction surveys TOS IT outsourced providers surveys TOS benchmarking surveys/results	Customer
Employee performance	TOS staff progress reporting TOS staff performance contract TOS staff learning/growth reporting TOS staff meetings/communications TOS staff retention/retraining/reward reporting	Employee

Roles → *Results Areas* ↓	*EBM* *CEO*	*EPM* *CPO*	*EITM* *CIO*	*PSC* *Sponsor*	*PDM*	*PMM*	*PST*
Strategic Management							
IT goal statement	I	C	A	C	R	R	R
IT strategic framework	I	C	A	C	R	R	R
IT strategic directives	I	C	A	C	R	R	R
IT policy framework	I	C	A	C	R	R	R
IT governance framework	I	C	A	C	R	R	R
IT value-based performance measurements	I	C	A	C	R	R	R

(a)

Roles → *Results Areas* ↓	*EBM* *CEO*	*EPM* *CPO*	*EITM* *CIO*	*PSC* *Sponsor*	*PDM*	*PMM*	*PST*
Performance Management							
Performance management standards	I	A	C	C	R	R	R
Performance measurement systems	I	A	C	C	R	R	R
Performance management reporting	I	A	C	C	R	R	R
Performance improvement management	I	A	C	C	R	R	R
Performance change management	I	A	C	C	R	R	R
HR performance management	I	A	C	C	R	R	R
Financial performance management	I	A	C	C	R	R	R

(b)

Figure 6.9 (a) Strategic management accountability matrix: technology operations services (TOS). (b) Performance management accountability: TOS. *Legend*: R, responsible; A, accountable; C, consulted; I, informed. *(Continued)*

Roles → *Results Areas* ↓	*EBM* *CEO*	*EPM* *CPO*	*EITM* *CIO*	*PSC* *Sponsor*	*PDM*	*PMM*	*PST*
IT Operations Management							
Financial accountability	I	C	A	C	C	R	R
HR accountability	I	C	A	C	C	R	R
Operational accountability	I	C	C	C	A	R	R
Project accountability	I	C	C	C	A	R	R
Applications accountability	I	C	C	C	A	R	R
Technology accountability	I	C	A	C	C	R	R

(c)

Figure 6.9 (*Continued*) (c) Information technology operations management accountability matrix: TOS. *Legend*: R, responsible; A, accountable; C, consulted; I, informed.

For each functional area, the strategic directives are provided with highlighted end results and alignment to outputs, outcomes, and performance measures in the integrated performance measurement dashboard. It also shows a responsible, accountable, consulted, informed (RACI) matrix representation for each functional area that shows how the results area of strategic management, performance management, and IT operational management are integrated, using the roles and accountabilities. Real-world problems and recommended solutions, for each functional area, are also discussed to provide the readers with scenarios of situations for proactive actions.

The real-world implementation of a client-centric outsourced model shows how ITS are managed, measured, and monitored using an RBM framework of strategic directives, end results, outputs, outcomes, and performance measures, with predictive analytics evidence-based decision-making culture. Performance management enables better decision making that is evidence based and measured by outputs and outcomes.

IT organizations whose goals are toward managing and delivering ITS that enforces accountability for results (RBM) in a client-centric outsourced/in-sourced environment should consider the following recommendations, as a framework, to guide them toward successful management and delivery of ITS, during the IT SDLC processes:

- Establish executive leadership/governance services (ELS) functional area, which consists of key strategic directives, results, outputs, outcomes, and performance measures that align with the integrated IT performance measurement dashboard and integrate with strategic management, IT operational management, and performance management results areas, similar to the model presented in Section 6.2. Executive leadership establishes a governance framework of accountability for results in a performance measurement culture that contributes to the success of IT governance and ITS delivery. It is not only about communications, it is about leadership that builds trust and improves performance results.
- Establish a PAS functional area, which consists of key strategic directives, results, outputs, outcomes, and performance measures that align with the integrated IT performance measurement dashboard and integrate with strategic management, IT operational management,

and performance management results areas, similar to the model presented in Section 6.3. Planning and administration establishes an RBB framework of accountability for results through alignment to the strategic plan that is executed using an IT operational plan and an IT budget plan based on output, outcomes, and performance measures. IT is not about ABB with traditional financial coding structure, it is about RBB that aligns with strategic and IT operation plans and optimizes the utilization of IT financial resources.

- Establish an enterprise architecture services (EAS) functional area, which consists of key strategic directives, results, outputs, outcomes, and performance measures that align with the integrated IT performance measurement dashboard and integrate with strategic management, IT operational management, and performance management results areas, similar to the model presented in Section 6.4. Enterprise architecture establishes an architectural framework of accountability for results in a performance measurement culture of predictive analytics (*big data and analytics*).[18] It is about aligning architectures (business, data, applications, technology [security/privacy]) with strategies and executing using IT operating plans, outputs, outcomes, and performance measures. IT data centers have traditionally consumed high technology resources, which have been ongoing concerns of EM. IT infrastructure and business projects using traditional software development processes have failed miserably to provide any form of meaningful transition to meet the expectations of both the business requirements and the IT design solution. In most cases, the architects or designers are forced to rework the analysis, and previous analysis was deemed to be a futile and wasted exercise.
- Establish a PPM functional area, which consists of key strategic directives, results, outputs, outcomes, and performance measures that align with the integrated IT performance measurement dashboard and integrate with strategic management, IT operational management, and performance management results areas, similar to the model presented in Section 6.5. Project management establishes a model-based iterative software development framework that aligns with architectures, strategic plans, and IT operational plans, using deliverables/output, outcomes, and performance success factors—accountability for results. It is not only about communications. It is about building win–win alliance and trust while improving performance results in a performance culture of accountability for results with proactive and predictive analytics, using earned value and trend analysis for insights on evidence-based decision making. One of the critical root causes of failures for ITS departments usually occur during project management.
- Establish an AMS functional area, which consists of key strategic directives, results, outputs, outcomes, and performance measures that align with the integrated IT performance measurement dashboard and integrate with strategic management, IT operational management, and performance management results areas, similar to the model presented in Section 6.6. Applications management establishes a client-centric outsourced framework in a performance-driven culture of accountability for results, with accurate and automated root cause analysis, proactive alerts, and predictive reports, using dashboard analytics for insights on evidence-based decision making for applications maintenance and enhancements. It is about communicating strategic directives and building win–win alliance and trust while improving performance results in a performance culture of accountability for results.
- Establish a TOS (AMS) functional area, which consists of key strategic directives, results, outputs, outcomes, and performance measures that align with the integrated IT performance measurement dashboard and integrate with strategic management, IT operational management, and performance management results areas, similar to the model presented in Section 6.6. Technology operations establish a client-centric outsourced framework in a

performance-driven culture of accountability for results, with accurate and automated root cause analysis, proactive alerts, and predictive reports, using dashboard analytics for insights on evidence-based decision making for technology operational support and operational efficiencies. The IT industry has struggled to balance innovations with stability and applicability. It is about communicating strategic directives and building win–win alliance and trust with improved IT asset performance and utilization and optimization in a performance culture of accountability for results.

6.9 Endnotes: Key Performance Management Terms

[1]*Results-driven, model-centric*: An approach to performance management that focuses on a results-oriented approach to support a client-centric outsourced model for managing and delivering IT services.

[2]*Results-driven, model-centric, analytical, integrated*: An approach to performance management that focuses on the four distinguishing characteristics of IPMF-IT framework.

[3]*In-house, contracted, or outsourced*: In-house delivery management and delivery of IT services are performed by clients/employees; contracted management and oversight are performed by the clients, while the delivery is contracted to external resources, using a time and materials contract type. The vendor may or may not assume the role of a project manager depending on the specifications by the client; outsourced oversight is performed by the clients, while the management and delivery are contracted to the IT outsourced provider, using a "fixed-priced" contract type, with contractual agreements that includes outsourced performance measures. The vendor or outsourced IT service provider assumes the role of the project manager because he or she is accountable for the delivery of performance or quality deliverables, as specified by the client.

[4]*Outsourced/in-sourced model*: Outsourced, similar to client-centric outsourced model; in-sourced, synonymous to in-house model.

[5]*Large to medium outsourced/in-sourced model*: An IT department with a storage capacity of over 200 terabytes and/or a budget in excess of $100,000/year.

[6]*Smaller-sized outsourced/in-sourced model*: An IT department with a storage capacity of less than 200 terabytes and/or an IT budget of less than $100,000/year.

[7]*Client-centric outsourced model*: A strategy that describes how IT services are managed and delivered, using in-house, contracted, and outsourced delivery methods, based on the functional area of the IT service delivery life cycle process, in a performance culture of accountability for results.

[8]*Stagg augmentation model*: When the client requires a pool of highly experienced IT professionals with a wide range of skill sets, the vendor may supply these dedicated resources to the projects. The vendor may be requested to provide a dedicated team trained on the client's line of business, systems, and processes. The client will assume the role as a project manager.

[9]*Fixed-priced request for proposal process*: Under this business model, the vendor or IT outsourced service provider ensures quality of the delivery of the final product within a prescheduled time frame, and the client pays a mutually agreed fixed price for the project implementation. The vendor assumes the role of a project manager because he or she is accountable for the performance of the delivery or quality of the deliverables, as specified by the client.

[10]*Time and materials request for proposal* (*RFP*): Under the time and materials option, the vendor offers its skilled resources, and the development effort is billed at the end of every month based on the prenegotiated and mutually agreed hourly rate for contracted work. The vendor may or may not assume the role of a project management depending on the specifications by the client.

[11]*Outsourced service providers*: Vendor who provides IT services based on a fixed-priced contractual agreements via a competitive RFP process.

[12]*Results-based management*: An approach to accountability for results that measures performance using strategic directives that align with outputs, outcomes, and performance measures.

[13]*Performance analytics*: Modern performance management culture that uses analytics to support rational evidence-based decision making.

[14]*KPI Institute, CMMI, COBIT, Six Sigma, PMI, ITIL, and Kaplan and Norton:* Performance management institutions/associations in the industry that provide research processes and best practices on performance management.

[15]*Chief information officer*: The individual accountable for the management and delivery of IT services in the organization.

[16]*Financial tracking system* (*FTS*): An automated system that tracks IT financials using results-based budgeting processes.

[17]*Executive steering committee*: An executive steering committee consisting of business, IT, finance, and human resource executives that provide approval and support for the management and delivery of IT services, similar to the performance steering committee.

[18]*Big data analytics*: Modern performance management culture that uses big data analytics to support rational evidence-based decision making.

[19]*IT infrastructure projects*: Projects that deliver improved performance, utilizations, and optimizations of IT assets—operating software, hardware, network, servers, storage, security, system management software, service catalog, and data center (cabling, power, and cooling).

[20]*Program/project steering committee*: A working steering committee consisting of business, IT, finance, and human resource managers that provide technical/business coordination, approval, and support for the management and delivery of IT services.

[21]PEA-A: Project expenditure approval process for managing and controlling IT expenditures.

[22]*Applications production service request* (*PSR*): A method of prioritizing changes to the applications for high severity requirements.

[23]*Innovative service requests*: A method of prioritizing changes to the applications for innovative operational requirements (operational excellence).

[24]*Monthy operating report*: A report that shows the performance results of applications and technology operational changes.

[25]*Managed operations*: An operational IT functional area that is managed by an outsourced IT service provider.

6.10 Questions to Think About: Management Perspectives

1. Think about how your organization manages, monitors, and measures IT services. How does your organization determine the key results of IT leadership/governance services (ELS)? What are the key rationales to building trust and improving performance in an IT department? What are the major functional areas of your IT SDLC? How do these functional areas relate to your ITS department? What are the views of your senior management on the SDLC model to manage and deliver IT services, using accountability for results (RBM)? How do you measure success of IT services? What are the views of your senior management on the need for client-centric outsourcing model?
2. Think about how your organization manages and determines the key services and results of planning and administration services (PAS)? What are the key results areas, results, outputs, and performance measures of PAS? How do these results areas and results relate to the deliverables of your IT PAS section? What are the views of your senior management on results-based budgeting (RBB)? How does your organization structure and manage IT budget plan? How does RBB relate to your IT budgeting process?
3. Think about how your organization manages and determines the key services and results of enterprise architecture services (EAS). What are the key results areas, results, outputs, and performance measures of EAS? How do these outputs/deliverables relate to the deliverables of your IT EAS section? What is the most frequent problem that occurs during EAS? What is the root cause? What is the recommended solution?
4. Think about how your organization manages and determines the key services and results of project portfolio management (PPM). What are the key results areas, results, outputs, and performance measures of PPM? How do these outputs/deliverables relate to the deliverables of your IT PPM section? What are the views of your senior management on model-based project developments? How does your organization manage projects? How do you measure success of projects? What is the most frequent problem that occurs during PPM? What is the root cause? What is the recommended solution?
5. Think about how your organization manages and determines the key services and results of applications management services (AMS). What are the key results areas, results, outputs, and performance measures of AMS? How do these outputs/deliverables relate to the deliverables of your IT AMS section? What are the views of your senior management on the performance culture of accountability for results? What are their view on automated predictive analytics and dashboard analytics for evidence-based decision making? How does your organization support and enhance applications? How do you measure success of AMS? How do you build trust with stakeholders while improving performance results? What is the most frequent problem that occurs during AMS? What is the root cause? What is the recommended solution?
6. Think about how your organization manages and determines the key services and results of technology operations services (TOS). What are the key results areas, results, outputs, and performance measures of TOS? How do these outputs/deliverables relate to the deliverables of your IT TOS section? How does your organization provide technology operational and operational efficiencies services? How do you measure success of TOS? How do you improve the performance, utilization, and optimization of IT technology assets? What is the most frequent problem that occurs during TOS? What is the root cause? What is the recommended solution?

6.11 Chapter Testing Questions

1. IPMF-IT has the following distinguishing characteristics *except*:
   a. Results driven
   b. Model centric
   c. Operational
2. Which of the following *client-centric outsourced* model delivers executive leadership/governance services (ELS)?
   a. In-house/in-sourced
   b. Outsourced
   c. Contracted
3. How does the integrated IT service delivery life cycle performance model integrate with the six (6) IT functional areas?
   a. Performance results
   b. Strategic directives
   c. Outcomes
4. Results-based budgeting has all of the following characteristics *except*:
   a. Activity-based budgeting, operating and capital, strategic projects
   b. Accountability for results, results-based management (RBM)
   c. IT financial, strategic projects, IT operational projects
5. Strategic directives align with IT performance measurement dashboard using which of the following:
   a. Results, outcomes, performance measures
   b. Results, outputs, outcomes
   c. Accountability for results, RBM
6. The performance measurement culture of predictive analytics (*big data and analytics*) is mostly the operational mind-set/values of staff in which IT functional area?
   a. Project portfolio management, executive leadership, PAS
   b. Enterprise architecture services, TOS, AMS
   c. Planning and administration (PAS), project management, EAS
7. What are the key rationales to building trust and improving performance in an IT department?
   a. Win–win, leadership, accountability, transparency
   b. Communications, accountability for results, integration
   c. People, politics, process, performance
8. Who is accountable for the day-to-day management and delivery of technology operations performance results?
   a. Chief information officer (CIO)
   b. Chief performance officer (CPO)
   c. Performance delivery manager (PDM)
9. Which of the following performance measures aligns with the outputs/deliverables of the "quality assurance" strategic directives?
   a. Operational, functional, service delivery, relationship management
   b. Service excellence, operational
   c. Financial, HR, operational process, customer

Recommended Readings

Performance Integration

Aguinis, H., *Performance Management*. New York: Pearson Education, 2012.

Bainey, K.R., *Integrated IT Project Management, A Model-Centric Approach*. New York: Artech House, 2004.

Batshalom, B., *Green Source, The Magazine of Sustainable Design*. Boston, MA: Sustainable Performance Institute, 2011.

Corkins, G., *Performance Management, Integrating Strategy, Execution, Methodologies, Risk, and Analytics*. Hoboken, NJ: John Wiley & Sons Inc., 2009.

Demartini, C., *Performance Management Systems: Design, Diagnosis and Use*. Berlin, Germany: Springer, 2013.

De Waal, A., *Strategic Performance Management: A Managerial and Behavioral Approach*. New York: Palgrave Macmillan, 2013.

Hall, D., *Corporate Governance: Ensuring Propriety for Performance: A Contemporary Themes in Strategic People Management*. New York: Palgrave Macmillan, 2013.

IBM Corporation, Latest insights from IBM Institute for business value, New York, 2012.

Kaplan, R.S. and Norton, D.P., *The Balanced Scorecard: Translating Strategy into Action*. Boston, MA: Harvard Business School Publishing, 1996.

KPI Institute, *The KPI Compendium: 20,000 Key Performance Indicators used in Practice*. Melbourne, Victoria, Australia: KPI Institute, 2013.

Marr, B., Strategic *Performance Management, Leveraging and Measuring Your Intangible Value Driver*. Burlington, MA: Elsevier Ltd., 2006.

Spitzer, D.R., *Transforming Performance Measurement, Rethinking the Way We Measure and Drive Organizational Success*. New York: AMACOM, 2007.

Chapter 7

Aligning IPMF-IT Framework with Industry Best Practices*

Customers require the effective integration of technologies to simplify their workflow and boost efficiency.

—Anne M. Mulcahy

7.1 Introduction

Some of the performance management methodologies that seem to be gaining widespread acceptance, applicable to the information technology (IT) industry, include The KPI Institute (KPI), Capability Maturity Model Integration (CMMI), Control Objectives for Information and Related Technology (COBIT), Six Sigma, Project Management Institute (PMI), Information Technology Infrastructure Library (ITIL), and Kaplan and Norton (K&N).[1] The foundation principle of these approaches to performance management is based on a life cycle process to control the dynamic environments and to optimize the utilization of resources. The *IPMF-IT* solution, discussed in Chapter 6, has similar characteristics as those of the specified industry best practices. The similarities include life cycle process framework, process optimization, and performance improvements. These specific industry performance frameworks integrate with IPMF-IT from the perspectives of strategic management, IT operational management, performance management results areas, and IT service delivery life cycle process framework. Table 7.1, IPMF-IT integration with industry best practices, provides a high-level representation. The objective of this chapter is to discuss industry best practices, performance trends, and performance measurement office (PMO) and to show the integration of IPMF-IT framework with industry performance measurement frameworks from accountability for results or outcome-driven perspective, *not* to describe the performance management processes, as advocated by these professional organizations. There are many excellent books on these new and exciting performance management and measurement methodologies, some of which are mentioned in the "Recommended Readings" section of this chapter.

---

* With appreciated assistance from Kristian Bainey, PMP, BS, MS (Information Systems).

Table 7.1 IPMF-IT Integration with Industry Best Practices

SDLC → *Results Areas ↓*	*ELS* *Strategy*	*PAS Plan*	*EAS* *Design*	*PPM Build*	*AMS* *Support*	*TOS* *Support/* *Services*
Strategic management	COBIT CMMI	COBIT CMMI	*Six Sigma* COBIT CMMI	*PMBOK* COBIT CMMI	*ITIL* COBIT CMMI	*ITIL* COBIT CMMI
Performance management	KPI K&N *Six Sigma*	KPI K&N *Six Sigma*	KPI K&N *Six Sigma*	KPI K&N *Six Sigma* *PMBOK*	KPI K&N *Six Sigma* *ITIL*	KPI K&N *Six Sigma* *ITIL*
IT operational management	ITIL *PMBOK*	PMBOK	*Six Sigma* *PMBOK*	*PMBOK*	ITIL	ITIL

IPMF-IT and the specified industry performance frameworks are integrated using *methods and tools* (*technologies*)[2] from industry best practices that support the major results areas of strategic management, performance management, and IT operational management within the context of IT service delivery life cycle. Effective performance management requires the integration of industry best practices to streamline processes, boost efficiencies, optimize the utilization of IT resources, and improve organizational excellence. Table 7.1 illustrates the integration, which is the theme of this book. This integration is based on these distinguishing characteristics: *performance framework–measurement driven*, *results driven*, *life cycle process driven*, *IT process framework*, and *performance analytics*.[3]

The IT service delivery life cycle process or functional area or stage, presented in Chapter 6 and replicated in Figure 7.1, is the foundation model used to define the strategic directives and linkages to the integrated performance management dashboard, using output, outcomes, and performance measures/metrics, with performance analytics. Appendices A through F provide a real-world implementation, using Microsoft Excel spreadsheet.

7.1.1 Merits of Understanding IPMF-IT with Industry Practices

During my extensive IT career, I am frequently confronted with misunderstandings by IT professionals, on the foundation knowledge needed to effectively apply performance management best practices methods, processes, and tools during the management of IT services in delivering the expected value and benefits. A major cause of these misunderstandings was the result of limited skills level of these IT decision makers, including chief information officers (CIOs). They seemed to lack strategic value integration (people, process, financials, and technology), transformational change (people, politics, process, and performance), and performance measurement (quality and risk management skills) to effectively apply these foundation concepts in executing these processes, tools, and technologies. The symptoms—not the root causes of these failures—are usually attributed to the technology and supporting process, not to IT management inefficiencies. The inefficient performance management process continues to prevail, without any understanding of how to monitor progress and measure the achievement of outcomes/outputs and accountability for results.

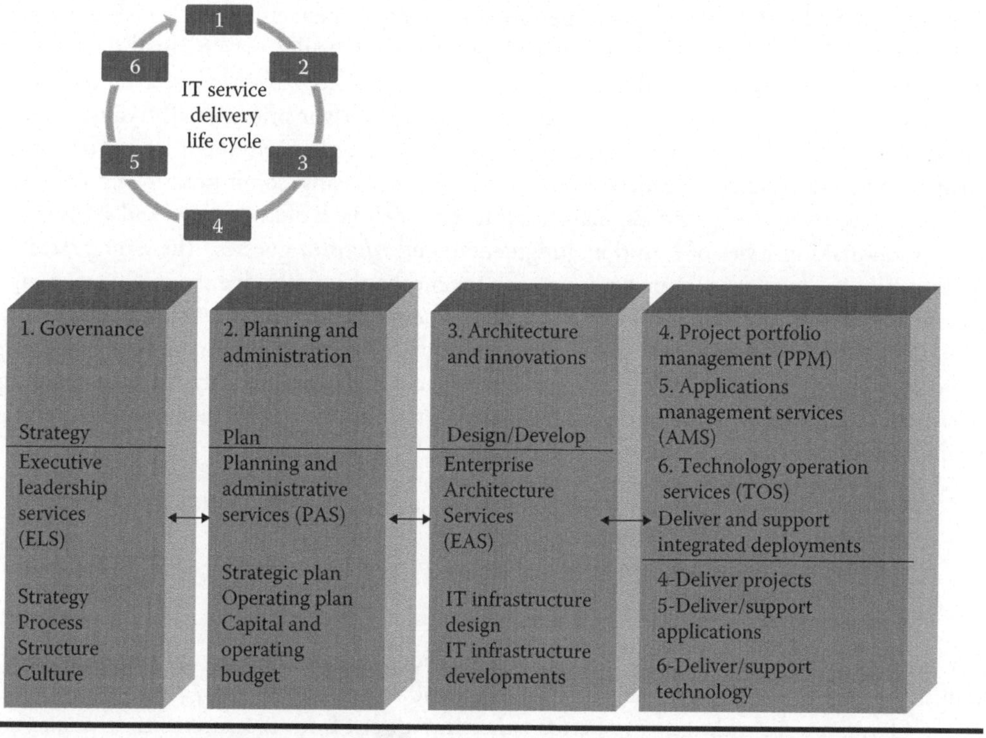

Figure 7.1 IT service delivery life cycle process.

One of the key functions of management is measuring and managing performance. Measuring the achievement of specific outcomes/outputs or evaluation of results is a subset of management. Effective management of IT services requires a basic understanding of *performance framework–measurement driven, results driven* (*results-based structure* [*RBS*]), *life cycle process driven, IT process framework*, and *performance analytics*. Performance measurement cannot be effectively implemented without an understanding of the basic RBS or results-driven concepts, as defined by *K&N balanced scorecard* (*BSC*) method. There are some IT leaders including CIOs, in medium to large IT departments, who manage IT services without applying performance measurement methods, tools, and technologies and who totally ignore concepts such as RBS. These IT leaders have the firm belief that concepts such as RBS and results-based management (RBM) and accountability for results are theoretical and have no place in the practical world.

IPMF-IT framework, for the delivery of IT services as defined in this book, is executed using a life cycle approach, illustrated in Figure 7.1.

Effective implementation of the IT service delivery life cycle process is the result of the proper execution of various methods, tools, and technologies to manage, measure, and monitor the achievements/results of specific outputs/outcomes for each of the IT functional areas. These industry performance management frameworks are mentioned because they fit the performance characteristics: *performance framework–measurement driven, results driven, life cycle process driven, IT process framework*, and *performance analytics*. It would be extremely difficult to effectively apply industry best practices to improve IT services without an understanding of how these methods fit within the IT functional areas or stages of the IT service delivery life cycle. Some IT leaders, including CIOs, manage the delivery of IT services, using data, applications, and technology development tools, and totally ignore performance management practices, which are measurement driven. They do not understand that IT performance results are measured to detect problems before it's too late. They do not ensure that internal controls are effective and efficient. Linking IT deliverables back to business goals is not one of their priorities. The value of measuring, monitoring, and improving risks, control processes, compliance standards, and performance results seems low. These IT leaders pronounced their not being committed to industry performance management best practices, mainly because of their lack of knowledge and skills resulting in decision-making styles of intuition, judgmental, and *educated* guesses. These integrated set of performance management frameworks provide the mechanism to bridge the intelligence gap and lack of knowledge and skills. In most cases, these leaders don't really know how well their function, their people, and their initiatives are performing. I am amazed how many IT leaders pursue the wrong initiatives, survive making the wrong decisions, and usually result in meaningless measures. Unbelievably, some of these IT departments continue to progressively function in this technologically advancing world.

> Incompetents invariably make trouble for people other than themselves.
>
> **Larry McMurtry (1936–)**
> *Lonesome Dove*

My main objective of writing this chapter is to provide an understanding on the applicability of industry performance management best practices and trends and to show the integration of the IPMF-IT framework with industry performance framework from measurement-driven, accountability for results, or outcome-driven perspectives. The materials are relevant to those IT leaders who have unconsciously contributed to IT service delivery failures of the past. These IT leaders and managers continue to unconsciously promote the need for ineffective traditional methods in the IT industry; some even disguised themselves as IT management consultants. I hope that these practicing IT leaders and professionals will fully accept the reality of technology advancements and applicability and improve their knowledge, skills, and practices to support the changing accountabilities and responsibilities of IT leaders and managers. One of the key functions of management is measuring and managing performance. Performance management best practices from the industry, some of which were mentioned in this chapter, can provide invaluable insights. These integrated set of performance management frameworks provide the mechanism to bridge the intelligence gap and lack of knowledge and skills and integrate these best practices within the IT functional areas of the IT service delivery life cycle process.

7.1.2 Key IT Performance Management Trends

Here are some key IT performance management trends in 2015, which can provide valuable insights into the knowledge and skill requirements of IT leaders, managers, and performance specialists, for the next few years. IT is a dynamically changing industry, resulting in the innovative nature of this industry. As a result, performance management processes, tools, and technologies will need to adapt to these dynamically changing IT environments. However, the fundamental principles of performance management such as accountability for results, outcome driven, measurement driven, performance culture of performance analytics, and the ability to predict future outcomes will not change—still fundamental. Business analytics is generally accepted as the science that involves analyzing data to reveal trends and/or develop insights that can be used to manage or predict future performance. These key IT performance management trends are the result of surveys and researches conducted by eG Innovations, published in *The Business Edge* and *KPI*, as well as my extensive experiences and researches:

- Predictive analytics
  - Big data and business analytics and KPI BSC
  - KPI used for measuring performance and improving organizational performance
  - Linking big data virtualization to the value of KPI
  - Usage of big data and analytics for insights on decision making and predictions
- Performance management software
  - Technological advancements related to performance management software
  - Domain-specific intelligence (dashboard) growing in importance for performance management
  - New technologies creating new opportunities
  - Automated performance management, transparency, and collaboration
  - Application performance management becoming virtualization aware
  - Virtualization vendors seeking to become application aware
  - Return on investments dominating decisions between performance management tools and processes
- Performance structure
  - "Holocracy"[4] structures to build win–win alliances between employees and organizations
  - Enterprise to shift from silos to collaborative management
  - Organizational performance to complement through personal performance
- Performance measures
  - Focus on soft performance measures and organizational culture, power distribution, and environmental, political climate, and social responsibilities
  - Hard performance management indicators—financial, productivity, and production
  - Benchmarking—comparing organizational performance and industry competitors and defining strengths and weaknesses
- Strategic alignment
  - Ethics in business—a performance culture of improvement
  - End users as a key success factor by which IT success will be measured
  - Flexibility as the key factor when it comes to performance management
- Performance management
  - Outcome-driven perspectives and accountability for results
  - Results-driven (RBM) and results-based budgeting (RBB)
  - Performance analytics, RBS, and integrated performance measurement dashboard

7.2 IPMF-IT Integration with Industry Best Practices

Table 7.1 matrix is an integrated representation on how industry best practices integrate with the major results areas from IPMF-IT and the stages or IT functional areas of the IT service delivery life cycle. The acronyms on the matrix are abbreviations for IT functional areas. K&N represents K&N BSC; ITIL—ITIL framework; KPI—The KPI Institute; Project Management Body of Knowledge (PMBOK)—PMI framework; COBIT, Control Objectives for Information and Related Technology framework; and CMMI, Capability Maturity Model Integration from CMMI Institute.

7.3 Strategic Management Integration

Table 7.2 matrix is an integrated representation on how the industry best practices integrate with the strategic management results areas from IPMF-IT and the stages or IT functional areas of the IT service delivery life cycle.

7.3.1 SM Integration with IT Service Delivery Life Cycle Process

COBIT, an acronym for "Control Objectives for Information and Related Technology," defines a set of generic processes for the management of IT, using a life cycle process. The framework defines each process together with process inputs and outputs, key process activities, process objectives, and performance measures. The framework supports the governance of IT by defining and aligning business goals, IT goals, and IT processes.

COBIT IT governance framework is business focused, process output, control based, and measurement driven, which uses accountability frameworks for assigning decision-making rights. It provides a set of recommended best practices for governance and control process of information systems and technologies with the essence of aligning IT with business. The business orientation of COBIT consists of linking business goals to IT goals, providing metrics and maturity models to measure their achievement, and identifying the associated responsibilities of business and IT process owners.

Table 7.2 IPMF-IT Integration with Industry Best Practices—Strategic Management

SDLC → *Results Areas ↓*	*ELS Strategy*	*PAS Plan*	*EAS Design*	*PPM Build*	*AMS Support*	*TOS Support*
Strategic Management						
IT goal statement	COBIT CMMI	COBIT CMMI	COBIT CMMI	COBIT CMMI	COBIT CMMI	COBIT CMMI
IT strategic framework	COBIT CMMI	COBIT CMMI	*Six Sigma* COBIT CMMI	PMBOK COBIT CMMI	ITIL COBIT CMMI	ITIL COBIT CMMI
IT strategic directives	COBIT CMMI	COBIT CMMI	*Six Sigma* COBIT CMMI	COBIT CMMI	COBIT CMMI	COBIT CMMI
IT policy framework	COBIT CMMI	COBIT CMMI	COBIT CMMI	COBIT CMMI	COBIT CMMI	COBIT CMMI
IT governance framework	COBIT CMMI	COBIT CMMI	*Six Sigma* COBIT CMMI	PMBOK COBIT CMMI	*ITIL* COBIT CMMI	*ITIL* COBIT CMMI
IT value-based performance measurement	COBIT CMMI	COBIT CMMI	Six Sigma COBIT CMMI	PMBOK COBIT CMMI	ITIL COBIT CMMI	ITIL COBIT CMMI

The purpose of the CMMI model is to assess the maturity of an organization's processes and to provide guidance on improving processes that will lead to improved products, especially in software developments. The model was designed to be used as the basis for a process improvement initiative, with its use in assessment only—a support system for measuring improvement. It was also designed to produce a map that identifies gaps in existing processes that may need to be streamlined. The fundamental building block of CMMI consists of process area that defines goals and several activities to support these process areas.

The strategic management results areas from IPMF-IT can apply COBIT framework and CMMI maturity model to streamline the processes and improve the results–outputs, outcomes, and performance measures for each of the IT functional areas of the IT service delivery life cycle. As a CIO, management consultant, and senior architect in the IT industry, I have found COBIT and CMMI best practices to be valuable and effective in improving the results–outputs, outcomes, and performance measures of strategic management—especially for IT governance framework, IT goal statement, and IT strategic framework, and in managing the delivery IT service delivery life cycle services, especially the executive leadership/governance and planning and administration. COBIT and CMMI can also be integrated with ITIL during the improvement of applications management and technology operations services (TOS), integrated with PMBOK during the improvement of .projects, and integrated with Six Sigma during the improvement of architecture services—streamlining of internal operational processes.

These industry best practices fit with the performance management trends, presented in this chapter, especially performance framework–measurement driven, results driven (streamlining RBS), life cycle process driven, and IT process framework. Figures 7.2 and 7.3 illustrate the life cycle process–driven characteristics.

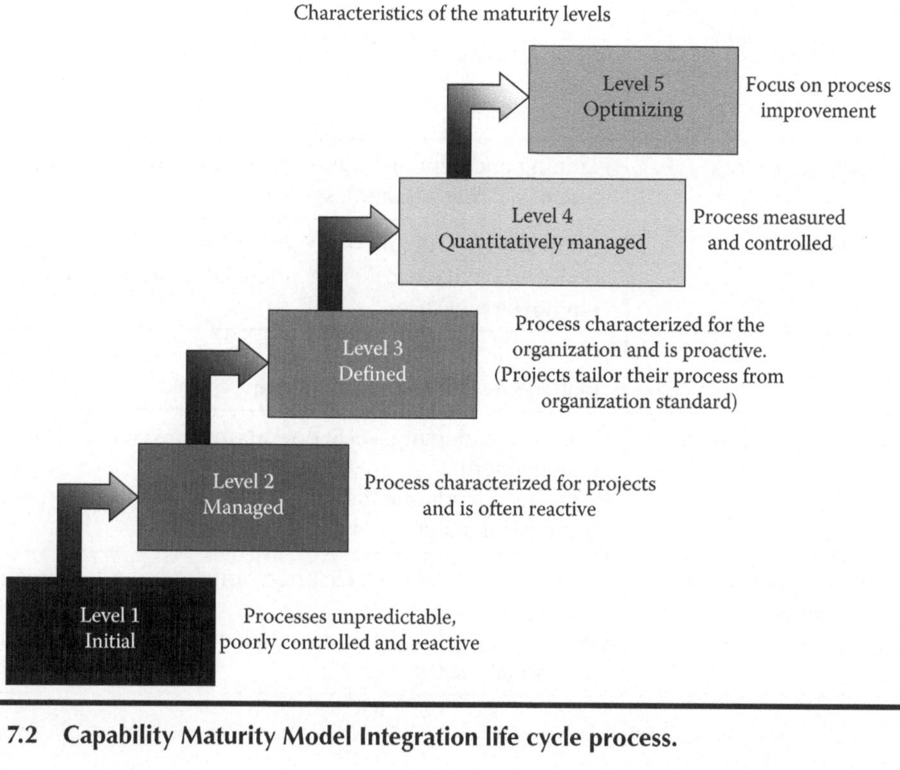

Figure 7.2 Capability Maturity Model Integration life cycle process.

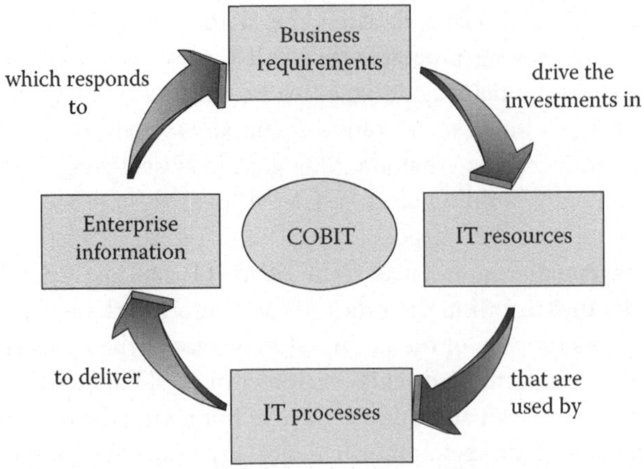

Figure 7.3 Control Objectives for Information and Related Technology life cycle process.

7.3.2 SM Integration with Performance Measurement Dashboard

In the preceding section, the value of using performance measurement processes such as COBIT and CMMI is discussed. In this section, the strategic value of measurement is highlighted to show how strategic management results areas, as defined in this book, integrate with the RBS, based on a modified version of Norton and Kaplan's (K&N) BSC. Table 7.3 matrix shows the integration of strategic management with performance measurement dashboard. Chapter 3 provides

Table 7.3 Service Management Integration with Performance Measurement Dashboard

Strategic Management	*Performance Measurement Dashboard*
IT goal statement	Executive leadership—ELS; operational measures—functional management
IT strategic framework	Planning and administration—PAS; operational measures—functional management, service excellence
IT strategic directives	Enterprise architecture—EAS; operational measures—service delivery, service excellence; financial, customer, and employee measures
IT policy framework	Executive leadership—ELS; operational measures—functional management, service excellence
IT governance framework	Executive leadership—ELS; operational measures—functional management Planning and administration—PAS; operational measures-(functional management)
IT value-based performance measurements	Executive leadership—ELS; operational measures—functional management Planning and administration—PAS; operational measures—functional management

real-world illustrations of this integration, using the integrated IT performance measurement dashboard, to guide decision making. The outputs and outcomes for the results areas are aligned with the outputs, outcomes, and performance measures in the integrated IT performance management dashboard. Chapter 6 provides real-world illustrations of how the end results of the strategic directives integrate with the outputs and outcomes for each of the IT functional areas or stages, within the IT service delivery life cycle. Appendices A through F provide a more detailed representation.

The key to success is measurement. Measurement is fundamental to high-performance improvement and, ultimately, success in business. Think about the critical role of measurement in your IT department to guide decision making. Accountability is measured responsibility. How do you hold someone accountable without measuring the expected results with the accomplished results? Do you understand what you measure? Some IT leaders use measurements to promote their self-serving hidden agenda. How (within what context) were the data in the dashboard interpreted, used, and applied?

7.4 Performance Management Integration

Table 7.4 matrix is an integrated representation on how the industry best practices integrate with the performance management results areas from IPMF-IT and the stages or IT functional areas of the IT service delivery life cycle process.

7.4.1 PM Integration with IT Service Delivery Life Cycle

KPI is the acronym for "The KPI Institute." The global authority *on key performance indicators'* (KPIs) research and education provides, through its publications and training courses, insights on how to measure and learn with KPIs. It developed the first *KPI Management Framework*[5] and operates several research programs dedicated to performance management, strategy, BSC and key performance indicators. It operates *smartKPIs.com*, where the results of the research program dedicated to documenting and cataloging how KPIs are used in practice can be found; it is an online portal containing the largest collection of well-documented KPI samples supported by a community of tens of thousands of members. KPI Management Framework is a performance measurement that is results focused, with the goal to monitor and manage outputs in order to produce measureable outcomes by linking objectives with scorecard/dashboard.

In 1992, K&N concept of the BSC revolutionized conventional thinking about performance metrics. By going beyond traditional measures of financial performance, the concept has given a generation of managers a better understanding of how their companies are really doing. These non-financial metrics are so valuable mainly because they predict future financial performance rather than simply report what's already happened. This article, first published in 1996, describes how the BSC can help senior managers systematically link current actions with tomorrow's goals, focusing on that place where, in the words of the authors, "the rubber meets the sky." The BSC supplemented traditional financial measures with criteria that measured performance from three additional perspectives—customers, internal business processes, and employees' learning and growth.

The fundamental objective of the Six Sigma methodology is the implementation of a measurement-based strategy that focuses on process improvement and streamlining through the

Table 7.4 IPMF-IT Integration with Industry Best Practices—Performance Management

Roles→ Results Areas ↓	*ELS Strategy*	*PAS Plan*	*EAS Design*	*PPM Build*	*AMS Support*	*TOS Support*
Performance Management						
Performance management standards	KPI K&N Six Sigma	KPI K&N Six Sigma	KPI K&N Six Sigma	KPI K&N Six Sigma PMBOK	KPI K&N Six Sigma ITIL	KPI K&N Six Sigma ITIL
Performance measurement systems	KPI K&N Six Sigma	KPI K&N Six Sigma	KPI K&N Six Sigma	KPI K&N Six Sigma PMBOK	KPI K&N Six Sigma ITIL	KPI K&N Six Sigma ITIL
Performance management reporting	KPI K&N Six Sigma	KPI K&N Six Sigma	KPI K&N Six Sigma	KPI K&N Six Sigma PMBOK	KPI K&N Six Sigma ITIL	KPI K&N Six Sigma ITIL
Performance improvement management	KPI K&N Six Sigma	KPI K&N Six Sigma	KPI K&N Six Sigma	KPI K&N Six Sigma PMBOK	KPI K&N Six Sigma ITIL	KPI K&N Six Sigma ITIL
Performance change management	KPI K&N Six Sigma	KPI K&N Six Sigma	KPI K&N Six Sigma	KPI K&N Six Sigma	KPI K&N Six Sigma	KPI K&N Six Sigma

application of Six Sigma improvement projects. This is accomplished through the use of two Six Sigma submethodologies: DMAIC and DMADV. The Six Sigma DMAIC process (define, measure, analyze, improve, and control) is an improvement system for existing processes falling below specifications and looking for incremental improvements. The Six Sigma DMADV process (define, measure, analyze, design, and verify) is an improvement system used to develop new processes or products at Six Sigma quality levels.

The performance management results areas from IPMF-IT apply a modified version of K&N BSC approach to performance measurement, KPI Management Framework, and Six Sigma measurement–based strategy for process improvement to streamline the processes and improve the results–outputs, outcomes, and performance measures for each of the IT functional areas of the IT service delivery life cycle. As a CIO, management consultant, and senior architect in the IT industry, I have found KPI, K&N, and Six Sigma best practices to be valuable and effective in improving the results–outputs, outcomes, and performance measures of performance management—especially for performance measurement systems, performance management reporting, and performance improvement in managing the IT service delivery life cycle services. KPI, K&N, and Six Sigma methods can also be integrated with ITIL during the improvement of applications management and TOS, integrated with PMBOK during the improvement of .projects, and integrated with Six Sigma during the improvement of architecture services—streamlining of internal operational processes.

These industry best practices fit with the performance management trends, presented in this chapter, especially performance framework–measurement driven, results driven (streamlining RBS), life cycle process driven, and IT process framework. Figures 7.4 through 7.6 illustrate the life cycle process–driven characteristics.

7.4.2 PM Integration with Performance Measurement Dashboard

In the preceding section, the value of using performance measurement processes such as KPI, K&N BSC, and Six Sigma was discussed. In this section, the value of performance analytics and business intelligence is highlighted to show how performance management results areas, as defined in this book, integrate with the RBS, based on a modified version of K&N BSC. Table 7.5 matrix shows the integration of performance management with performance measurement dashboard. Chapter 4 provides real-world illustrations of this integration, using the integrated IT performance measurement dashboard, to guide decision making. The outputs and outcomes for the results areas are aligned with the outputs, outcomes, and performance measures in the integrated IT performance management dashboard. Chapter 6 provides real-world illustrations of how the end results of the strategic directives integrate with the outputs and outcomes for each of the IT functional areas or stages, within the IT service delivery life cycle. Appendices A through F provide more detailed representation.

The key to evidence-based decision making is predictive analytics. Performance analytics is fundamental in the high-performance improvement and ultimately success of the business. Think about the critical function of business intelligence in your IT department to guide decision making. Think about end-to-end predictive analytics and *data mining*, *data integration*,

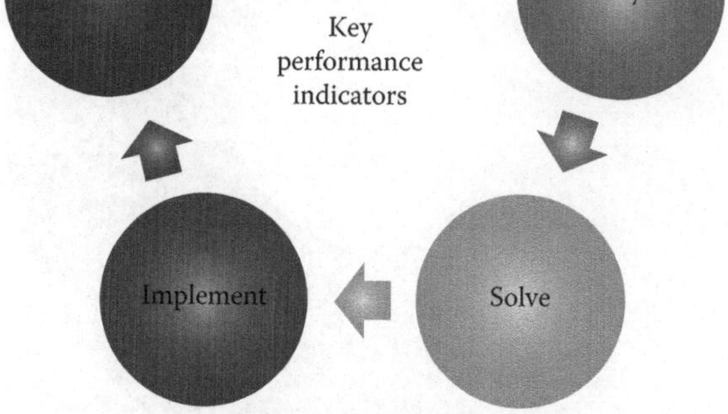

Figure 7.4 The KPI Institute life cycle process.

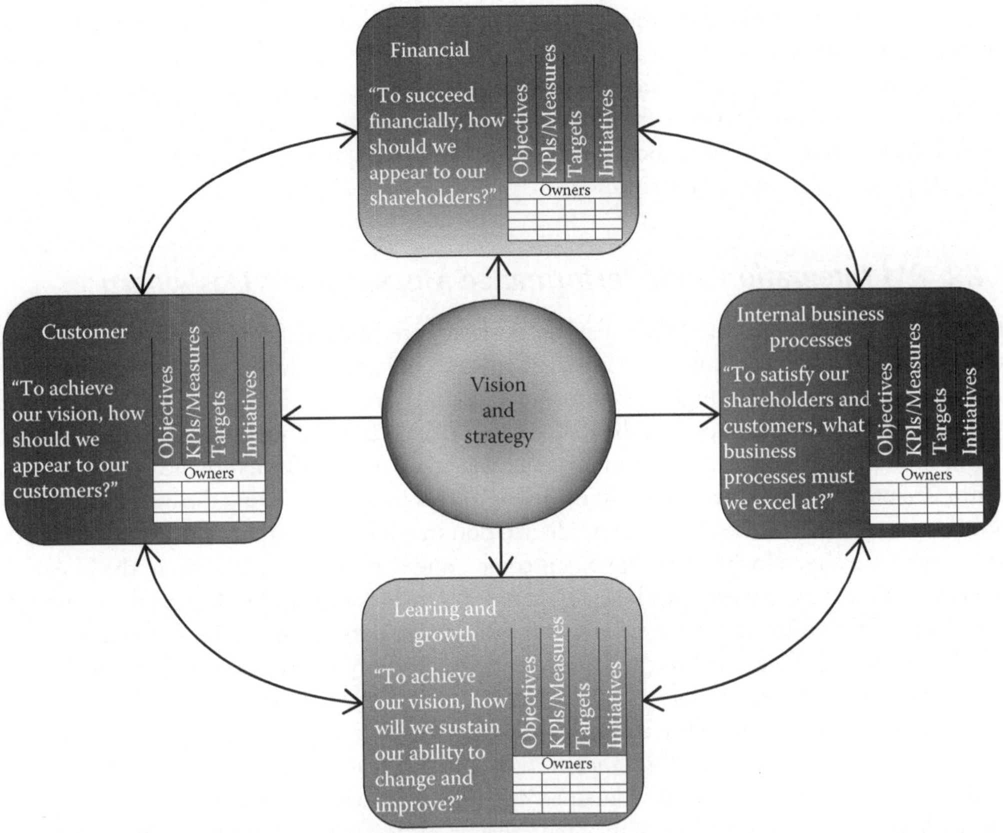

Figure 7.5 Kaplan and Norton's Balanced Scorecard.

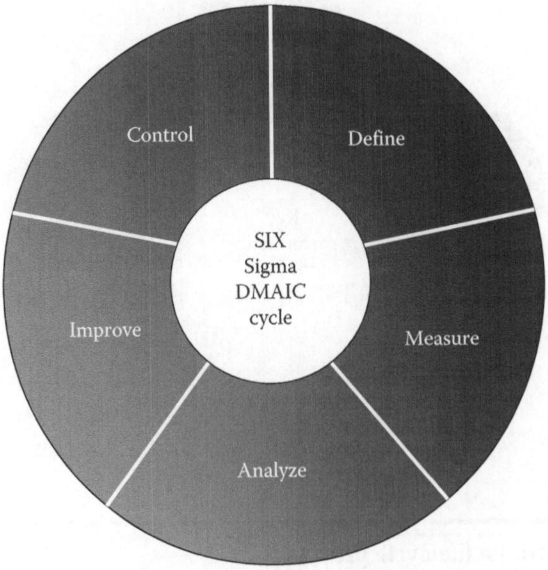

Figure 7.6 Six Sigma life cycle process.

Table 7.5 PM Integration with Performance Measurement Dashboard

Performance Management (PM)	*Performance Measurement Dashboard*
Performance management standards	Executive leadership—ELS; operational measures—service excellence
Performance measurement systems	Executive leadership—ELS; operational measures—service excellence
Performance management reporting	Performance analytics—business intelligence; operational, financial, customer, and employee measures
Performance improvement management	Executive leadership—ELS; operational measures—service excellence; financial, customer, and employee measures
Performance change management	Applications management services—AMS; operational measures—service delivery; service excellence Financial, customer, and employee measures
HR performance management	Employee measures
Financial performance management	Financial measures

big data, and *real-time analytics*[6] for assessing and predicting performance results and building your own dashboard or analytical tools. *TDWI Best Practices Report*[7] focuses on how organizations can use next-generation analytics. It provides in-depth analysis of current strategies and future trends for next-generation analytics across both organizational and technical dimensions, including organizational culture, infrastructure, data, and processes. It examines both the analytics and infrastructure necessary for next-generation analytics. On the other hand, many measurement systems are designed to justify the salary of top executives—people who use the measurement system to get ahead with appearance of success—producing results on the wrong measures of success.

7.5 IT Operational Management Integration

Table 7.6 matrix is an integrated representation on how the industry best practices integrate with IT operational management (IT-OM) results areas from IPMF-IT and the stages or IT functional areas of the IT service delivery life cycle process.

7.5.1 IT-OM Integration with IT Service Delivery Life Cycle

ITIL, the acronym for the Information Technology Infrastructure Library, is a framework for IT service management that strives for predictable, maintainable services that align with the needs of the corporation or organization. This framework defines the organizational structure and skill requirements of an IT organization and a set of standard operational management

Table 7.6 IPMF-IT Integration with Industry Best Practices—IT Operational Management

Roles→ *Results Areas ↓*	*ELS Strategy*	*PAS Plan*	*EAS Design*	*PPM Build*	*AMS Support*	*TOS Support*
IT Operations Management						
Financial accountability	ITIL *PMBOK*	PMBOK	*Six Sigma PMBOK*	*PMBOK*	ITIL	ITIL
HR accountability	ITIL *PMBOK*	PMBOK	*Six Sigma PMBOK*	*PMBOK*	ITIL	ITIL
Operational accountability	ITIL *PMBOK*	PMBOK	*Six Sigma PMBOK*	*PMBOK*	ITIL	ITIL
Project accountability	ITIL *PMBOK*	PMBOK	*Six Sigma PMBOK*	*PMBOK*	ITIL	ITIL
Applications accountability	ITIL *PMBOK*	PMBOK	*Six Sigma PMBOK*	*PMBOK*	ITIL	ITIL
Technology accountability	ITIL *PMBOK*	PMBOK	*Six Sigma PMBOK*	*PMBOK*	ITIL	ITIL

procedures and practices to allow the organization to manage an IT operation and associated infrastructure. It is the most widely accepted approach to IT service management in the world that helps individuals and organizations who use IT to realize business change, transformation, and growth.

ITIL focuses on cost and quality improvements in IT services to drive the cost and quality improvements in people, processes, and technologies. The fundamental characteristics are process oriented and customer-focused based on IT service management best practices.

PMBOK, the acronym for the Project Management Body of Knowledge, is a framework and preeminent global standard for project management. It provides project managers the fundamental practices needed to achieve organizational results and excellence in the practice of project management. The fundamental building block of PMBOK consists of process areas that defines a generic life cycle or phases consisting of initiation, planning, execution, monitoring and control, and closeout, 47 processes, and 10 knowledge areas that support these process areas.

The IT operational management results areas from IPMF-IT can apply ITIL service management framework and PMBOK project management framework to streamline the processes and improve the results–outputs, outcomes, and performance measures for the IT functional areas of the IT service delivery life cycle. As a CIO, management consultant, and senior architect in the IT industry, I have found ITIL and PMBOK best practices to be valuable and effective in improving the results–outputs, outcomes, and performance measures of applications and technology accountability and project accountability, respectively, and in managing the delivery IT service delivery life cycle services—TOS, applications management services (AMS), and project portfolio management (PPM). ITIL framework can also be integrated with PMBOK framework for the improvement of executive leadership services—strategy, and

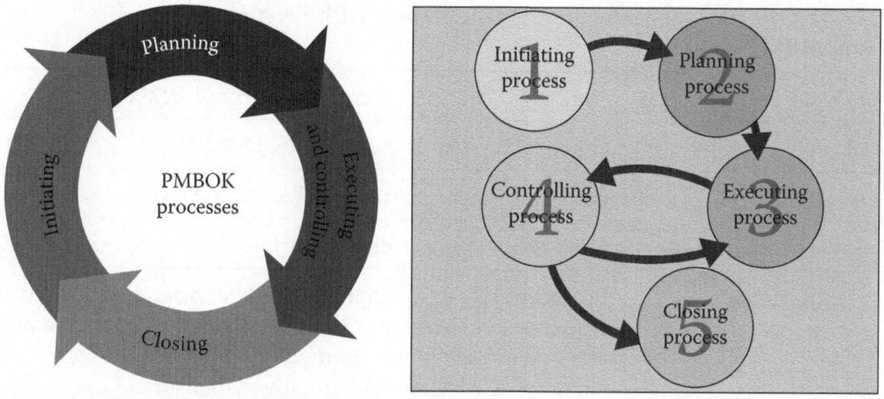

Figure 7.7 Project Management Body of Knowledge life cycle process.

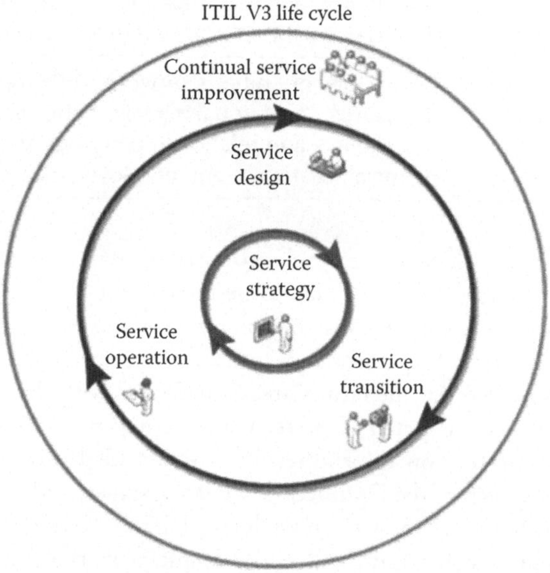

Figure 7.8 Information Technology Infrastructure Library life cycle process.

PMBOK framework can also be integrated with Six Sigma processes for the improvement of project delivery.

These industry best practices fit with the performance management trends, presented in this chapter, especially performance framework–measurement driven, results driven (streamlining RBS), life cycle process driven, and IT process framework. Figures 7.7 and 7.8 illustrate the life cycle process–driven characteristics.

7.5.2 IT-OM Integration with Performance Measurement Dashboard

In the preceding section, the value of using performance measurement processes such as PMBOK and ITIL was discussed. In this section, the implementation of performance measurement is

Table 7.7 IT Operational Management Integration with Performance Measurement Dashboard

IT Operational Management	*Performance Measurement Dashboard*
Financial accountability	Financial measures for ELS, PAS, EAS; PPM, ASM, and TOS
HR accountability	Employee measures for ELS, PAS, EAS; PPM, ASM, and TOS
Operational accountability	Operational measures for ELS, PAS, EAS; PPM, ASM, and TOS
Project accountability	Project portfolio management—PPM; operational measures—functional management, service delivery, service excellence, and relationship management Financial, customer, and employee measures
Applications accountability	Applications management services—AMS; operational measures—functional management, service delivery, service excellence, and relationship management Financial, customer, and employee measures
Technology accountability	Technology operations services—TOS; operational measures—functional management, service delivery, service excellence, and relationship management Financial, customer, and employee measures

highlighted to show why the elements of people–culture, process, and technology must be integrated to ensure success. Table 7.7 matrix shows the integration of IT operational management with performance measurement dashboard. Chapter 5 provides real-world illustrations of this integration, using the integrated IT performance measurement dashboard, to guide decision making. The outputs and outcomes for the results areas are aligned with the outputs, outcomes, and performance measures in the integrated IT performance management dashboard. Chapter 6 provides real-world illustrations of how the end results of the strategic directives integrate with the outputs and outcomes for each of the IT functional areas or stages, within the IT service delivery life cycle. Appendices A through F provide more detailed representation.

As a CIO, management consultant, and senior architect in the IT industry, I have found that successful implementation of ITIL and PMBOK performance measurement framework is constrained by how the processes and technologies are applied within the context of people or organizational culture—behaviors and social measures. I encountered an IT organization that enforced a policy to apply ITIL and PMBOK framework in a passive resistance culture of performance management—an organizational culture that seems to understand "blame game" to identify poor performers rather than poor performances. An organizational culture that is more interested to prove rather than improve, to use measurement system to get ahead with appearance of success, and to look good on the wrong measures of success (illusions of progress), with massive useless processes and data that confuse rather than clarify, which produces a performance measurement system of confusion. These IT leaders used measurement systems that were designed to please top executives—by highlighting good news and hiding bad news. My decision was to look at both the positive and negative sides of performance measurement. I understood that influencing and changing organizational culture to accountability for results and improvement mind-set is not easy and transformation to an outcome-driven or results-based culture is not immediate. From experience, I fully realized that people tend to behave in their own self-interest, especially when their self-interest is being generously rewarded by rewards and recognition systems that maintain the status quo, self-promotion, and self-protection. The major challenge of talent, trust, knowledge, and collaboration, amidst tensions between IT and business leadership, has forced new approaches to delivering processes and technologies, including ITIL and PMBOK frameworks.

My objective was to build a performance culture to ensure employees, *IT service providers, consultants*, and *vendors*[8] are more productive, creative, committed, and engaged. IT leaders must measure success based not only on the results of financial measures but also on increase in efficiencies and elimination of inefficiencies to resource utilization through process and process-enabling technology. IT must measure and track performance results to ensure that the organization is executing the strategy to producing the right operational performance results. Cost and quality measurements and improvements in IT services using the integrated IT performance measurement dashboard drive the cost and quality improvements in people, processes, and technologies. Figures 7.9 and 7.10 from *The Bridgespan Group©* represent the following characteristics: *performance framework–measurement driven, results driven, life cycle process driven, IT process framework*, and *performance analytics.*

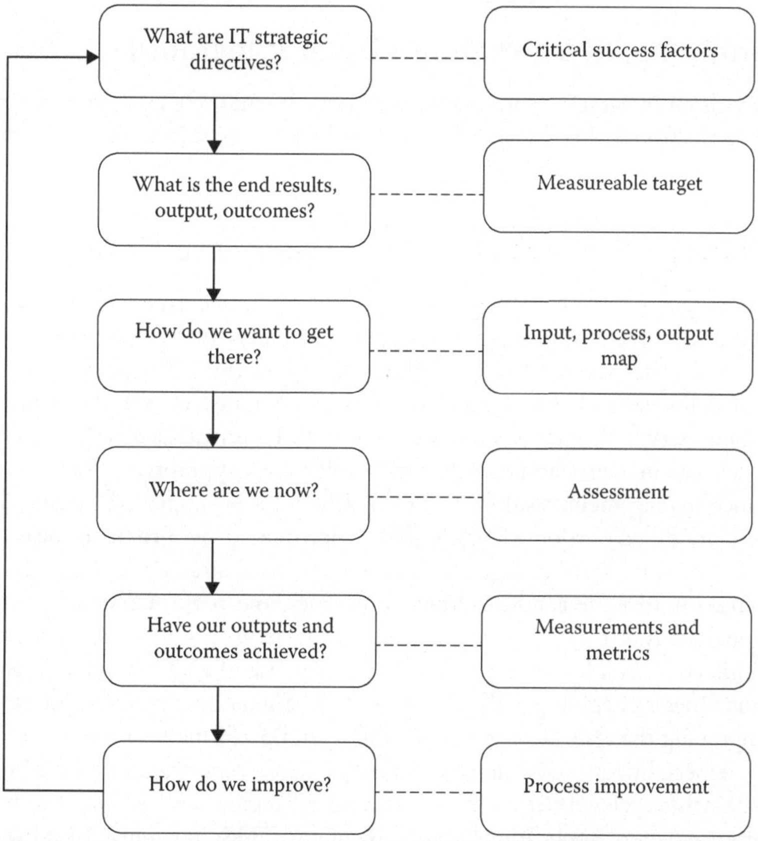

Figure 7.9 Project Management Body of Knowledge and Information Technology Infrastructure Library measurement framework implementation.

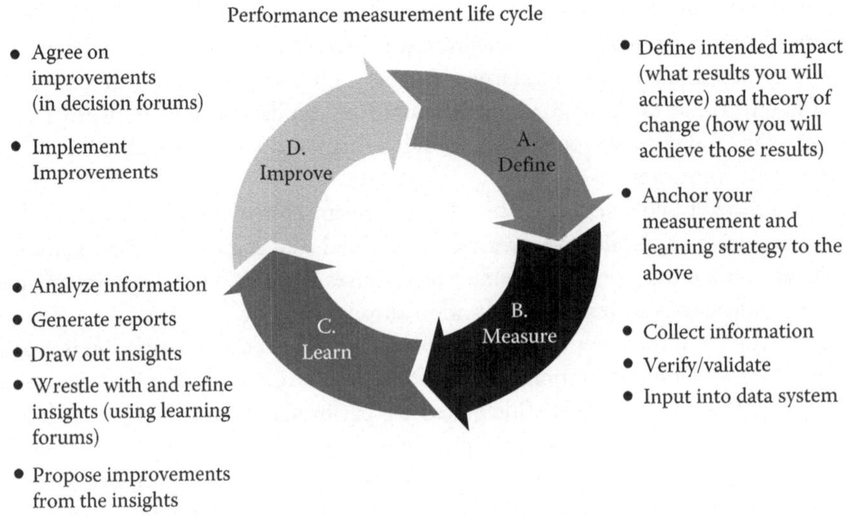

Figure 7.10 Performance measurement life cycle process.

7.6 Performance Measurement Office Integration

Table 7.8 matrix is an integrated representation on how the industry best practices integrate with the key PMO results from IPMF-IT and the stages or IT functional areas of the IT service delivery life cycle.

7.6.1 PMO Integration with IT Service Delivery Life Cycle

The performance measurement team, performance delivery manager, and PMO support staff will provide process and technical support in applying industry best practice processes and tools, according to PMO standards, policies, procedures, and guidelines. The performance reports and metrics generated for each IT functional area will be compiled by the PMO using the PMO repository and industry best practice processes and tools. Inconsistencies will be presented to the performance delivery manager and to other stakeholders, as appropriate, for corrective actions. The performance management results areas from IPMF-IT is supported by the PMO and the application of a modified version of K&N BSC approach to performance measurement, KPI Management Framework, and Six Sigma measurement–based strategy. The goal is to streamline the processes and improve the results–outputs, outcomes, and performance measures for each of the IT functional areas of the IT service delivery life cycle. As a CIO, management consultant, and senior architect in the IT industry, I have found the use of PMO standards, policies, procedures, and guidelines in applying KPI, K&N, and Six Sigma best practices to be valuable and effective in improving the results–outputs, outcomes, and performance measures of performance management—especially for PMO metrics and performance reporting, in managing the delivery IT service delivery life cycle services. KPI, K&N, and Six Sigma can also be integrated with ITIL during the improvement of applications management and TOS, integrated with PMBOK during the improvement of projects, and integrated with Six Sigma during the improvement of architecture services—streamlining of internal operational processes.

Table 7.8 IPMF-IT Integration with Industry Best Practices—Performance Measurement Office

Roles→ *Results Areas ↓*	*ELS Strategy*	*PAS Plan*	*EAS Design*	*PPM Build*	*AMS Support*	*TOS Support*
PMO						
PMO infrastructure support strategy	KPI K&N Six Sigma	KPI K&N Six Sigma	KPI K&N Six Sigma	KPI K&N Six Sigma PMBOK	KPI K&N Six Sigma ITIL	KPI K&N Six Sigma ITIL
PMO processes and structure	KPI K&N Six Sigma	KPI K&N Six Sigma	KPI K&N Six Sigma	KPI K&N Six Sigma PMBOK	KPI K&N Six Sigma ITIL	KPI K&N Six Sigma ITIL
PMO management plan	KPI K&N Six Sigma	KPI K&N Six Sigma	KPI K&N Six Sigma	KPI K&N Six Sigma PMBOK	KPI K&N Six Sigma ITIL	KPI K&N Six Sigma ITIL
PMO repository-PMIR and PMIS	KPI K&N Six Sigma	KPI K&N Six Sigma	KPI K&N Six Sigma	KPI K&N Six Sigma PMBOK	KPI K&N Six Sigma ITIL	KPI K&N Six Sigma ITIL

These industry best practices fit with the performance management trends, presented in this chapter, especially the following characteristics: performance framework–measurement driven, results driven (streamlining RBS), life cycle process driven, and IT process framework. Figure 7.10 illustrates the life cycle process–driven characteristics.

7.6.2 PMO Integration with Performance Measurement Dashboard

In the preceding section, the value of using the PMO standards, policies, procedures, and guidelines, in applying industry best practices such as KPI, K&N BSC, and Six Sigma, is discussed. In this section, the value of using PMO metrics and performance reporting for performance analytics and business intelligence is highlighted to show how performance management results areas, as defined in this book, integrate with the RBS, based on a modified version of K&N BSC. Table 7.9 matrix shows the integration of performance management with performance measurement dashboard. Section 4.3 provides real-world illustrations of this integration, using the integrated IT performance measurement dashboard, to guide decision making. The outputs and outcomes for the results areas are aligned with the outputs, outcomes, and performance measures in the integrated IT performance management dashboard. Chapter 6 provides real-world illustrations of how the end results of the strategic directives integrate with the outputs and outcomes for each of the IT functional areas, within the IT service delivery life cycle. Appendices A through F provide more detailed representation.

Table 7.9 Performance Measurement Office Integration with Performance Measurement Dashboard

Performance Measurement Office (PMO)	*Performance Measurement Dashboard*
PMO infrastructure support strategy	Performance measurement office (PMO); operational measures—FM, SD, SE, and RM
PMO processes and structure	Performance measurement office (PMO); operational measures—FM, SD, SE, and RM
PMO management plan	Performance measurement office (PMO); operational measures—FM, SD, SE, and RM
PMO repository-PMIR and PMIS	Performance measurement office (PMO); operational measures—FM, SD, SE, and RM
PMO metrics and performance reporting	Performance measurement office (PMO); operational measures—FM, SD, SE, and RM
PMO predictive analytics and informed decision making	Performance measurement office (PMO); operational measures—FM, SD, SE, and RM

The key to evidence-based decision making is predictive analytics. Performance analytics is fundamental in the high-performance improvement and ultimately success of the business. Think about the critical function of business intelligence in your IT department to guide decision making. How do you interpret the results? Is there measurement confusion? Do you understand what you measure? Are you producing results using the wrong measures of success? Are you looking good on the wrong measures of success—illusions of progress? Are you producing massive needless data that confuse rather than clarify? Do you understand the value of industry best practices? PMO standards, policies, procedures, and guidelines, in applying industry best practices, can provide the right answers, given the maturity of the organizational performance culture for performance analytics, results-driven, and accountability for results perspectives.

7.6.3 Performance Measurement Dashboard

The focus of this book is on the accountability for results (RBM) perspective, aligning strategies with IT operations using output, outcomes, and performance measures and metrics. The strategic directives for each of the IT function areas of the IT service delivery life cycle are linked to an integrated IT performance measurement dashboard, which generates reports and performance analytics for evidence-based decision-making and improvement actions. This book also provides real-world insights on the social, behavioral, cultural, and organizational aspects of performance management—so crucial to transforming performance measures in your organization. There are many books on performance management processes, which can be applied to the IT industry. As you may have realized, this book emphasizes transformational change, compliance, accountability for results, transparency, integration, and sustainability. These areas are critically important in good times to compete in a global economy and essential to the survival of a business in tough economic times. The focus is toward measuring and monitoring outcomes, *not* inputs or activities, % customer satisfaction, % policies and procedures established, % IT projects successfully completed, etc. Yes, I understand, there are cases where we will need to monitor performances of inputs and activities, such as the number of resources utilized and the number of processes streamlined.

The integration between organizations' financials (budget, investments, and expenses), customers (external stakeholders), operations (process, technology), and employee (internal stakeholders) performance results is *not* sufficiently addressed neither in theory nor in practice. Also, the integration between strategic, operational, and performance managements is not sufficiently addressed, neither in theory nor in practice. The lack of standards and integrated body of knowledge for performance management leaves room for interpretations, flawed assumptions, and confusions. The concept of performance management is perceived quite differently in practice and in academic research. It is still in the formation stages with no unified body of knowledge outlining its structures, results, processes, and boundaries.

This book provides that body of knowledge from the perspectives of integrating strategic, IT operational, and performance management results–outputs, outcomes, and processes. It uses a logic model to enhance performance through outcomes accountability, relationships among strategic directives, and accountability for results, outcomes, process flows, and performance measures that are guided by the interrogatives: Input, what is invested? Output, what is done? Outcome (impact), what is the result? What difference are we making?

The IT industry has struggled to balance innovations with stability and applicability. To exploit innovation, we need to better understand the outputs, outcomes, and processes used toward the development of a consistent framework. To drive consistency and effectiveness of performance across an organization, the best efforts must come together in an integrated performance management framework. This innovative IT performance management framework provides that balance with stability, applicability, and consistency. I am sure you all will be amazed with the insightful, innovative concepts and applicability.

Here are some practical suggestions that you should consider to start transforming performance management in your organization that could be applicable to your IT department. These tips are categorized based on the elements of transformational change, as defined in this book: people (organizational culture), process, politics, and performance.

7.6.3.1 Suggestions for Understanding/Improving Organizational Culture (People)

Organizational culture is defined as the system of management styles, decision-making strategies and processes, and the ability to change mind-set, shared values/beliefs, attitudes, and behaviors of your organization leaders and employees:

- Promote a performance culture to ensure employees and service providers are more productive, creative, committed, and engaged. IT must measure success based not only on the results of financial measures but also on increase in efficiencies and elimination of inefficiencies of resource utilization through process and process-enabling technology.
- Encourage an organizational culture that promotes and endorses the importance and necessity for accountability for results, integrity, and ethics—culture of feedback and follow-up.
- Build an organizational culture that influences IT governance performance with regard to the process and structure by measuring the impact and success of decision making. Understand the organizational cultural factors adopted by the organization that contributed to the success or failures of IT governance model.

- Transform a command and control hierarchical structure to a collaborative structure of decision making; build win–win alliances between employees and customer service providers, vendors, etc., through shared purpose and goals of performance measurements.
- Build a performance culture, mind-set, and value system of improvements to operational organizational excellence that will satisfy both good and tough economic times by understanding the trends, predictive analytics, and next-generation performance management.
- Traditional performance management is viewed as the reward for few, punishment for many, and search for the guilty. Measurement should be used for the purpose of improving rather than making judgments or placing blame toward poor performers. Technological advancements have enabled innovative cultural solution for the next-generation performance management: *enterprise data grids—culture of performance analytics.*[9] The next generation of performance management will assess the performance culture, either static, reactive, proactive, or predictive of an organization, and integrate performance culture with trust and transparency, that is, leadership + transparency = trust; therefore, trust and transparency are always linked.

7.6.3.2 Suggestions for Understanding/Improving Organizational Politics

Politics from this perspective is defined as self-interest, conflicting goals, loss of power, and hidden agenda.

- Always remember that people tend to behave in their own self-interest, especially when their self-interest is being generously recompensated by rewards and recognition systems that maintain the status quo, self-promotion, and self-protection (loss of power). The major challenges of maintaining talent, trust, knowledge, and collaboration, amidst tensions between IT and business leadership, have forced innovative approaches to delivering processes and technologies, including performance measurement dashboards, IT governance, and operational frameworks such as ITIL and PMBOK. Understanding organizational political climate to produce win–win decisions, trust, and consensus agreements with shared values/beliefs is a challenge of soft measures, which generally results in stable and sustained decision-making processes, that is, accountability + transparency = trust.
- The behavioral side of measurement—the social aspect of measurement—is sounding impressive rather than being effective. Many measurement systems are designed to build the ego of top executives—I am sure you know of people who use measurement system to move ahead with appearance of success, highlighting good news and hiding bad news. I know leaders who use measurement systems to promote their self-serving hidden agenda, normally with secrecy style of leadership-hiding and covering-up mistakes.
- I am sure that many of you know of executives, including IT leaders, who have hired management consulting firms to produce performance measurement metrics that will justify their self-serving hidden agenda. Some of these management consulting firms, with heavy political connections to executives and IT leaders, market their services as futurist's transformation change agents, emphasizing the use of the greatest hyped performance management solutions on the market.

7.6.3.3 Suggestions for Understanding/Improving Organizational Process

The organizational process from performance management context is defined as the internal processes and controls used to measure and streamline how services are performed to achieve the results—what (outputs) and why (outcomes):

- Build the framework of performance management process using the concepts of performance measures, input measures, and data sources (customer, employee, operations, financials); outputs/outcomes measure the results (what/why), while the process measures how the services are performed.
- Optimize the effectiveness and efficiencies of internal processes by benchmarking—comparison with similar industries/organizations, client satisfaction surveys and feedbacks from internal and external stakeholders, and comparisons with industry best practices.
- To drive consistency and effectiveness of performance across an organization, the best efforts must come together in an integrated performance management framework. This innovative IT performance management framework, defined in this book, provides that balance with stability, applicability, and consistency, using suggested processes and industry best practices. Does management ensure that internal controls are effective and efficient?

7.6.3.4 Suggestions for Understanding/Improving Organizational Performance

Organizational performance is what you do with the information you've developed from measuring performance. Performance management means using performance measurement information to manage your IT resources—people, processes, technologies, and financials. Performance means to perform and account for results. Accountability means effectiveness/efficiencies of services using quality/quantity of management to change/improve services.

- Performance management is the use of performance measure information to establish performance goals and success factors, allocate and prioritize resources, inform managers to either confirm or change current processes, assess your organization asset capacity, assign and assess accountability, improve work quality, track progress, and report success. Reporting–continuous communications for improvement to service delivery.
- Focus on soft performance measures—organizational culture, power distribution, political climate, social accountabilities and responsibilities, leadership, trust, transparency, and other cultural factors.
- Establish hard performance management indicators—financial, productivity, internal process effectiveness/efficiencies, quality/quantity of production, and management.
- Research and understand performance management trends and automation of performance management—transparency reporting and collaboration tools and technologies.
- Focus on managing, monitoring, and measuring IT performance based on strategic alignment with IT operational execution, using *accountability for results—RBM and RBB*[10]—with predictive performance analytic tools and technologies.
- Do not develop metrics in a vacuum—metrics that do not show how IT is performing against a goal—with many useless and meaningless metrics that sound impressive.
- Build foundation measurement process and structure on how to interpret the metrics; *not* many metrics, many meetings; poorly designed metrics that lack baseline; misleading and useless measures.
- Align strategic directive measures with operational execution measures using an integrated measurement dashboard, with metrics to show not only where IT is trending-proactive and predictive but also where IT has been reactive and static.

- Integration of performance management with the IT service delivery life cycle performance model and industry best practices.
- *Performance management body of knowledge*[11] and PMO as the framework for managing the delivery of IT services, using integration and applicability of intellectual/cognitive intelligence (logic model), emotional intelligence (culture/people), and economic intelligence (IT resource utilizations).

7.6.3.5 Suggestions for Understanding/Improving IT Leaders

We live in a globalized economy with technological advancements—dynamically changing organizations that still use antiquated organizational change management practices. Resistance to change continues to prevail because many IT leaders promote a culture that maintains the status quo, self-promotion, and self-protection (loss of power). We should realize that change is inevitable and an entire cultural change (mind-set, shared values/beliefs, attitudes/behaviors) is needed, not a transformational change initiative, delegated to an internal or external (consulting firm) team, sponsored by an executive to satisfy his or her self-serving hidden agenda.

This dynamically changing IT industry needs a set of next-generation leaders who understand why change is important to the business and who is accountable in implementing it, using accountability for results. These next-generation leaders must understand the culture of their employees relative to mobile computing and the ability to transform to productivity tools such as cloud computing and predictive analytics and ability to transform from measuring activities to measuring outputs (what) and outcomes (why).

Do you believe that your traditional human resource annual performance review process is an effective measure of your performance? Do you believe that improvements are needed for this reward and recognition system? Are you one of those who are generously rewarded each year for successes because you satisfy an egoistic and politically attractive executive?

I believe most organizations, including IT departments, need to revisit the ways they measure success. They need to radically transform the traditional human resource annual performance review process to one that measures the strategic directives/goals of the organization that is linked to employees, customers, internal processes, and financial measures.

IT leaders need to truly understand the opportunity that technological advancements provide and its importance in creating the next-generation performance management environment. They need to rely less on these services of futurist's transformation change agents who emphasize the need for the greatest hyped solution on the market, in their management consulting practice. They need to transform from the traditional antiquated change management practices to a transformation change model of people, politics, process, and performance, as suggested in this performance management framework. CIOs need to analyze performance management trends and prepare their leaders for the next-generation performance measurement practices, not the greatest hyped performance management best practices.

A repeating theme throughout this book has been the need for effectively managing, measuring, and monitoring IT leadership to ensure successful delivery of IT services, using accountability for results—RBM. An integrated IT performance management framework was defined, within the context of strategic, IT operational, and performance management. The applicability of this framework within the IT service delivery life cycle, using an innovative *client-centric outsourced* model and specified industry best practices, is provided with real-world illustrations.

I hope this book helped you start thinking about what you are doing and the transformation you need to make. I leave you with one question: Are you ready to look at the management of IT resources—people, processes, technologies, and financials—from the accountability for results perspectives? Are you ready to link IT strategic directives to IT operational execution, using an integrated IT performance measurement dashboard? Are you ready to adopt the client-centric outsourced model to the management and delivery of IT services, using the IT service delivery life cycle? Are you ready to integrate industry best practices in the IT service delivery life cycle? Are you ready to apply performance predictive analytics for evidence-based decision making? Are you ready to start transforming your organization and IT department to a results-driven performance management and measurement culture? What do you think of the 4 Ps to transformational change?

Whatever you do, think big, start small, and gain momentum through repeated successes. Always use a logic model that fits the *organizational culture—integration of emotional, intellectual,* and *economic intelligence. Economic intelligence*[12] is the optimized utilization of IT resources. Please send me your feedback on how you are implementing these ideas? I would be most willing to clarify any confusion, with immediate follow-up. You can contact me at www.IPMF-IT.com or ken.bainey@shaw.ca. My website www.IPMF-IT.com contains many practical articles, white papers, presentations, and dashboards that you will find useful, informative, and insightful. Good luck in your search for IT organizational excellence. This is the start of an exciting journey on IT performance management, measurement, and improvement.

7.7 Summary

The IPMF-IT alignment with specified industry best practices presented in this chapter describes how the components of IPMF-IT framework and specified industry best practices are aligned, based on the IT functional areas or stages of the IT service delivery life cycle process. For each of the major results area of IPMF-IT, the integration with IT service delivery life cycle is demonstrated, based on the methods and tools of the specified industry best practices. Also, the integration of the results areas with integrated IT performance measurement dashboard is also demonstrated. Performance management trends and recommended solutions for PMO support services, using real-world scenarios, are also discussed to provide the readers with scenarios of situations for proactive actions. Suggestions for transforming performance management in your organization based on people, politics, process, and performance understanding/improvement are presented to provide readers and IT leaders, including CIOs, tips on how to transform to a performance management organizational culture of excellence.

Leaders at IT organizations or departments who plan to start transforming performance management in their organization should consider the suggestions provided on transformational change model—people, politics, process, and performance—as presented in this book. The suggestions provide practical insights on when and how to transform to performance management to ensure a high probability of success during the management and delivery of IT services. The value of aligning specified industry best practices with each of the IT functional areas will provide decision makers with an understanding of how and when these methods and tools fit within the context of the IT service delivery life cycle. The purpose of integrating evidence-based decisions of industry best practices is to prepare IT leaders for the next-generation performance measurement practices, not hyped performance management best practices.

- Strategic management integration with industry best practices suggests specified best practices and illustrates how they should be applied during the strategy and planning stages of the IT service delivery life cycle. It also shows the integration with integrated IT performance measurement dashboard. This integration will form the baseline to better manage, monitor, and measure the delivery of IT service with the focus toward strategic organizational excellence linked to IT operational excellence.

- Performance management integration with industry best practices suggests specified best practices and illustrates how they should be applied during all stages of the IT service delivery life cycle. It also shows the integration with integrated IT performance measurement dashboard. This integration will form the baseline to better manage, monitor, and measure the delivery of IT service with the focus toward performance management organizational excellence linked to strategic and operational excellence.
- IT operational management integration with industry best practices suggests specified best practices and illustrates how they should be applied during the design, build, and support services stages of the IT service delivery life cycle. It also shows the integration with integrated IT performance measurement dashboard. This integration will form the baseline to better manage, monitor, and measure the delivery of IT service with the focus toward IT operational excellence linked to strategic and performance excellence.
- PMO integration with industry best practices suggests specified best practices and illustrates how they should be applied during all stages of the IT service delivery life cycle but resides in the PPM IT functional area. It also shows the integration with integrated IT performance measurement dashboard. This integration will form the baseline to provide integrated performance measurement services to measure the delivery of IT service with the focus toward strategic, IT operational, and performance management excellence.
- Transforming performance management provides suggestions for transforming performance management in your organization, which might be applicable to IT organizations or departments. These suggestions provide practical tips based on the transformational change model people/culture, politics, process, and performance, as outlined in this book. Suggestions on the next-generation IT leaders are also provided to prepare CIOs and their leaders for the next-generation performance measurement practices, not the greatest hyped performance management best practices.

7.8 Endnotes: Key Performance Management Terms

[1]*The KPI Institute, CMMI, COBIT, Six Sigma, PMI, ITIL, and Kaplan and Norton*: Industry best practices for the implementation of performance management strategies and processes. These are the major themes of this chapter.

[2]*Methods and tools* (*technologies*): Processes and supporting technologies to support industry best practices.

[3]*Performance framework–measurement driven, results driven, life cycle process driven, IT process framework, and performance analytics*: Integration characteristics of IPMF-IT framework with industry best practices—wherein integration is the key theme of this book.

[4]*Holocracy*: A comprehensive practice of structuring, governing, and running an organization. It replaces today's top-down command and control paradigm with a new way of achieving control by distributing power. It is a new *operating system* that instills rapid revolution in the core process of an organization.

[5]*KPI Management Framework*: A framework from *The KPI Institute* that provides KPI processes and structures to support performance measurements.

[6]*Data mining, data integration, big data, and real-time analytics*: Performance predictive analytical tools to support evidence-based decision making. Big data is the use of predictive analytics or other certain advanced methods to extract value from data using data mining and data integration processes to support evidenced-based decision making.

[7]*TDWI Best Practices Report*: The Data Warehouse Institute (TDWI) is a professional association that provides education, conferences, and researches in business intelligence and data warehousing.

[8]*IT service providers, consultants, and vendors*: External outsourced service/solution providers of IT services and vendors provide the technology products for distribution.

[9]*Enterprise data grids—culture of performance analytics*: Next-generation performance management practices to support predictive analytics, using an integrated data analysis solution.

[10]*Accountability for results—RBM and RBB*: Accountability for results based on results-based management (RBM), that is, output and outcome–driven measures. RBB is an output (what) and outcome (why) approach to financial management that aligns with the strategic directives and goals of the organization.

[11]*Performance management body of knowledge*: An integrated framework or body of knowledge for performance management that defines the outputs, outcomes, processes, and performance measures that align with the results of strategic directives and are acquired using an integrated IT performance measurement dashboard. The focus of this book is on the IPMF-IT framework.

[12]*Organizational culture—integration of emotional, intellectual, and economic intelligence*: Successful transformation to a performance management culture is dependent on an integrated understanding of emotional intelligence (heart), intellectual intelligence (mind and logic), and economic intelligence (optimized utilization of IT resources/asset capacities).

7.9 Questions to Think About: Management Perspectives

1. Think about how your organization makes decisions on when and how to apply industry best practices in managing, monitoring, and measuring IT services. How does your organization integrate these best practices within your IT service delivery life cycle? How does your organization integrate these best practices in your IT performance measurement dashboard? What are the major components of IPMF-IT alignment? How do these components relate to your IT service environment? What is the perception of senior IT leaders in integrating your IT delivery framework with industry best practices methods and tools?
2. Think about how your organization makes decision on optimizing governance and planning strategies and processes? What are the suggested industry best practices? How do these best practices relate to your approach to IT governance and IT planning in your IT organization?
3. Think about how your organization makes decision on optimizing architectural (business, data, applications, technology security) strategies and processes? What are the suggested industry best practices? How do these best practices relate to your approach to architecture delivery in your IT organization?

4. Think about how your organization makes decision on optimizing project delivery strategies and processes? What are the suggested industry best practices? How do these best practices relate to your approach to project delivery in your IT organization?
5. Think about how your organization makes decision on optimizing applications management strategies and processes? What are the suggested industry best practices? How do these best practices relate to your approach to applications management delivery in your IT organization?
6. Think about how your organization makes decision on optimizing technology operations strategies and processes? What are the suggested industry best practices? How do these best practices relate to your approach to technology operations delivery in your IT organization?
7. Think about how your organization ensures consistency, completeness, and integration of IT performance measurement outputs, outcomes, and performance measures. What are the services of the PMO in measuring IT service delivery? How do these services relate to your organization? What is the perception of your senior management on the value of PMO for the management and delivery of IT services? What are the major causes of PMO failures? What are the key suggested industry best practices solutions? How do these best practices relate to your IT organization?
8. Think about how you plan to start transforming performance management in your organization. What are the key trends of IT performance management? What are the key components of transformation change? How does this approach relate to your approach to change management? What are the key suggestions for improvements in starting performance management? How do these suggestions relate to your approach to performance management in your organization?

7.10 Chapter Testing Questions

1. Which one of the following is *not* a major results area of integrating IPMF-IT with IT industry best practices?
   a. Strategic, IT operational, and performance managements
   b. Strategic, IT operational, and performance measures
   c. Operational processes, strategic management, and performance management
2. What are the best suggested industry best practices for IT governance?
   a. CMMI, KPI, PMBOK, and ITIL
   b. CMMI, COBIT, K&N, and Six Sigma
   c. PMBOK, ITIL, COBIT, and CMMI
3. The IT department wants to implement a measurement-based strategy that focuses on streamlining and improving processes? Which of these should the IT leader select?
   a. Six Sigma, CMMI, and COBIT
   b. KPI, K&N, and CMMI
   c. PMBOK, ITIL, and Six Sigma
4. IT operational management integration with industry best practices will occur during which stage of SDLC?
   a. All stages
   b. Strategy, support services, and plan
   c. Build, design, and support services

5. What is the key results area of PMO in measuring IT service delivery?
   a. PMO metrics and performance reporting
   b. Business intelligence
   c. Predictive analytics
6. You decided to start transforming your organization to performance management. What would you most likely examine?
   a. Process, culture, and structure
   b. Are we doing the right things? Right way? Getting benefits? How well?
   c. People, politics, process, and performance
7. Successful implementation of ITIL and PMBOK performance measurement framework is constrained by which of the following? What is the best solution?
   a. Organizational culture—behaviors and social measures
   b. Process and best practices
   c. Technology and predictive analytics
8. Building a sustained trustful environment requires what?
   a. Credibility, integrity, and best practices
   b. People, process, and technology
   c. Leadership, transparency, and accountability
9. Which one of the following best practices is process oriented and customer focused that support IT service management?
   a. ITIL
   b. PMBOK
   c. K&N

Recommended Readings

IPMF-IT Alignment with Industry Best Practices

Aguinis, H., *Performance Management*. New York: Pearson Education, 2012.

Bainey, K.R., *Integrated IT Project Management, A model-Centric Approach*. New York: Artech House, 2004.

Bathshalom, B., *Green Source, The Magazine of Sustainable Design*. Boston, MA, Sustainable Performance Institute, 2011.

Corkins, G., *Performance Management, Integrating Strategy, Execution, Methodologies, Risk, and Analytics*. Hoboken, NJ: John Wiley & Sons Inc., 2009.

Demartini, C., *Performance Management Systems: Design, Diagnosis and Use*. Berlin, Germany: Springer, 2013.

Hall, D., *Corporate Governance: Ensuring Propriety for Performance: A Contemporary Themes in Strategic People Management*. New York: Palgrave Macmillan, 2013.

Info-Tech Research Group, *IT Management and Governance Diagnostics*. Toronto, Ontario, Canada, http://www.infotech.com, 1997–2015.

Kaplan, R.S. and Norton, D.P., *The Balanced Scorecard: Translating Strategy into Action*. Boston, MA: Harvard Business School Publishing, 1996.

KPI Institute, *The KPI Compendium: 20,000 Key Performance Indicators used in Practice*. Melbourne, Victoria, Australia: KPI Institute, 2013.

Marr, B., *Strategic Performance Management, Leveraging and Measuring Your Intangible Value Driver*. Burlington, MA: Elsevier Ltd., 2006.

NAI, Nouri Associates Inc., *IT Metrics*. San Francisco, CA, http://www.nouriassociates.com, 2002.

Spitzer, D.R., *Transforming Performance Measurement, Rethinking the Way We Measure and Drive Organizational Success*. New York: AMACOM, 2007.

Waal, A.D., *Strategic Performance Management: A Managerial and Behavioral Approach*. New York: Palgrave Macmillan, 2013.

Appendix A: Integrated IT Performance Measurement Dashboard—Executive Leadership Services (ELS)*

A real-world illustration of the integrated IT performance measurement dashboard is provided using a Microsoft Excel spreadsheet to demonstrate implementation of this results breakdown structure (RBS). It shows the practical applicability of using this RBS as the foundation structure, during the management and delivery of IT services, for each IT functional area within the IT service delivery life cycle. The end results or deliverables of the strategic directives framework defined in Chapter 6 link with the outputs, outcomes, indicators, and performance measures/metrics in the integrated IT performance dashboard, using a modified version of Kaplan and Norton's Balanced Scorecard performance measurement framework. An example of progress analytics is illustrated in the executive leadership dashboard, and an example of performance measures/metrics is illustrated in the planning and administration dashboard.

My website www.IPMF-IT.com contains more details on the implementation of this integrated IT performance measurement dashboard. It also includes many presentations, practical articles, white papers, and dashboards that I am sure you will find useful, informative, and insightful. This framework can be used as the fundamental structure in the design and implementation of performance management software systems or the start of a new performance management body of knowledge—performance excellence body of knowledge (PEBOK, performance management body of knowledge).

* With appreciated assistance from Ana Drummond, Bsc.

IT EXECUTIVE LEADERSHIP

OPERATIONAL-FM	Start Date	End Date	Status	% Complete	Indicator
IT Governance Accountability Framework	4/1/2011	12/31/2011	In-Progress	60%	G
HR Performance Contract Alignment	4/1/2011	9/30/2011	In-Progress	80%	G
Executive Management (EM) Progress Status	4/1/2011	3/31/2012	In-Progress	40%	G
Executive Management Presentation/Approvals	4/1/2011	3/31/2012	In-Progress	60%	G
IT Policies and Procedures	4/1/2011	3/31/2012	In-Progress	60%	G
IT Operational Accountability Framework	4/1/2011	3/31/2012	In-Progress	40%	G
OPERATIONAL-FM Summary	4/1/2011	3/31/2012	In-Progress	57%	G

OPERATIONAL-SD	StartDate	End Date	Status	% Complete	Indicator
IT Contract Accountability Framework	4/1/2011	9/30/2011	In-Progress	80%	G
IT Consultants NDA	4/1/2011	9/30/2011	In-Progress	70%	Y
CIO Approvals-RFP	4/1/2011	3/31/2012	In-Progress	35%	Y
CIO Approvals-IT Infrastructure Impact	4/1/2011	9/30/2011	In-Progress	80%	G
IT Equipment Purchases Records	4/1/2011	12/31/2011	In-Progress	50%	G
CIO Approvals-Business Projects	4/1/2011	9/30/2011	In-Progress	90%	G
CIO Approvals-Technology Infrastructure Projects	4/1/2011	3/31/2012	Not-Started	40%	G
CIO Approvals-IT Equipment Expenditures	4/1/2011	3/31/2012	In-Progress	40%	G
CIO Approvals-IT Outsourced/Consulting Services	4/1/2011	8/31/2011	In-Progress	80%	R
CIO/CEO Approvals-Special Business Projects	4/1/2011	9/30/2011	In-Progress	80%	G
CIO/CEO Approvals-Special Technology Projects	4/1/2011	12/31/2011	In-Progress	50%	G
OPERATIONAL-SD Summary	4/1/2011	3/31/2012	In-Progress	63%	G

OPERATIONAL-SE	Start Date	End Date	Status	% Complete	Indicator
IT Management Policies Framework	4/1/2011	3/31/2012	In-Progress	30%	Y
IT Management Procedures	4/1/2011	3/31/2012	In-Progress	30%	Y
IT Business Council Accountability Framework	4/1/2011	9/30/2011	In-Progress	80%	G
IT Compliance - Industry Performance Measures	4/1/2011	3/31/2012	Not-Started	30%	Y
IT Benchmarking Metrics	4/1/2011	6/30/2011	Complete	100%	Black
OPERATIONAL-SE Summary	4/1/2011	3/31/2012	In-Progress	54%	G

Figure A.1 Integrated IT performance measurement dashboard: governance (ELS), part 1.

OPERATIONAL-RM	Start Date	End Date	Status	% Complete	Indicator
Executive Management Relations/Feedback	4/1/2011	3/31/2012	In-Progress	30%	Y
Business Areas Relations/Feedback	4/1/2011	3/31/2012	In-Progress	30%	Y
Vendors Relations/Feedback	4/1/2011	9/30/2011	In-Progress	80%	G
IT Outsourced Providers Relations/Feedback	10/1/2011	3/31/2012	Not-Started	0%	
IT Contracted Resources Relations/Feedback	4/1/2011	6/30/2011	Complete	100%	Black
OPERATIONAL-RM Summary	4/1/2011	3/31/2012	In-Progress	48%	G

FINANCIAL	Start Date	End Date	Status	% Complete	Indicator
IT Capital Costs	4/1/2011	3/31/2012	In-Progress	30%	Y
IT Operational Costs	4/1/2011	3/31/2012	In-Progress	30%	Y
IT Outsourced/Consulting Costs	4/1/2011	9/30/2011	In-Progress	80%	G
IT Staff Costs	10/1/2011	3/31/2012	Not-Started	0%	
Major Business Projects Costs	4/1/2011	6/30/2011	Complete	100%	Black
Major Technology Infrastructure Project Costs	4/1/2011	6/30/2011	Complete	100%	Black
FINANCIAL Summary	4/1/2011	3/31/2012	In-Progress	57%	G

CUSTOMER	Start Date	End Date	Status	% Complete	Indicator
Client Relationships/Satisfaction Surveys	4/1/2011	3/31/2012	In-Progress	30%	Y
IT Business Council Meetings	4/1/2011	3/31/2012	In-Progress	30%	Y
Vendor Relationships/Satisfaction Surveys	4/1/2011	9/30/2011	In-Progress	80%	G
IT Outsourced Providers Performance Measures	10/1/2011	3/31/2012	Not-Started	0%	
IT Benchmarking Surveys/Results	4/1/2011	6/30/2011	Complete	100%	Black
CUSTOMER Summary	4/1/2011	3/31/2012	In-Progress	48%	G

EMPLOYEE	Start Date	End Date	Status	% Complete	Indicator
IT Progress Reporting	4/1/2011	6/30/2011	Complete	100%	Black
IT Staff Performance Contract	4/1/2011	3/31/2012	In-Progress	35%	Y
Staff Learning/Growth	4/1/2011	3/31/2012	In-Progress	35%	Y
Staff Meetings/Communications	4/1/2011	3/31/2012	In-Progress	35%	Y
Staff Retention/Retraining/Reward Reporting	4/1/2011	7/31/2011	In-Progress	100%	Black
EMPLOYEE Summary	4/1/2011	3/31/2012	In-Progress	61%	G
IT EXECUTIVE LEADERSHIP SUMMARY	4/1/2011	3/31/2012	In-Progress	55%	G

Figure A.2 Integrated IT performance measurement dashboard: governance (ELS), part 2.

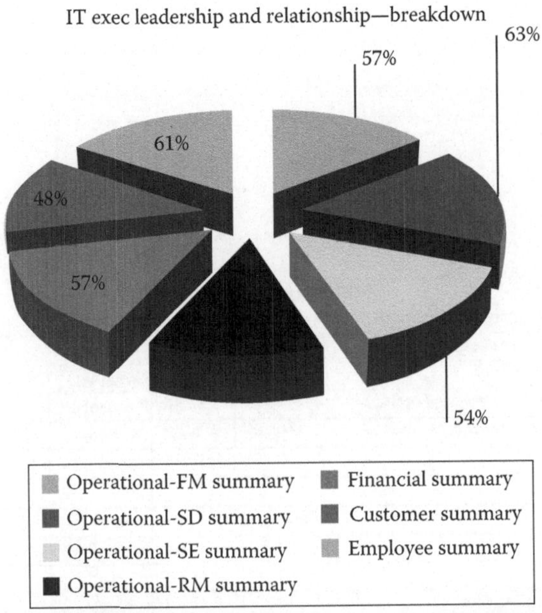

Figure A.3 Integrated IT performance measurement dashboard: governance (ELS), part 3.

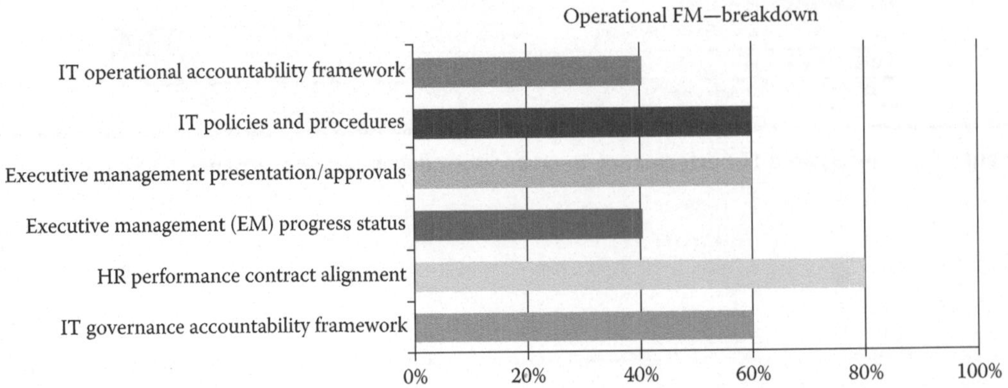

Figure A.4 Integrated IT performance measurement dashboard: governance (ELS), part 4.

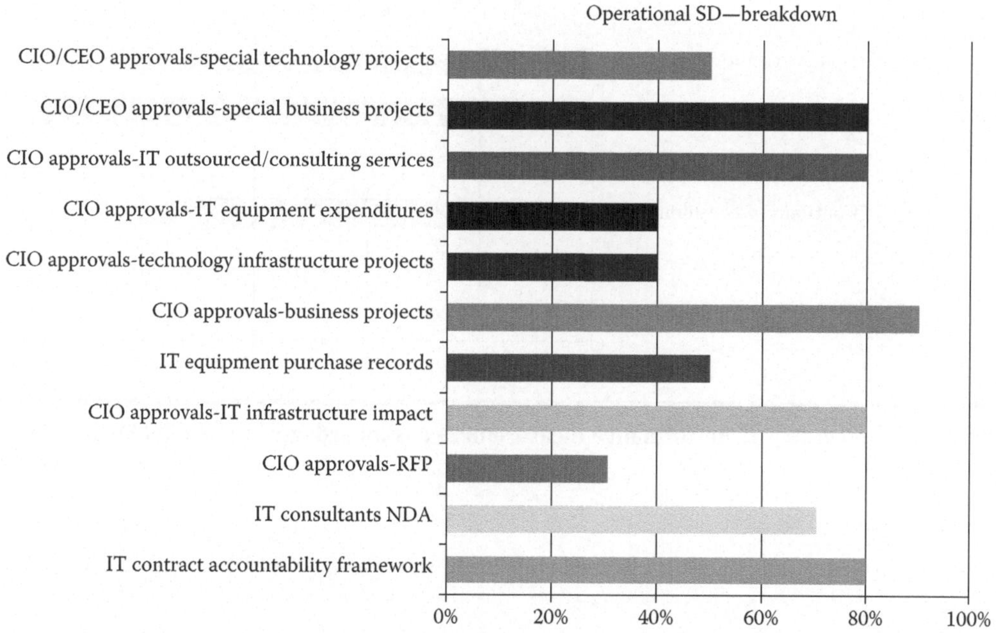

Figure A.5 Integrated IT performance measurement dashboard: governance (ELS), part 5.

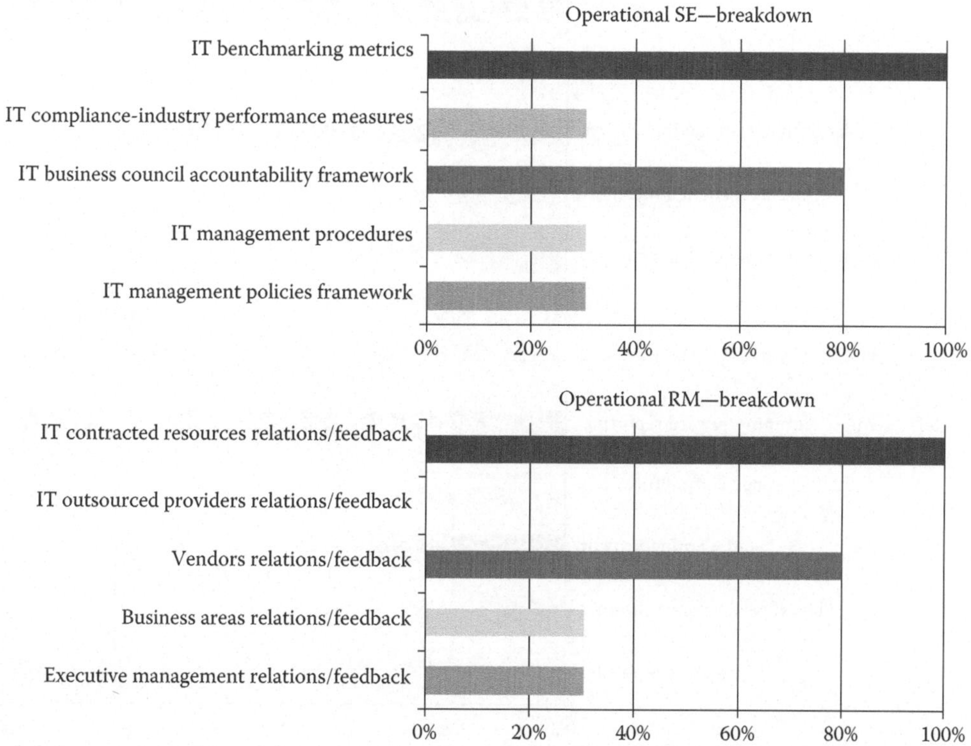

Figure A.6 Integrated IT performance measurement dashboard: governance (ELS), part 6.

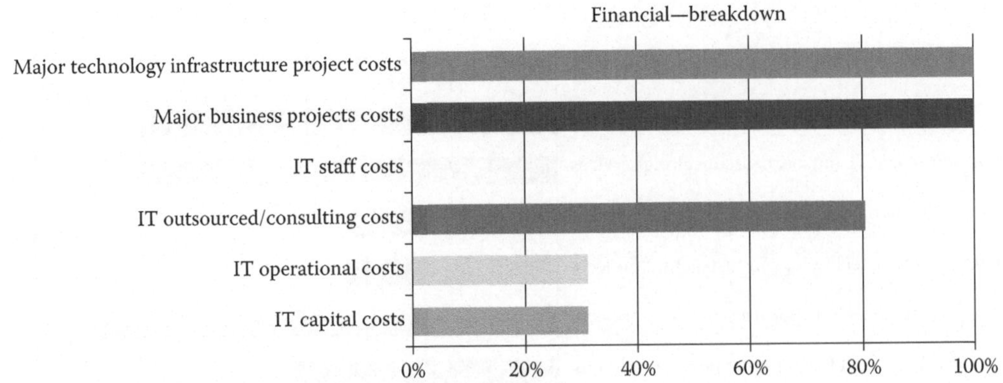

Figure A.7 Integrated IT performance measurement dashboard: governance (ELS), part 7.

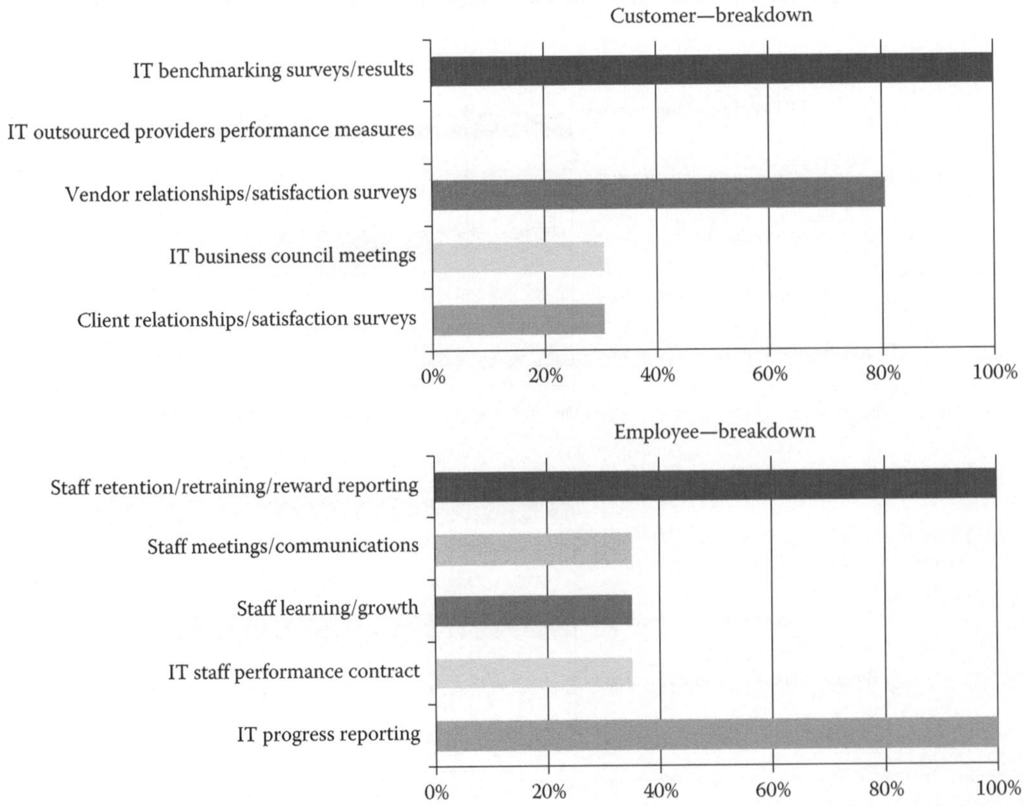

Figure A.8 Integrated IT performance measurement dashboard: governance (ELS), part 8.

Appendix B: Integrated IT Performance Measurement Dashboard—Planning and Administration Services (PAS)

IT PLANNING & ADMINISTRATION SERVICES (PAS)					
OPERATIONAL-FM	Start Date	End Date	Status	% Complete	Indicator
IT Strategic Planning Framework	4/1/2011	9/30/2011	In-Progress	100%	Black
IT Operating Planning Framework	4/1/2011	3/31/2012	In-Progress	35%	Y
IT Budgeting Planning Framework	4/1/2011	12/31/2011	In-Progress	30%	R
OPERATIONAL-FM Summary	4/1/2011	3/31/2012	In-Progress	55%	G

% IT staff performing IT Strategic Planning ; # Improvements completed
% IT staff performing IT Operating Planning ; # Improvements completed
% IT staff performing IT Budget Planning ; # Improvements completed

Figure B.1 Integrated IT performance measurement dashboard: planning (PAS), part 1.

OPERATIONAL-SD	Start Date	End Date	Status	% Complete	Indicator
IT Strategic and Operating Plan	4/1/2011	4/30/2011	In-Progress	100%	Black
IT Budget Plan	4/1/2011	12/31/2011	In-Progress	50%	G
IT Budget Plan status/ progress/forecasts	1/1/2012	3/31/2012	Not-Started	0%	
IT Capital/Operating Expenditures Coding	4/1/2011	3/31/2012	In-Progress	45%	G
IT Invoice Processing & Financial Admin	4/1/2011	3/31/2012	In-Progress	45%	G
IT Contract Agreement Status	4/1/2011	6/30/2011	In-Progress	55%	Past Due
Stakeholders Financial Support	4/1/2011	3/31/2012	In-Progress	45%	G
Finance and HR collaborations	4/1/2011	3/31/2012	In-Progress	45%	G
OPERATIONAL-SD Summary	4/1/2011	3/31/2012	In-Progress	48%	G

% IT staff delivering IT Strategic/Operating Plans ; # Improvements completed
% IT staff delivering IT Budget Plans ; # Improvements completed
% IT staff delivering IT Budget Plan status ; # Improvements completed
% IT staff delivering IT Capital/Operating Expenditures ; # Improvements completed
% IT staff delivering IT Invoicing ; # Improvements completed
% IT staff delivering IT Contract Agreement Status ; # Improvements completed
% IT staff delivering Stakeholders Financial Support ; # Improvements completed
% IT staff delivering Finance and HR Collaborations ; # Improvements completed

Figure B.2 Integrated IT performance measurement dashboard: planning (PAS), part 2.

OPERATIONAL-SE	Start Date	End Date	Status	% Complete	Indicator
IT Strategic/Operating Plan-Guidelines	4/1/2011	6/30/2011	In-Progress	80%	Past Due
IT Financial Accountability Framework	4/1/2011	6/30/2011	In-Progress	80%	Past Due
IT Financial Guidelines	4/1/2011	6/30/2011	In-Progress	90%	Past Due
IT Financial Compliance-Financial Measures	4/1/2011	6/30/2011	In-Progress	100%	Black
IT Financial Benchmarking Metrics	4/1/2011	6/30/2011	In-Progress	90%	Past Due
OPERATIONAL-SE Summary	4/1/2011	6/30/2011	In-Progress	88%	Past Due

% IT staff performing IT Strategic/Operating Guidelines ; # Improvements completed
% IT staff performing IT Financial Accountability Framework ; # Improvements completed
% IT staff performing IT Financial Guidelines ; # Improvements completed
% IT staff performing IT Financial Measures ; # Improvements completed
% IT staff performing IT Financial Benchmarking Metrics ; # Improvements completed

Figure B.3 Integrated IT performance measurement dashboard: planning (PAS), part 3.

OPERATIONAL-RM	Start Date	End Date	Status	% Complete	Indicator
Financial Management Relations/Feedback	4/1/2011	3/31/2012	In-Progress	45%	G
Vendors PAS Relations/Fedback	4/1/2011	3/31/2012	In-Progress	45%	G
IT Outsourced Providers PAS Relations/Feedback	4/1/2011	3/31/2012	In-Progress	45%	G
OPERATIONAL-RM Summary	4/1/2011	3/31/2012	In-Progress	45%	G

% IT staff performing Financial Relations ; # Improvements completed
% IT staff performing Vendors Relations ; # Improvements completed
% IT staff performing Outsourced Providers Relations ; # Improvements completed

Figure B.4 Integrated IT performance measurement dashboard: planning (PAS), part 4.

FINANCIAL	Start Date	End Date	Status	% Complete	Indicator
IT Planning Costs	4/1/2011	3/31/2012	In-Progress	30%	Y
IT Administration Costs	4/1/2011	3/31/2012	In-Progress	30%	Y
FINANCIAL Summary	4/1/2011	3/31/2012	In-Progress	30%	Y

% IT staff managing IT Capital Costs; # Improvements completed
% IT staff managing IT Operational Costs Mgnt; # Improvements completed

Figure B.5 Integrated IT performance measurement dashboard: planning (PAS), part 5.

CUSTOMER	Start Date	End Date	Status	% Complete	Indicator
PAS Client Relationships/Satisfaction Surveys	4/1/2011	3/31/2012	In-Progress	30%	Y
PAS Committee Meetings	4/1/2011	3/31/2012	In-Progress	30%	Y
PAS Vendors Relationships/Satisfaction Surveys	4/1/2011	9/30/2011	In-Progress	80%	G
PAS IT Outsourced Providers Surveys	10/1/2011	3/31/2012	Not-Started	0%	
PAS Benchmarking Surveys/Results	4/1/2011	6/30/2011	Complete	100%	Black
CUSTOMER Summary	4/1/2011	3/31/2012	In-Progress	48%	G

% IT staff performing Client Satisfaction Surveys; # Improvements completed
% IT staff attending IT Business Council Meetings; # Improvements completed
% IT staff performing Vendor Satisfaction Surveys; # Improvements completed
% IT staff performing IT Vendors Performance Measures; # Improvements completed
% IT staff performing PAS Benchmarking ; # Improvements completed

Figure B.6 Integrated IT performance measurement dashboard: planning (PAS), part 6.

EMPLOYEE	Start Date	End Date	Status	% Complete	Indicator
PAS Progress Reporting	4/1/2011	6/30/2011	Complete	100%	Black
PAS Staff Performance Contract	4/1/2011	3/31/2012	In-Progress	35%	Y
PAS Staff Learning/Growth Reporting	4/1/2011	3/31/2012	In-Progress	35%	Y
PAS Staff Meetings/Communications	4/1/2011	3/31/2012	In-Progress	35%	Y
PAS Staff Retention/Retraining/Reward Reporting	4/1/2011	7/31/2011	In-Progress	50%	Past Due
EMPLOYEE Summary	4/1/2011	3/31/2012	In-Progress	51%	G
IT PLANNING & ADMINISTRATION SUMMARY	4/1/2011	3/31/2012	In-Progress	52%	G

% IT staff performing Progress Reporting ; # Improvements completed
% IT Staff performing Staff Performance Contract ; # Improvements completed
% IT staff performing Learning/Growth sessions; # Improvements completed
% IT staff performing staff communications/meetings ; # Improvements completed
% IT staff performing IT Benchmarking/retention/retraining ; # Improvements completed

Figure B.7 Integrated IT performance measurement dashboard: planning (PAS), part 7.

Appendix C: Integrated IT Performance Measurement Dashboard—Enterprise Architecture Services (EAS)

IT ENTERPRISE ARCHITECTURE SERVICES (EAS)					
OPERATIONAL-FM	Start Date	End Date	Status	% Complete	Indicator
IT Enterprise Architecture Framework	4/1/2011	9/30/2011	In-Progress	25%	R
Information Management Framework	4/1/2011	9/30/2011	In-Progress	25%	R
Technology Project Management Governance	4/1/2011	3/31/2012	In-Progress	25%	Y
OPERATIONAL-FM Summary	4/1/2011	3/31/2012	In-Progress	25%	Y
OPERATIONAL-SD	Budget	YTD Actual	Status	% Complete	Indicator
Business Systems Planning Support	4/1/2011	3/31/2012	In-Progress	25%	Y
Business Case/Architecture Support	4/1/2011	3/31/2012	In-Progress	25%	Y
IT Enterprise Architectures	4/1/2011	3/31/2012	In-Progress	35%	Y
IT Enterprise Architecture Standards	4/1/2011	3/31/2012	In-Progress	30%	Y
IT Security Plans	4/1/2011	9/30/2011	In-Progress	80%	G
IT Security Implementation	4/1/2011	3/31/2012	In-Progress	30%	Y
Innovative Communications tools	4/1/2011	3/31/2012	In-Progress	35%	Y
Technology Projects Contract Management	4/1/2011	3/31/2012	In-Progress	35%	Y
Technology Program/Project Management	4/1/2011	9/30/2011	In-Progress	90%	G
IT Productivity Tools and Framework	4/1/2011	9/30/2011	In-Progress	40%	R
Technology Infrastructure Delivery/Support	4/1/2011	9/30/2011	In-Progress	35%	R
Technology Research/Trends	4/1/2011	3/31/2012	In-Progress	35%	Y
OPERATIONAL-SD Summary	4/1/2011	3/31/2012	In-Progress	41%	G

Figure C.1 Integrated IT performance measurement dashboard: architecture (EAS), part 1.

OPERATIONAL-SE	Start Date	End Date	Status	% Complete	Indicator
Technology Infrastructure Project Plan QA	4/1/2011	6/30/2011	In-Progress	75%	Past Due
IT Security and Privacy Compliance/Approval	4/1/2011	7/31/2011	In-Progress	80%	Past Due
Infrastructure Projects Financial Measures	4/1/2011	9/30/2011	In-Progress	60%	R
Technology Infrastructure Compliance	4/1/2011	3/31/2012	In-Progress	35%	Y
Technology Infrastructure Optimization	4/1/2011	3/31/2012	In-Progress	35%	Y
Technology Infrastructure Benchmarking	4/1/2011	9/30/2011	In-Progress	80%	G
OPERATIONAL-SE Summary	4/1/2011	3/31/2012	In-Progress	61%	G
OPERATIONAL-RM	Start Date	End Date	Status	% Complete	Indicator
EAS Client Management Relations/Feedback	4/1/2011	3/31/2012	In-Progress	100%	Black
Vendors EAI Relations/Feedback	4/1/2011	3/31/2012	In-Progress	40%	G
IT Outsourced Providers EAI Relations/Feedback	4/1/2011	3/31/2012	In-Progress	25%	Y
OPERATIONAL-RM Summary	4/1/2011	3/31/2012	In-Progress	55%	G
FINANCIAL	Start Date	End Date	Status	% Complete	Indicator
IT Infrastructure Project Costs	4/1/2011	3/31/2012	In-Progress	35%	Y
IT Enterprise Architecture Costs	4/1/2011	3/31/2012	In-Progress	25%	Y
FINANCIAL Summary	4/1/2011	3/31/2012	In-Progress	30%	Y

Figure C.2 Integrated IT performance measurement dashboard: architecture (EAS), part 2.

CUSTOMER	Start Date	End Date	Status	% Complete	Indicator
EAS Client Relationships/Satisfaction Surveys	4/1/2011	3/31/2012	In-Progress	40%	G
EAS Committee Meetings	4/1/2011	3/31/2012	In-Progress	40%	G
EAS Vendors Relationships/Satisfaction Surveys	4/1/2011	3/31/2012	In-Progress	40%	G
EAS IT Outsourced Providers Surveys	4/1/2011	3/31/2012	In-Progress	40%	G
EAS Benchmarking Surveys/Results	4/1/2011	3/31/2012	In-Progress	40%	G
CUSTOMER Summary	4/1/2011	3/31/2012	In-Progress	40%	G
EMPLOYEE	**Start Date**	**End Date**	**Status**	**% Complete**	**Indicator**
EAS IT Progress Reporting	4/1/2011	6/30/2011	Complete	100%	Black
EAS IT Staff Performance Contract	4/1/2011	3/31/2012	In-Progress	35%	Y
EAS Staff Learning/Growth Reporting	4/1/2011	3/31/2012	In-Progress	35%	Y
EAS Staff Meetings/Communications	4/1/2011	3/31/2012	In-Progress	35%	Y
EAS Staff Retention/Retraining/Reward Reporting	4/1/2011	7/31/2011	In-Progress	100%	Black
EMPLOYEE Summary	4/1/2011	3/31/2012	In-Progress	61%	G
IT ENTERPRISE ARCHITECTURE	4/1/2011	3/31/2012	In-Progress	45%	G

Figure C.3 Integrated IT performance measurement dashboard: architecture (EAS), part 3.

Appendix D: Integrated IT Performance Measurement Dashboard—Project Portfolio Management (PPM)

IT PROJECT PORTFOLIO MANAGEMENT (PPM)					
OPERATIONAL-FM	Start Date	End Date	Status	% Complete	Indicator
IT PPM Governance Framework	4/1/2011	12/31/2011	In-Progress	50%	G
IT PPM Innovative Technical Direction	4/1/2011	3/31/2012	In-Progress	45%	G
PPM Projects Outsourcing Framework	4/1/2011	9/30/2011	In-Progress	65%	Y
OPERATIONAL-FM Summary	4/1/2011	3/31/2012	In-Progress	53%	G
OPERATIONAL-SD	Start Date	End Date	Status	% Complete	Indicator
IT Business Projects Monitoring/Reporting	4/1/2011	3/31/2012	In-Progress	25%	Y
Innovative PMO Communications tools	4/1/2011	9/30/2011	In-Progress	75%	Y
IT PPM Productivity Tools and Processes	4/1/2011	9/30/2012	In-Progress	40%	G
PPM Systems and Regression Testing	4/1/2011	3/31/2012	In-Progress	40%	G
IT Project Management /Delivery	4/1/2011	3/31/2012	In-Progress	40%	G
IT Business Projects RFP/Contracts	4/1/2011	3/31/2012	In-Progress	40%	G
IT Business Projects Program/Projects Plan	4/1/2011	3/31/2012	In-Progress	40%	G
IT Business Project Architecture/Design	4/1/2011	3/31/2012	In-Progress	40%	G
IT PMO Support	4/1/2011	3/31/2012	In-Progress	40%	G
IT Business Project Requirements Specifications	4/1/2011	3/31/2012	In-Progress	40%	G
OPERATIONAL-SD Summary	4/1/2011	3/31/2012	In-Progress	42%	G

Figure D.1 Integrated IT performance measurement dashboard: projects (PPM), part 1.

OPERATIONAL-SE	Start Date	End Date	Status	% Complete	Indicator
Business Projects Plan QA	4/1/2011	6/30/2011	In-Progress	75%	Past Due
IT Project Management Compliance/Approval	4/1/2011	7/31/2011	In-Progress	80%	Past Due
Business Projects Financial Measures	4/1/2011	9/30/2011	In-Progress	60%	R
PMO Compliance	4/1/2011	3/31/2012	In-Progress	35%	Y
Project Management Optimization	4/1/2011	3/31/2012	In-Progress	35%	Y
Business Projects Benchmarking Metrics	4/1/2011	9/30/2011	In-Progress	80%	G
OPERATIONAL-SE Summary	4/1/2011	3/31/2012	In-Progress	61%	G
OPERATIONAL-RM	Start Date	End Date	Status	% Complete	Indicator
PPM Client Management Relations/Feedback	4/1/2011	3/31/2012	In-Progress	100%	Black
Vendors PPM Relations/Feedback	4/1/2011	3/31/2012	In-Progress	40%	G
IT Outsourced Providers PPM Relations/Feedback	4/1/2011	3/31/2012	In-Progress	25%	Y
OPERATIONAL-RM Summary	4/1/2011	3/31/2012	In-Progress	55%	G
FINANCIAL	Start Date	End Date	Status	% Complete	Indicator
IT Business Project Costs	4/1/2011	3/31/2012	In-Progress	35%	Y
IT PPM Costs	4/1/2011	3/31/2012	In-Progress	25%	Y
FINANCIAL Summary	4/1/2011	3/31/2012	In-Progress	30%	Y

Figure D.2 Integrated IT performance measurement dashboard: projects (PPM), part 2.

CUSTOMER	Start Date	End Date	Status	% Complete	Indicator
PPM Client Relationships/Satisfaction Surveys	4/1/2011	3/31/2012	In-Progress	30%	Y
PPM Committee Meetings	4/1/2011	3/31/2012	In-Progress	30%	Y
PPM Vendors Relationships/Satisfaction Surveys	4/1/2011	9/30/2011	In-Progress	80%	G
PPM IT Outsourced Providers Surveys	10/1/2011	3/31/2012	Not-Started	0%	
PPM Benchmarking Surveys/Results	4/1/2011	6/30/2011	Complete	100%	Black
CUSTOMER Summary	4/1/2011	3/31/2012	In-Progress	48%	G

EMPLOYEE	Start Date	End Date	Status	% Complete	Indicator
PPM IT Progress Reporting	4/1/2011	6/30/2011	Complete	100%	Black
PPM IT Staff Performance Contract	4/1/2011	3/31/2012	In-Progress	35%	Y
PPM Staff Learning/Growth Reporting	4/1/2011	3/31/2012	In-Progress	35%	Y
PPM Staff Meetings/Communications	4/1/2011	3/31/2012	In-Progress	35%	Y
PPM Staff Retention/Retraining/Reward Reporting	4/1/2011	7/31/2011	In-Progress	100%	Black
EMPLOYEE Summary	4/1/2011	3/31/2012	In-Progress	61%	G
IT PROJECT PORTFOLIO SUMMARY	4/1/2011	3/31/2012	In-Progress	50%	G

Figure D.3 Integrated IT performance measurement dashboard: projects (PPM), part 3.

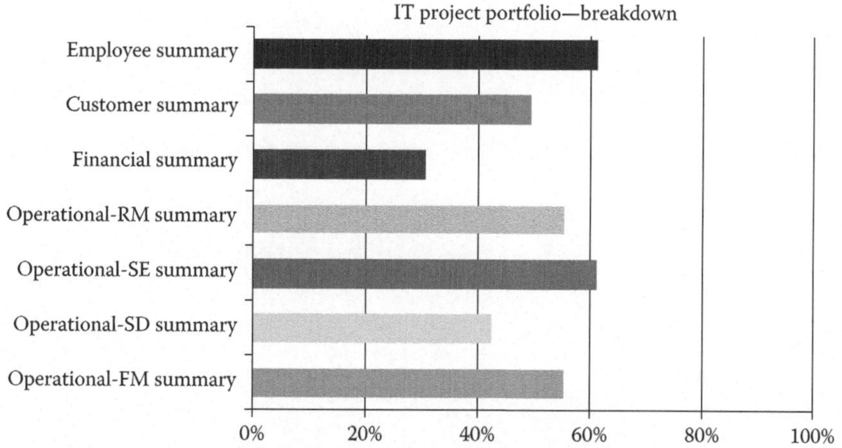

Figure D.4 Integrated IT performance measurement dashboard: projects (PPM), part 4.

Appendix E: Integrated IT Performance Measurement Dashboard—Applications Management Services (AMS)

IT APPLICATIONS MANAGEMENT SERVICES (AMS)					
OPERATIONAL-FM	**Start Date**	**End Date**	**Status**	**% Complete**	**Indicator**
IT AMS Governance Framework	4/1/2011	12/31/2011	In-Progress	50%	G
IT AMS Innovative Technical Direction	4/1/2011	3/31/2012	In-Progress	45%	G
AMS Outsourcing Framework	4/1/2011	9/30/2011	In-Progress	65%	Y
OPERATIONAL-FM Summary	4/1/2011	3/31/2012	In-Progress	53%	G
OPERATIONAL-SD	**Budget**	**YTD Actual**	**Status**	**% Complete**	**Indicator**
AMS Services & SLA mgmt	4/1/2011	3/31/2012	In-Progress	45%	G
AMS SLA Support	4/1/2011	3/31/2012	In-Progress	45%	G
Web-Services Policy/Strategy Development	4/1/2011	6/30/2011	In-Progress	50%	Past Due
Innovative Communications tools	4/1/2011	3/31/2012	In-Progress	45%	G
AMS RFP/Contract Mgnt	4/1/2011	3/31/2012	In-Progress	45%	G
AMS Committee Meetings	4/1/2011	3/31/2012	In-Progress	45%	G
AMS Migrations	4/1/2011	3/31/2012	In-Progress	45%	G
AMS Change Management	4/1/2011	3/31/2012	In-Progress	45%	G
OPERATIONAL-SD Summary	4/1/2011	3/31/2012	In-Progress	46%	G

Figure E.1 Integrated IT performance measurement dashboard: applications (AMS), part 1.

OPERATIONAL-SE	**Start Date**	**End Date**	**Status**	**% Complete**	**Indicator**
AMS QA	4/1/2011	6/30/2011	In-Progress	75%	Past Due
AMS Compliance/Approval	4/1/2011	7/31/2011	In-Progress	80%	Past Due
AMS Financial Measures	4/1/2011	9/30/2011	In-Progress	60%	
AMS SLA Compliance	4/1/2011	3/31/2012	In-Progress	35%	Y
AMS Optimization	4/1/2011	3/31/2012	In-Progress	35%	Y
AMS Benchmarking Metrics	4/1/2011	9/30/2011	In-Progress	80%	G
OPERATIONAL-SE Summary	4/1/2011	3/31/2012	In-Progress	61%	G
OPERATIONAL-RM	**Start Date**	**End Date**	**Status**	**% Complete**	**Indicator**
AMS Client Management Relations/Feedback	4/1/2011	3/31/2012	In-Progress	100%	Black
Vendors AMS Relations/Feedback	4/1/2011	3/31/2012	In-Progress	40%	G
IT Outsourced Providers AMS Relations/Feedback	4/1/2011	3/31/2012	In-Progress	25%	Y
OPERATIONAL-RM Summary	4/1/2011	3/31/2012	In-Progress	55%	G
FINANCIAL	**Start Date**	**End Date**	**Status**	**% Complete**	**Indicator**
IT AMS Innovative Initiative Costs-Capital	4/1/2011	12/31/2011	In-Progress	50%	G
IT AMS Operating Costs	4/1/2011	3/31/2012	In-Progress	15%	
FINANCIAL Summary	4/1/2011	3/31/2012	In-Progress	33%	Y

Figure E.2 Integrated IT performance measurement dashboard: applications (AMS), part 2.

CUSTOMER	Start Date	End Date	Status	% Complete	Indicator
AMS Client Relationships/Satisfaction Surveys	4/1/2011	3/31/2012	In-Progress	30%	Y
AMS Committee Meetings	4/1/2011	3/31/2012	In-Progress	30%	Y
AMS Vendors Relationships/Satisfaction Surveys	4/1/2011	9/30/2011	In-Progress	80%	G
AMS IT Outsourced Providers Surveys	10/1/2011	3/31/2012	Not-Started	0%	
AMS Benchmarking Surveys/Results	4/1/2011	6/30/2011	Complete	100%	Black
CUSTOMER Summary	4/1/2011	3/31/2012	In-Progress	48%	G
EMPLOYEE	**Start Date**	**End Date**	**Status**	**% Complete**	**Indicator**
AMS Progress Reporting	4/1/2011	6/30/2011	Complete	100%	Black
AMS Staff Performance Contract	4/1/2011	3/31/2012	In-Progress	35%	Y
AMS Staff Learning/Growth Reporting	4/1/2011	3/31/2012	In-Progress	35%	Y
AMS Staff Meetings/Communications	4/1/2011	3/31/2012	In-Progress	35%	Y
AMS Staff Retention/Retraining/Reward Reporting	4/1/2011	7/31/2011	In-Progress	100%	Black
EMPLOYEE Summary	4/1/2011	3/31/2012	In-Progress	61%	G
IT APPLICATIONS SERVICES SUMMARY	4/1/2011	3/31/2012	In-Progress	51%	G

Figure E.3 Integrated IT performance measurement dashboard: applications (AMS), part 3.

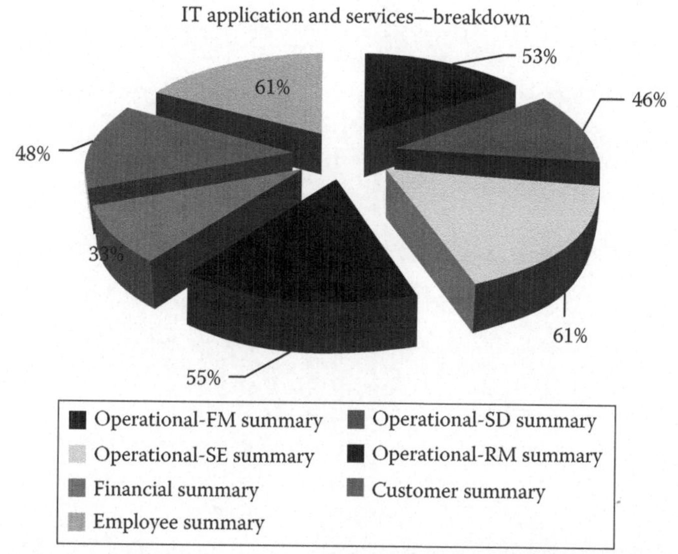

Figure E.4 Integrated IT performance measurement dashboard: applications (AMS), part 4.

Appendix F: Integrated IT Performance Measurement Dashboard—Technology Operations Services (TOS)

IT OPERATIONS SERVICES (TOS)					
OPERATIONAL-FM	**Start Date**	**End Date**	**Status**	**% Complete**	**Indicator**
TOS Governance Framework	4/1/2011	12/31/2011	In-Progress	50%	G
TOS Innovative Technical Direction	4/1/2011	3/31/2012	In-Progress	45%	G
TOS Outsourcing Framework	4/1/2011	9/30/2011	In-Progress	65%	Y
TOS Data Centre Technology Direction	4/1/2011	3/31/2012	In-Progress	45%	G
OPERATIONAL-FM Summary	4/1/2011	3/31/2012	In-Progress	51%	G
OPERATIONAL-SD	**Budget**	**YTD Actual**	**Status**	**% Complete**	**Indicator**
TOS Services & SLA Management	4/1/2011	3/31/2012	In-Progress	45%	G
TOS SLA Support	4/1/2011	3/31/2012	In-Progress	45%	G
Data Centre Policy/Strategy Development	4/1/2011	6/30/2011	In-Progress	50%	Past Due
Innovative Communications tools	4/1/2011	3/31/2012	In-Progress	45%	G
TOS RFP/Contract Mgnt	4/1/2011	3/31/2012	In-Progress	45%	G
TOS Committee Meetings	4/1/2011	3/31/2012	In-Progress	45%	G
TOS Migrations	4/1/2011	3/31/2012	In-Progress	45%	G
TOS Change Management	4/1/2011	3/31/2012	In-Progress	45%	G
Managed Operations Support	4/1/2011	3/31/2012	In-Progress	45%	G
Technology Infrastructure Delivery	4/1/2011	6/30/2011	In-Progress	50%	Past Due
TOS Innovative Productivity tools	4/1/2011	3/31/2012	In-Progress	45%	G
OPERATIONAL-SD Summary	4/1/2011	3/31/2012	In-Progress	46%	G

Figure F.1 Integrated IT performance measurement dashboard: technology (TOS), part 1.

OPERATIONAL-SE	**Start Date**	**End Date**	**Status**	**% Complete**	**Indicator**
TOS QA	4/1/2011	6/30/2011	In-Progress	75%	Past Due
TOS Compliance/Approval	4/1/2011	7/31/2011	In-Progress	80%	Past Due
TOS Financial Measures	4/1/2011	9/30/2011	In-Progress	60%	
TOS SLA Compliance	4/1/2011	3/31/2012	In-Progress	35%	Y
TOS Asset Optimization	4/1/2011	3/31/2012	In-Progress	35%	Y
TOS Benchmarking Metrics	4/1/2011	9/30/2011	In-Progress	80%	G
IT Infrastructure Purchases Approvals	4/1/2011	5/31/2011	In-Progress	75%	Past Due
OPERATIONAL-SE Summary	4/1/2011	3/31/2012	In-Progress	63%	G
OPERATIONAL-RM	**Start Date**	**End Date**	**Status**	**% Complete**	**Indicator**
TOS Client Management Relations/Feedback	4/1/2011	3/31/2012	In-Progress	100%	Black
Vendors TOS Relations/Feedback	4/1/2011	3/31/2012	In-Progress	40%	G
IT Outsourced Providers TOS Relations/Feedback	4/1/2011	3/31/2012	In-Progress	25%	Y
OPERATIONAL-RM Summary	4/1/2011	3/31/2012	In-Progress	55%	G
FINANCIAL	**Start Date**	**End Date**	**Status**	**% Complete**	**Indicator**
IT TOS Innovative Initiative Costs-Capital	4/1/2011	12/31/2011	In-Progress	50%	G
IT TOS Operating Costs	4/1/2011	3/31/2012	In-Progress	15%	
FINANCIAL Summary	4/1/2011	3/31/2012	In-Progress	33%	Y

Figure F.2 Integrated IT performance measurement dashboard: technology (TOS), part 2.

CUSTOMER	Start Date	End Date	Status	% Complete	Indicator
TOS Client Relationships/Satisfaction Surveys	4/1/2011	3/31/2012	In-Progress	30%	Y
TOS Committee Meetings	4/1/2011	3/31/2012	In-Progress	30%	Y
TOS Vendors Relationships/Satisfaction Surveys	4/1/2011	9/30/2011	In-Progress	80%	G
TOS IT Outsourced Providers Surveys	10/1/2011	3/31/2012	Not-Started	0%	
TOS Benchmarking Surveys/Results	4/1/2011	6/30/2011	Complete	100%	Black
CUSTOMER Summary	4/1/2011	3/31/2012	In-Progress	48%	G
EMPLOYEE	**Start Date**	**End Date**	**Status**	**% Complete**	**Indicator**
TOS Staff Progress Reporting	4/1/2011	6/30/2011	Complete	100%	Black
TOS Staff Performance Contract	4/1/2011	3/31/2012	In-Progress	35%	Y
TOS Staff Learning/Growth Reporting	4/1/2011	3/31/2012	In-Progress	35%	Y
TOS Staff Meetings/Communications	4/1/2011	3/31/2012	In-Progress	35%	Y
TOS Staff Retention/Retraining/Reward Reporting	4/1/2011	7/31/2011	In-Progress	100%	Black
EMPLOYEE Summary	4/1/2011	3/31/2012	In-Progress	61%	G
IT OPERATIONS SERVICES SUMMARY	4/1/2011	3/31/2012	In-Progress	51%	G

Figure F.3 Integrated IT performance measurement dashboard: technology (TOS), part 3.

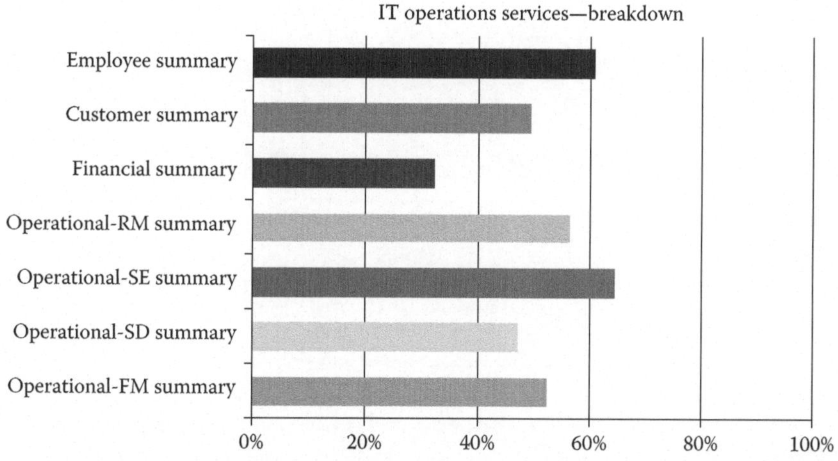

Figure F.4 Integrated IT performance measurement dashboard: technology (TOS), part 4.

Index

F

H

I

K

V